Professional SQL Server 2000 XML

Paul J. Burke
Sam Ferguson
Denise Gosnell
Paul Morris
Jan D. Narkiewicz
J. Michael Palermo IV
Jon D. Reid
Darshan Singh
Brian Smith
Karli Watson
Carvin Wilson
Warren Wiltsie

Wrox Press Ltd. ®

Professional SQL Server 2000 XML

First Printed June, 2001

Published by Wrox Press Ltd,
Arden House, 1102 Warwick Road, Acocks Green,
Birmingham, B27 6BH, UK
Printed in the United States
ISBN 1861005466

Credits

Authors
Paul J. Burke
Sam Ferguson
Denise Gosnell
Paul Morris
Jan D. Narkiewicz
J. Michael Palermo IV
Jon D. Reid
Darshan Singh
Brian Smith
Karli Watson
Carvin Wilson
Warren Wiltsie

Additonal Material
Hope Hatfield

Technical Architect
Kate Hall

Technical Editors
Victoria Blackburn
Claire Brittle
Benjamin Egan
Paul Jeffcoat
Douglas Paterson

Category Manager
Bruce Lawson

Project Administrator
Rob Hesketh

Author Agents
Sarah Bowers
Avril Corbin

Additional Artwork
Chris Matterface

Technical Reviewers
Ramesh Balaji
Martin Beaulieu
Maxime Bombardier
Beth Breidenbach
Robert Chang
David Faour
Jeff Gabriel
Scott Hanselman
Mark Horner
Daniel Kent
Shaun McAravey
Gleydson de Macedo
Jon D. Reid
David M. Scott
Robert Vieira
Larry Wall
Jonathan Winer
Donald Xie
Sakhr Youness

Production Manager
Simon Hardware

Production Project Coordinator
Mark Burdett

Production Assistant
Abbie Forletta

Illustrations
Shabnam Hussain
Paul Grove

Cover
Chris Morris

Index
Adrian Axinte

About the Authors

Paul J. Burke

Paul J Burke is a senior developer for a financial institution in the City of London. He specializes in distributed N-Tier applications using COM/MTS, COM+ & J2EE.

He has written several magazine articles on XML and COM+ various aspects of database technology and is a contributor to Microsoft's 'members helping members' on topics such as SQL Server, Visual Basic, and XML. He can be contacted via the experts in IT web site: http://www.experts-in-it.com/.

Thanks to my parents who got me started, Richard Waldstein for keeping me one step ahead, Alistair Lowe-Norris for the same, Michael Lewis and Andrew Parry for the constant Microsoft bashing that meant I really had to know my stuff :-) and keeping me sharp. Thanks also to Brian Randall, Andrew Gaytor, and Paul Kirby of Developmentor.

To my wife Jo for letting me do this.

To my daughter Rosie for putting the spaces in all the right places.

Sam Ferguson

Sam is an IT consultant and developer with API software, based in Glasgow, Scotland. Sam, who lives in Ayrshire, specialises in all .NET-oriented technologies. In what little spare time he has, he is also a keen golfer.

He is soon to marry his angel Jacquie, in the idyllic surroundings of Zel Am See in Austria. He also has two cats, The Leg and Chick, and a wonderful mother Kathleen.

For all my friends and colleagues.

Denise Gosnell

Denise Gosnell, a Microsoft Certified Solution Developer, works for Microsoft as a consultant in the MCS National Retail Consulting Group. Denise has a unique background in both law and technology and she hopes to find unique ways to utilize her diverse background.

She received a bachelor's degree in Computer Science – Business (summa cum laude) from Anderson University and a Doctor of Jurisprudence from Indiana University in Indianapolis. Denise is an attorney licensed to practice law in Indiana and is an active member of the Indiana and Indianapolis Bar Associations.

Denise has worked in the computer industry for over 7 years and has recently co-authored the MSDE Bible published by IDG Books in December 2000. Prior to joining Microsoft, she worked in a variety of positions ranging from systems engineer, programmer, IS Manager, and senior consultant.

When Denise isn't working or studying, she and her husband Jake enjoy traveling around the globe to places such as Russia, Poland, and China.

To my wonderful husband Jake for his patience and encouragement when I spent my weekends writing and working instead of spending time with him.

Paul Morris

Paul is a database architect and consultant based in South West London, UK. He has over fifteen years experience in IT, the last ten immersed in Microsoft technologies. He specialises in designing and building e-commerce solutions for clients of all sizes. Currently he is designing a major e-recruitment solution for a UK-based publisher.

He is a Microsoft certified database administrator (MCDBA), solution developer (MSCD), and systems engineer (MCSE+I).

Jan D. Narkiewicz

Jan D. Narkiewicz is Chief Technical Officer at Software Pronto, Inc (jann@softwarepronto.com). Jan began his career as a Microsoft developer thanks to basketball star, Michael Jordan. In the early 90's Jan noticed that no matter what happened during a game, Michael Jordan's team won. Similarly, no matter what happened in technology Microsoft always won (then again this strategy is ten years old and may need some revamping). Clearly there was a bandwagon to be jumped upon. Over the years Jan managed to work on an email system that resided on 17 million desktops, helped automate factories that make blue jeans you have in your closet (trust me you own this brand) and kept the skies over the Emirate of Abu Dhabi safe from enemy aircraft. All this was achieved using technology such as COM/DCOM, COM+, C++, VB, C#, ADO, SQL Server, Oracle, DB2, ASP.Net, ADO.Net, Java, Linux and XML. In his spare time Jan is Academic Coordinator for the Windows curriculum at U.C. Berkeley Extension, teaches at U.C. Santa Cruz Extension, writes for ASPToday, and occasionally plays some football (a.k.a soccer).

J. Michael Palermo IV

J. Michael Palermo IV is currently a consultant for Cunningham Consulting – a Microsoft GOLD Certified Partner. His passions for technology are XML, SQL Server, ASP, and the upcoming .NET framework. He is an MCT, MCSE, MCDBA, and MCSD. In his spare time he enjoys coral reef aquariums.

I really want to thank the Wrox team for giving me the opportunity to contribute to such an exciting project. I also want to thank my wife Toshia for the sacrifices she made during my 'disappearances' from the family.

Jon D. Reid

Jon is the Chief Technology Officer for the database and development toolmaker, Micro Data Base Systems, Inc. (www.mdbs.com). He is the editor for the C++ and Object Query Language (OQL) components of the Object Data Management Group (ODMG) standard, and has contributed to previous Wrox titles including *Professional SQL Server 2000 Programming* and *Professional Windows DNA 2000 Development*. When not working, writing, or bicycling, he enjoys spending time with his wife and two young sons.

Darshan Singh

Darshan Singh is a Senior Developer with InstallShield Software Corp., where he works with DigitalWizard team to build Internet software using ATL/COM+ and XML. In the course of his professional career he has worked for Microsoft, Talisma, PSPL (India), and Spectrum (India), with major focus on database and component technologies.

Darshan also manages XML community Web site: www.PerfectXML.com and can be reached at darshan@PerfectXML.com.

I would like to thank my parents without whom I would have never been able to achieve what I have today. I must also thank my beloved wife, Satwant – I simply love her smile. Big thanks to wonderful team at Wrox: James Robinson, Avril Corbin, Beckie Stones, Kate Hall, and Rob Hesketh.

Brian Smith

Brian Smith is currently working as Chief Technical Architect for Tempo Ltd, an independent electrical retailer in the UK. He has been a professional software developer for more years than he cares to mention, first catching the 'bug' writing assembly language diagnostic code for the Intel 8080 8-bit micro-processor. He has been a VB and SQL Server developer for 10 years, and considers that the life of a developer has never been more interesting, stimulating, or rewarding than at present.

He is an avid cinema goer, and a keen amateur photographer, although he says that the invention of Photoshop has made this particular pursuit as much a desk-bound activity as an outdoor one (but better than being locked in a smelly darkroom!).

Writing for this book has been an interesting and intensive experience. I'd chiefly like to thank my wife Moira for persevering with my vacant moods, and my dog Sam for being such an appreciative participant in our discussions on form and content while we trudged through the soggy Surrey countryside.

Karli Watson

Karli Watson is an in-house author for Wrox Press with a penchant for multicolored clothing. He started out with the intention of becoming a world famous nanotechnologist, so perhaps one day you might recognize his name as he receives a Nobel Prize. For now, though, Karli's computing interests include all things mobile, and upcoming technologies such as C#. He can often be found preaching about these technologies at conferences, as well as after hours in drinking establishments. Karli is also a snowboading enthusiast, and wishes he had a cat.

Thanks go to the Wrox team, both for helping me get into writing, and then dealing with the results when I started. Finally, and most importantly, thanks to my wife, Donna, for continuing to put up with me.

Carvin Wilson

Carvin Wilson owns a small software consulting company in Gig Harbor, WA specializing in Component Object Model, Visual Basic, SQL Server, Access, server-side Web programming, .NET, and Delphi. He has worked with Microsoft and Borland technologies for nearly 10 years. He freely gives his advice and opinions to anyone who will listen. You can visit Carvin's web site at www.harborviewsolutions.com.

Warren Wiltsie

Warren is currently an Adjunct Professor of Computer Science at Fairleigh Dickinson University where he has taught computer science courses for over 18 years. His current focus is on developing and teaching Graduate-level course on Internet programming topics. Prior to his retirement from AT&T, Warren held a number of positions in the technology areas including managing the UNIX System V Technical Support organization, auditing the networks and systems within AT&T, running MS NT-based client-server systems for Internal Audit department, and introducing Web-based applications into Internal Auditing.

Thanks to Avril, Kate, and Rob at Wrox for helping a first-time author, the technical reviewers for their insightful and positive comments, and my wife Diane who has put up with the "I go can't gos" and the "I don't have time to do its" over the years.

Table of Contents

Introduction

One of the biggest new features of SQL Server 2000 is that it provides direct integration with XML. Microsoft has recognized that the next generation of Web and Enterprise applications will use XML to provide their data transfer functionality and, consequently, is keen to incorporate XML into SQL Server.

The standard SQL Server 2000 install includes the following XML features:

- The `FOR XML` clause in `SELECT` statements
- `OPENXML`
- XML Views

The World Wide Web Consortium (W3C) is creating standards for XML related technologies so rapidly now that Microsoft has resorted to releasing updates to SQL Server 2000 over the Web. In mid February 2001, Microsoft announced the XML for SQL Server Web Release 1. This increases SQL Server's XML abilities substantially, providing the following additional functionality:

- Updategrams
- XML Bulkload

At the end of April, just as this book was going to press, Microsoft released Beta 1 of XML for Microsoft SQL Server 2000 Web Release 2. This web release largely increases SQL Server's support for XSD schemas.

What's Covered in this Book

We will start with an introduction to XML to bring you up to speed with the technology if you are a novice, or to give you a recap if you have some XML experience.

Chapter 2 gives quick examples of SQL Server's standard XML functionality.

Chapter 3 covers the `SELECT` command's `FOR XML` clause. `FOR XML` allows us to produce XML documents from our relational database tables by adding as few as eleven characters to the end of our query. `RAW`, `AUTO`, and `EXPLICIT` sub-clauses provide increasing control over the level of structure within the XML output. We also examine how to produce XML schemas and how to handle binary data.

Chapter 4 looks at the reverse process – extracting relational data from XML documents using `OPENXML`. The resultsets produced can be used in exactly the same way as standard SQL Server resultsets such as tables or views. We have the ability to control the final structure of the `OPENXML` resultset, and can use it to update or delete records from the database.

XDR schemas are covered in Chapter 5. These enable us to structure XML documents and control the data types used within them. They also allow us to retrieve results through HTTP requests, avoiding the need to establish explicit connections to SQL Server.

Chapter 6 covers XSD schemas and compares them with XDR schemas. XSD is a platform independent W3C standard for XML schemas, which provides wider functionality than XDR. Microsoft is already rushing to incorporate XSD into SQL Server 2000, as reflected in Web Release 2.

XML views and templates are examined in Chapter 7. XML views provide a way of describing how a SQL Server table looks from an XML standpoint. XML templates give us the ability to standardise queries and enhance security.

Chapter 8 looks at XPath. A limitation of XML is that it is impossible to navigate through or query an XML document with XML alone. XPath is a navigational query language specified by the W3C for locating data within XML documents.

Updategrams are installed with Web Release 1 and are covered in Chapter 9. They consist of blocks of special XML tags that describe what the data looks like now and what we want it to look like once the Updategram is executed. They enable us to seamlessly and transparently update our database in real-time over HTTP, with minimal programming and maximum performance.

Chapter 10 describes XML Bulk Load, another addition from Web Release 1. XML Bulk Load enables the quick and efficient import of potentially millions of records into the database from XML documents.

These ten main chapters are followed by five case studies which should give you some good ideas as to how all this XML functionality can be incorporated into your SQL Server projects. Finally, we round off the book with three appendices. Appendix A describes how to configure virtual directories, Appendix B looks at the XML View Mapper, and Appendix C details what's provided in Web Release 2.

Who is this Book For?

This book is for developers with experience of SQL Server 2000, and T-SQL in particular.

XML experience would be beneficial, although Chapter 1 is aimed at those who are complete novices in this area.

What You Need to Use this Book

For the main book, you will need:

- SQL Server 2000.
- XML for SQL Server Web Release 1. Chapter 9 explains how to download this.
- Microsoft XML View Mapper 1.0. Appendix B describes from where this can be downloaded.

For the case studies, you will require VB 6, ASP, C++ 6 and C#. Note, though, that the case studies are not central to the book itself.

Source Code

The complete source code from the book is available for download at: http://www.wrox.com.

Conventions

To help you get the most from the text and keep track of what's happening, we've used a number of conventions throughout the book.

For instance:

> **These boxes hold important, not-to-be forgotten information that is directly relevant to the surrounding text.**

The background style is used for asides to the current discussion.

As for styles in the text:

- When we introduce them, we **highlight** important words.
- We show keyboard strokes like this: *Ctrl-A*.
- We show filenames and code within the text like so: `SELECT *`
- Text on user interfaces and URLs is shown like this: Menu.

We present code in several different ways. Definitions of methods and functions are shown as follows:

```
OPENXML(iDoc int [in],RowPattern nvarchar[in],[Flags byte[in]])
[WITH (SchemaDeclaration | TableName)]
```

Example code is shown like so:

```
In our code examples, the code foreground style shows new, important,
    pertinent code...
While code background shows code that's less important in the present context,
    or code that has been seen before.
```

Customer Support

We want to know what you think about this book: what you liked, what you didn't like, and what you think we can do better next time. You can send your comments, either by returning the reply card in the back of the book, or by e-mail (to feedback@wrox.com). Please be sure to mention the book title in your message.

Errata

We've made every effort to make sure that there are no errors in the text or the code. However, to err is human and, as such, we recognize the need to keep you informed of any mistakes as they're spotted and corrected. Errata sheets are available for all of our books at http://www.wrox.com. If you find an error that hasn't already been reported, please let us know.

E-mail Support

If you wish to directly query a problem in the book with an expert who knows the book in detail, then e-mail support@wrox.com with the title of the book and the last four numbers of the ISBN in the subject field of the e-mail. A typical e-mail should include the following things:

- The **name**, **last four digits of the ISBN**, and **page number** of the problem in the Subject field.
- Your **name**, **contact info**, and the **problem** in the body of the message.

We *won't* send you junk mail. We need the details to save your time and ours. When you send an e-mail, it will go through the following chain of support:

- Customer Support – Your message is delivered to our customer support staff who are the first people to read it. They have files on the most frequently asked questions and will answer anything general immediately. They answer general questions about the book and the web site.
- Editorial – Deeper queries are forwarded to the technical editor responsible for that book. They have experience with the programming language or particular product and are able to answer detailed technical questions on the subject. Once an issue has been resolved, the editor can post the errata to the web site.
- The Authors – Finally, in the unlikely event that editors can't answer your problem, they will forward the request to the author. We try to protect the author from any distractions from writing. However, we are quite happy to forward specific requests to them. All Wrox authors help with the support on their books. They'll mail the customer and the editor with their response, and again all readers should benefit.

P2P.WROX.COM

For author and peer support, join the SQL Server mailing lists. Our unique system provides **programmer to programmer™ support** on mailing lists, forums, and newsgroups – all *in addition* to our one-to-one e-mail system. Be confident that your query is not just being examined by a support professional, but by the many Wrox authors and other industry experts present on our mailing lists. At p2p.wrox.com, you'll find a number of different lists aimed at SQL Server programmers that will support you, not only while you read this book, but also as you develop your own applications.

Why this System Offers the Best Support

You can choose to join the mailing lists or you can receive them as a weekly digest. If you don't have the time or facility to receive the mailing list, then you can search our online archives. Junk and spam mails are deleted, and your own e-mail address is protected by the unique Lyris system. Any queries about joining or leaving lists, or the lists in general, should be sent to listsupport@p2p.wrox.com.

1

An Introduction to XML

Since computing began, there has been a need to exchange data. In the past people have used many different formatting techniques, usually specialized to the specific application. Other applications running on different operating systems often found this formatting indecipherable. There is nothing inherently wrong with this approach, and there are certainly situations when a proprietary data exchange format could be the best choice.

However, there are times, particularly in enterprise scale applications, where there is an attractive alternative. Having a well-defined specification for data formatting can make things a lot easier in large teams of developers, where complex exchange schemes may increase development times dramatically. In addition, further development of so-called "legacy" code becomes easier if it is simpler to come to grips with an application and its data exchanges. There are many techniques we can use to achieve these rather general aims, and one that has received universal acclaim in recent years is the use of **XML**, or the **eXtensible Markup Language**.

XML is a specification created by the W3C (the World Wide Web Consortium, http://www.w3c.org/) in 1998 in an effort to standardize text markup. It is, in fact, a subset of SGML – Standard Generalized Markup Language, detailed in ISO 8879 published in 1986 – but is much simpler and requires no knowledge of this standard. Perhaps the best way to explain what is meant by the term "text markup" is to consider an annotated section of text:

> Earlier in the day Jenkins had met Smith in Fenchurch Street. He was a tall man with striking features and eyes that always seemed to be looking at you in an unnerving way. The spark of devious intelligence was obvious, and most people quickly learned to choose their words with care around him. Not Jenkins, though, who had discovered his weakness. He had always carried a bar of chocolate with him when he knew he would encounter this strange individual.
>
> Now, Smith was dead. It was up to Jenkins to find out how – and why.

If this paragraph were to appear on a piece of paper, it would be possible to "mark up" the text:

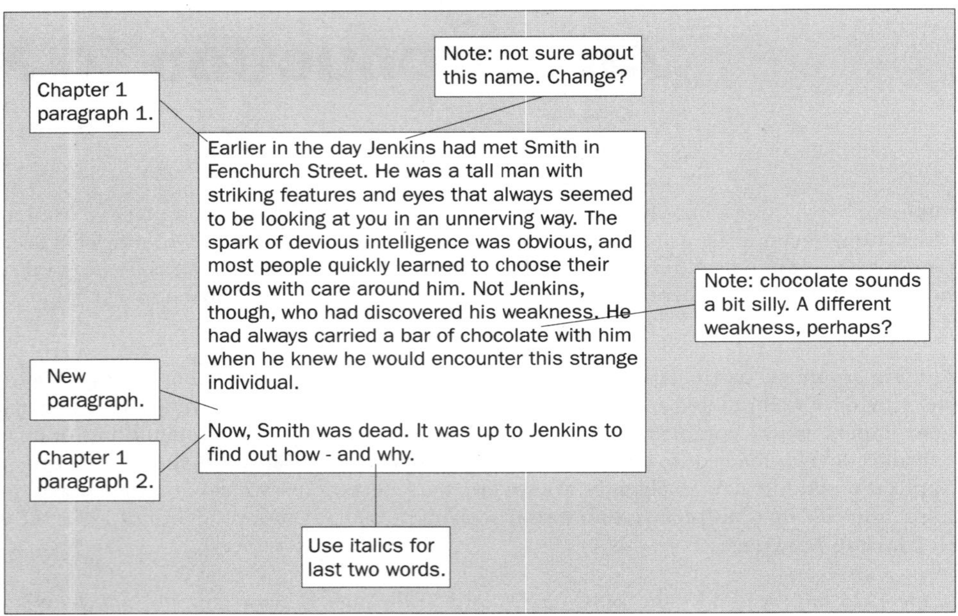

In a markup language it is possible to do this sort of thing in-line with the text, such that extra information is encapsulated along with it. HTML is an excellent example of this, where the text for display in a browser is often contained with all the information concerning how to display it in a single file. For example, to write the last two words of the above example in italics using HTML, we'd simply enclose them in opening and closing `<I>` tags:

```
Now, Smith was dead. It was up to Jenkins to find out how - <I>and why</I>.
```

The second tag starts with a forward slash (/) character to signify that it is a closing tag. Using this syntax, an appropriately capable text reader – such as an HTML browser – can render the text, including the additional information it contains.

XML is similar to HTML, although there is an important difference. HTML is intended for display purposes – text formatting, embedded graphics etc. XML is intended purely to give structural and contextual information concerning the data it contains. This shift in emphasis makes it ideal for exchanging data in a standard manner, though it is possible for XML to be used in a more traditional text markup way, as we will see later.

In this chapter, we will look at:

- The basics of XML
- The Document Object Model representation of an XML file
- Creating XML files according to a defined grammar using DTDs and schemas
- XML namespaces
- The basics of transforming XML using XSLT
- Using XML for data storage as opposed to text markup

The Basics of XML

In this section, we'll introduce the syntax of XML along with the rules we must obey, and discuss the difference between text and data storage in more detail.

XML Documents

XML files are known as **documents** and they consist of the following sections:

- An optional **XML declaration** to say that the document *is* XML, along with the version of XML being used, character encoding type, and possibly some additional information if required.
- An optional **document type definition** (**DTD**), detailing the structure of the XML document and what syntax is allowed. DTDs may be specified internally or consist of a reference to an external specification.
- The document body.

The declaration will usually look something like:

```
<?xml version="1.0"?>
```

This is an example of a processing instruction – a specialized form of tag that is enclosed in `<?` and `?>` delimiters and is intended to give instructions to processing applications. Here we are just saying that we're using XML version 1.0 (currently the only option, but this is subject to later expansion). The method of specifying this version information involves the use of an **attribute** called `version`. We'll discuss attributes in more detail in a moment.

For now we'll skip the DTD section of the file, and come back to this later in the chapter. In order to explain DTDs it is necessary to understand the structure of XML documents in more detail.

The document body consists of a single **document element** (or **root element**). There must be one and only one root element.

XML documents can be viewed in two ways: by a human in a text editor etc., or by an application. When an application loads an XML document it is usually **parsed**, which means that it will undergo several checks to make sure that it is OK. In the next sections we will take a closer look at the pieces that make up an XML document and the rules that we must conform to for a parser to accept our documents.

To start with, let's take a closer look at what we mean by an element.

Elements

In XML terms an **element** consists of a start tag delimiter, element contents, and an end tag delimiter. Both start and end tag delimiters look similar to HTML tags in that they consist of text enclosed in *greater than* and *less than* symbols (< and >), with an additional forward slash at the start of the end tag (/>). Each element must be complete, which (with the exception of empty elements, see below) means that each start tag *must* be matched with an end tag. The name of the element is used in both start and end tags for additional characterization, placed just inside the tags. For example, an element might look like the following:

```
<MyElement>
   ...
</MyElement>
```

Elements can contain any of the following:

- Other elements
- Text data
- A mix of the above

In addition, an element may be **empty** – that is, it can contain nothing. Such elements may still represent information via attributes, as we will see in the next section, but may also simply be structural in nature. Empty elements may be expressed using start and end tags as normal, but may also use the shorthand empty element syntax, which consists of a single tag with a forward slash at the end, for example:

```
<IAmEmpty/>
```

Note that elements *cannot* overlap. That is to say that if one element contains the start tag of another element then it must also include the end tag for that element. This is different to HTML, where it is possible to overlap elements like so:

```
This text is a mix of normal, <I>italic and <B>bold italic</I></B> text.
```

This would result in an error in XML.

Elements that are contained by other elements are said to be **nested**. In addition, elements are often referred to as **children**, **parents**, or **siblings** of other elements, which simply represents their relative position in the **document hierarchy**. This is illustrated by the following structure:

```
<Element1>
   <Element2>
      <Element3/>
   </Element2>
   <Element4>
      <Element5/>
   </Element4>
</Element1>
```

Here, `<Element2>` has `<Element1>` as a parent, `<Element3>` as a child, and `<Element4>` as a sibling.

Attributes

Elements may also include **attributes** in their start tag, which are name-value pairs. We specify these by a name followed by an *equals* sign (=) then a value in quotes (single or double, the choice is often determined by the value content such that if a single quote exists in the content, then double quotes will be used to delimit it, and vice versa). For example:

```
<MyElement myAttribute1="myValue1" myAttribute2="myValue2">
   ...
</MyElement>
```

Names in XML

The names of attributes and elements must follow these rules (making up XML **names**):

- The first character must be a letter or underscore character
- Subsequent characters may be letters, underscores, numbers, dots, or dashes

Valid names include:

```
_Person
Root-Element
Section42
```

Invalid names include:

```
69Dude
-F1
```

Note also that XML names are *case sensitive.* That is to say that it is possible to have different elements named `<Book>` and `<book>` in the same document – although this may not be desirable.

Comments

It is possible to place comments in XML documents much like you would in a programming language such as C++. Comments are intended to provide information for a human reader, not to give any information to an application using XML. Comment syntax in XML is identical to that in HTML, and looks like the following:

```
<!-- Comment Text -->
```

Everything between the opening `<!--` and the closing `-->` is ignored by the parser, even if these tags are on different lines.

Comments may be placed outside of the root element (but not before the XML declaration, which must be the first thing in an XML file), allowing global level descriptive text if required.

Note that comments are also parsed in an XML document. This means that excessive amounts of lengthy comments could potentially cause a performance hit. However, this doesn't mean you should avoid comments completely, merely that you should use them judiciously and keep them short. Well commented documents definitely have their advantages when human consumption is required.

Special Characters

By now it has become obvious that certain characters in XML have a specific meaning to parsers, such as < and >. The question therefore arises, "How do we use these characters in text?" We have two options. We can either use **character references** or **CDATA sections**.

Character references are sequences of characters that will be interpreted by the parser as other characters. The following table lists those available:

Character Reference String	Resultant Character
`&`	&
`>`	>
`<`	<
`'`	'
`"`	"

All of these references start with an "&" and end with a ";". They are, in fact, a special case of XML **entities** (which we'll look at in more detail later). The above table shows only the small set of named characters available – it is possible to use the more general form enabling characters from the complete ISO\IEC 10646 character set. To do this, we build up our character reference by starting with "&#", typing the number of the character in the character set (in hexadecimal if desired, specified with a preceding "x" character), and then adding a closing ";". For example, the text content:

```
You &amp; me are &#3C; him.
```

would be parsed as:

```
You & me are > him.
```

Alternatively, we can specify explicitly that a region of text does not contain anything that should be interpreted as markup by using CDATA sections. This involves enclosing text in "<![CDATA[" and "]]>" delimiters. Anything after the first of these will be interpreted exactly as-is, with the single restriction that we mustn't include the string "]]>" because this sequence is considered to end the CDATA block. For example:

```
<![CDATA[You &amp; me]]>
```

would be parsed as:

```
You &amp; me
```

Example

As an example, consider the following XML document, which conforms to all the rules we've seen so far:

```
<?xml version="1.0"?>
<!-- Here is a comment outside the root element -->
<MyRootElement>
   This is some text inside the root element.
   <MyContainedElement myAttribute="myValue">
      This text is inside an element contained by the root.
   </MyContainedElement>
   Here is some more text inside the root element.
   <MyEmptyElement myOtherAttribute="myOtherValue"/>
   <!-- Here is a comment in the root element -->
</MyRootElement>
```

To summarize:

- There is a *single* root element, `<myRootElement>`
- The root element may contain a mix of text and other elements, and none of the elements overlap
- Every element is complete, either using start and end tags, or being empty
- All names used (for elements and attributes) are valid

A document that conforms to these rules is known as a **well-formed document**.

DOM Representation

The structure of XML is hierarchical and it is often necessary to take this into consideration at a fundamental level. One such conceptual representation of this, known as the **Document Object Model** (**DOM**), involves looking at an XML document as a set of **nodes** in a tree. Nodes might be elements, attributes, text nodes, comments, or processing instructions.

In the DOM model there is a single node known as the **document node** that contains everything in an XML document. This is *not* the same thing as the document *element* in our XML document, which is contained inside the document node at the same hierarchical level as the XML declaration, etc.

Using the DOM concept we can represent the XML document in our last section graphically, as follows:

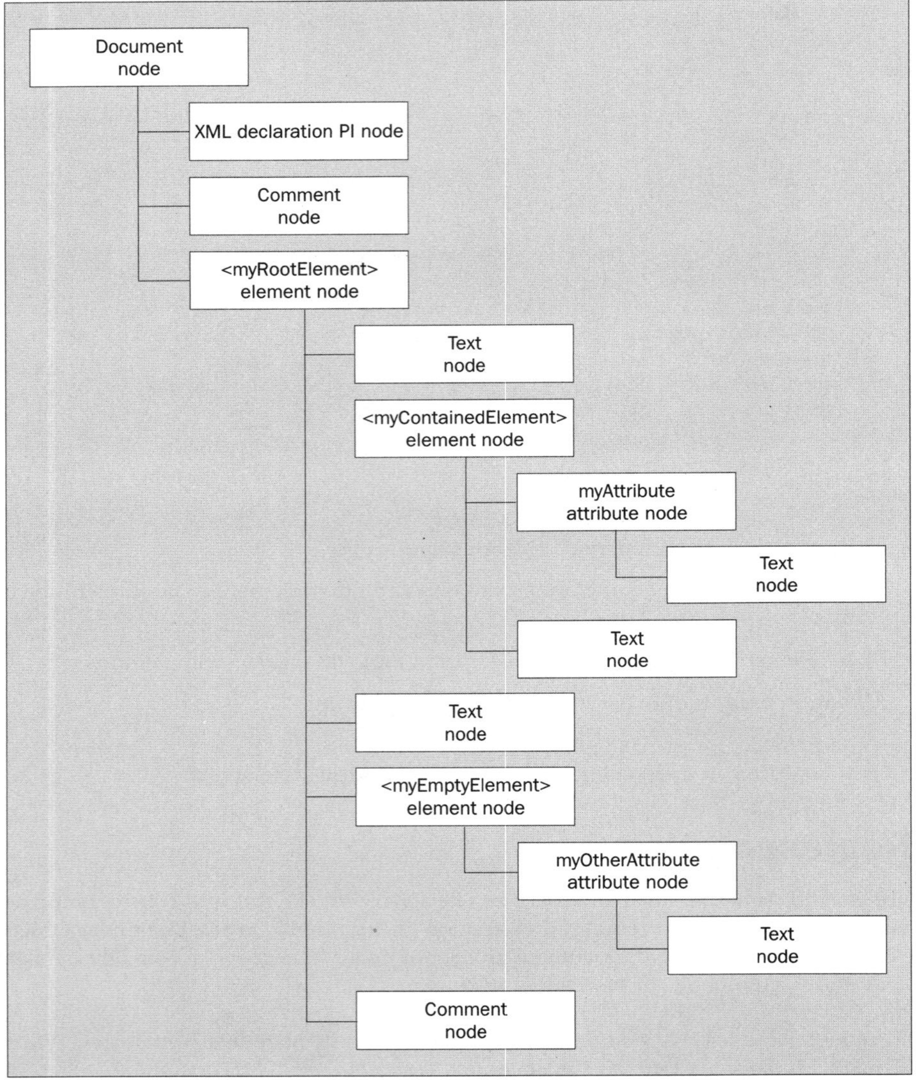

This visualization will become important later on, when we look at XSLT.

Document Order

Note that the DOM representation of an XML document preserves document order. This means that nodes in the tree structure represent the document exactly, such that we can refer to elements via their names or via their positions (for example, "the second element child of `<myRootElement>`").

Note that this ordering doesn't apply to attributes – we cannot assume that the order of attributes in an element will be preserved as this behavior is not included in the XML specification.

Valid XML

All the XML we have seen so far in this chapter has been well-formed XML. This means that the XML document complies with all the syntactical rules of XML and may be understood by a parser. In this section, we will consider **valid** XML, which is not the same thing.

Valid XML is well-formed XML that conforms to an additional set of rules, which may be specified in the XML document or elsewhere. A **validating parser** is a parser that is capable of checking that these additional rules have been kept to, and rejecting XML documents that fail this check.

The concept of valid XML is an important one. Simply knowing that an XML document we obtain from a business partner is well-formed is not enough. Let's say that we ask for a document showing customer details, and obtain the following:

```
<Customers>
   <Customer>
      <Name>Billy Robertson</Name>
      <Age>13</Age>
      ...
   </Customer>
   ...
</Customers>
```

Another partner might send the following:

```
<Customers>
   <Customer>
      <FirstName>Billy</FirstName>
      <LastName>Robertson</LastName>
      <Age>13</Age>
      ...
   </Customer>
   ...
</Customers>
```

These are both well-formed XML documents, but they may take some effort to reconcile. If we validate these documents by providing rules as to how the XML should be structured, we can avoid this problem. In effect we say something like "<Customer> elements must include complete names in <Name> elements", thus invalidating the second document above. However, we can do this in a far more rigid way than simply phoning up our partners and telling them rules.

Currently, there are two widely accepted ways of specifying XML validation rules:

- **Document Type Definitions** (**DTDs**)
- **XML Schemas**

In the next two sections we'll look at these methods.

Document Type Definitions (DTDs)

DTDs, often referred to as **doctypes**, consist of a series of declarations for elements and associated attributes that may appear in the documents they validate. If this target document contains other elements or attributes, or uses included elements and attributes in the wrong way, then validation will fail. In effect, the DTD defines a *grammar* for the documents it validates.

DTDs may either be stored internally as part of the XML document or externally in a separate file, accessible via a URL. A DTD is associated with an XML document by means of a `<!DOCTYPE>` declaration within the document. This declaration specifies a name for the doctype (which should be the same as the name of the root element in the XML document) along with either a URL reference to a remote DTD file, or the DTD itself.

> *It is possible to reference both external and internal DTDs, in which case the internal DTD is processed first, and duplicate definitions in the external file may cause errors.*

To specify an external DTD we use either the `SYSTEM` or `PUBLIC` keyword as follows:

```
<!DOCTYPE docTypeName SYSTEM "http://www.somewhere.com/docTypeFile.dtd">
```

Using `SYSTEM` as shown above allows the parser to load the DTD from the specified location. If we use `PUBLIC` then the named DTD should be one that is familiar to the parser being used, which may have a store of commonly used DTDs. In most cases, we'll want to use our own and use `SYSTEM`. This method enables the parsing application to make its own decisions as to what DTD to use, which may result in a performance increase. However, specific implementation of this is down to individual parsers, which might limit the usefulness of this technique.

Internal DTDs are enclosed in square brackets:

```
<!DOCTYPE docTypeName [ ... ]>
```

The syntax for the DTD, whether it is external or internal, is identical, with the exception that external DTDs may have conditionally processed sections. However, these are rarely used and we won't look at them here.

Element Definitions

DTDs allow element definitions to specify what content a given element can have, using `<!ELEMENT>` declarations. In general, element content will fall into one of the following four categories:

- **Empty** – the element cannot contain any content
- **Element** – the element contains other elements
- **Mixed** – the element contains other elements and/or text data
- **Any** – the element may contain anything

Elements that are empty or can contain anything may be specified using the `EMPTY` or `ANY` keywords in the following way, respectively:

```
<!ELEMENT emptyElementName EMPTY>
<!ELEMENT anyContentElement ANY>
```

Mixed and element content elements require a slightly more in-depth assignment. Basically, we list each of the children that the element can have either by element name (for element children) or #PCDATA for text. The simplest way to do this is to specify a list of children separated by commas, for example:

```
<!ELEMENT myElement (myChild1, myChild2)>
```

This would mean that <myElement> must have two children, <myChild1> and <myChild2>, in the order specified. We can declare a mixed content element in the same way:

```
<!ELEMENT myMixedElement (myChild1, #PCDATA, myChild2)>
```

Here there must be text in between <myChild1> and <myChild2> in the content of <myMixedElement>.

In addition to declaring a set list of children using commas, we can use the | operator to specify that one of a selection of elements is allowed, for example:

```
<!ELEMENT myElement (myChild1 | myChild2)>
```

This means that <myElement> may contain a single <myChild1> element *or* a single <myChild2> element.

There are times when we need to specify how many times an element should occur in the child list of its parent element. DTD syntax includes three **cardinality operators** that may be applied to elements to specify this:

- ? to specify that a child appears either once or not at all
- * to specify that a child can appear any number of times (including not at all)
- + to specify that a child appears any number of times except not at all

For example:

```
<!ELEMENT myElement (myChild1+ | myChild2*)>
```

This means that <myElement> can contain either one or more <myChild1> elements or zero or more <myChild2> elements.

There are limitations in this system. We can't specify a minimum amount of children other than zero or one, for example, and we can't specify an upper amount other than infinite. This is one of the problems addressed by XML schemas.

> *For more information on DTDs, see* Beginning XML *by David Hunter et al. (Wrox Press, ISBN 1861003412)*

XML Schemas

As an alternative to DTDs, we can use XML schemas to define the structure of XML files. XML schemas are a more recent addition to the XML toolkit, and address many of the failings of DTDs. In particular:

- Schemas are written in XML, so it is not necessary to learn a completely different syntax to use them
- Schemas provide many more powerful techniques for building structures, particularly with the use of **types** to simplify situations when standard structures are desired
- Schemas allow for extra flexibility in cardinality, and are not limited to the three operators used in DTDs
- Schemas allow data typing of elements

The schema specification on the W3C web site (http://www.w3c.org) is currently a Proposed Recommendation, dated March 2001, and contains three parts. The first is a primer explaining the purpose of schemas and how they differ from DTDs, the second details how XML structural information is defined, and the third discusses data types.

The schemas specification is very complex, and we would not do it justice if we tried to go through even the key points here. We will examine schemas in detail in Chapters 5 and 6. Note, though, that the data type portion of the schema specification will come in handy when moving data from databases into XML, as it allows us to restrict values in the same way as the database does, so that a suitably validated XML document could be placed into a database without fear of values being lost or changed in the process.

Namespaces

XML namespaces allow documents to make use of names from multiple DTDs and/or schemas at the same time. They also allow for name qualification, such that identical names in different DTDs or schemas may be differentiated.

As an example, consider two DTDs for product list XML files, one for rodents and one for computer equipment. Both of these DTDs might include an entry for a `<Mouse>` element. Here is the relevant section from `Rodents.dtd`:

```
<!ELEMENT Mouse EMPTY>
<!ATTLIST Mouse
   name         CDATA                                  #Required
   age          CDATA                                  #Required
   color        CDATA (white | brown | pink | gray)    #Required
>
```

And here is the section from `ComputingEquipment.dtd`:

```
<!ELEMENT Mouse EMPTY>
<!ATTLIST Mouse
   manufacturer IDREF                                  #Required
   model        CDATA                                  #Required
   modelID      ID                                     #Required
>
```

Another XML document, perhaps an invoice, might want to reference products using both of these DTDs. The question arises: how?

Namespaces provide the solution by associating elements with DTDs and schemas, for example. We do this using the xmlns attribute, which may be applied to any element. For example, to associate an <Invoice> element with Rodents.dtd we might write the following:

```
<Invoice xmlns="Rodents.dtd">
   ...
</Invoice>
```

All elements within this element will then have access to names in Rodents.dtd so, if we had a <Mouse> element here it would be defined by the entry in this DTD.

In the more general case, we can associate name prefixes with namespaces. The following code creates two name prefixes, rodent and comp, referring to our two DTDs:

```
<Invoice xmlns:rodent="Rodents.dtd"
         xmlns:comp="ComputingEquipment.dtd">
   ...
</Invoice>
```

If we want to use names from these namespaces we must use their **fully qualified** version, which simply involves using the name prefix followed by a colon, followed by the name:

```
<Invoice xmlns:rodent="Rodents.dtd"
         xmlns:comp="ComputingEquipment.dtd">
   <rodent:Mouse name="Jerry" age="1 year" color="gray"/>
   <comp:Mouse manufacturer="manufacturer0001" model="Stupidimouse MkIV"
               modelID="mouse0001"/>
</Invoice>
```

Note that xmlns declarations have a limited scope: they are only valid for the element that they are applied to and any elements contained thereof. Elements further out of the hierarchy than <Invoice> will not have access to the rodent and comp namespaces.

If a namespace contains global attributes (possible in schemas, but not in DTDs) then we can also use qualified names for these, to apply them to any elements where the namespace is in scope. For example, let's say we had a schema containing the global attribute color. We could use it as follows:

```
<Products xmlns:global="http://www.wrox.com/schemas/global/">
   <Item type="cube" global:color="yellow"/>
   ...
</Products>
```

XML for Data

In this book, we are primarily concerned with XML as a means of exchanging data. In contrast, many XML applications are used in the more traditional markup way as text annotation. A good example of this is XHTML, which is basically a modified version of HTML that complies with the XML standard. A section of XHTML might read:

```
<html>
   <h1>My Page</h1>
   <br/>
   Welcome one and all! <b>This</b> is the page you've been looking for!
</html>
```

The exact arrangement of data within this file is important. Changing the order of contained elements and text nodes could destroy the result of processing the file:

```
<html>
   is the page you've been looking for!
   <h1>My Page</h1>
   <b>This</b>
   <br/>
   Welcome one and all!
</html>
```

XML files used for data are often a lot more forgiving. With the following document:

```
<Invoice>
   <Originator name="Bob"
               address="addr1"
               phone="555-1234"/>
   <Items>
      <Item ID="item001"
            category="car"
            description="Big blue gas guzzler."
            costUSD="15000"
            catalogReference="CAR00042"/>
      <Item ID="item002"
            category="furniture"
            description="Black leather recliner."
            costUSD="45"
            catalogReference="CHR00321"/>
   </Items>
</Invoice>
```

rearranging the nodes doesn't change the information contained, and processing applications should work fine:

```
<Invoice>
   <Items>
      <Item ID="item002"
            category="furniture"
            description="Black leather recliner."
            costUSD="45"
            catalogReference="CHR00321"/>
      <Item ID="item001"
            category="car"
            description="Big blue gas guzzler."
            costUSD="15000"
            catalogReference="CAR00042"/>
   </Items>
   <Originator name="Bob"
               address="addr1"
               phone="555-1234"/>
</Invoice>
```

Data Points

Note that the sample document above uses attributes to represent data points, that is, the actual data information in the document as opposed to its structure. It would be equally possible to modify the structure to use elements:

```
<Invoice>
   <Originator>
      <Name>Bob</Name>
      <Address>addr1</Address>
      <Phone>555-1234</Phone>
   </Originator>
   <Items>
      <Item>
         <ID>item001</ID>
         <Category>car</Category>
         <Description>Big blue gas guzzler.</Description>
         <CostUSD>15000</CostUSD>
         <CatalogReference>CAR00042</CatalogReference>
      </Item>
      <Item>
         <ID>item002</ID>
         <Category>furniture</Category>
         <Description>Black leather recliner.</Description>
         <CostUSD>45</CostUSD>
         <CatalogReference>CHR00321</CatalogReference>
      </Item>
   </Items>
</Invoice>
```

This document contains exactly the same information, although formatted in a different way. Let's take a brief look at the issues and considerations involved with **element-centric** versus **attribute-centric** forms.

To start with, although rearranging the above document does not change the information stored in any way, it could cause problems in applications that address data points by their position (for example, requesting the third child of the second `<Item>` element). A rearrangement here could break such a routine. Using attributes for data makes things a bit easier, as the order of attributes is completely arbitrary (no XML addressing system can ask for "the third attribute of X", for example). In addition, using ID attributes also allows easy selection of different elements.

Attributes also have the advantage that they can be "typed" more easily than elements. It is possible to restrict permissible attribute values to an enumerated set. This might be useful in some data storage applications involving user input, for example.

If you do decide to use an attribute data point model you may find that your data maps better into databases, as structure and content are kept separate. When you have some structural elements (such as `<Item>` above) and some data point holding elements (such as `<Description>` above) it can become slightly more confusing to store.

In addition, using attribute storage can result in smaller documents, as fewer elements are required.

However, using attributes might make transformations (see the next section) more awkward, should they be required, as the syntax for addressing attributes is slightly more convoluted.

Having said all this, there are no earth-shattering arguments one way or the other. In most cases, the choice of whether to represent data points as elements or attributes is a purely personal one.

Using XSLT to Transform XML

Using DTDs and schemas to rigidly structure XML documents is all very well, but the case often arises where business partners (or even other departments in your enterprise) might represent the same data in a different way, as we saw earlier. In situations like this, it is not always desirable (or even possible) to reconcile differences and for multiple parties to agree on the same structure. Even if a compromise is reached, there is still the problem of converting existing data to different structures.

Luckily there is a technique that comes to our rescue. One of the W3C specifications concerns **XSL**, or **eXstensible Stylesheet Language**, which provides ways to transform XML either from one structure to another, or into a rendition language such as HTML. There are two XSL approaches for dealing with these conceptually different issues. The first of these, XSLF (XSL Formatting), is intended purely to convert XML into formatting objects, which can then be converted into a rendition format, such as HTML or PDF. The other XSL technique, and the one that is more relevant to us, is XSLT (XSL Transformations).

XSLT is capable of transforming XML into a different structure using a supplied stylesheet. The end result of this transformation may be XML, but might also be plain text, HTML, or anything else you'd like to format. In fact, XSLF makes use of XSLT to perform some of its formatting magic.

In this section, though, we'll concentrate on transforming XML into other XML vocabularies.

How XSLT Works

XSLT works using the DOM structure of an XML document, as detailed earlier in this chapter. To start with, source XML is loaded into a **source node tree** and the XSLT stylesheet (which is also written in XML) is loaded into a **stylesheet node tree**. These are then combined to create a **result node tree**. The combination involves a series of **templates** in the stylesheet, each of which tells the XSLT processor how to reformat a node from the source node tree into the result node tree.

Each template in the stylesheet matches one or more nodes in the source node tree. This matching, as we will see shortly, uses **XPath** syntax (detailed later in this book, but we'll see enough of the basics to use it here). XSLT processing commences with the processor looking for a template that matches the document node of our source XML (remember that the document node is *not* the same thing as the document element of the source XML document – the document node contains the whole XML document, including the XML declaration etc.). The template for the document node will then start to write nodes into the result node set, which may involve applying other templates along the way.

Once all templates have been applied, the result node tree is completed and may be saved to disk. Note that this isn't the same thing as saying, "Once all nodes in the source tree have been transformed". It is often the case that we will only use sections of the source tree nodes, filtering out the information we require.

XSLT Elements

Now we've had a brief overview of the process, let's take a look at the structure of XSLT stylesheets.

As mentioned above, XSLT stylesheets are written in XML. As such, they all start with the standard XML declaration:

```
<?xml version="1.0"?>
```

Next we have the root element for the stylesheet:

```
<xsl:stylesheet version="1.0"
                xmlns:xsl="http://www.w3.org/1999/XSL/Transform">
   ...
</xsl:stylesheet>
```

This element, taken from the xsl namespace declared here, simply specifies the XSLT version to use, which will always be 1.0 for now.

Inside this element, we specify the output format for the result node tree. For structural XML transformations, this will always be XML:

```
   <xsl:output method="xml"/>
```

The rest of the stylesheet will consist of <xsl:template> elements containing the templates to be used in the transformation. Each of these templates has a match attribute that specifies, in XPath syntax, the node(s) to match. In general, the first template will be the one matching the root element, using the simple XPath expression "/". For example:

```
   <xsl:template match="/">
      ...
   </xsl:template>
```

Within this template, we can specify literal XML to output, such as:

```
   <xsl:template match="/">
      <Invoice>
         <Item ID="CAR0001"/>
      </Invoice>
   </xsl:template>
```

It would be perfectly legal to use the above code as a complete XSLT transformation, although it wouldn't be that useful. Regardless of the source XML, the following would appear in the result tree:

```
<?xml version="1.0"?>
<Invoice>
   <Item ID="CAR0001"/>
</Invoice>
```

There are many more elements and constructs that we can use in XSLT to make things more interesting. The purpose of this chapter is to give more of an overview than a complete reference, so perhaps the best way to illustrate more of the features of XSLT is to give an example and discuss it.

An XSLT Example

Consider the two different invoice structures shown in the last section, one of which used attributes for data points, while the other used element-centric content. Let's imagine that our company uses attributes and we would like to read in an invoice using element content supplied by a partner. One way of doing this would be to use the following XSLT stylesheet to convert the XML into our desired format:

```
<?xml version="1.0"?>
<xsl:stylesheet version="1.0"
                xmlns:xsl="http://www.w3.org/1999/XSL/Transform">

   <xsl:output method="xml"/>

   <xsl:template match="/">
      <Invoice>
         <xsl:apply-templates select="//Originator"/>
         <Items>
            <xsl:apply-templates select="//Item"/>
         </Items>
      </Invoice>
   </xsl:template>

   <xsl:template match="Originator">
      <Originator>
         <xsl:attribute name="name">
            <xsl:value-of select="Name"/>
         </xsl:attribute>
         <xsl:attribute name="address">
            <xsl:value-of select="Address"/>
         </xsl:attribute>
         <xsl:attribute name="phone">
            <xsl:value-of select="Phone"/>
         </xsl:attribute>
      </Originator>
   </xsl:template>

   <xsl:template match="Item">
      <Item>
         <xsl:attribute name="ID">
            <xsl:value-of select="ID"/>
         </xsl:attribute>
         <xsl:attribute name="category">
            <xsl:value-of select="Category"/>
         </xsl:attribute>
         <xsl:attribute name="description">
            <xsl:value-of select="Description"/>
         </xsl:attribute>
         <xsl:attribute name="costUSD">
            <xsl:value-of select="CostUSD"/>
         </xsl:attribute>
         <xsl:attribute name="catalogReference">
            <xsl:value-of select="CatalogReference"/>
         </xsl:attribute>
      </Item>
   </xsl:template>

</xsl:stylesheet>
```

The easiest way to test this out for yourself is to use the XT XSLT processor written by Jim Clark, available at http://www.jclark.com/xml/xt.html. If you do so, you should find that the end result is exactly what we were after.

Let's break it down and look at how it works. First off, the template that matches the document root:

```
<xsl:template match="/">
   <Invoice>
      <xsl:apply-templates select="//Originator"/>
      <Items>
         <xsl:apply-templates select="//Item"/>
      </Items>
   </Invoice>
</xsl:template>
```

Most lines of code here simply write XML directly into the result tree, but on two lines we use the `<xsl:apply-templates>` element. This tells the processor to apply templates to whatever nodes are specified using the `select` attribute, which provides an XPath selection. Here we simply name the elements we want to process using the XPath "`//`" operator, meaning "select all elements with this name in the whole source node tree". We can also use relative paths here, where the origin is the point in the source node tree where the XSLT processor is currently working. This is an important point – during the processing of any template, the XSLT is working at a certain point in the source node tree. This point is known as the **context**. The context is the document root during the processing of the document root template so, if we were to use relative addressing, we'd need to supply the following:

```
<xsl:template match="/">
   <Invoice>
      <xsl:apply-templates select="/Invoice/Originator"/>
      <Items>
         <xsl:apply-templates select="/Invoice/Items/Item"/>
      </Items>
   </Invoice>
</xsl:template>
```

This works just as well (you can think of these simple XPath expressions as if they were pathnames to a file), but involves more typing. However, this might be essential if there were multiple elements with the same name throughout the source document. There might be `<Item>` elements that are children of `<Originator>` for example – in which case, using "`//Item`" would select these as well.

Moving on, then, the first `<xsl:apply-templates>` element results in the processor trying to match `<Originator>` element nodes with a template. Further down we see the template found:

```
<xsl:template match="Originator">
   <Originator>
      <xsl:attribute name="name">
         <xsl:value-of select="Name"/>
      </xsl:attribute>
      <xsl:attribute name="address">
         <xsl:value-of select="Address"/>
      </xsl:attribute>
      <xsl:attribute name="phone">
         <xsl:value-of select="Phone"/>
      </xsl:attribute>
   </Originator>
</xsl:template>
```

This template writes out an <Originator> element and assigns several attributes to it using <xsl:attribute> elements. Each of these elements provides an attribute name using its name attribute, and attribute value via its contents. Here we are extracting the text content of named elements using <xsl:value-of> elements, each of which has a select attribute providing an XPath expression pointing to the required node. Note that we can use relative addressing here – the context in this template is the <Originator> node being processed, so writing "Name" is interpreted as "the <Name> child of the current context", that is, "the <Name> child of <Originator>".

This attribute adding process is repeated for each element that we wish to convert to an attribute. Then we close the <Originator> element and the template is complete.

The template matching <Item> elements works in exactly the same way.

We've barely scratched the surface of XSLT in this chapter. If you want to learn more about using it, please see *XSLT Programmer's Reference* (Wrox Press, ISBN 1861003129).

Summary

In this chapter we've looked at the basics of XML and some of the technologies surrounding it. In the rest of the book we will be making use of this knowledge and, in particular, drawing on and expanding the techniques presented here.

In the next chapter we'll look at how we can use XML alongside SQL Server, and summarize the available methods before going into more detail concerning their usage later in the book.

2

Overview of XML in SQL Server

In the last chapter we took a look at XML and some of its related technologies. In this chapter we'll start to look at the XML capabilities of SQL Server 2000. Specifically, we will look at:

- The `FOR XML` clause in `SELECT` statements
- Simple HTTP URL queries
- Updategrams
- XML Bulkload
- `OPENXML`

Some of these techniques are not available with the basic SQL Server 2000 install. Instead we need to install **XML for SQL Server 2000 Web Release 1**, which is available to download free of charge at http://msdn.microsoft.com/downloads/. For more on this, see Chapter 9.

Note also that many of the techniques require Internet Information Server 5 (IIS) or above to work. However, this should be a fairly standard installation package on the systems of users with SQL Server 2000, so we'll assume that IIS is being used throughout this chapter.

The FOR XML Clause

The most basic way of extracting XML data from SQL Server databases is to use the `FOR XML` clause with SQL queries. This instructs SQL Server that the response should be an XML document.

When we use this clause we also have to specify one of the following three modes to use:

- RAW – gives a simple XML result with little formatting
- AUTO – gets an XML result with more formatting options
- EXPLICIT – allows you to explicitly format the XML result returned

In the following sections we will look at the modes available in a bit more detail. The techniques developed here will be expanded on in Chapter 3.

RAW Mode

If we ask for RAW XML then we will get several <row> elements, each signifying a table row. These elements will have attributes for each column in the table containing data content.

For example, we could query the SQL Server Northwind database in the following way:

```
SELECT CategoryName,Description FROM Categories FOR XML RAW
```

This would return the following XML:

```
<row CategoryName="Beverages" Description="Soft drinks, coffees, teas, beers, and ales"/>
<row CategoryName="Condiments" Description="Sweet and savory sauces, relishes, spreads,
      and seasonings"/>

...

<row CategoryName="Produce" Description="Dried fruit and bean curd"/>
<row CategoryName="Seafood" Description="Seaweed and fish"/>
```

Some queries won't run properly in this mode. For example:

```
SELECT * FROM Categories FOR XML RAW
```

Results in:

Server: Msg 6829, Level 16, State 1, Line 1
"FOR XML EXPLICIT and RAW modes currently do not support addressing binary data as URLs in column 'Picture'. Remove the column, or use the BINARY BASE64 mode, or create the URL directly using the 'dbobject/TABLE[@PK1="V1"]/@COLUMN' syntax".

This is because the Picture field required extra processing, and not because of the * syntax which works in simpler situations.

As hinted at by the error report, in order to get this query to work for us, we need to use...

AUTO Mode

AUTO mode results in extra formatting being added to the resultant XML. The most noticeable result of this is that <row> elements are replaced by elements with context aware names. For example, running the first query from the last section in AUTO mode:

```
SELECT CategoryName,Description FROM Categories FOR XML AUTO
```

returns the following:

```
<Categories CategoryName="Beverages" Description="Soft drinks, coffees, teas, beers,
        and ales"/>
<Categories CategoryName="Condiments" Description="Sweet and savory sauces, relishes,
       spreads, and seasonings"/>
...
<Categories CategoryName="Produce" Description="Dried fruit and bean curd"/>
<Categories CategoryName="Seafood" Description="Seaweed and fish"/>
```

The only difference is that we have `<Categories>` elements – named by the table name – for each row, instead of `<row>` elements.

Using `AUTO` mode also allows extra processing, such as was required in the second example from the last section:

```
SELECT * FROM Categories FOR XML AUTO
```

This time we will get the following result:

```
<Categories CategoryID="1"
            CategoryName="Beverages"
            Description="Soft drinks, coffees, teas, beers, and ales"
            Picture="dbobject/Categories[@CategoryID='1']/@Picture"/>
...
```

This time, a series of URLs are generated that give us access to the binary content of the `Picture` column. We'll take a closer look at this and how we can use the returned URL later.

In most simple cases, `AUTO` mode provides as much functionality as we're likely to require, but we can also use...

EXPLICIT Mode

`EXPLICIT` mode allows us much more control over the formatting of the XML returned, but requires more complicated syntax to work, involving transforming the XML rows into **universal table** format. This special format allows you to specify exact nesting of elements and how data will be placed into attributes and/or elements.

For example, to replicate the behavior of one of the simple queries we saw above, we'd need to use the following query:

```
SELECT
   1            AS Tag,
   NULL         AS Parent,
   CategoryName AS [Category!1!CategoryName],
   Description  AS [Category!1!Description]
   FROM Categories
   FOR XML EXPLICIT
```

resulting in:

```
<Category CategoryName="Beverages"
          Description="Soft drinks, coffees, teas, beers, and ales"/>
...
```

The only difference here is that the `<Category>` element has been specifically named in the query.

XMLDATA and ELEMENTS Options

We can specify XMLDATA for any of the modes discussed above to view the schema created. For example, we could use it as follows:

```
SELECT CategoryName,Description FROM Categories FOR XML RAW,XMLDATA
```

This gives us the schema as follows:

```
<Schema name="Schema1"
      xmlns="urn:schemas-microsoft-com:xml-data"
      xmlns:dt="urn:schemas-microsoft-com:datatypes">
  <ElementType name="row" content="empty" model="closed">
    <AttributeType name="CategoryName" dt:type="string"/>
    <AttributeType name="Description" dt:type="string"/>
    <attribute type="CategoryName"/>
    <attribute type="Description"/>
  </ElementType>
</Schema>
<row xmlns="x-schema:#Schema1"
    CategoryName="Beverages"
    Description="Soft drinks, coffees, teas, beers, and ales"/>
...
```

This shows how each data column maps to an attribute in the XML data result we obtain, in terms of schemas (which we saw briefly in the last chapter). The schema is found between the opening and closing <Schema> tags. The remaining lines are produced as a result of the query.

If we are using AUTO mode we can change things a little and specify that the resultant XML should have data formatted in elements rather than attributes. We do this by using the ELEMENTS option. We can see this very well by combining it with the XMLDATA option:

```
SELECT CategoryName,Description FROM Categories FOR XML AUTO,XMLDATA,ELEMENTS
```

This time we see a different schema, as follows:

```
<Schema name="Schema1"
      xmlns="urn:schemas-microsoft-com:xml-data"
      xmlns:dt="urn:schemas-microsoft-com:datatypes">
  <ElementType name="Categories"
          content="eltOnly"
          model="closed"
          order="many">
    <element type="CategoryName"/>
    <element type="Description"/>
  </ElementType>
  <ElementType name="CategoryName"
          content="textOnly"
          model="closed"
          dt:type="string"/>
```

```
  <ElementType name="Description"
           content="textOnly"
           model="closed"
           dt:type="string"/>
</Schema>
<Categories xmlns="x-schema:#Schema1">
  <CategoryName>Beverages</CategoryName>
  <Description>Soft drinks, coffees, teas, beers, and ales</Description>
</Categories>
...
```

`CategoryName` and `Description` have both been formatted as elements instead of attributes.

Again, the `<Categories>` elements have been produced as a result of the query and are not a part of the schema.

HTTP Database Access

Another addition to SQL Server 2000 is the ability to perform queries via HTTP, simply by tagging them onto the end of URLs. We can also provide XPath queries in a similar way. It is not advisable to permit this in production level applications, however. This syntax allows any query to be executed, which is a potential security risk if the database is exposed over the Internet. It can be useful at design time to test things out, though.

As well as this simple URL access, it is possible to restrict the queries available to those stored in **template** files on the web server connected to the SQL Server instance being used. Templates also allow more freedom with the queries available and the formatting of results, as well as cutting down on the amount of typing that you have to do to execute identical queries multiple times. Templates can also be specified directly in the URL used to access the database, although this has the same security risks as simple HTTP queries.

One other thing that is possible using templates is the use of **updategrams** to modify data in a database. These are really extensions to the template syntax and work in much the same way. One slight difference, though, is the ability to specify updategram parameters that may be passed to an updategram file via the URL. Also, complete updategrams may be sent to the server using `HTTP POST`, although again, this may expose a security risk.

Simple HTTP URL Queries

Create a virtual directory called `northwind` that maps to the `Northwind` database using IIS Virtual Directory for SQL Server. In order to execute simple URL queries we need to configure our virtual directory to Allow sql=... or template=... URL queries, the first option on the Securities tab in the New Virtual Directory Properties window. Switching this option on automatically enables the second option, Allow posted updategrams, which will provide no additional security risk. However, this option can be enabled independently.

The name of this option pretty much gives away how this technique works. We simply specify a SQL query by appending it to a URL after sql=, or a template after template=.

For help in setting up the virtual directory and virtual names, please read Appendix A.

SQL Queries in URLs

If you have a virtual directory configured (as above) for the `Northwind` database, you should be able to execute a query as follows:

```
http://localhost/northwind?sql=SELECT+*+FROM+Categories+WHERE+CategoryID=1+FOR+
XML+AUTO
```

Here we have simply changed spaces into + signs and tagged the `sql=` query onto the URL as a query string parameter (which is why there is a `?` in the URL – anything placed after one of these is interpreted as a query string parameter). We can leave spaces as they are, but they get replaced with escape strings ("`%20`" for a space), which can make the URLs difficult to read.

You can try this out simply by typing it into the address bar of a web browser capable of viewing XML, such as Microsoft Internet Explorer 5 and above. This will give you the following:

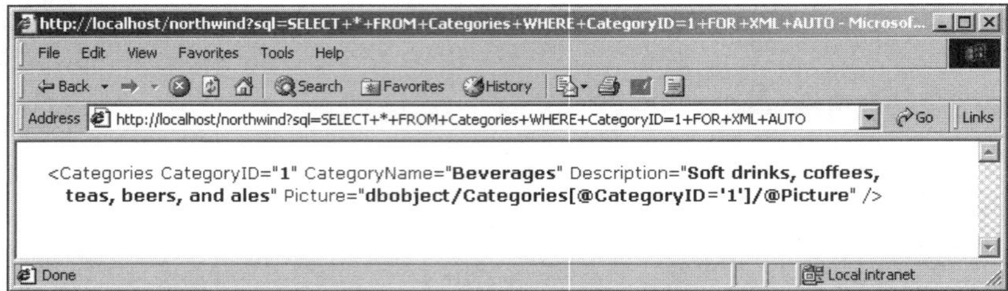

If you try a query that returns multiple rows (such as the above query without the `WHERE` clause) you may find that the XML isn't displayed. This is because, as we saw in the last chapter, well-formed XML requires one and only one root element. Multiple rows will result in several root elements, and a parsing error. Fortunately, there is a solution to this.

Specifying a Root Element

To specify a root element we add an extra parameter to our HTTP query: `root`. We can specify the name of the root element to use here. For example:

```
http://localhost/northwind?sql=SELECT+*+FROM+Categories+FOR+XML+AUTO&root=ROOT
```

Results in:

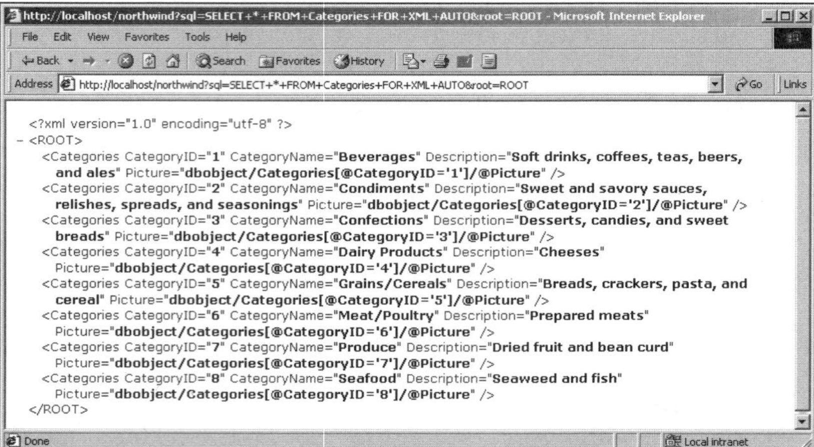

This solves the multiple root element problem.

It is well worth doing this if we use the XMLDATA option, as there will be at least one extra root level element if we don't.

Templates

If we want a more involved hierarchy, or a document that returns the result of several queries, we can use a template to format our results. We'll see templates used throughout the book and Chapter 7 is devoted to them, but we'll look at the basics here.

A template is basically an XML file with queries placed in <query> elements, which come from the urn:schemas-microsoft-com:xml-sql namespace. Within these elements we can place full SQL queries, and even insert the results of stored procedures.

The following is a simple template using a now familiar query:

```
<?xml version="1.0"?>
<Root xmlns:sql="urn:schemas-microsoft-com:xml-sql">
   <sql:query>
      SELECT * FROM Categories FOR XML AUTO
   </sql:query>
</Root>
```

This template instructs SQL Server to place the result of the query directly into the XML structure specified.

We can run this template by placing the whole thing in a URL, such as:

```
http://localhost/northwind?template=<Root+xmlns:sql="urn:schemas-microsoft-com:xml-sql"><sql:query>SELECT+*+FROM+Categories+FOR+XML+AUTO</sql:query></Root>
```

This quickly becomes difficult to understand, and suffers from the same security problems as running straight SQL queries in the same manner. It is usually better to store queries on the web server and call them as necessary.

In order to try this out, we need to do a little more configuration. First, we need to ensure that the Allow Template Queries option is enabled. We also need to create a **virtual name** that tells IIS and SQL Server where we have our templates stored. In effect, this is another virtual directory, just like the one we have set up for the database itself.

So, create a new subdirectory of the northwind database directory called templates, and then create a virtual name of type Template that points at it.

Once this is configured, saving the template file above as `template1.xml` in this new directory and pointing the browser at http://localhost/northwind/templates/template1.xml, will give us the following:

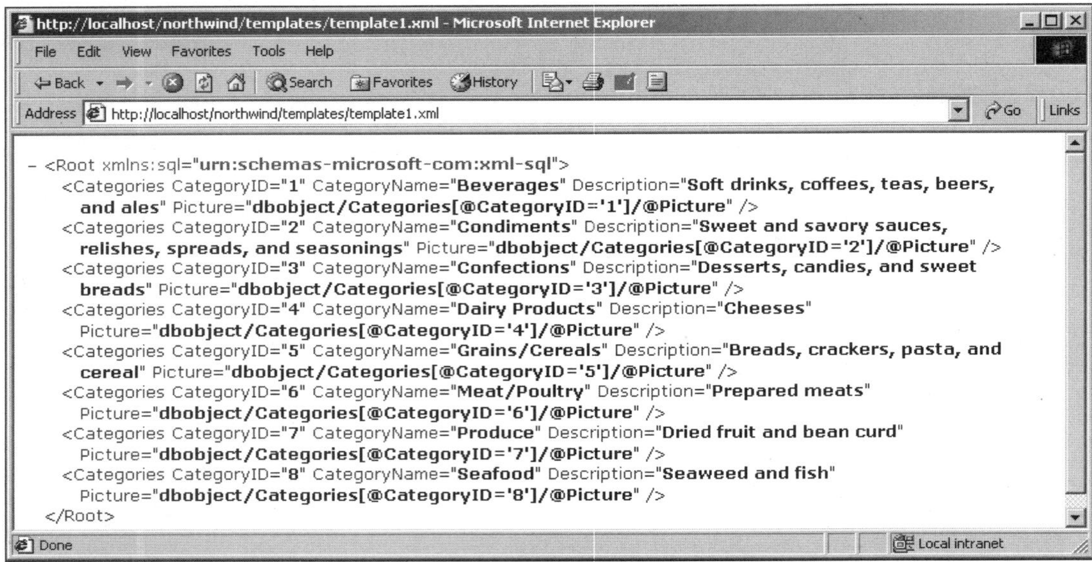

This is pretty much the same result we saw earlier, but with a lot less typing in the URL.

> *Note that using this technique may result in many template files on your server. It can be worth having multiple virtual names for template directories with common functionality, and it's certainly worth naming templates in a slightly more involved way than just "`templateX.xml`".*

As mentioned above, we can use templates to execute multiple queries, supplying structure for all of them. For example:

```
<?xml version="1.0"?>
<Root xmlns:sql="urn:schemas-microsoft-com:xml-sql">
   <CategoryList>
      <sql:query>
         SELECT CategoryName FROM Categories FOR XML AUTO
      </sql:query>
   </CategoryList>
   <ProductList>
      <sql:query>
         SELECT ProductName FROM Products FOR XML AUTO
      </sql:query>
   </ProductList>
</Root>
```

Save the above code as `template2.xml` and then navigate to it in IE. This will give us two recordsets nested in different regions of the resultant XML:

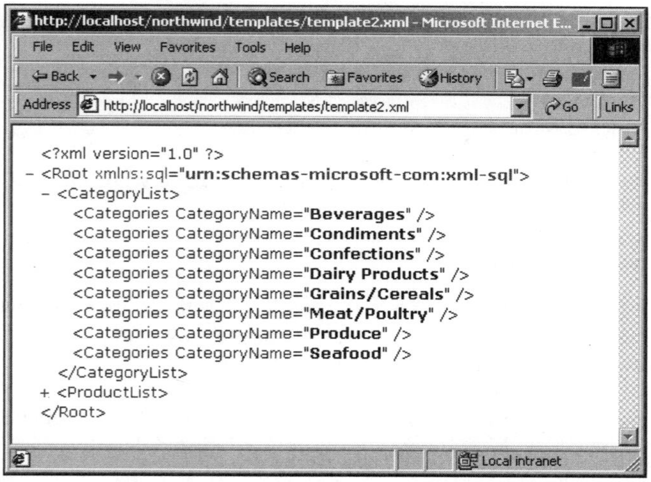

```
<?xml version="1.0" ?>
- <Root xmlns:sql="urn:schemas-microsoft-com:xml-sql">
  - <CategoryList>
      <Categories CategoryName="Beverages" />
      <Categories CategoryName="Condiments" />
      <Categories CategoryName="Confections" />
      <Categories CategoryName="Dairy Products" />
      <Categories CategoryName="Grains/Cereals" />
      <Categories CategoryName="Meat/Poultry" />
      <Categories CategoryName="Produce" />
      <Categories CategoryName="Seafood" />
    </CategoryList>
  + <ProductList>
  </Root>
```

Specifying Parameters for Templates

From the above discussion, it may seem that templates are basic static files which may not be that useful unless identical queries are run often. However, it is possible to pass parameters to templates, giving them more functionality but still restricting the operations that users can perform on your database.

To use a parameter in a template we need to declare it with a `<param>` element inside a `<header>` element in our template (both elements come from the namespace we saw earlier). We use the `name` attribute of `<param>` to name the parameter, and its contents to supply a default value to use if none is passed to the template. For example:

```
<?xml version="1.0"?>
<Root xmlns:sql="urn:schemas-microsoft-com:xml-sql">
   <sql:header>
      <sql:param name="ID">1</sql:param>
   </sql:header>
   ...
</Root>
```

Here we are specifying a parameter called `ID` with a default value of 1.

We can use parameters in our queries simply by typing the `@` character followed by the name of the parameter, for example:

```
<?xml version="1.0"?>
<Root xmlns:sql="urn:schemas-microsoft-com:xml-sql">
   <sql:header>
      <sql:param name="ID">1</sql:param>
   </sql:header>
   <sql:query>
      SELECT CategoryName FROM Categories WHERE CategoryID=@ID FOR XML AUTO
   </sql:query>
   <ProductList>
      <sql:query>
         SELECT * FROM Products WHERE CategoryID=@ID FOR XML AUTO
      </sql:query>
   </ProductList>
</Root>
```

Next, we just have to pass the parameter to the template and execute it. We can do this simply by using query string parameters in a URL, such that, if the above template were saved in our `templates` directory as `template3.xml`, we could use a URL like:

http://localhost/northwind/templates/template3.xml?ID=4

This shows us the relevant rows in `Categories` and `Products` where the `CategoryID` column is 4.

Updategrams

Updategrams are a special sort of template (covered in Chapter 9) that are specifically designed to add or modify data in a database. This is done in a very simple way using three elements from the urn:schemas-microsoft-com:xml-updategram namespace:

- `<after>` – specifies how the row to be modified should look after modification, or what data to place in a new row. May be empty if a row is being deleted.
- `<before>` – locates the row to be modified according to what data is in it before applying a modification. May be empty if a new row is being added.
- `<sync>` – parent tag for `<before>` and `<after>` pairs.

So, to add a row we provide an empty `<before>` element and an `<after>` element containing the row data to add, and to modify a row we specify its data before and after the modification. `<sync>` can contain multiple modifications, each specified using a pair of `<before>` and `<after>` elements.

For example, we could use the following updategram:

```
<?xml version="1.0"?>
<Root xmlns:udg="urn:schemas-microsoft-com:xml-updategram">
   <udg:sync>
      <udg:before>
      </udg:before>
      <udg:after>
         <Territories TerritoryID="44121"
                      TerritoryDescription="Birmingham (UK)"
                      RegionID="1"/>
      </udg:after>
   </udg:sync>
</Root>
```

This would add a new row to the `Territories` table in the `Northwind` database.

We can run this updategram in the same way as other templates by placing it in the `Templates` directory we created earlier and calling it by filename. We can also pass parameters to updategrams, although the syntax is slightly different:

```
<?xml version="1.0"?>
<Root xmlns:udg="urn:schemas-microsoft-com:xml-updategram">
   <udg:header>
      <udg:param name="TID"/>
      <udg:param name="TD"/>
      <udg:param name="RID"/>
   </udg:header>
```

```
    <udg:sync>
      <udg:before>
      </udg:before>
      <udg:after>
        <Territories TerritoryID="$TID"
                     TerritoryDescription="$TD"
                     RegionID="$RID"/>
      </udg:after>
    </udg:sync>
  </Root>
```

We place $ symbols in front of parameter names when we refer to them, instead of @ symbols. Other than that, everything works the same (note that no default values have been specified in the above example).

We would then access the above updategram using URL syntax, such as this, which would add one record:

http://localhost/northwind/templates/updategram1.xml?TID=44121&TD=Birmingham+(UK)&RID=1

The interpreter for `<before>` and `<after>` elements is quite versatile, and lets us specify data points as attributes or elements, so we could rewrite the above `<after>` element as:

```
      <udg:after>
        <Territories>
          <TerritoryID>$TID</TerritoryID>
          <TerritoryDescription>$TD</TerritoryDescription>
          <RegionID>$RID</RegionID>
        </Territories>
      </udg:after>
```

This would not affect the functionality of the updategram.

XPath Queries

Earlier on we saw that one of the values generated by an `AUTO` query looked like the following:

```
<Categories CategoryID="1"
       CategoryName="Beverages"
       Description="Soft drinks, coffees, teas, beers, and ales"
       Picture="dbobject/Categories[@CategoryID='1']/@Picture"/>
```

The `Picture` attribute looks like a very strange URL. In fact, it is a relative URL based on our `northwind` virtual directory that executes an XPath query. This isn't the place to get into XPath syntax (see Chapter 8), but let's look at how we can make the above string do something.

To execute XPath queries we need to create a new virtual name in the configuration tool that has the type **dbobject**. We can just call this `dbobject` for now, and we don't have to provide a path:

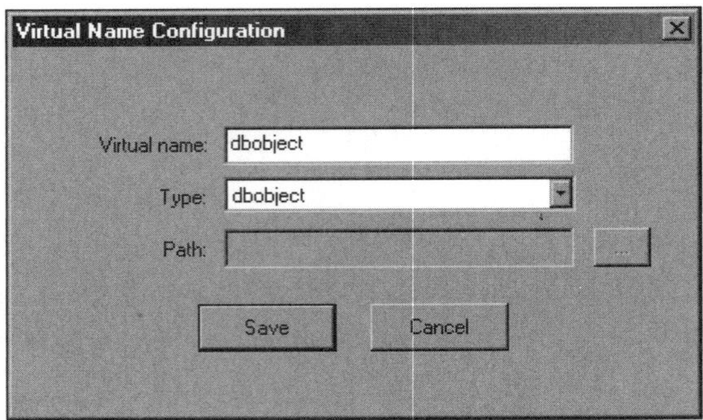

Once this is done, we can tag the above query onto a URL and see what happens:

http://localhost/northwind/dbobject/Categories[@CategoryID='1']/@Picture

On most computers, depending on your browser and helper applications, you should get the option to download a picture file, which looks like the following:

XPath queries can do more than just get binary data, though. For example:

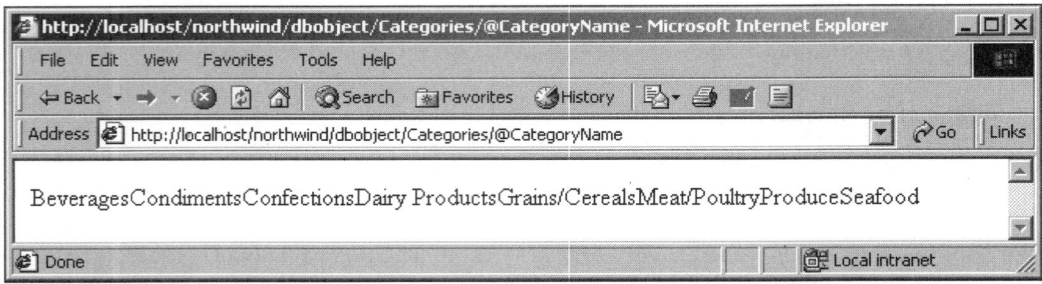

Here we have just obtained the text from all `CategoryName` values in `Categories`, as specified in the XPath structure at the end of the URL.

XML Bulkload

XML Bulkload is a technique that you can use to populate database tables with large amounts of data stored in XML files. This is something that you are likely to want to do on the server itself rather than over the Web, perhaps when you receive a large amount of data from a partner in XML format.

In order to achieve all this we need to make use of the `SQLXMLBulkLoad` object, which we can create from a scripting language such as VBScript as follows:

```
set BulkLoadObj = CreateObject("SQLXMLBulkLoad.SQLXMLBulkLoad")
```

Once we have this object we need to provide it with:

- Connection details so it has access to the SQL Server database to populate
- The XML containing the data to upload
- An annotated schema file detailing the mapping between the XML data and the database

There are many other options that we can use, but the above is all we need for a simple upload. For more details, see Chapter 10.

OPENXML

`OPENXML` is a new rowset accessor that enables XML data to be viewed and treated as a rowset. This means that we can execute queries against XML data as if it were already stored in a database. Using `OPENXML` is, again, quite programmatically intensive and so detailed coverage will be left to Chapter 4.

In an example application, we might load some XML data into memory, either straight from a disk or some other application, and then want to perform a query on it. To do this, we can execute a SQL query using the `OPENXML` clause. This clause is used in the place of a table name after the `FROM` clause, for example:

```
SELECT * FROM OPENXML(...)
```

The parameters of this clause enable us to specify some in-memory XML data, along with an XPath to provide an initial dataset within this data, and various other options.

One place where we might use `OPENXML` is in stored procedures using Transact-SQL.

Summary

In this chapter we've looked at some of the XML-specific tools available to us in SQL Server 2000 with the XML web release patch. The intention here has been to introduce some of the techniques before getting down and using them more intensively in the rest of the book. As has been pointed out in several places, many of these techniques would actually require a lot more space for a thorough treatment – so don't worry if you feel that you wouldn't be confident using them just yet.

We'll kick this process off in the next chapter, by spending some more time looking at the `FOR XML` clause in SQL queries.

SQL SQL SQL SQL SQL SQL SQL
XML XML XML XML XML

3
FOR XML

Rowsets have traditionally been returned by queries run against a SQL Server database. SQL Server 2000 provides a new mechanism that can be used to return XML as the result of a query, instead of a rowset. This mechanism is the SELECT command's FOR XML clause.

The FOR XML clause is powerful but, importantly, straightforward to use. Consider the following SELECT statement, which is executed against SQL Server's Northwind database:

```
SELECT * FROM Shippers FOR XML RAW
```

The results of this query (after adding a few carriage returns) are as follows:

```
<row ShipperID="1" CompanyName="Speedy Express" Phone="(503) 555-9831"/>
<row ShipperID="2" CompanyName="United Package" Phone="(503) 555-3199"/>
<row ShipperID="3" CompanyName="Federal Shipping" Phone="(503) 555-9931"/>
```

We have XML generation simply by typing in eleven extra characters after the query!

This chapter will present the various types of FOR XML clause. By fine-tuning the form of this clause, different styles of XML rowsets can be generated. This chapter will also present a comprehensive overview of the limitations and restrictions associated with the FOR XML clause.

It should be noted that all queries within this chapter will be executed against the Northwind database.

Using FOR XML with Query Analyzer

When executing queries that use the FOR XML clause, you will probably find it quite useful to adjust some of the default settings in SQL Server 2000's Query Analyzer.

First of all, XML is normally returned as a continuous string without carriage returns. The length of this row can easily exceed the default maximum number of characters, in which case Query Analyzer will truncate your results. Select Tools | Options and the Results tab. Change the Maximum characters per column value to a large number, say 8192.

It is also useful to change the Default results target setting in this window. The default is Results to Grid, which works well with tabular data. For XML, it is advantageous to change this setting to Results to Text:

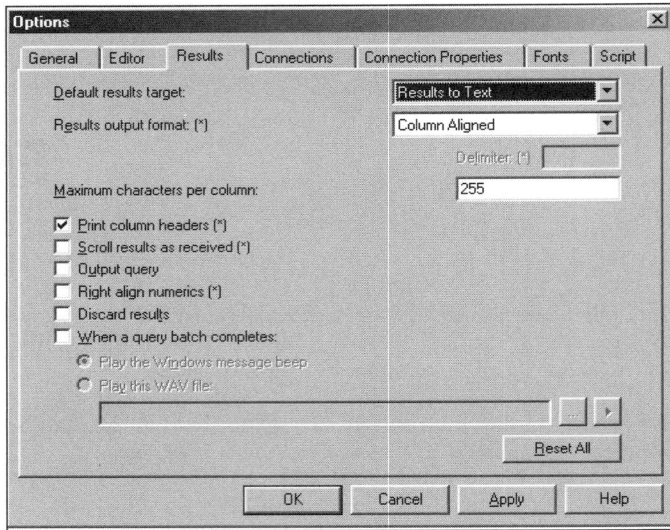

The query results shown in this chapter are not cut-and-pasted exactly from Query Analyzer. Carriage returns and spaces are added for readability and the superfluous text generated by Query Analyzer is removed. Consider the query that we have already executed, `SELECT * FROM Shippers FOR XML RAW`. In Query Analyzer, the result appears as follows:

```
XML_F52E2B61-18A1-11d1-B105-00805F49916B
----------------------------------------------------------------------------------------------------
<row ShipperID="1" CompanyName="Speedy Express" Phone="(503) 555-9831"/>
<row ShipperID="2" CompanyName="United Package" Phone="(503) 555-3199"/>
<row ShipperID="3" CompanyName="Federal Shipping" Phone="(503) 555-9931"/>

(3 row(s) affected)
```

Here, we are informed that three rows were affected. This will obviously vary depending on the modifications that you have already made to your database, so the number of rows affected will not be included with each example XML document shown in this chapter. Additionally, the first line of text returned (`XML_F52E...`) is also not directly germane to understanding FOR XML. This line is simply a GUID prefixed by the text XML_, and is actually a placeholder for the name of the column in the rowset returned by the FOR XML query.

The contents of this column and the rowset's single row *are* relevant to our discussion. The single row of the single column is the XML document in its entirety. The XML document contains (in attributes or elements) the name of columns associated with the query. The name of the rowset's lone column is actually arbitrary.

FOR XML Syntax

Here is the syntax of the `FOR XML` clause (remember that arguments in square brackets are optional):

```
FOR XML xmlmode [, XMLDATA] [, ELEMENTS] [, BINARY BASE64]
```

The arguments are defined as follows:

- *`xmlmode`* – an *`xmlmode`* must be associated with each `FOR XML` clause to specify the form of XML retrieved by the query. Valid values for *`xmlmode`* are:
  - `AUTO` – builds a tree based on the tables in the `FROM` clause
  - `EXPLICIT` – you specify the shape of the tree
  - `RAW` – resultset rows are mapped to elements with columns mapped to attributes
- `XMLDATA` – this argument causes the schema associated with the XML rowset to be returned. The schema is pre-pended to the returned XML rowset.
- `ELEMENTS` – when `ELEMENTS` is specified, the columns of the returned XML rowset are in the form of XML sub-elements. If `ELEMENTS` is not specified, the columns are in the form of XML attributes. The `ELEMENTS` argument may only be specified when the *`xmlmode`* is `AUTO`.
- `BINARY BASE64` – this argument dictates the form of the XML rowset when binary data is represented. When `BINARY BASE64` is specified, the binary data values are encoded as base64. If the *`xmlmode`* is either `EXPLICIT` or `RAW`, `BINARY BASE64` must be specified, but the argument is optional if the *`xmlmode`* is `AUTO`. In the latter case, not specifying `BINARY BASE64` causes binary data in the XML rowset to be represented by reference (URL-encoded data). Obviously, if no binary data is contained in the rowset, `BINARY BASE64` should not be specified.

FOR XML RAW

When the `RAW` `xmlmode` is specified, the XML rowset returned has the following form:

- Each row in the resultset is represented by an XML element named `row`.
- The column values associated with each row are represented by attributes. The exceptions to this are columns containing `NULL` values. `NULL` columns are not returned and no placeholders are provided.

Let's look at an example to better understand the `RAW` option:

```
SELECT CustomerID, Region FROM Customers WHERE CustomerID LIKE 'BO%'
```

This query returns the following rowset:

```
CustomerID    Region
------------- ----------
BOLID         NULL
BONAP         NULL
BOTTM         BC
```

Appending FOR XML RAW to the previous query generates the following XML resultset:

```
<row CustomerID="BOLID"/>
<row CustomerID="BONAP"/>
<row CustomerID="BOTTM" Region="BC"/>
```

Notice that each row is represented by an XML element named row. The non-NULL columns returned are represented by attributes: CustomerID and Region. For the customers with CustomerIDs of BOLID and BONAP, no Region attribute is returned because they have NULL values in the Region column of the Customers table.

Alias Names in FOR XML RAW Queries

Each attribute generated as part of a query containing FOR XML RAW is named after the corresponding column in the query. The column name given in the query is either the name of the corresponding column in the underlying table, or an alias name for the corresponding column. The following query demonstrates the use of alias names within a FOR XML RAW query:

```
SELECT ProductID AS ID, ProductName AS Name, UnitPrice AS Price
FROM   Products
FOR XML RAW
```

Here are the results:

```
<row ID="1" Name="Chai" Price="18.0000"/>
<row ID="2" Name="Chang" Price="19.0000"/>
<row ID="3" Name="Aniseed Syrup" Price="10.0000"/>

...

<row ID="75" Name="Rhönbräu Klosterbier" Price="7.7500"/>
<row ID="76" Name="Lakkalikööri" Price="18.0000"/>
<row ID="77" Name="Original Frankfurter grüne Soße" Price="13.0000"/>
```

We see that the use of column aliases has affected the attribute names. ProductID is now the ID attribute, rather than the default ProductID attribute. Likewise, we have Name and Price attributes instead of ProductName and UnitPrice attributes.

XMLDATA in FOR XML RAW Queries

Run the following query:

```
SELECT ProductID AS ID, ProductName AS Name, UnitPrice AS Price
FROM   Products
FOR XML RAW, XMLDATA
```

Here are the results:

```
<Schema name="Schema1" xmlns="urn:schemas-microsoft-com:xml-data"
                       xmlns:dt="urn:schemas-microsoft-com:datatypes">
      <ElementType name="row" content="empty" model="closed">
                 <AttributeType name="ID" dt:type="i4"/>
                 <AttributeType name="Name" dt:type="string"/>
                 <AttributeType name="Price" dt:type="fixed.14.4"/>
                 <attribute type="ID"/>
                 <attribute type="Name"/>
 <attribute type="Price"/>
      </ElementType>
</Schema>

<row xmlns="x-schema:#Schema1" ID="1" Name="Chai" Price="18.0000"/>
<row xmlns="x-schema:#Schema1" ID="2" Name="Chang" Price="19.0000"/>
<row xmlns="x-schema:#Schema1" ID="3" Name="Aniseed Syrup" Price="10.0000"/>

...

<row xmlns="x-schema:#Schema1" ID="77" Name="Original Frankfurter grüne Soße"
Price="13.0000"/>
```

Using XMLDATA causes the XML-Data schema to be pre-pended to the XML rowset returned by the query. Note that this will use more server resources than normal and may result in reduced performance.

The schema provides a definition of the data types for the elements returned by the query. This definition can be used to validate the data. The ID associated with the schema is Schema1 (the value of the name attribute for the <Schema> element).

The attribute and value xmlns="urn:schemas-microsoft-com:xml-data" specify the default schema for the <Schema> element. The attribute xmlns:dt specifies that dt is shorthand for the namespace urn:schemas-microsoft-com:datatypes. Notice that type information for each attribute in the query is specified using this shorthand notation (dt:type="i4", dt:type="string", and dt:type="fixed.14.4"). The namespace referred to by dt (urn:schemas-microsoft-com:datatypes) contains information used to validate the data types in the document. The types "string" and "i4" correspond to a string data type and a four byte integer, respectively. The type "fixed.14.4" specifies a fixed-point number with fourteen digits to the left of the decimal point and four digits to the right.

Each row in the resultset contains a default namespace x-schema:#Schema1. An astute observer would be concerned about collisions given that this namespace does not appear to be unique. Actually, the namespace used is of the form SchemaN. The first query executed using FOR XML with XMLDATA is named Schema1. Run the query again and you will see Schema1 becomes Schema2, and so on.

Retrieving Binary Data with FOR XML RAW

It is possible to retrieve binary data by using FOR XML RAW and specifying BINARY BASE64. Northwind's Category table contains a Picture column of type image. Run the following query:

```
SELECT CategoryID AS ID, CategoryName AS Name, Picture
FROM   Categories
FOR XML RAW, BINARY BASE64
```

The result of this query is a lot of base64-encoded data (Picture) and a little bit of ID and Name data. Notice once again that alias column names were used. An excerpt from the XML document generated by this query is as follows:

<row ID="1" Name="Beverages" Picture="FRwvAAIA ... ADHrQX+"/>
<row ID="2" Name="Condiments" Picture="FRwvAAI ... YXAgrQX+"/>
<row ID="3" Name="Confections" Picture="FRwvAAI ... AADhrQX+"/>
<row ID="4" Name="Dairy Products" Picture="FRwv ...

Here, the strings like "FRwvAAIA ... ADHrQX+" are reams of non-human-readable, base64-encoded data that represent the photo. One of the reasons why XML has gained such wide support is its readability. If the XML is to be read by humans, it is better (where possible) to generate a URL referring to the binary data instead of an illegible string. There are tradeoffs to be considered when base64 encoding is not used, as discussed below.

The following query uses the virtual name `dbobject` to retrieve the photo as a URL for each row of the `Categories` table:

```
SELECT CategoryID, CategoryName,
       'dbobject/Categories[@CategoryID='+CAST(CategoryID AS
       NVARCHAR (4000))+']/@Picture' Picture
FROM   Categories
FOR XML RAW
```

A portion of the XML document generated by the previous query is as follows:

<row CategoryID="1" CategoryName="Beverages"
    Picture="dbobject/Categories[@CategoryID=1]/@Picture"/>
<row CategoryID="2" CategoryName="Condiments"
    Picture="dbobject/Categories[@CategoryID=2]/@Picture"/>
<row CategoryID="3" CategoryName="Confections"
    Picture="dbobject/Categories[@CategoryID=3]/@Picture"/>

This XML snippet contains URL-encoded binary data, and is more human-readable than the previous query's illegible, base64-encoded data. Each `Picture` attribute contains a URL relative to the database's virtual root. In an XML document, base64 encoding allows simple transport of the binary content and not merely references to such content.

It must be recognized that the consumer of an XML document may not be able to resolve reference attributes. The reference generated requires access to an Internet Information Server (IIS) that has been correctly configured to access SQL Server (not all environments support this specific configuration).

Notice in the previous XML snippet that the consumer of the XML document requires knowledge of the database schema and clearly some form of access to the database. Using base64 encoding or references represents a classic dilemma for any designer – readability with significant restrictions (references) versus portability with increased size (base64 encoding). Most developers will likely choose base64 encoding because it generates the most portable form of XML document containing binary data.

> *Chapter 8 discusses XPath and linking to binary data in detail.*

FOR XML AUTO

Specifying AUTO as the *xmlmode* causes the resultset to be returned in the following form:

- Each table in the FROM clause of the query is represented in the XML resultset by an element. The name of this element corresponds to the name of the table or the table's alias if an alias is specified.
- By default, the column values are represented by attributes contained within the element corresponding to the column's table name. The name associated with this attribute is the name of the column, or the column's alias if an alias is specified.
- Column values can be returned as elements using the ELEMENT argument of the FOR XML clause. The column elements returned are nested within the element corresponding to the column's table. The name of a column's element is the same as the name of the column, or the column's alias if an alias is specified.

The following query demonstrates FOR XML AUTO:

```
SELECT Employees.EmployeeID, TerritoryID
FROM   Employees, EmployeeTerritories
WHERE  Employees.EmployeeID=EmployeeTerritories.EmployeeID
FOR XML AUTO
```

Here are the results:

```
<Employees EmployeeID="3">
    <EmployeeTerritories TerritoryID="30346"/>
    <EmployeeTerritories TerritoryID="31406"/>
    <EmployeeTerritories TerritoryID="32859"/>
    <EmployeeTerritories TerritoryID="33607"/>
</Employees>
<Employees EmployeeID="4">
    <EmployeeTerritories TerritoryID="20852"/>
    <EmployeeTerritories TerritoryID="27403"/>
    <EmployeeTerritories TerritoryID="27511"/>
</Employees>
<Employees EmployeeID="8">
    <EmployeeTerritories TerritoryID="19428"/>
    <EmployeeTerritories TerritoryID="44122"/>
    <EmployeeTerritories TerritoryID="45839"/>
    <EmployeeTerritories TerritoryID="53404"/>
</Employees>

...
```

Now, for a comparison, run the same query with RAW specified instead of AUTO. You will get the following:

```
<row EmployeeID="3" TerritoryID="30346"/>
<row EmployeeID="3" TerritoryID="31406"/>
<row EmployeeID="3" TerritoryID="32859"/>
<row EmployeeID="3" TerritoryID="33607"/>
```

```
<row EmployeeID="4" TerritoryID="20852"/>
<row EmployeeID="4" TerritoryID="27403"/>
<row EmployeeID="4" TerritoryID="27511"/>
<row EmployeeID="8" TerritoryID="19428"/>
<row EmployeeID="8" TerritoryID="44122"/>
<row EmployeeID="8" TerritoryID="45839"/>
<row EmployeeID="8" TerritoryID="53404"/>

...
```

In contrast to the RAW mode, the AUTO *xmlmode* addresses the need to represent the data in hierarchal form. Even so, AUTO does not produce a root node, so we still don't have a well-formed XML document.

Take a close look at the results from the AUTO query. The top element is an <Employees> element, which corresponds directly to the Employees table. Each column value selected from the Employees table is returned as an attribute of the <Employees> element – for example, EmployeeID="...". The second table that returns column data as part of the query is EmployeeTerritories. This data is contained in the <EmployeeTerritories> elements, which are sub-elements of <Employees>. Again, the column values associated with the EmployeeTerritories table are returned as attributes of the <EmployeeTerritories> elements – for example, TerritoryID="...".

AUTO mode also exploits the one-to-many relationship between the Employees and EmployeeTerritories tables. One <Employees> element contains many <EmployeeTerritories> sub-elements. If RAW mode had been used, the information for each employee would be duplicated for each employee territory. Consequently, the use of AUTO can reduce the size of the XML document generated. The issue at hand is hierarchy (AUTO mode) versus grid with data duplication (RAW mode).

If the columns in the query are reversed, the XML resultset returned is radically different. Try the following query:

```
SELECT TerritoryID, Employees.EmployeeID
FROM   EmployeeTerritories, Employees
WHERE  EmployeeTerritories.EmployeeID=Employees.EmployeeID
FOR XML AUTO
```

Now we get:

```
<EmployeeTerritories TerritoryID="30346">
    <Employees EmployeeID="3"/>
</EmployeeTerritories>
<EmployeeTerritories TerritoryID="31406">
    <Employees EmployeeID="3"/>
</EmployeeTerritories>
<EmployeeTerritories TerritoryID="32859">
    <Employees EmployeeID="3"/>
</EmployeeTerritories>
<EmployeeTerritories TerritoryID="33607">
    <Employees EmployeeID="3"/>
</EmployeeTerritories>
<EmployeeTerritories TerritoryID="20852">
    <Employees EmployeeID="4"/>
```

```
</EmployeeTerritories>
<EmployeeTerritories TerritoryID="27403">
    <Employees EmployeeID="4"/>
</EmployeeTerritories>
<EmployeeTerritories TerritoryID="27511">
    <Employees EmployeeID="4"/>
</EmployeeTerritories>
<EmployeeTerritories TerritoryID="19428">
    <Employees EmployeeID="8"/>
</EmployeeTerritories>

...
```

The top element of the altered query is `<EmployeeTerritories>` and each of these elements contains a single `<Employees>` element. This is because the XML resultset is formed through the many-to-one relationship between the `EmployeeTerritories` and `Employees` tables. The hierarchy in this case is not nearly as elegant. Consequently, be sure to take care when specifying the order of fields.

ELEMENTS in FOR XML AUTO Queries

The previous query can be modified to use the `FOR XML` option, `ELEMENTS`. This option causes the query's columns in the resulting XML document to be represented as XML elements rather than attributes. The modified form of the query is as follows:

```
SELECT Emps.EmployeeID AS EmpID, TerritoryID AS TerID
FROM   Employees AS Emps, EmployeeTerritories AS Territories
WHERE  Emps.EmployeeID=Territories.EmployeeID
FOR XML AUTO, ELEMENTS
```

A snippet from the XML document generated by this query is as follows:

```
<Emps>
    <EmpID>3</EmpID>
    <Territories>
        <TerID>30346</TerID>
    </Territories>
    <Territories>
        <TerID>31406</TerID>
    </Territories>
    <Territories>
        <TerID>32859</TerID>
    </Territories>
    <Territories>
        <TerID>33607</TerID>
    </Territories>
</Emps>
<Emps>
    <EmpID>4</EmpID>
    <Territories>
        <TerID>20852</TerID>

...
```

Alias Names in FOR XML AUTO Queries

Remember that XML documents generated by the AUTO *xmlmode* contain table names as elements and column names as attributes (default behavior) or elements (specifying the FOR XML ELEMENTS option). XML documents generated in RAW mode only contain column names as attributes.

This difference is significant when it comes to the use of aliases. An alias for a table produces an element with the alias's name when using AUTO mode. When RAW mode is used, each row of the resultset is referred to as element <row>, and an aliased table name is not reflected in the XML generated. Using AUTO mode, the alias for a column produces an attribute or element with the alias's name. Using RAW mode only generates attributes for each column but, again, this attribute would be named for the column name or the alias.

To demonstrate how a FOR XML AUTO query is affected by aliases, consider the following query:

```
SELECT Emps.EmployeeID AS EmpID, TerritoryID AS TerID
FROM   Employees AS Emps, EmployeeTerritories AS Territories
WHERE  Emps.EmployeeID=Territories.EmployeeID
FOR XML AUTO
```

The XML document generated from this query looks like this:

```
<Emps EmpID="3">
      <Territories TerID="30346"/>
      <Territories TerID="31406"/>
      <Territories TerID="32859"/>
      <Territories TerID="33607"/>
</Emps>
<Emps EmpID="4">
      <Territories TerID="20852"/>
      <Territories TerID="27403"/>
      <Territories TerID="27511"/>
</Emps>
<Emps EmpID="8">
      <Territories TerID="19428"/>
      <Territories TerID="44122"/>
      <Territories TerID="45839"/>
      <Territories TerID="53404"/>
</Emps>

...
```

Looking at these results, we see that the table alias Emps, which corresponds to the Employees table, is the outermost element. This is because data from this table is in the left-hand column of the resultset – the Query Analyzer identifies the Employees table in the SELECT before it identifies the EmployeeTerritories table.

The <Territories> child element is named with an alias and corresponds to the EmployeeTerritories table. Similarly, the EmpID attribute is named with an alias for the EmployeeID column, and the TerID attribute is named with an alias for the TerritoryID column.

A great many SQL developers are used to specifying terse aliases with respect to columns and tables, such as A, B, or C. Such aliases result in nearly unreadable XML documents because the elements and attributes of the document will be named A, B, and C. One of the ten tenets of XML, as listed at the W3C, is that, "Terseness in XML is of minimal importance".

We have already discussed why the outermost XML element is Emps and not Territories. A curious reader might wonder what would happen if the SELECT used a wild card (*) instead of specifying individual column names. Under such circumstances, the XML element hierarchy would be based on the column ordering generated by the Query Analyzer.

XMLDATA in FOR XML AUTO Queries

Any of the queries demonstrating FOR XML AUTO could have used the XMLDATA option. For example:

```
SELECT  Emps.EmployeeID AS EmpID, TerritoryID AS TerID
FROM    Employees AS Emps, EmployeeTerritories AS Territories
WHERE   Emps.EmployeeID=Territories.EmployeeID
FOR XML AUTO, ELEMENTS, XMLDATA
```

As we saw when reviewing FOR XML RAW, XMLDATA returns schema information for the XML resultset, pre-pended to the data. The question that remains is, "Is the use of XMLDATA a positive or a negative thing?" Clearly it is advantageous to ship the schema as part of an XML document. The schema allows the document's contents to be validated. Clearly the size of the XML document dictates the cost in pre-pending the schema. A schema of five thousand bytes, associated with an XML document containing a single element referring to a byte of data, might not be a good candidate for the XMLDATA option.

Retrieving Binary Data with FOR XML AUTO

It is possible to base64 encode binary data by using BINARY BASE64 with FOR XML AUTO. As we saw with the RAW mode, this produces long strings in the resultsets which are illegible to human readers. An alternative technique involves using the dbobject virtual name – references being used to specify the location of the binary data instead of including the data in encoded form. Consider the following query:

```
SELECT  CategoryID, CategoryName,
        'dbobject/Categories[@CategoryID='+CAST(CategoryID AS
        NVARCHAR (4000))+']/@Picture' Picture
FROM    Categories
FOR XML AUTO, ELEMENTS
```

In actual fact, this behavior – including a reference (**URL-encoding**) to binary objects rather than using base64-encoding – is encapsulated as the default behavior with FOR XML AUTO queries. The following query, which is far simpler to read, produces an identical XML document to the previous query:

```
SELECT  CategoryID, CategoryName, Picture
FROM    Categories
FOR XML AUTO, ELEMENTS
```

A portion of the XML that would be generated by either query is as follows:

```
<Categories>
      <CategoryID>1</CategoryID>
      <CategoryName>Beverages</CategoryName>
      <Picture>dbobject/Categories[@CategoryID=1]/@Picture</Picture>
</Categories>
<Categories>
      <CategoryID>2</CategoryID>
      <CategoryName>Condiments</CategoryName>
      <Picture>dbobject/Categories[@CategoryID=2]/@Picture</Picture>
</Categories>
<Categories>
      <CategoryID>3</CategoryID>
      <CategoryName>Confections</CategoryName>
      <Picture>dbobject/Categories[@CategoryID=3]/@Picture</Picture>
</Categories>

...
```

The readability of by-reference binary data should be weighed against portability of using `BINARY BASE64` to encode the data.

Restrictions When Using `FOR XML AUTO`

Restrictions must be taken into account when using `FOR XML AUTO` with:

- `GROUP BY` or aggregate functions
- Binary data
- Computed columns

Restrictions with `GROUP BY` or Aggregate Functions

> **The `FOR XML AUTO` mode does not support queries that contain `GROUP BY` or aggregate functions.**

Recall that aggregate functions take a set of data and generate a single value, and include such functions as `AVG`, `COUNT`, `MAX`, `MIN`, and `SUM`. The following query generates an error because of the use of `GROUP BY` and the aggregate function `SUM`:

```
SELECT Orders.OrderID AS OID, SUM(UnitPrice * Quantity) AS Costs
FROM   Orders, [Order Details]
WHERE  Orders.OrderID=[Order Details].OrderID
GROUP BY Orders.OrderID
ORDER BY Costs
FOR XML AUTO
```

By generating a temporary table, it is possible to work around this restriction and use aggregate functions with `FOR XML AUTO`. The previous query can be rewritten in order to generate a temporary table, `OrderTotals`:

```
SELECT OID, Costs FROM
   (SELECT Orders.OrderID AS OID, SUM(UnitPrice * Quantity) AS Costs
    FROM   Orders, [Order Details]
    WHERE  Orders.OrderID=[Order Details].OrderID
    GROUP BY Orders.OrderID) OrderTotals
ORDER BY Costs
FOR XML AUTO
```

The `GROUP BY` and `SUM` are associated with the generation of the temporary table, `OrderTotals`. The `FOR XML AUTO` clause works with `OrderTotals` and never sees either the `GROUP BY` or `SUM` – hence there is no error in executing this query. When a temporary table is generated, most database developers get nervous. This nervousness is because temporary tables incur overhead to the database engine and cause performance degradation. Performance aside, without the temporary table, the `FOR XML AUTO` would fail.

Restrictions with Binary Data

Including binary data by reference is a useful feature of `FOR XML AUTO`, but this feature does incur a set of subtle restrictions. Recall that each reference to binary data contains a URL relative to the database's virtual root. This URL contains the required information to retrieve the binary data, provided that IIS is set up accordingly to support this URL. The information in this URL includes:

- The name of the column associated with the binary image
- The primary key associated with the row containing the binary image

> **In order to provide the required information for the URL-encoding, it is imperative that the column containing the binary image is not referenced by an alias.**
>
> **Similarly, it is imperative that the table or view from which an image is retrieved contains a primary key.**

The alias restriction is quite straightforward. When a query uses an alias to specify a column, the alias exists for the life of the query. If an alias name were used to generate a reference, there would be no way to resolve this reference. The reference would not contain a valid column name but would instead contain an alias that was only valid in the context of the query which generated the alias name.

Let's look at the primary key restriction. It is possible to generate a view using a SQL statement that contains either `TOP` or `DISTINCT`. `TOP` (specifically `TOP n`) limits the number of rows in the view to `n`. `DISTINCT` removes duplicate entries from the view. In either case, the primary key associated with the view's underlying table(s) is not retained, and attempting a query using `FOR XML AUTO` on such a view results in an error. This is a limitation to `FOR XML AUTO` and the best plan is simply to avoid this situation because there is no magical work-around. To further clarify, consider the following view, created using a `SELECT` statement that contains `TOP 5`:

```
CREATE VIEW BestWorkers AS
  SELECT Top 5 EmployeeID, FirstName, LastName, HireDate, Photo
  FROM   Employees
  ORDER BY HireDate DESC
```

The BestWorkers view contains a binary column, Photo. The following query results in an error because there is no primary key associated with the BestWorkers view:

```
SELECT Top 1 EmployeeID GoodByeID, FirstName, LastName, HireDate, Photo
FROM   BestWorkers
ORDER BY HireDate DESC
FOR XML AUTO
```

If, in the previous query, the Employees table is named instead of the BestWorkers view, the FOR XML AUTO query would succeed because its primary key is intact (the Employees table has a primary key called EmployeeID).

Restrictions with Computed Columns

Computed columns present an interesting issue with respect to FOR XML AUTO. Each computed column must have a name associated with it. The following query fails because there is no name associated with the computed column:

```
SELECT CompanyName, ContactTitle + ' ' + ContactName, OrderID
FROM   Customers, Orders
ORDER BY Companyname
FOR XML AUTO
```

Adding AS ComboName results in the following query, which can be successfully executed:

```
SELECT CompanyName, ContactTitle + ' ' + ContactName AS ComboName, OrderID
FROM   Customers, Orders
WHERE  Customers.CustomerID=Orders.CustomerID
ORDER BY Companyname
FOR XML AUTO
```

A portion of the XML document returned by this query is as follows:

```
<Customers CompanyName="Alfreds Futterkiste"
           ComboName="Sales Representative Maria Anders">
    <Orders OrderID="10643"/>
    <Orders OrderID="10692"/>
    <Orders OrderID="10702"/>
    <Orders OrderID="10835"/>
    <Orders OrderID="10952"/>
    <Orders OrderID="11011"/>
</Customers>
<Customers CompanyName="Ana Trujillo Emparedados y helados"
           ComboName="Owner Ana Trujillo">
    <Orders OrderID="10308"/>
    <Orders OrderID="10625"/>

...

<Customers CompanyName="Wolski Zajazd"
           ComboName="Owner Zbyszek Piestrzeniewicz">
```

```
    <Orders OrderID="10374"/>
    <Orders OrderID="10611"/>
    <Orders OrderID="10792"/>
    <Orders OrderID="10870"/>
    <Orders OrderID="10906"/>
    <Orders OrderID="10998"/>
    <Orders OrderID="11044"/>
</Customers>
```

The computed column is placed as an attribute of the innermost element of the document when the attribute's value is computed. In this case, the innermost element is `Customers` when the `ComboName` attribute is computed. It just so happens that, in this document, `Customers` is also the outermost element.

Modifying the query as follows (by removing `CompanyName` from the `SELECT`) presents some interesting results:

```
SELECT ContactTitle + ' ' + ContactName AS ComboName, OrderID
FROM   Customers, Orders
WHERE  Customers.CustomerID=Orders.CustomerID
ORDER BY Companyname
FOR XML AUTO
```

The results look like the following:

```
<Orders ComboName="Sales Representative Maria Anders" OrderID="10643"/>
<Orders ComboName="Sales Representative Maria Anders" OrderID="10692"/>
<Orders ComboName="Sales Representative Maria Anders" OrderID="10702"/>

...

<Orders ComboName="Owner Zbyszek Piestrzeniewicz" OrderID="10906"/>
<Orders ComboName="Owner Zbyszek Piestrzeniewicz" OrderID="10998"/>
<Orders ComboName="Owner Zbyszek Piestrzeniewicz" OrderID="11044"/>
```

We now have no innermost element because the hierarchy of elements is only one deep. The XML document generated is just a sequence of `<Orders>` elements with attributes. `ComboName` will be an attribute of the `<Orders>` element, even though `ComboName` was constructed from columns found in the `Customers` table.

In the previous XML document, there are no `<Customers>` elements because there is no data retrieved from the `Customers` table. A rather elaborate solution to this problem (as recommended by MSDN at http://msdn.microsoft.com/library/psdk/sql/ac_openxml_03xh.htm; in section D, entitled Specify computed columns in the AUTO mode) is to use an inner `SELECT` to create a temporary table, `CustomersOuter`, and then join that table with `Orders`. An example of this is as follows:

```
SELECT CustomersOuter.ComboName, Orders.OrderID
FROM   (SELECT ContactTitle + ' ' + ContactName AS ComboName, CustomerID
        FROM Customers) CustomersOuter
LEFT OUTER JOIN Orders ON CustomersOuter.CustomerID=Orders.CustomerID
FOR XML AUTO
```

This query generates an outermost element named `<CustomersOuter>` and child elements named `<Orders>`:

```
<CustomersOuter ComboName="Sales Representative Maria Anders">
    <Orders OrderID="10643"/>
    <Orders OrderID="10692"/>
    <Orders OrderID="10702"/>
    <Orders OrderID="10835"/>
    <Orders OrderID="10952"/>
    <Orders OrderID="11011"/>
</CustomersOuter>
<CustomersOuter ComboName="Owner Ana Trujillo">
    <Orders OrderID="10308"/>
    <Orders OrderID="10625"/>
    <Orders OrderID="10759"/>

...

<CustomersOuter ComboName="Marketing Manager Eduardo Saavedra">
    <Orders OrderID="10366"/>
    <Orders OrderID="10426"/>
    <Orders OrderID="10568"/>
    <Orders OrderID="10887"/>
    <Orders OrderID="10928"/>
</CustomersOuter>
```

This extra effort was required because no column from the `Customers` table was specified in the `SELECT`. A less dedicated developer would skip the complicated query, place a column from `Customers` as the first element of the `SELECT`, and then just ignore this first column.

Encoding Issues

Both XML and URLs view certain characters as having special significance. There are several interesting situations that arise if these characters are encountered when `FOR XML AUTO` is used to generate an XML document:

- By default, binary data is represented by a reference. This reference is a URL that contains a table name and column names. How does `FOR XML AUTO` handle special characters when they are part of the table or column names that make up the URL? (Remember that references to binary data cannot contain aliases.)
- Table and column names or aliases are used as the names of an XML document's attributes and elements. How does `FOR XML AUTO` handle special characters when they occur in element and/or attribute names?
- How does `FOR XML AUTO` handle special characters when they occur in element or attribute values?

The characters that XML views as special are not placed literally in an XML document. Instead, such characters are placed in the document using an alternative representation. Converting special characters to this alternative representation is referred to as **entity encoding**. The following table presents the special XML characters subject to entity encoding, and the entity encoding representation:

Name	Character	Entity Encoding	XML context
Ampersand	&	`&`	Marks entity encoding
Apostrophe	'	`'`	Marks string literals
Less than	<	`<`	Marks tag's beginning
Greater than	>	`>`	Marks tag's end
Quotation mark	"	`"`	Marks string literals

URLs can also contain special characters that need to be entity encoded. Any character within a URL can be represented as a hexadecimal value. The hexadecimal character representation is specified using a prefix – the `%` character – followed by the numeric hexadecimal value. The list of URL special characters and their hexadecimal representations is as follows:

Name	Character	Hex Value	URL context
Ampersand	&	`%26`	Parameter separator
Forward slash	/	`%2F`	Directory separator
Percent	%	`%25`	Marks hex representation
Plus	+	`%20`	Marks a space
Pound	#	`%23`	Indicates a bookmark
Question mark	?	`%3F`	Separates the URL from its parameters

In order to explore how `FOR XML AUTO` handles special URL and XML characters, we need to enhance Northwind's `Categories` table as follows:

```
ALTER TABLE [Categories] ADD [Extra/.Stuff] IMAGE
```

The `Extra/.Stuff` column added in this `ALTER TABLE` statement is of type `IMAGE`. When this column is accessed using a `FOR XML AUTO` query, the default behavior will be for the XML document to contain references to such data values.

Now that we have added a tainted column, we can add some tainted data. This data contains special XML characters and is inserted into the `Categories` table as follows:

```
INSERT INTO [Categories]
  ([CategoryName], [Description], [Extra/.Stuff])
VALUES ('I Am >= You', 'You&Me', 0x8)
INSERT INTO [Categories]
  ([CategoryName], [Description], [Extra/.Stuff])
VALUES ('I Am < You', '"Lets just be friends"', 0x9)
```

The `CategoryName` and `Description` columns now contain special XML characters, including the greater than, less than, and apostrophe characters. A `FOR XML AUTO` query that retrieves the tainted column name, `Extra/.Stuff`, and the tainted data values is as follows:

```
SELECT [CategoryID], [CategoryName], [Description], [Extra/.Stuff]
FROM [Categories]
WHERE [CategoryName] LIKE 'I Am%'
FOR XML AUTO
```

The XML document generated by this `FOR XML AUTO` query is as follows:

```
<Categories CategoryID="23"
   CategoryName="I Am &lt; You"
   Description="&quot;Lets just be friends&quot;"
   Extra_x002F_.Stuff=
   "dbobject/Categories[@CategoryID='23']/@Extra_x002F_.Stuff"/>
<Categories CategoryID="22"
   CategoryName="I Am &gt;= You"
   Description="You&amp;Me"
   Extra_x002F_.Stuff=
   "dbobject/Categories[@CategoryID='22']/@Extra_x002F_.Stuff"/>
```

Let's look at this output in detail:

- CategoryName – the value associated with this attribute includes entity encoding, for example. "I Am < You", where the < was replaced by <.
- Extra_x002F_.Stuff – this attribute name contains a URL hexadecimal value, x002F, representing the URL special character, /. If this column and, hence, attribute name contained XML special characters, these characters would also be hexadecimal encoded.
- dbobject/Categories[@CategoryID='22']/@Extra_x002F_.Stuff – this URL includes a column name, Extra_x002F_.Stuff, that contains a URL hexadecimal value, x002F, representing the XML special character, /. If this column and, hence, attribute name contained XML special characters, these characters would also be hexadecimal encoded.

FOR XML EXPLICIT

`FOR XML RAW` is simple and easy to use, but the XML generated lacks sophistication and flexibility. With `FOR XML RAW`, developers have to be satisfied with grids which potentially contain repeated data.

Developers craving more flexibility can use `FOR XML AUTO`, where hierarchy is the name of the game, and column values can be specified to generate attributes or elements. However, the style of XML generation (attribute or element) applies to every column in the query. The `FOR XML AUTO` mechanism is straightforward and relatively easy to use, but the XML document generated cannot be fine tuned at the column level. For example, there is no mechanism to specify that some columns will be mapped to elements and other columns will be mapped to attributes.

For better control over the shape of the XML document generated, use the `EXPLICIT` mode of `FOR XML`. However, this extra flexibility comes at a cost, which can be measured in terms of complexity and query performance. Consider a `FOR XML EXPLICIT` query containing seven columns, each of type `text`. Using `FOR XML EXPLICIT`, the columns of the query could be tuned as follows:

- The data associated with column 1 is placed in an XML `CDATA` section.
- The data associated with column 2 is placed within an XML element named `ElementX`.
- The data associated with column 3 is placed within an XML attribute named `AttributeX`.
- The data associated with column 4 is of XML schema type `ID`.
- The data associated with column 5 is of XML schema type `IDREF`.
- The data associated with column 6 is entity encoded.
- The data associated with column 7 is not entity encoded.

This list is just a subset of the permissible per-column manipulations supported by `FOR XML EXPLICIT`.

The hierarchy of the XML document generated could also be fine-tuned. Queries that utilize `FOR XML EXPLICIT` contain additional information that dictates the type and level of nesting in the resulting XML document. A query containing `FOR XML EXPLICIT` creates a rowset in a specific form known as a **universal table**. The universal table is not actually a persisted database table. It is used solely to generate the XML document and can be viewed by executing the `FOR XML EXPLICIT` query and leaving off the actual "`FOR XML EXPLICIT`".

An example of a `FOR XML EXPLICIT` query is as follows:

```
SELECT 999 AS Tag,
       0 AS Parent,
       FirstName AS [EmployeeTable!999!FirstName]
FROM Employees
FOR XML EXPLICIT
```

This SQL statement is certainly not a practical example of a `FOR XML EXPLICIT` query because it does not generate a hierarchy of data. This example simply serves to demonstrate the basic requirements that must be met in order to generate a `FOR XML EXPLICIT` query. The columns are defined as follows:

- `Tag` – this column is of the integer data type and is required to be the first column of a query containing `FOR XML EXPLICIT`. The `Tag` column is a metadata column and does not correspond to a column found in any of the table names specified in the `FROM` clause of the query. The `Tag` column represents a tag number which corresponds to a level within the hierarchy of the XML document generated. In other words, this tag number indicates at what level of the XML tree data from a column resides. In the example query, the value of `Tag` is `999`. This does *not* mean that this is the 999th level of the XML data hierarchy. This means that all data associated with tag value `999` will reside at a particular level, as determined by the parent of this tag. Typically `1` is used, rather than `999`, for the first tag value of such a query.
- `Parent` – this column is also an integer and is required to be the second column of a query containing `FOR XML EXPLICIT`. The `Parent` column is also a metadata column and does not correspond to a column found in any of the table names specified in the `FROM` clause of the query. The `Parent` column represents the tag number of an element's parent. Each element within a query has a parent. The elements that are outermost in an XML document contain a `Parent` value of `0` or `NULL`. This is because such elements are at the top of the data hierarchy and have no parents. In the previous example query, note that the value of `FirstName`'s `Parent` was `0`.

- `FirstName` – this column *does* correspond to a column found within a table in the `FROM` clause of the query. In this example, `FirstName` is a member of the `Employees` table. This column contains the generated XML's element name and attribute name, the information being specified by the alias, `[EmployeeTable!999!FirstName]`. This style of alias is required for each column associated with a `FOR XML EXPLICIT` query. The simplest part of this alias is the number `999`. This numeric value indicates at what level of the data hierarchy the data associated with the column `FirstName` will reside. All columns with the tag value `999` will reside at the same level of the XML hierarchy. This column's data will be placed in the top tier of the data hierarchy (the first level), because the `Parent` of `Tag` value `999` is `0`. With respect to this alias, `EmployeeTable` is the element in which the value for the attribute `FirstName` will reside. It would have been possible to specify `Employees` instead of `EmployeeTable` as part of this alias. This would mean that the XML element generated would be named `Employees`. The name `Employees` also happens to be the name of the database table in which column `FirstName` resides. In addition to using this style of alias, it would also have been possible to specify data transform information for this column using directives. This is explained in more detail later.

The columns `Tag` and `Parent` ultimately specify the shape of the XML tree generated by the query. This is because the `Tag` and `Parent` columns specify the parent-child relationship of each element. The output generated by our example query is as follows:

```
<EmployeeTable FirstName="Nancy"/>
<EmployeeTable FirstName="Andrew"/>
<EmployeeTable FirstName="Janet"/>
<EmployeeTable FirstName="Margaret"/>
<EmployeeTable FirstName="Steven"/>
<EmployeeTable FirstName="Michael"/>
<EmployeeTable FirstName="Robert"/>
<EmployeeTable FirstName="Laura"/>
<EmployeeTable FirstName="Anne"/>
```

From the previous XML snippet, it should be clear that the `FirstName` attribute was contained in the `EmployeeTable` element. It should also be clear that the `EmployeeTable` element (corresponding to a `Tag` value of `999`) was at the first level of the data hierarchy because the `Parent` of this tag level was of value `0`.

The source files associated with this chapter include a SQL script called `ExplicitExtra01.sql`. This script is too long to present here, but a trimmed down portion of the script is as follows:

```
SELECT 1 AS Tag,
       0 AS Parent,
       EmployeeID AS [EmployeeTable!1!EmployeeID],
       Firstname AS [EmployeeTable!1!FirstName],
       LastName AS [EmployeeTable!1!LastName],
       NULL AS [EmployeeTerritoriesTable!2!TerritoryID],
       0 AS [EmployeeTerritoriesTable!2!EmployeeID],
       ' ' AS [OrdersTable!3!OrderID],
       ' ' AS [OrdersTable!3!EmployeeID],
       ' ' AS [CustomersTable!4!CustomerID],
       ' ' AS [CustomersTable!4!OrderID]
       ...
UNION ALL
```

```
SELECT 2, -- EmployeeTerritoriesTable level
       1, -- Parent, EmployeeTable level
       ...
UNION ALL

SELECT 3, -- OrdersTable Level
       1, -- Parent, EmployeeTable level
       ...
UNION ALL

SELECT 4, -- CustomersTable level
       3, -- Parent OrdersTable Level
       ...
FOR XML EXPLICIT, XMLDATA
```

The "..." sequences in this code represent missing components of the SQL statement. The values of all data marked by a tag value `1` (`EmployeeID`, `FirstName`, and `LastName`) will reside at this level of the data hierarchy. Similarly, the values of all data marked by tag value `2` (`TerritoryID` and `EmployeeID`) will reside at that specific level of the data hierarchy. The `ExplicitExtra01.sql` script demonstrates a more complicated data hierarchy (with 3 levels):

Element Name	Parent Value	Tag Value	Level in Hierarchy
`Employees`	0	1	1
`EmployeeTerritories`	1	2	2
`Orders`	1	3	2
`Customers`	3	4	3

Notice that `Orders` (`Tag` = `3`) has a parent value of `1`. This means that `Orders` are in the second level of the XML hierarchy.

The basic layout of the XML generated by `ExplicitExtra01.sql` is as follows:

```
<EmployeeTable>
  <EmployeeTerritoriesTable> <\EmployeeTerritoriesTable>
  <OrdersTable>
    <CustomersTable><\CustomersTable>
  <\OrdersTable>
<\EmployeeTable>
```

Column Elements, Attributes, and Transforms

Our first `FOR XML EXPLICIT` query contained:

```
FirstName AS [EmployeeTable!999!FirstName]
```

This first `FOR XML EXPLICIT` example demonstrated how an element name (`EmployeeTable`), tag number (`999`), and attribute name (`FirstName`) are specified within the XML document. The generic form for representing this information is as follows:

```
ElementName!TagNumber!AttributeName!Directive
```

Our first example did not demonstrate a **directive** so, clearly, directives are optional when it comes to specifying the columns associated with a universal table. Directives specify data encoding or how string data is represented in XML.

In order to understand where a directive might be useful, consider a database table – called `HelpDocumentation` – that is used to store the help text for an application. This table contains an integer column called `HelpID` that identifies which help string is being looked up, and a text column called `HelpInfo`. This latter column contains the help information being retrieved. The data inside the `HelpInfo` column is formatted as an XML document. What is needed here is a directive that forces the data found in `HelpInfo` to be treated as *data* contained in an XML document, and not to be treated as *part of* the XML document. This could be achieved by placing the data associated with the `HelpInfo` column inside an XML `CDATA` section. The `FOR XML EXPLICIT` directive `cdata` specifies that the data associated with a column will be placed in an XML `CDATA` section. Similarly, other directives allow the XML data format to be specified on a column by column basis.

The permissible values for directives include: `ID`, `IDREF`, `IDREFS`, `hide`, `element`, `xml`, `xmltext`, and `cdata`. An astute observer may have noticed that certain directives are named identically to certain XML attribute types (`ID`, `IDREF`, `IDREFS`, and `cdata`). This is a less than subtle hint as to what type of data a specific directive manipulates and generates. Each permissible directive value will be presented in detail later in this section.

The rules dictating when a particular portion of a column-specifying clause is required or is optional are as follows:

- Attribute name specified – the directive is optional. This was the case with our first `FOR XML EXPLICIT` example, `[EmployeeTable!1!FirstName]`.
- Attribute name not specified, directive not specified – in this case, the directive is interpreted to be `element`. With respect to our example, this would be represented as `EmployeeTable!1!!element`, or `EmployeeTable!1` since `element` is the default. The specific features of the `element` directive are presented below.

The directives that specify how string data is to be represented are as follows:

- `cdata` – when this directive is specified, the column data being represented as an XML string must be one of the following types: `ntext`, `nvarchar`, `text`, or `varchar`. The `cdata` directive causes the column data to be placed in a `CDATA` section. The data itself is not entity encoded. This means that less-than characters (<) are left as-is and are not encoded as `<`, and ampersand characters (&) are left as-is and not encoded as `&`. The same applies to greater-than, apostrophe, and quotation mark characters. If the `cdata` directive is used, an attribute name cannot be specified (for example, `EmployeeTable!1!!cdata` is valid). It is permissible to use the `cdata` directive in conjunction with the `hide` directive.
- `element` – when the `element` directive is specified, the data for the column is contained in an element rather than an attribute. The name of the element that contains the data is taken from the attribute name specified – for example, `EmployeeTable!1!EStyleFirstName!element`, where the element is named `EStyleFirstName`. If no attribute name is provided, the data values will be contained inside elements named after the element name specified as part of the directive clause. So, if the attribute name `EStyleFirstName` was not specified, the data values would be contained in elements named `EmployeeTable`. The data associated with an `element` directive is entity encoded. It is permissible to use the `element` directive in conjunction with the `hide`, `ID`, `IDREF`, and `IDREFS` directives.

- hide – columns that specify the hide directive are not included in the XML document generated.
- xml – this directive behaves identically to the element directive, save that data is not entity encoded. It is permissible to use the xml directive in conjunction with the hide directive.
- xmltext – the xmltext directive handles **overflow**. When using OPENXML, the database table has a set number of columns that should correspond to the elements and attributes of the XML document. If there are more elements and/or attributes than columns, the **unconsumed** elements and attributes get tossed into a column created by OPENXML to specifically handle this extra data. This **overflow column** must be of type char, nchar, ntext, nvarchar, text, or varchar. The xmltext directive was specifically designed to retrieve unconsumed XML from this overflow column. Be aware that, if the data residing in the column is junk (not well-formed XML) there is no guarantee that this directive will execute properly. In formal terms, invalid XML leads to undefined behavior. The xmltext directive can be used with the hide directive, and its behavior is fairly complicated. For more information, see the section of this chapter entitled *The xmltext Directive.*

The directives that specify how links within a document are to be encoded make sense only if used in a FOR XML EXPLICIT query that specifies XMLDATA. The links between data values are specified as part of an XML document's schema, which is, of course, generated when XMLDATA is specified. The schema has knowledge of such links and can therefore be used to ensure that such intra-document references are valid. Such links within a document are often referred to as **intra-document links** and are created by using XML attribute data of type ID, IDREF, and IDREFS. The FOR XML EXPLICIT directives that specify how to encode such links are:

- ID – a column can be mapped to an ID type attribute. Such an attribute can be referenced by IDREF and IDREFS attributes, thus supporting links within a document. The corresponding XML attribute type, ID, refers to a unique value (identity value) within an XML document.
- IDREF – the IDREF directive creates an attribute that can refer to an attribute of type ID. The corresponding XML attribute type, IDREF, specifies a reference to a unique value within an XML document (a reference to an attribute of type ID).
- IDREFS – the IDREFS directive creates an attribute that contains a list of references to attributes of type ID. The corresponding XML attribute type, IDREFS, specifies a white space delimited list of references to a unique value within an XML document (a list of references to attributes of type ID).

An Example of a Two-Level Hierarchy

The Northwind database contains a table called Employees. Each employee is associated with one or more employee territories that can be found in the table EmployeeTerritories. This relationship could be elegantly represented by an XML document containing a two level data hierarchy. To more precisely control the generation of this XML document, the following FOR XML EXPLICIT query will be used:

```
SELECT 1 AS Tag,
       0 AS Parent,
       Firstname AS [EmployeeTable!1!FirstName],
       LastName AS [EmployeeTable!1!LastName],
       NULL AS [EmployeeTerritoriesTable!2!TerritoryID]
FROM Employees
```

```
UNION ALL

SELECT 2,
       1,
       FirstName,
       LastName,
       TerritoryID
FROM Employees, EmployeeTerritories
WHERE Employees.EmployeeId = EmployeeTerritories.EmployeeID
ORDER BY [EmployeeTable!1!LastName],
         [EmployeeTable!1!FirstName],
         [EmployeeTerritoriesTable!2!TerritoryID]
FOR XML EXPLICIT
```

The query uses a UNION ALL to combine the results of two queries. The data from one query is placed in separate rows to the data in the other query. For this reason, the columns in both queries must be compatible. This is why both sub-queries have the same columns (Tag, Parent, FirstName, LastName, and TerritoryID). Notice in the first sub-query that the fifth column is specified as:

```
       NULL AS [EmployeeTerritoriesTable!2!TerritoryID]
```

Each row of this sub-query will contain a value of NULL in the fifth column. This always-NULL column ensures compatibility between the five columns of the two sub-queries that are combined using UNION.

Behind the scenes, the previous query generates a result set in universal table form. This resultset is ultimately used to generate the XML document. A subset of this universal table is as follows:

Tag	**Parent**	**EmployeeTable !1!FirstName**	**EmployeeTable !1!LastName**	**EmployeeTerritoriesTable !2!TerritoryID**
1	NULL	Steven	Buchanan	NULL
2	1	Steven	Buchanan	02903
2	1	Steven	Buchanan	07960
2	1	Steven	Buchanan	08837
2	1	Steven	Buchanan	10019
2	1	Steven	Buchanan	10038
2	1	Steven	Buchanan	11747
2	1	Steven	Buchanan	14450
1	NULL	Laura	Callahan	NULL
2	1	Laura	Callahan	19428
2	1	Laura	Callahan	44122

Each row starting with a Tag column value of 1 is at the top of the XML tree generated by this query, because the Parent column has a value of 0. Each row starting with a Tag column value of 2 and, hence, Parent column value of 1, is at the second level of the XML tree. All employees are at the top of the XML tree. The employee territories are found in the second level of the tree. A portion of the XML document generated by this query is as follows:

```
<EmployeeTable FirstName="Steven" LastName="Buchanan">
    <EmployeeTerritoriesTable TerritoryID="02903"/>
    <EmployeeTerritoriesTable TerritoryID="07960"/>
    <EmployeeTerritoriesTable TerritoryID="08837"/>
    <EmployeeTerritoriesTable TerritoryID="10019"/>
    <EmployeeTerritoriesTable TerritoryID="10038"/>
    <EmployeeTerritoriesTable TerritoryID="11747"/>
    <EmployeeTerritoriesTable TerritoryID="14450"/>
</EmployeeTable>
<EmployeeTable FirstName="Laura" LastName="Callahan">
    <EmployeeTerritoriesTable TerritoryID="19428"/>
    <EmployeeTerritoriesTable TerritoryID="44122"/>
```

There is a clear elegance to the XML document generated above. Much of this can be attributed to one specific clause of the query – the `ORDER BY` clause:

```
ORDER BY [EmployeeTable!1!LastName],
         [EmployeeTable!1!FirstName],
         [EmployeeTerritoriesTable!2!TerritoryID]
```

Without the `ORDER BY` clause, the XML document generated would contain all of the `EmployeeTable` elements followed by all of the `EmployeeTerritoriesTable` elements. There would be no nice interleaving within the XML tree.

Notice that, in the `ORDER BY` clause, the alias (`[ElementName!Tag!AttributeName]`) for each column is specified. The first query does not contain a `TerritoryID` column but it does contain the alias `[EmployeeTerritoriesTable!2!TerritoryID]`. The alias name is common to both queries so it must be specified as part of the `ORDER BY` clause. This is not necessary for the `LastName` and `FirstName` columns since both queries contain `LastName` and `FirstName`. The alias names were specified because it is a safe habit to get into when writing extremely complicated `FOR XML EXPLICIT` queries.

The `hide` Directive

When the `hide` directive is specified, the column associated with this directive is not contained in the XML document generated by the `FOR XML EXPLICIT` query. In order to understand this directive, consider an XML document ordered with some key. For this hypothetical scenario, the XML document does not contain an attribute or element representing this key. The key is only used for the purposes of ordering and, hence, should be hidden.

A query that uses the `hide` directive is as follows:

```
SELECT 1 AS Tag,
       0 AS Parent,
       Employees.EmployeeID AS [EmployeeTable!1!EmployeeID!hide],
       Firstname AS [EmployeeTable!1!FirstName],
       Lastname AS [EmployeeTable!1!LastName],
       NULL AS [EmployeeTerritoriesTable!2!TerritoryID]
FROM Employees

UNION ALL
```

```
SELECT 2,
       1,
       EmployeeTerritories.EmployeeID,
       NULL,
       NULL,
       TerritoryID
FROM Employees, EmployeeTerritories
WHERE Employees.EmployeeId = EmployeeTerritories.EmployeeID
ORDER BY [EmployeeTable!1!EmployeeID!hide],
         [EmployeeTerritoriesTable!2!TerritoryID]
FOR XML EXPLICIT
```

In this query, the value of `EmployeeID` in conjunction with `TerritoryID` determines the order of elements. Although `EmployeeID` is critical in determining order, it is not ultimately contained in the XML document generated by this query. This omission occurs because the `hide` directive was specified for the `EmployeeID` column of the query. Consider the following portion of the universal table that would be generated by this query:

Tag	**Parent**	**EmployeeTable !1!FirstName**	**EmployeeTable !1!LastName**	**EmployeeTerritoriesTable !2!TerritoryID**
1	NULL	Nancy	Davolio	NULL
2	1	NULL	NULL	06897
2	1	NULL	NULL	19713
1	NULL	Andrew	Fuller	NULL
2	1	NULL	NULL	01581
2	1	NULL	NULL	01730
2	1	NULL	NULL	01833
2	1	NULL	NULL	02116

Notice in the table that each element with a `Tag` value of `2` contains `NULL` for the value of `FirstName` and `LastName`. The columns are not used in the `ORDER BY` clause so they do not need to appear in the sub-query that selects employee territories.

A portion of the XML document produced by this query is as follows:

```
<EmployeeTable FirstName="Nancy" LastName="Davolio">
   <EmployeeTerritoriesTable TerritoryID="06897"/>
   <EmployeeTerritoriesTable TerritoryID="19713"/>
</EmployeeTable>
<EmployeeTable FirstName="Andrew" LastName="Fuller">
   <EmployeeTerritoriesTable TerritoryID="01581"/>
   <EmployeeTerritoriesTable TerritoryID="01730"/>
   <EmployeeTerritoriesTable TerritoryID="01833"/>
   <EmployeeTerritoriesTable TerritoryID="02116"/>
```

Although the value of `EmployeeID` dictated the order in which the elements are displayed, we do not see this element anywhere in the document.

The `element` and `xml` Directives

The `element` directive is specified as part of a `FOR XML EXPLICIT` query when the data is to be placed in an element rather than an attribute. Let's look at an example:

```
SELECT 1 AS Tag, 0 AS Parent,
       Firstname AS [EmployeeTable!1!FirstName!element]
FROM Employees
FOR XML EXPLICIT
```

In this query the `element` directive is associated with the `FirstName` column. A portion of the XML document generated by this query is as follows:

```
<EmployeeTable>
   <FirstName>Nancy</FirstName>
</EmployeeTable>
<EmployeeTable>
    <FirstName>Andrew</FirstName>
</EmployeeTable>
```

Note that the XML document contains the data associated with `FirstName` inside an element rather than an attribute.

Running the same query with the `xml` directive instead of the `element` directive will not change the output. If the `SELECT`ed data includes a character that requires entity encoding, it would be automatically encoded with `element`, but would be passed straight into the resulting XML output if the `xml` directive is used.

The `xmltext` Directive

The `xmltext` directive has as slight incompatibility with the Northwind database, namely that Northwind contains no columns that hold unconsumed XML. In order to demonstrate the `xmltext` directive we will alter the Northwind database by adding an additional column to the `Employees` table. This `LeftOvers` column will contain unconsumed XML and will be created as follows:

```
ALTER TABLE EMPLOYEES ADD LeftOvers NVARCHAR (1000)
```

Before we invent some overflow data, let's be clear as to why a column such as `LeftOvers` would exist in the real world. The next chapter will introduce the SQL keyword `OPENXML`. This keyword allows XML documents to act like SQL Server rowsets. When `OPENXML` is used, a column can be specified (byte flag value of 8) as being the place where unconsumed XML is placed. If an `INSERT` or `UPDATE` takes place in conjunction with `OPENXML`, then the unconsumed data is placed in this column.

Imagine that Northwind hires several temporary workers from a staffing agency. The agency provides an XML document that contains the details of the temporary employees. A portion of this XML is as follows:

```
< EmployeeTable FirstName="Jasmine" LastName="Smith"
    Title="Web Designer" ComputerPreference="PC">
</ EmployeeTable>

< EmployeeTable FirstName="Jamila" LastName="Cruz"
    Title="GUI Architect" ComputerPreference="Mac">
        <HomeOfficeInfo> Walls painted magenta <HomeOfficeInfo>
</ EmployeeTable>
```

Using OPENXML, the two employees hired from the staffing agency could be easily added to our Northwind Employees table. Certain attributes provided by the staffing agency's XML can be placed directly in our Employees table: FirstName, LastName, and Title. However, our Employees table does not contain a column that could be used to specify ComputerPreference or HomeOfficeInfo. For this reason, the XML associated with the ComputerPreference attribute and the HomeOfficeInfo element would remain unconsumed. Luckily, we created the LeftOvers column that can be used to store such overflow (unconsumed) XML.

Now that we know how overflow occurs and have a place to hold it (LeftOvers), we can invent some overflow data (elements with content, elements with attributes, and elements with sub-elements). The following UPDATE statements show some of the XML overflow being injected into the LeftOvers column:

```
UPDATE Employees SET LeftOvers = '<joelement attr="something" />'
WHERE EmployeeID=1;
UPDATE Employees
SET LeftOvers = '<joelement> some content </joelement>'
WHERE EmployeeID=2;
UPDATE Employees
SET LeftOvers = '<joelement> attrsomename="Wu" some content</joelement>'
WHERE EmployeeID=3;
UPDATE Employees
SET LeftOvers = '<joelement> attrsomename="Susan" </joelement>'
WHERE EmployeeID=4;
UPDATE Employees
SET LeftOvers =
  '<joelement> <janelement attr1="hi mom"/> Joe content </joelement>'
WHERE EmployeeID=5;
UPDATE Employees
SET LeftOvers = '<joelement> <janelement> Other Jane content</janelement> Other
Joe content </joelement>'
WHERE EmployeeID=6;
```

Note that we do not specify an empty value ('') when developing mock overflow data. An empty string is not considered valid when a FOR XML EXPLICIT query is executed using the xmltext directive.

There are two ways to use the xmltext directive – with or without an attribute name. An example *without* an attribute name is as follows:

```
LeftOvers AS [EmployeeTable!1!!xmltext]
```

Here is an example that specifies an attribute name (SomeAttr):

```
LeftOvers AS [EmployeeTable!1!SomeAttr!xmltext]
```

In both of these examples, the LeftOvers column is assumed to contain unconsumed XML. This XML is assumed to be well-formed and so is enclosed in a tag. When an attribute name is specified, the value of this attribute name replaces the tag associated with the unconsumed XML. To demonstrate this point, consider the following examples of unconsumed XML that reside in the LeftOvers column:

	LeftOvers
1	<joelement attr="something" />
2	<joelement> some content </joelement>

Executing a `FOR XML EXPLICIT` query – using the `xmltext` directive in conjunction with an attribute name – will alter this unconsumed XML. The XML document ultimately produced will contain no references to `joelement` but, instead, will contain a tag name that is the same as the attribute name specified. Using our example:

```
LeftOvers AS [EmployeeTable!1!SomeAttr!xmltext]
```

in conjunction with the previous unconsumed XML, would result in the following being generated as part of the query's XML document (`joelement` will be replaced by `SomeAttr`):

```
<SomeAttr attr="something"/>
<SomeAttr> some content </SomeAttr>
```

What happens when the `xmltext` directive has no specified attribute name? Under this scenario, the current element of the XML document being generated will now contain the attributes of the unconsumed XML column. The content of the column in which the unconsumed XML resides will not be entity encoded, and will be placed foremost in the containing element (the current element of the XML document being generated).

Here is an example. The `LeftOvers` column in the following query is associated with the `xmltext` directive. Notice that there is no attribute name associated with the `LeftOvers` column:

```
SELECT 1 AS Tag, 0 AS Parent,
       Firstname AS [EmployeeTable!1!FirstName!element],
       LeftOvers AS [EmployeeTable!1!!xmltext]
FROM Employees
FOR XML EXPLICIT
```

Here is a portion of this query's output:

```
<EmployeeTable attr="something">
    <FirstName>Nancy</FirstName>
</EmployeeTable>
<EmployeeTable> some content
    <FirstName>Andrew</FirstName>
</EmployeeTable>
<EmployeeTable> attrsomename="Wu" some content
    <FirstName>Janet</FirstName>
</EmployeeTable>
<EmployeeTable> attrsomename="Susan"
    <FirstName>Margaret</FirstName>
</EmployeeTable>
<EmployeeTable>
    <janelement attr1="hi mom"/> Joe content
    <FirstName>Steven</FirstName>
</EmployeeTable><EmployeeTable>
    <janelement> Other Jane content</janelement> Other Joe content
    <FirstName>Michael</FirstName>
</EmployeeTable>
```

The XML overflow that was added to the Employees table included content, attributes, and sub-elements. Each of these XML components was contained in an element referred to as joelement. Notice in the previous snippet of output that there is no sign of the joelement element. The content, attributes, and sub-elements are all associated with the current element as specified by the query. For our query, EmployeeTable is the current element and so the unconsumed XML is associated with EmployeeTable.

Breaking the results of this query down in more detail, recall that the unconsumed XML included:

```
<joelement attr="something" />
<joelement> some content </joelement>
```

The first line of unconsumed XML appeared in the generated XML document as:

```
<EmployeeTable attr="something">
```

As we noted before, the current element of the XML document being generated contains the attributes of the unconsumed XML column. Here, the current element is EmployeeTable and the unconsumed XML column's attribute is attr="something".

The second line of unconsumed XML appeared in the generated XML document as:

```
<EmployeeTable> some content
```

Again, we said before that the content of the column in which the unconsumed XML resides is placed foremost in the containing element. Here, the containing element is EmployeeTable and the unconsumed XML column's content is some content.

Using xmltext and specifying an attribute name is more straightforward. An example of such a query is as follows:

```
SELECT 1 AS Tag, 0 AS Parent,
       Firstname AS [EmployeeTable!1!FirstName],
       LeftOvers AS [EmployeeTable!1!SomeAttr!xmltext]
FROM Employees
FOR XML EXPLICIT
```

Each tag in the unconsumed XML LeftOvers column will be replaced by the attribute name specified – SomeAttr. The tag in our example was joelement. A portion of the output from this query is as follows:

```
<EmployeeTable FirstName="Nancy">
   <SomeAttr attr="something"/>
</EmployeeTable>
<EmployeeTable FirstName="Andrew">
   <SomeAttr> some content </SomeAttr>
</EmployeeTable>
<EmployeeTable FirstName="Janet">
   <SomeAttr> attrsomename="Wu" some content</SomeAttr>
</EmployeeTable>
<EmployeeTable FirstName="Margaret">
   <SomeAttr> attrsomename="Susan" </SomeAttr>
</EmployeeTable>
```

The cdata Directive

The cdata directive is not complex to use from a FOR XML EXPLICIT standpoint. Using this directive causes the data to be placed in a CDATA section within the XML document generated. A CDATA section is used to mark sections of an XML document that are to be left unparsed by the XML parser. These sections may encompass XML markup; the markup will be ignored. An excellent overview of the CDATA section's pros, cons, and limitations can be found in *Professional XML* from Wrox Press, ISBN 1861003110.

In order to better understand why CDATA is required, recall when the HelpDocumentation table was discussed previously in this chapter. This table contained the help text for an application (HelpInfo column). This help text was formatted using XML. Placing this data in a CDATA section ensures that the data is treated as "data", and is not consumed as part of the XML document generated by a FOR XML EXPLICIT query.

To demonstrate the cdata directive, a data column is needed that contains XML markup. We can use the LeftOvers column for this purpose. An example query that exploits LeftOvers and demonstrates the cdata directive is as follows:

```
SELECT 1 AS Tag, 0 AS Parent,
       Firstname AS [EmployeeTable!1!FirstName],
       LeftOvers AS [EmployeeTable!1!!cdata]
FROM Employees
FOR XML EXPLICIT
```

The LeftOvers column in the previous query will be placed in a CDATA section because the cdata directive is specified for this column. A portion of the XML document generated by this query is as follows:

```
<EmployeeTable FirstName="Nancy">
<![CDATA[<joelement attr="something" />]]>
</EmployeeTable>
<EmployeeTable FirstName="Andrew">
<![CDATA[<joelement> some content </joelement>]]>
</EmployeeTable>
```

XMLDATA in FOR XML EXPLICIT Queries

Any of the queries demonstrating FOR XML EXPLICIT could have taken advantage of the XMLDATA option. For example, the following is permissible:

```
SELECT 1 AS Tag,
       0 AS Parent,
       EmployeeID AS [EmployeeTable!1!EmployeeID],
       FirstName AS [EmployeeTable!1!FirstName]
FROM Employees
FOR XML EXPLICIT, XMLDATA
```

By generating a schema in this query using the XMLDATA clause, the data associated with the XML document can be verified. This is because the XML-Schema both describes and constrains the data. For instance, if the XML document contains an EmployeeID of "abc", as opposed to the integer specified in the schema, the parser will produce an error when it validates the document.

The tradeoffs associated with returning schema information using XMLDATA were thoroughly discussed earlier in this chapter when we looked at FOR XML RAW.

We will see in the next section that the XMLDATA option has special significance with the ID, IDREF, and IDREFS directives.

The ID, IDREF, and IDREFS Directives

The ID, IDREF, and IDREFS directives combine to support links within a document, so we'll refer to them as **intra-document links** for the rest of the chapter. These directives are used to give an XML document knowledge of a database's primary keys (ID type) and foreign keys (IDREF or IDREFS type).

The ID, IDREF, and IDREFS directives are used in conjunction with FOR XML's XMLDATA option. This is because these directives assign specific type information within the XML-Data schema. The attribute type specified by each directive is self-documenting: ID, IDREF, and IDREFS.

The data generated by the ID, IDREF, and IDREFS directives is strongly typed and subject to schema dictated restrictions. The fundamental type of these directives is text. The value of each ID must be unique within the XML document generated. Note that the previous sentence did *not* read, "Each ID is unique for the element type it identifies."

The following query demonstrates the use of the ID and IDREF directives. This query uses the XMLDATA option to generate an XML-Data schema. The ID directive in the query indicates that the value of the Employees.EmployeeID column (primary key) will be placed in the XML document and defined as attribute type ID. The IDREF directive in the query indicates that the value of the EmployeeTerritories.EmployeeID column (foreign key) will be placed in the XML document and defined as attribute type IDREF:

```
SELECT 1 AS Tag,
       0 AS Parent,
       EmployeeID AS [EmployeeTable!1!EmployeeID!id],
       Firstname AS [EmployeeTable!1!FirstName],
       LastName AS [EmployeeTable!1!LastName],
       NULL AS [EmployeeTerritoriesTable!2!TerritoryID],
       0 AS [EmployeeTerritoriesTable!2!EmployeeID!idref]
FROM Employees

UNION ALL

SELECT 2,
       1,
       0,
       FirstName,
       LastName,
       TerritoryID,
       EmployeeTerritories.EmployeeID
FROM Employees, EmployeeTerritories
WHERE Employees.EmployeeId = EmployeeTerritories.EmployeeID
ORDER BY [EmployeeTable!1!FirstName],
         [EmployeeTable!1!LastName],
         [EmployeeTerritoriesTable!2!TerritoryID]
FOR XML EXPLICIT, XMLDATA
```

A portion of the output generated by this query, including the schema in its entirety, is as follows:

```
<Schema name="Schema1" xmlns="urn:schemas-microsoft-com:xml-data"
     xmlns:dt="urn:schemas-microsoft-com:datatypes">
  <ElementType name="EmployeeTable" content="mixed" model="open">
    <AttributeType name="EmployeeID" dt:type="id"/>
    <AttributeType name="FirstName" dt:type="string"/>
    <AttributeType name="LastName" dt:type="string"/>
    <attribute type="EmployeeID"/>
    <attribute type="FirstName"/>
    <attribute type="LastName"/>
  </ElementType>
  <ElementType name="EmployeeTerritoriesTable" content="mixed" model="open">
    <AttributeType name="TerritoryID" dt:type="string"/>
    <AttributeType name="EmployeeID" dt:type="idref"/>
    <attribute type="TerritoryID"/>
    <attribute type="EmployeeID"/>
  </ElementType>
</Schema>
<EmployeeTable xmlns="x-schema:#Schema1" EmployeeID="2"
         FirstName="Andrew" LastName="Fuller">
  <EmployeeTerritoriesTable TerritoryID="01581" EmployeeID="2"/>
  <EmployeeTerritoriesTable TerritoryID="01730" EmployeeID="2"/>
  <EmployeeTerritoriesTable TerritoryID="01833" EmployeeID="2"/>
  <EmployeeTerritoriesTable TerritoryID="02116" EmployeeID="2"/>
  <EmployeeTerritoriesTable TerritoryID="02139" EmployeeID="2"/>
```

Within the previous snippet of XML, two specific lines were highlighted in bold. The first:

```
<AttributeType name="EmployeeID" dt:type="id"/>
```

specifies that, within the `EmployeeTable` element, the `EmployeeID` attribute is of `ID` attribute type. The second highlighted portion of the schema is:

```
<AttributeType name="EmployeeID" dt:type="idref"/>
```

This portion of the XML schema specifies that, within the `EmployeeTerritoriesTable` element, the `EmployeeID` attribute is of `IDREF` attribute type. There is nothing in the schema that says, "`EmployeeTerritoriesTable.EmployeeID` refers back to an `ID` found in `EmployeesTable.EmployeeID`." This is precisely the reason why the value of each `ID` must be unique within the XML document generated.

Thus far, we have demonstrated an attribute of type `IDREF` referring to an attribute of type `ID`. The `IDREFS` directive facilitates the referencing of multiple attributes of type `ID` (a list of `ID`s). The following query demonstrates the usage of `FOR XML EXPLICIT`'s `ID` and `IDREFS` directives:

```
-- Sub-query 1
SELECT 1 AS Tag,
       NULL AS Parent,
       CustomerID AS [Customers!1!CustomerID],
       ContactName AS [Customers!1!ContactName!element],
       CompanyName AS [Customers!1!CompanyName!element],
       NULL AS [Customers!1!OrderIDs!IDREFS],
       NULL AS [Orders!2!OrderID!ID],
       NULL AS [Orders!2!OrderDate!element]
FROM Customers
```

```
UNION ALL

-- Sub-query 2
SELECT 1 AS Tag,
       NULL AS Parent,
       C.CustomerID,
       C.ContactName,
       C.CompanyName,
       'ID-'+CAST(O.OrderID AS VARCHAR(10)),
       NULL,
       NULL
FROM Customers AS C, Orders AS O
WHERE O.CustomerID = C.CustomerID

UNION ALL

-- Sub-query 3
SELECT 2 AS tag,
       1 AS parent,
       C.CustomerID,
       NULL,
       NULL,
       NULL,
       'ID-'+CAST(O.OrderID AS VARCHAR(10)),
       O.OrderDate
FROM Customers AS C, Orders AS O
WHERE O.CustomerID = C.CustomerID
ORDER BY [Customers!1!CustomerID],
         [Orders!2!OrderID!ID],
         [Customers!1!OrderIDs!IDREFS]
FOR XML EXPLICIT, XMLDATA
```

This query generates an XML document that contains a `Customers` element with a `Tag` value of `1` and `Parent` value of `0` (so it's the outermost element). The `Customers` element contains an attribute, `OrderIDs` (attribute type `IDREFS`). The value of this attribute is a space-delimited list of references to lower-level elements of type `Orders`. The specific reference of each list element within the `OrderIDs` attribute is to an attribute of `Orders` called `OrderID` (attribute type `ID`).

In order to facilitate explanation of this lengthy query, three comments are included that identify the sub-queries of the overall query. These sub-queries can be broken down as follows:

- Sub-query 1 – this sub-query selects all customers, including the value of a customer's `CustomerID`, `ContactName`, and `CompanyName`. This sub-query generates data contained in the outermost level of the generated XML document (`Tag` value of `1` with `Parent` value of `0`). The `element` directive is specified for `ContactName` and `CompanyName` and, hence, these will be included in the generated XML document as elements as opposed to attributes.
- Sub-query 2 – this sub-query creates the list of `OrderIDs` associated with a particular customer. This query generates data contained in the outermost level of the generated XML document (`Tag` value of `1` with `Parent` value of `0`). The specific SQL text that generates each element in the `IDREFS` list is `'ID-'+CAST(O.OrderID AS VARCHAR(10))`. This SQL snippet generates an attribute of type `IDREFS` because the `IDREFS` directive was previously specified (`[Customers!1!OrderIDs!IDREFS]`) in conjunction with this column. The mechanism used to create each `ID` in the `IDREFS` list may seem a bit ornate but there is method to the madness. Each `ID` is prefixed by `'ID-'` and the value of the `ID` is cast from SQL `integer` type to SQL `varchar` type. The rationale for this intricate name mangling is that each `ID` must be unique and of `string` type.

- Sub-query 3 – this sub-query creates data contained in the second level of the generated XML document (Tag value of 2 with Parent value of 1). This data is contained in the Orders element and includes the ID associated with each order. The OrderID attribute contains the ID of each Orders element and is generated using 'ID-'+CAST(O.OrderID AS VARCHAR(10)).

The XML-Data schema is pre-pended to the XML document generated. Of interest in this schema are the following AttributeType elements, containing name attributes of OrderIDs and OrderID, respectively:

```
<AttributeType name="OrderIDs" dt:type="idrefs"/>
<AttributeType name="OrderID" dt:type="id"/>
```

The reason why these attributes were generated as part of the XML-Data schema should be obvious. The IDREFS directive ([Customers!1!OrderIDs!IDREFS]) caused the name attribute of the OrderIDs value to be generated. The ID directive ([Orders!2!OrderID!ID]) caused the name attribute of the OrderID value to be generated.

A portion of the XML generated by this query is as follows (without the XML-Data schema):

```
<Customers xmlns="x-schema:#Schema12"
        CustomerID="ALFKI"
        OrderIDs="ID-10643 ID-10692 ID-10702 ID-10835 ID-10952 ID-11011">
  <ContactName>Maria Anders</ContactName>
  <CompanyName>Alfreds Futterkiste</CompanyName>
  <Orders OrderID="ID-10643">
    <OrderDate>1997-08-25T00:00:00</OrderDate>
  </Orders>
  <Orders OrderID="ID-10692">
    <OrderDate>1997-10-03T00:00:00</OrderDate>
  </Orders>
  <Orders OrderID="ID-10702">
    <OrderDate>1997-10-13T00:00:00</OrderDate>
  </Orders>
```

Notice that the data associated with ContactName, CompanyName, and OrderDate is contained in elements rather than attributes. This is because the element directive was used with each of these columns in the FOR XML EXPLICIT query. The Customers element contains an OrderIDs attribute. The value of this attribute:

```
"ID-10643 ID-10692 ID-10702 ID-10835 ID-10952 ID-11011"
```

is of attribute type IDREFS and each member of this list references an attribute of type ID. The attribute data was generated in this form because the OrderID column:

```
'ID-'+CAST(O.OrderID AS VARCHAR(10))
```

was associated with the IDREFS directive. An example of an ID attribute referenced by a member of the OrderIDs attribute can be found in the Orders element – specifically the attribute:

```
OrderID="ID-10643"
```

This was a fairly complicated query so why bother with:

```
'ID-'+CAST(O.OrderID AS VARCHAR(10))
```

Remember that every ID must be unique. What if this query contained more than one ID type: OrderID, CategoryID, and ShipperID? Each of these would have to be unique within the XML document. It would make sense to perform some type of uniqueness conversion, such as:

- 'OrID-'+CAST(OrderID AS VARCHAR(10))
- 'CaID-'+CAST(CatetoryID AS VARCHAR(10))
- 'ShID-'+CAST(ShipperID AS VARCHAR(10))

BINARY BASE64 in FOR XML EXPLICIT Queries

When binary data is included in a query containing FOR XML EXPLICIT, the BINARY BASE64 argument must be specified to encode the data. The section on FOR XML RAW covered this topic in detail.

Regardless of the FOR XML query type executed, binary data has a huge number of uses. An installation program for a software package could be shipped in XML. Each element might refer to a library that is either required or optional. The library (the actual DLL) could be included as binary data (Module attribute). The installation program could display the library names (Name attribute), what the library does (Desc attribute), and prompt whether or not to install the DLL:

```
<DLL> Name="MerryDiskUtil.DLL" Desc="Optimizes Disk Speed" Optional="Y"
 Module="LMQRZAIA … ADHrDD+"</DLL>
```

Imagine shipping a car dealership's catalog as an XML document. The catalog could include XML designed to entice a buyer to purchase a car:

```
<CAR> Color="Red" Speed="Fast"/>
```

We are not going to sell a lot of cars with this representation of a Ferrari. If we add binary data – such as a photograph of the car – our sales would rocket:

```
<CAR> Color="Red" Speed="Fast" Picture="FRwvAAIA … ADHrQX+"/>
```

An Example of a Three-Level Hierarchy

We conclude our discussion of FOR XML EXPLICIT with a three-level hierarchy. The motivation for this example is to emphasize the flexibility of the EXPLICIT form of the FOR XML query, and that developing such queries takes some careful thought and planning. The query that generates an example three-level XML document is as follows:

```
SELECT 1 AS Tag,
       0 AS Parent,
       Firstname AS [EmployeeTable!1!FirstName],
       LastName AS [EmployeeTable!1!LastName],
       0 AS [EmployeeTerritoriesTable!2!TerritoryID],
       NULL AS [EmployeeTerritoriesTable!2!TerritoryDesc],
       0 AS [RegionTable!3!RID],
       NULL AS [RegionTable!3!RDesc]
FROM Employees
```

```
UNION ALL

SELECT 2,
       1,
       FirstName,
       LastName,
       ET.TerritoryID,
       RTRIM(TerritoryDescription),
       0,
       NULL
FROM Employees, EmployeeTerritories AS ET, Territories AS T
WHERE Employees.EmployeeId = ET.EmployeeID AND
      Et.TerritoryID = T.TerritoryID

UNION ALL

SELECT 3,
       2,
       FirstName,
       LastName,
       ET.TerritoryID,
       NULL,
       R.RegionID,
       RTRIM(R.RegionDescription)
FROM Employees, EmployeeTerritories AS ET, Territories AS T,
      Region AS R
WHERE Employees.EmployeeId = ET.EmployeeID AND
      Et.TerritoryID = T.TerritoryID

ORDER BY [EmployeeTable!1!FirstName],
         [EmployeeTable!1!LastName],
         [EmployeeTerritoriesTable!2!TerritoryID],
         [RegionTable!3!RID]
FOR XML EXPLICIT
```

The `RTRIM` function was used in this query because the `TerritoryDescription` and `RegionDescription` columns are of `nchar` SQL type, which represents fixed-length Unicode character data. Such columns generate fixed-length XML and `RTRIM` was used here to remove the trailing spaces. The query also indirectly utilizes the relationship between tables in order to generate a three-level SQL hierarchy. The table relationships exploited are:

- `Employees` and `EmployeeTerritories`
- `EmployeeTerritories` and `Territories`
- `Territories` and `Region`

A portion of the XML generated by this query is as follows:

```
<EmployeeTable FirstName="Andrew" LastName="Fuller">
  <EmployeeTerritoriesTable TerritoryID="1581" TerritoryDesc="Westboro">
    <RegionTable RID="1" RDesc="Eastern"/>
    <RegionTable RID="2" RDesc="Western"/>
    <RegionTable RID="3" RDesc="Northern"/>
    <RegionTable RID="4" RDesc="Southern"/>
  </EmployeeTerritoriesTable>
```

```
<EmployeeTerritoriesTable TerritoryID="1730" TerritoryDesc="Bedford">
  <RegionTable RID="1" RDesc="Eastern"/>
  <RegionTable RID="2" RDesc="Western"/>
  <RegionTable RID="3" RDesc="Northern"/>
  <RegionTable RID="4" RDesc="Southern"/>
</EmployeeTerritoriesTable>
<EmployeeTerritoriesTable TerritoryID="1833" TerritoryDesc="Georgetown">
  <RegionTable RID="1" RDesc="Eastern"/>
  <RegionTable RID="2" RDesc="Western"/>
```

The process for writing a `FOR XML EXPLICIT` query is not as complicated as it might appear. The query in this example is composed of three sub-queries. Keep in mind that each sub-query contains a union of every column of every other sub-query. In simpler terms, every query contains every column. A column will only be reflected as an attribute or an element at its own specific level, where the value of `Tag` indicates the level number. For this reason, a good portion of the columns at any level can be specified as having a `0` or `NULL` value. Be aware also that the additional information required by `FOR XML EXPLICIT` needs only to be specified for the first sub-query.

Calling `FOR XML` Queries with ADO

Thus far in this chapter, we've presented a variety of different ways to use `FOR XML` – namely with `RAW`, `AUTO`, and `EXPLICIT`. We have yet to show how to call such queries from Microsoft's standard data access API – ADO. The ADO example presented here is written in Visual Basic 6.0 and uses version 2.6 of MDAC and ADO (automatically installed with SQL Server 2000).

Data is typically accessed with ADO via its `Recordset` object. ADO recordsets are stored in a proprietary format – **Advanced Data TableGram format** or **ADTG** for short. What has this to do with `FOR XML` queries? It means that you cannot just execute a `FOR XML` query and have the XML document magically appear in an ADO recordset. Run `Project1.vbp` from the source code for Chapter 3, which contains the following:

```
Dim strQuery, strConn As String
Dim conn As New Connection
Dim rs As New Recordset

strConn = "PROVIDER=SQLOLEDB;DATA SOURCE=localhost;" & _
        "DATABASE=NorthWind;USER ID=sa;PASSWORD=sa;"
'Set conn = New ADODB.Connection
Set conn.Open strConn
strQuery = "SELECT * FROM SHIPPERS FOR XML AUTO"
' Set rs = New ADODB.Recordset
rs.Open strQuery, conn, , , adCmdText ' This won't work
textResult.Text = rs.Fields(0).Name & vbCrLf & rs.Fields(0).Value

Set rs = Nothing
conn.Close
Set conn = Nothing
```

This VB code is executed when the Won't Work button is clicked on `Project1`'s dialog:

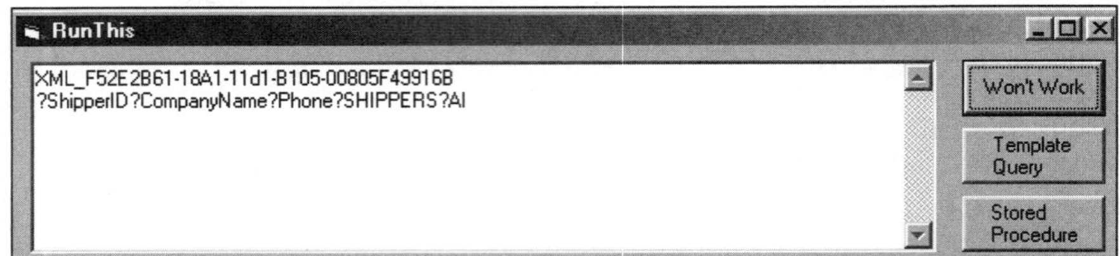

The first line of text displayed is the name of the field. Remember that, every time we execute a FOR XML query, we see this column name: XML_F52E2B61-18A1-11d1-B105-00805F49916B. The data – the second line displayed – is clearly not the XML document we were attempting to generate!

Developers familiar with ADO will know that XML can be retrieved from ADO using:

- Recordset.Save(filename, adPersistXML) – a recordset can be persisted to a file and stored as XML. This is because a persistence format of adPersistXML is specified in conjunction with the file name. It would also be possible to persist to a proprietary binary format – Advanced Data TableGram (ADTG) – by specifying a persistence format of adPersistADTG.
- Recordset.Save(stream, adPersistXML) – a recordset can be persisted to an ADO Stream object and stored as XML. This is because a persistence format of adPersistXML is specified in conjunction with an ADO Stream object.

Saving the XML version of a recordset to a text file is *not* an optimal way to transport an XML document. A large percentage of the time, the Save method is used to associate a Recordset object with a Stream object containing XML. Given what we know about the functionality of the Save method, it should be no surprise that ADO supports FOR XML style queries using the Stream object.

ADO and Template Queries

An example code snippet that retrieves an XML document from a FOR XML query is as follows:

```
Private Sub Command2_Click()
    strConn = "PROVIDER=SQLOLEDB;DATA SOURCE=localhost;" & _
              "DATABASE=NorthWind;USER ID=sa;PASSWORD=sa;"
    Dim strQuery, strConn As String
    Dim conn As New Connection
    Dim streamOut As New Stream
    Dim streamIn As New Stream
    Dim cmd As New Command

    strConn = "PROVIDER=SQLOLEDB;DATA SOURCE=localhost;" & _
              "DATABASE=NorthWind;USER ID=sa;PASSWORD=sa;"
    conn.Open strConn

    strQuery = "<ROOT xmlns:sql='urn:schemas-microsoft-com:xml-sql'>" & _
               "<sql:query>" & _
               "SELECT * FROM Shippers FOR XML AUTO" & _
               "</sql:query></ROOT>"
    streamIn.Open
    streamIn.WriteText strQuery, adWriteChar
    streamIn.Position = 0

    Set cmd.CommandStream = streamIn
    Set cmd.ActiveConnection = conn
    cmd.Dialect = "{5D531CB2-E6Ed-11D2-B252-00C04F681B71}"

    streamOut.Open
    cmd.Properties("Output Stream") = streamOut
    cmd.Execute , , adExecuteStream

    streamOut.Position = 0
    textResult.Text = streamOut.ReadText(adReadAll)
```

```
    Set cmd = Nothing
    Set StreamIn = Nothing
    Set StreamOut = Nothing
    conn.Close
    Set conn = Nothing

End Sub
```

Observant readers may have noticed that a special form of SQL query was used. This form of query is not in the standard (default) SQL dialect executed by the OLE DB provider for SQL Server. This type of query is referred to as a **template query**:

```
<ROOT xmlns:sql='urn:schemas-microsoft-com:xml-sql'>
<sql:query>
SELECT * FROM Shippers FOR XML AUTO
</sql:query></ROOT>
```

The query itself is written in XML and uses the `urn:schemas-microsoft-com:xml-sql` namespace. This is the namespace associated with SQL Server template queries. The abbreviation specified for this namespace is `sql`. The `FOR XML` query itself is enclosed by the tag, `<sql:query>`. Let's now walk through this code:

- We create an instance of an ADO `Stream` object. This will be the input stream containing the template query (in our example, `streamIn` is the `Stream` object):

```
    Dim streamIn As New Stream
```

- Call the `Stream` object's `Open` method:

```
    streamIn.Open
```

- Write the template query previously discussed to the input stream, using the `Stream` object's `WriteText` method:

```
    streamIn.WriteText strQuery, adWriteChar
```

- Set the `Position` property of `streamIn` to `0`, representing an offset of zero bytes into the stream. This ensures that the `Command` reads from the beginning of the template query we specified (position zero in the stream):

```
    streamIn.Position = 0
```

- Create an instance of an ADO `Command` object. This `Command` object will ultimately execute the query (in our example, `cmd` is the `Command` object):

```
    Dim cmd As New Command
```

- Set the `Command` object's `CommandStream` property to be equal to the `Stream` object previously set up. In order to execute a `FOR XML` style query, `Command.CommandText` is not used but, instead, we use `Command.CommandStream` in conjunction with setting up the command's dialect.

```
    Set cmd.CommandStream = streamIn
```

- Set the Command object's Dialect property to be equal to "{5D531CB2-E6Ed-11D2-B252-00C04F681B71}":

```
cmd.Dialect = "{5D531CB2-E6Ed-11D2-B252-00C04F681B71}"
```

  The Command object can execute one or more language dialects. By default, the Dialect property is set to {C8B521FB-5CF3-11CE-ADE5-00AA0044773D}. This default dialect allows the OLE DB provider for SQL Server to execute traditional (non-FOR XML style) SQL commands. The dialect specified by the GUID value "{5D531CB2-E6Ed-11D2-B252-00C04F681B71}" is that of the XML Template Query dialect. We specified an XML Template Query when we called the Stream object's WriteText method, so it makes sense to set the Dialect property in this manner.

- Associate the Command object with a connection to a SQL Server 2000 database accessed using the OLE DB provider for SQL Server:

```
Set cmd.ActiveConnection = conn
```

Those who are curious as to the origins of the dialect GUID should look at C/C++ header file that ships with version 2.6 of SQL Server's OLE DB provider. This header file, sqloledb.h, contains the following declaration:

```
extern const GUID  DBGUID_MSSQLXML =
    {0x5d531cb2L,0xe6ed,0x11d2,{0xb2,0x52,0x00,0xc0,0x4f,0x68,0x1b,0x71}};
```

Thus far we have managed to set up the Command object but we do not quite have a way to retrieve the data. To execute the query specified and retrieve the data, we performed the following steps:

- Create an instance of an ADO Stream object. This will be the output stream containing the XML document generated by the query (in our example, streamOut is the output Stream object):

```
Dim streamOut As New Stream
```

- Call the output Stream object's Open method:

```
streamOut.Open
```

- Set the Command object's Output Stream property to the value of the output Stream object just created and opened. This sounds like a rather strange way to code unless you have actually implemented an OLE DB provider. The properties collection serves as a mechanism that can be used to pass data between client and OLE DB provider. The Output Stream property is a way for a client to pass data to SQL Server's OLE DB Provider. The Output Stream property of the Command object is found in its Properties collection, as follows:

```
cmd.Properties("Output Stream") = streamOut
```

- Call the Command object's Execute method and make sure to specify the command type as adExecuteStream:

```
cmd.Execute , , adExecuteStream
```

- The XML document generated by the query can be retrieved using the output Stream object's ReadText method:

```
textResult.Text = streamOut.ReadText(adReadAll)
```

In our example, we use the value returned from `ReadText` to set the `Text` property of a text box called `textResult`. This allows the XML document to be displayed in a text box.

When the Template Query button is pressed, the `FOR XML AUTO` query is executed and the XML document is displayed in the text box:

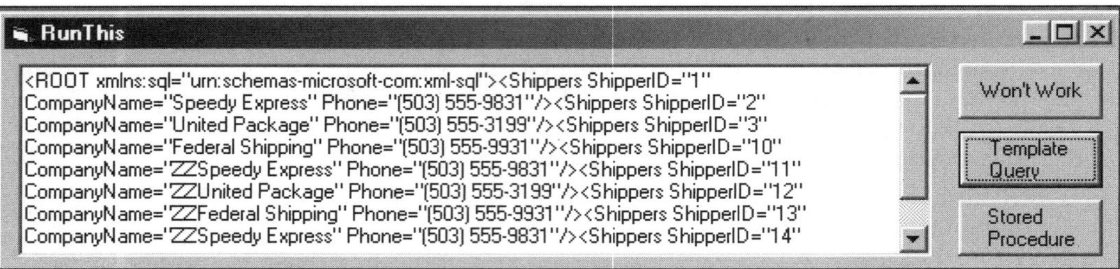

ADO and Stored Procedure Calls

Setting up an input `Stream` object and setting the `Dialect` to `"{5D531CB2-E6Ed-11D2-B252-00C04F681B71}"` is certainly not difficult but it can be tedious. A simpler way to access `FOR XML` queries from ADO is through the use of stored procedure calls. Not only is this simpler to code but it has a major advantage over using template SQL directly in the code. The source code can be written to use the stored procedure call. In the event that the SQL changes, the code never has to be modified. The stored procedure can be modified and the business logic remain untouched, provided that the parameters to the stored procedure call remain unchanged. An example stored procedure call, `GetShippersRaw`, is created as follows:

```
CREATE PROCEDURE GetShippersRaw @companyName NVARCHAR(40) AS
  SELECT '<ROOT xmlns:sql="urn:schemas-microsoft-com:xml-sql">'
  IF LEN(@companyName) > 0
    SELECT * FROM Shippers
    WHERE CompanyName LIKE (@companyName+'%')
    FOR XML RAW
  ELSE
    SELECT * FROM Shippers FOR XML RAW
  SELECT '</ROOT>'
```

The stored procedure call uses a query of type `FOR XML RAW`. If a company name is passed to the stored procedure call (`@companyName` parameter), a `WHERE` clause is used to retrieve all companies `LIKE` the one specified. If no company name is specified, then all shippers are retrieved. The stored procedure call is executed when the Stored Procedure button is pressed. The `Command_Click1` method is executed when this button is clicked. The code associated with this method is as follows:

```
Private Sub Command1_Click()
    Dim strQuery, strConn As String
    Dim conn As New Connection
    Dim streamOut As New Stream
    Dim cmd As New Command

    strConn = "PROVIDER=SQLOLEDB;DATA SOURCE=localhost;" & _
              "DATABASE=NorthWind;USER ID=sa;PASSWORD=sa;"
    conn.Open strConn
```

```
    cmd.CommandText = "GetShippersRaw"
    cmd.CommandType = adCmdStoredProc
    Set cmd.ActiveConnection = conn

    streamOut.Open
    cmd.Properties("Output Stream") = streamOut
    cmd.Parameters("@companyName") = ""
    cmd.Execute , , adExecuteStream + adCmdStoredProc

    streamOut.Position = 0
    textResult.Text = streamOut.ReadText(adReadAll)

    Set cmd = Nothing
    Set streamOut = Nothing
    conn.Close
    Set conn = Nothing

End Sub
```

The setup of the command has been simplified because a `Stream` object is no longer required in order to specify the `FOR XML` query. The `Command` object is created and its `CommandText` property is associated with the name of stored procedure call, `GetShippersRaw`. The `Command` object's `CommandType` property is set to `adCmdStoredProc`. The lone parameter of the stored procedure call, `@companyName`, is set to an empty string: `cmd.Parameters("@companyName") = ""`. The query is executed when the `Command` object's `Execute` method is called. The `adExecuteStream` option is passed as a parameter to the `Execute` method:

```
cmd.Execute , , adExecuteStream
```

Developers experienced in ADO specify the command type (for example `adCmdStoredProc`) as the third parameter to the `Execute` method. Specifying the `adCmdStoredProc` command type without also specifying the `adExecuteStream` execute option results in the query failing to return data correctly. The `adExecuteStream` option must be specified in order to return an XML document as a stream. It would be perfectly legal to not set the `CommandType` property separately and to call `Execute` as follows (with execution option and command type specified):

```
cmd.Execute , , adExecuteStream + adCmdStoredProc
```

Developers unfamiliar with stored procedure calls, the execute options, and the command options should consider honing their skills with *ADO 2.6 Programmer's Reference* from Wrox Press, ISBN 186100463x.

The output generated when the Stored Procedure button is clicked is as follows:

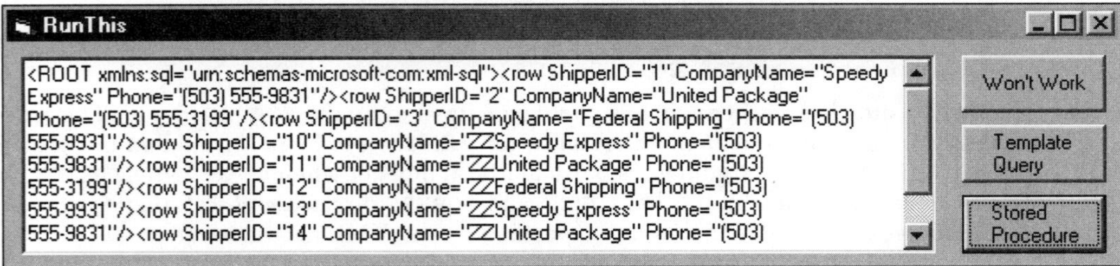

When it comes to ADO and the generation of XML, developers have a variety of options:

- The Recordset's Save method to a file – simple to use but there is no customization of the XML and performance is slowed because the XML document is persisted.
- The Recordset's Save method to a stream – simple to use but there is no customization of the XML generated.
- FOR XML query using template query in source code – using an input stream, output stream, Recordset property, and specifying a command dialect is not a style of programming used by most ADO developers. However, this approach is highly customizable because it is as customizable as FOR XML. In the event that the query is changed, the code must be recompiled.
- FOR XML query using stored procedure call – using an output stream and Recordset property is as customizable as FOR XML is – that is, very customizable! The huge benefit is that the SQL code is stored in a SQL Server database. If the SQL query needs to be altered, the source code does not have to be recompiled. The SQL associated with a stored procedure call is already prepared for use by SQL Server. Using this form of FOR XML query should result in the highest level of performance.

Summary

This chapter has concentrated on the RAW, AUTO, and EXPLICIT clauses of FOR XML. To summarize:

- If you want nice square grids of data, use FOR XML RAW. Remember, each row will be contained in an element called <row> and all data values will be contained in attributes.
- If you prefer trees of hierarchical data, use FOR XML AUTO. Data for the entire query can be specified as being contained in attributes or elements.
- If you would like explicit control over the generation of the XML document, and don't mind some complexity being added to the query, use FOR XML EXPLICIT. The shape of the hierarchy can be specified using the Tag and Parent schema columns. Directives can be used to specify the format of each column of data (attribute or element, CDATA, entity encoded, etc.).

From a performance standpoint, be aware that FOR XML EXPLICIT generates at least one temporary table.

We examined the use of FOR XML's optional arguments:

- ELEMENTS – this only applies to FOR XML AUTO and causes the data in the XML document to be contained in elements rather than attributes (the default). This applies to all data in the query. For column by column control, the only alternative is FOR XML EXPLICIT.
- XMLDATA – attaches a schema before the data extracted by the FOR XML query. The schema increases the size of the data but does allow for validation to be performed on the contents of the data. The XMLDATA argument is particularly significant when a FOR XML EXPLICIT query is used in conjunction with the ID, IDREF, and IDREFS directives. Recall that it is the schema that enforces the intra-document links specified by the XML data generated.

- `BINARY BASE64` – using this option, binary data is encoded and embedded in the XML document. This option is required for `FOR XML` queries of types `RAW` and `EXPLICIT`. By default, `FOR XML AUTO` queries contain references to binary data. In order to resolve these references, an entirely Microsoft-specific infrastructure must be used – recall that such references make the documents non-portable.

The restrictions associated with the use of `FOR XML AUTO` were reviewed in detail, as were all of the `FOR XML EXPLICIT` directives. `FOR XML EXPLICIT` may appear daunting at first. However, the layout is quite straightforward and it allows XML to be generated that matches nearly any reasonable specification.

With respect to generating XML using ADO, `FOR XML` queries are more versatile than ADO's native support for XML generation. When using `FOR XML` with ADO, a strong case has been made for calling such queries from stored procedure calls. Doing so results in better performance and allows the SQL to be modified without changing the source code and recompiling.

The most import thing to remember from this chapter is that we can generate XML by adding as few as eleven characters (with `FOR XML RAW`) to the ends of our queries. There are some subtle nuances to `FOR XML`, but it remains relatively simple to use and is extremely powerful.

4

OPENXML

In Chapter 3, we saw how to retrieve relational data from the database and render it as XML. OPENXML facilitates the opposite functionality. It exposes an XML document as a relational resultset that can be used anywhere that a resultset provider, such as a table or view, can be used.

In this chapter, we will see how:

- OPENXML provides a relational resultset over in-memory XML documents
- We can specify the structure of the resulting resultset
- We use the resultant resultset to insert, update, and delete from the database
- To retrieve metadata from the original XML document and utilize it
- ADO 2.6 can be used to manipulate the database using an XML document from various environments

Throughout the course of this chapter, there will be plenty of chances to get our hands dirty in code, but first let's get a handle on what OPENXML is, what it can and can't do, and how we use it.

OPENXML Overview

OPENXML is a SQL Server 2000 extension to Transact-SQL which can generate resultsets from an XML stream for use in other SQL statements. These resultsets can also be stored in the database, just as if we were using a table name in the FROM clause of a SELECT INTO statement. For example:

```
SELECT *
INTO XML_Result_Table
FROM
OPENXML (@hDoc, '/ROOT/Customers', 1)
```

We can see here the similarities to selecting records from a table or view. Don't worry about the syntax and parameters just yet – we will go through these in subsequent sections.

Although OPENXML can be used within a SELECT statement, the main use of OPENXML is to insert new records, update existing records, or delete data from a database – based on the data in source XML documents. This is a very powerful feature and perhaps the most important extension to SQL Server 2000's XML support.

For example, say we have two companies who are engaged in mutual exchange of data. The companies could send XML transactions in files to and from each other (maybe using Microsoft BizTalk 2000), and update their data store with the data contained in these files. As long as the companies have a know data format, this would be a very simple process. As the data is sent in XML, it would also be easy for transient applications to use this data, such as in a web report or validation tool.

We will concentrate on how to use OPENXML to facilitate the updating of the database by manipulating an XML stream, in this chapter.

We are not limited with regard to the amount of records or tables that are affected by executing an OPENXML statement. We can also use a WHERE clause with OPENXML to specify a filter on columns in the resultset produced. Again, the WHERE clause can be used anywhere that a WHERE clause can be used in normal resultset providers.

There is a lot more to OPENXML than merely providing relational data from the underlying values in an XML document. We can employ OPENXML to specify how we want the resultset produced to be structured, that is, to define how we want to map the XML components to the columns in the resultset. We could also use an existing table to act as a template for the mapping from the source XML to the resultset. Finally, we can query properties that describe the various components of the document, such as entities, attributes, and IDRefs.

The Syntax of OPENXML

Let's work through all of the various options we have, and look at some examples of each.

The basic syntax of OPENXML is shown below:

```
OPENXML(iDoc int [in],RowPattern nvarchar[in],[Flags byte[in]])
[WITH (SchemaDeclaration | TableName)]
```

The iDoc Parameter

This is the internal representation of the XML stream that we wish to produce a resultset from. This internal representation is produced by the sp_xml_preparedocument system stored procedure. We will discuss the use of this procedure in subsequent sections.

The RowPattern Parameter

This specifies the nodes of the preceding iDoc document that are to be processed by OPENXML. An XPath expression is used to specify the nodes.

We will look at XPath in detail in Chapter 8 but, for the purposes of this chapter, XPath allows us to specify a route through the XML. For example, given the following XML:

```
<ROOT>
<Name>Bob</Name>
</ROOT>
```

an XPath expression such as:

```
ROOT/Name
```

will retrieve the name from the XML. XPath is used quite a bit in this chapter but, in the majority of cases, the intention is very clear.

The Flags Parameter

This dictates the format of the resultset produced by the `OPENXML` statement. This parameter also allows us to indicate how we want to handle overflow information. Overflow columns are used to store unconsumed data from the source XML document. Examples for the uses of overflow columns are discussed in the *Writing Queries Using OPENXML* section later in this chapter.

The table below shows the accepted values for the *`Flags`* parameter:

Flags Byte Value	Description
0	Default. Attribute-centric mapping.
1	Explicitly indicates that the source XML should be mapped to the resultset using an attribute-centric mapping.
2	Explicitly indicates that the source XML should be mapped to the resultset using an element-centric mapping.
8	This value explicitly states that only unconsumed data should be copied to the overflow property, `@mp:xmltext`.

Attribute- and element-centric mappings dictate how the mapping between the source XML document, the `RowPattern` XPath expression, and the output resultset are tied together. Basically, attribute-centric pulls the column data from attributes of selected entities, while element-centric pulls the information from the sub elements of the selected entities. We will look at this in more detail later in the next and subsequent sections.

OPENXML Column Mapping – RowPattern Rules

There are rules that govern how combinations of these `Flags` parameters are handled. We can concatenate the `Flags` values using logical `OR` to perform multiple processing of the source XML document. For example, we can specify attribute- and element-centric processing by performing `1` (attribute-centric) `OR` `2` (element-centric). The result of this `OR` is `3`, so we can insert `3` into the `OPENXML` statement to specify that we want to perform both attribute- and element-centric mappings of the XML source to the resultset.

The possible values are shown in this diagram – which shows the path through the processing of an `OPENXML` statement – and are explained in the subsequent text.

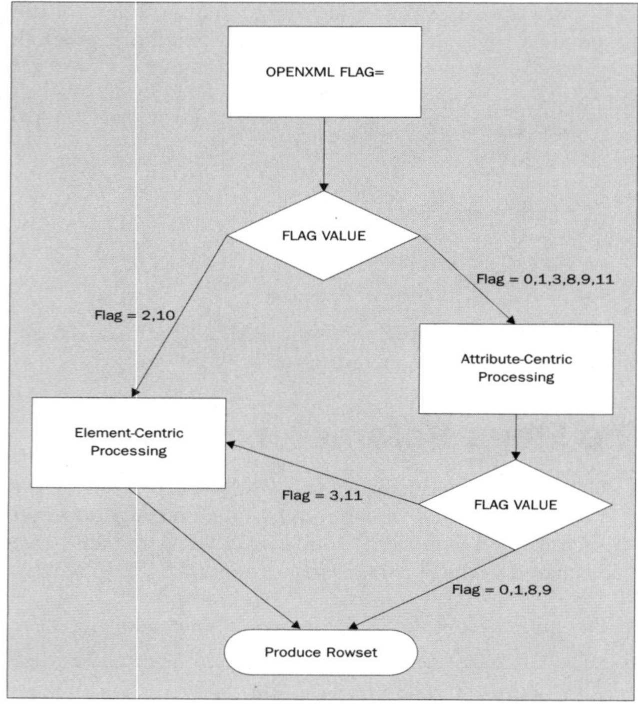

The diagram above shows how `OPENXML` handles the mapping values. If the value passed to `OPENXML` is `0`, `1`, `3`, `8`, `9`, or `11`, `OPENXML` knows that an attribute-centric mapping has been specified. Also, if the value is `3` or `11`, `OPENXML` applies element-centric mapping to the source XML. If, however, the flag value is `2` or `10`, element-centric mapping is the only mapping specified.

Note that the path through the diagram above indicates that attribute-centric mappings, if specified, are always performed before element-centric mappings.

When we use logical `OR` to concatenate the `Flags` values, we can produce values that specify the multiple processing steps we require. The table below lists the possible values and their purpose:

Flags Byte Value	Mapping Description
`0`	Default. Attribute-centric.
`1`	Attribute-centric.
`2`	Element-centric.
`3`	Both attribute- and element-centric.
`8`	Unconsumed data only stored in `@mp:xmltext`, defaults to attribute-centric.
`9`	Unconsumed data only stored in `@mp:xmltext`, explicit attribute-centric.
`10`	Unconsumed data only stored in `@mp:xmltext`, element-centric.
`11`	Unconsumed data only stored in `@mp:xmltext`, both attribute- and element-centric.

From this table, we can deduce that attribute-centric mapping is always used unless element-centric is specified. From the diagram, we can see that attribute-centric processing is always performed before element-centric processing if both mappings are specified.

The WITH Clause

The `Flags` parameter gives us a quick and easy way to extract a resultset from source XML but, sometimes, we need to extract the data in a formal and selective way. The `WITH` clause allows us to specify what columns we want to appear in the resultset, their data types, and what node the column should be mapped to from the source XML.

There are three options with the `WITH` clause:

- `WITH TableName` – to associate the resultset with an existing table.
- `WITH (Name varchar(20), 'ROOT/Name')` – to specify the columns, their data types, and (optionally) the XPath expression that directs the processor to the source XML node to map to.
- Omit the clause altogether.

We shall now look at these three possible options in more detail.

Associate with an Existing Table

If we have XML that has been structured to represent a table in our database, we can use the `WITH` clause to specify the table that the XML represents. `OPENXML` will then use this table as the template for associating the nodes in our source XML to the columns of the resultset.

This is especially useful if we have XML data that represents entities in our database, but is stored in a non-relational fashion. For example, if we have XML to insert into our database which lists artists, albums, and tracks, these would be stored as individual tables in our database and related by key fields. This being the case, we need some way of identifying the individual entities in our source to map to the tables on an insert.

Specify the Columns

Assuming the XML was in the correct structure, we can use `OPENXML` and the `WITH` clause to specify the tables that portions of the source XML map to. Consider the following XML data snippet:

```
<Artist Name="David Gray">
   <Media Type="Album">
      <Name>White Ladder</Name>
      <TrackList NoOfTracks="10">
         <Track Pos="1">Please Forgive Me</Track>
         <Track Pos="2">Babylon</Track>
         <Track Pos="3">My Oh My</Track>
         <Track Pos="4">Were Not Right</Track>
         <Track Pos="5">Nightblindness</Track>
         <Track Pos="6">Silver Lining</Track>
         <Track Pos="7">White Ladder</Track>
         <Track Pos="8">This Years Love</Track>
         <Track Pos="9">Sail Away</Track>
         <Track Pos="10">Say Hello Wave Goodbye</Track>
      </TrackList>
   </Media>
</Artist>
```

We will see more detailed examples of this in the next section but, for now, the following code fragment shows how we can use tables as templates for the mapping of the source XML data to a resultset:

```
INSERT Artists
SELECT *
FROM OPENXML(@iDoc, N'/ROOT/Artist')
   WITH Artist

INSERT Albums
SELECT *
FROM OPENXML(@iDoc, N'/ROOT/Artist/Albums')
   WITH Album
```

Here, `Artist` and `Album` are existing tables in our database, and `@iDoc` is a handle to our source XML data. Don't worry about this handle at the moment, all will be revealed soon.

This technique could be used for replicating disconnected or disparate databases over the Internet or some other medium. We could send the XML and a script for the entities we want to replicate, then use this technique to publish the data.

In the method used in the code snippet above, the assumption was that the structure of the source XML was such that we could relate the elements in the source to those of existing tables in our database. Unfortunately, this will not always be the case, so we need some means of manipulating the source data to allow us to map the source XML to table columns.

We can map the source XML nodes to columns in the resultset by explicitly specifying the column name and data type, and the XPath expression which identifies the source node to retrieve the value from.

The following code snippet shows how we use the `WITH` clause to do this:

```
SELECT *
FROM OPENXML(@iDoc, '/ROOT/Artist/Album/Track')
   WITH(
      ArtistID int '../../@ArtistID',
      ArtistName varchar(30) '../../@ArtistName',
      Album varchar(30) '../Name',
      Track varchar(30) '@TrackNo')
```

We will not worry about how this example works just yet, but note the way that we can use XPath to specify the nodes of the XML and associate them with columns in the resultset. Also note that we haven't specified a `Flags` parameter. We could have passed a value for the `Flags` parameter but the value is overridden by the column pattern in the `WITH` clause.

This method presents us with a very powerful way of pulling data from an XML source and manipulating the XML to update a database.

Omit the WITH Clause – Edge Tables

The final option is to omit the `WITH` clause altogether. You might think that `OPENXML` will return garbage if we do this, but we actually get an **edge table**.

An edge table is so called because every edge in the source XML is mapped to a row in the resultset. By this we mean that the XML is broken down into its constituent elements, and each element is described by a row of metadata. Given the following XML data snippet:

```
<Track Pos="1">Zoo Station</Track>
<Track Pos="2">Even Better Than The Real Thing</Track>
```

we can generate the sample edge table shown below:

	id	parentid	nodetype	localname	prefix	namespaceuri	datatype	prev	text
1	8	5	1	Track	NULL	NULL	NULL	7	NULL
2	9	8	2	TrackNo	NULL	NULL	NULL	NULL	NULL
3	14	9	3	#text	NULL	NULL	NULL	NULL	1
4	10	8	3	#text	NULL	NULL	NULL	NULL	Zoo Station
5	11	5	1	Track	NULL	NULL	NULL	8	NULL
6	12	11	2	TrackNo	NULL	NULL	NULL	NULL	NULL
7	15	12	3	#text	NULL	NULL	NULL	NULL	2
8	13	11	3	#text	NULL	NULL	NULL	NULL	Even Better

In this screenshot, each of the records presents information about a node in the source XML. This will make much more sense with a description of the columns in the edge table.

Column	Description
`ID`	Uniquely identifies the XML component. An XML component could be an element, an attribute, a textual value, a processing instruction, etc. In our album example, this would relate to the first column of the screenshot.
`ParentID`	The ID of the parent component. Note that this is not necessarily the parent node. The parent could be an attribute, the child, a text node value, etc. The parentid column in our screenshot shows this. Notice that the record with an id of 10 has a parentid of 8. This is the relationship between the album track node and the track's name.
`NodeType`	The type of node that the component belongs to. There are twelve possible values for this column: ❑ element node ❑ attribute node ❑ text node ❑ CDATA section node ❑ entity reference node ❑ entity node ❑ processing instruction node ❑ comment node ❑ document node ❑ document type node ❑ document fragment node ❑ notation node In our example above, the record with id 8 is an element node – in this case representing a `Track` element.

Column	Description
LocalName	The local name of the node. The LocalName is used in conjunction with the Prefix and NamespaceURI properties to name element and attribute nodes. From the screenshot, we can see that this field maps to element or attribute names, and the special name #text which indicates the text node type from the list of NodeTypes above.
Prefix	The prefix used to identify the namespace of the node. NULL in all the cases in our example, but would be shown if the element that the record is associated with had a namespace prefix assigned to it.
NamespaceURI	The URI of the namespace of the node. Again, NULL in our example but would be populated if the element that the record is representing had a namespace associated with it.
DataType	The node's data type. This is derived from the DTD of the XML source. NULL in our example, but this field would contain the data type of the element if a DTD had been specified for the source XML data.
Prev	If the node has a previous sibling, this node holds the ID property of the sibling. If we look at the record with id 11, the prev field has the value 8. This is the ID of the previous element on the same level as the element represented in this record.
Text	The element's value, if available. In the example above, this field stores the value for our attribute and element nodes.

In our example screenshot, the edge table shows us the hierarchy of the source XML by mapping out each element in the source XML data, informing us of the element's position in the source by using ParentID and Prev. The edge table also shows us the attributes and elements of the XML, and their values. There are only three types of nodes in the portion of the edge table shown in this screenshot, but there are more in the rest of the table, which we will see later. The important thing to note here is the power of the edge table. We can virtually recreate the source from this table, and the properties held within it allow us to make decisions on how to manipulate the source.

You might be wondering why all this would be useful! Well, the edge table gives us a lot more information than is available from viewing the source XML data, such as element IDs and data types. For example, given the XML data shown below:

```
<ROOT>
   <CUSTOMER>
      <NAME>Glen Harding</NAME>
   </CUSTOMER>
   <CUSTOMER>
      <NAME>Angus Gilmour</NAME>
   </CUSTOMER>
</ROOT>
```

we could insert these records into a CustomerName table with the structure:

```
[ID] INT,
[Name] VARCHAR(50)
```

by executing the following OPENXML script:

```
DECLARE @idoc INT

EXEC sp_xml_preparedocument  @idoc OUTPUT,'
<ROOT>
   <CUSTOMER>
      <NAME>Glen Harding</NAME>
   </CUSTOMER>
   <CUSTOMER>
      <NAME>Angus Gilmour</NAME>
   </CUSTOMER>
</ROOT>
'

INSERT CustomerName(ID, Name)
SELECT *
FROM OPENXML (@idoc,'/ROOT/CUSTOMER')
      WITH (ID int '@mp:id',
            [Name] Varchar(50) 'NAME')
```

Don't worry too much about the specifics of the example, except for the OPENXML statement. We have specified the @mp:id metaproperty – which maps to the ID column of the edge table – as the ID column of the table in the WITH clause. This will always be unique within a particular document. We will take a look at metaproperties and their uses later in this chapter.

Writing Queries Using OPENXML

After wading through the syntax of OPENXML, let's now put it to use. Specifically, we will examine the following:

- sp_xml_preparedocument and sp_xml_removedocument
- Attribute-centric, element-centric, and mixed mapping
- Explicit column mapping
- OPENXML metaproperties
- Overflow columns
- ADO and OPENXML

First, let's have a look at the test dataset that we are going to use throughout this section. We will be using this data to examine the OPENXML statement and its primary uses. This will include adding, updating, and deleting data from existing tables.

The code below is the XML for a library of music.

```
<?xml version="1.0" encoding="UTF-8"?>
<ROOT>
   <Artist Name="U2">
      <Media Type="CD">
         <Name>Achtung Baby</Name>
         <TrackList NoOfTracks="12">
            <Track Pos="1">Zoo Station</Track>
```

```
            <Track Pos="2">Even Better Than The Real Thing</Track>
            <Track Pos="3">One</Track>
            <Track Pos="4">Till The End Of The World</Track>
            <Track Pos="5">Whose Gonna Ride Your Wild Horses</Track>
            <Track Pos="6">So Cruel</Track>
            <Track Pos="7">The Fly</Track>
            <Track Pos="8">Mysterious Ways</Track>
            <Track Pos="9">Trying To Throw Your Arms Around The World</Track>
            <Track Pos="10">Ultra Violet(Light My Way)</Track>
            <Track Pos="11">Acrobat</Track>
            <Track Pos="12">Love Is Blindness</Track>
         </TrackList>
      </Media>
      <Media Type="Album">
         <Name>All That You Cant Leave Behind</Name>
         <TrackList NoOfTracks="12">
            <Track Pos="1">Beautiful Day</Track>
            <Track Pos="2">Stuck In A Moment You Cant Get Out Of</Track>
            <Track Pos="3">Elevation</Track>
            <Track Pos="4">Walk On</Track>
            <Track Pos="5">Kite</Track>
            <Track Pos="6">In A Little While</Track>
            <Track Pos="7">Wild Honey</Track>
            <Track Pos="8">Peace On Earth</Track>
            <Track Pos="9">When I Look At The World</Track>
            <Track Pos="10">New York</Track>
            <Track Pos="11">Grace</Track>
            <Track Pos="12">The Ground Beneath Her Feet</Track>
         </TrackList>
      </Media>
   </Artist>
   <Artist Name="David Gray">
      <Media Type="Album">
         <Name>White Ladder</Name>
         <TrackList NoOfTracks="10">
            <Track Pos="1">Please Forgive Me</Track>
            <Track Pos="2">Babylon</Track>
            <Track Pos="3">My Oh My</Track>
            <Track Pos="4">Were Not Right</Track>
            <Track Pos="5">Nightblindness</Track>
            <Track Pos="6">Silver Lining</Track>
            <Track Pos="7">White Ladder</Track>
            <Track Pos="8">This Years Love</Track>
            <Track Pos="9">Sail Away</Track>
            <Track Pos="10">Say Hello Wave Goodbye</Track>
         </TrackList>
      </Media>
   </Artist>
   <Artist Name="Alanis Morissette">
      <Media Type="CD">
         <Name>Supposed Former Infatuation Junkie</Name>
         <TrackList NoOfTracks="17">
            <Track Pos="1">Front Row</Track>
            <Track Pos="2">Baba</Track>
            <Track Pos="3">Thank You</Track>
            <Track Pos="4">Are You Still Mad</Track>
            <Track Pos="5">Sympathetic Character</Track>
            <Track Pos="6">That I Would Be Good</Track>
            <Track Pos="7">The Couch</Track>
            <Track Pos="8">Cant Not</Track>
            <Track Pos="9">UR</Track>
            <Track Pos="10">I Was Hoping</Track>
```

```
            <Track Pos="11">One</Track>
            <Track Pos="12">Would Not Come</Track>
            <Track Pos="13">Unsent</Track>
            <Track Pos="14">So Pure</Track>
            <Track Pos="15">Joining You</Track>
            <Track Pos="16">Heart Of The House</Track>
            <Track Pos="17">Your Congratulations</Track>
         </TrackList>
      </Media>
   </Artist>
</ROOT>
```

This sample code is very straightforward. After the root, there is a collection of `<Artist>` elements which contain media types, names of the recordings, and lists of the tracks that the recordings contain. This code will be used throughout the rest of this section, with only slight changes in order to highlight important concepts.

In the examples we have seen so far, the `iDoc` parameter has not been declared or assigned a value. As stated in the syntax section, the `iDoc` parameter is a handle to the XML stream that we want to process with `OPENXML`. In order to obtain this handle, we use a system stored procedure called `sp_xml_preparedocument`. The following section discusses this procedure, as well as its sibling procedure `sp_xml_removedocument`.

sp_xml_preparedocument

`sp_xml_preparedocument` is used to prepare the XML for use with `OPENXML`. An example of this procedure is shown below:

```
EXEC sp_xml_preparedocument @hDoc OUTPUT, @DocIn,
     '<root xmlns:xyz="run:MyNamespace"/>'
```

`@hDoc` is a handle to the processed document and `@DocIn` is the XML stream to be processed. There is also a third parameter which allows us to specify namespace declarations. This parameter is optional and, if omitted, the following default value is used:

```
<root xmlns:mp="urn:schemas-microsoft-com:xml-metaprop">
```

`@hDoc` is an integer value which points to the in-memory internal representation of the document specified by the `@DocIn` parameter. The `@DocIn` parameter is the textual representation of the source XML data. Note that the `@hDoc` parameter is an `OUPUT` parameter, as the integer handle is returned into the parameter by the `sp_xml_preparedocument` procedure.

`sp_xml_preparedocument` takes the source XML, parses it, and creates an in-memory internal representation of the document. This representation is a tree structure defining the nodes of the XML. For example, given the statement:

```
   sp_xml_preparedocument @hDoc OUTPUT, @DocIn
```

where the `@DocIn` variable has been assigned to the following XML:

```
<ROOT>
   <Artist Name="U2">
      <Media Type="CD">
         <Name>Achtung Baby</Name>
         <TrackList NoOfTracks="12">
```

```
            <Track Pos="1">Zoo Station</Track>
            <Track Pos="2">Even Better Than The Real Thing</Track>
            <Track Pos="3">One</Track>
            <Track Pos="4">Till The End Of The World</Track>
            <Track Pos="5">Whose Gonna Ride Your Wild Horses</Track>
            <Track Pos="6">So Cruel</Track>
            <Track Pos="7">The Fly</Track>
            <Track Pos="8">Mysterious Ways</Track>
            <Track Pos="9">Tryin' To Throw Your Arms Around The World</Track>
            <Track Pos="10">Ultra Violet(Light My Way)</Track>
            <Track Pos="11">Acrobat</Track>
            <Track Pos="12">Love Is Blindness</Track>
         </TrackList>
      </Media>
   </Artist>
</ROOT>
```

the source XML data would be blown out to produce the following tree structure:

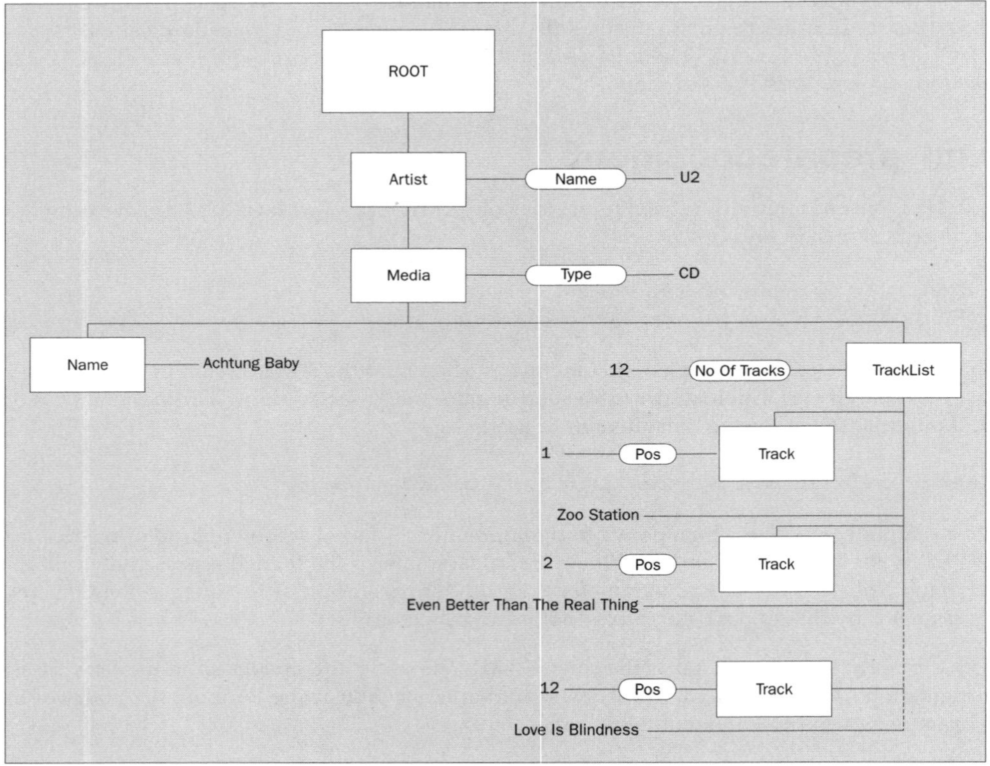

As we can see, each element and attribute of the source XML is broken out into its constituent elements. For illustration purposes, the boxes represent elements, the "sausage" shapes represent attributes, and values are displayed as borderless snippets of text.

After representing the source XML in this way, OPENXML now uses this representation to perform the many functions we can ask of it. The rest of this chapter will highlight these functions and how we may use them.

> **`sp_xml_preparedocument` uses `Msxml2.dll` as the source for the MSXML Parser which creates this processed output.**

The document handle returned by `sp_xml_preparedocument` is available to be used in code until one of the following two events occurs:

- The current session ends
- There is a call to `sp_xml_removedocument`

sp_xml_removedocument

When the current session ends, the in-memory representation of the source XML is de-allocated and the reference to the document is destroyed. As programmers who have used COM, SQL cursors, and the like, we know that garbage collection is an important part of memory management. To this end, SQL Server 2000 provides the system stored procedure `sp_xml_removedocument`. This procedure handles the clean-up process for us.

> **Garbage collection is very important because the MSXML parser can consume around an eighth of the total memory allocation of SQL Server. This is due to storage of the internal representation created by `sp_xml_preparedocument`.**

The syntax for this procedure is very simple. Just pass the handle to the document produced by `sp_xml_preparedocument`:

```
EXEC sp_xml_removedocument @hDoc
```

where `@hDoc` is the handle to the document we wish to remove. This will remove the in-memory representation of the source XML, and render the document handle `@hDoc` invalid.

Attribute-Centric Mapping

Now that we know how to prepare the source XML for processing by `OPENXML`, let's do it! Firstly, we shall have a look at how we map attribute-centric source XML to a relational resultset using `OPENXML`. The tables that we need for this example are scripted below:

```
CREATE TABLE [dbo].[Album] (
   [ArtistID] [int] NULL ,
   [AlbumID] [int] IDENTITY (1, 1) NOT NULL ,
   [MediaID] [int] NULL ,
   [Name] [varchar] (50) NULL ,
   [NoOfTracks] [int] NULL
) ON [PRIMARY]
GO

CREATE TABLE [dbo].[Artist] (
   [ArtistID] [int] IDENTITY (1, 1) NOT NULL ,
   [Name] [nvarchar] (100) NULL
) ON [PRIMARY]
GO
```

```
CREATE TABLE [dbo].[Media] (
   [MediaID] [int] IDENTITY (1, 1) NOT NULL ,
   [Type] [varchar] (20) NULL
) ON [PRIMARY]
GO

CREATE TABLE [dbo].[Track] (
   [AlbumID] [int] NULL ,
   [Pos] [int] NULL ,
   [Name] [varchar] (50) NULL
) ON [PRIMARY]
GO

 CREATE  UNIQUE  INDEX [ind_AlbumID] ON [dbo].[Album]([AlbumID]) ON [PRIMARY]
GO

 CREATE  UNIQUE  INDEX [ind_ArtistID] ON [dbo].[Artist]([ArtistID]) ON [PRIMARY]
GO

 CREATE  UNIQUE  INDEX [ind_MediaID] ON [dbo].[Media]([MediaID]) ON [PRIMARY]
GO
```

Don't forget that this code is available for download from www.wrox.com. You will notice that the tables we have created mirror reasonably the example XML data for this chapter. As this is the case, we can use these tables to specify the mappings from the source XML data to the generated resultset.

Now that we have the tables in place, we can use OPENXML to use these tables as templates for the columns in the resultset. Run the following code:

```
-- First declare some variables to hold the XML stream and the handle
-- returned from sp_xml_preparedocument.

DECLARE @hDoc int,
        @cDoc varchar(8000)

-- Now load the source XML into the @cDoc variable.

SET @cDoc = '
<ROOT>
   <Artist Name="U2">
      <Media Type="CD">
         <Name>Achtung Baby</Name>
         <TrackList NoOfTracks="12">
            <Track Pos="1">Zoo Station</Track>
            <Track Pos="2">Even Better Than The Real Thing</Track>
            <Track Pos="3">One</Track>
            <Track Pos="4">Till The End Of The World</Track>
            <Track Pos="5">Whose Gonna Ride Your Wild Horses</Track>
            <Track Pos="6">So Cruel</Track>
            <Track Pos="7">The Fly</Track>
            <Track Pos="8">Mysterious Ways</Track>
            <Track Pos="9">Trying To Throw Your Arms Around The World</Track>
            <Track Pos="10">Ultra Violet(Light My Way)</Track>
            <Track Pos="11">Acrobat</Track>
            <Track Pos="12">Love Is Blindness</Track>
         </TrackList>
      </Media>
      <Media Type="Album">
         <Name>All That You Cant Leave Behind</Name>
         <TrackList NoOfTracks="12">
```

```
            <Track Pos="1">Beautiful Day</Track>
            <Track Pos="2">Stuck In A Moment You Cant Get Out Of</Track>
            <Track Pos="3">Elevation</Track>
            <Track Pos="4">Walk On</Track>
            <Track Pos="5">Kite</Track>
            <Track Pos="6">In A Little While</Track>
            <Track Pos="7">Wild Honey</Track>
            <Track Pos="8">Peace On Earth</Track>
            <Track Pos="9">When I Look At The World</Track>
            <Track Pos="10">New York</Track>
            <Track Pos="11">Grace</Track>
            <Track Pos="12">The Ground Beneath Her Feet</Track>
         </TrackList>
      </Media>
   </Artist>
   <Artist Name="David Gray">
      <Media Type="Album">
         <Name>White Ladder</Name>
         <TrackList NoOfTracks="10">
            <Track Pos="1">Please Forgive Me</Track>
            <Track Pos="2">Babylon</Track>
            <Track Pos="3">My Oh My</Track>
            <Track Pos="4">Were Not Right</Track>
            <Track Pos="5">Nightblindness</Track>
            <Track Pos="6">Silver Lining</Track>
            <Track Pos="7">White Ladder</Track>
            <Track Pos="8">This Years Love</Track>
            <Track Pos="9">Sail Away</Track>
            <Track Pos="10">Say Hello Wave Goodbye</Track>
         </TrackList>
      </Media>
   </Artist>
   <Artist Name="Alanis Morissette">
      <Media Type="CD">
         <Name>Supposed Former Infatuation Junkie</Name>
         <TrackList NoOfTracks="17">
            <Track Pos="1">Front Row</Track>
            <Track Pos="2">Baba</Track>
            <Track Pos="3">Thank You</Track>
            <Track Pos="4">Are You Still Mad</Track>
            <Track Pos="5">Sympathetic Character</Track>
            <Track Pos="6">That I Would Be Good</Track>
            <Track Pos="7">The Couch</Track>
            <Track Pos="8">Cant Not</Track>
            <Track Pos="9">UR</Track>
            <Track Pos="10">I Was Hoping</Track>
            <Track Pos="11">One</Track>
            <Track Pos="12">Would Not Come</Track>
            <Track Pos="13">Unsent</Track>
            <Track Pos="14">So Pure</Track>
            <Track Pos="15">Joining You</Track>
            <Track Pos="16">Heart Of The House</Track>
            <Track Pos="17">Your Congratulations</Track>
         </TrackList>
      </Media>
   </Artist>
</ROOT>
'

-- We now call sp_xml_preparedocument to render the source XML in a
-- fashion consumable by OPENXML.
```

```
EXEC sp_XML_preparedocument @hdoc OUTPUT, @cDoc

-- Now call the OPENXML function to select a list of the artists from
-- the source XML. We shall SELECT artist [Name] from OPENXML, using
-- table Artist as the template.

SELECT [Name]
FROM OPENXML (@hdoc, '/ROOT/Artist',1)
WITH Artist

EXEC sp_xml_removedocument @hDoc
```

The lines of code *without* gray shading are taken from the XML source document. Note the use of the `WITH` clause, towards the end, that we discussed in the earlier section on the syntax of `OPENXML`.

The resultset is shown below:

```
Name
------------------------
U2
David Gray
Alanis Morissette

(3 row(s) affected)
```

Easy, isn't it? Let's quickly go through how the example works. We first load the source XML into a variable, which is passed to `sp_xml_preparedocument`. The resultant handle to the processed source is used with an XPath expression to pull back various nodes in the source. We then use an existing table as a template for the mapping between the source XML and the resultset.

The definition of the `Artist` table has two columns. If we had used `SELECT *` rather than `SELECT [Name]`, we would still have produced the same result. This is because we are not allowed to specify identity columns in the `SELECT` list of a `FROM OPENXML` statement. So, in the case of `SELECT *`, the identity column `ArtistID` is ignored.

The XPath expression in the example is `'/ROOT/Artist'`, which instructs `OPENXML` to loop through all the `Artist` nodes in our source XML. We have also specified that the mapping type be set to 1, that is, attribute-centric. This means that our `SELECT` statement pulls back only the name attribute of all the `Artist` elements.

To expand on this, let's use the other tables we created to get the attribute values for the other nodes in the source. Append the following code after the `Artist` select and before the remove document procedure, and execute the script:

```
SELECT *
FROM OPENXML (@hdoc, '/ROOT/Artist/Media',1)
WITH Media

SELECT *
FROM OPENXML (@hdoc, '/ROOT/Artist/Media/TrackList',1)
WITH Album

SELECT *
FROM OPENXML (@hdoc, '/ROOT/Artist/Media/TrackList/Track',1)
WITH Track
```

The resultsets are shown below:

```
Name
----------------------------
U2
David Gray
Alanis Morissette

(3 row(s) affected)

Type
--------------------
CD
Album
Album
CD

(4 row(s) affected)

ArtistID    MediaID     Name                                              NoOfTracks
----------- ----------- ------------------------------------------------- ----------------
NULL        NULL        NULL                                              12
NULL        NULL        NULL                                              12
NULL        NULL        NULL                                              10
NULL        NULL        NULL                                              17

(4 row(s) affected)

AlbumID     Pos         Name
----------- ----------- ----------------
NULL        1           NULL
NULL        2           NULL
NULL        3           NULL

...

NULL        15          NULL
NULL        16          NULL
NULL        17          NULL

(51 row(s) affected)
```

There are a lot of NULLs in these results. This is due to the SELECT * statements and the fact that the tables used in the WITH clause specify columns which are not modeled as attributes in the source XML. We shall see how to retrieve element values in the next set of examples.

So, to recap, we can use the value 1 to direct OPENXML to retrieve attribute values from the source XML, based on the XPath expression. In this example, we used a table to specify the columns to map the source XML to. Identity columns cannot be specified in the SELECT list, and are not returned in the resultset if all columns are specified.

Element-Centric Mapping

Let's concentrate on the Media, Name, TrackList, and Track elements. We will use two different styles of WITH clause to map the columns to the resultset, for reasons that we shall see later. To run this example, simply replace the SELECT statements in the attribute-centric example with the following:

```
SELECT *
FROM OPENXML (@hdoc, '/ROOT/Artist/Media', 2)
WITH Album --([Name] varchar(100))

SELECT Track 'Name'
FROM OPENXML (@hdoc, '/ROOT/Artist/Media/TrackList/Track', 2)
WITH (Track varchar(100) '.')
```

Let's have a look at the results of these statements before we discuss them:

```
ArtistID    MediaID     Name                                NoOfTracks
----------- ----------- ----------------------------------- -----------
NULL        NULL        Achtung Baby                        NULL
NULL        NULL        All That You Cant Leave Behind      NULL
NULL        NULL        White Ladder                        NULL
NULL        NULL        Supposed Former Infatuation Junkie  NULL

(4 row(s) affected)

Name
--------------------------------------------------
Zoo Station
Even Better Than The Real Thing
One

...

Joining You
Heart Of The House
Your Congratulations

(51 row(s) affected)
```

The first SELECT is as you might expect, using the Media table as the template for the mapping to the XML source. We set the flag on the OPENXML statement to 2, specifying element-centric mapping, and the rest of the columns in the returned resultset are NULL.

You will notice that, in the second SELECT statement, we are not using a table as a template for the column mapping. This is because the Track table and the source XML Track element do not have the same column names. The table has a field called Name, but the source XML element is called Track. So we explicitly map the source XML column to the resulting row in the resultset, using XPath and the WITH clause:

```
SELECT Track 'Name'
FROM OPENXML (@hdoc, '/ROOT/Artist/Media/TrackList/Track', 2)
WITH (Track varchar(100) '.')
```

What we have done here is set the XPath to the node that we want to expose. We then specify the column name, data type, and the XPath of the node that we want to map to. In this case it is the current node, so we use the dot notation as the XPath.

Mixed Mapping

Our source XML data may not be in a format which allows us to use attribute- or element-centric mappings to retrieve the resultset that we require. In some cases we will need to use a mixture of both attribute- and element-centric. We can use both types of mapping in one `SELECT` statement by specifying the logical `OR` of the `Flags` value for attribute- and element-centric mappings. An example is shown below:

```
DECLARE @hDoc int
DECLARE @cDoc varchar(8000)

SET @cDoc = '
<ROOT>
   <Artist Name="U2">
      <Media Type="CD">
         <Name>Achtung Baby</Name>
         <TrackList NoOfTracks="12">
            <Track Pos="1">
               <Name>Zoo Station</Name>
            </Track>
            <Track Pos="2">
               <Name>Even Better Than The Real Thing</Name>
            </Track>
            <Track Pos="3">
               <Name>One</Name>
            </Track>
            <Track Pos="4">
               <Name>Till The End Of The World</Name>
            </Track>
            <Track Pos="5">
               <Name>Whose Gonna Ride Your Wild Horses</Name>
            </Track>
            <Track Pos="6">
               <Name>So Cruel</Name>
            </Track>
            <Track Pos="7">
               <Name>The Fly</Name>
            </Track>
            <Track Pos="8">
               <Name>Mysterious Ways</Name>
            </Track>
            <Track Pos="9">
               <Name>Trying To Throw Your Arms Around The World</Name>
            </Track>
            <Track Pos="10">
               <Name>Ultra Violet(Light My Way)</Name>
            </Track>
            <Track Pos="11">
               <Name>Acrobat</Name>
            </Track>
            <Track Pos="12">
               <Name>Love Is Blindness</Name>
            </Track>
         </TrackList>
      </Media>
   </Artist>
</ROOT>
'
-- Create an internal representation of the XML document.
EXEC sp_XML_preparedocument @hdoc OUTPUT, @cDoc
```

```
-- SELECT the appropriate fields using a table to map to
-- the source XML
SELECT *
FROM OPENXML (@hdoc, '/ROOT/Artist/Media/TrackList/Track', 3)
WITH Track

EXEC sp_XML_removedocument @hdoc
```

When this code is run, the following output is produced:

```
AlbumID      Pos         Name
------------ ----------- ------------------------------------------------------
NULL         1           Zoo Station
NULL         2           Even Better Than The Real Thing
NULL         3           One
NULL         4           Till The End Of The World
NULL         5           Whose Gonna Ride Your Wild Horses
NULL         6           So Cruel
NULL         7           The Fly
NULL         8           Mysterious Ways
NULL         9           Trying To Throw Your Arms Around The World
NULL         10          Ultra Violet(Light My Way)
NULL         11          Acrobat
NULL         12          Love Is Blindness

(12 row(s) affected)
```

Explicit Column Mapping

This is all very well, but using attribute, element, or mixed mappings with tables as templates, or specifying column definitions explicitly, will not always meet our requirements. Take our running example, for instance. Imagine that we want to know everything about an album – the artist, album name, number of tracks, track positions, and track names. To achieve this using the method above requires a list of `SELECT` statements, which bring back the results in separate resultsets.

The most effective way of bringing back a single resultset with all the information that we require is by explicitly mapping the columns of the desired resultset to elements and attributes in the source XML. To do this, we specify the XPath expression which identifies the value that we want to retrieve. The code below shows how this is done:

```
-- SELECT the appropriate fields using an explicit mapping to
-- the source XML

SELECT *
FROM OPENXML (@hdoc, '/ROOT/Artist/Media/TrackList/Track', 1)
WITH (Artist          varchar(30)   '../../../@Name',
      [Media Type]    varchar(10)   '../../@Type',
      [No Of Tracks]  int           '../@NoOfTracks',
      [Album Name]    varchar(50)   '../../Name',
      [Track Pos]     int           '@Pos',
      [Track Name]    varchar(100)  '.')
```

Let's have a look at how this works. The XPath passed to the `OPENXML` statement points to the very last node that we want to retrieve a value from. This is done so that we can easily select parent nodes in the `WITH` clause. The `WITH` clause itself contains the definitions for the columns that we want to retrieve, plus the XPath expression of the value that we want to pull from the source XML. The first of these is the `Artist`, which is at the top level of the repeating group in the source XML. From this node we want the artist's name, so we select the `@Name` attribute. Then we go to the next level, which is media type, and retrieve the value for the `@Type` attribute, and so on. The columns can be specified in any order, and the `"../"` notation in XPath instructs the parser to go up one level from the current position, that is, go to the node's parent.

The result of running this `SELECT` statement against the XML source given at the beginning of the *Attribute-Centric Mapping* section is shown below:

```
Artist           Media Type       No Of Tracks      Album Name        Track Pos     Track Name
---------------- ---------------- ----------------- ----------------- ------------- ---------------------------------
U2               CD               12                Achtung Baby      1             Zoo Station
U2               CD               12                Achtung Baby      2             Even Better Than The...
U2               CD               12                Achtung Baby      3             One
U2               CD               12                Achtung Baby      4             Till The End Of The World
U2               CD               12                Achtung Baby      5             Whose Gonna Ride...
U2               CD               12                Achtung Baby      6             So Cruel
U2               CD               12                Achtung Baby      7             The Fly
U2               CD               12                Achtung Baby      8             Mysterious Ways
U2               CD               12                Achtung Baby      9             Trying To Throw Your...
U2               CD               12                Achtung Baby      10            Ultra Violet(Light My Way)
U2               CD               12                Achtung Baby      11            Acrobat
U2               CD               12                Achtung Baby      12            Love Is Blindness
David Gray       Album            10                White Ladder      1             Please Forgive Me
David Gray       Album            10                White Ladder      2             Babylon
David Gray       Album            10                White Ladder      3             My Oh My
...
(51 row(s) affected)
```

OPENXML Metaproperties

`OPENXML` metaproperties provide information about DOM elements contained in the source XML. The information is not textually represented in the source; the `OPENXML` statement provides this meta-information as part of normal processing.

We can use these metaproperties in generated resultsets to make processing decisions, track parentage, provide a unique key, etc.

Metaproperty	Description
`@mp:id`	The unique ID of the node within the source XML. The ID of the root node is zero (0). The ID is valid for as long as the document is loaded in-memory. So, if the document is reloaded, the same node may not have the same ID as when it was loaded initially.
`@mp:parentid`	The unique ID of the current node's parent. The root node has an `@mp:parentid` of `NULL`.

Metaproperty	Description
@mp:localname	The current node's name. So, if the node is <Customer>, the node's @mp:localname is Customer.
@mp:parentlocalname	The name of the current node's parent.
@mp:namespaceuri	The namespace URI of the current element.
@mp:parentnamespaceuri	The namespace URI of the current element's parent.
@mp:prefix	Provides the prefix of the namespace URI above. This is set to NULL if there is no namespace URI. There is no prefix if the namespace in @mp:namespaceuri is the default namespace.
@mp:parentprefix	The prefix relating to the current node's parent namespace URI. The same rules apply to this metaproperty as to @mp:prefix.
@mp:prev	Used to determine node order, this property specifies the @mp:id of the current node's previous sibling. If the node is the first sibling, the value of @mp:prev is NULL.
@mp:XMLtext	This node is used mainly for overflow columns. We will look at overflow columns in more detail in the next section.

With the exception of @mp:XMLtext, we won't go any further into these metaproperties because they are described in great detail in the SQL Server Books Online section called *Specifying Metaproperties in OPENXML.*

Overflow Columns

The metaproperty @mp:XMLtext aids us with a feature of OPENXML called **overflow columns**. Overflow columns allow us to store data that has not already been used in the OPENXML statement, hence the word "overflow". The unconsumed data spills over into the @mp:XMLtext property, and is available for us to utilize in the same way that any other column included in the WITH clause is available. Let's have a look at a small example before we look at some of the possible uses of this feature.

If we load our music library example as before, and run the following SELECT FROM OPENXML statement:

```
SELECT *
FROM OPENXML (@hdoc, '/ROOT/Artist/Media/TrackList',8)
WITH ([Album Name]   varchar(50)    '../Name',
      [No Of Tracks] int            '@NoOfTracks',
      [OverflowCol]  varchar(8000) '@mp:XMLtext')
```

we will get a resultset which contains the name of the album, the number of tracks, and an XML list of the tracks on the album, as shown below (note the line wrap because of the width of this page):

```
Album Name                             No Of Tracks  OverflowCol
-------------------------------------- ------------  ----------------------------------------
Achtung Baby                           12            <TrackList><Track Pos="1">Zoo
  Station</Track><Track Pos="2">Even Better Than The Real Thing</Track><Track ...
All That You Cant Leave Behind         12            <TrackList><Track Pos="1">Beautiful
  Day</Track><Track Pos="2">Stuck In A Moment You Cant Get Out Of</Track><Track ...
White Ladder                           10            <TrackList><Track Pos="1">Please Forgive
  Me</Track><Track Pos="2">Babylon</Track><Track Pos="3">My Oh My</Track><Track ...
Supposed Former Infatuation Junkie     17            <TrackList><Track Pos="1">Front
  Row</Track><Track Pos="2">Baba</Track><Track Pos="3">Thank You</Track><Track ...

(4 row(s) affected)
```

We can see in the overflow column that there is a top level `<TrackList>` element, but notice the fact that the `NoOfTracks` attribute is not present. This is because the `NoOfTracks` attribute is present in the `WITH` clause and is therefore consumed. The `@mp:XMLtext` property only holds unconsumed data; no reference to the consumed attribute will be held.

Now, what can we possibly use this for? Well, as we can see from the example above, we could use the overflow column to hold the unconsumed data for reference or audit reasons, or just to provide summary information rather than normalizing the data. We could also use this overflow to store the whole of the source XML data, either with or without the XML header. This would be useful for document management systems.

ADO Support for OPENXML

In the previous sections of this chapter, we saw how to use `OPENXML` directly from a SQL-oriented environment such as Query Analyzer. Obviously, this will not always suffice. We will probably want to execute the `OPENXML` statements through code, such as in a Visual Basic application. In order to integrate the new functionality in SQL Server 2000 with our favorite development environments, Microsoft have provided support for `OPENXML` through ActiveX Data Objects (ADO).

To fully utilize ADO support for XML, we must use ADO version 2.6 which is installed as part of the SQL Server 2000 installation. ADO 2.6 is part of the Microsoft Data Access Components 2.6 component, which can be downloaded from http://www.microsoft.com/data/download_260rtm.htm. The reason for the use of version 2.6 is that an important part of writing and retrieving XML from SQL Server 2000 using ADO involves the use of the `Stream` object, which was introduced with this version. We will not use the Stream object heavily in this section but several case studies will use this object extensively and should be referred to for more information.

> *For a comprehensive look at ADO 2.6, read David Sussman's* ADO 2.6 Programmer's Reference *(Wrox Press, ISBN 186100463X).*

ADO and OPENXML Examples

We will primarily use VBScript in our examples because it is easy to see the objects being created and no development environment is required, although the script can also be easily modified to work in a VBA or Visual Basic environment. Experienced script developers will also be able to quickly convert the scripts to JavaScript or JScript.

We will not go into the grizzly details of ADO and its various components, but will assume that you know the basic techniques for retrieving data from a SQL Server database.

The examples in this section will concentrate on executing `OPENXML` statements that simply return the source XML in an ADO `Recordset` object. Some of the examples in the next section will show how to update the SQL Server using ADO and `OPENXML`.

For all of the following examples, the data source is the music library XML in the *Writing Queries Using OPENXML* section. Wherever the variable `cXMLDoc` is used, this source XML should be assigned prior to use – save it as `MusicLibrary.xml`.

Example 1

The first example creates the appropriate ADO objects and executes an `OPENXML` statement against the source XML. The `OPENXML` statement will generate a resultset, which contains the albums held in our music library. The result set is then written to a file for easy viewing.

```
Option Explicit

Call Main

Sub Main()
Dim oADOConn
Dim oADORec
Dim cSQL
Dim oFSO
Dim oTS
Dim cXMLDoc
Dim oField

'DB connection constants.
Const SERVER_NAME = "(local)"
Const DATABASE_NAME = "Northwind"   ' Or wherever you chose to create the
                                    ' tables for the previous examples.
Const USER_ID = "sa"
Const PASSWORD = ""

'File system constants.
Const FOR_WRITING = 2
Const FOR_READING = 1
Const INPUT_FILE = "C:\Wrox\SQL 2000 XML\Code\MusicLibrary.xml"
Const OUTPUT_FILE = "C:\Wrox\SQL 2000 XML\Data\ADOExample1.txt"

'Other constants.
Const COL_NULL = "NULL"

On Error Resume Next

'Create the FSO to access the file system.
Set oFSO = CreateObject("Scripting.FileSystemObject")
'Open a text stream for the file containing the source XML.
Set oTS = oFSO.OpenTextFile(INPUT_FILE, FOR_READING, False, -2)

'Store the XML in a variable.
cXMLDoc = oTS.ReadAll

'Create the ADO objects to access the database.
Set oADOConn = CreateObject("ADODB.Connection")
Set oADORec = CreateObject("ADODB.Recordset")
```

```
'Build the SQL which will execute the OPENXML statement.
cSQL = "DECLARE @hDoc int " & vbCrLf
cSQL = cSQL & "EXEC sp_xml_preparedocument @hDoc OUTPUT, '" & _
                                   cXMLDoc & "'" & vbCrLf
cSQL = cSQL & "SELECT Name 'Album Name' FROM OPENXML(@hDoc, 'ROOT/Artist/Media',
2)" & vbCrLf
cSQL = cSQL & "WITH Album"

'Open the connection to the database.
oADOConn.Open "Provider=SQLOLEDB;Server=" & SERVER_NAME & _
                                   ";Database=" & DATABASE_NAME & _
                                   ";UID=" & USER_ID & _
                                   ";pwd=" & PASSWORD

'Execute the OPENXML statement.
Set oADORec = oADOConn.Execute(cSQL)

'Hopefully not needed!
If Err.Number <> 0 Then
        Dim oErr, cErrMsg
            For Each oErr In oADOConn.Errors
                cErrMsg = cErrMsg & oErr.Number & vbCrLf
                cErrMsg = cErrMsg & oErr.Description & vbCrLf
                cErrMsg = cErrMsg & oErr.Source & vbCrLf
            Next
            MsgBox cErrMsg
        Exit Sub
End If

'Reset the text stream and recreate as writable file.
Set oTS = Nothing
Set oTS = oFSO.CreateTextFile(OUTPUT_FILE, FOR_WRITING, True)

'Loop through the fields for column headers.
For Each oField In oADORec.Fields
        oTS.write oField.Name
        oTS.write vbTab
Next

oTS.write vbCrLf
oTS.Write "___________________________" & vbcrlf

'For each records and each field, write the field values to file.
If Not isNull(oADORec) Then
   oADORec.MoveFirst
   Do While Not oADORec.EOF
        For Each oField In oADORec.Fields
                If Not IsNull(oField.Value) Then
                    oTS.write oField.Value
                Else
                    oTS.write COL_NULL
                End If
                oTS.write vbTab
        Next
        oTS.write vbCrLf
        oADORec.MoveNext
   Loop
End If

oADORec.Close
oADOConn.Close
oTS.Close
```

```
'Clean Up
Set oFSO = Nothing
Set oTS = Nothing
Set oADOConn = Nothing
Set oADORec = Nothing
Set oField = Nothing

End Sub
```

After changing the input file, output file, and database connectivity constants as necessary, save this script as a visual basic script (`.vbs`) file. Running the script will produce the following:

```
Album Name
______________________________
Achtung Baby
All That You Cant Leave Behind
White Ladder
Supposed Former Infatuation Junkie
```

Let's go through this example in a little bit more detail. Firstly, we set up the objects required to open the file that contains the source XML, and which will finally write the results to a file. These objects are based on the File System Objects provided by Microsoft. We then create the ADO objects. For our example, we only require a `Connection` object and a `Recordset` object.

We then set up the constants required for file and database access. These are used to direct the opening of a file in a certain mode, or for specifying connection information. If we were using a real development environment such as Visual Basic 6, most of the previous information would be either intelligently sensed, or provided through references.

Then we retrieve the source XML from the file. A simple call to open the text file and read the data into a variable is all that is required here.

We now build the `OPENXML` statement, which will be passed to the ADO `Connection` object that will generate the `Recordset`. The statement has been broken into separate lines for clarity, but the statement that is passed to the `Connection` object is shown below:

```
DECLARE @hDoc int
EXEC sp_xml_preparedocument @hDoc OUTPUT, '{SourceXML Stream}'

SELECT Name 'Album Name'
FROM OPENXML(@hDoc, 'ROOT/Artist/Media', 2)
WITH Album
```

where `{SourceXML Stream}` is the XML stored in the `cXMLDoc` variable.

The `OPENXML` statement is then passed as an argument to the `Connections Execute` method. This method passes a `Recordset` back to the caller, based on the passed SQL statement.

The `Connection` object holds an error collection, which, if this statement was to fail, we could traverse to pull back the error generated by the provider.

If all is well, we traverse the `Recordset`, pulling the field names as column headers, and then each of the field values, writing the results to the output file that we opened previously.

Finally, we clean up the objects that we created.

Example 2

Now let's have a look at a more complex example. Here, we shall use ADO to execute an `OPENXML` statement that produces a resultset holding all possible information from the source XML data.

```
Option Explicit

Call Main

Sub Main()
Dim oADOConn
Dim oADORec
Dim cSQL
Dim oFSO
Dim oTS
Dim cXMLDoc
Dim oField

'DB connection constants.
Const SERVER_NAME = "(local)"
Const DATABASE_NAME = "Northwind"  ' Or wherever you chose to create the
                                   ' tables for the 'previous examples.
Const USER_ID = "sa"
Const PASSWORD = ""

'File system constants.
Const FOR_WRITING = 2
Const FOR_READING = 1
Const INPUT_FILE = "c:\Wrox\SQL 2000 XML\Code\MusicLibrary.xml"
Const OUTPUT_FILE = "c:\Wrox\SQL 2000 XML\Data\ADOExample2.txt"
Const TRISTATE_MIXED = -2

'Other constants.
Const COL_NULL = "NULL"

'Create the FSO to access the file system.
Set oFSO = CreateObject("Scripting.FileSystemObject")
'Open a text stream for the file containing the source XML.
Set oTS = oFSO.OpenTextFile(INPUT_FILE, FOR_READING, False, TRISTATE_MIXED)

'Store the XML in a variable.
cXMLDoc = oTS.ReadAll

'Create the ADO objects to access the database.
Set oADOConn = CreateObject("ADODB.Connection")
Set oADORec = CreateObject("ADODB.Recordset")

'Build the SQL which will execute the OPENXML statement.
cSQL = "DECLARE @hDoc int " & vbCrLf
cSQL = cSQL & "EXEC sp_xml_preparedocument @hDoc OUTPUT, '" & _
                                cXMLDoc & "'" & vbCrLf
cSQL = cSQL & "SELECT [Artist Name] , [Media Type], [No of Tracks], "
cSQL = cSQL & "[Album Name], [Track Pos], [Track Name]"
cSQL = cSQL & "FROM OPENXML (@hdoc, '/ROOT/Artist/Media/TrackList/Track', 1)"
cSQL = cSQL & "WITH ( [Artist Name] varchar(30)  '../../../@Name',"
cSQL = cSQL & "[Media Type]         varChar(10)  '../../@Type', "
cSQL = cSQL & "[No Of Tracks]       int          '../@NoOfTracks',"
cSQL = cSQL & "[Album Name]         varChar(50)  '../../Name',"
cSQL = cSQL & "[Track Pos]          int          '@Pos',"
cSQL = cSQL & "[Track Name]         varChar(100) '.')"
```

```
'Open the connection to the database.
oADOConn.Open "Provider=SQLOLEDB;Server=" & SERVER_NAME & _
                                ";Database=" & DATABASE_NAME & _
                                ";UID=" & USER_ID & _
                                ";pwd=" & PASSWORD

'Execute the OPENXML statement.
Set oADORec = oADOConn.Execute(cSQL)

'Hopefully this is not needed!
If Err.Number <> 0 Then
        Dim oErr, cErrMsg
            For Each oErr In oADOConn.Errors
                cErrMsg = cErrMsg & oErr.Number & vbCrLf
                cErrMsg = cErrMsg & oErr.Description & vbCrLf
                cErrMsg = cErrMsg & oErr.Source & vbCrLf
            Next
            MsgBox cErrMsg
        Exit Sub
End If

'Reset the text stream and recreate as writable file.
Set oTS = Nothing
Set oTS = oFSO.CreateTextFile(OUTPUT_FILE, FOR_WRITING, True)

'Loop through the fields for column headers.
For Each oField In oADORec.Fields
        oTS.write oField.Name
        oTS.write vbTab
Next

oTS.write vbCrLf

'For each records and each field, write the field values to file.
oADORec.MoveFirst
Do While Not oADORec.EOF
        For Each oField In oADORec.Fields
                If Not IsNull(oField.Value) Then
                    oTS.write oField.Value
                Else
                    oTS.write COL_NULL
                End If
                oTS.write vbTab
        Next
        oTS.write vbCrLf
        oADORec.MoveNext
Loop

oADORec.Close
oADOConn.Close
oTS.Close

'Clean up.
Set oFSO = Nothing
Set oTS = Nothing
Set oADOConn = Nothing
Set oADORec = Nothing

End Sub
```

Importing the resulting document into Microsoft Excel produces the following:

Artist Name	Media Type	No of Tracks	Album Name	Track Pos	Track Name
U2	CD	12	Achtung Baby	1	Zoo Station
U2	CD	12	Achtung Baby	2	Even Better Than The Real Thing
U2	CD	12	Achtung Baby	3	One
U2	CD	12	Achtung Baby	4	Till The End Of The World
U2	CD	12	Achtung Baby	5	Whose Gonna Ride Your Wild Horses
U2	CD	12	Achtung Baby	6	So Cruel
U2	CD	12	Achtung Baby	7	The Fly
U2	CD	12	Achtung Baby	8	Mysterious Ways
U2	CD	12	Achtung Baby	9	Trying To Throw Your Arms Around The World
U2	CD	12	Achtung Baby	10	Ultra Violet(Light My Way)
U2	CD	12	Achtung Baby	11	Acrobat
U2	CD	12	Achtung Baby	12	Love Is Blindness
U2	Album	12	All That You Cant Leave Behind	1	Beautiful Day
U2	Album	12	All That You Cant Leave Behind	2	Stuck In A Moment You Cant Get Out Of
U2	Album	12	All That You Cant Leave Behind	3	Elevation
U2	Album	12	All That You Cant Leave Behind	4	Walk On
U2	Album	12	All That You Cant Leave Behind	5	Kite
U2	Album	12	All That You Cant Leave Behind	6	In A Little While
U2	Album	12	All That You Cant Leave Behind	7	Wild Honey
U2	Album	12	All That You Cant Leave Behind	8	Peace On Earth
U2	Album	12	All That You Cant Leave Behind	9	When I Look At The World
U2	Album	12	All That You Cant Leave Behind	10	New York
U2	Album	12	All That You Cant Leave Behind	11	Grace
U2	Album	12	All That You Cant Leave Behind	12	The Ground Beneath Her Feet
David Gray	Album	10	White Ladder	1	Please Forgive Me
David Gray	Album	10	White Ladder	2	Babylon
David Gray	Album	10	White Ladder	3	My Oh My
David Gray	Album	10	White Ladder	4	Were Not Right
David Gray	Album	10	White Ladder	5	Nightblindness
David Gray	Album	10	White Ladder	6	Silver Lining
David Gray	Album	10	White Ladder	7	White Ladder
David Gray	Album	10	White Ladder	8	This Years Love
David Gray	Album	10	White Ladder	9	Sail Away
David Gray	Album	10	White Ladder	10	Say Hello Wave Goodbye

This example works in exactly the same way as the previous example, except for the SQL statement that is passed to the ADO `Connection` object. The SQL used is shown below:

```
DECLARE @hDoc int
EXEC sp_xml_preparedocument @hDoc OUTPUT, '{SourceXML Stream}'

SELECT [Artist Name] , [Media Type], [No of Tracks],
       [Album Name], [Track Pos], [Track Name]
FROM OPENXML (@hdoc, '/ROOT/Artist/Media/TrackList/Track', 1)
WITH ([Artist Name]  varchar(30)   '../../../@Name',
      [Media Type]   VarChar(10)   '../../@Type',
      [No Of Tracks] int           '../@NoOfTracks',
      [Album Name]   VarChar(50)   '../../Name',
      [Track Pos]    int           '@Pos',
      [Track Name]   VarChar(100)  '.')
```

where `{SourceXML Stream}` is the XML stored in the `cXMLDoc` variable.

As you can see, the `OPENXML` statement is using a `WITH` clause with explicit mapping. The section on *Explicit Column Mapping* earlier in this chapter covers this topic in more detail.

To get the most out of this section, we should now go and play with the code and the source XML, to gain a thorough understanding of how we pass the XML about and how it is rendered in the resultset.

For example, we could change the XPath passed to the OPENXML statement to pull back particular nodes:

```
'/ROOT/Artist/Media/TrackList/Track[@Pos=1]'
```

This will return only the first track of the recordings. Alternatively, we could add WHERE clauses to the SELECT statement to achieve the same result:

```
"WHERE [Track Pos] = 1"
```

So now we can work with an XML source as if it were an ADO Recordset. This will be useful to developers who are more familiar with ADO than an XML based process like the Microsoft XML Document Object Model.

However, the main purpose of the OPENXML statement is to allow the updating of SQL Server 2000 databases. The next section shows how to perform this procedure in detail, using all of the techniques we have employed previously.

Using OPENXML to Update the SQL Server

As we have seen, we can use OPENXML to generate a relational resultset from an XML document. So far, we have been simply selecting and viewing the resultset, but the most powerful aspect of OPENXML is the fact that we can use the returned resultset to update data in the database.

Using OPENXML, we can update multiple tables in a database using one stored procedure. This procedure would take a parameter of type TEXT which holds the XML to process. The procedure would then process the XML as before, and manipulate it into updating tables in our database.

Updating the database in this way saves processing time in round trips to the database. Additionally, it might be possible to construct the update in such a way that the procedure mirrors business processes that could be wrapped in a transaction within the procedure.

Once again, the examples in this section will be primarily based on the music library XML from the *Writing Queries Using OPENXML* section. This source XML will allow us to highlight the majority of the functionality exposed by OPENXML.

We will look at each type of database update separately, and then look at how we can make data decisions based on the source XML and the values currently held in the database.

Inserting New Records Using OPENXML

The first example we will look at populates the lookup tables in our music library, namely Media and Artist. We shall use the values in the source XML to locate entries for these tables, and insert records accordingly. By running this example, the lookup tables will be populated with all possible values, which we will then use to populate the Album table. The source code for the example is shown below:

```
DECLARE @hDoc int
DECLARE @cDoc varchar(8000)

SET @cDoc = '
<ROOT>
```

```
<Artist Name="U2">
   <Media Type="CD">
      <Name>Achtung Baby</Name>
      <TrackList NoOfTracks="12">
         <Track Pos="1">Zoo Station</Track>
         <Track Pos="2">Even Better Than The Real Thing</Track>
         <Track Pos="3">One</Track>
         <Track Pos="4">Till The End Of The World</Track>
         <Track Pos="5">Whose Gonna Ride Your Wild Horses</Track>
         <Track Pos="6">So Cruel</Track>
         <Track Pos="7">The Fly</Track>
         <Track Pos="8">Mysterious Ways</Track>
         <Track Pos="9">Trying To Throw Your Arms Around The World</Track>
         <Track Pos="10">Ultra Violet(Light My Way)</Track>
         <Track Pos="11">Acrobat</Track>
         <Track Pos="12">Love Is Blindness</Track>
      </TrackList>
   </Media>
   <Media Type="Album">
      <Name>All That You Cant Leave Behind</Name>
      <TrackList NoOfTracks="12">
         <Track Pos="1">Beautiful Day</Track>
         <Track Pos="2">Stuck In A Moment You Cant Get Out Of</Track>
         <Track Pos="3">Elevation</Track>
         <Track Pos="4">Walk On</Track>
         <Track Pos="5">Kite</Track>
         <Track Pos="6">In A Little While</Track>
         <Track Pos="7">Wild Honey</Track>
         <Track Pos="8">Peace On Earth</Track>
         <Track Pos="9">When I Look At The World</Track>
         <Track Pos="10">New York</Track>
         <Track Pos="11">Grace</Track>
         <Track Pos="12">The Ground Beneath Her Feet</Track>
      </TrackList>
   </Media>
</Artist>
<Artist Name="David Gray">
   <Media Type="Album">
      <Name>White Ladder</Name>
      <TrackList NoOfTracks="10">
         <Track Pos="1">Please Forgive Me</Track>
         <Track Pos="2">Babylon</Track>
         <Track Pos="3">My Oh My</Track>
         <Track Pos="4">Were Not Right</Track>
         <Track Pos="5">Nightblindness</Track>
         <Track Pos="6">Silver Lining</Track>
         <Track Pos="7">White Ladder</Track>
         <Track Pos="8">This Years Love</Track>
         <Track Pos="9">Sail Away</Track>
         <Track Pos="10">Say Hello Wave Goodbye</Track>
      </TrackList>
   </Media>
</Artist>
<Artist Name="Alanis Morissette">
   <Media Type="CD">
      <Name>Supposed Former Infatuation Junkie</Name>
      <TrackList NoOfTracks="17">
         <Track Pos="1">Front Row</Track>
         <Track Pos="2">Baba</Track>
         <Track Pos="3">Thank You</Track>
         <Track Pos="4">Are You Still Mad</Track>
         <Track Pos="5">Sympathetic Character</Track>
```

```
            <Track Pos="6">That I Would Be Good</Track>
            <Track Pos="7">The Couch</Track>
            <Track Pos="8">Cant Not</Track>
            <Track Pos="9">UR</Track>
            <Track Pos="10">I Was Hoping</Track>
            <Track Pos="11">One</Track>
            <Track Pos="12">Would Not Come</Track>
            <Track Pos="13">Unsent</Track>
            <Track Pos="14">So Pure</Track>
            <Track Pos="15">Joining You</Track>
            <Track Pos="16">Heart Of The House</Track>
            <Track Pos="17">Your Congratulations</Track>
         </TrackList>
      </Media>
   </Artist>
</ROOT>
'
-- Create an internal representation of the XML document.
EXEC sp_xml_preparedocument @hdoc OUTPUT, @cDoc
-- INSERT into the lookup tables from the generate resultset.
INSERT Media(Type)
SELECT DISTINCT [Media Type]
FROM OPENXML (@hdoc, '/ROOT/Artist/Media',1)
WITH ([Media Type] varchar(10) '@Type')

INSERT Artist(Name)
SELECT DISTINCT [Artist Name]
FROM OPENXML (@hdoc, '/ROOT/Artist',1)
WITH ([Artist Name] varchar(20) '@Name')

EXEC sp_xml_removedocument @hdoc
```

If we now look at the data held in the `Media` and `Artist` tables, we should see the following series of entries:

```
MediaID     Type
----------- --------------------
1           Album
2           CD

(2 row(s) affected)

ArtistID    Name
----------- --------------------
1           Alanis Morissette
2           David Gray
3           U2

(3 row(s) affected)
```

Let's have a look at the code which inserts these records into the two tables:

```
INSERT Media(Type)
SELECT DISTINCT [Media Type]
FROM OPENXML (@hdoc, '/ROOT/Artist/Media',1)
WITH ([Media Type] varchar(10) '@Type')

INSERT Artist(Name)
SELECT DISTINCT [Artist Name]
FROM OPENXML (@hdoc, '/ROOT/Artist',1)
WITH ([Artist Name] varchar(20) '@Name')
```

As stated at the beginning of the chapter, the OPENXML statement can be used anywhere that a resultset provider, such as a table, can be used. As we can see here, the INSERT...SELECT...FROM series works in exactly the same way with OPENXML as it would with a table.

Now that we have the lookup tables in place, we can process the source XML and insert into all the other relevant tables, namely Track and Album. If you remember, the schema for these tables – which will be the main store for the music library – is:

```
CREATE TABLE [dbo].[Album] (
   [ArtistID] [int] NULL ,
   [AlbumID] [int] IDENTITY (1, 1) NOT NULL ,
   [MediaID] [int] NULL ,
   [Name] [varchar] (50),
   [NoOfTracks] [int] NULL) ON [PRIMARY]

CREATE TABLE [dbo].[Track] (
   [AlbumID] [int] NULL ,
   [Pos] [int] NULL ,
   [Name] [varchar] (50)) ON [PRIMARY]
```

In order to insert the album and track data into the tables, we will firstly insert the album information, pulling relational data from the lookup tables, and then insert the tracks for each of the albums. The source for inserting the data is the same as that which was used initially in this section, with the following SQL after the XML string:

```
-- Generate a handle to the XML document.
EXEC sp_XML_preparedocument @hdoc OUTPUT, @cDoc
-- Insert the albums first.
INSERT Album(
      ArtistID,
      MediaID,
       [Name],
       [NoOfTracks])
SELECT ArtistID, MediaID, o.[Album Name], o.[No Of Tracks]
FROM Artist a, Media m, (
SELECT    DISTINCT
   [Artist],
   [Media Type],
   [Album Name],
   [No Of Tracks]
FROM OPENXML (@hdoc, '/ROOT/Artist/Media/TrackList/Track',1)
WITH (Artist          varchar(30) '../../../@Name',
       [Media Type]   varchar(10) '../../@Type',
       [No Of Tracks] int         '../@NoOfTracks',
       [Album Name]   varchar(50) '../../Name'
)) o
where a.Name = o.Artist
and m.Type = o.[Media Type]

--Now insert the tracks
INSERT Track(
      AlbumID,
      Pos,
       [Name])
SELECT AlbumID, o.[Track Pos], o.[Track Name]
FROM Album a, (
SELECT
   [Track Pos],
   [Track Name],
   [Album Name]
```

```
FROM OPENXML (@hdoc, '/ROOT/Artist/Media/TrackList/Track',1)
WITH (   [Track Pos]   int      '@Pos',
    [Track Name]   varchar(100)   '.',
    [Album Name]   varchar(50)    '../../Name'
)) o
where a.Name = o.[Album Name]

--Remove the document handle from memory
EXEC sp_XML_removedocument @hdoc
```

If we now look at joining all of our tables together, by executing the following SQL:

```
SELECT
   art.[Name]      'Artist',
   med.Type        'Media Type',
   alb.NoOfTracks 'No Of Tracks',
   alb.[Name]      'Album Name',
   tra.Pos         'Track Pos',
   tra.[Name]      'Track Name'
FROM
   Artist art,
   Album  alb,
   Media  med,
   Track  tra
WHERE
   alb.ArtistID = art.ArtistID
AND alb.MediaID = med.MediaID
AND tra.AlbumID = alb.AlbumID
```

We can form the resultset that we generated before in the *Explicit Column Mapping* section.

If we look at the `INSERT...SELECT...FROM OPENXML` statement used to insert the album and track data, we use the `OPENXML` statement in a derived table in the `FROM` clause. You may be wondering why we don't use a cursor to loop through the records generated by the `OPENXML` statement. We could easily change the code to include a cursor because, unlike the `FOR XML` function described in Chapter 3, `OPENXML` can be used readily with SQL cursors. We can also assign values to variables in the same way that we could if we were using an existing table. To illustrate this, have a look at the following code:

```
-- Generate a handle to the XML document.
EXEC sp_XML_preparedocument @hdoc OUTPUT, @cDoc
-- Update the length field of the track based on source XML values.

DECLARE @Error int                  -- Holds error values.
DECLARE @Fetch_Status int           -- Holds the cursor fetch status.
DECLARE @ArtistName varchar(50)     -- ArtistName and AlbumName are used in
DECLARE @AlbumName varchar(50)      -- conjunction with the cursor fetch.

-- Declare the cursor.
DECLARE CUR_TEST CURSOR
   FOR(
   SELECT [Name] FROM OPENXML(@hDoc, 'ROOT/Artist',1)
   WITH ([Name] varchar(20) '@Name'))
SELECT @Error = @@ERROR
```

```
-- Open the cursor.
OPEN CUR_TEST
SELECT @Error = @@ERROR

SELECT @Fetch_Status = 0
--Loop through each of the artists in the table.
WHILE @Fetch_Status = 0 AND @Error = 0
BEGIN
   FETCH NEXT FROM CUR_TEST INTO @ArtistName
   SELECT @Fetch_Status = @@FETCH_STATUS
   IF @Fetch_Status = 0 SELECT @ArtistName 'Artist Name'
END

--Clean up
CLOSE CUR_TEST
DEALLOCATE CUR_TEST

--Use a variable to hold the value from the generated resultset.
SELECT @AlbumName = [Name] FROM OPENXML(@hDoc, 'ROOT/Artist[@Name="David
Gray"]/Media/Name',1)
WITH ([Name] varchar(20) '.')

SELECT @AlbumName 'Album Name'
--Remove the document handle from memory.
EXEC sp_XML_removedocument @hdoc
```

Assuming that we have loaded the source XML as before, and declared the appropriate variables (`@Fetch_Status`, `@Error`, `@ArtistName`, and `@AlbumName`), then running the above code would generate the following results:

```
Artist Name
--------------------------------------------------
U2

(1 row(s) affected)

Artist Name
--------------------------------------------------
David Gray

(1 row(s) affected)

Artist Name
--------------------------------------------------
Alanis Morissette

(1 row(s) affected)

Album Name
--------------------------------------------------
White Ladder

(1 row(s) affected)
```

As we can see, using OPENXML we can build a relational view from the hierarchical structure of an XML document. This is obviously extremely useful in many scenarios, the most obvious one being the transfer of data to disparate sources. We could send a SQL script and the XML document to other users, and they could import the information using the method shown above.

Updating Existing Records Using OPENXML

We have seen how to insert new records into our databases using OPENXML, but what about updating existing records? This is just as simple as inserting records with OPENXML. As an example, imagine we have added a length attribute to the <Track> element which denotes the playing time of the track. To update the Track table with this information, we first need to add a column to the table:

```
ALTER TABLE Track
   ADD TrackLength varchar(5) NULL
```

Now run the following SQL script to update the new field with the values stored in the source XML document:

```
DECLARE @hDoc int
DECLARE @cDoc varchar(8000)

SET @cDoc = '
<ROOT>
   <Artist Name="U2">
      <Media Type="CD">
         <Name>Achtung Baby</Name>
         <TrackList NoOfTracks="12">
            <Track Pos="1" Length="4:01">Zoo Station</Track>
            <Track Pos="2" Length="4:32">Even Better Than The Real Thing</Track>
            <Track Pos="3" Length="5:15">One</Track>
            <Track Pos="4" Length="4:58">Till The End Of The World</Track>
            <Track Pos="5" Length="5:04">Whose Gonna Ride Your Wild Horses</Track>
            <Track Pos="6" Length="5:20">So Cruel</Track>
            <Track Pos="7" Length="4:44">The Fly</Track>
            <Track Pos="8" Length="5:18">Mysterious Ways</Track>
            <Track Pos="9" Length="5:32">Trying To Throw Your Arms Around The
World</Track>
            <Track Pos="10" Length="4:34">Ultra Violet (Light My Way)</Track>
            <Track Pos="11" Length="5:26">Acrobat</Track>
            <Track Pos="12" Length="3:59">Love Is Blindness</Track>
         </TrackList>
      </Media>
   </Artist>
</ROOT>
'
-- Generate a handle to the XML document.
EXEC sp_XML_preparedocument @hdoc OUTPUT, @cDoc
-- Update the length field of the track based on source XML values
UPDATE Track
SET TrackLength = o.Length
FROM    (
   SELECT Length, AlbumName, TrackName
   FROM OPENXML (@hdoc, '/ROOT/Artist/Media/TrackList/Track',1)
   WITH (   Length        varchar(5)     '@Length',
      AlbumName    varchar(50)    '../../Name',
      TrackName    varchar(50)    '.')
   ) o,
```

```
        Album a
    WHERE     o.AlbumName = a.[Name]
    AND    Track.AlbumID = a.AlbumID
    AND    o.TrackName = Track.[Name]

    --Remove the document handle from memory
    EXEC sp_XML_removedocument @hdoc
```

If we now look at the `Track` table, we see that the `TrackLength` field has been updated with the values of the `Length` attributes of the `Track` nodes in the source XML.

```
AlbumID   Pos   Name                                              TrackLength
--------- ----- ------------------------------------------------- -----------
3         1     Zoo Station                                       4:01
3         2     Even Better Than The Real Thing                   4:32
3         3     One                                               5:15
3         4     Till The End Of The World                         4:58
3         5     Whose Gonna Ride Your Wild Horses                 5:04
3         6     So Cruel                                          5:20
3         7     The Fly                                           4:44
3         8     Mysterious Ways                                   5:18
3         9     Trying To Throw Your Arms Around The World        5:32
3         10    Ultra Violet(Light My Way)                        4:34
3         11    Acrobat                                           5:26
3         12    Love Is Blindness                                 3:59
2         1     Beautiful Day                                     NULL
2         2     Stuck In A Moment You Cant Get Out Of             NULL

(51 row(s) affected)
```

The `UPDATE...SET...FROM` statement here is similar to the way that we inserted the track and album records in the previous section. We derive a table using the `OPENXML` statement and join all the key fields to update the correct record.

Remember that the format of the source XML document does not need to be the same as when it was first inserted. The `WITH` clause of the `OPENXML` statement allows you to specify the XPath of the mapping between source XML elements and the resultset.

Deleting Records Using OPENXML

In order to demonstrate the deletion of records using `OPENXML`, let's add a new component to the XML structure – `<Available>`. Obviously, if this node's value is `No`, the particular recording is unavailable and cannot be borrowed from the library. We add this element as a child of the `<Media>` element and a sibling to `<Name>` and `<TrackList>`.

Imagine we are looking through the source XML and we find a record that is unavailable and needs deleting. How do we cascade the delete? If we delete an album and cascade the delete to the artist entry, what happens if the artist still has other recordings associated with them? This problem can be managed by using triggers to enforce the integrity of the data. However, this is beyond the scope of this book and we shall only demonstrate here how to remove the album and use a trigger to delete the associated tracks.

> *For more information on triggers, see* Professional SQL Server 2000 Programming *by Robert Vieira (Wrox Press, ISBN 1-861004-48-6).*

Unlike the update example, this <Available> element does not have to be stored anywhere – the element is meta-information, if you like. Therefore, we can execute the following SQL script to delete the album "All That You Can't Leave Behind":

```
CREATE TRIGGER trg_Track ON [dbo].[Album]
FOR DELETE
AS

   DELETE
   FROM Track
   WHERE AlbumID IN(
      SELECT AlbumID
      FROM deleted)

GO

DECLARE @hDoc int
DECLARE @cDoc varchar(8000)
DECLARE @ArtistName varchar(20)
DECLARE @AlbumName varchar(20)
DECLARE @Fetch_Status int
DECLARE @Error int

SET @cDoc = '
   <ROOT>
      <Artist Name="U2">
      <Media Type="CD">
         <Name>Achtung Baby</Name>
         <Available>Yes</Available>
         <TrackList NoOfTracks="12">
            <Track Pos="1">Zoo Station</Track>
            <Track Pos="2">Even Better Than The Real Thing</Track>
            <Track Pos="3">One</Track>
            <Track Pos="4">Till The End Of The World</Track>
            <Track Pos="5">Whose Gonna Ride Your Wild Horses</Track>
            <Track Pos="6">So Cruel</Track>
            <Track Pos="7">The Fly</Track>
            <Track Pos="8">Mysterious Ways</Track>
            <Track Pos="9">Trying To Throw Your Arms Around The World</Track>
            <Track Pos="10">Ultra Violet(Light My Way)</Track>
            <Track Pos="11">Acrobat</Track>
            <Track Pos="12">Love Is Blindness</Track>
         </TrackList>
      </Media>
      <Media Type="Album">
         <Name>All That You Cant Leave Behind</Name>
         <Available>No</Available>
         <TrackList NoOfTracks="12">
            <Track Pos="1">Beautiful Day</Track>
            <Track Pos="2">Stuck In A Moment You Cant Get Out Of</Track>
            <Track Pos="3">Elevation</Track>
            <Track Pos="4">Walk On</Track>
            <Track Pos="5">Kite</Track>
            <Track Pos="6">In A Little While</Track>
            <Track Pos="7">Wild Honey</Track>
            <Track Pos="8">Peace On Earth</Track>
            <Track Pos="9">When I Look At The World</Track>
            <Track Pos="10">New York</Track>
            <Track Pos="11">Grace</Track>
            <Track Pos="12">The Ground Beneath Her Feet</Track>
         </TrackList>
      </Media>
   </Artist>
   <Artist Name="David Gray">
      <Media Type="Album">
```

```
            <Name>White Ladder</Name>
            <Available>Yes</Available>
            <TrackList NoOfTracks="10">
               <Track Pos="1">Please Forgive Me</Track>
               <Track Pos="2">Babylon</Track>
               <Track Pos="3">My Oh My</Track>
               <Track Pos="4">Were Not Right</Track>
               <Track Pos="5">Nightblindness</Track>
               <Track Pos="6">Silver Lining</Track>
               <Track Pos="7">White Ladder</Track>
               <Track Pos="8">This Years Love</Track>
               <Track Pos="9">Sail Away</Track>
               <Track Pos="10">Say Hello Wave Goodbye</Track>
            </TrackList>
         </Media>
      </Artist>
      <Artist Name="Alanis Morissette">
         <Media Type="CD">
            <Name>Supposed Former Infatuation Junkie</Name>
            <Available>Yes</Available>
            <TrackList NoOfTracks="17">
               <Track Pos="1">Front Row</Track>
               <Track Pos="2">Baba</Track>
               <Track Pos="3">Thank You</Track>
               <Track Pos="4">Are You Still Mad</Track>
               <Track Pos="5">Sympathetic Character</Track>
               <Track Pos="6">That I Would Be Good</Track>
               <Track Pos="7">The Couch</Track>
               <Track Pos="8">Cant Not</Track>
               <Track Pos="9">UR</Track>
               <Track Pos="10">I Was Hoping</Track>
               <Track Pos="11">One</Track>
               <Track Pos="12">Would Not Come</Track>
               <Track Pos="13">Unsent</Track>
               <Track Pos="14">So Pure</Track>
               <Track Pos="15">Joining You</Track>
               <Track Pos="16">Heart Of The House</Track>
               <Track Pos="17">Your Congratulations</Track>
            </TrackList>
         </Media>
      </Artist>
   </ROOT>
   '
   -- Generate a handle to the XML document.
   EXEC sp_xml_preparedocument @hdoc OUTPUT, @cDoc

   DELETE
   FROM Album
   WHERE AlbumID IN(
      SELECT   AlbumID
      FROM   Album, (
         SELECT Available, AlbumName
         FROM OPENXML (@hdoc, '/ROOT/Artist/Media',1)
         WITH (Available varchar(3)  'Available',
               AlbumName varchar(50) 'Name')
         ) o
      WHERE    ltrim(rtrim(Album.[Name])) = ltrim(rtrim(o.AlbumName))
      AND   o.Available = 'No')

   --Remove the document handle from memory
   EXEC sp_xml_removedocument @hdoc
```

If we now check the `Album` and `Track` tables, the entries for `albumID 2` have been deleted from the tables.

Mixed Example

Now that we have seen all of the database update functions in action, let's have a look at a more comprehensive example. We will look at some of the data held for a veterinary surgery, using an `Owner` table, a `Pets` table (which holds the `OwnerID`), and a `Type` table (for dog, cat, etc.).

Firstly, run the SQL that builds the schema for these tables:

```
CREATE TABLE [dbo].[Owner] (
    [OwnerID] [int] NOT NULL ,
    [OwnerName] [varchar] (50) NULL ,
    [Address] [varchar] (50) NULL
) ON [PRIMARY]
GO

CREATE TABLE [dbo].[Pets] (
    [PetID] [int] NOT NULL ,
    [OwnerID] [int] NOT NULL ,
    [PetType] [varchar] (50) NULL ,
    [PetName] [varchar] (20) NULL
) ON [PRIMARY]
GO

CREATE TABLE [dbo].[Type] (
    [TypeID] [int] NOT NULL ,
    [Type] [varchar] (50) NULL
) ON [PRIMARY]
GO

SET QUOTED_IDENTIFIER OFF
GO
SET ANSI_NULLS ON
GO

CREATE TRIGGER trg_Owner ON [dbo].[Owner]
FOR DELETE
AS

    DELETE FROM Pets
    WHERE OwnerID in(
       SELECT OwnerID
       FROM DELETED)

GO
SET QUOTED_IDENTIFIER OFF
GO
SET ANSI_NULLS ON
GO
```

What we are going to show here is how we use the `OPENXML` statement to make the information held in the database reflect that held in the source XML document. To this end, the initial XML document looks like this:

```
<ROOT>
   <OWNER ID="1">
      <NAME>Sam</NAME>
      <ADDRESS>25 Hillfoot Dr, Howwod</ADDRESS>
      <PETS>
         <PET ID="2">
            <NAME>Peggy</NAME>
            <TYPE ID="2">Cat</TYPE>
         </PET>
      </PETS>
   </OWNER>
   <OWNER ID="2">
      <NAME>Jacquie</NAME>
      <ADDRESS>3 Station Court, Glengarnock</ADDRESS>
      <PETS>
         <PET ID="3">
            <NAME>Chick</NAME>
            <TYPE ID="2">Cat</TYPE>
         </PET>
         <PET ID="4">
            <NAME>Louis</NAME>
            <TYPE ID="3">Reptile</TYPE>
         </PET>
      </PETS>
   </OWNER>
   <OWNER ID="3">
      <NAME>Glen</NAME>
      <ADDRESS>21 Corseford Ave, Wishaw</ADDRESS>
      <PETS>
         <PET ID="1">
            <NAME>Max</NAME>
            <TYPE ID="1">Dog</TYPE>
         </PET>
      </PETS>
   </OWNER>
</ROOT>
```

Our aim is to facilitate updates to the database which will reflect changes in this source XML. To do this we shall create three stored procedures, called `sp_UpdateOwners`, `sp_UpdatePets`, and `sp_UpdatePetType`. These procedures will take the XML source as a parameter.

We can use these procedures with the XML shown above to create the initial load of the pets and owners data. The procedures will use `OPENXML` to generate the resultset to work with. The owners procedure will check if the owner record exists and, if not, the owner will be added. If the owner record already exists, the procedure will perform an update.

When the inserts and updates to the tables have taken place, the owner procedure will check to see if any owners in the database now do not exist in the source XML.

The exact same process will then take place for the pets and pet types, although the delete trigger on the `Owner` table will take care of the deletions of pets if their owner is no longer present.

The source for these procedures is shown below:

```
CREATE PROCEDURE sp_UpdateOwners    @cDoc   text
AS

DECLARE @hDoc int
```

```
-- Create an internal representation of the XML document.
EXEC sp_xml_preparedocument @hdoc OUTPUT, @cDoc
-- INSERT the owner if they do not already exist.

INSERT Owner
SELECT OwnerID, OwnerName, OwnerAddress
FROM OPENXML(@hDoc, 'ROOT/OWNER', 1)
WITH (OwnerID      int          '@ID',
      OwnerName    varchar(50) 'NAME',
      OwnerAddress varchar(50) 'ADDRESS')
WHERE OwnerID Not In    (
         SELECT OwnerID
         FROM Owner)

--UPDATE all owner details.
UPDATE Owner
SET    OwnerName = o.OwnerName,
       Address = o.OwnerAddress
FROM (
     SELECT OwnerID, OwnerName, OwnerAddress
     FROM OPENXML(@hDoc, 'ROOT/OWNER', 1)
     WITH (OwnerID      int          '@ID',
           OwnerName    varchar(50) 'NAME',
           OwnerAddress varchar(50) 'ADDRESS')
     )o
WHERE
   Owner.OwnerID = o.OwnerID

--DELETE any redundant owners.
DELETE
FROM   Owner
WHERE   OwnerID NOT IN(
   SELECT OwnerID
   FROM OPENXML(@hDoc, 'ROOT/OWNER', 1)
   WITH (OwnerID int '@ID'))
GO
CREATE PROCEDURE sp_UpdatePets    @cDoc   text
AS

DECLARE @hDoc int

-- Create an internal representation of the XML document.
EXEC sp_xml_preparedocument @hdoc OUTPUT, @cDoc
-- INSERT the owner if they do not already exist.

INSERT Pets
SELECT PetID, OwnerID, PetType, PetName
FROM OPENXML(@hDoc, 'ROOT/OWNER/PETS/PET', 1)
WITH (PetID   int           '@ID',
      OwnerID int           '../../@ID',
      PetType varchar(50)  'TYPE',
      PetName varchar(50)  'NAME')
WHERE PetID Not In    (
         SELECT PetID
         FROM Pets)

--UPDATE all pet details.
UPDATE Pets
SET    PetType = o.PetType,
   PetName = o.PetName
FROM (
   SELECT PetID, OwnerID, PetType, PetName
```

```
   FROM OPENXML(@hDoc, 'ROOT/OWNER/PETS/PET', 1)
   WITH (PetID   int          '@ID',
         OwnerID int          '../../@ID',
         PetType varchar(50) 'TYPE',
         PetName varchar(50) 'NAME')
   )o
WHERE
   Pets.PetID = o.PetID

--DELETE redundant pet records.
DELETE
FROM   Pets
WHERE   PetID NOT IN(
   SELECT PetID
   FROM OPENXML(@hDoc, 'ROOT/OWNER/PETS/PET', 1)
   WITH (PetID int '@ID'))
GO
CREATE PROCEDURE sp_UpdatePetType    @cDoc   text
AS

DECLARE @hDoc int

-- Create an internal representation of the XML document.
EXEC sp_xml_preparedocument @hdoc OUTPUT, @cDoc
-- INSERT the owner if they do not already exist.

INSERT Type
SELECT DISTINCT *
FROM OPENXML(@hDoc, 'ROOT/OWNER/PETS/PET/TYPE')
WITH (TypeID   int          '@ID',
      Type varchar(20)      '.')
WHERE TypeID Not In   (
         SELECT TypeID
         FROM Type)

--UPDATE all pet details.
UPDATE Type
SET    Type = o.Type
FROM (
   SELECT TypeID, Type
   FROM OPENXML(@hDoc, 'ROOT/OWNER/PETS/PET/TYPE')
   WITH (TypeID   int          '@ID',
         Type      varchar(20) '.')
   )o
WHERE
   Type.TypeID = o.TypeID

--DELETE redundant pet records.
DELETE
FROM   Type
WHERE   TypeID NOT IN(
   SELECT TypeID
   FROM OPENXML(@hDoc, 'ROOT/OWNER/PETS/PET/TYPE')
   WITH (TypeID int '@ID'))
```

After running this SQL, we can now execute these stored procedures:

```
EXEC sp_UpdateOwners 'Source XML'
EXEC sp_UpdatePets 'Source XML'
EXEC sp_UpdatePetType 'Source XML'
```

With the initial source XML document shown above (insert the source XML data between the single quotes in the EXECs immediately above):

We can now test out our maintenance of the data by changing the source XML data and executing the stored procedures again. An example of amended XML data is shown below:

```
<ROOT>
   <OWNER ID="1">
      <NAME>Sam</NAME>
      <ADDRESS>25 Hillfoot Dr, Howwod</ADDRESS>
      <PETS>
         <PET ID="2">
            <NAME>The Leg</NAME>
            <TYPE ID="2">Cat</TYPE>
         </PET>
      </PETS>
   </OWNER>
   <OWNER ID="2">
      <NAME>Jacquie</NAME>
      <ADDRESS>3 Station Court, Glengarnock</ADDRESS>
      <PETS>
         <PET ID="3">
            <NAME>Chick</NAME>
            <TYPE ID="2">Cat</TYPE>
         </PET>
         <PET ID="4">
            <NAME>Louis</NAME>
            <TYPE ID="3">Reptile</TYPE>
         </PET>
      </PETS>
   </OWNER>
   <OWNER ID="4">
      <NAME>Sue</NAME>
      <ADDRESS>7 Station Court, Glengarnock</ADDRESS>
      <PETS>
         <PET ID="5">
            <NAME>Chico</NAME>
            <TYPE ID="2">Cat</TYPE>
         </PET>
      </PETS>
   </OWNER>
</ROOT>
```

Executing these procedures will update our tables accordingly.

Summary

OPENXML is the means by which we can generate resultsets from an XML source. We can use this function anywhere that we can use any other resultset providers, such as tables or views. The source XML document components can be mapped to the created resultset by specifying the type of mapping that we wish to use in the OPENXML statement (attribute- or element-centric), or by explicitly defining the mapping in the WITH clause.

We can also specify tables as templates for the created resultset's columns to be mapped to, along with the attribute- or element-centric parameter.

Explicitly defining the mappings is the most flexible option. This allows us to specify the column names, column types, and the XPath expression which select the node that we want to map the column to.

If we do not specify a `WITH` clause, `OPENXML` will render an edge table which allows us to view information about each of the nodes in the source XML. This functionality is complemented by `OPENXML` metaproperties, which can be used to provide unique identifiers and ancestry information about source XML nodes.

We can use ADO 2.6 to execute `OPENXML` statements and return the produced resultset as an ADO `Recordset` object.

The main benefit of the `OPENXML` function in SQL Server 2000 is the ability to update the database, using information contained in a source XML document. We can perform all the normal functions using the `OPENXML` statement – inserting, updating, and deleting data from the source. We can also use `SELECT INTO`s, declare cursors, and assign values to variables, based on the results from an `OPENXML` statement.

Hopefully, this chapter has introduced you to the wealth of opportunities that this new functionality in SQL Server 2000 provides. The fact that a common mode of communication can be used to influence enterprise data is something which should ensure that the use of `OPENXML` – along with the other XML support features provided in SQL Server 2000 – will become commonplace in the development of interfacing applications.

5

XDR Schemas

We have seen how SQL query features such as `FOR XML` and `OPENXML` can be used to return data as XML. **Annotated XDR** (**XML-Data Reduced**) schemas can also provide this functionality, and allow us to retrieve the results through HTTP requests, bypassing the need to establish an explicit connection to SQL Server and to issue complex queries. It is likely that you will find designing schemas to be less complex than writing a query using `FOR XML EXPLICIT`.

In this chapter, we will examine:

- What XML schemas are
- How to design and use XDR schemas in SQL Server 2000
- Annotations to XDR schemas to enable data mapping
- XML data types vs. SQL data types
- Schema caching
- Key points to remember when using annotated XDR schemas

What are Schemas?

One of the goals of XML is to allow the open exchange of information between organizations and applications. This can only be possible if the format of XML documents can be defined and agreed upon. This is where schemas play an important role. Quite simply, a schema is the definition of a *valid* XML document, agreed between participants. An XML document or fragment may be well-formed, but will it adhere to business rules or logic? Schemas provide an XML-based syntax for defining what elements and attributes are allowed in a given document. Once the set of common tags is defined and agreed upon, the schema provides the common vocabulary that is used to give a framework for communication between the parties. For example, a manufacturer in the USA might refer to a data item as being an "inventory" item while, in the UK, this data item might be referred to as a "stock" item. By agreeing a schema, the manufacturers can establish data item definition rules, and arrange for both parties to use a single term. They now share a common vocabulary and can safely communicate using the same schema.

Let's have a look at a code example. Imagine a situation where different high schools maintain separate XML records of students' grade point averages (GPAs). One school's records might look like this:

```
<?xml version="1.0"?>
   <Students>
      <Student>
         <ID>12345</ID>
         <GPA>3.5</GPA>
      </Student>
      <Student>
          <ID>67890</ID>
         <GPA>4.0</GPA>
      </Student>
   </Students>
```

Another school's records might have this format:

```
<?xml version="1.0"?>
   <Students>
      <Student ID="12345">
            <GPA>3.5</GPA>
      </Student>
      <Student ID="67890">
            <GPA>4.0</GPA>
      </Student>
   </Students>
```

If these details need to be communicated between schools, a standard format must be agreed – this is the schema.

If the schools agreed upon the first example as the proper format, then here is what a simple schema to enforce this "contract" would look like:

```
<?xml version="1.0"?>
   <Schema name="StudentsSchema"
   xmlns="urn:schemas-microsoft-com:xml-data">
      <ElementType name="ID" content="textOnly"/>
      <ElementType name="GPA" content="textOnly"/>
      <ElementType name="Student" content="eltOnly">
         <element type="ID"/>
         <element type="GPA"/>
      </ElementType>
      <ElementType name="Students" content="eltOnly">
         <element type="Student"/>
      </ElementType>
   </Schema>
```

We will dissect the contents of a schema a little later. For now, let's observe some basic concepts. First of all, the schema itself is an XML document. Next, the definition of the acceptable elements is found within the `<Schema>` element. In this case, only elements are declared, through the use of `<ElementType>` and `<element>` tags. The `<Student>` element contains two children: `<ID>` and `<GPA>`. Finally, the `<Students>` element contains a `<Student>` element.

Schemas vs. DTDs

Schemas were not the first definition language on the scene. Early in the life of XML, there was only one accepted standard for defining a document – a **DTD** (**Document Type Definition**). The DTD language was used in W3C XML 1.0 to provide a way to validate the structure of XML documents. It was actually invented (prior to XML) specifically for SGML (Standard Generalized Markup Language) documents. Since XML is really a simplified subset of SGML, DTDs can be used to define validation rules for XML documents also.

Let's look at a DTD describing the structure of the first student data example cited earlier:

```
<!ELEMENT Students (Student+)>
<!ELEMENT Student (ID, GPA)>
<!ELEMENT ID (#PCDATA)>
<!ELEMENT GPA (#PCDATA)>
```

The DTD defines the document element of `<Students>` and indicates (with a plus sign, +) that it may have one or many `<Student>` elements within it. `<Student>` elements contain two child elements: `<ID>` and `<GPA>`; both of which contain `#PCDATA` (parsed character data – basically, any character data). If this definition were saved in a file named `Students.dtd`, it could be referenced in an XML document in this way:

```
<?xml version="1.0"?>
<!DOCTYPE Students SYSTEM "Students.dtd">
   <Students>
      <Student>
         <ID>12345</ID>
         <GPA>3.5</GPA>
      </Student>
      <Student>
          <ID>67890</ID>
         <GPA>4.0</GPA>
      </Student>
   </Students>
```

How does this approach differ from using schemas? First, observe how DTDs use a non-XML syntax for defining grammatical rules. For a developer, this is yet another language and syntax to remember. Second, DTDs do not support data types (although "attribute-types" such as enumerations are supported). In the DTD shown above, the `<GPA>` element contains `#PCDATA`. Therefore, in our students example, the following fragment is valid against the DTD even though the data is confusing:

```
<Student>
   <ID>12345</ID>
   <GPA>Hello!</GPA>
</Student>
```

Another noteworthy difference between DTDs and schemas is that only one DTD can be attached to an XML document, whereas multiple schemas can be applied throughout elements of an XML document. Schemas are also extensible in that one schema can reference another, thus avoiding duplicate definitions of common elements or attributes.

Because of the advantages offered by schemas over DTDs, many developers have quickly embraced these features and incorporated schemas in their environment.

XDR Schemas

An XML-Data Reduced or XDR schema is a subset of XML-Data schemas. XDR schemas were introduced to overcome the drawbacks of DTDs, and offer more features to developers. Here is a brief summary of the key features of an XDR schema document:

- XDR schemas *are* XML documents, so you don't have to learn another syntax to use them, unlike with DTDs
- XDR schemas allow undefined elements or tags to exist within an XML document, unlike DTDs, thus giving an "open" content model
- Data types can be specified for an element or attribute
- XDR schemas offer extensibility by allowing one schema to reference the definition of another
- Although, in most cases, XDR schemas would apply at the root element of an XML document, they can be applied to individual elements

XDR schemas define the format, content, and data of an XML document. When the Microsoft XML Parser (MSXML) validates a document that references an XDR schema, for instance, it confirms whether or not the document meets the criteria defined in the schema. If the validation fails, an error occurs.

Designing XDR Schemas

Let's return to our students example. Each student has an ID and GPA. How could this document be expressed as an XDR schema? Let's identify some of the necessary requirements to define our own XDR schema.

XML Declaration

Remember, an XDR schema is an XML document, so the first line can be a standard XML declaration:

```
<?xml version="1.0"?>
```

In this example, `version` is the only attribute expressed in the declaration. Other attributes – such as `encoding` and `standalone` – determine which encoding is used to represent characters, or if the document relies on an external source.

<Schema>

The next line in our XDR schema defines the root element itself. For XDR schemas, the root element is always `<Schema>`. To identify the root element of the schema to the MSXML parser as an XDR schema, a specific namespace is referenced as an attribute in the `<Schema>` element. The namespace for XDR schemas is `urn:schemas-microsoft-com:xml-data`. Namespaces uniquely identify an element or attribute to a parser for special processing. Therefore, `<Schema>` declared with the Microsoft XDR namespace is processed differently than `<Schema>` with a namespace for XSD (which is covered in the next chapter).

The following example is a typical declaration of the `<Schema>` element with the XDR namespace as the default namespace:

```
<?xml version="1.0"?>
   <Schema name="StudentsSchema"
   xmlns="urn:schemas-microsoft-com:xml-data">
   </Schema>
```

In the example above, the default namespace for the XML document designates the root element and all of its children as belonging to the XDR schema namespace. Note that the `<Schema>` element also allows us to specify a name for the schema.

<ElementType>

The `<ElementType>` element determines the characteristics of an element by the use of the following attributes:

- `name`

  Required. This is the name of the element.

- `content`

  This attribute determines what kind of value the element will contain. Here are the possible values:

Value	Description
`mixed`	The default – the element can contain any mixture of child elements and values (free text).
`textOnly`	The element contains a value, no child elements.
`eltOnly`	The element contains only child elements, no value.
`empty`	The element cannot contain any values or child elements. Attributes are allowed.

- `model`

  This attribute determines whether or not the document will allow for extra content. There are two possible values:

Value	Description
open	The default – the element allows for content not defined in the schema.
closed	The element only allows content defined in the schema.

- order

  This attribute defines how child elements are ordered, selected, or combined within the element. There are three possible values:

Value	Description
many	The default – the element may include all, none, or some of the child elements in any order.
seq	The element must contain all child elements in the sequence specified.
one	The element must contain *only one* of the possible child elements.

Before looking at how our example XDR schema is building up, we must consider the <element> element, a close relative to <ElementType>.

<element>

The <element> element refers to an instance of a declared <ElementType> and can appear within the scope of another <ElementType>. Assigning values to the following attributes can modify the behavior of the element:

- type

  Required. Refers to the name of a declared <ElementType>.

- minOccurs

  This attribute determines if the element is optional. There are two possible values that may be assigned here:

Value	Description
0	The element is optional.
1	The element must occur at least once.

- maxOccurs

  This attribute determines how many elements are allowed. There are two possible values:

Value	Description
1	Only one element can appear at most.
*	The element may appear an unlimited amount of times.

With this understanding of <ElementType> and <element>, let's take a look at our updated schema example:

```
<?xml version="1.0"?>
   <Schema name="StudentsSchema"
   xmlns="urn:schemas-microsoft-com:xml-data">
      <ElementType name="ID" content="textOnly"/>
      <ElementType name="GPA" content="textOnly"/>
      <ElementType name="Student" content="eltOnly">
         <element type="ID" minOccurs="1" maxOccurs="1"/>
         <element type="GPA" minOccurs="1" maxOccurs="1"/>
      </ElementType>
      <ElementType name="Students" content="eltOnly" model="closed">
         <element type="Student" minOccurs="0" maxOccurs="*"/>
      </ElementType>
   </Schema>
```

Looking at the schema, we notice the following definitions and rules:

- The only elements that contain free text values are <ID> and <GPA>
- The <Student> element must contain only one <ID> and <GPA> element
- The <Students> element may have unlimited <Student> elements, or none at all
- No additional elements or attributes are allowed outside of the schema definition

In other words, we have defined that documents adhering to this schema may list as many students as necessary, as long as an ID and GPA are provided for each student. This contract can now allow multiple parties to share student information in an agreed format. In the case of our example, how does an XML document apply the schema? In most cases, it is referenced in a namespace in the root element. It could, however, be applied to just a single element or an XML fragment. Here is an XML document example in which the above schema is assumed to reside in the same directory:

```
<?xml version="1.0"?>
   <Students
   xmlns="x-schema:StudentsSchema1.xdr">
      <Student>
         <ID>12345</ID>
         <GPA>3.5</GPA>
      </Student>
      <Student>
          <ID>67890</ID>
         <GPA>4.0</GPA>
      </Student>
   </Students>
```

In this case, our schema is saved in a file named StudentsSchema1.xdr.

This example is element-centric – void of any attributes. Suppose it was decided that <ID> should be an *attribute* of <Student>, instead of a child element. This might be done to reduce the size of the overall document or to conform to technical specifications. Nevertheless, we will probably implement the use of attributes in a document at some point. What changes need to be made to our schema? Let's take a look at other elements in the XDR schema that define attributes in an XML document.

<AttributeType>

Defining attributes in an XDR schema is very similar to defining elements. First, we need to declare our attribute with the <AttributeType> element, and then determine behaviors by providing values for attributes within the element. Unlike elements, attributes either appear once in a given element or do not, and the order of attributes in an element is not constrained. Here is the list of attributes that are associated with the <AttributeType> element:

- name

  Required. This is the name of the attribute.

- required

Value	Description
yes	The attribute must appear in the element.
no	The attribute is optional.

- default

  This allows for a default value to be provided.

An <AttributeType> declared within an <ElementType> defines the attribute within the scope of the <ElementType> that contains it. Multiple <ElementType> elements can reference an <AttributeType> not declared within a specific <ElementType>. In other words, declare an <AttributeType> within an <ElementType> if the attribute should only be used within that specific type of element.

Here is an example of a typical <AttributeType> declaration:

```
<AttributeType name="ID" required="yes"/>
```

Once we have declared an <AttributeType>, we can now reference it with its counterpart – <attribute>.

<attribute>

The relationship between <attribute> and <AttributeType> is similar to <element> and <ElementType>. The <attribute> element will reference a declared <AttributeType> within the scope of an <ElementType>. The behaviors of the <attribute> element are almost identical to the ones just discussed in <AttributeType>. Here is the list of attributes that can be used with this element:

- type

  Required. This attribute refers to a declared <AttributeType>. The value of this attribute corresponds with the name attribute of the <AttributeType>.

- required

  This determines whether the attribute must appear in the element. This is optional if the value has been set in the referenced <AttributeType>.

Value	Description
yes	The attribute must appear in the element.
no	The attribute is optional.

- `default`

  This allows for a default value to be provided. Note that this value takes precedence over the value specified in `default` attribute of the `<AttributeType>`.

A combination of `<attribute>` values can have an interesting effect on the validation of the XML document. For instance, if, within the `<attribute>` element, we set `required="yes"` and provide a default value, the effect is that the default value must be used. This combination essentially creates a constant, and any other values will not validate.

Now let's apply this knowledge to our ongoing example. If we want the `<ID>` element to be an attribute of the `<Student>` element, modifications to the schema would produce this new look:

```
<?xml version="1.0"?>
   <Schema name="StudentsSchema"
   xmlns="urn:schemas-microsoft-com:xml-data">
      <ElementType name="GPA" content="textOnly"/>
      <ElementType name="Student" content="eltOnly" model="closed">
         <AttributeType name="ID"/>
         <attribute type="ID" required="yes"/>
         <element type="GPA" minOccurs="1" maxOccurs="1"/>
      </ElementType>
      <ElementType name="Students" content="eltOnly">
         <element type="Student" minOccurs="0" maxOccurs="*"/>
      </ElementType>
   </Schema>
```

The revisions now indicate the following requirements:

- The `<Student>` element must contain an `ID` attribute
- The `ID` attribute cannot be used in any other elements as it is declared within the `<ElementType>` element for `<Student>`

If, later, we introduced other elements to the schema that could use an `ID` attribute, we could simply declare the `<AttributeType>` outside of any `<ElementType>` to make it accessible to the schema.

If we saved the schema above in a file named `StudentSchema2.xdr`, our XML document example of students could now be expressed in this way:

```
<?xml version="1.0"?>
   <Students
   xmlns="x-schema:StudentSchema2.xdr">
      <Student ID="12345">
         <GPA>3.5</GPA>
      </Student>
      <Student ID="67890">
```

```
        <GPA>4.0</GPA>
    </Student>
</Students>
```

The previous examples illustrate the basics of defining simple XDR schemas using elements and attributes.

At this point however, there is still nothing validating the *data* within the elements or attributes. As was highlighted earlier with DTDs, any free text can be placed within an attribute or element. What if we wanted to prevent illogical data like:

```
<GPA>Hello!</GPA>
```

The solution to this issue is the introduction of **data types** to our schema.

Data Types

Clearly, the support for data types in XDR schemas is a much-desired feature. Data types can be defined for elements or attributes. This allows for a deeper level of validation and proper formatting. XDR schemas support a wide range of data types in addition to the "attribute types" defined in a DTD. And as we will see later, most XDR data types naturally map to SQL Server 2000 data types.

Data Type Namespace

To use data types within an XDR schema, declare the data type namespace within the schema document, like so:

```
<?xml version="1.0"?>
   <Schema name="StudentsSchema"
   xmlns="urn:schemas-microsoft-com:xml-data"
   xmlns:dt="urn:schemas-microsoft-com:datatypes">
```

dt:type

Once the namespace is declared, we can associate XML data types with `<ElementType>` or `<AttributeType>` elements in the schema. We do so by using the `dt:type` attribute. The qualifier `dt` identifies the attribute name `type` as belonging to the data type namespace. Let's examine a listing of the possible data types that can be assigned to `dt:type`:

XDR Data Type	Description
`bin.base64`	MIME-style Base64 encoded binary data.
`bin.hex`	Hexadecimal-encoded binary data.
`boolean`	1 (true) or 0 (false).
`char`	Number corresponding to the Unicode representation of the character.
`date`	Date in a subset of the ISO 8601 format. Example: 2001-04-06

DR Data Type	Description
`dateTime`	Date in a subset of the ISO 8601 format. Time is optional. Example: 2001-04-06T11:45:33
`dateTime.tz`	Date in a subset of the ISO 8601 format. Time and zone are optional. Example: 2001-04-06T11:45:33-04:00 (-04:00 = 4 hours behind GMT)
`enumeration`	Explicit list of allowed values separated by whitespace. Example: Breakfast Lunch Dinner
`fixed.14.4`	Floating-point number. Not to exceed 14 digits to the left of the decimal point and no more than 4 to the right.
`float`	Floating-point number. Approximate. Range 2.2250738585072014E–308 to 1.7976931348623157E+308
`i1`	Integer (one-byte). Sign is optional. Range –128 to 127
`i2`	Integer (two-byte). Sign is optional. Range –32768 to 32767
`i4`	Integer (four-byte). Sign is optional. Range –2147483648 to 2147483647
`i8`	Integer (eight-byte). Sign is optional. Range –9223372036854775808 to 9223372036854775807
`id`	The `id` values must be unique throughout all elements in the XML document. This attribute is referenced by other attributes such as `idref` and `idrefs`.
`idref`	References the value in an `id` attribute within the XML document.
`idrefs`	References multiple `id` type values separated by whitespace.
`int`	Integer. Sign is optional. Range –9223372036854775808 to 9223372036854775807
`nmtoken`	Name token value. String consisting of one word.
`nmtokens`	List of name tokens separated by whitespace.
`number`	Floating-point number. Approximate. Range 2.2250738585072014E–308 to 1.7976931348623157E+308
`r4`	Floating-point number. Approximate. Range 1.17549435E-38F to 3.40282347E+38F

Table continued on following page

DR Data Type	Description
`r8`	Floating-point number. Approximate. Range 2.2250738585072014E–308 to 1.7976931348623157E+308
`string`	String of character data.
`time`	Time in a subset of the ISO 8601 format. Example: 11:45:33
`time.tz`	Time in a subset of the ISO 8601 format. Zone optional. Example: 08:15:27-05:00 (-05:00 = 5 hours behind GMT)
`ui1`	Unsigned integer (one-byte). Range 0 to 255
`ui2`	Unsigned integer (two-byte). Range 0 to 65535
`ui4`	Unsigned integer (four-byte) Range 0 to 4294967296
`ui8`	Unsigned integer (eight-byte) Range 0 to 18446744073709551615
`uri`	Uniform Resource Identifier (URI). This is not a data type for URLs, although URLs can be used for unique identification. Example: `urn:schemas-microsoft-com:xml-data`
`uuid`	Hexadecimal digits representing octets. Optional embedded hyphens ignored. This is the same data type as SQL Server's `uniqueidentifier`. Example: C8337F13-E9D7-4607-A1F8-A68341FF446C

Now let's see an example of the `dt:type` in action. To invalidate the string "Hello!" as content for the `<GPA>` element, our schema can define a floating-point number as the only valid data type. Here is how it looks:

```
<?xml version="1.0"?>
   <Schema name="StudentsSchema"
   xmlns="urn:schemas-microsoft-com:xml-data"
   xmlns:dt="urn:schemas-microsoft-com:datatypes">
      <ElementType name="GPA" content="textOnly" dt:type="r4"/>
      <ElementType name="Student" content="eltOnly" model="closed">
         <AttributeType name="ID"/>
         <attribute type="ID" required="yes"/>
         <element type="GPA" minOccurs="1" maxOccurs="1"/>
      </ElementType>
      <ElementType name="Students" content="eltOnly">
         <element type="Student" minOccurs="0" maxOccurs="*"/>
      </ElementType>
   </Schema>
```

Now, if an XML document references this schema and it contains this element:

```
<GPA>Hello!</GPA>
```

the MSXML parser will generate an error indicating a conflict in the data types. However, limiting the data type to a floating point number would still allow for GPA to contain data such as 9999.9999. The data type in this case is valid, although clearly not appropriate.

Although most of the data types are simple to implement, let's take some time to review a few examples that will provide a better understanding of concepts we will need when covering annotations later in this chapter.

id, idref, and idrefs

Since we will revisit id, idref, and idrefs when discussing the SQL Server annotations shortly, it is a good idea to get a good understanding of why we would use them. Put simply, these data types are really mechanisms for supporting intra-document referential integrity. Instead of nesting duplicate data throughout the XML document, we can "normalize" the data by making references to it. To demonstrate, examine the following schema:

```
<?xml version="1.0"?>
   <Schema name="CustOrdSchema"
   xmlns="urn:schemas-microsoft-com:xml-data"
   xmlns:dt="urn:schemas-microsoft-com:datatypes">
      <ElementType name="OrderHistory" content="textOnly" dt:type="idrefs"/>
      <ElementType name="Customer" content="eltOnly">
         <AttributeType name="custID" dt:type="id"/>
         <attribute type="custID" required="yes"/>
         <element type="OrderHistory" minOccurs="1" maxOccurs="1"/>
      </ElementType>
      <ElementType name="Order" content="empty">
         <AttributeType name="ordID" dt:type="id"/>
         <attribute type="ordID" required="yes"/>
         <AttributeType name="custID" dt:type="idref"/>
         <attribute type="custID" required="yes"/>
      </ElementType>
      <ElementType name="Orders" content="eltOnly">
         <element type="Order" minOccurs="1" maxOccurs="*"/>
      </ElementType>
      <ElementType name="Customers" content="eltOnly">
         <element type="Customer" minOccurs="1" maxOccurs="*"/>
      </ElementType>
      <ElementType name="CustomerOrders" content="eltOnly">
         <element type="Customers" minOccurs="1" maxOccurs="1"/>
         <element type="Orders" minOccurs="1" maxOccurs="1"/>
      </ElementType>
   </Schema>
```

This schema makes use of id, idref, and idrefs. It defines an attribute named custID in the <Customer> element and an attribute named ordID in the <Order> element, both of the id data type. The <Customer> element contains one child element named <OrderHistory>, which is declared with a data type of idrefs. This element could therefore reference the ordID attribute of the Order element, allowing a one-to-many relationship between <Customer> and <Order> elements. Note that the Order element contains an attribute named custID declared with a data type of idref. This also associates <Order> elements with <Customer> elements.

If the above example was saved to a file named CustOrdSchema.xdr, an example of an XML document that references the schema looks like this:

```
<?xml version="1.0" ?>
<CustomerOrders
xmlns="x-schema:CustOrdSchema.xdr">
   <Customers>
      <Customer custID="Cust-1">
         <OrderHistory>
            Ord-1 Ord-3 Ord-5
         </OrderHistory>
      </Customer>
      <Customer custID="Cust-2">
         <OrderHistory>
            Ord-2 Ord-4
         </OrderHistory>
      </Customer>
   </Customers>
   <Orders>
      <Order ordID="Ord-1" custID="Cust-1"/>
      <Order ordID="Ord-2" custID="Cust-2"/>
      <Order ordID="Ord-3" custID="Cust-1"/>
      <Order ordID="Ord-4" custID="Cust-2"/>
      <Order ordID="Ord-5" custID="Cust-1"/>
   </Orders>
</CustomerOrders>
```

Notice the values provided for ordID and custID. The prefixes of Ord – and Cust – are not accidental. When assigning values to elements or attributes of data type id, the *value* must be unique throughout the *entire* document. Therefore, ordID="1" and custID="1" would not be valid. Using prefixes makes it easier to maintain uniqueness across the XML document.

Date and Time

What if we wanted to know the date and time an order was placed? We can define an attribute in the <Order> element named orderDate and declare it with a dateTime data type. The schema definition for the <Order> element would be:

```
<ElementType name="Order" content="empty">
   <AttributeType name="orderDate" dt:type="dateTime"/>
   <attribute type="orderDate" required="yes"/>
   <AttributeType name="ordID" dt:type="id"/>
   <attribute type="ordID" required="yes"/>
   <AttributeType name="custID" dt:type="idref"/>
   <attribute type="custID" required="yes"/>
</ElementType>
```

Now the orders XML fragment could look like this:

```
<Orders>
   <Order orderDate="2001-03-26T09:56:15" ordID="Ord-1" custID="Cust-1"/>
   <Order orderDate="2001-03-28T13:05:33" ordID="Ord-2" custID="Cust-2"/>
   <Order orderDate="2001-03-29T15:34:49" ordID="Ord-3" custID="Cust-1"/>
   <Order orderDate="2001-04-02T11:13:03" ordID="Ord-4" custID="Cust-2"/>
   <Order orderDate="2001-04-06T12:40:22" ordID="Ord-5" custID="Cust-1"/>
</Orders>
```

According to the XML fragment, the order with an `ordID` attribute of `Ord-4` was placed at 11:13 AM on April 2nd, 2001.

Design Techniques

As we design our own schemas, we should keep the following issues in mind:

- **Scope**

  Before we declare elements and attributes, we should consider the reuse of any node within the document. For instance, if we create an `ID` attribute for a `<Customer>` element, and the `<Supplier>` element also needs an `ID` attribute of the same definition, declare the `ID` attribute outside the scope of any `<ElementType>` tags. This will allow multiple elements to reuse the same attribute definition.

- **Brevity**

  Several techniques can be used to reduce the physical size of an XML document. One way is by using attributes when these values have a one-to-one relationship with a given element. Another way to reduce file size is to avoid duplicate data. For example, many orders might reference the same customer. Instead of nesting all of the customer information under each order, we can design our schemas with `id`, `idref`, and `idrefs` to make references to the data without duplicating it.

- **Extensibility**

  Schemas can reference other schemas for common declarations. For instance, if one schema needed an `<Address>` element – with children such as `<Street>`, `<City>`, `<State>`, `<Country>`, and `<Postal Code>` – that was already declared in another schema, the first schema could simply reference the other for the declaration. If the name of the schema that contained the address information was `Info.xdr`, here is how another schema in the same directory would reference it:

```
<?xml version="1.0" ?>
<Schema xmlns="urn:schemas-microsoft-com:xml-data"
        xmlns:dt="urn:schemas-microsoft-com:datatypes">
<ElementType name="Student" xmlns:a="Info.xdr">
   <element type="a:Address"/>
</ElementType>
...
</Schema>
```

- **Documentation**
  Designing schemas requires forethought and planning. When completed, it would be very helpful for you as the designer – and for anyone else, for that matter – to have comments within the schema to clarify or explain each node's use. These can be inserted using the <document> tag. Here is a brief example:

```
<ElementType name="Student" xmlns:a="Info.xdr">
   <document>
   This is the student element!
   </document>
...
</ElementType>
```

Everything we have learned up to this point is specific to XDR schemas, and serves as a review for developers new to schema definitions. The next section discusses how XDR schemas are supported in SQL Server 2000.

Designing Annotated XDR Schemas

SQL Server 2000 introduced annotations to the XDR schema language, enabling data to be retrieved in the form of XML in a precise format. The annotations allow for an XDR schema to define a mapping of elements and attributes to database tables and columns. This is why XDR schemas that employ such annotations are known as **mapping schemas**. We can apply our knowledge of XDR schemas and easily define the structure of the document that we want returned, populated with data from the database.

Schema vs. Mapping Schema

A key difference between a simple XDR schema and one marked-up with annotations is the role the schema plays. Mapping schemas *form* the data in an XML document, while schemas without annotations validate existing structure and data types. Both types of schemas still form a "contract" for how the data should be presented.

Annotations allow for XML documents to represent a view of the relational data. Queries can be specified against mapping schemas by using XPath (see Chapter 8 for a full discussion of XPath).

IIS Virtual Directory Management for SQL Server

To demonstrate the features of mapping schemas, it will be necessary to create a virtual directory to execute XPath queries against.

> *For help in setting up the virtual directory and virtual names, please read Appendix A – Configuring Virtual Directories.*

For the examples in this chapter, create a virtual directory named `NW` to access the `Northwind` sample database. Then create a virtual name of type **schema** named `XDR`. The directory associated with the virtual name `XDR` is where our mapping schemas will be saved. To demonstrate templates (as one example requires) create another virtual name of type **template** named `Template`, and associate it with the same directory. The associated file directory you choose will be the working directory for all of the examples in this chapter.

When configuring the NW virtual directory, make sure to Allow XPath and Allow template queries. Optionally, you may want to Disable caching of mapping schemas, as changes made to schemas are not reflected for approximately two minutes when caching is turned on. During development, this can be annoying when testing the schemas.

Namespace for Annotations

In order to create our own mapping schemas, we need to specify a new namespace. We also need to understand default mapping behavior and cover the available annotations for explicit mappings.

To annotate an XDR schema, we must specify this namespace – urn:schemas-microsoft-com:xml-sql. Like the data type namespace, this is typically done in the <Schema> element. An example of declaring a namespace for annotations looks like this:

```
<?xml version="1.0"?>
<Schema
xmlns="urn:schemas-microsoft-com:xml-data"
xmlns:sql="urn:schemas-microsoft-com:xml-sql">
</Schema>
```

In our example, the sql namespace prefix is used to distinguish annotations in this namespace from those in other namespaces.

List of Annotations

By merely declaring the namespace for annotations, simple data mapping from tables or views to elements and attributes is possible. The following list of annotations is available to control the mapping behavior:

Annotation	Description
sql:relationship	Defines relationships between XML elements. The effect of this annotation is similar to using a JOIN in T-SQL. The use of the following attributes establishes the relationship: key, key-relation, foreign-key, and foreign-relation.
sql:field	Mapping between an XML element or attribute and the database field. This allows for element or attribute names to be different from the underlying column. This annotation is also used if the name of the column contains spaces or characters not valid in an XML schema.
sql:id-prefix	Concatenates a prefix to a database field to create valid id, idref, and idrefs. The effect of the annotation prevents data conflicts within the XML document.
sql:is-constant	Used when you want an item to appear in the XML document but the item is not linked to a column or table. Adding this annotation to an element and setting it to "1" (True) generates a constant value in the query output.
sql:key-fields	Specifies a field (or fields) that uniquely identifies the rows in a table. This assures proper nesting in the resulting XML.

Table continued on following page

Annotation	Description
sql:limit-field	This annotation is used to identify a column in the underlying table to filter the resulting XML. Similar to a WHERE clause in T-SQL, this annotation represents the column name in the equation. This is used with sql:limit-value to provide the filtering value in the equation.
sql:limit-value	Used with sql:limit-field, this provides the filtering value.
sql:map-field	Allows schema items to be excluded from the result. To exclude a node from the resulting XML, add this annotation and set it to "1" (True).
sql:overflow-field	Used to specify the column where overflow data is stored.
sql:relation	Mapping between an XML element or attribute to the database table. This allows for element or attribute names to be different from the underlying table. This annotation is also used if the name of the table contains spaces or characters not valid in an XML schema.
sql:target-namespace	Used to put the query results in a namespace that is not the default namespace.
sql:url-encode	Used to supply a URI to get BLOB data.
sql:use-cdata	Allows the specifying of CDATA sections to be used for certain elements in the XML document.

All of these annotations will be covered in depth throughout the rest of this chapter.

Default Mappings

Once an XDR schema specifies the annotations namespace, default mapping behavior is already present. With default mapping, an element name automatically maps to a table or view with the same name, and attribute names map to columns with corresponding names.

Here is an example of an XDR schema with default mappings:

```
<?xml version="1.0"?>
<Schema name="CategoriesSchema1"
   xmlns="urn:schemas-microsoft-com:xml-data"
        xmlns:sql="urn:schemas-microsoft-com:xml-sql">
   <ElementType name="Categories">
      <AttributeType name="CategoryID"/>
      <AttributeType name="CategoryName"/>
      <attribute type="CategoryID"/>
      <attribute type="CategoryName"/>
   </ElementType>
</Schema>
```

Save this schema as a file named CategoriesSchema1.xdr in the directory associated with the virtual name XDR. Open Internet Explorer and type the following URL (localhost can be replaced by the name of the IIS server):

http://localhost/NW/XDR/CategoriesSchema1.xdr/Categories?root=root

The result set appears this way:

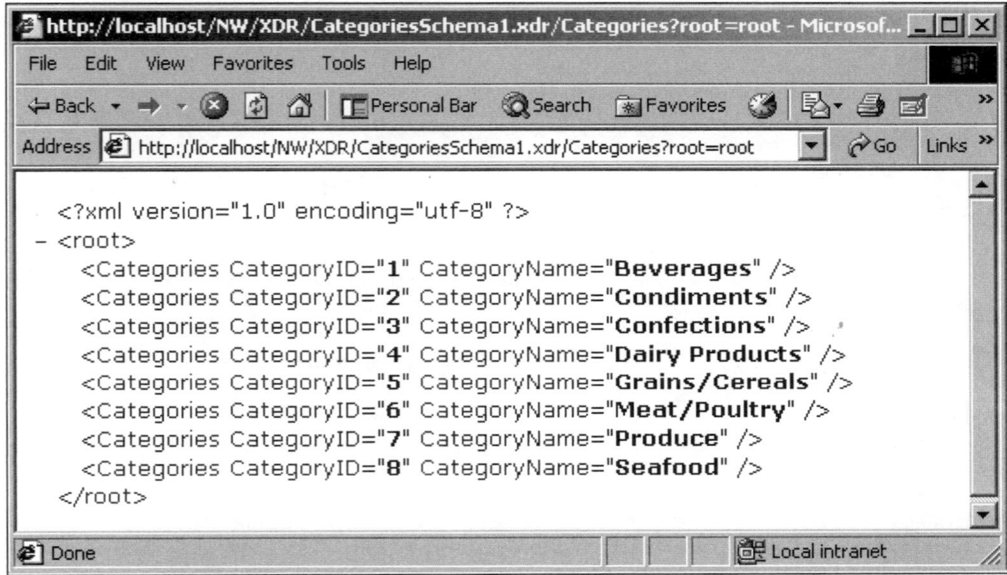

The URL specified an XPath query against the `CategoriesSchema1.xdr` schema. The XPath query in this example was simply `Categories`. The `?root=root` following the query indicated that the root element should be named `root`. The root element can be named whatever you prefer. A root query string assignment is necessary when multiple elements are returned. If the URL is changed to:

http://localhost/NW/XDR/CategoriesSchema1.xdr/Categories[@CategoryID=4]

the resultset appears like this:

```
<Categories CategoryID="4" CategoryName="Dairy Products" />
```

The XPath query in this case is `Categories [@CategoryID=4]`. In other words, retrieve a child element named `Categories` containing an attribute named `CategoryID` with a value of `4`. Because only one element is being returned, it is not necessary to append the query string with the `?root=root` assignment.

XPath queries are covered in more detail in Chapter 8.

This mapping schema was easy to design, as it required nothing other than the annotations namespace and the proper mapping of elements and attributes to their corresponding database objects. The `<Categories>` element mapped to the `Categories` table in the `Northwind` database. Likewise the `CategoryID` and `CategoryName` attributes mapped to columns in the `Categories` table.

Let's look at another example. In this case we would like to see a listing of Northwind employees. Suppose we wanted to list the last name, first name, and city. The XDR schema can be defined as follows:

```
<?xml version="1.0"?>
<Schema name="EmployeesSchema1"
   xmlns="urn:schemas-microsoft-com:xml-data"
        xmlns:sql="urn:schemas-microsoft-com:xml-sql">
   <ElementType name="Employees">
      <AttributeType name="LastName"/>
      <AttributeType name="FirstName"/>
      <AttributeType name="City"/>
      <attribute type="LastName"/>
      <attribute type="FirstName"/>
      <attribute type="City"/>
   </ElementType>
</Schema>
```

Save this schema into a file named `EmployeesSchema1.xdr` in our working directory. Open Internet Explorer and type the following URL:

http://localhost/NW/XDR/EmployeesSchema1.xdr/Employees?root=root

This is the resultset:

```
<?xml version="1.0" encoding="utf-8" ?>
<root>
    <Employees LastName="Davolio" FirstName="Nancy" City="Seattle" />
    <Employees LastName="Fuller" FirstName="Andrew" City="Tacoma" />
    <Employees LastName="Leverling" FirstName="Janet" City="Kirkland" />
    <Employees LastName="Peacock" FirstName="Margaret" City="Redmond" />
    <Employees LastName="Buchanan" FirstName="Steven" City="London" />
    <Employees LastName="Suyama" FirstName="Michael" City="London" />
    <Employees LastName="King" FirstName="Robert" City="London" />
    <Employees LastName="Callahan" FirstName="Laura" City="Seattle" />
    <Employees LastName="Dodsworth" FirstName="Anne" City="London" />
</root>
```

What if we don't want to use this attribute-centric mapping approach? We can redefine our schema to use elements for column values as well. Note the use of the `content` attribute in the `<ElementType>` elements in this schema:

```
<?xml version="1.0"?>
<Schema name="EmployeesSchema2"
   xmlns="urn:schemas-microsoft-com:xml-data"
        xmlns:sql="urn:schemas-microsoft-com:xml-sql">
   <ElementType name="LastName" content="textOnly"/>
   <ElementType name="FirstName" content="textOnly"/>
   <ElementType name="City" content="textOnly"/>
   <ElementType name="Employees">
      <element type="LastName"/>
      <element type="FirstName"/>
      <element type="City"/>
   </ElementType>
</Schema>
```

By specifying the `content` to be `textOnly`, these elements will map to their corresponding column names. Save this new schema as `EmployeesSchema2.xdr`. This time, execute the XPath query to return only London-based employees, like this:

```
http://localhost/NW/XDR/EmployeesSchema2.xdr/Employees[City="London"]?root=root
```

The element-centric result set is:

```
<?xml version="1.0" encoding="utf-8" ?>
<root>
    <Employees>
        <LastName>Buchanan</LastName>
        <FirstName>Steven</FirstName>
        <City>London</City>
    </Employees>
    <Employees>
        <LastName>Suyama</LastName>
        <FirstName>Michael</FirstName>
        <City>London</City>
    </Employees>
    <Employees>
        <LastName>King</LastName>
        <FirstName>Robert</FirstName>
        <City>London</City>
    </Employees>
    <Employees>
        <LastName>Dodsworth</LastName>
        <FirstName>Anne</FirstName>
        <City>London</City>
    </Employees>
</root>
```

Suppose we want to name the elements and attributes differently from their corresponding database objects? How can we specify a target namespace? What if we want more control over how the resulting XML document will be structured? What if we want to represent data relationships in our XML output? Explicit mappings provide functionality that lets us tackle all of these questions.

Explicit Mappings

Annotated XDR schemas offer control over the way our XML documents are shaped. The various annotations supported by XDR schemas allow for explicit mapping of the data stored in SQL Server 2000 to nodes in the XML document, and other valuable features. Let's begin our review with a look at how we can define a target namespace for the resulting XML document.

Specifying the Target Namespace

It may be a requirement for the resulting XML to be associated with a specific namespace. The `sql:target-namespace` annotation allows us to place elements and attributes from the default namespace into a namespace that we specify. The value assigned to the `sql:target-namespace` attribute is the URI (Uniform Resource Identifier) applied to all elements and attributes in the resulting XML document.

The `sql:target-namespace` can only be used in the `<Schema>` element of the XDR schema.

Here is a revision to our schema returning categories from the `Northwind` database. The schema filename has been changed to `CategoriesSchema2.xdr`:

```
<?xml version="1.0"?>
<Schema name="CategoriesSchema2"
   xmlns="urn:schemas-microsoft-com:xml-data"
        xmlns:sql="urn:schemas-microsoft-com:xml-sql"
   sql:target-namespace="urn:my-namespace">
   <ElementType name="Categories">
      <AttributeType name="CategoryID"/>
      <AttributeType name="CategoryName"/>
      <attribute type="CategoryID"/>
      <attribute type="CategoryName"/>
   </ElementType>
</Schema>
```

The URI specified as the target namespace is `urn:my-namespace`. Let's access this data by executing a template file in the URL.

Template Files

Template files contain references to mapping schemas and XPath queries. To make our own template, create a file in the working directory named `CategoriesTemplate.xml`, containing the following markup:

```
<ROOT
xmlns:sql="urn:schemas-microsoft-com:xml-sql">
   <sql:xpath-query mapping-schema="CategoriesSchema2.xdr"
              xmlns:x="urn:my-namespace" >
      /x:Categories
   </sql:xpath-query>
</ROOT>
```

Note that the `<sql:xpath-query>` element specifies the `urn:my-namespace`. The `x` prefix is used to qualify `Categories` in the XPath query.

To execute the template in the URL, open Internet Explorer and enter the following:

http://localhost/NW/Template/CategoriesTemplate.xml

Notice that we are now referencing the `Template` virtual name in the URL rather than `XDR`. We cannot just reference the XDR file directly in the URL because we can't specify the namespace in the URL. We have to use templates to reference the namespace in the `<sql:xpath-query>` annotation. The resultset should appear like this:

```
<ROOT xmlns:sql="urn:schemas-microsoft-com:xml-sql">
  <y0:Categories xmlns:y0="urn:my-namespace" CategoryID="1" CategoryName="Beverages" />
  <y0:Categories xmlns:y0="urn:my-namespace" CategoryID="2" CategoryName="Condiments" />
  <y0:Categories xmlns:y0="urn:my-namespace" CategoryID="3" CategoryName="Confections" />
  <y0:Categories xmlns:y0="urn:my-namespace" CategoryID="4" CategoryName="Dairy Products" />
  <y0:Categories xmlns:y0="urn:my-namespace" CategoryID="5" CategoryName="Grains/Cereals" />
  <y0:Categories xmlns:y0="urn:my-namespace" CategoryID="6" CategoryName="Meat/Poultry" />
```

```
  <y0:Categories xmlns:y0="urn:my-namespace" CategoryID="7" CategoryName="Produce" />
  <y0:Categories xmlns:y0="urn:my-namespace" CategoryID="8" CategoryName="Seafood" />
</ROOT>
```

Each `<Categories>` element specifies the `urn:my-namespace` namespace. The prefix, however, is not `x` as you might have expected. Instead, an arbitrary prefix – in this case, `y0` – is generated.

Controlling the Naming of Elements and Attributes

The `sql:relation` annotation is used to map XML nodes to tables or views. This means we can name our elements or attributes differently to the names used in the underlying data source. We can add `sql:relation` to either `<ElementType>`, `<element>`, or `<attribute>` elements. The `sql:relation` annotation is ignored in the `<AttributeType>` element.

> **Using `sql:relation` also resolves naming issues in the XDR schema. Whereas SQL Server allows spaces in names of tables and views, spaces are not valid in XML identifiers. So we could not use default mappings for the `[Order Details]` table in the `Northwind` database.**

When we use this annotation in `<ElementType>`, the mapping scope applies to all elements and attributes specified in the element. If it is used in `<element>`, the scope applies to all the specified attributes.

The following example uses the `sql:relation` annotation to resolve the naming issue with mapping to the `[Order Details]` table:

```
<?xml version="1.0"?>
<Schema name="ODSchema1"
   xmlns="urn:schemas-microsoft-com:xml-data"
        xmlns:sql="urn:schemas-microsoft-com:xml-sql">
   <ElementType name="OrderDetail" sql:relation="[Order Details]">
      <AttributeType name="OrderID"/>
      <AttributeType name="ProductID"/>
      <AttributeType name="UnitPrice"/>
      <attribute type="OrderID"/>
      <attribute type="ProductID"/>
      <attribute type="UnitPrice"/>
   </ElementType>
</Schema>
```

This schema maps the `<OrderDetail>` element to the `[Order Details]` table. It's good to remember that the squared brackets `[]` are still required to qualify the table name to SQL Server. Save the schema to our working directory as `ODSchema1.xdr`. The following URL executes an XPath query that returns all elements with a `UnitPrice` attribute value of `4.8`:

http://localhost/NW/XDR/ODSchema1.xdr/OrderDetail[@UnitPrice=4.8]?root=root

Here is the resultset:

```
<?xml version="1.0" encoding="utf-8" ?>
<root>
    <OrderDetail OrderID="10276" ProductID="13" UnitPrice="4.8" />
```

```
    <OrderDetail OrderID="10291" ProductID="13" UnitPrice="4.8" />
    <OrderDetail OrderID="10325" ProductID="13" UnitPrice="4.8" />
    <OrderDetail OrderID="10383" ProductID="13" UnitPrice="4.8" />
    <OrderDetail OrderID="10391" ProductID="13" UnitPrice="4.8" />
    <OrderDetail OrderID="10394" ProductID="13" UnitPrice="4.8" />
    <OrderDetail OrderID="10420" ProductID="13" UnitPrice="4.8" />
    <OrderDetail OrderID="10462" ProductID="13" UnitPrice="4.8" />
</root>
```

Another option available with this annotation is the ability to assign fully qualified database object names to the attribute. We could, for example, have assigned the value like this:

```
<ElementType name="OrderDetail" sql:relation="[ServerName].Northwind.dbo.[Order
Details]">
```

Mapping XML Nodes to Columns

The `sql:field` annotation is used to map XML nodes to columns in a database. The value assigned to this attribute is, therefore, the name of the column. Like `sql:relation`, `sql:field` can be used in the `<ElementType>`, `<element>`, and `<attribute>` elements. Unlike `sql:relation`, fully qualified database object names are not allowed. Only a valid column name can be assigned to `sql:field`.

Use of this annotation is an alternative to setting the `content` attribute of `<ElementType>` to `textOnly`. We can still set the `content` attribute to `textOnly` and override the default behavior by explicitly mapping the element to a column with a different name.

In the following schema example, we will generate an element-centric document that maps to the `[Category Sales for 1997]` view:

```
<?xml version="1.0"?>
<Schema name="CSViewSchema1"
   xmlns="urn:schemas-microsoft-com:xml-data"
        xmlns:sql="urn:schemas-microsoft-com:xml-sql">
   <ElementType name="Category" sql:field="CategoryName"/>
   <ElementType name="Total" sql:field="CategorySales"/>
   <ElementType name="Sales" sql:relation="[Category Sales for 1997]">
      <element type="Category"/>
      <element type="Total"/>
   </ElementType>
</Schema>
```

Save this schema as `CSViewSchema1.xdr` in our working directory. Execute the following XPath query in the URL:

http://localhost/NW/XDR/CSViewSchema1.xdr/Sales?root=root

This is a partial resultset:

```
<?xml version="1.0" encoding="utf-8" ?>
<root>
    <Sales>
            <Category>Beverages</Category>
            <Total>102074.31</Total>
```

```
    </Sales>
    <Sales>
            <Category>Condiments</Category>
            <Total>55277.6</Total>
    </Sales>
    <Sales>
            <Category>Confections</Category>
            <Total>80894.14</Total>
    </Sales>
    <Sales>
            <Category>Dairy Products</Category>
            <Total>114749.78</Total>
    </Sales>

...

</root>
```

Note how each element is identified differently from the underlying database table or column name (we have used `Category` and `Total` instead of `CategoryName` and `CategorySales`).

Representing Data Relationships in the XML Output

Up to this point, we have designed annotated XDR schemas that map to either a single table or view. In T-SQL terms, the equivalent would be a `SELECT` statement against one table or view. In many cases, however, joins are added to `SELECT` statements to combine data so that the resulting information presents a relationship of entities. We may, for instance, want to retrieve a list of products and the category name it falls under. Since the `Products` table in `Northwind` doesn't have a column for category name, we would need to join the `Products` table to the `Categories` table to get this result. The primary key column in `Categories` is named `CategoryID`, and this is used in the join to the `Products` table, on its foreign key column of the same name. Here is what the join looks like from a T-SQL perspective:

```
SELECT     c.CategoryName, p.ProductName
FROM       Categories c
INNER JOIN Products p
ON         c.CategoryID = p.CategoryID
```

To accomplish joins in mapping schemas, we use the `<sql:relationship>` *element* (as opposed to attribute). This annotation provides us the means to nest the schema elements hierarchically, based on the primary key and foreign key relationships among the underlying tables to which the elements map. In order to specify the necessary join information, the `<sql:relationship>` element contains the following four required attributes:

Attribute	Description
`key-relation`	Primary table.
`key`	Primary key of the `key-relation`. Composite key values are separated with spaces. Must match the positional sequence of `foreign-key`.

Table continued on following page

Attribute	Description
`foreign-relation`	Foreign table.
`foreign-key`	Foreign key of the `foreign-relation`. Composite key values are separated with spaces. Must match the positional sequence of `key`.

The `<sql:relationship>` in the XDR schema is used only in `<element>` and `<attribute>` elements.

Joining Two Tables

We'll explore several examples of this annotation using simple and complex relationships. Let's start by creating a relationship between categories and products. Since many products can share one category, the `Category` table is our `key-relation`, and the `Products` table is our `foreign-relation`. `CategoryID` is the value for both `key` and `foreign-key`. The following XDR schema creates the hierarchal relationship:

```
<?xml version="1.0"?>
<Schema name="CPJoinSchema1"
   xmlns="urn:schemas-microsoft-com:xml-data"
        xmlns:sql="urn:schemas-microsoft-com:xml-sql">
   <ElementType name="Product" sql:relation="Products" sql:field="ProductName"/>
   <ElementType name="Category" sql:relation="Categories">
      <AttributeType name="Name"/>
      <attribute type="Name" sql:field="CategoryName"/>
      <element type="Product">
         <sql:relationship
         key-relation="Categories"
         key="CategoryID"
         foreign-relation="Products"
         foreign-key="CategoryID"
         />
      </element>
   </ElementType>
</Schema>
```

Save this schema in the working directory as `CPJoinSchema1.xdr`, and then execute the following XPath query in the URL:

http://localhost/NW/XDR/CPJoinSchema1.xdr/Category?root=root

This is a partial resultset:

```
<?xml version="1.0" encoding="utf-8" ?>
<root>
    <Category Name="Beverages">
            <Product>Chai</Product>
            <Product>Chang</Product>
            <Product>Guaraná Fantástica</Product>
            <Product>Sasquatch Ale</Product>
            <Product>Steeleye Stout</Product>
            <Product>Côte de Blaye</Product>
            <Product>Chartreuse verte</Product>
```

```
                <Product>Ipoh Coffee</Product>
                <Product>Laughing Lumberjack Lager</Product>
                <Product>Outback Lager</Product>
                <Product>Rhönbräu Klosterbier</Product>
                <Product>Lakkalikööri</Product>
        </Category>
        <Category Name="Condiments">
                <Product>Aniseed Syrup</Product>
                <Product>Chef Anton's Cajun Seasoning</Product>
                <Product>Chef Anton's Gumbo Mix</Product>
                <Product>Grandma's Boysenberry Spread</Product>
                <Product>Northwoods Cranberry Sauce</Product>
                <Product>Genen Shouyu</Product>
                <Product>Gula Malacca</Product>
                <Product>Original Frankfurter grüne Soße</Product>
                <Product>Louisiana Fiery Hot Pepper Sauce</Product>
                <Product>Louisiana Hot Spiced Okra</Product>
                <Product>Sirop d'érable</Product>
                <Product>Vegie-spread</Product>
        </Category>

...

</root>
```

The relationships are defined by nesting "foreign" elements into "key" elements.

Joining Three Tables

The previous example was a demonstration of only joining two tables. What if our join is more complex? Let's add another entity – orders. If we want the list to reveal the order ID that each product has been placed on, we now need to join three tables: `Categories`, `Products`, and `[Order Details]`. We already know that `Categories` joins `Products` on the `CategoryID` column. `Products` joins `[Order Details]` on the `ProductID` column. The following schema maps this complex relationship:

```
<?xml version="1.0"?>
<Schema name="CPODJoinSchema1"
   xmlns="urn:schemas-microsoft-com:xml-data"
        xmlns:sql="urn:schemas-microsoft-com:xml-sql">
   <ElementType name="OrderID" sql:relation="[Order Details]"
sql:field="OrderID"/>
   <ElementType name="Product" sql:relation="Products">
      <AttributeType name="ProductName"/>
      <attribute type="ProductName" sql:field="ProductName"/>
      <element type="OrderID">
         <sql:relationship
         key-relation="Products"
         key="ProductID"
         foreign-relation="[Order Details]"
         foreign-key="ProductID"
         />
      </element>
   </ElementType>
   <ElementType name="Category" sql:relation="Categories">
```

```
        <AttributeType name="CategoryName"/>
        <attribute type="CategoryName" sql:field="CategoryName"/>
        <element type="Product">
          <sql:relationship
          key-relation="Categories"
          key="CategoryID"
          foreign-relation="Products"
          foreign-key="CategoryID"
          />
        </element>
      </ElementType>
    </Schema>
```

Save this schema as `CPODJoinSchema1.xdr` in the working directory, and then execute this XPath query in the URL:

http://localhost/NW/XDR/CPODJoinSchema1.xdr/Category?root=root

This is a partial resultset (with some nodes collapsed):

```
<?xml version="1.0" encoding="utf-8" ?>
<root>
    – <Category CategoryName="Beverages">
    + <Product ProductName="Chai">
    + <Product ProductName="Chang">
    + <Product ProductName="Guaraná Fantástica">
    + <Product ProductName="Sasquatch Ale">
    + <Product ProductName="Steeleye Stout">
    + <Product ProductName="Côte de Blaye">
    + <Product ProductName="Chartreuse verte">
    + <Product ProductName="Ipoh Coffee">
    – <Product ProductName="Laughing Lumberjack Lager">
    <OrderID>10284</OrderID>
    <OrderID>10502</OrderID>
    <OrderID>10544</OrderID>
    <OrderID>10670</OrderID>
    <OrderID>10775</OrderID>
    <OrderID>10864</OrderID>
    <OrderID>10911</OrderID>
    <OrderID>10923</OrderID>
    <OrderID>10939</OrderID>
    <OrderID>11054</OrderID>
    </Product>

...

</root>
```

Look at the output above. `<OrderID>` elements are children of `<Product>` elements, which are children of `<Category>` elements. The hierarchal structure was accomplished by specifying `<sql:relationship>` in two different elements in our mapping schema.

Specifying Indirect Relationships

What if we want to join two different entities indirectly? Suppose that we now want a list of orders identifying the customer ID and the product names ordered. There is no direct relationship between the `Orders` and `Products` tables. However, we could link them indirectly through the `[Order Details]` table. `Orders` joins `[Order Details]` on `OrderID`, and `[Order Details]` joins `Products` on `ProductID`. We don't actually need a value in `[Order Details]`; we just need it to get from `Orders` to `Products`.

The following schema demonstrates how to specify indirect relationships:

```
<?xml version="1.0" ?>
<Schema name="OPJoinSchema1" xmlns="urn:schemas-microsoft-com:xml-data"
xmlns:dt="urn:schemas-microsoft-com:datatypes"
xmlns:sql="urn:schemas-microsoft-com:xml-sql">
   <ElementType name="Product" sql:relation="Products" sql:field="ProductName"/>
   <ElementType name="Order" sql:relation="Orders" >
      <AttributeType name="OrderID" />
          <attribute type="OrderID" />
          <AttributeType name="CustomerID" />
          <attribute type="CustomerID" />
          <AttributeType name="EmployeeID" />
          <attribute type="EmployeeID" />
          <element type="Product" >
                   <sql:relationship
                      key-relation="Orders"
                      key="OrderID"
                      foreign-relation="[Order Details]"
                      foreign-key="OrderID"
               />
               <sql:relationship
                      key-relation="[Order Details]"
                      key="ProductID"
                      foreign-relation="Products"
                      foreign-key="ProductID"
               />
      </element>
   </ElementType>
</Schema>
```

The schema specifies an indirect join by repeating the `<sql:relationship>` element twice in the `<element>` declaration for `"Product"`.

Save the schema as `OPJoinSchema1.xdr` in the working directory, and then execute the following XPath query in the URL:

http://localhost/NW/XDR/OPJoinSchema1.xdr/Order?root=root

This is a partial resultset:

```
<?xml version="1.0" encoding="utf-8" ?>
<root>
    <Order OrderID="10248" CustomerID="VINET" EmployeeID="5">
            <Product>Mozzarella di Giovanni</Product>
```

```
            <Product>Queso Cabrales</Product>
            <Product>Singaporean Hokkien Fried Mee</Product>
            </Order>
    <Order OrderID="10249" CustomerID="TOMSP" EmployeeID="6">
            <Product>Manjimup Dried Apples</Product>
            <Product>Tofu</Product>
    </Order>
    <Order OrderID="10250" CustomerID="HANAR" EmployeeID="4">
            <Product>Jack's New England Clam Chowder</Product>
            <Product>Louisiana Fiery Hot Pepper Sauce</Product>
            <Product>Manjimup Dried Apples</Product>
    </Order>

...

</root>
```

We will see other examples of <sql:relationship> throughout the rest of this chapter.

Filtering Data

So far, the only filtering of data has been done in our XPath queries. We can also limit our results on relational data by the use of two annotations: sql:limit-field and sql:limit-value. These attributes are specified on <element> or <attribute> elements containing the <sql:relationship> annotation.

The role of sql:limit-field is to identify the column with the limiting value. The sql:limit-value contains the filtering value. If sql:limit-value is not specified, the default is NULL.

When these annotations are used, the behavior of the filter will return nodes that satisfy the match criteria. Let's revisit the OPJoinSchema1.xdr. Make the following changes and save the schema as OPJoinSchema2.xdr:

```
<?xml version="1.0" ?>
<Schema name="OPJoinSchema2"

   xmlns="urn:schemas-microsoft-com:xml-data"
        xmlns:dt="urn:schemas-microsoft-com:datatypes"
        xmlns:sql="urn:schemas-microsoft-com:xml-sql">

   <ElementType name="Product" sql:relation="Products" sql:field="ProductName"/>
   <ElementType name="Order" sql:relation="Orders" >
      <AttributeType name="OrderID" />
          <attribute type="OrderID" />
          <AttributeType name="CustomerID" />
          <attribute type="CustomerID" />
          <AttributeType name="EmployeeID" />
          <attribute type="EmployeeID" />

          <element type="Product"
      sql:limit-field="ProductName"
      sql:limit-value="Tofu">

                      <sql:relationship
                          key-relation="Orders"
                          key="OrderID"
```

```
                              foreign-relation="[Order Details]"
                              foreign-key="OrderID"
              />
              <sql:relationship
                              key-relation="[Order Details]"
                              key="ProductID"
                              foreign-relation="Products"
                              foreign-key="ProductID"
              />
          </element>
       </ElementType>
   </Schema>
```

The schema has been modified so that the `<product>` element is returned only if the product name is `Tofu`.

Execute the following XPath query in the URL:

http://localhost/NW/XDR/OPJoinSchema2.xdr/Order?root=root

This is a partial resultset:

```
<?xml version="1.0" encoding="utf-8" ?>
<root>
     <Order OrderID="10248" CustomerID="VINET" EmployeeID="5" />
     <Order OrderID="10249" CustomerID="TOMSP" EmployeeID="6">
            <Product>Tofu</Product>
     </Order>
     <Order OrderID="10250" CustomerID="HANAR" EmployeeID="4" />
     <Order OrderID="10251" CustomerID="VICTE" EmployeeID="3" />

...

     <Order OrderID="11077" CustomerID="RATTC" EmployeeID="1">
            <Product>Tofu</Product>
     </Order>
</root>
```

Controlling Structure in the XML Output

The `sql:key-fields` annotation indicates the column(s) that uniquely identify the rows of the relation specified in the `<ElementType>` element. If more than one column is used to uniquely identify the rows, use a space to separate column names. This annotation can be used in either `<ElementType>` or `<element>` elements.

Using `sql:key-fields` provides key information necessary to obtain the proper nesting result. This can be explained with the following example:

```
<?xml version="1.0" ?>
<Schema name="EmployeesSchema3"
xmlns="urn:schemas-microsoft-com:xml-data"
xmlns:dt="urn:schemas-microsoft-com:datatypes"
xmlns:sql="urn:schemas-microsoft-com:xml-sql">
   <ElementType name="City" content="textOnly">
```

```
    <AttributeType name="EmployeeID" />
          <attribute type="EmployeeID" />
    </ElementType>
    <ElementType name="Employees" >
          <element type="City" />
    </ElementType>
</Schema>
```

This schema uses default mappings so that the `<Employees>` element will map to the `Employees` table. The child element of `<Employees>` is `<City>`, which contains the `EmployeeID` attribute. Save the schema as `EmployeesSchema3.xdr` in the working directory and execute the following XPath query in the URL:

http://localhost/NW/XDR/EmployeesSchema3.xdr/Employees?root=root

This is the resultset:

```
<?xml version="1.0" encoding="utf-8" ?>
<root>
    <Employees />
    <Employees />
    <Employees />
    <Employees />
    <Employees />
    <Employees />
    <Employees />
    <Employees />
    <Employees>
          <City EmployeeID="1">Seattle</City>
          <City EmployeeID="2">Tacoma</City>
          <City EmployeeID="3">Kirkland</City>
          <City EmployeeID="4">Redmond</City>
          <City EmployeeID="5">London</City>
          <City EmployeeID="6">London</City>
          <City EmployeeID="7">London</City>
          <City EmployeeID="8">Seattle</City>
          <City EmployeeID="9">London</City>
    </Employees>
</root>
```

The correct information has been provided, but the elements are not nested properly. A simple change in the schema can resolve this problem. Add the `sql:key-fields` annotation to the `<ElementType>` for `<Employees>` like this:

```
<ElementType name="Employees" sql:key-fields="EmployeeID">
          <element type="City" />
</ElementType>
```

Save the changes and execute the XPath query again. The result set now looks like this:

```
<?xml version="1.0" encoding="utf-8" ?>
<root>
```

```
    <Employees>
        <City EmployeeID="1">Seattle</City>
    </Employees>
    <Employees>
        <City EmployeeID="2">Tacoma</City>
    </Employees>
    <Employees>
        <City EmployeeID="3">Kirkland</City>
    </Employees>
    <Employees>
        <City EmployeeID="4">Redmond</City>
    </Employees>
    <Employees>
        <City EmployeeID="5">London</City>
    </Employees>
    <Employees>
        <City EmployeeID="6">London</City>
    </Employees>
    <Employees>
        <City EmployeeID="7">London</City>
    </Employees>
    <Employees>
        <City EmployeeID="8">Seattle</City>
    </Employees>
    <Employees>
        <City EmployeeID="9">London</City>
    </Employees>
</root>
```

Why the difference? Because specifying the `EmployeeID` column as a key column forced the nesting of `<City>` elements (which contain the `EmployeeID` attribute) with each occurrence of `<Employees>`. This gives us control over the nesting behavior.

Let's consider another example. This schema defines a complex relationship where products are grouped by categories, and each product identifies its supplier:

```
<?xml version="1.0"?>
<Schema name="CPSJoinSchema1"
   xmlns="urn:schemas-microsoft-com:xml-data"
        xmlns:sql="urn:schemas-microsoft-com:xml-sql">
   <ElementType name="Supplier" sql:relation="Suppliers" sql:field="CompanyName"/>
   <ElementType name="Product" sql:relation="Products">
      <AttributeType name="ProductName"/>
      <attribute type="ProductName"/>
      <element type="Supplier">
         <sql:relationship
         key-relation="Products"
         key="SupplierID"
         foreign-relation="Suppliers"
         foreign-key="SupplierID"
         />
      </element>
   </ElementType>
   <ElementType name="Category" sql:relation="Categories">
      <AttributeType name="CategoryName"/>
      <attribute type="CategoryName"/>
```

```
        <element type="Product">
          <sql:relationship
          key-relation="Categories"
          key="CategoryID"
          foreign-relation="Products"
          foreign-key="CategoryID"
          />
        </element>
      </ElementType>
    </Schema>
```

Save this schema as `CPSJoinSchema1.xdr` in the working directory. Execute the following XPath query in the URL:

http://localhost/NW/XDR/CPSJoinSchema1.xdr/Category?root=root

This is a partial result set:

```
<?xml version="1.0" encoding="utf-8" ?>
<root>
    <Category CategoryName="Beverages">
        <Product ProductName="Chai" />
        <Product ProductName="Chang">
            <Supplier>Exotic Liquids</Supplier>
            <Supplier>Exotic Liquids</Supplier>
        </Product>

...

</root>
```

The data returned is not properly nested. The supplier Exotic Liquids should appear as a child element for Chai and Chang, not twice under Chang. It appears twice because Exotic Liquids supplies two products in the Beverages category. To obtain the correct nesting behavior, add the `sql:key-fields` annotation like this:

```
<ElementType name="Product" sql:relation="Products" sql:key-fields="ProductID">
```

Save the changes and execute the XPath query again. This is a partial resultset:

```
<?xml version="1.0" encoding="utf-8" ?>
<root>
    <Category CategoryName="Beverages">
        <Product ProductName="Chai">
            <Supplier>Exotic Liquids</Supplier>
        </Product>
        <Product ProductName="Chang">
            <Supplier>Exotic Liquids</Supplier>
        </Product>

...

</root>
```

Each product now properly identifies its respective supplier.

> **To produce proper nesting in the result, it is recommended that `sql:key-fields` be specified in all schemas.**

Elements that Do Not Map to the Database

Annotated XDR schemas are also known as mapping schemas for a good reason – all the elements and attributes in the schema map to either a table or view, or column. What if we wanted to introduce an element into the resulting XML document that maps to nothing in the database? This is where the `sql:is-constant` annotation comes in handy. We can only use this annotation in the `<ElementType>` element. Valid assignments to this attribute are either `1` (`True`) or `0` (`False`). The following schema demonstrates a typical use of the `sql:is-constant` annotation:

```
<?xml version="1.0"?>
<Schema name="EmployeesSchema4"
   xmlns="urn:schemas-microsoft-com:xml-data"
        xmlns:sql="urn:schemas-microsoft-com:xml-sql">
   <ElementType name="Employee" sql:relation="Employees">
      <AttributeType name="LastName"/>
      <AttributeType name="FirstName"/>
      <AttributeType name="City"/>
      <attribute type="LastName"/>
      <attribute type="FirstName"/>
      <attribute type="City"/>
   </ElementType>
   <ElementType name="Employees" sql:is-constant="1">
      <element type="Employee"/>
   </ElementType>
</Schema>
```

The `sql:is-constant="1"` is just a flag to mark the element as a constant.

Save the schema as `EmployeesSchema4.xdr` in the working directory. Execute the following XPath query in the URL:

http://localhost/NW/XDR/EmployeesSchema4.xdr/Employees

Notice anything different with the query above? It wasn't necessary to append the query string with `?root=root`. Why? Because the `<Employees>` element doesn't map to the database and thus appears only once in the XML document returned. However, the `<Employee>` element does map to the `Employees` table, and is repeated within the `<Employees>` element, as shown in the resultset:

```
<Employees>
     <Employee LastName="Davolio" FirstName="Nancy" City="Seattle" />
     <Employee LastName="Fuller" FirstName="Andrew" City="Tacoma" />
     <Employee LastName="Leverling" FirstName="Janet" City="Kirkland" />
     <Employee LastName="Peacock" FirstName="Margaret" City="Redmond" />
     <Employee LastName="Buchanan" FirstName="Steven" City="London" />
     <Employee LastName="Suyama" FirstName="Michael" City="London" />
     <Employee LastName="King" FirstName="Robert" City="London" />
     <Employee LastName="Callahan" FirstName="Laura" City="Seattle" />
     <Employee LastName="Dodsworth" FirstName="Anne" City="London" />
</Employees>
```

Preventing Elements from Appearing in the XML Output

The sql:map-field annotation is similar to sql:is-constant in that it prevents mapping behavior. Where does it differ? There might be situations that call for the declaration of nodes in the mapping schema that should not manifest in the returning XML document. To exclude an attribute or element from the result, specify the sql:map-field on either <ElementType>, <element>, or <attribute>, where the content attribute is set to textOnly (<attribute> is always textOnly). By setting this annotation to 0 (False), the node will not map to the database or appear in the XML document.

What situations would call for the use of sql:map-field? Perhaps we have been given an XDR schema from another source in which the business rules cannot be changed. The schema may define elements with no counterparts in the database. Since the schema may be used by other sources for validation, we can exclude the non-database nodes from participating in the mapping schema.

Here is an example of a schema that excludes an attribute from the resultset by specifying the sql:map-field annotation:

```
<?xml version="1.0"?>
<Schema name="EmployeesSchema5"
   xmlns="urn:schemas-microsoft-com:xml-data"
        xmlns:sql="urn:schemas-microsoft-com:xml-sql">
   <ElementType name="Employee" sql:relation="Employees">
      <AttributeType name="LastName"/>
      <AttributeType name="FirstName"/>
      <AttributeType name="EmailAddress"/>
      <attribute type="LastName"/>
      <attribute type="FirstName"/>
      <attribute type="EmailAddress" sql:map-field="0"/>
   </ElementType>
   <ElementType name="Employees" sql:is-constant="1">
      <element type="Employee"/>
   </ElementType>
</Schema>
```

The Employees table does not contain a column value for EmailAddress, so the schema excludes the attribute from the resultset by specifying sql:map-field="0".

Save the schema as EmployeesSchema5.xdr, and execute the following XPath query:

http://localhost/NW/XDR/EmployeesSchema5.xdr/Employees

This is the resultset:

```
<Employees>
    <Employee LastName="Davolio" FirstName="Nancy" />
    <Employee LastName="Fuller" FirstName="Andrew" />
    <Employee LastName="Leverling" FirstName="Janet" />
    <Employee LastName="Peacock" FirstName="Margaret" />
    <Employee LastName="Buchanan" FirstName="Steven" />
    <Employee LastName="Suyama" FirstName="Michael" />
    <Employee LastName="King" FirstName="Robert" />
    <Employee LastName="Callahan" FirstName="Laura" />
    <Employee LastName="Dodsworth" FirstName="Anne" />
</Employees>
```

The <Employee> elements lack any EmailAddress attributes.

Data Types in Annotated XDR Schemas

As we learned earlier this chapter, XDR schemas support data types. This is true in mapping schemas as well. When data is retrieved from the database using annotated schemas, the appropriate data type is output in the resulting XML document. We can also control (to a certain degree) mapping between SQL Server data types to XML data types, with `dt:type` and `sql:datatype`.

dt:type

If `dt:type` is specified in the schema, the XML document resulting from an XPath query will adhere to the XML data type conversion if possible. An example of how `dt:type` can be used is seen in the schema below. The `OrderDate` column (which has a SQL Server data type of `datetime`) in the `Orders` table has been "split" into two attributes: `OrderDate` and `OrderTime`.

```
<?xml version="1.0" ?>
<Schema name="OrdersSchema1"
   xmlns="urn:schemas-microsoft-com:xml-data"
        xmlns:dt="urn:schemas-microsoft-com:datatypes"
        xmlns:sql="urn:schemas-microsoft-com:xml-sql">
   <ElementType name="Order" sql:relation="Orders" >
      <AttributeType name="OrderID" />
          <attribute type="OrderID" />
          <AttributeType name="OrderDate" dt:type="date"/>
          <attribute type="OrderDate" />
      <AttributeType name="OrderTime" dt:type="time"/>
          <attribute type="OrderTime" sql:field="OrderDate" />
   </ElementType>
   <ElementType name="Orders" sql:is-constant="1" >
      <element type="Order"/>
   </ElementType>
</Schema>
```

Save the schema as `OrdersSchema1.xdr`, and execute the following XPath query:

```
http://localhost/NW/XDR/OrdersSchema1.xdr/Orders
```

This is a partial resultset:

```
<Orders>
     <Order OrderID="10248" OrderDate="1996-07-04" OrderTime="00:00:00" />
     <Order OrderID="10249" OrderDate="1996-07-05" OrderTime="00:00:00" />
     <Order OrderID="10250" OrderDate="1996-07-08" OrderTime="00:00:00" />
     <Order OrderID="10251" OrderDate="1996-07-08" OrderTime="00:00:00" />

...

</Orders>
```

The `OrderDate` attribute was set to `dt:date`, and `OrderTime` was set to `dt:time`. Both attributes map to the same column. However, the values returned conform to the data type specified in the schema.

Without explicit mapping, the following table describes the natural mapping process between SQL Server data types and XML data types:

SQL Server Data Type	XML Data Type
Bigint	i8
Binary	bin.base64
Bit	boolean
Char	char
Datetime	datetime
Decimal	r8
Float	r8
Image	bin.base64
Int	int
Money	r8
Nchar	string
Ntext	string
Nvarchar	string
Numeric	r8
Real	r4
Smalldatetime	datetime
Smallint	i2
Smallmoney	fixed.14.4
Sysname	string
Text	string
Timestamp	ui8
Tinyint	ui1
Varbinary	bin.base64
Varchar	string
Uniqueidentifier	uuid

sql:datatype

According to the listing above, the XML data type `bin.base64` maps to several different SQL data types, such as `binary`, `varbinary`, and `image`. Now, if the XDR schema is used in an Updategram (covered in Chapter 9) or an XML Bulk Load (covered in Chapter 10), the returning data must be stored in the appropriate SQL Server data type. Therefore…

> **To explicitly map from the XML data type `bin.base64` to the proper SQL Server data type, use the `sql:datatype` annotation.**

The valid assignment of data types to the `sql:datatype` annotation depends on the configuration of SQL Server 2000. Without the installation of Web Release 1, `sql:datatype` can only be assigned to the `text`, `ntext`, `image`, and `binary` data types. If Web Release 1 has been installed, `sql:datatype` can be assigned to any of the SQL Server built-in data types.

The following schema explicitly states the SQL Server data type for the `Picture` attribute:

```
<?xml version="1.0"?>
<Schema name="CategoriesSchema3"
   xmlns="urn:schemas-microsoft-com:xml-data"
        xmlns:sql="urn:schemas-microsoft-com:xml-sql">
   <ElementType name="Categories">
      <AttributeType name="CategoryID"/>
      <AttributeType name="CategoryName"/>
      <AttributeType name="Picture"/>
      <attribute type="CategoryID"/>
      <attribute type="CategoryName"/>
      <attribute type="Picture" sql:datatype="image"/>
   </ElementType>
</Schema>
```

BLOB Columns

This example mapped an attribute of `Picture` to a column with a SQL Server data type of `image`. When the data is extracted, the XML data type is `bin.base64`. Having this value may not be useful in the returning XML document. However, it may be useful to have the URI returned so that the binary data can be retrieved at a later time. This is what `sql:url-encode` can do for us in the mapping schema. By setting this annotation to `1` (`True`), we are requesting a reference to the BLOB column, not the data itself.

The `sql:url-encode` attribute cannot be used on attributes with a `dt:type` of either `id`, `idref`, `idrefs`, `nmtoken`, or `nmtokens`. It cannot be used in conjunction with the `sql:use-cdata` annotation (covered later this chapter).

A key identifier for the row is also needed for the URI to specify the exact instance of the data needed. This can be accomplished with either `<sql:relationship>` or `sql:key-fields` annotations.

Here is an example of a mapping schema using the `sql:url-encode` annotation:

```
<?xml version="1.0"?>
<Schema name="CategoriesSchema3"
   xmlns="urn:schemas-microsoft-com:xml-data"
        xmlns:sql="urn:schemas-microsoft-com:xml-sql">
   <ElementType name="Categories" sql:key-fields="CategoryID">
      <AttributeType name="CategoryID"/>
      <AttributeType name="CategoryName"/>
      <AttributeType name="Picture"/>
      <attribute type="CategoryID"/>
      <attribute type="CategoryName"/>
      <attribute type="Picture" sql:url-encode="1"/>
   </ElementType>
</Schema>
```

Save this schema as `CategoriesSchema3.xdr` and execute the following XPath query:

http://localhost/NW/XDR/CategoriesSchema3.xdr/Categories?root=root

Here is the resultset:

```
<?xml version="1.0" encoding="utf-8" ?>
<root>
    <Categories CategoryID="1" CategoryName="Beverages"
Picture="dbobject/Categories[@CategoryID="1"]/@Picture" />
    <Categories CategoryID="2" CategoryName="Condiments"
Picture="dbobject/Categories[@CategoryID="2"]/@Picture" />
    <Categories CategoryID="3" CategoryName="Confections"
Picture="dbobject/Categories[@CategoryID="3"]/@Picture" />
    <Categories CategoryID="4" CategoryName="Dairy Products"
Picture="dbobject/Categories[@CategoryID="4"]/@Picture" />
    <Categories CategoryID="5" CategoryName="Grains/Cereals"
Picture="dbobject/Categories[@CategoryID="5"]/@Picture" />
    <Categories CategoryID="6" CategoryName="Meat/Poultry"
Picture="dbobject/Categories[@CategoryID="6"]/@Picture" />
    <Categories CategoryID="7" CategoryName="Produce"
Picture="dbobject/Categories[@CategoryID="7"]/@Picture" />
    <Categories CategoryID="8" CategoryName="Seafood"
Picture="dbobject/Categories[@CategoryID="8"]/@Picture" />
</root>
```

Notice in the output above how the URI returned a reference uniquely identifying `Picture` by use of the `CategoryID` key field. If the schema did not reference this primary key column in the `sql:key-fields` annotation, the query would have failed.

Retrieving Overflow Column Data

In Chapter 4, we learned that inserts to a database from an XML document using `OPENXML` might contain unconsumed data that can be trapped in an overflow column. To retrieve this data, we can use the `sql:overflow-field` annotation. The value assigned to `sql:overflow-field` is the name of the column storing the overflow data. Specify `sql:overflow-field` on the `<ElementType>` element.

The data returned from an overflow column appears in one of two ways:

- If an attribute exists in the overflow column, it becomes an attribute of the element that `sql:overflow-field` is specified on
- All elements or children thereof become sub-elements of the element that `sql:overflow-field` is specified on

As an example, create the following table using this script:

```
CREATE TABLE [Contractors] (
    [ContractorID] [int]       IDENTITY (1, 1) NOT NULL ,
    [LastName]     [nvarchar]           (20)   NOT NULL ,
    [FirstName]    [nvarchar]           (10)   NOT NULL ,
    [OverFlow]     [nvarchar]           (200)  NULL )
```

Now insert the following row using this script:

```
INSERT INTO [Northwind].[dbo].[Contractors]
([LastName], [FirstName], [OverFlow])
VALUES('Doe', 'John', '<Data><Company>XYZ</Company><Rate>100</Rate></Data>')
```

Here is an example of defining a mapping schema for the `Contractors` table using the `sql:overlflow-field` on the `OverFlow` column:

```
<?xml version="1.0" ?>
<Schema name="ContractorSchema1"
   xmlns="urn:schemas-microsoft-com:xml-data"
        xmlns:dt="urn:schemas-microsoft-com:datatypes"
        xmlns:sql="urn:schemas-microsoft-com:xml-sql">
  <ElementType name="Contractors" sql:overflow-field="Overflow" >
    <AttributeType name="ContractorID" />
    <AttributeType name="LastName" />
    <AttributeType name="FirstName" />
    <attribute type="ContractorID" />
    <attribute type="LastName"/>
    <attribute type="FirstName" />
  </ElementType>
</Schema>
```

Save the above schema as `ContractorSchema1.xdr`, and execute the following XPath query in the URL:

http://localhost/NW/XDR/ContractorSchema1.xdr/Contractors?root=root

This is the resultset:

```
<?xml version="1.0" encoding="utf-8" ?>
<root>
     <Contractors ContractorID="1" LastName="Doe" FirstName="John">
               <Company>XYZ</Company>
               <Rate>100</Rate>
     </Contractors>
</root>
```

The mark-up in the `OverFlow` column became children of the `<Contractors>` element, as defined in the schema.

Default Values for Attributes

Earlier this chapter, we learned that `<AttributeType>` elements allow for a default value to be specified. When used in a mapping schema, the default value is used when the data returned from the database is `NULL`. The default values will *not* appear in the XML document that is returned; rather the validating parser uses this value whenever the attribute is not present.

The following schema defines a default value of `NONE` when the `Region` column in the `Employees` table returns a `NULL` value:

```
<?xml version="1.0"?>
<Schema name="EmployeesSchema6"
   xmlns="urn:schemas-microsoft-com:xml-data"
   xmlns:dt="urn:schemas-microsoft-com:datatypes"
        xmlns:sql="urn:schemas-microsoft-com:xml-sql">
   <ElementType name="Employee" sql:relation="Employees">
      <AttributeType name="LastName" />
      <AttributeType name="FirstName"/>
      <AttributeType name="Region" default="NONE"/>
      <attribute type="LastName"/>
      <attribute type="FirstName"/>
      <attribute type="Region"/>
   </ElementType>
   <ElementType name="Employees" sql:is-constant="1">
      <element type="Employee"/>
   </ElementType>
</Schema>
```

Ensuring Unique ids

If the mapping schema uses id, idref, or idrefs, the sql:id-prefix makes sure such references are valid. What if we define a relationship between the Categories and Products tables where the primary key values are equal? This is true in the Northwind database, where both CategoryID and ProductID can equal 1. If we map the key values to the id data type, conflicts will occur. Remember, the value assigned to id must be unique across the XML document. Using sql:id-prefix concatenates a constant value to the beginning of each id to enable uniqueness.

The schema below creates a relationship between the Categories and Product tables, mapping the key columns in each table to id data types. The <Category> element contains a ProductList attribute, of type idrefs, that references a valid ProductID attribute:

```
<?xml version="1.0"?>
<Schema name="CPJoinSchema2"
   xmlns="urn:schemas-microsoft-com:xml-data"
   xmlns:dt="urn:schemas-microsoft-com:datatypes"
        xmlns:sql="urn:schemas-microsoft-com:xml-sql">
   <ElementType name="Product" sql:relation="Products" sql:field="ProductName"
sql:key-fields="CategoryID">
      <AttributeType name="ProductID" dt:type="id" sql:id-prefix="PRD-"/>
      <attribute type="ProductID"/>
         <sql:relationship
         key-relation="Products"
         key="CategoryID"
         foreign-relation="Categories"
         foreign-key="CategoryID"
         />
   </ElementType>
   <ElementType name="Category" sql:relation="Categories" sql:key-
fields="CategoryID">
      <AttributeType name="CategoryID" dt:type="id" sql:id-prefix="CTG-"/>
      <AttributeType name="Name"/>
      <AttributeType name="ProductList" dt:type="idrefs" sql:id-prefix="PRD-"/>
      <attribute type="CategoryID"/>
      <attribute type="Name" sql:field="CategoryName"/>
      <attribute type="ProductList" sql:relation="Products" sql:field="ProductID">
         <sql:relationship
         key-relation="Categories"
```

```
            key="CategoryID"
            foreign-relation="Products"
            foreign-key="CategoryID"
            />
         </attribute>
      </ElementType>
      <ElementType name="Categories" sql:is-constant="1">
         <element type="Category"/>
      </ElementType>
      <ElementType name="Products" sql:is-constant="1">
         <element type="Product"/>
      </ElementType>
      <ElementType name="ProductCategories" sql:is-constant="1">
         <element type="Categories"/>
         <element type="Products" />
      </ElementType>
   </Schema>
```

Save this schema as `CPJoinSchema2.xdr`, and execute the following XPath query:

http://localhost/NW/XDR/CPJoinSchema2.xdr/ProductCategories

This is a partial resultset:

```
<ProductCategories>
      <Categories>
            <Category CategoryID="CTG-1" Name="Beverages" ProductList="PRD-1 PRD-2 PRD-
      24 PRD-34 PRD-35 PRD-38 PRD-39 PRD-43 PRD-67 PRD-70 PRD-75 PRD-76" />
            <Category CategoryID="CTG-2" Name="Condiments" ProductList="PRD-15 PRD-3
      PRD-4 PRD-44 PRD-5 PRD-6 PRD-61 PRD-63 PRD-65 PRD-66 PRD-77 PRD-8" />
            <Category CategoryID="CTG-3" Name="Confections" ProductList="PRD-16 PRD-19
      PRD-20 PRD-21 PRD-25 PRD-26 PRD-27 PRD-47 PRD-48 PRD-49 PRD-50 PRD-62 PRD-68"
      />
            <Category CategoryID="CTG-4" Name="Dairy Products" ProductList="PRD-11 PRD-12
      PRD-31 PRD-32 PRD-33 PRD-59 PRD-60 PRD-69 PRD-71 PRD-72" />
            <Category CategoryID="CTG-5" Name="Grains/Cereals" ProductList="PRD-22 PRD-
      23 PRD-42 PRD-52 PRD-56 PRD-57 PRD-64" />
            <Category CategoryID="CTG-6" Name="Meat/Poultry" ProductList="PRD-17 PRD-29
      PRD-53 PRD-54 PRD-55 PRD-9" />
            <Category CategoryID="CTG-7" Name="Produce" ProductList="PRD-14 PRD-28 PRD-
      51 PRD-7 PRD-74" />
            <Category CategoryID="CTG-8" Name="Seafood" ProductList="PRD-10 PRD-13 PRD-
      18 PRD-30 PRD-36 PRD-37 PRD-40 PRD-41 PRD-45 PRD-46 PRD-58 PRD-73" />
      </Categories>
      <Products>
            <Product ProductID="PRD-1">Chai</Product>
            <Product ProductID="PRD-2">Chang</Product>
            <Product ProductID="PRD-24">Guaraná Fantástica</Product>

...

            <Product ProductID="PRD-37">Gravad lax</Product>
      </Products>
</ProductCategories>
```

Dealing with Markup

The data returned by SQL Server may contain characters that represent markup to the MSXML parser. To avoid unwanted results, we could maintain the state of the data as it is stored in the database by wrapping it in an XML CDATA section. CDATA sections ignore markup characters such as <, >, <=, and &. The `sql:use-cdata` annotation wraps the column value specified in either `<ElementType>` or `<element>` elements in a CDATA section.

The following schema specifies the contents of the `PhotoPath` field to be wrapped in a CDATA section:

```
<?xml version="1.0"?>
<Schema name="EmployeesSchema7"
   xmlns="urn:schemas-microsoft-com:xml-data"
   xmlns:dt="urn:schemas-microsoft-com:datatypes"
        xmlns:sql="urn:schemas-microsoft-com:xml-sql">
   <ElementType name="PhotoPath" sql:field="PhotoPath"/>
   <ElementType name="Employee" sql:relation="Employees">
      <AttributeType name="LastName" />
      <AttributeType name="FirstName"/>
      <attribute type="LastName"/>
      <attribute type="FirstName"/>
      <element type="PhotoPath" sql:use-cdata="1"/>
   </ElementType>
   <ElementType name="Employees" sql:is-constant="1">
      <element type="Employee"/>
   </ElementType>
</Schema>
```

Save this schema as `EmployeesSchema7.xdr` and execute the following XPath query:

http://localhost/NW/XDR/EmployeesSchema7.xdr/Employees

This is a partial result set:

```
<Employees>
    <Employee LastName="Davolio" FirstName="Nancy">
            <PhotoPath>
                    <![CDATA[
                    http://accweb/employees/davolio.bmp
                    ]]>
            </PhotoPath>
    </Employee>
    <Employee LastName="Fuller" FirstName="Andrew">
            <PhotoPath>
                    <![CDATA[
                    http://accweb/employees/fuller.bmp
                    ]]>
            </PhotoPath>
    </Employee>
    <Employee LastName="Leverling" FirstName="Janet">
            <PhotoPath>
                    <![CDATA[
                    http://accweb/employees/leverling.bmp
                    ]]>
```

```
            </PhotoPath>
        </Employee>

    ...

    </Employees>
```

XPath Queries and Annotated XDR Schemas

Although Chapter 8 will cover XPath queries in more detail, let's give some attention to the role of annotated XDR schemas in queries. There are several ways to extract data with mapping schemas.

XPath Query in the URL

This has been the primary means by which most examples in this chapter have been presented. The annotated XDR schema is saved in a directory associated with a virtual name of type **schema**. Access to the data is achieved by referencing the schema file name, followed by the XPath query. Here is an example:

http://localhost/NW/XDR/ODSchema1.xdr/OD[@UnitPrice=4.8]?root=root

By now, it should be well understood that the name of the virtual directory in this example is `NW` and the virtual name is `XDR`. The name of the XDR schema is `ODSchema1.xdr`. The XPath query is `OD [@UnitPrice=4.8]`, which is asking for all `<OD>` elements with an attribute named `UnitPrice` containing a value of `4.8`. Finally, since there may be more than one `<OD>` element returned in the results, the query string has been appended with `?root=root`, which creates a root element with the name of `root`.

Template in the URL

We explored one example of this earlier in this chapter. We can create an XML document that will identify the mapping schema and contain the XPath query. To access the data, we simply specify the template in the URL. Here is an example of a template query:

http://localhost/NW/Template/CategoriesTemplate.xml

We know that `NW` is the virtual directory. `Template` is a virtual name that just happens to be configured as type **template**. `CategoriesTemplate.xml` is the name of the template. Here is the basic content of a template:

```
<ROOT
xmlns:sql="urn:schemas-microsoft-com:xml-sql">
  <sql:xpath-query
  mapping-schema="mappingschema.xdr">
    Categories
  </sql:xpath-query>
</ROOT>
```

The `<sql:xpath-query>` annotation contains two important pieces of information. First, the `mapping-schema` attribute contains the path or name of the annotated XDR schema. In the example above, this attribute is set to `mappingschema.xdr`, a fictitious schema name presumed to reside in the same directory as the template. Second, the content of the `<sql:xpath-query>` contains the XPath query – which, in this case, is `Categories`.

Inline Mapping Schema in the URL

This option has not been used in any of the examples so far. Imagine merging a template and schema together – the result is an inline mapping schema. In other words, the template references an annotated XDR schema defined within the same XML document. The URL reference is to the template file, as seen in this example:

http://localhost/NW/Template/InlineCategories.xml

Inline mapping schemas need to be accessed through a virtual name of type **template**. This is what the `InlineCategories.xml` looks like:

```
<ROOT xmlns:sql="urn:schemas-microsoft-com:xml-sql">
<Schema name="InlineCategories"
   xmlns="urn:schemas-microsoft-com:xml-data"
        xmlns:sql="urn:schemas-microsoft-com:xml-sql"
   sql:is-mapping-schema="1"
   sql:id="InlineCategories">
   <ElementType name="Categories">
      <AttributeType name="CategoryID"/>
      <AttributeType name="CategoryName"/>
      <attribute type="CategoryID"/>
      <attribute type="CategoryName"/>
   </ElementType>
</Schema>
<sql:xpath-query mapping-schema="#InlineCategories">
   Categories
</sql:xpath-query>
</ROOT>
```

Notice two new annotations specified in the `<Schema>` element: `sql:is-mapping-schema` and `sql:id`. The `sql:is-mapping-schema` specifies that the schema is an inline mapping schema. The `sql:id` annotation provides the unique name of the schema to be referenced in the `mapping-schema` attribute of the `<sql:xpath-query>` element.

Schema Caching

Near the outset of the chapter, it was recommended that you disable the schema caching option during development and testing. The reason given was that changes to the schema wouldn't take effect for approximately two minutes. What wasn't explained was why the changes would take that long.

The first time an XPath query is executed against an annotated XDR schema, the schema is stored in memory, and the necessary data structures are built there. The schema remains in memory if schema caching is enabled, thereby improving performance for subsequent XPath queries. If changes are made to the schema while cached in memory, it takes about two minutes before the new schema replaces the old.

To enable or disable schema caching, set the Disable caching of mapping schemas option when configuring the virtual directory. You can set the schema cache size by adding the following key in the registry:

HKEY_LOCAL_MACHINE\SOFTWARE\Microsoft\MSSQLServer\Client\SQLXMLX\SchemaCacheSize.

The default value for `SchemaCacheSize` is 31. The recommendation is to set the value higher than the number of mapping schemas used. To increase performance, increase the cache size. To reduce memory usage, decrease the size.

Summary

Annotated XDR schemas provide a great way to extract XML data from SQL Server 2000. Let's review some of the key points highlighted in this chapter.

- XDR schemas are a powerful alternative to other technologies. Unlike DTDs, XDR schemas support data types and are designed with XML syntax.
- A mapping schema can be used not only for validation, but also for returning an XML document, which maps to the database as the result of an XPath query.
- Annotations grant the developer control over data mapping, structure, relationships, and data types.

As you will probably agree, annotated XDR schemas are rather straightforward and easy to use. With very little investment of time, a mapping schema can be designed and implemented to return XML data in whatever format is deemed appropriate. The possibilities are exciting!

One constant in this industry is change. XML standards are no exception to the rule. Our next chapter will cover a new emerging definition language – XSD schemas.

6

XSD Schemas

XSD is the commonly used name for the proposed XML Schema Definition standard of the World Wide Web Consortium (W3C). In the previous chapter, we saw how to use XDR schemas to return data as XML. Microsoft created XDR so that it could start using XML schemas as soon as possible, even though the W3C's work on XSD was not near completion. As such, XDR is based on a snapshot of the W3C's schema activity from March 1999, and is purely a Microsoft product. The W3C has made progress on XSD since then, and it now provides a much richer set of functionality than XDR. Consequently, although the XSD schema syntax is not presently supported in SQL Server, it is important enough for us to cover.

This chapter will examine the following:

- What XSD schemas are
- The present status of XSD with the W3C
- How XSD schemas compare to XDR schemas
- How to design and use XSD schemas
- How to validate your XSD schema
- SQL Server and XSD
- Some translation tools available to convert from XDR to XSD

What are XSD Schemas?

New standards for defining XML documents have become desirable because of the limitations imposed by Document Type Definitions (DTDs). The W3C XML Schema Definition (XSD) standards were promoted from the Candidate Recommendation Phase to the Proposed Recommendation Phase in March 2001. Once the W3C's director approves the standards, they will become a full Recommendation. Until the XSD standards reach the full Recommendation phase, however, they are subject to further review and changes. Thus, the information contained in this chapter is subject to change. However, according to members of the Schema group, this last step is almost purely administrative and the proposed recommendation is good enough for software development.

Please consult the W3C's web site at http://www.w3.org *for current documentation and up-to-date information about the status of XSD. For a good overview of XSD, please see the XSD primer document on the W3C's web site at* http://www.w3.org/TR/xmlschema-0.

XSD Schemas vs. XDR Schemas

In the previous chapter, we learned that schemas provide an XML-based syntax for defining what elements and attributes are allowed in a given document. We saw examples of how to create schemas using the XDR schema syntax. So how does XDR compare to XSD? As we said earlier, XDR is Microsoft's own version of the W3C's early 1999 work-in-progress version of XSD. XSD provides a richer set of functionality than XDR and is vendor neutral.

Let's take a quick look at an example of how XSD compares to XDR. Don't worry yet about understanding the details of the XSD syntax. Consider the following XML document from the XDR chapter:

```
<?xml version="1.0"?>
   <Students>
      <Student>
         <ID>12345</ID>
         <GPA>3.5</GPA>
      </Student>
      <Student>
          <ID>67890</ID>
         <GPA>4.0</GPA>
      </Student>
   </Students>
```

Suppose that the XML shown above represents the proper syntax for the document. A valid XDR schema for this document could look like this:

```
<?xml version="1.0"?>
   <Schema name="StudentsSchema"
   xmlns="urn:schemas-microsoft-com:xml-data">
      <ElementType name="ID" content="textOnly"/>
      <ElementType name="GPA" content="textOnly"/>
      <ElementType name="Student" content="eltOnly">
         <element type="ID" minOccurs="1" maxOccurs="1"/>
         <element type="GPA" minOccurs="1" maxOccurs="1"/>
      </ElementType>
      <ElementType name="Students" content="eltOnly" model="closed">
         <element type="Student" minOccurs="0" maxOccurs="*"/>
      </ElementType>
   </Schema>
```

To define the same schema following the XSD syntax, on the other hand, the schema definition might look like:

```
<?xml version="1.0"?>
 <xsd:schema xmlns:xsd="http://www.w3.org/2001/XMLSchema">
  <xsd:element name="Student" minOccurs="0" maxOccurs="unbounded">
    <xsd:complexType>
     <xsd:sequence>
     <xsd:element name="ID" type="xsd:string" minOccurs="1" maxOccurs="1"/>
     <xsd:element name="GPA" type="xsd:string" minOccurs="1" maxOccurs="1"/>
     </xsd:sequence>
    </xsd:complexType>
  </xsd:element>
 </xsd:schema>
```

As you can see from a quick glimpse at these two examples, there are distinct differences in the syntax between XDR and XSD. The XSD syntax will be explained in greater detail later in this chapter.

Key Features

XSD schemas offer the capabilities of XDR schemas, DTDs, and much more. Here is a brief summary of the key features of an XSD schema document:

- Like XDR schemas, XSD schemas *are* XML documents, so you don't have to learn another syntax to use them (unlike with DTDs).
- As with XDR schemas, data types in XSD schemas can be specified for an element or attribute.
- XSD schemas allow you to define your own data types, or use one of the 44+ pre-defined data types.
- XSD schemas offer the ability to define keys on data elements for uniqueness.
- XSD schemas support object-oriented style inheritance where one schema can inherit from another. This is a huge benefit and allows you to create re-usable schemas.
- XSD schemas allow you to define elements that can be substituted for each other.
- XSD schemas allow you to define elements with Null content.

Like XDR, XSD schemas define the format, content, and data of an XML document. When a document that references an XSD schema is validated by a parser that supports XSD, it confirms whether or not the document meets the criteria defined in the schema. If the validation fails, an error occurs.

Designing XSD Schemas

Let's walk through the details of the student XSD schema presented earlier to see how it works.

XML Declaration

An XSD schema is an XML document, so the first line can be a typical XML declaration:

```
<?xml version="1.0"?>
```

In this example, version is the only attribute expressed in the declaration. Other attributes, such as encoding, can be specified to determine which encoding is used to represent characters.

<schema>

The next line in our XSD schema is the root element itself. For XSD schemas, the root element is always <schema>. To identify the root element to an XML parser as an XSD schema, a specific namespace is referenced in the <schema> element. Here is an example:

```
<?xml version="1.0"?>
  <xsd:schema xmlns:xsd="http://www.w3.org/2001/XMLSchema">
  </xsd:schema>
```

The namespace in the declaration is referencing the W3C's Proposed Recommendation version of XSD from 2001. In older examples, you may see the Candidate Recommendation version of XSD referenced, as shown below:

```
<?xml version="1.0"?>
  <xsd:schema xmlns:xsd="http://www.w3.org/2000/10/XMLSchema">
  </xsd:schema>
```

Note the xsd: prefix used in the above examples. This prefix is used to designate that an XSD schema is being used, although any prefix can actually be specified. The prefix must match the one specified prior to the namespace declaration, as shown below:

```
<xsd:schema xmlns:xsd="http://www.w3.org/2001/XMLSchema">
```

The purpose of using the prefixes throughout the schema is to show that the contents of the schema belong to the vocabulary of the designated namespace (XSD), versus that of another schema author.

It is worth noting that, if you make this namespace the default, then you don't have to use the prefixes at all. However, you should be aware that using default namespaces can lead to problems later, especially when you import schemas. Even the W3C's examples use the xsd: prefix throughout the code rather than setting the default namespace.

<element>

After identifying the schema, we then move on to the heart of the schema – the elements. We learned a lot about elements in the XDR chapter. So let's dive right into the syntax for creating elements with XSD.

Assigning values to the following attributes can modify the behavior of the element:

- name

  Required. Refers to the name of the element.

- type

  Refers to a simple type (for example xsd:string) or the name of a complex type. The type attribute can be used in the declaration of a simple type (when it is not being restricted) but not with a complex type, as will be demonstrated in this section.

- `minOccurs`

  This attribute determines if the element is optional. This attribute is not required. If unspecified, the default is `1`. The table below shows the possible values that may be assigned:

Value	Description
`0`	The element is optional.
`Integer > 0`	The element must occur at least the specified number of times.

- `maxOccurs`

  This attribute determines how many elements are allowed. This attribute is not required. If unspecified, the default is `1`. The table below shows the possible values that may be assigned:

Value	Description
`Integer > 0`	The element can only appear up to the specified number of times.
`Unbounded`	The element may appear an unlimited amount of times.

With this understanding of `<element>`, let's take a closer look at our schema example:

```
<?xml version="1.0"?>
<xsd:schema xmlns:xsd="http://www.w3.org/2001/XMLSchema">
 <xsd:element name="Student" minOccurs="0" maxOccurs="unbounded">
  <xsd:complexType>
    <xsd:sequence>
     <xsd:element name="ID" type="xsd:string" minOccurs="1" maxOccurs="1"/>
     <xsd:element name="GPA" type="xsd:string" minOccurs="1" maxOccurs="1"/>
    </xsd:sequence>
  </xsd:complexType>
</xsd:element>
</xsd:schema>
```

Looking at the schema, we notice the following definitions and rules:

- The `<ID>` and `<GPA>` contain string values.
- The `<Student>` element must contain only one `<ID>` and `<GPA>` element (the `<ID>` and `<GPA>` have a `minOccurs` and `maxOccurs` of `1`). Note that the `minOccurs` and `maxOccurs` attributes were not necessary in the above example because `1` is the default value if they are not specified.
- There can be unlimited `<Student>` elements or none at all (`minOccurs` is `0` and `maxOccurs` is unbounded).
- By specifying `<sequence>`, the `<ID> and <GPA>` elements are required to appear in the order listed in the schema.

In other words, we have defined that documents adhering to this XSD schema may list as many students as needed, as long as an ID and GPA are provided for each student. This "contract" can now allow multiple parties to share student information in an agreed format.

Now let's look at the detailed syntax of these element declarations.

<complexType> vs. <simpleType>

In the previous chapter, we saw how to use the <ElementType> element in XDR to describe characteristics – such as whether the element can contain child elements – by simply changing the values of the element attributes (for example textOnly, eltOnly, etc.). XSD takes a different approach. With XSD, you explicitly declare an element to be either a **complex type** or a **simple type**. When do you use each one?

The <complexType> element should be used:

- When your element will contain child elements, *and/or*
- When your element will contain attributes.

The <simpleType> element should be used:

- When you want to create a new data type from a built-in simple type, *and/or*
- When your element will *not* contain child elements or attributes.

To illustrate the differences, let's take a look at some examples. In the student example we have been using, each student has an ID and a GPA. Thus, if student is an element, then ID and GPA would be considered children of that element. Because the student element has child elements, we have to declare it as a complex type, as shown below:

```
<?xml version="1.0"?>
<xsd:schema xmlns:xsd="http://www.w3.org/2001/XMLSchema">
 <xsd:element name="Student" minOccurs="0" maxOccurs="unbounded">
  <xsd:complexType>
    <xsd:sequence>
     <xsd:element name="ID" type="xsd:string" minOccurs="1" maxOccurs="1"/>
     <xsd:element name="GPA" type="xsd:string" minOccurs="1" maxOccurs="1"/>
    </xsd:sequence>
  </xsd:complexType>
</xsd:element>
</xsd:schema>
```

Now let's modify our example to demonstrate the simple type element concept. Remember that we cannot use a simple type if there are children or attributes of the element. Suppose that we want to create a new data type called StudentGPA that would define the proper format for the GPA. In this scenario, we want to extend an existing simple data type (for example xsd:string) and customize it for our own purposes. These customizations are referred to as restrictions on the existing data type. We want to restrict the string so that the GPA has to be in a format like 4.00, for example. That is, we want there to be an integer followed by a decimal point and then two more integers. The code to declare this looks like:

```
<xsd:simpleType name="StudentGPA" minOccurs="1" maxOccurs="1">
  <xsd:restriction base="xsd:string">
    <xsd:length value="4"/>
    <xsd:pattern value="\d{1}.\d{2}"/>
  </xsd:restriction>
</xsd:simpleType>
```

Following the simple type element declaration are the restrictions. Notice first how the `base` data type that we are starting with is the `string` data type. Next, the restrictions that are being placed on the `string` data type are specified. In this case, we are requiring the `length` of the `StudentGPA` to be `4` characters and the `pattern` to be one digit, then a decimal, and then two more digits. It is important to know that this `pattern` is written in the Unicode **Regular Expression** language, which is similar in its syntax to the Perl programming language.

Let's digress for a moment to take a look at the regular expression language in more detail and then we'll come back to the `pattern` of our specific example, and see if it makes more sense. The table below summarizes some of the most common uses of regular expressions:

Regular Expression	Explanation	Valid Example(s)
`\d`	Digit	1, 2, 3, etc.
`[a-z]`	Lower case ASCII characters	a, b, c, etc.
`[A-Z]`	Upper case ASCII characters	A, B, C, etc.
`*`	Wildcard	A*Z = ABZ, ABCZ, ABCCZ, etc.
`?`	Single placeholder	A?Z = ABZ, ACZ, ADZ, etc.
`+`	Inclusive of at least the specified values, but more are allowed	A+Z = AZ, ABZ, ABCZ, etc.
`(value1|value2)`	`OR`	(A|Z)+Q = AQ, ZQ, ABQ, ZBQ, etc.
`[abcde]`	Another way to specify `OR`, but with single characters only	[abc] = a, b, or c
`[^0-9]`	Any non-digit character	A, B, C, a, b, c, etc.
`{integer}`	The number of occurrences that there must be of the previous value	az{2} = azz \d{3} = 123, 456, 789, 444, etc. (az){2} = azaz

Now, back to our example from before:

```
<xsd:pattern value="\d{1}.\d{2}"/>
```

The `\d{1}` is specifying that there must be one and only one digit prior to the decimal point. Then, after the decimal point, there must be two more digits, as specified by the `\d{2}` syntax.

This is just one of the many possible ways that regular expressions can be used to specify `patterns`. A detailed explanation of regular expressions is beyond the scope of this chapter. For more information about regular expressions, please consult Appendix D of the W3C's primer document at http://www.w3.org/TR/xmlschema-0.

Let's get back on track with our working example of declaring a custom data type called `StudentGPA`, which is shown again here to refresh your memory:

```
<xsd:simpleType name="StudentGPA" minOccurs="1" maxOccurs="1">
  <xsd:restriction base="xsd:string">
    <xsd:length value="4"/>
    <xsd:pattern value="\d{1}.\d{2}"/>
  </xsd:restriction>
</xsd:simpleType>
```

When declaring the complex type `<Student>` element with `<ID>` and `<GPA>` as children, we can make use of our new `StudentGPA` simple type by defining the GPA to be of this type instead of just a simple string type. Here's an example:

```
<?xml version="1.0"?>
<xsd:schema xmlns:xsd="http://www.w3.org/2001/XMLSchema">
 <xsd:element name="Student" minOccurs="0" maxOccurs="unbounded">
  <xsd:complexType>
    <xsd:sequence>
     <xsd:element name="ID" type="xsd:string" minOccurs="1" maxOccurs="1"/>
     <xsd:element name="GPA" type="StudentGPA"/>
    </xsd:sequence>
  </xsd:complexType>
 </xsd:element>
<xsd:simpleType name="StudentGPA" minOccurs="1" maxOccurs="1">
  <xsd:restriction base="xsd:string">
    <xsd:length value="4"/>
    <xsd:pattern value="\d{1}.\d{2}"/>
  </xsd:restriction>
</xsd:simpleType>
</xsd:schema>
```

We could put the `simpleType` declaration format for the `<GPA>` element inline with the `<GPA>` element itself, to accomplish basically the same result. Here's how:

```
<?xml version="1.0"?>
<xsd:schema xmlns:xsd="http://www.w3.org/2001/XMLSchema">
 <xsd:element name="Student" minOccurs="0" maxOccurs="unbounded">
  <xsd:complexType>
    <xsd:sequence>
     <xsd:element name="ID" type="xsd:string" minOccurs="1" maxOccurs="1"/>
     <xsd:element name="GPA" type="xsd:string" minOccurs="1"
                  maxOccurs="1"/>
       <xsd:simpleType>
         <xsd:restriction base="xsd:string">
          <xsd:length value="4"/>
          <xsd:pattern value="\d{1}.\d{2}"/>
         </xsd:restriction>
          </xsd:simpleType>
    </xsd:sequence>
  </xsd:complexType>
 </xsd:element>
</xsd:schema>
```

In this second version, the simple type declaration and the restrictions immediately follow the <GPA> element declaration line.

> **The difference between these two methods is that the first allows you to access the StudentGPA data type in multiple places in the schema. With the second example, the restrictions are specific to the <GPA> element and cannot be re-used by name outside that element.**

Now that we have seen some examples of the different ways to declare elements as simple and complex types, let's summarize what we have learned. There are actually three ways to declare elements. Under the first method, you list the name, type, minOccurs, and maxOccurs attributes. This method is actually an implied way of defining simple type elements without specifying the <simpleType> element syntax explicitly. You don't have to explicitly state that it is a simple type because you are using one of the built-in simple types already:

```
<xsd:element name="name" type="type" minOccurs="int" maxOccurs="int"/>
```

Remember that the values of the attributes are merely placeholders.

This syntax should look familiar to you. We declared the <ID> and <GPA> elements this way in one of our previous examples:

```
<?xml version="1.0"?>
<xsd:schema xmlns:xsd="http://www.w3.org/2001/XMLSchema">
 <xsd:element name="Student" minOccurs="0" maxOccurs="unbounded">
  <xsd:complexType>
    <xsd:sequence>
     <xsd:element name="ID" type="xsd:string" minOccurs="1" maxOccurs="1"/>
     <xsd:element name="GPA" type="xsd:string" minOccurs="1" maxOccurs="1"/>
    </xsd:sequence>
  </xsd:complexType>
 </xsd:element>
</xsd:schema>
```

With the second method for declaring an element, the name, minOccurs, and maxOccurs attributes are specified for the parent, which is then declared as a complexType so that it can have child elements:

```
<xsd:element name="name" minOccurs="int" maxOccurs="int"/>
  <xsd:complexType>
  </xsd:complexType>
</xsd:element>
```

The <Student> element in the same example was declared with name, minOccurs, and maxOccurs attributes, and as a complexType with <ID> and <GPA> as children:

```
<?xml version="1.0"?>
<xsd:schema xmlns:xsd="http://www.w3.org/2001/XMLSchema">
 <xsd:element name="Student" minOccurs="0" maxOccurs="unbounded">
  <xsd:complexType>
    <xsd:sequence>
     <xsd:element name="ID" type="xsd:string" minOccurs="1" maxOccurs="1"/>
     <xsd:element name="GPA" type="xsd:string" minOccurs="1" maxOccurs="1"/>
    </xsd:sequence>
  </xsd:complexType>
 </xsd:element>
</xsd:schema>
```

With the third method, the `name`, `minOccurs`, and `maxOccurs` attributes are specified, and then a `simpleType` is declared to describe the element restrictions:

```
<xsd:element name="name" minOccurs="int" maxOccurs="int"/>
  <xsd:simpleType>
    <xsd:restriction base = "type">
    </xsd:restriction>
  </xsd:simpleType>
</xsd:element>
```

An example of this was shown in our custom-defined GPA example:

```
<?xml version="1.0"?>
<xsd:schema xmlns:xsd="http://www.w3.org/2001/XMLSchema">
 <xsd:element name="Student" minOccurs="0" maxOccurs="unbounded">
  <xsd:complexType>
    <xsd:sequence>
     <xsd:element name="ID" type="xsd:string" minOccurs="1" maxOccurs="1"/>
     <xsd:element name="GPA" type="StudentGPA"/>
    </xsd:sequence>
  </xsd:complexType>
 </xsd:element>
<xsd:simpleType name="StudentGPA" minOccurs="1" maxOccurs="1">
  <xsd:restriction base="xsd:string">
    <xsd:length value="4"/>
    <xsd:pattern value="\d{1}.\d{2}"/>
  </xsd:restriction>
</xsd:simpleType>
</xsd:schema>
```

The ability to create your own data types, as in the example above, is a very powerful feature of XSD. We will walk through more examples of how to create your own data types in the *Data Types* section of this chapter.

Have you noticed how the student example we have been working with is element-centric? Suppose that we decided that `<ID>` should be an **attribute** of `<Student>`, instead of a child element. What changes need to be made to our schema? Let's take a look at other parts in the XSD schema that define attributes in an XML document.

<attribute>

Defining attributes in an XSD schema is very similar to defining elements. Here is the list of attributes that are associated with the `<attribute>` element:

- `name`
  Required. This is the name of the attribute.
- `type`
  Any simple type such as `xsd:string`, `xsd:integer`, `StudentGPA` (the custom simple type we created above), etc. can be specified. This identifies the data type of the attribute.

- use

Value	Description
Required	The attribute must appear in the element.
Default	The attribute will use the default value if none is specified. (See the value attribute).
Fixed	The attribute contains a fixed value that will never change. (See the value attribute).
Optional	The attribute is optional.
Prohibited	The attribute is prohibited.

- value

  Specifies the value of the attribute. This is only used when the use attribute is Default or Fixed.

We learned earlier that complex types can contain children or attributes. So we already know that an attribute has to be declared within a complex type. However, attributes themselves can only have simple types. They cannot contain child elements.

There are two ways to define an attribute. The first method is done on one line and is used in scenarios when the attribute is based on an existing simple type (either a built-in simple type or a simple type defined elsewhere in the document). The syntax for this method is shown below (again, using placeholders):

```
<xsd:attribute name="name" type="simple type" use="how used" value="value"/>
```

The second method for defining an attribute allows you to specify explicit restrictions on the attribute, such as the format that it must be in to be valid:

```
<xsd:attribute name="name" use="how used" value="value">
  <xsd:simpleType>
    <xsd:restriction base="simple type">
      <xsd:facet value="value"/>
    </xsd:restriction>
  </xsd:simpleType>
</xsd:attribute>
```

Facets will be discussed in greater detail in the *Data Types* section. In place of facet above, you can specify any particular facet available for a given simple type (for example length, pattern, enumeration, etc. for xsd:string). For now, let's move on to seeing how each of these methods can be used, by modifying our ongoing example.

Suppose we want the <ID> element to be an attribute of the <Student> element. The schema would then look something like this:

```
<?xml version="1.0"?>
<xsd:schema xmlns:xsd="http://www.w3.org/2001/XMLSchema">
 <xsd:element name="Student" minOccurs="0" maxOccurs="unbounded">
  <xsd:complexType>
     <xsd:element name="GPA" type="xsd:string" minOccurs="1" maxOccurs="1"/>
```

```
        <xsd:attribute name="ID" type="xsd:string" use="required"/>
      </xsd:complexType>
    </xsd:element>
  </xsd:schema>
```

There are a couple of important aspects to take note of here. First, notice how the attribute is defined within the <complexType> element. We recall from before that attributes can only exist within a complex type. In this instance, we have made ID an attribute of the <Student> element, instead of an element itself. Secondly, note how the ID declaration now follows the GPA declaration instead of coming before it. Attributes need to be declared as the last items in the complex type, following all the elements.

These revisions now indicate the following requirements:

- The <Student> element must contain an ID attribute.
- The ID attribute cannot be used in any other elements, as it is declared within the <Student> element.

If we later introduced other elements to the schema that could use an ID attribute, we could simply declare the attribute outside of any element to make it accessible to the schema as a whole.

What if we decide that we want to require the ID to be a fixed length string of 5 characters that can only contain numeric values? In this instance, we want to place restrictions on the values and format the ID will contain. The following example shows how we can do this:

```
<?xml version="1.0"?>
<xsd:schema xmlns:xsd="http://www.w3.org/2001/XMLSchema">
 <xsd:element name="Student" minOccurs="0" maxOccurs="unbounded">
  <xsd:complexType>
     <xsd:element name="GPA" type="xsd:string" minOccurs="1" maxOccurs="1"/>
     <xsd:attribute name="ID" use="required">
       <xsd:simpleType>
         <xsd:restriction base="xsd:string">
           <xsd:length value="5"/>
           <xsd:pattern value="\d{5}"/>
         </xsd:restriction>
       </xsd:simpleType>
     </xsd:attribute>
  </xsd:complexType>
 </xsd:element>
</xsd:schema>
```

Notice how, in this instance, we have declared the attribute and then declared a simple type with the restrictions that we want to implement. We specify in the length facet that the ID must be 5 characters long and in the pattern facet that it must contain five digits.

Now that we have a basic understanding of how to declare elements and attributes, let's take a look at how to reference an XSD schema from an XML document. We learned how to do this by referencing an XDR schema in the previous chapter. Now let's take a look at how to do this with XSD. Here is an XML document example with the XSD schema assumed to reside in the main directory on the www.mycollege.org namespace:

```
<?xml version="1.0"?>
   <Students xmlns = "http://www.mycollege.org"
             xmlns:xsi="http://www.w3.org/2001/XMLSchema-instance"
           xsi:schemaLocation="http://www.mycollege.org/StudentSchema1.xsd">
      <Student>
         <ID>12345</ID>
         <GPA>3.5</GPA>
      </Student>
      <Student>
         <ID>67890</ID>
         <GPA>4.0</GPA>
      </Student>
   </Students>
```

Save the schema as a file named `StudentSchema1.xsd`. Notice how a separate namespace, `http://www.w3.org/2001/XMLSchema-instance`, is used with the `xsi:` prefix. The W3C actually created this separate namespace to allow you to tie a document to its schema. If the XML document above is validated by an XML parser that supports XSD, it will succeed.

If you aren't using a namespace, then there is another way to reference the schema in your XML document. An example is shown below:

```
<?xml version="1.0"?>
   <Students xmlns:xsi="http://www.w3.org/2001/XMLSchema-instance"
             xsi:noNameSpaceSchemaLocation="StudentSchema1.xsd">
      <Student>
         <ID>12345</ID>
         <GPA>3.5</GPA>
      </Student>
      <Student>
         <ID>67890</ID>
         <GPA>4.0</GPA>
      </Student>
   </Students>
```

Thus, if the author of a document makes use of namespaces to indicate the intended interpretation of names in the document, the `xsi:schemaLocation` attribute should be used to specify the location of the XSD schema that can be used to validate the document (which, in this case, is assumed to reside in the same directory as the XML document itself).

If the author does not need or want a namespace, the `xsi:noNameSpaceSchemaLocation` attribute can be used to locate the XSD schema used to validate the document.

So far, we have illustrated the basics of defining simple XSD schemas using elements and attributes and have seen how to reference those schemas from XML documents. The next section will look at some alternative ways to structure the syntax, so we can accomplish better results.

Structure Alternatives

There are a few different ways to structure an XSD schema. One way is to define elements and their attributes within the complex type declaration itself. Another way to define elements is to declare them as immediate children of `<schema>` (that is, outside the complex type itself) and then just make reference to the elements within the complex type. By declaring the elements nested within the complex type declarations, their scope is local to that complex type – they are only available to that complex type and cannot be referenced by other elements in that schema, or in any other schema for that matter. By declaring the elements outside the complex type, on the other hand, their scope is global. This has the effect of allowing those elements to be utilized from anywhere within the schema or from other schemas.

So, in situations where you do not need the elements to be referenced from within the same schema or from other schemas, it is perfectly fine to declare them nested within other elements. However, in situations where you want to be able to *re-use* a specific element, you should define that element as a child of <schema>.

Let's walk through some examples to further clarify these concepts. Recall our example from earlier:

```
<?xml version="1.0"?>
<xsd:schema xmlns:xsd="http://www.w3.org/2001/XMLSchema">
 <xsd:element name="Student" minOccurs="0" maxOccurs="unbounded">
  <xsd:complexType>
    <xsd:sequence>
     <xsd:element name="ID" type="xsd:string" minOccurs="1" maxOccurs="1"/>
     <xsd:element name="GPA" type="xsd:string" minOccurs="1" maxOccurs="1"/>
    </xsd:sequence>
  </xsd:complexType>
 </xsd:element>
</xsd:schema>
```

First, notice how the <Student> element is declared as a child of the root element <schema>. This means that the <Student> element is global in scope and can be referenced from this or other schemas.

The <ID> and <GPA> elements, on the other hand, are declared within the Student complex type itself:

```
<?xml version="1.0"?>
<xsd:schema xmlns:xsd="http://www.w3.org/2001/XMLSchema">
 <xsd:element name="Student" minOccurs="0" maxOccurs="unbounded">
  <xsd:complexType>
    <xsd:sequence>
     <xsd:element name="ID" type="xsd:string" minOccurs="1" maxOccurs="1"/>
     <xsd:element name="GPA" type="xsd:string" minOccurs="1" maxOccurs="1"/>
    </xsd:sequence>
  </xsd:complexType>
 </xsd:element>
</xsd:schema>
```

This means that the <ID> and <GPA> are local in scope to the <Student> element and cannot be re-used anywhere else.

But what if we really need to re-use ID and GPA? For instance, we might also have to track professor credentials, which could also consist of an ID and GPA of the same data types. Let's take a look at how we could declare the ID and GPA globally so that we can reference them in other places, including in a <Professor> element.

First, we will start by modifying our previous example to define ID and GPA globally, and then have the <Student> element reference the global declarations:

```
<?xml version="1.0"?>
<xsd:schema xmlns:xsd="http://www.w3.org/2001/XMLSchema">
 <xsd:element name="Student" minOccurs="0" maxOccurs="unbounded">
  <xsd:complexType>
    <xsd:sequence>
      <xsd:element ref="ID" minOccurs="1" maxOccurs="1"/>
      <xsd:element ref="GPA" minOccurs="1" maxOccurs="1"/>
    </xsd:sequence>
  </xsd:complexType>
 </xsd:element>
<xsd:element name="ID" type="xsd:string"/>
<xsd:element name="GPA" type="xsd:string"/>
</xsd:schema>
```

In the above example, the ref attribute refers to the <ID> and <GPA> elements that are declared outside the Student complexType declaration as children of the root <schema> element. This takes two extra lines of code to accomplish, but the benefit of code re-use far outweighs the extra lines required.

So, if we also want to implement the <Professor> element using these global elements, it might look something like this:

```
<?xml version="1.0"?>
<xsd:schema xmlns:xsd="http://www.w3.org/2001/XMLSchema">
 <xsd:element name="Student" minOccurs="0" maxOccurs="unbounded">
  <xsd:complexType>
    <xsd:sequence>
      <xsd:element ref="ID" minOccurs="1" maxOccurs="1"/>
      <xsd:element ref="GPA" minOccurs="1" maxOccurs="1"/>
    </xsd:sequence>
  </xsd:complexType>
 </xsd:element>
<xsd:element name="Professor" minOccurs="0" maxOccurs="unbounded">
  <xsd:complexType>
    <xsd:sequence>
      <xsd:element ref="ID" minOccurs="1" maxOccurs="1"/>
      <xsd:element ref="GPA" minOccurs="1" maxOccurs="1"/>
    </xsd:sequence>
  </xsd:complexType>
</xsd:element>
<xsd:element name="ID" type="xsd:string"/>
<xsd:element name="GPA" type="xsd:string"/>
</xsd:schema>
```

Now, in the event that we want to modify the <ID> or <GPA> elements, we only have to change them in *one* place and both the <Student> and <Professor> elements will automatically reference the updates. Imagine the extra work required if we had duplicated the declarations in both places and then needed to modify them. Or, worse yet, what if we had duplicated them everywhere in multiple schemas? This could turn into a maintenance nightmare.

The fact that XSD provides you with a mechanism for re-using code in an efficient way is an incredible advantage. It is also a critical concept to master, so let's look at a few more examples to further fix it in your mind.

Recall when we looked at the two different syntaxes for declaring the StudentGPA restrictions. In one example, the restrictions on the GPA were nested within the element declaration itself:

```
<?xml version="1.0"?>
<xsd:schema xmlns:xsd="http://www.w3.org/2001/XMLSchema">
 <xsd:element name="Student" minOccurs="0" maxOccurs="unbounded">
  <xsd:complexType>
    <xsd:sequence>
     <xsd:element name="ID" type="xsd:string" minOccurs="1" maxOccurs="1"/>
     <xsd:element name="GPA" type="xsd:string" minOccurs="1"
                  maxOccurs="1"/>
       <xsd:simpleType>
         <xsd:restriction base="xsd:string">
          <xsd:length value="4"/>
```

```
            <xsd:pattern value="\d{1}.\d{2}"/>
          </xsd:restriction>
          </xsd:simpleType>
      </xsd:sequence>
    </xsd:complexType>
  </xsd:element>
</xsd:schema>
```

In this instance, the restrictions on the GPA are declared within the GPA element itself and are local in scope. Thus, they cannot be re-used. However, recall how the StudentGPA was declared separately in the other example, and then referenced as the type attribute for the <GPA> element:

```
<?xml version="1.0"?>
<xsd:schema xmlns:xsd="http://www.w3.org/2001/XMLSchema">
  <xsd:element name="Student" minOccurs="0" maxOccurs="unbounded">
    <xsd:complexType>
      <xsd:sequence>
        <xsd:element name="ID" type="xsd:string" minOccurs="1" maxOccurs="1"/>
        <xsd:element name="GPA" type="StudentGPA"/>
      </xsd:sequence>
    </xsd:complexType>
  </xsd:element>
<xsd:simpleType name="StudentGPA" minOccurs="1" maxOccurs="1">
    <xsd:restriction base="xsd:string">
      <xsd:length value="4"/>
      <xsd:pattern value="\d{1}.\d{2}"/>
    </xsd:restriction>
</xsd:simpleType>
</xsd:schema>
```

In this example, the <StudentGPA> element is global and can be re-used from within this schema or from other schemas. So, if we have another schema that needs to make use of the <StudentGPA> element, we can import the above schema and reference it, just as if it were declared within the same schema. Pay close attention as this is really useful.

Referencing External Schemas

The first step in making use of another schema is to **import** or **include** that schema into the one you're working with. You include schemas that are in the *same* namespace as the one you are working in:

```
<?xml version="1.0"?>
<xsd:schema xmlns:xsd="http://www.w3.org/2001/XMLSchema"
   targetNamespace="URIgoeshere">
<xsd:include schemaLocation="XSDFileNameGoesHere"/>
...
</xsd:schema>
```

On the other hand, you import schemas that are in a *different* namespace from the one you are working in:

```
<?xml version="1.0"?>
<xsd:schema xmlns:xsd="http://www.w3.org/2001/XMLSchema"
   targetNamespace="URIgoeshere">
<xsd:import namespace="URIgoeshere"
     schemaLocation="XSDFileNameGoesHere"/>
...
</xsd:schema>
```

So, let's suppose that we are creating a new schema for professors and want to make use of the global `<StudentGPA>` element (forgive the inappropriate name) from a (hypothetical) `StudentGPA1.xsd` file in our new `<Professor>` element. Further, suppose that we want to extend the `<Professor>` element to include an additional element for the university that professor graduated from. The code to accomplish this looks like:

```
<?xml version="1.0"?>
<xsd:schema xmlns:xsd="http://www.w3.org/2001/XMLSchema"
  targetNamespace="http://www.xsdrocks.com/students">
<xsd:include schemaLocation="StudentGPA1.xsd"/>
<xsd:element name="Professor" minOccurs="0" maxOccurs="unbounded">
  <xsd:complexType>
    <xsd:sequence>
     <xsd:element ref="StudentGPA" minOccurs="1" maxOccurs="1"/>
     <xsd:element name="University" type="xsd:string"/>
    </xsd:sequence>
  </xsd:complexType>
</xsd:element
</xsd:schema>
```

Note that the `include` statement references the `StudentGPA1.xsd` document that must be present in the same location as the target namespace. Once included in this schema, the `<Professor>` element references the `<StudentGPA>` global element in exactly the same manner as if it had been declared within this document itself. Think of it as though you were typing them all into the same schema to begin with, since that is actually the net effect of an `include` statement. Then, the additional `<University>` element, which is unique to the `<Professor>` element, is defined after the reference to the `<StudentGPA>` element.

What if the `StudentGPA1.xsd` document is not saved in the same location as the target namespace? In that case, you use the `import` statement instead of the `include` statement:

```
<?xml version="1.0"?>
<xsd:schema xmlns:xsd="http://www.w3.org/2001/XMLSchema"
  targetNamespace="http://www.xsdrocks.com/professors">
<xsd:import namespace="http://www.xsdrocks.com/students/"
     schemaLocation="StudentGPA1.xsd"/>
<xsd:element name="Professor" minOccurs="0" maxOccurs="unbounded">
  <xsd:complexType>
    <xsd:sequence>
     <xsd:element name="ProfessorGPA" type="StudentGPA1:StudentGPA"
        minOccurs="1" maxOccurs="1"/>
     <xsd:element name="University" type="xsd:string"/>
    </xsd:sequence>
  </xsd:complexType>
</xsd:element
</xsd:schema>
```

Notice that the `import` statement above specifies the namespace to import from, as well as the name of the schema to import. Further note that the `<ProfessorGPA>` element is defined as `StudentGPA1:StudentGPA`, with `StudentGPA1:` being the prefix as defined in the schema location.

If you would like more information about XSD structures, please see the XSD structures document on the W3C's web site at http://www.w3.org/TR/xmlschema-1.

Now that we have learned the basics of creating elements and attributes, and the varying ways to structure the code, we will take a look at how to document the schema so that it is easier to understand.

Annotations

Documenting your code is as important as writing the core functionality itself. If you do not describe what is happening so that you and others will be able to understand it later, then what good is it? XSD provides you with a way to document your schemas in a very clean and comprehensible way – **annotations**.

The <annotation> element can be used to document your schemas. You should use its <documentation> child element to provide comments to people, and use the <appinfo> child element to provide comments to applications. Here's an example of how an annotation might look:

```
<?xml version="1.0"?>
<xsd:schema xmlns:xsd="http://www.w3.org/2001/XMLSchema">
 <xsd:element name="Student" minOccurs="0" maxOccurs="unbounded">
  <xsd:complexType>
    <xsd:sequence>
     <xsd:element name="ID" type="xsd:string" minOccurs="1" maxOccurs="1"/>
      <xsd:annotation>
       <xsd:documentation>The Student ID uniquely identifies a student
       </xsd:documentation>
       <xsd:appInfo>Student Identification Number
       </xsd:appInfo>
      </xsd:annotation>
     <xsd:element name="GPA" type="xsd:string" minOccurs="1" maxOccurs="1"/>
    </xsd:sequence>
  </xsd:complexType>
 </xsd:element>
</xsd:schema>
```

Notice how the <annotation> for the ID immediately follows the element declaration line itself. The <documentation> and <appInfo> elements must be children of the <annotation> element. You can use either of them individually or both of them together.

> **It is important to note that you cannot put annotations anywhere you want in the schema. You can only put annotations at the beginning of the content model that you are annotating (for example immediately after a schema declaration or after an element declaration).**

The purpose of the <documentation> element is to describe what the code is doing for people looking at the source code. On the other hand, the purpose of the <appInfo> element is to display helpful information to the end user in the application. The <appInfo> element data is typically transformed and displayed to the user using a stylesheet, whereas the <documentation> element is simply left as-is.

Now that you have a good handle on creating and annotating schemas, let's take a look at the data types of XSD.

Data Types

Data type support is an extremely valuable feature of XSD. Data types allow for a deeper level of validation and proper format of elements and attributes. XSD schemas support a wide range of data types in addition to allowing you to define your own data types.

Simple Data Types

There are presently 44 simple data types in XSD that you can take advantage of. Some of these types are built into XSD, while others are derived from these built-in types. Both simple types and their derivations can be used in element and attribute declarations. We have already seen examples of this when we looked at how to declare elements and attributes. In doing so, we learned that you can specify the data type that you want the element or attribute to be by assigning a value to the `type` attribute, as shown below:

```
<?xml version="1.0"?>
<xsd:schema xmlns:xsd="http://www.w3.org/2001/XMLSchema">
 <xsd:element name="Student" minOccurs="0" maxOccurs="unbounded">
  <xsd:complexType>
    <xsd:sequence>
     <xsd:element name="ID" type="xsd:string" minOccurs="1" maxOccurs="1"/>
     <xsd:element name="GPA" type="xsd:string" minOccurs="1" maxOccurs="1"/>
    </xsd:sequence>
  </xsd:complexType>
 </xsd:element>
</xsd:schema>
```

Notice how `xsd:string` is specified for the `type` attribute of both the `ID` and `GPA`. This means that both of these elements will accept string values. We discussed at the beginning of this chapter the reason for including the `xsd:` prefix throughout your schema – so that the parser knows that the syntax you are using belongs to the XSD language.

In building your schemas, you can assign the `type` attribute to any of the valid simple data types shown in the table below. Or, as we will discuss in more detail shortly, you can create your own data types to extend these simple types.

XSD Data Type	Description
`anyUri`	Uniform Resource Identifier (URI). Examples: http://www.sample.com, http://www.sample.com/index.html#ID2
`base64Binary`	MIME-style Base64 encoded binary data.
`hexBinary`	Hexadecimal-encoded binary data.
`boolean`	True (1) or False (0).
`byte`	-128 to 127.
`dateTime`	Date in a subset of the ISO 8601 format. Time is optional. Time Zone is optional. Example: 2001-04-06T11:45:33.000-05:00

Table continued on following page

XSD Data Type	Description
`date`	Date in a subset of the ISO 8601 format. Example: 2001-04-06
`decimal`	Positive or negative arbitrary precision decimal value. Note that, in the Candidate Recommendation version of XSD, this was called `Number` instead. Examples: -5.34, 0, 5.34, 5000.00
`double`	Equivalent to double-precision 64-bit floating point.
`duration`	Duration of time specified in years, months, days, hours, minutes, and seconds format, as defined in the ISO 8601 standards extended format P*n*Y*n* M*n*DT*n*H *n*M*n*S. nY is the number of years, nM is the number of months, and so on. The P is required but the other items are optional. For example, to specify a duration of 1 year and 2 months, you would specify: P1Y2M. To specify a duration of 1 year, 2 months, 3 days, 10 hrs, 30 minutes, and 12.3 seconds, you would specify: P1Y2M3DT10H30M12.3S
`ENTITIES`	XML 1.0 `ENTITIES` attribute type. `ENTITIES` contain a set of `ENTITY` values. To retain compatibility between XSD and XML DTD 1.0s, these should only be used with attributes.
`ENTITY`	XML 1.0 `ENTITY` attribute type. To retain compatibility between XSD and XML DTD 1.0s, these should only be used with attributes.
`float`	Equivalent to single-precision 32-bit floating point.
`gDay`	Day in Gregorian format. Example: `--31` (every 31st day, regardless of month)
`gMonth`	Month in Gregorian format. Example: `--06--` (every May)
`gMonthDay`	Month and day in Gregorian format. Example: `--07-31` (every July 31st)
`gYear`	Year in Gregorian format. Example: 2000
`gYearMonth`	Year and month in Gregorian format. Example: 2000-02
`ID`	The `ID` values must be unique throughout all elements in the XML document. This attribute is referenced by other attributes such as `idref` and `idrefs`. To retain compatibility between XSD and XML DTD 1.0s, these should only be used with attributes.
`IDREF`	References the value in an `ID` attribute within the XML document. To retain compatibility between XSD and XML DTD 1.0s, these should only be used with attributes.
`IDREFS`	References multiple `ID` type values separated by whitespace. To retain compatibility between XSD and XML DTD 1.0s, these should only be used with attributes.

XSD Data Type	Description
`Int`	Integer. Sign is optional. Range: -2147483648 to 2147483647.
`Integer`	The standard mathematical concept of integer numbers. Range: an infinite set of negative or positive numbers.
`Language`	Any valid XML `Language` value as defined by RFC 1766. Example: en-US
`Long`	Integer. Range: -9223372036854775808 to 9223372036854775807.
`Name`	XML 1.0 `Name` type.
`NCName`	XML Namespace `NCName` (an XML `Name` without the prefix and colon).
`negativeInteger`	Range: negative infinity to –1.
`NMTOKEN`	Name token value. String consisting of one word in a set of letters, digits, and other characters in any combination. To retain compatibility between XSD and XML DTD 1.0s, these should only be used with attributes.
`NMTOKENS`	List of name tokens separated by whitespace. To retain compatibility between XSD and XML DTD 1.0s, these should only be used with attributes.
`nonNegativeInteger`	Range: 0 to infinity.
`nonPositiveInteger`	Range: Negative infinity to 0.
`normalizedString`	String of character data. Newline, tab, and carriage-return characters are converted to spaces before schema processing.
`NOTATION`	XML 1.0 `NOTATION` attribute type. To retain compatibility between XSD and XML DTD 1.0s, these should only be used with attributes.
`positiveInteger`	Range: 1 to infinity.
`QName`	XML Namespace `QName`.
`Short`	Range: -32768 to 32767.
`String`	String of character data (characters that match `Char` from XML 1.0).
`Time`	Time in hh:mm:ss.sss-TimeZone format. Time Zone is optional. The time zone is based on the number of hours ahead or behind Coordinated Universal Time (as defined in ISO 8601). Example: 11:45:33.20-05:00 where 05:00 means 5 hours behind Universal time

Table continued on following page

XSD Data Type	Description
Token	String of character data. Like normalizedString, the newline, tab, and carriage-return characters are converted to spaces before schema processing. In addition, adjacent space characters are collapsed to a single space and leading and trailing spaces are removed.
unsignedByte	Unsigned byte. Range: 0 to 255.
unsignedInt	Unsigned integer. Range: 0 to 4294967295.
unsignedLong	Unsigned long. Range: 0 to 18446744073709551615.
unsignedShort	Unsigned short. Range: 0 to 65535.

Now let's see an example of these data types in action. To invalidate the string "XSD is great!!" as content for the <GPA> element, our schema can define a floating-point number as the only valid data type. Here is how it looks:

```
<?xml version="1.0"?>
<xsd:schema xmlns:xsd="http://www.w3.org/2001/XMLSchema">
 <xsd:element name="Student" minOccurs="0" maxOccurs="unbounded">
  <xsd:complexType>
    <xsd:sequence>
     <xsd:element name="ID" type="xsd:string" minOccurs="1" maxOccurs="1"/>
     <xsd:element name="GPA" type="xsd:float" minOccurs="1" maxOccurs="1"/>
    </xsd:sequence>
  </xsd:complexType>
 </xsd:element>
</xsd:schema>
```

Now, if an XML document references this schema and it contains this element:

```
<GPA>XSD is great!!</GPA>
```

An XSD Parser will generate an error indicating a problem with the data type.

You can make use of the other data types in this same manner. As you can see, it is very easy to take advantage of these data types. Since this is a relatively straightforward concept, let's move on to the more complicated details of creating your own data types.

Creating Your Own Data Types

You can create a simple data type by deriving from any one of the 44 listed on the previous table. We already saw an example of this concept with our StudentGPA data type that restricts the GPA to a certain format:

```
<?xml version="1.0"?>
<xsd:schema xmlns:xsd="http://www.w3.org/2001/XMLSchema">
 <xsd:element name="Student" minOccurs="0" maxOccurs="unbounded">
  <xsd:complexType>
    <xsd:sequence>
     <xsd:element name="ID" type="xsd:string" minOccurs="1" maxOccurs="1"/>
     <xsd:element name="GPA" type="StudentGPA"/>
    </xsd:sequence>
  </xsd:complexType>
 </xsd:element>
<xsd:simpleType name="StudentGPA" minOccurs="1" maxOccurs="1">
  <xsd:restriction base="xsd:string">
    <xsd:length value="4"/>
    <xsd:pattern value="\d{1}.\d{2}"/>
  </xsd:restriction>
</xsd:simpleType>
</xsd:schema>
```

Facets

In the example above, we created a new data type called `StudentGPA` as an extension of the existing `xsd:string` simple type. We then specified the **facets** (`length` and `pattern`) that we wanted to implement to make the data type meet our objective.

In XSD, there are a number of different facets that can be specified to further restrict or define your new data type. The available facets vary depending on the data type you are deriving your new type from. For example, the `string` data type has the following facets:

- `enumeration`
- `length`
- `minLength`
- `maxLength`
- `pattern`
- `whitespace`

Our `StudentGPA` data type used the `length` facet to specify that the `GPA` must contain 4 characters, and the `pattern` facet to specify that the `GPA` must follow the particular format (for example 3.93):

```
<xsd:simpleType name="StudentGPA" minOccurs="1" maxOccurs="1">
  <xsd:restriction base="xsd:string">
    <xsd:length value="4"/>
    <xsd:pattern value="\d{1}.\d{2}"/>
  </xsd:restriction>
</xsd:simpleType>
```

Suppose that we wanted to restrict the `GPA` to be one of the following values: 2.0, 2.5, 3.0, 3.5, or 4.0. In such an instance, we could use the `enumeration` facet. Here's how that would look:

```
<xsd:simpleType name="StudentGPA" minOccurs="1" maxOccurs="1">
  <xsd:restriction base="xsd:string">
    <xsd:enumeration value="2.0"/>
    <xsd:enumeration value="2.5"/>
    <xsd:enumeration value="3.0"/>
    <xsd:enumeration value="3.5"/>
    <xsd:enumeration value="4.0"/>
  </xsd:restriction>
</xsd:simpleType>
```

The enumeration facet requires a document to contain one of its specified values for it to be valid. Note that, in this instance, there must be a 2.0, *or* a 2.5, *or* a 3.0, and so on. Yet, in the previous example, we required the length to be 4 *and* the pattern to follow the specified format. How can we tell when AND is being enforced, versus when OR is being enforced? The answer is simple: patterns and enumerations create OR scenarios. When you use a pattern or enumeration facet, the value must be one of those specified for the document element to be valid. All other facets create AND scenarios, which means that all values must be present for the document element to be valid.

Now, let's take a look at some examples using the int data type. For starters, you should know that the int data type has the following facets:

- enumeration
- fractionDigits
- maxExclusive
- maxInclusive
- minExclusive
- minInclusive
- pattern
- totalDigits
- whitespace

Suppose that we want to create a new data type to validate the course numbers that students are enrolled in. Each student can be enrolled in 0 to 10 classes a semester. Further, suppose that all course numbers are numbered in the following range: 1000 to 3000. We can use the int data type as our base type and then restrict the range of valid values using the minInclusive and maxInclusive facets:

```
<xsd:simpleType name="CourseNumber" minOccurs="0" maxOccurs="10">
  <xsd:restriction base="xsd:integer">
    <xsd:minInclusive value="1000"/>
    <xsd:maxInclusive value="3000"/>
  </xsd:restriction>
</xsd:simpleType>
<xsd:element name="Course" type="CourseNumber"/>
```

Now, if an XML document references this schema and it contains this element:

```
<Course>4000</Course>
```

an XSD parser will generate an error indicating a problem with the data type, because the number is out of the allowed range.

In this section, we have only begun to scratch the surface of the ways we can use the existing XSD data types or create our own.

> **For more information about XSD simple data types, or creating your own data types, please see the XSD data types document on the W3C's web site at http://www.w3.org/TR/xmlschema-2.**

Validating and Using XSD Schemas

Everything we have learned up to this point concerns the basics of writing XSD schemas. But how are XSD schemas supported in SQL Server 2000 and other applications? What parsers are available for validating XSD today? How can you translate existing XDR schemas into XSD? Those topics will be covered in this section.

SQL Server Support of XSD

Presently, SQL Server 2000 only supports the XDR schema standard. It does not support the XSD standard. However, Microsoft has announced plans to make support for XSD part of its core XML services at some point after XSD becomes a Recommendation from the W3C. In fact, in April 2001, Microsoft announced the availability of the MSXML Parser 4.0 Technology Preview, which supports the Proposed Recommendation version of XSD. Thus, the official MSXML 4.0 release will have an XSD schema validator, and a future release of Microsoft SQL Server will also support the XSD schema.

Microsoft Office XP and the Beta 2 version of Microsoft Visual Studio.Net already have some support for XSD, so all of these factors are very good evidence that Microsoft will be providing future support for XSD as it becomes finalized.

Validating XSD Schemas

As mentioned previously, the MSXML Parser 4.0 Technology Preview supports XSD schema validation. There are also some validators that have been created by other parties. A number of validators presently available can be found on the W3C's web site at http://www.w3.org/XML/Schema.html.

So you can either go to the Microsoft web site and download the MSXML Parser 4.0 Technology Preview (or the release version of MSXML 4.0, once it is available) or work with one of the other validators. The bottom line is that you have plenty of resources available to start working with and validating your XSD schemas today.

Translating XDR Schemas into XSD Schemas

It is not possible to go from XSD to XDR with a translation tool, because of the functionality that wouldn't be supported. However, it is possible to translate from XDR into XSD, which is most likely what you would want to do anyway. There are already a few such translation tools available in beta formats today. Since the XSD schema itself is not finalized, however, these tools are far from being complete. One example of a tool to convert XDR to XSD is listed in the Microsoft .Net Framework beta documentation. It lists an XML Schema Definition Tool (`xsd.exe`) with a variety of features, including one that converts XDR to XSD. As at the writing of this book, information about the tool was present at the following link:

http://msdn.microsoft.com/library/dotnet/cptools/cpconxmlschemadefinitiontoolxsdexe.htm

Once XSD is finalized, there will likely be some very comprehensive conversion tools available to help users migrate from XDR to XSD.

> **Important Note: On May 2, 2001, the W3C promoted XML Schema Definitions (XSD) to the Recommendation Stage. Now that XSD is a full Recommendation, it is effectively the worldwide standard for XML Schemas. Please consult the W3C's web site at http://www.w3.org for the latest documentation.**
>
> **Additionally, on April 30, 2001, Microsoft released the Beta 1 Version of SQL Server 2000 Web Release 2. This version of Web Release 2 provides support for XSD in SQL Server. More information about this beta release can be found in Appendix C.**

Summary

XSD schemas provide a great way to define valid instances of XML documents. They are very powerful and more flexible than DTDs and XDR schemas. Let's review some of the key points highlighted in this chapter:

- XSD schemas are a powerful alternative to other technologies. They provide much richer functionality than DTDs and XDR schemas.
- XSD schemas allow you to create your own data types.
- XSD schemas allow you to implement object-oriented style inheritance.
- MSXML 4.0 will support XSD, and a technology preview of MSXML 4.0 that supports XSD was made available for download on Microsoft's web site in April 2001.
- You can begin working with XSD today and can validate your schemas using the MSXML 4.0 Technology Preview, as well as a number of other schema validators.
- There are some translation tools in beta versions right now that allow you to translate from XDR to XSD.
- XSD is the new worldwide vendor neutral standard for schema definitions, so you should start becoming familiar with it today!

XSD will have a great future. The only questions that remain regard what exact syntax it will employ. The industry has been anxiously awaiting a formal schema with this level of power and flexibility for a long time. If all goes well, XSD will be a full Recommendation by the end of 2001. Once it becomes a full Recommendation, more and more XSD support will be offered by applications like SQL Server. We are already seeing XSD support in the latest software tools being developed by Microsoft today, like Microsoft Office XP, Microsoft Visual Studio.Net, and MSXML 4.0.

Our next chapter gets us back on the SQL Server track, exploring how XML templates can be used and why they are so beneficial.

SQL SQL SQL SQL SQL SQL
Server Server
XML XML XML XML XML
XML XML XML XML XML

7

XML Templates and Views

This chapter discusses XML templates and views. **XML views** are a way of describing how SQL Server tables look from an XML standpoint. These XML views can then be used within an XML template and queried using XPath queries.

However, before we can go into the details of describing the use of XML views we need to describe what **XML templates** are, as these piece together everything that's needed to actually perform the queries. XML templates also allow standard SQL queries to be performed and we also go through how to do this.

We'll then bring together the material introduced in Chapter 5 on annotated XDR schemas to discuss XML views.

Finally, we'll discuss the new XML View Mapper utility that was released by Microsoft after the initial release of SQL Server 2000. This allows you to connect to a SQL Server database, and then drag and drop the mappings of tables and columns on to an XDR schema to create an annotated XDR schema that can be used within template queries.

Introduction to XML Templates

An XML template is a well-formed XML document that can contain one or more SQL or XPath queries. We've had a basic introduction to XPath already in previous chapters, but just to recap, XPath is an XML querying language that allows you to return parts of an XML document in a similar way to how a SQL query acts against a table.

> *XPath is described in detail in Chapter 8.*

You can execute an XML template within an HTTP request to return the results of the queries. The template can even specify an XSL stylesheet to format the returned HTML.

We could specify a query directly within a URL instead of using a template. However, a user can modify the URL before submitting it. Keeping the query out of the URL and in a template abstracts it from the user's view, hence adding a layer of security (because templates are stored on the server rather than coming from a client request and so, in theory, they can't be viewed to see the details of the query).

With a template we can:

- Specify SQL or XPath queries. When using SQL, any valid SQL statement is allowed. For XPath, the query is executed against the annotated XDR schema that is specified within the template.
- Add parameters that are passed into the template. This allows passing of values into the SQL query or stored procedures that are within the template.
- Set the top-level element of the returned XML document. This is normally the `ROOT` tag but may be changed to another name as required.
- Declare namespaces. This is the only required part of the template and is used to determine how the other template elements are defined.
- Set an XSL stylesheet to apply to the returned document.

As XML templates are referenced by HTTP requests, IIS needs to be set up specifically to allow this. XML templates are stored in IIS in a special virtual directory that is set up with the IIS Virtual Directory Management for SQL Server utility. Therefore, before we look at how to use XML templates, we must configure the IIS Virtual Directory correctly in order to allow XML templates to be run.

Setting Up the IIS Virtual Directory

There are many different options that can be set when creating the virtual directory for SQL Server. We will only go through those settings that are required for this chapter. For full details of all the options that are available, please refer to Appendix A.

First of all we need to create two folders. The first maps the virtual directory – for the examples in this chapter we'll call it, imaginatively, XMLTemplates. The second folder is a child of XMLTemplates and is where the template files are stored – call it Template. Your installation may require the use of different folders, so change these names accordingly.

Start the IIS Virtual Directory Management for SQL Server utility by choosing Configure SQL XML Support in IIS within the Microsoft SQL Server group on the Start menu. You will be presented with a screen similar to this (although RSL005 will be replaced with the name of your server). This is from Windows 2000 Server and differs slightly for other versions of Windows:

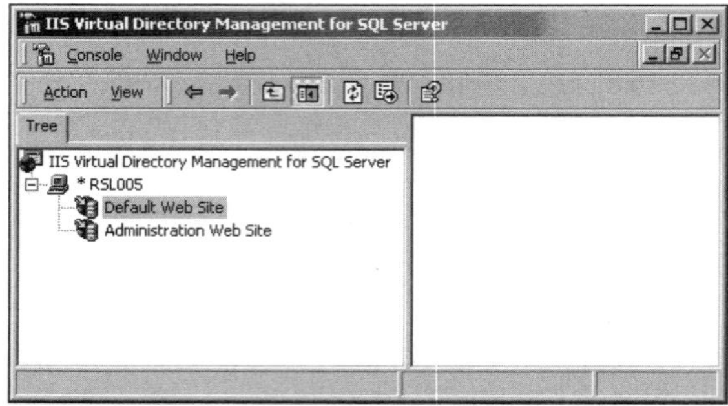

Right-click on the Default Web Site node and choose New | Virtual Directory. The New Virtual Directory Properties dialog appears. On the General tab, type XMLTemplates as the Virtual Directory Name and C:\XMLTemplates as the Local Path.

On the Security tab, select the appropriate authentication method for your machine.

> **In a production environment, the account that is used here is critical. Make sure that you use an account that has the absolute minimum permissions needed to run the queries within the templates, and no more. A standard approach is to use an account that is set up specifically for this purpose and the only thing that it has permissions to do is run the queries that are exposed through the virtual directory. Otherwise you will be inviting hackers into your database.**
>
> **For more information on security issues, see Appendix A.**

Next, on the Data Source tab, we choose (local) for the server name (provided you are working on the SQL Server machine – otherwise specify the server's name) and Northwind for the database. All the examples in this chapter will use `Northwind`.

Be sure to select Allow XPath as we'll be needing this later on in the chapter. Allow template queries should be selected by default.

Finally – and this is the important bit for templates – we need to configure the Virtual Names tab to define where the templates are actually stored within the virtual directory. To do this, click on the New button, and then fill in the details as in the dialog box below:

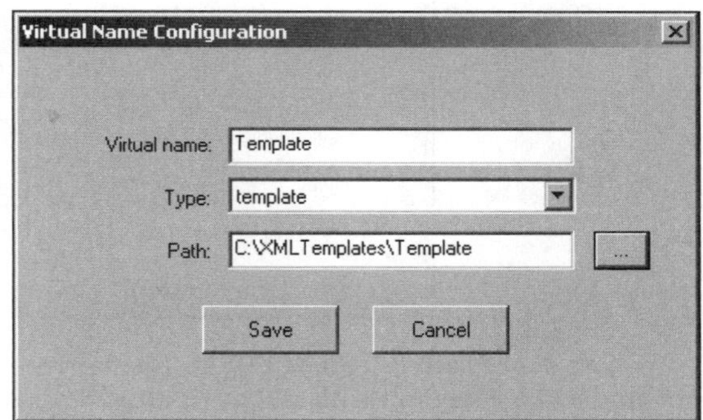

Then hit Save and OK. We have now configured our default web site to be able to use XML templates. We can put the templates that we develop into the folder `C:\XMLTemplates\Template` and then run them using URLs in the form:

```
http://localhost/xmltemplates/template/nameoftemplate.xml
```

Overview of the Parts of a Template

As the template is a standard well-formed XML document, it begins and ends with the usual root tags:

```
<ROOT xmlns:sql="urn:schemas-microsoft-com:xml-sql" >
. . .
</ROOT>
```

Between these root tags can come any combination of header, query, and XPath query tags. Let's begin by looking at SQL query tags.

SQL Query Tags

A SQL query tag is a SQL query bounded by <sql:query> and </sql:query> tags. The SQL query can be any valid SQL statement; you can even call stored procedures or use DDL (CREATE, DROP, ALTER). SQL query tags are placed within the opening and closing root tags, like so:

```
<ROOT xmlns:sql="urn:schemas-microsoft-com:xml-sql">
  <sql:query>
    SELECT EmployeeID, FirstName, LastName
    FROM   Employees
    ORDER BY LastName, FirstName
    FOR XML AUTO
  </sql:query>
</ROOT>
```

Save this code as employees.xml and put it inside the Template directory we created earlier. We can then execute the query by browsing to it, returning a list of employees:

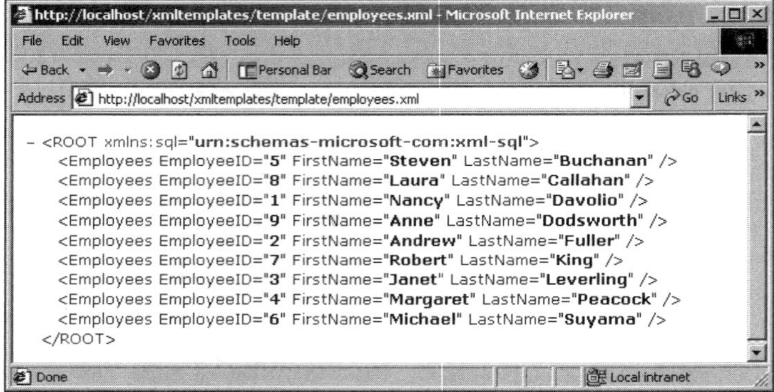

The query takes any standard SELECT statement – whether something simple like above, or a complicated statement with JOINs, GROUP BYs, etc. The only requirement is that you must have the FOR XML clause at the end, or you will get the following friendly message:

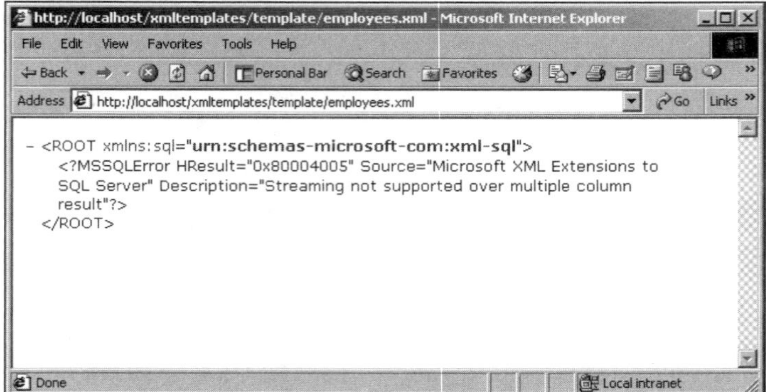

You can use any of the RAW, AUTO, and EXPLICIT options that were described in Chapter 3.

Calling Stored Procedures from within Query Tags

As well as executing a simple query, we can also call a stored procedure from within the query tags. This gives increased security benefits. For example, if an intruder gains access to the files on the web server, and reads `employees.xml`, he/she can glean potentially valuable information about our `Employees` table. If the query contains a stored procedure rather than a query, this information remains hidden.

Create the following stored procedure `OrdersByEmployee`, which returns a count of the number of orders taken by each employee:

```
CREATE PROCEDURE OrdersByEmployee
AS
   SELECT LastName,
          FirstName,
          TotalOrders = (SELECT COUNT(*)
                         FROM Orders
                         WHERE EmployeeId = Employees.EmployeeId)
   FROM Employees
   ORDER BY LastName, FirstName
   FOR XML AUTO
```

> **Make sure that you give execute permission on the stored procedure to the account that the virtual directory is connecting to the database with, otherwise you will get an error.**

Then create a file called `OrdersByEmployee.xml` within the `Template` directory, and put the code below into it:

```
<ROOT xmlns:sql="urn:schemas-microsoft-com:xml-sql">
  <sql:query>
    EXEC OrdersByEmployee
  </sql:query>
</ROOT>
```

Browsing to this XML template gives us this result:

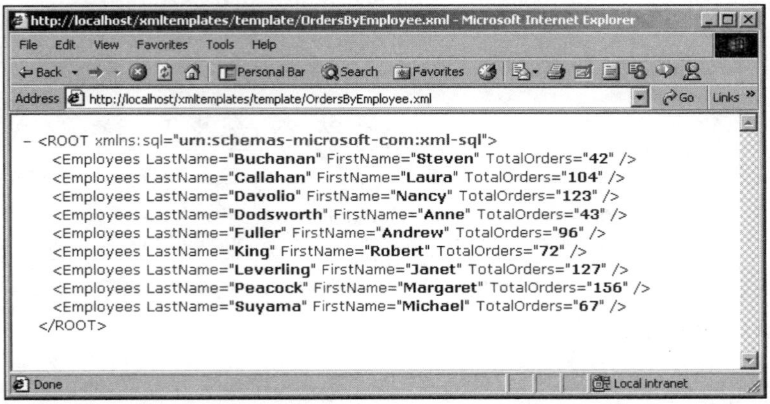

```
- <ROOT xmlns:sql="urn:schemas-microsoft-com:xml-sql">
    <Employees LastName="Buchanan" FirstName="Steven" TotalOrders="42" />
    <Employees LastName="Callahan" FirstName="Laura" TotalOrders="104" />
    <Employees LastName="Davolio" FirstName="Nancy" TotalOrders="123" />
    <Employees LastName="Dodsworth" FirstName="Anne" TotalOrders="43" />
    <Employees LastName="Fuller" FirstName="Andrew" TotalOrders="96" />
    <Employees LastName="King" FirstName="Robert" TotalOrders="72" />
    <Employees LastName="Leverling" FirstName="Janet" TotalOrders="127" />
    <Employees LastName="Peacock" FirstName="Margaret" TotalOrders="156" />
    <Employees LastName="Suyama" FirstName="Michael" TotalOrders="67" />
  </ROOT>
```

> **However, we are not limited to just executing stored procedures or queries. We can execute virtually any SQL statement that we want from within the template. You could even use `DROP DATABASE` statements in a query tag so, again, make sure that you lock down the rights of the account that will run them. Also, make sure that only authorized people can edit the templates. These is no way of restricting what will be run within the template other than these two ways, so make sure that the security requirements are carefully planned and implemented.**

Using Multiple Query Tags

It is possible to have more than one SQL statement between a set of query tags. Additionally, it is possible to have more than one set of query tags between the root tags.

Everything within one set of query tags is executed as one batch and, therefore, implicitly as a single transaction – in the same way that, in Query Analyzer, everything before a `GO` command is executed as one batch. We cannot use the `GO` command within a template, so the only way to execute statements separately from each other is to place them within separate query tags.

Let's go through a couple of examples to illustrate all this. Let's use the following template to discontinue a product, and also show its before and after status (call it `discontinue.xml`):

```
<ROOT xmlns:sql="urn:schemas-microsoft-com:xml-sql">
  <sql:query>
      SELECT   ProductID, ProductName, Discontinued
      FROM     Products ProductsBeforeUpdate
      WHERE    ProductID = 3 FOR XML AUTO

      UPDATE   Products
      SET      Discontinued = 1
      WHERE    ProductID = 3

      SELECT   ProductID, ProductName, Discontinued
      FROM     Products ProductsAfterUpdate
      WHERE    ProductID = 3 FOR XML AUTO
  </sql:query>
</ROOT>
```

Running this template gives the following results. As you can see each of the three statements have been run and then the two `SELECT` statements results consolidated into one set:

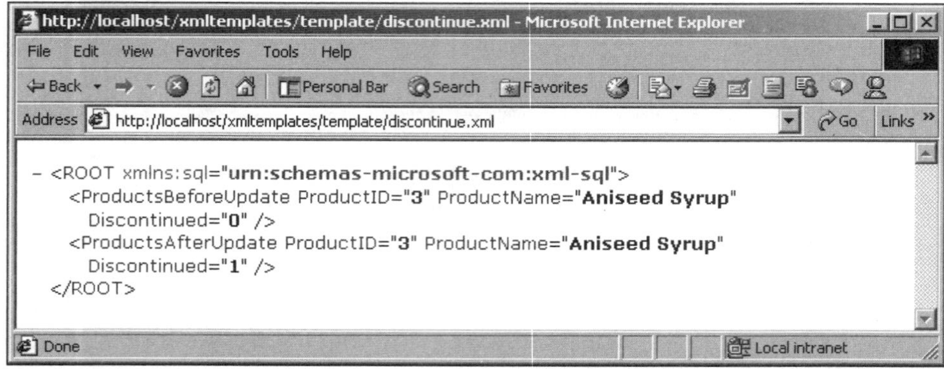

This all works fine in this case as all three statements are executed as one batch within SQL Server. The problem comes about when one of the statements fails for any reason. For example the update could time out if the server is busy. Here we change the update to an invalid value (it's a lot simpler to illustrate this than trying to make the query time out!):

```
<ROOT xmlns:sql="urn:schemas-microsoft-com:xml-sql">
  <sql:query>
      SELECT   ProductID, ProductName, Discontinued
      FROM     Products ProductsBeforeUpdate
      WHERE    ProductID = 3 FOR XML AUTO

      UPDATE   Products
      SET      Discontinued = 'yes'
      WHERE    ProductID = 3

      SELECT   ProductID, ProductName, Discontinued
      FROM     Products ProductsAfterUpdate
      WHERE    ProductID = 3 FOR XML AUTO
  </sql:query>
</ROOT>
```

Save this template as `discontinuefail.xml` and try to run it. You'll get the following output, which shows that the first statement ran but that the update gave an error that caused the third statement not to be run at all:

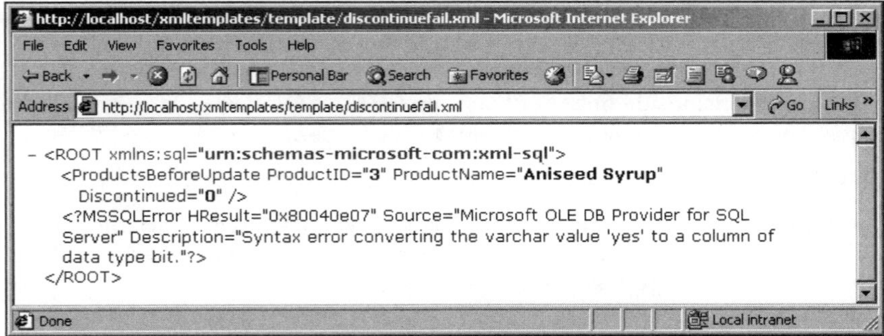

Note that we've reset the `Discontinued` value of `ProductID=3` to `0` again before running this new XML template.

To get around this kind of problem, we can separate the statements out into their own `<sql:query>` tags:

```
<ROOT xmlns:sql="urn:schemas-microsoft-com:xml-sql">
  <sql:query>
      SELECT   ProductID, ProductName, Discontinued
      FROM     Products ProductsBeforeUpdate
      WHERE    ProductID = 3 FOR XML AUTO
  </sql:query>
  <sql:query>
      UPDATE   Products
      SET      Discontinued = 1
      WHERE    ProductID = 3
  </sql:query>
```

```
    <sql:query>
        SELECT    ProductID, ProductName, Discontinued
        FROM      Products ProductsAfterUpdate
        WHERE     ProductID = 3 FOR XML AUTO
    </sql:query>
</ROOT>
```

This template (called `discontinue-multitags.xml`) gives exactly the same results back as in the first case. It is only after we change the `UPDATE` statement again to fail that we see a difference:

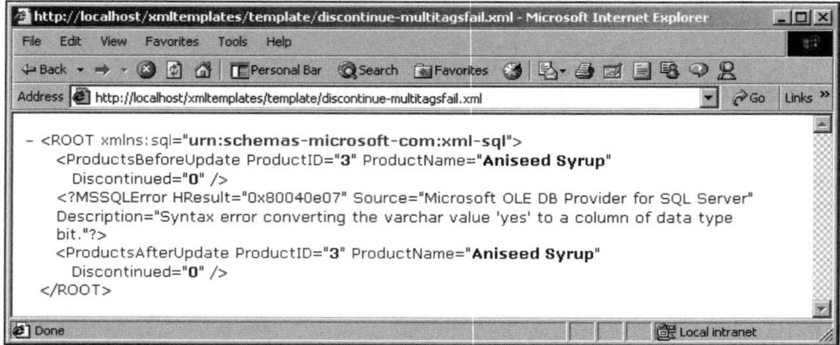

Here, the last statement is still run even though the second one failed. So what, in practice are the reasons to use single `<sql:query>` tags or multiple ones?

- All the statements inside one set of tags are sent to SQL Server in one batch, so it is quicker to use just one as there are less round trips to the server.
- If you require every statement to be run then use separate tags.
- Everything within a tag is local to that tag, so if you declared a variable within a tag it wouldn't be available to the other tags. If you need to use variables in multiple statements then they all need to go inside one tag.

Header and Parameter Tags

The next section of code creates a stored procedure, called `SalesForEmployee`, which reports the total sales for a given sales person:

```
CREATE PROCEDURE SalesForEmployee
   @EmployeeID int

AS

SELECT LastName,
       FirstName,
       TotalSales = (SELECT SUM(CAST (UnitPrice * Quantity *
                    (1 - Discount) AS money))
                    FROM Orders
                    JOIN [Order Details]
```

```
                        ON Orders.OrderID = [Order Details].OrderID
                        WHERE    Employees.EmployeeID = Orders.EmployeeID)
    FROM Employees
   WHERE Employees.EmployeeID = @EmployeeID
  FOR XML AUTO
```

To execute this stored procedure from within a template, we need to be able to pass in the relevant value for the `EmployeeID` parameter to select the desired employee. To do this, we need to use header and parameter tags. The general form of the template becomes:

```
<ROOT xmlns:sql="urn:schemas-microsoft-com:xml-sql" >
   <sql:header>
      <sql:param>..</sql:param>
      <sql:param>..</sql:param>...n
   </sql:header>
   <sql:query>
      sql statement (s)
   </sql:query>
. . .
</ROOT>
```

There can be one set of header tags at the top of the template, immediately below the root, and, within this, there can be one or more parameter tags. So, in order that we can execute the `SalesForEmployee` stored procedure, we need to create the following template:

```
<ROOT xmlns:sql="urn:schemas-microsoft-com:xml-sql">
   <sql:header>
      <sql:param name='EmployeeID'> </sql:param>
   </sql:header>
  <sql:query>
    EXEC SalesForEmployee @EmployeeID
  </sql:query>
</ROOT>
```

Save this as `SalesForEmployee.xml` and browse to:

http://localhost/xmltemplates/template/SalesForEmployee.xml?EmployeeID=2

This gives the following:

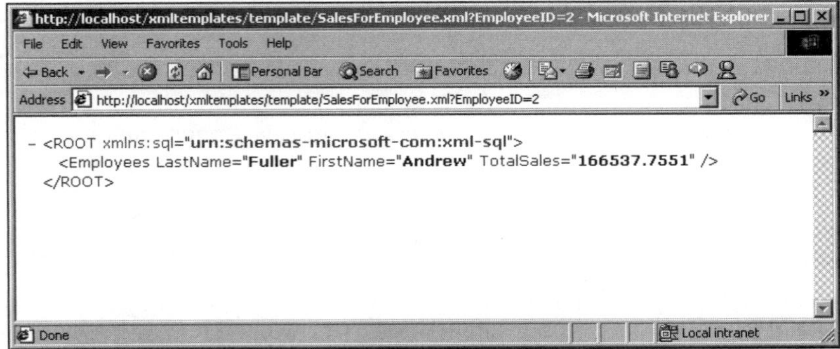

As you can see, the `EmployeeID` parameter value is passed in at the end of the URL in the format of `?parametername=value`.

Multiple Parameters

We can also pass multiple parameters to the template. To illustrate this, create the following stored procedure that allows us to limit the employee's sales to a particular country:

```
CREATE PROCEDURE SalesForEmployeeForCountry
   @EmployeeID int,
   @ShipCountry nvarchar(15)

AS

SELECT LastName,
       FirstName,
       TotalSales = (SELECT SUM(CAST (UnitPrice * Quantity *
                    (1 - Discount) AS money))
                    FROM Orders
                    JOIN [Order Details]
                    ON Orders.OrderID = [Order Details].OrderID
                    WHERE Employees.EmployeeID = Orders.EmployeeID
                    AND ShipCountry = @ShipCountry)
FROM Employees
WHERE Employees.EmployeeID = @EmployeeID
FOR XML AUTO
```

The template required to execute this stored procedure looks like:

```
<ROOT xmlns:sql="urn:schemas-microsoft-com:xml-sql">
  <sql:header>
    <sql:param name='EmployeeID'></sql:param>
    <sql:param name='ShipCountry'></sql:param>
  </sql:header>
  <sql:query>
    EXEC SalesForEmployeeForCountry @EmployeeID, @ShipCountry
  </sql:query>
</ROOT>
```

Save this as `SalesForEmployeeForCountry.xml` and browse to it, you should see this:

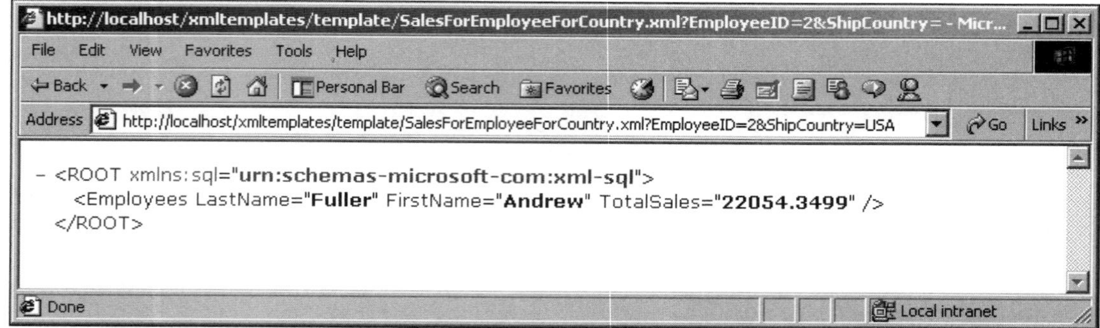

Note that, to pass multiple parameters in the URL, each one is separated by an ampersand in the same way as this would be done when passing values in the URL with ASP.

Default Parameter Values

We can provide a default value for a parameter by inserting the value between the opening and closing parameter tags, like so:

```
<ROOT xmlns:sql="urn:schemas-microsoft-com:xml-sql">
  <sql:header>
    <sql:param name='EmployeeID'></sql:param>
      <sql:param name='ShipCountry'>UK</sql:param>
  </sql:header>
  <sql:query>
    EXEC SalesForEmployeeForCountry @EmployeeID, @ShipCountry
  </sql:query>
</ROOT>
```

Whenever we run this template (`SalesForEmployeeForCountryUK.xml`) without specifying the `ShipCountry` parameter, it will always show the sales for the UK. However, we must still pass the `EmployeeID` parameter for it to work:

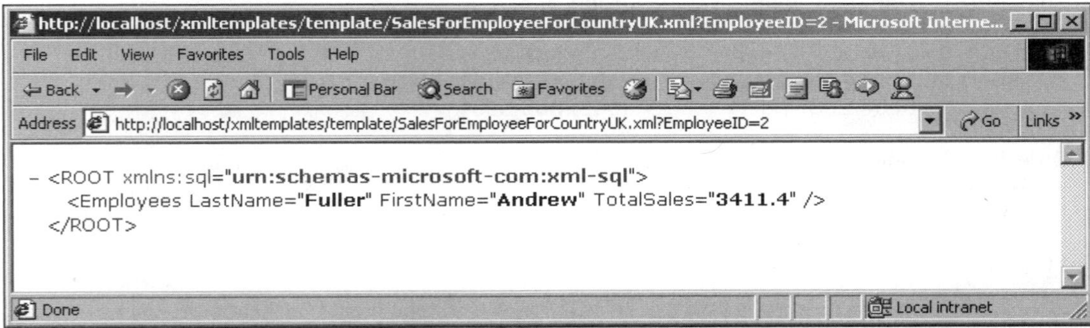

Passing Values between Statements

We can also pass values between statements using parameter tags. Say, for example, that we have a stored procedure that creates a new shipper and returns the new `ShipperID` as an output parameter. We want to update all open orders that have not yet shipped so that they use this new shipper – and all from within a single template. To do this, we add an extra parameter tag, pass in the value from the call to the stored procedure, and then pass this into the update statement. Here's the code for the stored procedure that creates the new shipper:

```
CREATE PROCEDURE CreateShipper
   @ShipperID int OUTPUT,
   @CompanyName nvarchar(40),
   @Phone nvarchar(24)
AS
   INSERT INTO Shippers
     (CompanyName, Phone)
   VALUES (@CompanyName, @Phone)

SET @ShipperID = @@IDENTITY
```

And here is the template that executes this and then updates the open orders:

```
<ROOT xmlns:sql="urn:schemas-microsoft-com:xml-sql">
   <sql:header>
      <sql:param name='ShipperID'></sql:param>
      <sql:param name='CompanyName'></sql:param>
      <sql:param name='Phone'></sql:param>
   </sql:header>
  <sql:query>
    EXEC CreateShipper @ShipperID OUTPUT, @CompanyName, @Phone
    UPDATE Orders
    SET ShipVia = @ShipperID
    WHERE ShippedDate IS NULL
  </sql:query>
</ROOT>
```

Save this as `createshipper.xml`. Here's what the `Shippers` table and open orders look like prior to running this template (this is on a new copy of `Northwind`, if yours may look different if you've been trying things):

```
ShipperID   CompanyName                  Phone
---------   --------------------------   ---------------------
1           Speedy Express               (503) 555-9831
2           United Package               (503) 555-3199
3           Federal Shipping             (503) 555-9931

OrderId     ShipVia
---------   -----------
11008       3
11019       3
11039       2
...
11077       2
```

Use the following URL in your browser to execute the template:

http://localhost/XMLTemplates/Template/createshipper.xml?CompanyName=Wrox%20Couriers&Phone=503%20555%201111

If we now run a query to test if our new shipper has been created, and to show which shipper is handling the open orders, we see:

```
ShipperID   CompanyName                  Phone
---------   --------------------------   ---------------------
1           Speedy Express               (503) 555-9831
2           United Package               (503) 555-3199
3           Federal Shipping             (503) 555-9931
4           Wrox Couriers                503 555 1111

OrderId     ShipVia
---------   -----------
11008       4
11019       4
11039       4
...
11077       4
```

XPath Query Tags

The general idea to how XPath query tags work is that XPath queries are run against an annotated XDR schema file that you specify as the mapping schema. An XPath query returns results from an XML document in much the same way as a SQL statement queries a database and returns results. Annotated XDR schemas within a template are referred to as **XML views**. They provide a mapping of the database to expose it to XPath as XML.

Let's start by looking at the syntax for using XPath queries. The XML template takes the following form:

```
<ROOT xmlns:sql="urn:schemas-microsoft-com:xml-sql" >
  <sql:header>
    <sql:param>..</sql:param>
    <sql:param>..</sql:param>...n
  </sql:header>
  <sql:query>
    sql statement(s)
  </sql:query>
   <sql:xpath-query mapping-schema="SchemaFileName.xml">
      XPath query
   </sql:xpath-query>
</ROOT>
```

Now let's look at a simple example. Say, for instance, we wanted to make a query against the `Employees` table to bring back all the details for `EmployeeID 1`, we would then use this template:

```
<ROOT xmlns:sql="urn:schemas-microsoft-com:xml-sql">
  <sql:xpath-query mapping-schema="EmployeesSchema.xml">
      Employees[@EmployeeID=1]
  </sql:xpath-query>
</ROOT>
```

Call this XML template `EmployeesXPath.xml` and save it in your `Template` directory. The next step is to create the mapping schema file (`EmployeesSchema.xml`) referenced in this template.

Using XML View Mapper

The simplest way to create the mapping schema file is to use the new XML View Mapper utility that Microsoft introduced as a free web download after the launch of SQL Server 2000. For details of where to download it and how it works, see Appendix B.

To create the mapping schema for this example, start up XML View Mapper (via Start | Programs | Microsoft SQL Server XML Tools | XML View Mapper) and select the option to create a new XML View Mapper project. You are then presented with two parts to XML View Mapper: the main Map Editor window and the Project Explorer window:

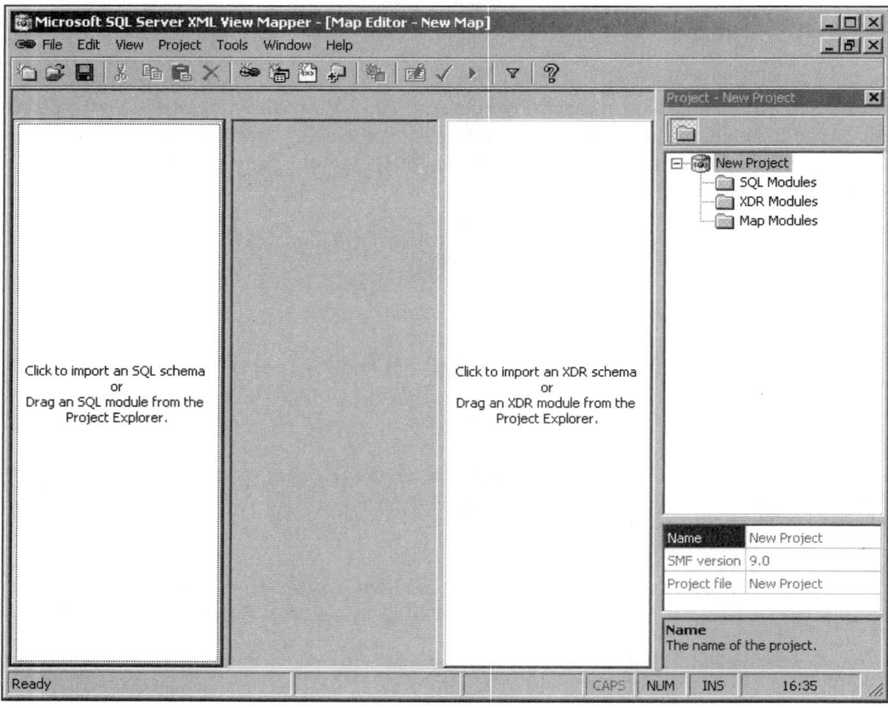

Unless you've altered your default settings for the XML View Mapper, it should look identical to this – with the Click to import an SQL schema ... pane on the left of the Map Editor. This is where we define our database schema. Click this to bring up the Data Link Properties dialog box. Connect to the Northwind database in the Connection tab and click on OK:

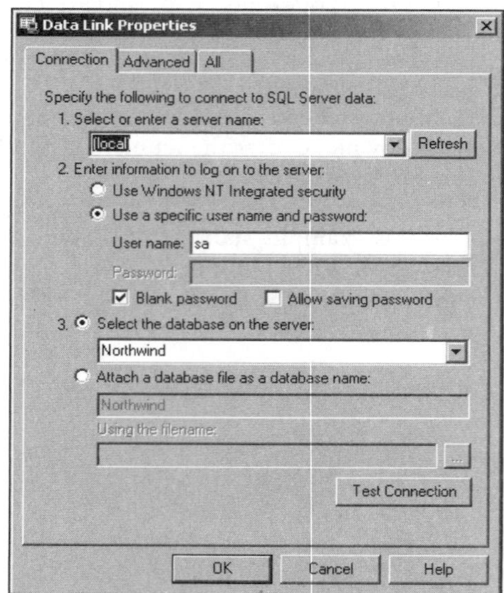

Now select the Employees table from the New Database Tables window and click on OK:

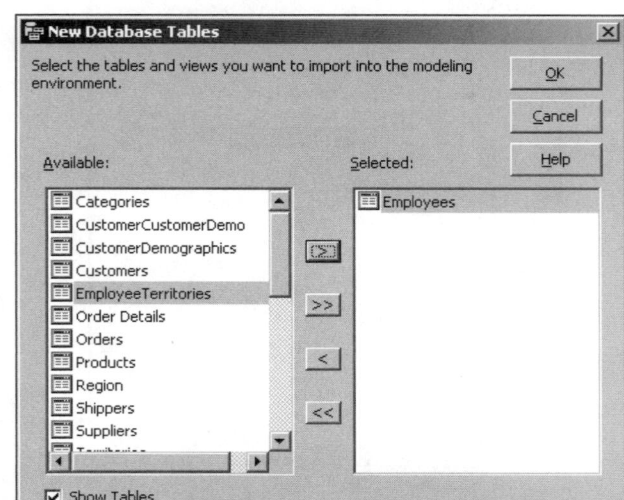

Your Map Editor window should now look like this:

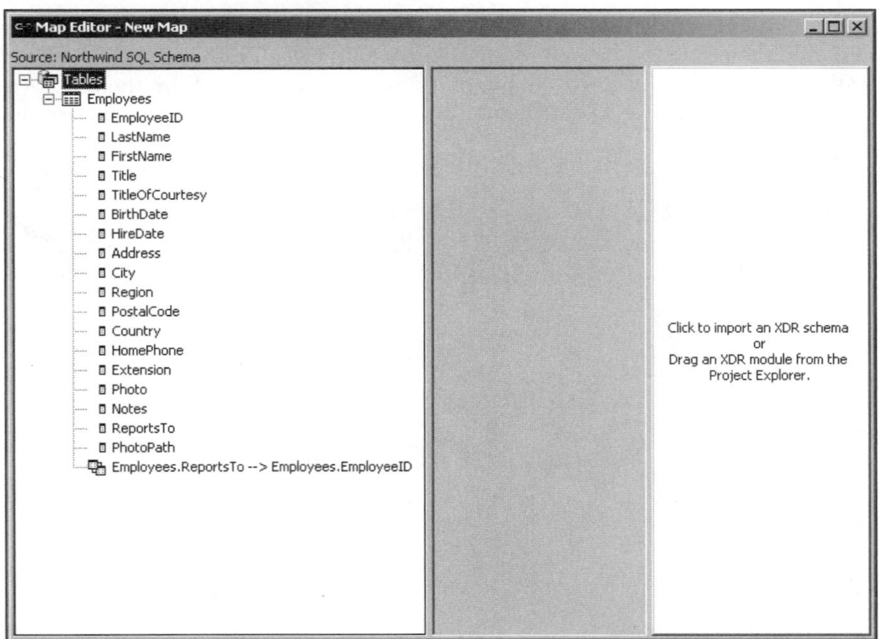

We now need to generate our XDR file to map against this schema. From the Tools menu, select Utilities and then Generate XDR Module. A new XDR module called Northwind should have appeared in the Project Explorer window:

Click on this and then drag it into the right-hand pane of the Map Editor. XML View Mapper will automatically create links (which are the mappings) between the fields from the Employees table across to its corresponding field in the XDR schema. Your Map Editor should now look like this:

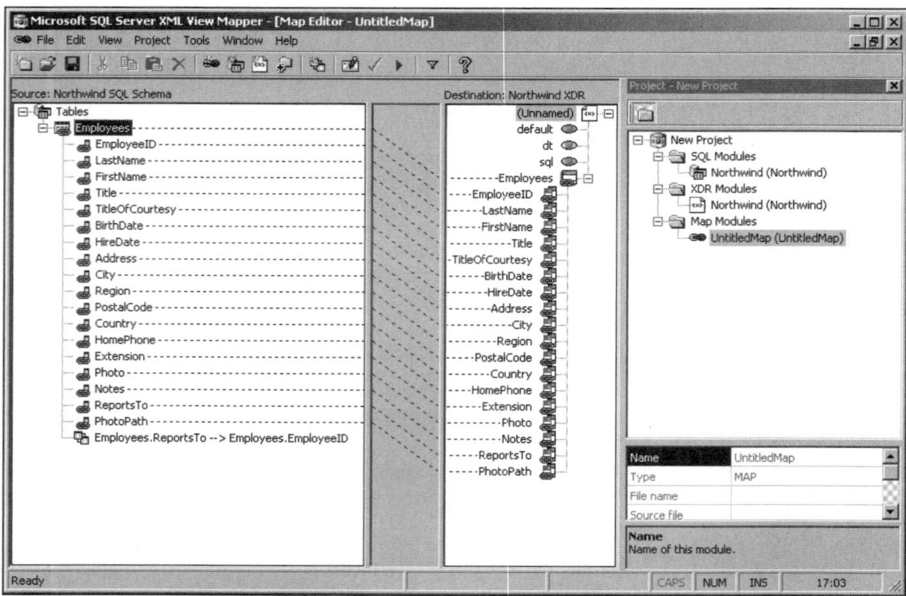

Finally, right-click on the new map module (UntitledMap) in the Project Explorer window and select Export XDR Schema from the menu. Save this map module as `EmployeesSchema.xml` in the `Template` directory.

Now run the `EmployeesXPath.xml` template we created at the beginning of this section and you should get results similar to those below:

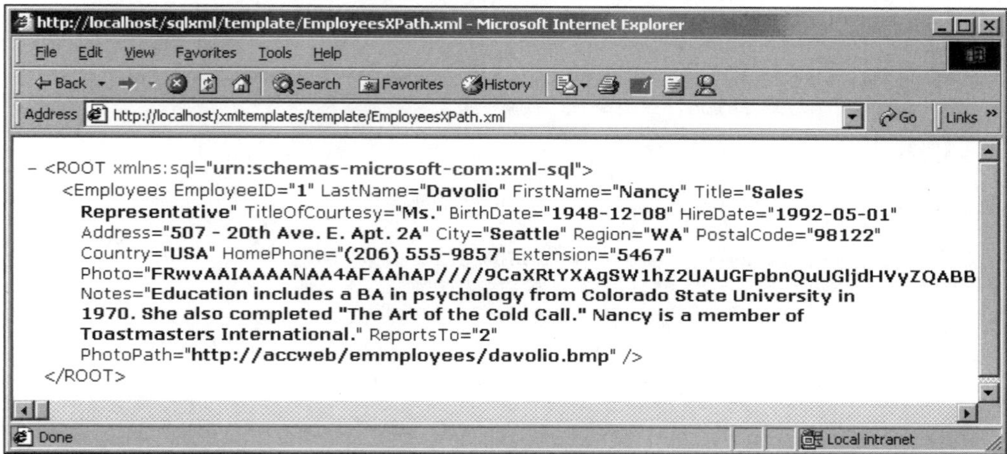

Applying XSL to the Template

We can apply an XSL stylesheet directly from within the template simply by putting its name in as part of the root tag, as shown in the general form below:

```
<ROOT xmlns:sql="urn:schemas-microsoft-com:xml-sql"
    sql:xsl="XSL FileName">
  <sql:header>
    <sql:param>..</sql:param>
    <sql:param>..</sql:param>...n
  </sql:header>
  <sql:query>
    sql statement (s)
  </sql:query>
  <sql:xpath-query mapping-schema="SchemaFileName.xml">
    XPath query
  </sql:xpath-query>
</ROOT>
```

The use of an XSL stylesheet allows the formatting of the output, so that you can return HTML back to the user rather than the raw XML that we have seen in the examples in this chapter up to this point. As we're not really discussing the ins and outs of XSL here, we'll just give a very simple example.

Save the following template as `ViewShippers.xml`.

```
<ROOT xmlns:sql="urn:schemas-microsoft-com:xml-sql"
      sql:xsl="ViewShippers.xsl">
  <sql:query>
   SELECT ShipperID, CompanyName, Phone
```

```
    FROM Shippers
    ORDER BY CompanyName
    FOR XML AUTO
  </sql:query>
</ROOT>
```

Here's the `ViewShippers.xsl` stylesheet, which is applied to our template:

```
<?xml version='1.0' encoding='UTF-8'?>
<xsl:stylesheet xmlns:xsl="http://www.w3.org/1999/XSL/Transform"
                version="1.0">
<xsl:template match = '*'>
   <xsl:apply-templates />
</xsl:template>
<xsl:template match = 'Shippers'>
   <TR>
      <TD><xsl:value-of select = '@ShipperID' /></TD>
      <TD><xsl:value-of select = '@CompanyName' /></TD>
      <TD><xsl:value-of select = '@Phone' /></TD>
   </TR>
</xsl:template>
<xsl:template match = '/'>
   <HTML>
      <HEAD>
         <STYLE>th { background-color: #CCCCCC }</STYLE>
      </HEAD>
   <BODY>
      <TABLE border='1' style='width:600;'>
      <TR><TH colspan='3'>Shippers</TH></TR>
      <TR><TH >Shipper ID</TH><TH>Company Name</TH><TH>Phone</TH></TR>
      <xsl:apply-templates select = 'root' />
      </TABLE>
   </BODY>
   </HTML>
</xsl:template>
</xsl:stylesheet>
```

Save `ViewShippers.xsl` in the same `Template` directory as the template itself. This stylesheet presents the results as a simple formatted table, like so:

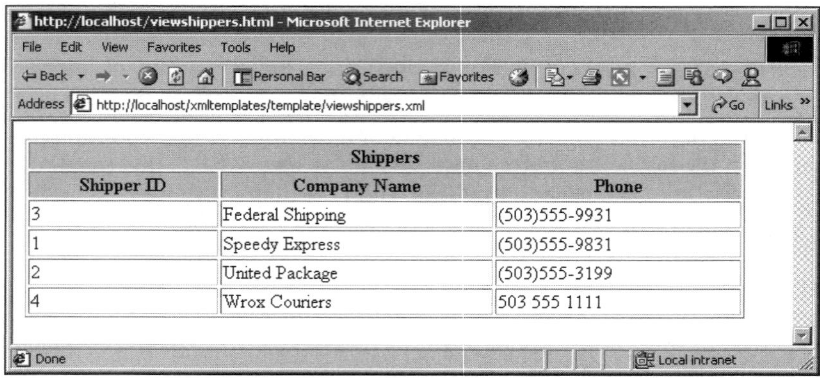

There is an error that arises on some machines when applying XSL to a template that says:

Cannot view XML input using XSL style sheet. Please correct the error and then click the Refresh button, or try again later. End tag 'HEAD' does not match the start tag 'META'.

The reason for this error is unknown at the time of writing, but a bug report has been raised with Microsoft.

That covers all the different options that can be used within XML templates, but Microsoft have not stood still with this technology as they have now updated the functionality that is available for XML template queries. This was released in Web Release 1 in January 2001 and is discussed in the next section.

Web Release of SQL Server Updates

With changes happening so fast in the XML world, Microsoft has decided that it can't wait for a whole release or service pack of SQL Server before introducing updates. The XML part of SQL Server has been built separately from the core product in order that updates can be slotted in without affecting anything else. At the time of writing, the first web release is complete and available from the Microsoft web site at www.microsoft.com/downloads/. Apart from the usual set of general bug fixes, Microsoft has introduced the following enhancements for templates.

Template Caching

When an XML template is first used it is now cached in memory so that, in future, it does not need to be read from the disk. This can give significant performance improvements over having to read the template from disk each time it is executed.

Unfortunately, in the first web release at least, the configuration of the cache size and how long the templates remain in the cache is all done through the registry.

To set the template cache size add the following key to the registry:

```
HKEY_LOCAL_MACHINE\SOFTWARE\Microsoft\MSSQLServer\Client\SQLXMLX\
TemplateCacheSize.
```

Without this key being present, the cache size defaults to storing 31 templates. You might want to increase this value if you are going to be using a large number of XML templates so that more of them can fit into memory. You need to weigh the effects of having less memory for other things against this though, as you may gain template speed at the expense of something else. The maximum size that it can be set to is 128.

You can also change how often templates are refreshed in memory. By default they are refreshed every 30 minutes, but adding the following registry key can change this:

```
HKEY_LOCAL_MACHINE\SOFTWARE\Microsoft\MSSQLServer\Client\SQLXMLX\
TemplateCacheExpiration
```

You might want to change this value to a larger one if the templates are not being changed.

> **The usual warnings apply here about editing the registry. Doing so can be dangerous and may leave the machine in a no-bootable state. Make changes with care and make a back-up first.**

is-xml

The `is-xml` attribute is a new attribute that can be set as part of a parameter to say whether the parameter value is a string of text or whether it can contain XML. This allows XML or HTML characters to be passed to SQL Server without them being translated first. The attribute can take a value of 0 or 1, and is used like so:

```
<sql:param name=parameter1 is-xml=0></sql:param>
```

When set to `1`, the parameter value may contain XML and should be used without any translation. When set to `0`, the parameter value is treated as a string – in other words, it is treated as it would have been prior to the Web Release.

For example, if you wanted to pass the string `"£5000"` to SQL Server, it would have first been translated to `"£5000"` before being passed. By using `is-xml=1` it will be passed unchanged.

NULL Attributes

The `nullvalue` attribute is another new attribute that can be set, as part of the header, to allow `NULL` values to be passed in parameters. It is used in the form:

```
<sql:header sql:nullvalue='IsNULL'>
```

When this is set in the header, you can then pass `NULL` parameter values within the URL – for example:

http://.../mytemplate.xml?myparm=IsNULL

This will be translated by the template into the value `NULL`. Before Web Release 1, we would have had to use a magic value, and then make our stored procedures or SQL statements interpret this value and translate it to `NULL` themselves.

For example, if we wanted to create a new `Categories` record but didn't know what the `Picture` field was for it yet, before the Web Release we would have had to code our template along the lines of:

```
<ROOT xmlns:sql="urn:schemas-microsoft-com:xml-sql">
   <sql:header>
      <sql:param name='CategoryName'> </sql:param>
      <sql:param name='Description'> </sql:param>
      <sql:param name='Picture'> </sql:param>
   </sql:header>

  <sql:query>
      IF @Picture = 'NULLMagicValue'
         INSERT INTO Categories
         VALUES (@CategoryName,@Description,NULL)
      ELSE
         INSERT INTO Categories
         VALUES (@CategoryName,@Description,CONVERT(varbinary, @Picture))
  </sql:query>
</ROOT>
```

We could then pass in the parameters using the following URL:

http://localhost/xmltemplates/template/NewCategory.xml?CategoryName=Specialities&
Description=Speciality+Foods&Picture=NULLMagicValue

This has to specially test the value of the `@Picture` parameter for a special magic value and then translate this into a `NULL`. We can now greatly simplify this by using the `sql:nullvalue` attribute as below:

```
<ROOT xmlns:sql="urn:schemas-microsoft-com:xml-sql">
   <sql:header sql:nullvalue="IsNULL" >
      <sql:param name='CategoryName'> </sql:param>
      <sql:param name='Description'> </sql:param>
      <sql:param name='Picture'> </sql:param>
   </sql:header>
  <sql:query>
      INSERT INTO Categories
      VALUES (@CategoryName,@Description,CONVERT(varbinary, @Picture))
   </sql:query>
</ROOT>
```

Save it as `NewCategorynull.xml` and use this URL to execute it:

http://localhost/xmltemplates/template/NewCategorynull.xml?CategoryName=Specialities
&Description=Speciality+Foods&Picture=IsNULL

As you can see, the code within the template is much simpler and also more efficient to run.

Summary

In this chapter, we have taken an in-depth look at XML templates which allow the running of SQL queries directly from a URL but have the added security of not exposing the actual query to the user. We have described how to configure the IIS virtual directory for SQL Server to allow template queries to be run.

We then went through all the different types of queries that can be run from within an XML template. These included:

- Simple `SELECT` statements
- Executing stored procedures
- Running other types of SQL statements such as `UPDATE`s
- Passing parameters into the template to allow passing values into the SQL statements or stored procedures
- Running XPath queries against XML views
- Using XSL stylesheets to format the output from the query

We then went on to discuss all the new features and improvements that Microsoft has introduced in their Web Release 1 for SQL Server 2000.

In this chapter we only briefly looked at the use of XPath queries within templates. In the next chapter, XPath is discussed in much more detail.

8

XPath

XML is technically limited in that it is impossible to query or navigate through an XML document using XML alone. XPath overcomes this limitation. XPath is a navigational query language specified by the World Wide Web Consortium (W3C) for locating data within an XML document. It was created for use with XSLT and XPointer, as well as other components of XML like the upcoming XQuery specification. All of these technologies require some tool which enables querying and navigation within the structure of an XML document. XPath version 1.0 is now an official W3C Recommendation and is, therefore, a recognized standard web technology along with HTML, XHTML, and XML itself.

One of the most important uses of XPath is in combination with XSLT, as described briefly in Chapter 1. XPath is used to query XML documents, then XSLT is used to transform the resulting XML into an HTML document (for display in any format desired) or any other form of XML (for import into another program that may use a different set of XML tags).

> **Before going any further, a disclaimer: this chapter is not a definitive or complete XPath tutorial or reference. Rather it is a technical introduction specifically geared towards the XPath support in SQL Server.**

For a complete XPath tutorial, see the many examples on the web or Beginning XML *by David Hunter et al. (Wrox Press, ISBN 1861003412). For reference purposes, see the XPath document on the W3C web site at* http://www.w3c.org/TR/XPath.

Why the "Path"?

The word "path" refers to XPath's use of a **location path** to locate the desired parts of an XML document. This concept is similar to the path used to locate a file in the directories of a file system, or the path specified in a URL in a web browser to locate a specific page in a complex web site.

To explain a bit further, consider the tree representation of an XML document described in Chapter 1:

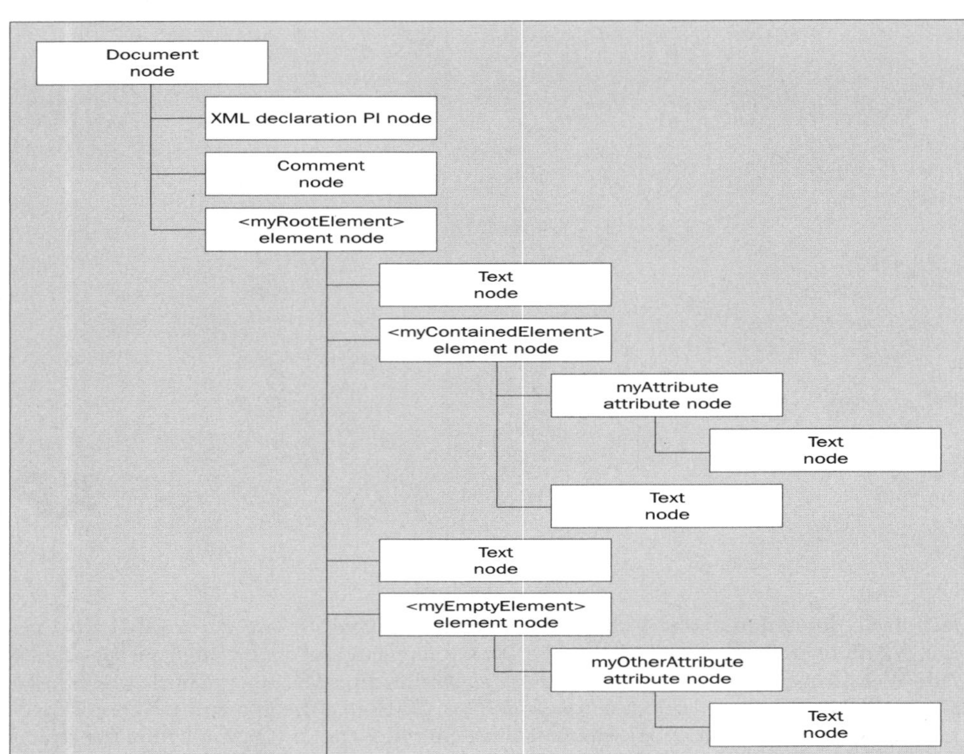

The tree begins at the root and **nodes** are located at the branches and leaves of the tree. An XPath query returns a **node set**, which is a set of nodes that match the query. The location path – the most basic form of XPath query – specifies a path through the branches of the tree. For example, this query conceptually navigates through the tree beginning at `Root` (note that `Root` is not a keyword; we could name the root anything), then travelling to `Element1`, and then to `Element2`:

```
/Root/Element1/Element2
```

The reality is a little more complicated since the query finds *all* `Element2` children having `Element1` parents deriving from `Root`. However, you get the basic idea and we'll explain a bit more of the detail when we're ready to show some sample queries.

SQL Server XPath Support

SQL Server 2000 implements a subset of the full W3C XPath 1.0 specification. For example, the root query (beginning with /) is one of the first operations mentioned in a typical XPath tutorial, but is not supported in SQL Server 2000.

While differences like these will seem strange at first if you have some existing XPath experience, you'll find there is still a tremendous amount that you can accomplish within the framework of XPath as it has been implemented in SQL Server 2000. We'll present more specifics of the unsupported features a little later on in this chapter.

The material in this chapter is based on SQL Server 2000 and XML for SQL Server Web Release 1 (download information is described in Chapter 9). XML for SQL Server Web Release 1 has only minor updates for XPath support, so it really doesn't make a lot of difference for the purposes of this chapter whether you've updated to Web Release 1 or not.

> *The subject of this chapter is XPath as it is used to query data in SQL Server. SQL Server has another facility for importing XML documents – the `OPENXML` function, described in Chapter 4. One of the arguments to `OPENXML` is an XPath query. `OPENXML` uses a different implementation of XPath, leveraging much more of the XPath 1.0 standard, because it is targeted at XML documents. This implementation is based directly on the MSXML parser, and its XPath support level will depend on what version of MSXML is installed. SQL Server 2000 shipped with MSXML 2.6. Don't confuse the various MSXML web releases with the XML For SQL web releases – they are different.*

Using XPath in SQL Server

There are several different ways of using XPath to query SQL Server data:

- Direct database object access from the URL, as described in Chapter 2
- Querying against annotated XDR schemas from the URL, described in detail in Chapter 5
- By embedding XPath queries in templates for use from the URL, as described in Chapters 2 and 7

We'll look at each of these with some examples but, first, let's review what is needed to set up XPath access.

Setting Up SQL Server for XPath

For all XPath usage except for `OPENXML`, the requirements for XPath are as follows:

- Set up a virtual directory named `NW` for URL access, as described in Chapter 5.
- Be sure to enable the Allow XPath option on the Settings tab for each virtual directory where XPath access is desired.
- Set up a virtual name of the proper type (`dbobject` for direct database object access, `schema` for annotated XDR schemas, and `template` for templates) for each virtual directory where XPath access is desired. We will use the following virtual names within the `NW` virtual directory:
    - `Dbobject` is the virtual name associated with direct database object access.
    - `XDR` is the virtual name associated with the schema.
    - `Template` is the virtual name associated with template access.

Sample XDR Schema

Most of the sample XPath queries in this chapter will be based on the following XDR schema, which creates an XML tree view of the customers, orders, and order details in the `Northwind` sample database. Save this code as `try_xpath.xdr`:

```
<?xml version="1.0" ?>
<Schema xmlns="urn:schemas-microsoft-com:xml-data"
        xmlns:dt="urn:schemas-microsoft-com:datatypes"
        xmlns:sql="urn:schemas-microsoft-com:xml-sql">
  <ElementType name="Customer" sql:relation="Customers">
    <AttributeType name="CustomerID" dt:type="id" />
    <AttributeType name="CompanyName" />
    <AttributeType name="ContactName" />
    <AttributeType name="Orders" dt:type="idrefs" sql:id-prefix="Order-"/>
    <attribute type="CustomerID" />
    <attribute type="CompanyName" />
    <attribute type="ContactName" />
    <attribute type="Orders" sql:relation="Orders" sql:field="OrderID">
      <sql:relationship key-relation="Customers" key="CustomerID"
                foreign-relation="Orders" foreign-key="CustomerID" />
    </attribute>
    <element type="Order">
      <sql:relationship key-relation="Customers" key="CustomerID"
               foreign-relation="Orders" foreign-key="CustomerID" />
    </element>
  </ElementType>
  <ElementType name="Order" sql:relation="Orders">
    <AttributeType name="OrderID" dt:type="id" sql:id-prefix="Order-" />
    <AttributeType name="OrderDate" />
    <attribute type="OrderID" />
    <attribute type="OrderDate" />
    <element type="OrderDetail">
      <sql:relationship key-relation="Orders" key="OrderID"
                foreign-relation="[Order Details]" foreign-key="OrderID" />
    </element>
  </ElementType>
  <ElementType name="OrderDetail" sql:relation="[Order Details]"
                                  sql:key-fields="OrderID ProductID">
    <AttributeType name="ProductID" dt:type="idref"
                                    sql:id-prefix="Product-" />
    <AttributeType name="UnitPrice"/>
    <AttributeType name="Quantity" />

    <attribute type="ProductID" />
    <attribute type="UnitPrice" sql:field="UnitPrice" />
    <attribute type="Quantity" />
    <element type="Discount"  sql:field="Discount"/>
  </ElementType>
  <ElementType name="Discount" dt:type="string"
                               sql:relation="[Order Details]"/>
</Schema>
```

To try out the queries, enter them at the web browser as follows:

http://localhost/NW/XDR/try_xpath.xdr/**xpathquery**?root=root

Where the actual XPath query is substituted in place of **xpathquery**.

SQL Server XPath Syntax

SQL Server 2000 supports the following XPath 1.0 features:

- Location paths
- Abbreviated and unabbreviated XPath syntax
- Child, parent (`..`), self (`.`), and attribute (`@`) directional axes
- Boolean-valued predicates
- Multiple and nested predicates
- Relational operators: `=`, `!=`, `<`, `<=`, `>`, `>=`
- Arithmetic operators: `+`, `-`, `*`, `div` (/ is used for root)
- Conversion functions: `number()`, `string()`, `boolean()`
- Boolean operators and functions: `AND`, `OR`, `true()`, `false()`, `not()`
- XPath data types
- XPath variables

These terms are explained below with examples of their use in SQL Server using the sample schema.

Location Path

This is the path to the nodes of interest within the XML document. A straight location path without qualifiers will return all the nodes (and their children) that satisfy the given path. Consider the XML tree view of the customers, orders, and order details created by `try_xpath.xdr`, showing just the elements for clarity:

```
<Customer>
  <Order>
    <OrderDetail>
      <Discount>
      </Discount>
    </OrderDetail>
  </Order>
</Customer>
```

This location path returns all the `Customer` nodes with their children, grandchildren, etc. elements:

```
Customer
```

Try it by entering this query in your browser:

http://localhost/NW/XDR/try_xpath.xdr/Customer?root=root

The results are:

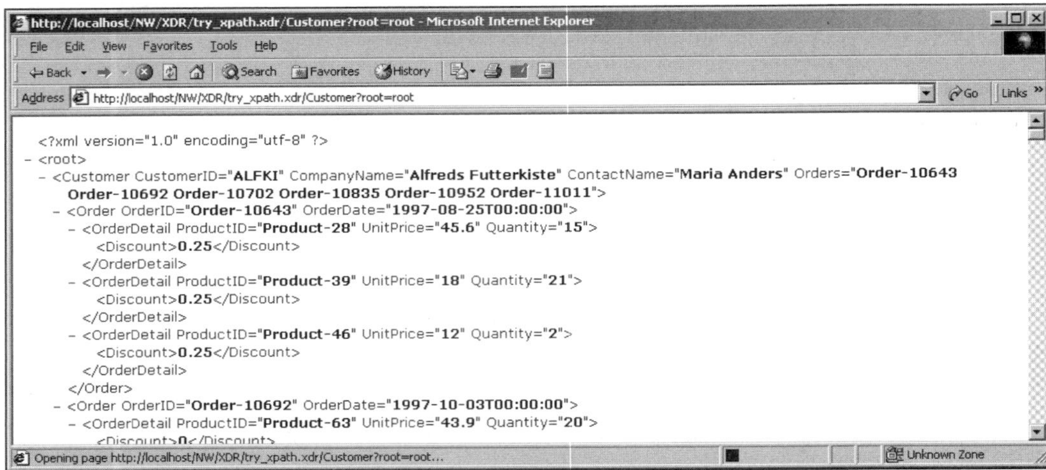

Now try this XPath query:

```
Customer/Order/OrderDetail
```

This returns the `OrderDetail` nodes (and `Discount` children of those nodes) having `Customer` grandparents and `Order` parents. Try it by entering:

http://localhost/NW/XDR/try_xpath.xdr/**Customer/Order/OrderDetail**?root=root

As shown here:

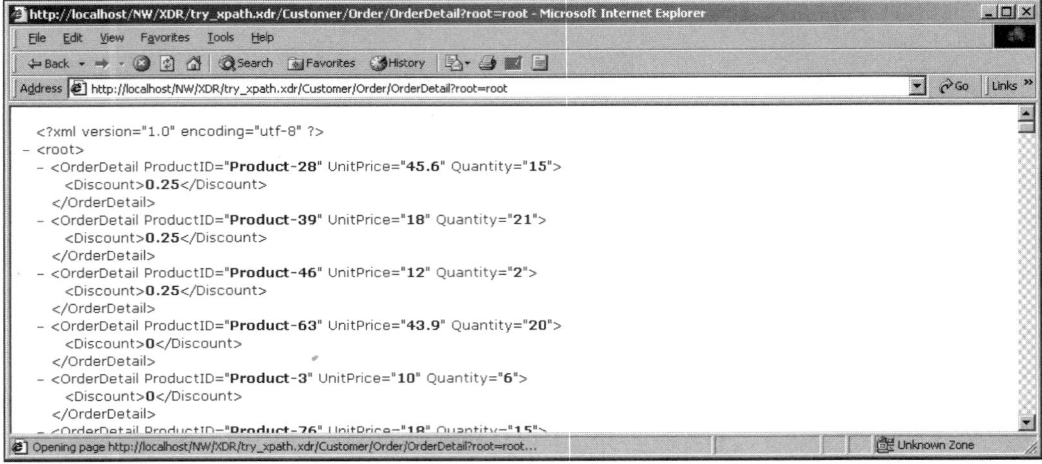

Finally, this XPath query:

```
Customer/Order/OrderDetail/Discount
```

returns only the `Discount` nodes, which have no children, as they are at the bottom level of the hierarchy defined in our schema:

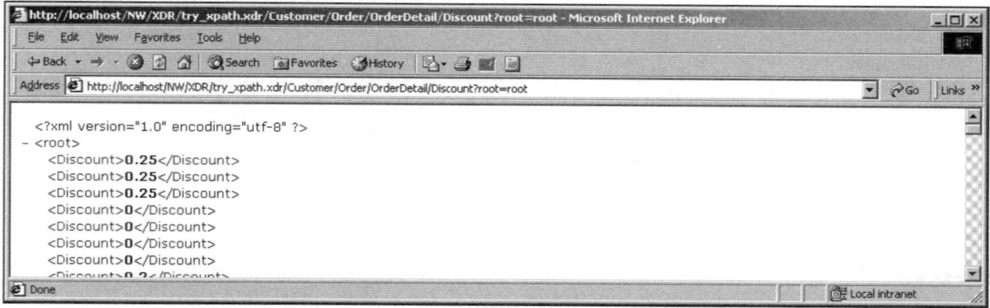

Abbreviated and Unabbreviated Syntax

XPath supports abbreviated and unabbreviated forms of query syntax. The queries shown so far are in the abbreviated form, which most people prefer to use because of its simplicity. The last query in the previous section could be written in the unabbreviated form as follows:

```
/child::ROOT/child::Customer/child::Order/child::OrderDetails/child::Discount
```

This quickly becomes tedious, as you can imagine. Most queries specify children, so XPath defaults to `child::` if the directional axis (see the next section) is not specified.

SQL Server 2000 supports the unabbreviated syntax for all implemented features of XPath, but we will use the abbreviated syntax throughout this chapter because it is what XML developers actually use in practice. Also, it is not clear that the unabbreviated form will be fully supported in future developments such as XQuery.

Directional Axes

Each node within an XML document has a directional relationship with other nodes. You can picture the relationships for a single node – the **context node** – using the following diagram:

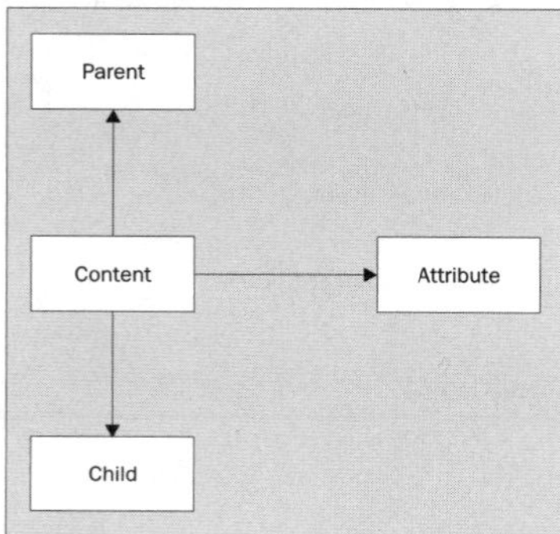

Each of the directions from the context node (up, down, sideways) is called an **axis**. All XPath navigation occurs along one of these axes. The up direction is the parent axis. The down direction is the child axis. The sideways direction, if the current node is an element, is the attribute axis.

This is simplified a bit as XPath specifies additional axes for preceding or following nodes, preceding or following siblings, etc. However, the support for these is limited in SQL Server 2000, so we'll not cover them here.

Context Node

The context node of an XPath navigation is the starting node, which may be the root or another node within the document. All XPath navigation starts from the context node if not otherwise specified. When accessing XML views of SQL Server data using any of the URL access modes (XDR schemas, direct database object, or templates), the context node may be any of the top-level elements or tables available in the schema.

Child Axis

The child axis is the default axis as previously noted, so it has no abbreviation (it is `child::` in the unabbreviated form). The abbreviated location path:

```
X/Y/Z
```

Is equivalent to the unabbreviated:

```
child::X/child::Y/child::Z
```

Parent Axis

The parent axis is specified with a double period (`..`) just as within a file system path (and is `parent::` in the unabbreviated form). This query:

```
Discount/../OrderDetail
```

Finds the parent of `Discount` and then navigates back to the `OrderDetail` elements:

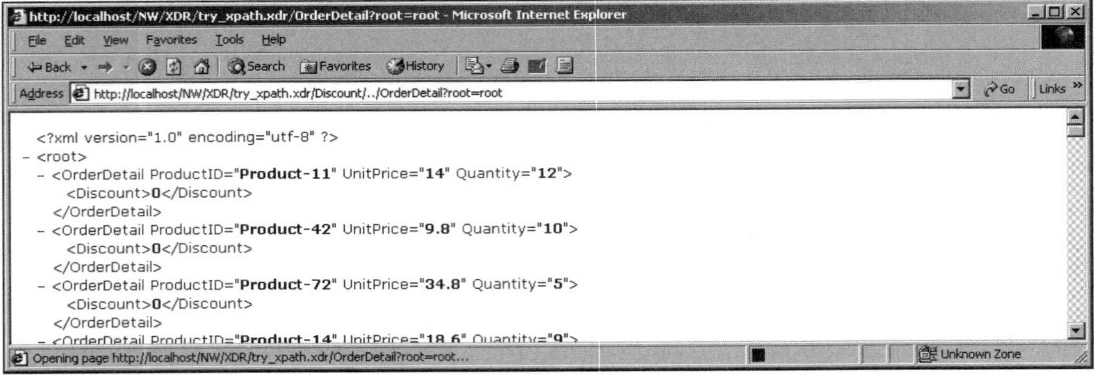

Self Axis

A single period (`.`) is a self-reference to the current node (and is an abbreviation for `self::`). As you can imagine, it is rarely used in XPath queries in SQL Server.

Attribute Axis

The attribute axis is specified with `@` (and is `attribute::` in the unabbreviated form). This query:

```
Customer/@ContactName
```

selects the `ContactName` attributes from the `Customer` elements in the sample schema. If we try it in the browser, we produce an error message, as shown:

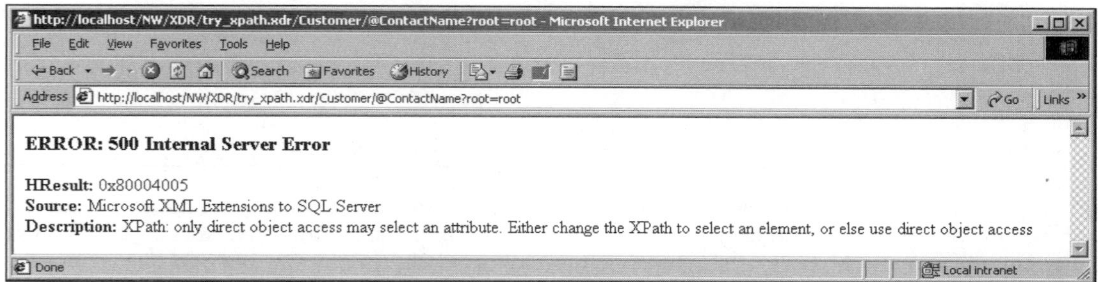

However, we can specify attributes in a direct database object query, as the message suggests. If we try this instead:

http://localhost/NW/dbobject/Customers/@ContactName?root=root

we get some results, but they don't look particularly useful:

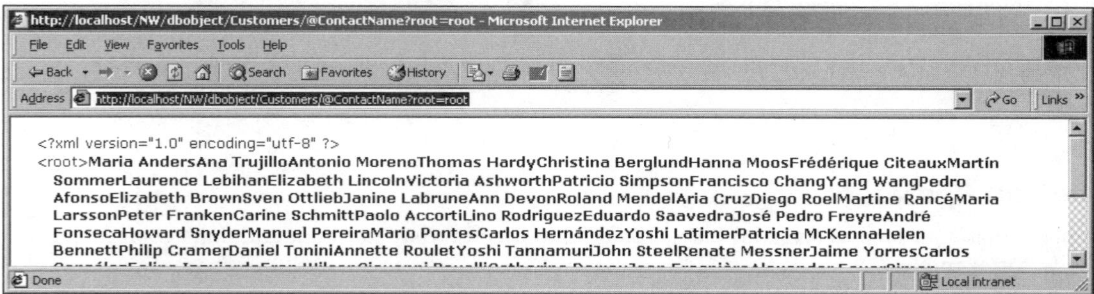

There is one very good reason to directly reference attributes. Doing this allows us to reference binary data such as pictures. This is described later in this chapter in the section entitled *Direct Linking to Binary Attributes*. Otherwise, to really do something useful with attributes, we need to use predicates.

Predicates

Location paths are a fairly limited query capability by themselves. To make queries interesting you need search conditions, or **predicates** as they are called in XPath. If you are familiar with SQL, an XPath predicate corresponds to the `WHERE` clause as a means of selecting data that matches specific criteria. You can specify predicates in XPath for each element in the location path, by specifying an expression within square brackets (`[]`). For example, this query finds the `Orders` with a `Quantity` attribute greater than `10`:

```
Customer/Order/OrderDetail[@Quantity>10]
```

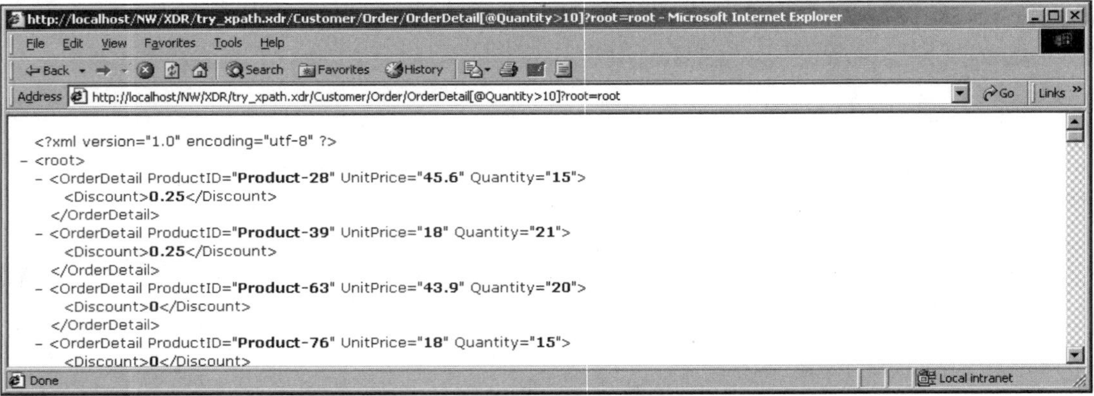

SQL Server 2000 specifically supports **Boolean predicates**. By Boolean predicates we mean that the expression within the square brackets must evaluate to `TRUE` or `FALSE`. The XPath specification allows numeric predicates – as in `Order[3]`, meaning the third order child element – but SQL Server does not support this as document order cannot always be guaranteed from the underlying relational data.

Relational Operators

Typical predicates use the relational operators (=, !=, <, <=, >, >=) to compare attribute values:

```
[@UnitPrice <= 50]
[@CustomerID='XXXXX']
```

If you're used to SQL or Visual Basic, remember that XPath uses != instead of <> for not equal:

```
[@Country != 'USA']
```

Boolean Operators

Boolean operators such as `AND` and `OR` can be used to specify what you want and don't want in query results, for example:

```
OrderDetail[@Quantity >10 and @UnitPrice < 5]
```

Watch out for issues with embedded spaces in some browsers. Microsoft Internet Explorer takes care of this automatically, converting:
http://localhost/NW/XDR/try_xpath.xdr/OrderDetail[@Quantity > 10 and @UnitPrice < 5]?root=root

into the following, with the %20 codes for embedded spaces:

http://localhost/NW/XDR/try_xpath.xdr/OrderDetail[@Quantity%20>%2010%20and%20@UnitPrice%20<%205]?root=root

Arithmetic Operators

While numeric-valued predicates are unsupported, you can still use the usual range of arithmetic operators (+, -, *, div) for calculations inside expressions, as long as the result resolves to a TRUE or FALSE value. Notice the use of div to avoid conflict with / as used for URL and path separators:

```
OrderDetail[(@Quantity div 10) < @UnitPrice]
```

While this particular query doesn't make a lot of sense, it shows what you can do. Note that parentheses for nesting are supported.

Multiple and Successive Predicates

Multiple predicates can be used in a single query. For example, this query returns only elements having both a particular CustomerID and ProductID:

```
Customer[@CustomerID='ALFKI']/Order/OrderDetail[@ProductID='Product-28']
```

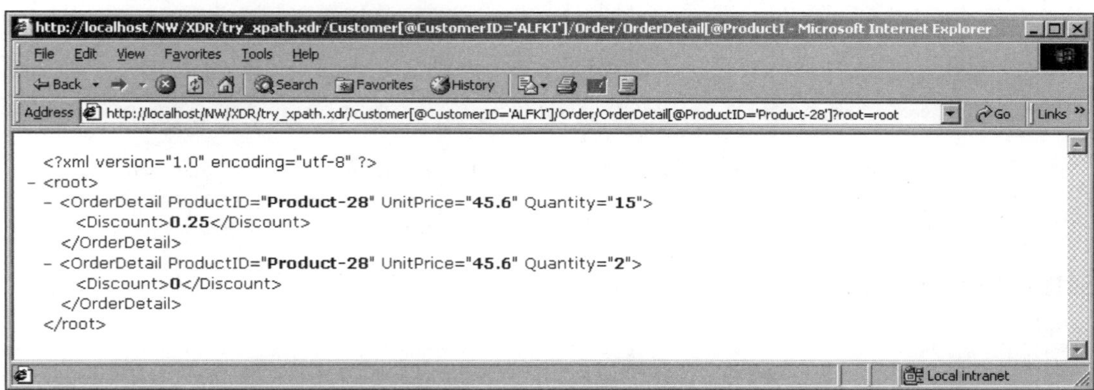

Successive predicates can also be used with several different predicates being applied to the same element in the path. For example, this query returns only elements having both a particular CustomerID and ProductID:

```
OrderDetail[@Quantity>10][@UnitPrice < 5]
```

This is equivalent to the same query made with an AND in the expression, as both predicates must evaluate to TRUE to satisfy the query.

Location Path Predicates

Predicates may contain location paths and these evaluate to TRUE or FALSE depending on the existence of nodes that satisfy the path. For example this returns all customers who have orders:

```
Customer[Order]
```

The path inside the predicate can have multiple elements just like any XPath location path. For instance, we previously executed a query to find `OrderDetails` with `Quantity` attributes greater than `10`. It is likely that you would want to see the `Order` that goes with each `OrderDetail`. Specifying a location path within the predicate can achieve this:

```
Customer/Order[OrderDetail/@Quantity>10]
```

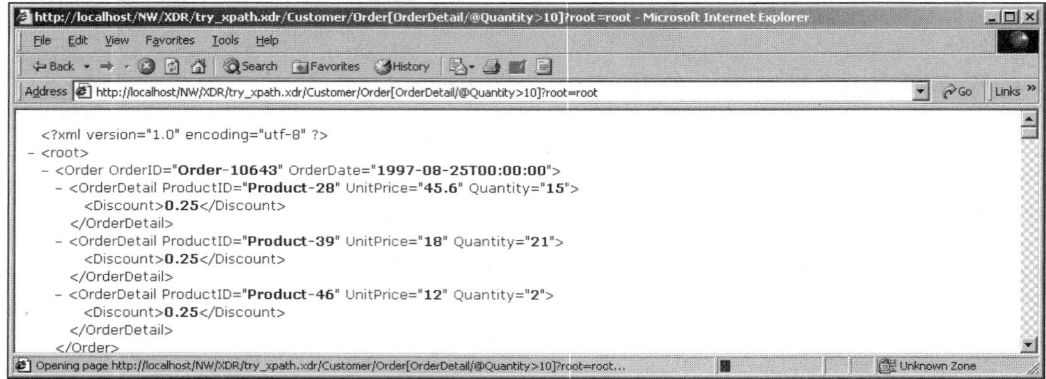

You might ask why the `OrderDetail` with a `Quantity` of 2 has been returned. SQL Server is doing what was asked of it. It has returned all `Orders` which have at least one `OrderDetail` with a `Quantity` greater than `10`.

Nested Predicates

Another way of specifying the previous query is to nest predicates within one another:

```
Customer/Order[OrderDetail[@Quantity>10]]
```

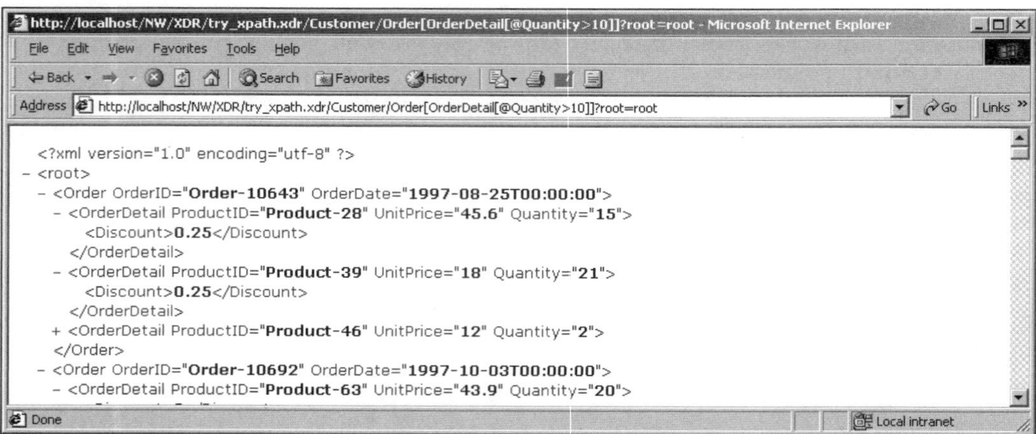

Functions

XPath provides a set of functions for use in queries. Functions in XPath look like functions in most programming languages – the function name followed by the function arguments in parentheses. The number of supported functions is currently limited in SQL Server 2000.

Boolean Functions

The Boolean functions `true()` and `false()` return `TRUE` and `FALSE` respectively. The `not()` Boolean function negates its argument expression. `not()` is especially handy with location path predicates. For example, recall this query:

```
Customer[Order]
```

It returns all customers who have orders. Most customers in the `Northwind` database have orders, so it's hard to tell whether this query's results are different to those that would have been generated if we had just asked for all of the customers. It is more interesting to find the customers who do not have orders, and this is easy with the `not()` function:

```
Customer[not(Order)]
```

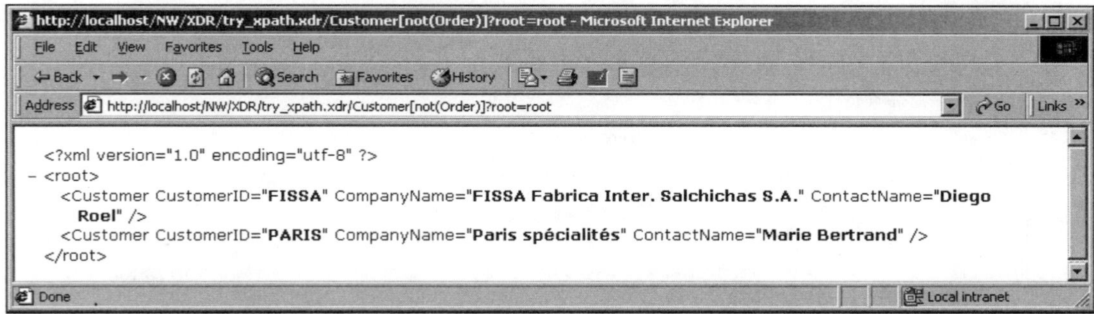

Conversion Functions

Conversion functions such as `number()`, `string()`, and `boolean()` convert their arguments to a value with a data type of number, string, and Boolean, respectively. Data type conversion is an issue worthy of more detailed discussion.

XPath Data Types and Type Conversions

The values manipulated in an XPath query always belong to these four data types:

- **Boolean** – a `TRUE` or `FALSE` value
- **number** – a floating point number
- **string** – character data
- **node-set** – a list of nodes (elements and attributes), such as the result of an XPath query

XPath converts liberally between data types during query processing. For example, the location path predicates depend on the type conversion from a node-set to Boolean. An empty node set is converted to a `FALSE` Boolean value, so the expression predicate in a query such as `Customer[Orders]` returns `FALSE` if there are no matching nodes. Similarly, an empty character string is converted to a `FALSE` Boolean value. A zero numeric value evaluates as `FALSE`. Non-zero numeric values evaluate as `TRUE`.

The set of XPath data types is quite limited when compared to the data types implemented in SQL Server and in XDR. There are no integer or fixed-decimal numbers, no dates or times, nor other complex data types. Instead, SQL Server and XDR data types are liberally converted to the basic data types during XPath query processing. In almost all cases, the implicit type conversions automatically happen and the query works transparently without intervention. However, some of the conversions are not obvious.

For example, dates and times are converted to strings within XPath. The string format chosen is specifically designed to allow string-based queries to give correct results most of the time. For example, we can issue an XPath query on `OrderDate` to find the orders placed after `1997`, as follows:

```
Order[@OrderDate>'1997']
```

The results of this XPath query are shown here (with some of the `Order` nodes collapsed so that several dates can be seen at once):

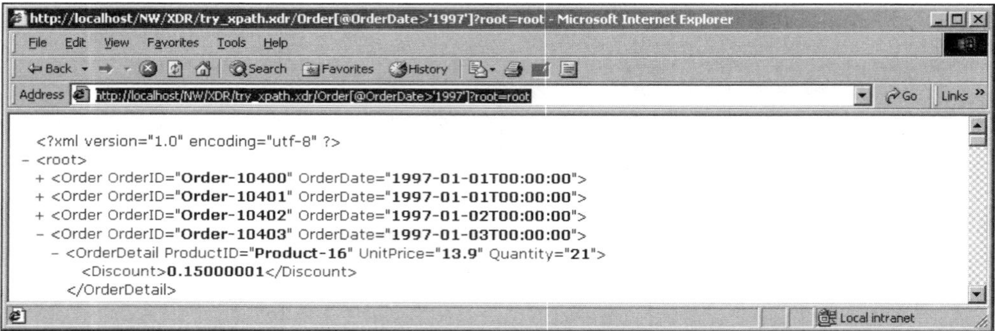

Because date and time columns are converted to strings in a YYYY-DD-MM format, we can issue more precise queries, such as:

```
Order[@OrderDate>'1997-08-15']
```

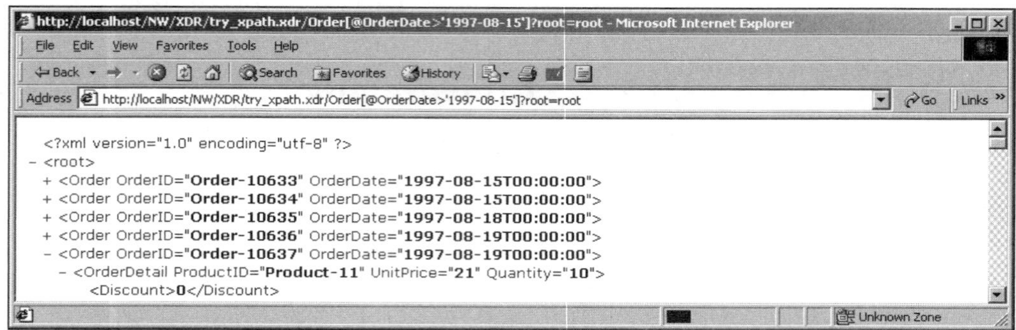

However, if you forget the quotation marks around the date, as in:

```
Order[@OrderDate>1997]
```

incorrect results will be returned:

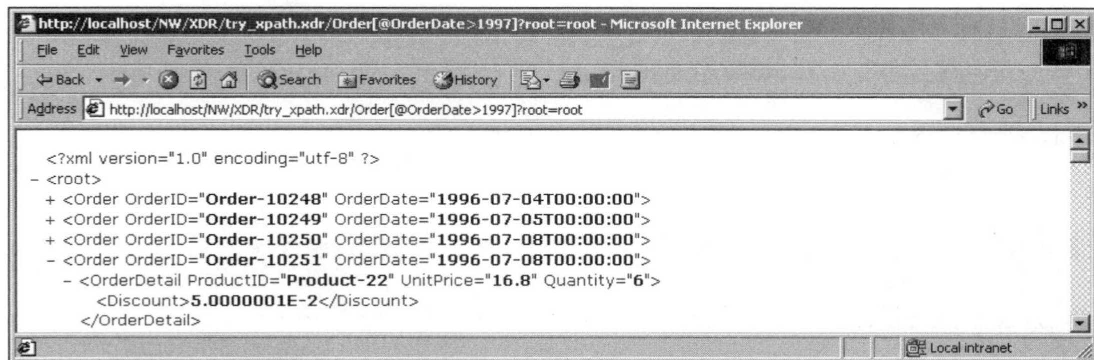

Data type conversions have a potential performance impact, especially for primary key columns. When an XPath query is processed, data is first converted from the SQL type to the XDR type, and then to the XPath type. In XML for SQL Server Web Release 1, XPath queries now use the `sql:datatype` tag to reduce the number of type conversions needed, improving performance for primary key columns. The `sql:datatype` tag can now be specified for all SQL Server data types.

XPath Variables

XPath variables are used in XPath queries within templates, to pass in query elements from the URL without requiring that the user enter an entire valid XPath query expression. By hiding the details of the query, this technique also enhances security.

Templates and template parameters were first introduced in Chapter 2. We'll look at a template like those in Chapters 2 and 7, with the addition of an embedded XPath query. Name the following template `try_xpath_var.xml` and save it in the `Template` virtual name of the `NW` virtual directory:

```
<ROOT xmlns:sql="urn:schemas-microsoft-com:xml-sql">
 <sql:header>
   <sql:param name='CID'>ALFKI</sql:param>
 </sql:header>
 <sql:xpath-query mapping-schema="../schemas/try_xpath.xdr">
  Customer[@CustomerID=$CID]
 </sql:xpath-query>
</ROOT>
```

Be sure to change the path of the `mapping-schema` attribute to match that to the folder containing your virtual name files.

The <sql:param> tag specifies an XPath variable, and the value between the opening and closing tags is the default value. Within the XPath query inside the template, variables are dereferenced with the dollar ($) prefix:

```
Customer[@CustomerID=$CID]
```

The value of the variable `CID` will be used as the search condition for the `CustomerID` attribute.

The URL to query this template with parameters is:

http://localhost/NW/Template/try_xpath_var.xml?CID=LINOD

Here are the results:

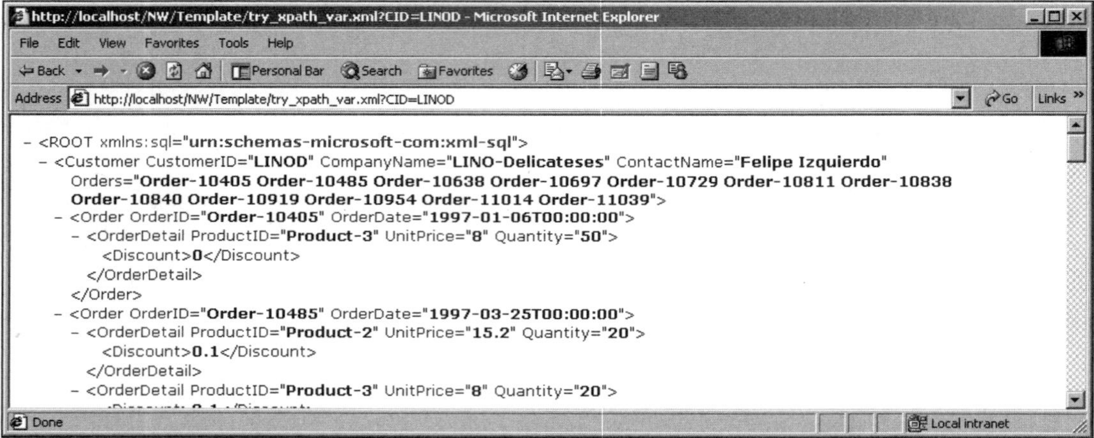

Unsupported Syntax

Not all of XPath 1.0 is supported in SQL Server 2000 or XML for SQL Server Web Release 1. Unsupported operations include:

- Wildcard (*) queries, as in `XXX/*/YYY`.
- The union operator (|).
- The root query (/). Every SQL Server XPath query must begin at a top-level `<ElementType>` in the schema.
- Positional selection, as in `XXX[3]`. Indeed, all numeric-valued predicates are unsupported.
- Axial operations that depend on document order: `following`, `following-sibling`, `namespace`, `preceding`, `preceding-sibling`.
- Axial ancestor operations other than parent-child: `ancestor`, `ancestor-or-self`, `descendant`, `descendant-or-self` (//).
- The `mod` arithmetic operator.

- String functions: string(), concat(), starts-with(), contains(), substring-before(), substring-after(), substring(), string-length(), normalize(), translate().
- The lang() Boolean function.
- The numeric functions: sum(), floor(), ceiling(), and round().
- Cross-product queries such as Customer[Order/@OrderDate=Order/@ShippedDate]. This query selects all customers with any order for which the OrderDate equals the ShippedDate of any order. However, SQL Server 2000 *does* support queries such as Customer[Order[@OrderDate=@ShippedDate]], which selects customers with any order for which the OrderDate equals its ShippedDate.

Most of these functions are supported in the XPath queries used in OPENXML, except for the document-order axial operations: following, following-sibling, preceding, preceding-sibling.

Other SQL Server XPath Topics

Before finishing the chapter, we'll take a quick run through the following issues:

- Errors
- Security
- XPath and FOR XML EXPLICIT
- Direct linking to binary attributes

Errors

What happens if an XPath query finds no data? The W3C XPath specification defines no error conditions. XPath queries that fail to select any nodes return an empty node-set. For example, this query finds no data and returns an empty node set, except for the root node specified directly on the URL:

```
Customer[@CustomerID='NotThere']
```

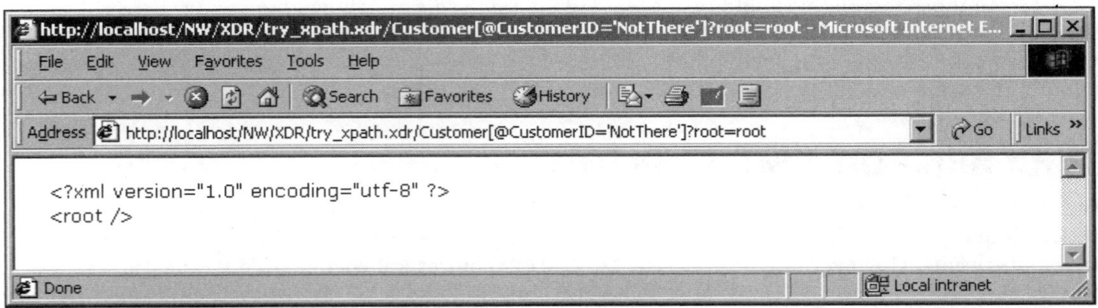

Many queries return actual error messages if the query specifies an unsupported syntax or a schema element that is missing. For example, this query:

```
Customers
```

returns the following:

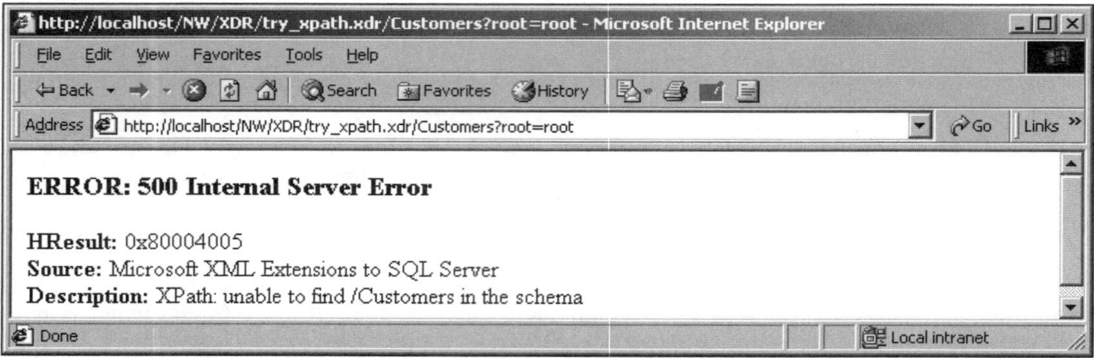

Actually, the error information returned here goes beyond the W3C specification. A compliant implementation could just return an empty node set for any error condition!

Security

The problem with allowing direct access to the database is security, of course. Any SQL Server data available to the login defined for the virtual directory is available on the Internet! Once a user sees how the XPath query is constructed for an operation like accessing an image, it's not hard for the user to figure out how to construct an XPath query to get at some other database object.

To prevent this, several levels of protection can be set up. You could just disallow XPath queries but that prevents XDR schema queries from working. At the database level, access could be restricted to just the tables and/or columns that are public, but this is inconvenient and may require involving more people than you want to add to the project.

In any case, make sure that the users identified in virtual directories have appropriate (for example read-only) access to the database.

The best practice is to use templates and to not provide direct database object access. Templates with embedded XPath queries hide the structure of the database from prying eyes. Template names and parameters to those templates should be all that URL-based users are allowed to see or change. XDR schemas also enable the hiding of the details. Support for XPath variables in SQL Server lets the user supply parameters for the query without the details of the query being visible (see the *XPath Variables* section in this chapter).

XPath and FOR XML EXPLICIT

XPath in SQL Server allows much of the flexibility that the SQL Server `FOR XML EXPLICIT` syntax offers. The XPath query processor with SQL Server 2000 actually creates a `FOR XML EXPLICIT` query internally to generate its results. However, use of `FOR XML EXPLICIT` requires knowledge of SQL and SQL Server Transact-SQL in particular. XPath is more familiar to Internet and XML developers, and some web users find XPath easier to use, especially in URL-based queries.

Direct Linking to Binary Attributes

In the recent past, an application using binary data from a database would require that some application code be written using ADO or a similar database API. This code would execute the query to locate the desired data and then extract it chunk by chunk into a memory buffer, where it could be written to a file or otherwise manipulated. Not fun!

The XPath direct database object support allows us to take a binary database object such as an image and put a direct link to it on a web page – no application code or storage in an intermediate file is required! Let's see this in action with a simple web page that shows the picture of Laura Callahan (employee number 8 in the `Northwind` database):

```
<html>
<body>
Hi, this is Laura!
<img src="NW/dbobject/Employees[@EmployeeID=8]/@Photo">
</body>
</html>
```

Save this text as `Laura.html` in the root directory of your web server (most likely `C:\Inetpub\wwwroot`) and then enter this URL:

http://localhost/Laura.html

Not bad for a one-liner:

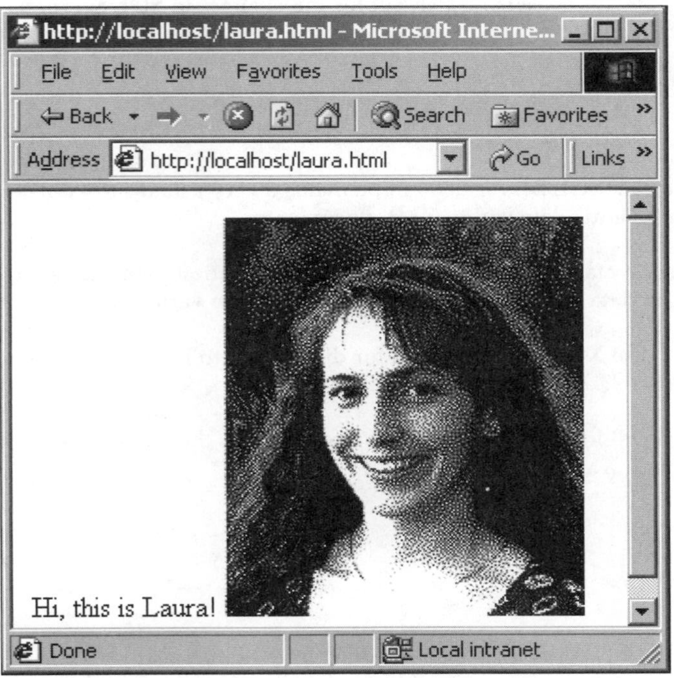

The Future of XPath

SQL Server's support for XPath will probably continue to evolve with performance enhancements and a more complete XPath 1.0 implementation.

XML for SQL Server Web Release 2, expected in late 2001, is likely to implement support for all of the XPath string functions and, indeed, most of the XPath 1.0 keywords and functions that have not yet been implemented. Because of the intrinsic data type differences between SQL Server and XPath, not every behavior or nuance is likely to be completely supported.

XPath itself will also continue to evolve. As this was written, requirements for version 2.0 of XPath were in working draft stage (http://www.w3c.org/TR/XPath20req.html). While it is extremely speculative to predict specifics from such an early draft, it is clear that XPath 2.0 will improve ease of use and add more functionality for supporting other XML components, with many of the new features directed to supporting XQuery and XML Schema. New SQL-like data query capabilities are likely, such as:

- Additional aggregation functions (`min()`, `max()`, and others – in addition to the existing `sum()` and `count()` in XPath 1.0)
- Set-oriented intersection and difference functions
- Additional string functions.

A stated goal of XPath 2.0 is to maintain as much backwards compatibility as possible with XPath 1.0.

XQuery (http://www.w3c.org/TR/XQuery) will add major new query capabilities to XML that will be of extreme interest to database users. Watch out for big changes to SQL Server as soon as the W3C XQuery standard stabilizes.

Summary

In this chapter we saw that SQL Server 2000 implements a very useful subset of XPath 1.0, the W3C standard language for locating data within XML documents.

We examined the basic syntax of XPath queries, including location paths, axes, predicates, operators, and functions. We discussed data types and type conversions, XPath variables, error handling, and security.

Finally, we saw how to use XPath in web pages for direct links to binary database data, and discussed the future of XPath and the related XQuery standard.

In the next chapter we will look at Updategrams. These give us the ability to modify the contents of a database directly through XML.

9

Updategrams

XML technologies are changing very quickly, and this is the reason why Microsoft has chosen to adopt a web release format for its XML component, MSXML. Microsoft uses this model to publish updates to MSXML on their web site (http://msdn.microsoft.com/xml/default.asp), as opposed to waiting to bundle it with other products or service packs, which have comparatively longer release cycles.

By now, we know that Microsoft has integrated XML into SQL Server 2000 to help developers build the next generation Web and Enterprise applications. SQL Server 2000 introduced several features for querying a database, receiving the results in XML format, or inserting and updating data through stored procedures and `OPENXML`, or the ability to access SQL Server data over HTTP through a URL or a template file. However, to enhance and keep SQL Server 2000 XML support up-to-date, like MSXML, here also Microsoft has decided to follow the Web Release model.

In mid-February 2001, Microsoft announced the XML for SQL Server Web Release 1 (WR1). The major highlights of this release include two new features: **Updategrams** and **Bulk Load**. In this chapter, we will take a detailed look at Updategrams and see how they can be used to seamlessly update our databases over HTTP. Let's first start with a quick overview of Web Release 1.

XML for SQL Server 2000 Web Release 1

SQL Server 2000 added a wide array of powerful XML features, for example, retrieving relational data using `FOR XML` clause with `SELECT` statement; ability to access SQL Server data directly over HTTP; writing XML data using `OPENXML` etc. Microsoft has now decided to use the web release format to update XML functionality inside SQL Server, so instead of providing new features and updated functionality through periodic service packs, Microsoft is making SQL Server XML enhancements available on its web site.

After making two betas, the final product release for Web Release 1 (WR 1) was announced in February 2001. This release is available for download at the MSDN download center (http://msdn.microsoft.com/downloads/default.asp). You'll find the download we need in the Microsoft SQL Server node of the Data Access and Databases section. Download and run `xmfosql.exe`, a self-extracting installation file. It is important to remember that the web release will almost always be installed on either the middle tier (web server) or on the client, and not on the SQL Server 2000 machine.

This web release updates the following files: SQL ISAPI extension DLL (`sqlisapi.dll`), IIS Virtual Directory Management for SQL Server (`sqlvdir.dll`), and installs XML Bulk Load for SQL Server (`xmlblkld.dll`) and XML extensions for SQL Server (`sqlxmlx.dll`). In addition, the web release also installs MSXML version 3.0.

> *Note that you can easily check if you already have Web Release 1 installed on your system by looking in* Add/Remove Programs *in Control Panel. There will be an entry* XML for SQL *if it is installed.*

This release also features several minor bug fixes, and enhancements to XML functionality. Let's move on, and learn about Updategrams, an important functionality in this web release.

Updategrams Overview

Updategrams refer to the ability to modify (insert, update, or delete the contents of) a database directly through XML. Updategrams consist of blocks of special XML tags that describe what the data looks like now, and what you want it to look like once the Updategram has been executed.

> *Some early SQL Server documentation, and indeed other documents, referred to Updategrams as "XML grams" or "Update grams" (note the space) or simply "Grams".*

Before Updategrams were introduced, the only way to use an XML document to directly modify a database was to use the `OPENXML` feature, which we looked at in Chapter 4.

Updategrams offer us a useful alternative to `OPENXML`. Apart from the performance benefits, they also streamline the use of schemas to perform database updates over HTTP. Updategrams also require less programming, and are much simpler to use than `OPENXML`. For example, with `OPENXML`, the syntax is a little complicated; we have to deal with document handles, and also worry about calling `sp_xml_removedocument` to remove internal representation of the XML document from memory.

Another point to note is that since `OPENXML` loads the entire XML document into memory (and keeps it there until we close the handle), it's not an efficient mechanism and is not suited to working with large XML documents, as it causes server resources to fill up when multiple such documents are loaded. The use of `OPENXML` requires dealing with other T-SQL or data access components; hence it is not a "pure" or "transparent" database update through XML. All of these limitations of `OPENXML` make Updategrams a perfect, and preferred, choice for making direct database updates over HTTP using XML. With Updategrams we can now build data-driven web applications without using any data access mechanism (for example, ADO) or T-SQL, but XML.

Finally, unlike `OPENXML`, which is natively available in SQL Server 2000, Updategrams are available as part of the XML for SQL Server web release. This means that the extra step of installing the web release is needed as part of deployment. However, the positive side of the web release approach is frequent, periodic releases, and hence faster availability of updated or new features and bug fixes.

Updategrams Syntax

Updategrams are nothing more than templates with a special set of tags. These tags permit the description of the current data state and the new state, based upon which the database modifications are executed. Being a template, an Updategram is also a well-formed XML document. Here's what the Updategram syntax looks like:

```
<ROOT xmlns:updg="urn:schemas-microsoft-com:xml-updategram">
  <updg:header [nullvalue="isNULL"] >
    <updg:param name="paramName"/>
    ...
  </updg:header>

  <updg:sync [mapping-schema="schemaFile.xml"]
             [updg:nullvalue="IsNULL"]>
    <updg:before>
      <ElementName attribute="value" attribute="value" ... />
      ...
    </updg:before>
    <updg:after [updg:returnid="iVar1 iVar2 ..."]>
      <ElementName [updg:id="value"] [updg:at-identity="iVar"]
                   [updg:guid="gVar"]
                   attribute="value" attribute="value" .../>
      ...
    </updg:after>
      ...
  </updg:sync>
  ...
</ROOT>
```

The above structure illustrates the complete syntax for XML Updategrams. Not all of the elements and attributes are compulsory; in fact, the simplest Updategram syntax would look something like this:

```
<ROOT xmlns:updg="urn:schemas-microsoft-com:xml-updategram">
  <updg:sync>
    <updg:before>
      ...
    </updg:before>

    <updg:after>
      ...
    </updg:after>
  </updg:sync>
</ROOT>
```

The three core blocks in an Updategram are the `<sync>`, `<before>`, and `<after>` blocks. Let's have a look at what each one does:

Block Tag	Description
`<sync>`	Wraps one or more `<before>` and `<after>` pairs to produce the modification as a single transaction
`<after>`	Represents the post modification, new state of the data
`<before>`	Represents the existing state of the data

When an Updategram is successfully executed, it can perform one of three actions: insert, delete, or update. The kind of modification performed is dependent upon the contents of `<before>` and `<after>` blocks.

If only the `<after>` data block is specified, without a corresponding `<before>` block, then an insert is performed

- If only a `<before>` data block is specified, without a corresponding `<after>` block, then a delete operation is performed
- If both a `<before>` and its corresponding `<after>` data block are specified, then an update operation is performed

For a single insert operation in a transaction, the `<before>` block can be left empty, or completely omitted. Similarly, for a single delete operation in a transaction, the `<after>` block can be left empty or omitted.

The `<sync>` block may contain multiple `<before>` and `<after>` blocks, indicating multiple modifications to the database. In such circumstances, the `<before>` and `<after>` blocks must be properly paired, even if they are empty. It is here that it is important to remember that if one modification block fails, then all of the other modifications inside that `<sync>` block are rolled back, since all of the `<before>` and `<after>` pairs inside the current `<sync>` block are executed as a single transaction.

> *A transaction is a unit of work that is done as a single, atomic operation; that is, the operation succeeds or fails as a whole. For example, transferring money from one bank account to the other involves two steps: withdrawing the money from the first account, and then depositing it in the second. It is important that both steps succeed; it is not acceptable for one step to succeed and the other to fail. A transaction ensures that sets of operations are either all completely done (transaction committed), or all are failed (transaction rolled back).*

Finally, an Updategram can have multiple `<sync>` blocks to specify multiple transactions. If one transaction (one `<sync>` block) fails, it does not affect the other transactions (the other `<sync>` blocks).

Having looked at the Updategram syntax, and its basic behavior, now is a good time to play around with a few very simple Updategrams. We'll continue to discuss Updategrams a little more after these short examples.

Three Simple Examples

The basic set of data manipulation operations that can be performed with the help of Updategrams includes inserts, updates, and deletes. In this section, we'll write some simple Updategrams to perform each of these three operations on the database. However, before we jump into these examples, let's first try to understand and build the environment needed to run the samples.

The Environment

To run all of the examples in this chapter, we'll use the `Northwind` sample database. If you have made any changes to this database, or if after running examples from this chapter (which will make changes to the database), you would like to rebuild the original database all you need do is run the `instnwnd.sql` script file from `MSSQL\Install` folder. Once executed, the database will be reinstated in its original form.

Next, we'll need a web server that we can use to store and execute the Updategram files. This chapter was written using Microsoft Internet Information Server (IIS) 5.0 on Windows 2000 Advanced Server, however, the examples should also run perfectly well on IIS 4.0 or PWS (Personal Web Server) on Windows NT or Win9x.

Finally, we'll have to create the IIS virtual directory on the web server using the IIS Virtual Directory Management for SQL Server tool. All requests to this virtual directory will be processed by the SQL ISAPI extension DLL. In this chapter, we'll be creating the virtual directory under the Default Web Site, however, you can create them under non-default web sites if you prefer (for instance, a separate web on a non-standard port). We'll also configure the IIS virtual directory to connect to SQL Server using the super-user, `sa`, login, but you can (and indeed *should* in real-life) create a separate account with proper access rights and permissions set. Since configuring IIS virtual directories for SQL Server 2000 is discussed in detail in Appendix A, we'll just briefly describe the steps involved, just enough for discussion in context.

Creating the IIS Virtual Directory

Create a sub-directory named `TestUpdg` under `C:\` and a sub-directory named `template` under it. In the IIS Virtual Directory Management utility, create a new virtual directory called `TestUpdg` and specify the physical directory path as `C:\TestUpdg`.

> *For simplicity in this example, we have chosen to have the same names for both the virtual directory and the physical directory, but you can have different names for virtual and actual, physical directories.*

As mentioned earlier, for simplicity, we are going to assume that you're using the `sa` SQL Server login in this chapter. On the Data Source tab, select your SQL Server and the database to be used with this virtual directory (in this case, we'll be using `Northwind` sample database).

On the Settings tab, check all the boxes except Allow sql=... or template=... URL queries. The options we have selected will allow us to post Updategrams to the URL, execute template files using a URL, execute XPath queries against the schema files, and use a HTTP `POST`, apart from the default `GET` and `HEAD`.

Finally, in the Virtual Names tab, click on the New button, and in the Virtual Name Configuration dialog box set the Virtual name to template, select template as the Type, and use Path to specify the physical location for this virtual name, C:\TestUpdg\template.

This completes the IIS virtual directories creation step. Now let's write our first three simple Updategrams (finally!), and then study them in detail.

Example 1: Insert

Just to recap, if only the `<after>` data block is specified (without a corresponding `<before>` block), an insert operation is performed. That's what we'll do here. Open Notepad, and create your first Updategram as shown in the following code fragment:

```
<ROOT xmlns:updg="urn:schemas-microsoft-com:xml-updategram">
  <updg:sync>

    <updg:before>
    </updg:before>
```

```
      <updg:after>
         <Shippers CompanyName="Sky Packages" Phone="(503) 555-1234" />
      </updg:after>

   </updg:sync>
</ROOT>
```

Save this code as insert1.xml in C:\TestUpdg\template. Be sure to save the file in the template subdirectory, and not in the virtual root TestUpdg directory. Before executing this Updategram, start Query Analyzer, select Northwind as your current database, and then execute the following query:

```
SELECT * FROM Shippers
```

You'll see three records from the Shippers table.

Now let's execute our insert Updategram, so begin by starting the Internet Explorer (or any other web browser that you have), and entering the following URL:

http://localhost/TestUpdg/template/insert1.xml

> *Notice that we are using localhost as our web server reference (and will be for all of the examples in this chapter). If your IIS web server is not installed locally on your machine, make changes accordingly.*

When you navigate to the above URL, you should see the following result, a single line in the browser, indicating that the Updategram executed successfully, and that no errors were generated:

<ROOT xmlns:updg="urn:schemas-microsoft-com:xml-updategram" />

When we navigated to the Updategram URL, the request for insert1.xml was sent to the web server. This request is handled by the SQL ISAPI extension DLL (sqlisapi.dll), which then looks at the <before> and <after> blocks, and makes internal database calls to perform the desired data modifications.

Go back to Query Analyzer and execute the SELECT * FROM Shippers query again. You should see a new record appended to the table, with fields having the values specified in the above Updategram. Now perhaps you can see just how easy and convenient it is to insert new records to the database using Updategrams!

Our Updategram started with the <ROOT ...> element, but you could have given any other legal name to this element. The Updategram keywords (for example: <sync>, <before>, <after>, etc.) are declared in the urn:schemas-microsoft-com:xml-updategram namespace, so it is necessary to include this namespace declaration in every Updategram. You can use any arbitrary name for the namespace prefix. In this chapter, we'll use updg prefix to indicate an Updategram namespace.

Following the <ROOT...> element is the <sync> tag, which indicates the start of transaction block. Since this is an insert operation, there is nothing in the <before> block, so you can omit it completely, if you wish.

The <Shippers...> element inside the <after> block indicates an insert operation. By default, the element name maps to the table name (Shippers), and attribute names map to columns (CompanyName and Phone).

If your SQL Server database is set to use case-sensitive collation, take special care to ensure that the element names, attributes names, etc. in your Updategrams are also in the same case as in the database.

We'll come back to insert Updategrams, and some other options with them later, but for now let's move on writing our second Updategram: to delete a record.

Example 2: Delete

The presence of a `<before>` block, without a corresponding `<after>` block (or an empty `<after>` block), indicates a delete operation.

The `Shippers` table has an identity column named `ShipperID`, which also happens to be the primary key for the table. The record we just inserted using our insert Updategram has a `ShipperID` value of `4` (so long as Sky Packages is the first new shipper you've inserted into the `Shippers` table). Let's now write a delete Updategram to remove this record. Once again, launch your favorite editor (I used Notepad), and enter the following delete Updategram:

```
<ROOT xmlns:updg="urn:schemas-microsoft-com:xml-updategram">
  <updg:sync>

    <updg:before>
       <Shippers ShipperID="4" />
    </updg:before>

    <updg:after>
    </updg:after>

  </updg:sync>
</ROOT>
```

Save the Updategram as `delete1.xml` in the subdirectory `C:\TestUpdg\template`. Execute this delete Updategram by using a browser to navigate to the following URL:

http://localhost/TestUpdg/template/delete1.xml

This should result in the same browser output as we saw from the insert Updategram, indicating a successful execution:

<ROOT xmlns:updg="urn:schemas-microsoft-com:xml-updategram" />

This time, the `<after>` block is empty (and again, can be omitted). The `<before>` block contains just one sub-element named `Shippers`, which again maps to the table with the same name in the `Northwind` database. This element has one attribute, `ShipperID`, and its specified value is `4`. This tells the SQL ISAPI extension DLL to delete a record from the `Shippers` table whose `ShipperID` equals `4`. One record should match. If multiple records are matched, or no record matches the criteria, an error is generated, and transaction aborts.

It is important to remember that if you want cascading deletes to happen you'll have to specify the cascading delete constraint on the table in the database. If you try to delete a record from the master table, without setting the cascading deletes option for the database table relationship, an error will be generated. Similarly, cascading updates needs to be set up at the database level, if a change in the master table needs to be reflected in the details table.

In this example, we have only used one condition (ShipperID=4) to match the record, however, you may specify multiple attribute name=value pairs to specify multiple conditions. All of the conditions will be tested in order for the record to qualify.

Finally, let's now see how to update our SQL Server database using an update Updategram!

Example 3: Update

This time, our Updategram will have a <before> as well as a corresponding <after> block. They indicate the original and updated states of the data.

In the Shippers table we have a fictitious shipper record with a CompanyName of Federal Shipping, with the contents of its Phone field being (503) 555-9931. Let's say they got an updated telephone number (503) 333-3715 (for 503-FED-ERAL), here's an Updategram that would make the necessary change to the database:

```
<ROOT xmlns:updg="urn:schemas-microsoft-com:xml-updategram">
  <updg:sync>

    <updg:before>
       <Shippers ShipperID="3" />
    </updg:before>

    <updg:after>
       <Shippers Phone="(503) 333-3715" />
    </updg:after>

  </updg:sync>
</ROOT>
```

Save the Updategram as update1.xml in the C:\TestUpdg\template subdirectory. Now, execute this Updategram, by browsing to the following URL:

http://localhost/TestUpdg/template/update1.xml

This should result in the same output in the browser as the insert or delete Updategrams, indicating a successful execution:

```
<ROOT xmlns:updg="urn:schemas-microsoft-com:xml-updategram" />
```

In order to perform the update operation, both the <before> and <after> blocks are specified. The <before> block identifies a single record to be updated, while the <after> block details how the new field data should look. As with the delete Updategram, we should also have one record that matches the criteria. If numerous or no records match the criteria specified in the <before> block, an error is generated.

So, what have we covered? Well, hopefully, with these three simple examples you now have an idea of what Updategrams are, and how they function. Let's continue on this path of learning by example, and see what other interesting things we can do with Updategrams.

More Examples

In this section, we'll look at some more examples to help you understand Updategrams a little better, and to prepare the ground for the next section. You may want to keep the SQL Query Analyzer open, so that once you execute the example Updategrams via the browser, it's a little easier to submit a `SELECT * FROM Shippers` query to see the changes.

Default Mapping

We saw earlier that to signify which database table to modify, the element name is used, and that the attributes indicate which data columns should be operated on. This is known as **attribute-based default mapping**. With this mapping, each element within the `<before>` and `<after>` blocks maps to a table, and each such element's attributes map to the data columns.

Element-Based Default Mapping

Instead of element attributes, you may write sub-elements to denote the data columns. This is called **element-based default mapping**. Here's an example to illustrate this:

```
<ROOT xmlns:updg="urn:schemas-microsoft-com:xml-updategram">
  <updg:sync>

    <updg:before>
    </updg:before>

    <updg:after>
       <Shippers>
          <CompanyName>Sky Packages</CompanyName>
          <Phone>(503) 555-1234</Phone>
       </Shippers>
    </updg:after>

  </updg:sync>
</ROOT>
```

Enter this code, and save it as `insert2.xml` in the `C:\TestUpdg\template` subdirectory. Now execute this Updategram by navigating to http://localhost/TestUpdg/template/insert2.xml using your browser. All being well, you'll be able to see that this Updategram produces the same result as `insert1.xml`, that is, the insertion of a new record into the `Shippers` table. The point of interest in this Updategram is that now `CompanyName` and `Phone` are sub-elements, rather than attributes.

Attribute and Element-Based Default Mapping

It is possible to write an Updategram that uses both attribute- and element-based default mapping. Let's look at the example to illustrate this:

```
<ROOT xmlns:updg="urn:schemas-microsoft-com:xml-updategram">
  <updg:sync>

    <updg:before>
    </updg:before>
```

```
      <updg:after>
         <Shippers CompanyName="Worldwide Shippers">
            <Phone>(503) 555-9988</Phone>
         </Shippers>
      </updg:after>

   </updg:sync>
</ROOT>
```

Save this code as insert3.xml in subdirectory C:\TestUpdg\template and browse to http://localhost/TestUpdg/template/insert3.xml. This Updategram inserts a new record into the Shippers table. Note how the attribute (CompanyName), and sub-element (Phone) are both used to specify which column to update.

Use of attributes versus sub-elements depends on personal taste and is a religious question, rather than technical. However, in some situations, it becomes necessary to use sub-elements instead of attributes (for example, you cannot have multiple attributes with the same name on an element). If you are keen to know when to use attributes versus sub-elements, visit http://www.oasis-open.org/cover/elementsAndAttrs.html to learn more about XML elements and attributes in general.

Until now, we have relied on the default mapping, where each element name within <before> and <after> blocks exactly matches the table name, and an attribute or sub-element dictates which columns to update. Very soon, we'll learn how we can specify our own schema with the Updategrams to perform the mapping of XML elements to database objects.

Handling Multiple Rows

In all of our examples so far, we have worked with a single row. In this section, we'll learn how to modify multiple rows from a single Updategram. We'll also see how to run multiple transactions.

Let's start with an example to insert multiple rows into the Shippers table:

```
<ROOT xmlns:updg="urn:schemas-microsoft-com:xml-updategram">
  <updg:sync>

    <updg:after>
       <Shippers CompanyName="Company One" Phone="(503) 111-1111" />
       <Shippers CompanyName="Company Two" Phone="(503) 222-2222" />
       <Shippers>
          <CompanyName>Company Three</CompanyName>
          <Phone>(503) 333-3333</Phone>
       </Shippers>
    </updg:after>

  </updg:sync>
</ROOT>
```

Save the code as insert4.xml in our C:\TestUpdg\template subdirectory. Again, to execute this Updategram, simply browse to its URL. This Updategram completely omits the <before> block, and has an <after> block enclosed inside a single <sync>, and is therefore an insert operation inside a single transaction. This Updategram inserts three records into the Shippers table. Note how attribute-based and element-based default mapping is used here.

In the above Updategram, all three of the `<Shippers>` elements were enclosed within a single `<after>` block. You may write each insert in a separate `<after>` block. This will not produce any different results or behavior, but this approach is useful if you are doing inserts, updates, and deletes inside a single transaction.

> **Remember that, if you are writing multiple `<before>` and `<after>` blocks under a single `<sync>`, they must be properly paired, even if they are empty.**

The following Updategram produces exactly the same results as `insert4.xml`, but it achieves this by employing multiple `<after>` blocks:

```
<ROOT xmlns:updg="urn:schemas-microsoft-com:xml-updategram">
  <updg:sync>

    <updg:before>
    </updg:before>

    <updg:after>
      <Shippers CompanyName="Company One" Phone="(503) 111-1111" />
    </updg:after>

    <updg:before>
    </updg:before>

    <updg:after>
      <Shippers CompanyName="Company Two" Phone="(503) 222-2222" />
    </updg:after>

    <updg:before>
    </updg:before>

    <updg:after>
      <Shippers>
        <CompanyName>Company Three</CompanyName>
        <Phone>(503) 333-3333</Phone>
      </Shippers>
    </updg:after>

  </updg:sync>
</ROOT>
```

To execute the above Updategram, again, we simply save the text as `insert5.xml` in the `C:\TestUpdg\template` subdirectory and then browse to the file using the following URL:

http://localhost/TestUpdg/template/insert5.xml

To see the real benefit of multiple `<before>` and `<after>` blocks, let's build an example to update and delete records in a single transaction:

```
<ROOT xmlns:updg="urn:schemas-microsoft-com:xml-updategram">
  <updg:sync>

    <updg:before>
      <Shippers ShipperID="6" />
    </updg:before>
```

```
      <updg:after>
         <Shippers CompanyName="Windy City Shippers" Phone="1-899-WIN-DCTY"/>
      </updg:after>

      <updg:before>
         <Shippers ShipperID="5" />
      </updg:before>

      <updg:after>
      </updg:after>

   </updg:sync>
</ROOT>
```

To execute this Updategram, save the text as `multiupdate1.xml` in the `C:\TestUpdg\template` subdirectory and then browse to http://localhost/TestUpdg/template/multiupdate1.xml.

This Updategram executes two modifications within the scope of a single transaction. First it updates the `CompanyName` and `Phone` for the record with a `ShipperID` equal to `6`. It then deletes the `Shipper` record where `ShipperID` is equal to `5`. If either of the two updates fails, the entire transaction is rolled back.

In the previous Updategram, we used multiple `<before>` and `<after>` block pairs to perform multiple modifications. However, it is possible to perform multiple modifications using a single `<before>` and `<after>` block. In such a case, we will need to have multiple elements within the `<before>` and `<after>` blocks. In order to match those sub-elements, we need to use the `updg:id` attribute. Let's have a look at an example of this:

```
<ROOT xmlns:updg="urn:schemas-microsoft-com:xml-updategram">
   <updg:sync>

      <updg:before>
         <Shippers updg:id="row1" ShipperID="1" />
         <Shippers updg:id="row2" ShipperID="6" />
      </updg:before>

      <updg:after>
         <Shippers updg:id="row1" Phone="(509) 444-1212"/>
         <Shippers updg:id="newRow"
                   CompanyName="Reliable Shippers"
                   Phone="(509) 123-6767" />
      </updg:after>

   </updg:sync>
</ROOT>
```

To execute this Updategram, save the text as `idexample1.xml` in the `C:\TestUpdg\template` subdirectory, and then browse to http://localhost/TestUpdg/template/idexample1.xml.

This Updategram performs all of the three modifications – update, delete, and insert. It updates the `Phone` field for a record with `ShipperID` equal to `1`, it then deletes the record with `ShipperID` equal to `6`, and finally, it then inserts a new record for `Reliable Shippers`.

The `updg:id` attribute and its value is used to pair the elements in the <before> and <after> blocks. In the above example, as the element with `id="row1"` is present in both the <before> and <after> blocks, it indicates an update. As there is no matching <after> element for `id="row2"`, it indicates a delete operation. Similarly, the absence of a matching `id="newRow"` in the <before> block indicates an insert operation. This particular Updategram will not work at all without the `updg:id` attribute.

It's fun to watch T-SQL statements being executed under the cover, when an Updategram is executed. Run SQL Profiler, and watch how SQL ISAPI extension DLL makes T-SQL calls to perform the operations specified in an Updategram.

Finally, to execute modifications in different transactions, we simply use multiple <sync> blocks. If one transaction fails, only that transaction is rolled back; the other transactions remain unaffected. Here's an example to illustrate the implementation of multiple transaction blocks:

```
<ROOT xmlns:updg="urn:schemas-microsoft-com:xml-updategram">

  <updg:sync>
    <updg:before>
      <Shippers ShipperID="999" />
    </updg:before>

    <updg:after>
    </updg:after>
  </updg:sync>

  <updg:sync>
    <updg:before>
      <Shippers ShipperID="3" />
    </updg:before>

    <updg:after>
      <Shippers CompanyName="Federal Shipping Inc."/>
    </updg:after>
  </updg:sync>

</ROOT>
```

Again, to execute the above Updategram, simply save the above code as, say, `multisync1.xml` in the `C:\TestUpdg\template` subdirectory, and then browse to it at http://localhost/TestUpdg/template/multisync1.xml.

This Updategram has two transactions, the first attempts to delete a record with a `ShipperID` equal to `999`, and then the second transaction updates the `CompanyName` field for a record with a `ShipperID` equal to `3`.

When you execute the above Updategram, the first transaction fails since there is no record with `ShipperID` equal to `999`, and you'll see the Empty delete, no deletable rows found Transaction aborted error message in the browser, but this does not affect the update transaction, and it continues to update the `CompanyName` field for the record with a `ShipperID` equal to `3`. If you check in Query Analyzer, you'll see that the second update transaction succeeded.

Special Cases

In all the insert Updategram examples so far, we have only specified values for the `CompanyName` and `Phone` fields; the other field, `ShipperID`, is an **identity** column, and SQL Server automatically assigns the value to it when an insert is performed. What if we wanted to know the value assigned to this identity column when an insert Updategram was executed? Well, in this section, we'll focus on such questions, and will address some of the other special cases that you should be aware of while working with Updategrams:

- Getting the identity column value
- Generating GUIDs
- Dealing with `NULL` values
- Characters valid in SQL Server, but illegal in XML
- Data type conversion issues

Let's start by dealing with identity column values.

Working with Identity Columns

When an insert operation is performed on a table having an identity column, SQL Server automatically assigns the value to this column. In an Updategram, you can capture this value and use it further in the Updategram and/or return the identity column value to the client. We'll see examples of both of these cases.

Capturing an Identity Column Value to Use It in the Updategram

In our first example, we'll learn how to capture identity column values and use them again in the subsequent code of the Updategram. The `ShipperID` identity column is a primary key of the `Shippers` table, and is also used as a foreign key in the `Orders` table, mapped to its `ShipVia` field. In the following example, we'll insert a new record to `Shippers` table, and update the `Orders` table with this value in its `ShipVia` field for the record having `Orders.OrderID` equal to `10248`:

```
<ROOT xmlns:updg="urn:schemas-microsoft-com:xml-updategram">
  <updg:sync>

    <updg:before>
    </updg:before>
    <updg:after>
       <Shippers updg:at-identity="varIden"
                 CompanyName="First Air" Phone="(509) 789-1234"/>
    </updg:after>


    <updg:before>
       <Orders OrderID="10248" />
    </updg:before>
    <updg:after>
       <Orders ShipVia="varIden"/>
    </updg:after>

  </updg:sync>
</ROOT>
```

To execute this Updategram, save the code as identity1.xml in the C:\TestUpdg\template subdirectory, and then browse to http://localhost/TestUpdg/template/identity1.xml.

This Updategram has two <before> <after> block pairs. The first <before> block is empty while the corresponding <after> block has a sub-element mapping to Shippers table, which specifies values for the CompanyName and Phone fields – indicating an insert operation. The important part in this sub-element is the updg:at-identity attribute, which is used to capture the identity column value. The identity value of the newly inserted record is temporarily saved to a variable called varIden. This variable is then later used in the Updategram to update the ShipVia field in the Orders table.

Remember that SQL Server only permits one identity column per table. It is for this reason that we did not have to specify the identity column name in the above Updategram. SQL Server automatically finds out about the only identity column in the table.

Returning Identity Column Values to the Client

Apart from using the identity column value in the Updategram, this value can also be returned to the client. This is done using the <after> block's updg:returnid attribute along with the updg:at-identity attribute. Here's an example to illustrate this:

```
<ROOT xmlns:updg="urn:schemas-microsoft-com:xml-updategram">
  <updg:sync>

    <updg:after updg:returnid="IdenVal">
       <Shippers updg:at-identity="IdenVal"
                 CompanyName="Rapid Shippers" Phone="(509) 555-8898"/>
    </updg:after>

  </updg:sync>
</ROOT>
```

To execute this Updategram, again, simply save the code as identity2.xml in the C:\TestUpdg\template subdirectory, and then browse to http://localhost/TestUpdg/template/identity2.xml.

This Updategram omits the <before> block and has just one <after> block specifying an insert operation into the Shippers table. This time, the <after> block uses the updg:returnid attribute, which results in returning the identity column value for the newly inserted record to the client. On execution of this Updategram, you should see an output similar to this in your browser:

```
<ROOT xmlns:updg="urn:schemas-microsoft-com:xml-updategram">
    <returnid>
            <IdenVal>15</IdenVal>
    </returnid>
</ROOT>
```

This is the first time that we've got a different output as a result of the execution of an Updategram since we started with three simple examples at the beginning of the chapter. The output now has a sub-element with the value of the identity column (15 for my Shippers table) enclosed within the parent <returnid> element.

The insert Updategram above inserted just a single row and hence we dealt with a single variable (IdenVal) as the value of the updg:returnid and updg:at-identity attributes. It is possible to use multiple placeholder variables, separated by a single space, in case of a multiple insert operation.

Applying a Stylesheet to the Updategram

We can now apply an XSL stylesheet on this output to present the results in a more visually pleasing manner. To see this working, save the following stylesheet text as `identity2.xsl` in your `c:\TestUpdg\template` directory:

```
<xsl:stylesheet xmlns:xsl="http://www.w3.org/1999/XSL/Transform"
                version="1.0"  >

   <xsl:output method="html" />
   <xsl:template match="/ROOT/returnid/IdenVal" >
      Your Shipper ID is: <xsl:value-of select="." />
   </xsl:template>

</xsl:stylesheet>
```

Now, to use this stylesheet with the output of `identity2.xml` Updategram, simply amend the URL to:

http://localhost/TestUpdg/template/identity2.xml?xsl=template/identity2.xsl

There is no magic here – Updategrams are templates just like we saw in Chapters 2 and 7, hence we can apply stylesheets to them. In fact, we can specify the XSL stylesheet reference in the Updategram `<ROOT>` node itself, instead of passing it as a parameter to the URL.

> *If you feel you would like to learn more about XSLT and stylesheets, we recommend that you read Michael Kay's excellent book* XSLT Programmer's Reference*, also published by Wrox Press, ISBN 1-861003-12-9.*

Generating GUIDs

GUID is an acronym for Globally Unique Identifier, and refers to a 16-byte binary value that is guaranteed to be a unique number across the world. GUIDs are used to create a unique identity for an entity (a record, in this case). SQL Server's `uniqueidentifier` data type supports storing GUID values.

Let's say that we had a table with a `uniqueidentifier` data type column, and that we wanted to perform an insert to that table using an Updategram. How do you think we could set the value for this `uniqueidentifier` column now? Well, the answer is to use the `updg:guid` attribute. Let's have a look at an example of this, and then we'll look at how exactly `updg:guid` operates.

Since there is no table in the `Northwind` sample database, which already has a `uniqueidentifier` data type column, we'll create a new table and use it in our example Updategram. Let's assume we are developing a web site and need a table to store user feedbacks, and that we are planning to use Updategrams to do database modifications. Let's first create the `WebFeedback` table.

Open up Query Analyzer, and create our feedback table by running the following T-SQL statement:

```
USE Northwind
Go

CREATE TABLE WebFeedback
   (FeedId UNIQUEIDENTIFIER,
    FeedText NTEXT)
Go
```

Let's now take a look at the code for the Updategram that will insert a row into this table:

```
<ROOT xmlns:updg="urn:schemas-microsoft-com:xml-updategram">
  <updg:sync>

    <updg:after>
       <WebFeedback updg:guid="gVal">
          <FeedId>gVal</FeedId>
          <FeedText>Great site! </FeedText>
       </WebFeedback>
    </updg:after>

  </updg:sync>
</ROOT>
```

To execute this Updategram, save the code as `insert6.xml` in the `C:\TestUpdg\template` subdirectory, and then browse to http://localhost/TestUpdg/template/insert6.xml.

This Updategram inserts a new row into the `WebFeedback` table. It uses the `updg:guid` attribute, which generates a GUID and saves it into temporary placeholder named `gVal`. This placeholder value is then assigned to the `FeedId` field. When the SQL ISAPI extension DLL sees the `updg:guid` attribute being used, it calls the `NEWID()` T-SQL function.

Like the identity column example we saw earlier, the GUID value also can be returned as output XML, using the `updg:returnid` attribute within the `<after>` block. Another point to remember is that the GUID variable (`gVal` in our case) is available throughout the scope of `<sync>` block, so you may use it anywhere within that scope.

Dealing with NULL Values

In SQL Server, `NULL` values usually indicate data that is unknown, not applicable, or data that is to be added at a later date. Remember that a `NULL` value is not the same as an empty string or zero value; it is just simply *Null*.

While with XML, you cannot natively denote `NULL` values, and if you specify empty values for an attribute or an element (for example, `Phone=""`), the result is an empty string, and not `NULL`.

With Updategrams however, in order to clearly indicate that the data column should have a `NULL` value, we have to use the `updg:nullvalue` attribute, as illustrated below.

Here is an example of inserting yet another row into `Shippers` table. This time we know the `CompanyName` value, but we are not sure of the `Phone` number, so we'll be assigning a `NULL` value to it. Here we go:

```
<ROOT xmlns:updg="urn:schemas-microsoft-com:xml-updategram">
  <updg:sync updg:nullvalue="NA">

    <updg:after >
       <Shippers CompanyName="Northwest Cargo" Phone="NA" />
    </updg:after>

  </updg:sync>
</ROOT>
```

To execute this Updategram, follow the (hopefully!) now familiar procedure of saving the code (as insert7.xml, in the C:\TestUpdg\template subdirectory), and then browsing to the file (http://localhost/TestUpdg/template/insert7.xml).

Note that updg:nullvalue is an attribute of the <sync> block tag, and can be assigned any arbitrary string as its value. In this case, we assigned "NA" to this attribute. Note how the same value is also assigned to the Phone field to indicate that it should have a NULL value.

We'll come back to nullvalue when we talk about passing parameters to Updategrams later on in this chapter.

The Handling of Special Characters

In SQL Server, it is possible to have two database objects with the same name, the only stipulation being that they must have different object owners. For example, we could have two tables with the same name, say, T1, and this would not be a problem provided that each of the tables had been created by distinct users, say, dbo and Joe. In such a case, it's suggested that we fully qualify the table name by prefixing them with the associated owner name, resulting in table names like [dbo].T1 or [Joe].T1.

Note that [and] are not legal characters for use in XML element names, and also that while table names in SQL Server can use the space character (for example, the Northwind sample database has a table named Order Details), the use of the space character is not permitted inside valid XML element names. So, bearing that in mind that we cannot use element names such as <Order Details...> or <[Joe].[T1]...>, how would we go about using Updategrams to update a table called <Order Details ...> or perhaps <[Joe].[T1] ...>?

The solution is that we simply use the **UCS-2 encoding** to convert special characters into _xHHHH_ format, where HHHH is the hexadecimal UCS-2 equivalent of each special character in context, in most significant bit-first order. As a result, a space character is converted to _x0020_, [is converted to _x005B_,] to _x005D_, and so on.

> *Visit http://www.unicode.org/charts/index.html if you are interested in learning more about UCS-2 codes, or Unicode in general.*

Let's take a look at an example to update the [Order Details] table in our Northwind sample database:

```
<ROOT xmlns:updg="urn:schemas-microsoft-com:xml-updategram">
  <updg:sync>

    <updg:before >
      <Order_x0020_Details OrderID="10248" ProductID="42" />
    </updg:before>

    <updg:after >
      <Order_x0020_Details Discount="0.575" />
    </updg:after>

  </updg:sync>
</ROOT>
```

Execute this Updategram by saving the text as update2.xml in the C:\TestUpdg\template subdirectory, and then browsing to http://localhost/TestUpdg/template/update2.xml.

The above Updategram matches a record with an OrderID of 10248 and a ProductID as 42. It then updates the matching record's Discount field with 0.575 (essentially 0.57499999, a nearest real number). Note how the space is converted to _x0020_ in the table (element) name.

Another important point to note in the Updategram above is that we are updating the Discount field, which is a real (floating point number) data type field. The value 0.575 is passed as a string to the middle-tier processor (SQL ISAPI extension DLL, sqlisapi.dll), and is then passed to SQL Server as an nvarchar (a Unicode character data type). Since SQL Server can implicitly convert an nvarchar to a real data type, the above Updategram succeeds, but what if you were to update some field (for example, a money data type field) for which explicit conversion is required? To try to answer this question, let's move on to our final sub-section, where we will discuss data conversion issues.

Data Type Conversion Issues

SQL Server Books Online has an excellent chart that illustrates the explicit and implicit data type conversions allowed for SQL Server system-supplied data types, which can be found under the heading CAST and CONVERT. According to this chart, SQL Server automatically converts nvarchar data to char, datetime, decimal, real, etc. But nvarchar to money or nvarchar to smallmoney, for instance, requires an explicit conversion using the CAST or CONVERT functions.

In an Updategram, any time such explicit conversion is needed, simply precede the attribute value with a $ symbol. How about an example? Let's amend our last Updategram (update2.xml), so that it modifies the UnitPrice field in the table, which is of money data type:

```
<ROOT xmlns:updg="urn:schemas-microsoft-com:xml-updategram">
  <updg:sync>

    <updg:before >
       <Order_x0020_Details OrderID="10248" ProductID="42" />
    </updg:before>

    <updg:after >
       <Order_x0020_Details UnitPrice="$11.04" />
    </updg:after>

  </updg:sync>
</ROOT>
```

Save the Updategram as update3.xml, and then execute it by browsing to http://localhost/TestUpdg/template/update3.xml.

The UnitPrice attribute value in this Updategram, is preceded by a $ symbol. Try removing the $ character, and notice how its removal results in a data type conversion error on execution.

Note that this is only required if you are using default mapping schemas (element and attribute/sub-element names directly matching the table and column names, respectively). Later in the chapter, we'll see how mapping schemas streamline data type mapping, in which case it would not be necessary to use the $ symbol in attribute values.

Passing Parameters

In all of the Updategram examples so far, we have hard-coded the data values. However, in real-life applications, we may want to pass parameters to the Updategram, and make it work on a different set of records, based upon these input parameters.

We learned earlier that Updategrams are nothing more than templates. They are run through templates, and in Chapter 2 we saw that by using <header> and <param> blocks, we can pass parameters to a template. Similarly, it is also possible to pass parameters to Updategrams. Let's look at a very simple example of passing parameters to an Updategram:

```
<ROOT xmlns:updg="urn:schemas-microsoft-com:xml-updategram">
   <updg:header>
      <updg:param name="ShID"/>
      <updg:param name="ShPhone" />
   </updg:header>

   <updg:sync>

    <updg:before>
       <Shippers ShipperID="$ShID" />
    </updg:before>

    <updg:after>
       <Shippers Phone="$ShPhone" />
    </updg:after>

  </updg:sync>
</ROOT>
```

Once again, to execute this Updategram, we simply save the above code as `param1.xml` in our `C:\TestUpdg\template` subdirectory, and then browse to:

http://localhost/TestUpdg/template/param1.xml?ShID=2&ShPhone=(509)%20123-4455

As with templates, when using Updategrams we also use the <header> and <param> blocks to pass parameters.

> **Remember that parameter names are case sensitive. So, for the above example, if we were to pass the parameter name as `SHID` instead of `ShID`, the Updategram will output an error, since it has no value for the `ShID` parameter, and no records are matched for update.**

The above Updategram accepts two parameters, `ShID` and `ShPhone`. It then updates the `Phone` field for the record matching the `ShipperID` value with the `ShID` parameter. These parameters can be passed as part of the URL (`GET` method), or as part of HTTP headers (`POST` method). Later in the chapter, we'll see how to pass parameters using the `POST` method when the web form is submitted to an Updategram.

If you are using SQL Profiler to watch what's going on behind the scenes when an Updategram is executed, you'll notice that as soon as SQL ISAPI extension DLL finds out that an Updategram has a parameters block, it calls the `sp_executesql` system stored procedure, instead of directly making T-SQL calls.

Finally, as with templates, Updategrams also permit passing `NULL` as a parameter value. To do this, we use the `nullvalue` attribute within the <header> block to specify that an Updategram can accept `NULL` as a parameter value. Let's make one small change to our `param1.xml` Updategram:

```
<ROOT xmlns:updg="urn:schemas-microsoft-com:xml-updategram">
  <updg:header nullvalue="NA">
    <updg:param name="ShID"/>
```

Now, save the text with this change as `param2.xml` in your `C:\TestUpdg\template` under subdirectory, and then browse to:

http://localhost/TestUpdg/template/param2.xml?ShID=1&ShPhone=NA

Note that unlike as in the `<sync>` block, the `nullvalue` is not fully qualified by using the `updg:namespace` qualifier. This is because the same attribute is used within the `<header>` block in `sql:namespace` in regular templates.

When you execute the above Updategram (`param2.xml`), and pass `ShPhone` as `NA`, it changes the `Phone` field for the record with `ShID=1`, to `NULL`.

Updategrams and Annotated XDR Schemas

In all of the Updategram examples so far, we have used default (also known as **implicit**) mapping, wherein the elements within the `<before>` and `<after>` blocks explicitly match the table (or view) name, and each such element's attribute or sub-element matches a column name in the table. This default mapping is not very useful when you are updating multiple tables having primary-foreign key relationships, or need to take care of data type conversion issues.

In this section, we'll focus on the use of mapping schemas with Updategrams to provide the necessary information to map Updategram XML elements and attributes to the corresponding database tables and columns.

To specify an annotated XDR schema in an Updategram, the `mapping-schema` attribute of the `<sync>` block is used. When we use this attribute, the Updategram does not use default mapping, but uses the specified mapping information to update the database tables and columns.

Let's modify our very first example (`insert1.xml`) to make use of an annotated XDR schema:

```
<ROOT xmlns:updg="urn:schemas-microsoft-com:xml-updategram">

  <updg:sync mapping-schema="sch1.xml">

    <updg:before>
    </updg:before>

    <updg:after>
      <ShipRec CN="Sky Packages" PH="(503) 555-1234" />
    </updg:after>

  </updg:sync>
</ROOT>
```

Save this code as insert8.xml in the C:\TestUpdg\template subdirectory. Note the addition of a mapping-schema attribute to the <sync> block. This attribute points to a file called sch1.xml, which is the annotated XDR schema file used for this Updategram. Let's have a look at the sch1.xml schema file (you should save this in your C:\TestUpdg\template subdirectory):

```
<Schema xmlns="urn:schemas-microsoft-com:xml-data"
        xmlns:dt="urn:schemas-microsoft-com:datatypes"
        xmlns:sql="urn:schemas-microsoft-com:xml-sql">
   <ElementType name="ShipRec" sql:relation="Shippers" >
      <AttributeType name="CN" />
      <AttributeType name="PH" />

      <attribute type="CN" sql:field="CompanyName" />
      <attribute type="PH" sql:field="Phone" />
   </ElementType>
</Schema>
```

It is clearly visible that this time the Updategram does not use default mapping, because there is no table in our Northwind database named ShipRec. So how does it know which table to work on? Well, it uses the mapping-schema attribute, and looks in the sch1.xml schema file to find out that the ShipRec element is mapped to Shippers table (using the sql:relation annotation). Similarly, using the sch1.xml schema file, the Updategram finds out that CN is mapped to CompanyName field (using the sql:field annotation), and PH is mapped to the Phone field.

Multi-Table Relationships and Data Types

The above example was a very basic illustration of how an annotated XDR Schema can be used with an Updategram. The real value of using an XDR schema comes into being when specifying multi-table relationships, and having the ability to specify data types. Let's look at the example of this now:

```
<?xml version="1.0" ?>
<Schema xmlns="urn:schemas-microsoft-com:xml-data"
        xmlns:dt="urn:schemas-microsoft-com:datatypes"
        xmlns:sql="urn:schemas-microsoft-com:xml-sql">

   <ElementType name="Product" sql:relation="Products" >
      <AttributeType name="PName" />
      <AttributeType name="CatID" />
      <AttributeType name="Price" dt:type="fixed.14.4" />

      <attribute type="PName" sql:field="ProductName"/>
      <attribute type="CatID" sql:field="CategoryID"/>
      <attribute type="Price" sql:field="UnitPrice"/>
   </ElementType>

   <ElementType name="Category" sql:relation="Categories">
      <AttributeType name="CategoryID" />
      <attribute type="CategoryID" />

      <element type="Product" >
         <sql:relationship
            key-relation="Categories" key="CategoryID"
            foreign-relation="Products" foreign-key="CategoryID"
         />
      </element>
   </ElementType>
</Schema>
```

Save this code as `sch2.xml` in your `C:\TestUpdg\template` subdirectory.

This schema file declares two elements: `Product` and `Category`, and a primary key/foreign key relationship between them using the `<sql:relationship>` annotation. Also note that, for the `Price` attribute we have specified the data type as `fixed.14.4`, which maps to the smallmoney SQL Server data type. Now we don't have to precede the data value in the Updategram with a `$` character to indicate explicit data conversion.

Let's take a look at the Updategram that uses the above schema file. This Updategram accepts a `CategoryID` parameter, and inserts a new record into the `Products` table with `CategoryID` field set to the parameter value that is passed in:

```
<ROOT xmlns:updg="urn:schemas-microsoft-com:xml-updategram">
  <updg:header>
     <updg:param name="CatID" />
  </updg:header>

  <updg:sync mapping-schema="sch2.xml" >

    <updg:before>
       <Category CategoryID="$CatID" />
    </updg:before>

    <updg:after>
      <Category CategoryID="$CatID" >
         <Product PName="Seattle Coffee" Price="10.50" />
      </Category>
    </updg:after>
  </updg:sync>
</ROOT>
```

To execute this Updategram, save the text as `insert9.xml` in the `C:\TestUpdg\template` subdirectory and then browse to http://localhost/TestUpdg/template/insert9.xml?CatID=1.

Important points to note about the above Updategram are how `<Product>` is a sub-element of the `<Category>` node, and that we do not specify a `CategoryID` attribute for the `<Product>` element. The Updategram understands the primary key/foreign key relationship and gets the `CategoryID` field value from parent `<Category>` element. Hence, when you run this Updategram, it inserts a new record into the `Products` table, and then sets the `ProductName`, `UnitPrice`, and `CategoryID`.

Using the LIKE Operator

Let's now look at another interesting example that illustrates situations where the use of an XDR schema is a must. The `Northwind` database has a table called `Categories`, and let's say that we want to find a record with a `Description` field with a value of `Cheeses`, and if found, we want to update the description to `Milk and Cheeses`. Here's an Updategram that is intended to make this data modification:

```
<ROOT xmlns:updg="urn:schemas-microsoft-com:xml-updategram">
   <updg:sync>
      <updg:before>
          <Categories Description="Cheeses"/>
      </updg:before>
```

```
        <updg:after>
            <Categories Description="Milk and Cheeses" />
        </updg:after>
    </updg:sync>
</ROOT>
```

Just as we've done many times already, execute this Updategram by saving the above code as `update4.xml` in the `C:\TestUpdg\template` subdirectory, and then browsing to http://localhost/TestUpdg/template/update4.xml.

The execution of this Updategram should produce an error with the following description: The text, ntext, and image data types cannot be compared or sorted, except when using IS NULL or LIKE operator. This error occurs because behind the scenes, SQL ISAPI extension DLL executes following T-SQL `UPDATE` statement:

```
UPDATE [Categories] SET [Description]=N'Milk and Cheeses'
WHERE  ( [Description]=N'Cheeses')
```

The `Description` field is of the ntext data type, and, as the error message suggests, the ntext data type cannot be compared. However, SQL Server has a `LIKE` operator, which can be used to work with ntext data types instead of using the equals character, =, to draw comparisons. So how do we tell the SQL ISAPI extension DLL to use the `LIKE` operator? Well, there's a straightforward solution – we simply use a schema, and describe the `Description` column as `ntext`, which then forces the SQL ISAPI extension DLL to use the `LIKE` operator as a replacement for the equals, =, operator:

```
<?xml version="1.0" ?>
<Schema xmlns="urn:schemas-microsoft-com:xml-data"
        xmlns:dt="urn:schemas-microsoft-com:datatypes"
        xmlns:sql="urn:schemas-microsoft-com:xml-sql">

   <ElementType name="Categories" sql:relation="Categories">
      <AttributeType name="Description" sql:datatype="ntext" />

      <attribute type="Description" sql:field="Description" />
   </ElementType>

</Schema>
```

Save the code fragment above as `sch3.xml`, in the `C:\TestUpdg\template` subdirectory.

Now take a look at the following Updategram. You'll see that it's actually the same as `update4.xml`, with a minor modification of having an added schema reference (to `sch3.xml`):

```
<ROOT xmlns:updg="urn:schemas-microsoft-com:xml-updategram">
   <updg:sync mapping-schema="sch3.xml">
      <updg:before>
          <Categories Description="Cheeses"/>
      </updg:before>

      <updg:after>
          <Categories Description="Milk and Cheeses" />
      </updg:after>
   </updg:sync>
</ROOT>
```

Once again, to execute this Updategram, save the text as `update5.xml` in the `C:\TestUpdg\template` subdirectory, and then browse to http://localhost/TestUpdg/template/update5.xml.

This time, you should find that execution of the Updategram succeeds, and the `Description` column is updated to a new value. If you run SQL Profiler while executing this Updategram, you'll notice that the `UPDATE` T-SQL statement now uses the `LIKE` operator to perform the comparison on the `Description` column.

Having looked at standalone Updategram examples, let's now move forward and learn how we can use Updategrams in applications.

Updategrams Integrated with Applications

In most of today's web applications, the database update forms are posted using the `POST` method, which means that the data is sent as part of HTTP headers, rather than passing it as part of URL. While other multi-tier applications use ADO calls to make database modifications. In this section, we'll look at some examples for using Updategrams integrated with such implementations.

Updategrams and HTML Forms

Earlier in the chapter we saw how to pass parameters to Updategrams using `<header> - <param>` blocks, and how to pass parameter values as part of a URL. Let's now extend that parameter passing capability, and see how we can use Updategrams with the `POST` method for form submission.

The following example facilitates the insertion of a new record into the `Shippers` table through an HTML form submitted using the HTTP `POST` method:

```
<HTML>
<HEAD>
<TITLE>Adding New Shippers Record</TITLE>
</HEAD>

<BODY>

<FORM ACTION="http://localhost/TestUpdg" METHOD="POST">

<INPUT TYPE="hidden" NAME="contenttype" VALUE="text/xml">

<INPUT TYPE="hidden" NAME="template" VALUE='
<ROOT xmlns:updg="urn:schemas-microsoft-com:xml-updategram">
<updg:header>
  <updg:param name="CN" />
  <updg:param name="Phone" />
</updg:header>
  <updg:sync>

    <updg:after>
      <Shippers CompanyName="$CN" Phone="$Phone" />
    </updg:after>
```

```
  </updg:sync>
</ROOT>
'>

<B> Company Name:</B>
<INPUT TYPE="text" NAME="CN" MAXLENGTH="40">

<BR>

<B> Phone Number:</B>
<INPUT TYPE="text" NAME="Phone" MAXLENGTH="24">

<BR><BR>
<INPUT TYPE="submit" VALUE="Submit Changes">

</FORM>

</BODY>

</HTML>
```

Save this HTML code as `C:\post1.html` (or in some other directory if you wish to) and then open this file directly in the browser. Enter some values for the Company Name and Phone Number fields, and verify that a new record is created when you submit the form.

There are a couple of important points to note about the above HTML code, and they are:

- The form is posted directly to the virtual root. Note the `ACTION` attribute in the `FORM` tag, and how the form is submitted to the `http://localhost/TestUpdg` virtual root, where the SQL ISAPI extension DLL is listening. All the requests to the `TestUpdg` virtual root are handled by `sqlisapi.dll`.
- The above form has two hidden fields: one to hold the `contenttype`, while the other contains the Updategram template text. The `contenttype` of `text/xml` tells the SQL ISAPI extension DLL that an XML document is being posted, which is essentially the value of the second hidden field, named `template`.

Let's look at a little variation on this example. This time, instead of posting the form data and Updategram directly to the virtual root, we'll call an Updategram XML file, and pass the form data to it as parameters:

```
<HTML>
<HEAD>
<TITLE>Adding New Shippers Record, version 2.0</TITLE>
</HEAD>

<BODY>

<FORM ACTION="http://localhost/TestUpdg/template/insert10.xml"
      METHOD="POST">

<B> Company Name:</B>
<INPUT TYPE="text" NAME="CN" MAXLENGTH="40">
```

```
<BR>

<B> Phone Number:</B>
<INPUT TYPE="text" NAME="Phone" MAXLENGTH="24">

<BR><BR>
<INPUT TYPE="submit" VALUE="Submit Changes">

</FORM>

</BODY>

</HTML>
```

Save this HTML code as c:\post2.html.

Now let's write the action handler (insert10.xml) for the above form:

```
<ROOT xmlns:updg="urn:schemas-microsoft-com:xml-updategram">
<updg:header>
  <updg:param name="CN" />
  <updg:param name="Phone" />
</updg:header>
  <updg:sync>

    <updg:after>
      <Shippers CompanyName="$CN" Phone="$Phone" />
    </updg:after>

  </updg:sync>
</ROOT>
```

Save this as insert10.xml in your c:\TestUpdg\template subdirectory. The above code is a very simple insert Updategram, accepting two parameters.

Now open c:\post2.html, and fill in the Company Name and Phone Number fields. When you submit the form, insert10.xml is called, which gets the form field data as parameters, and on execution it inserts a new record into the Shippers table.

Posting an Updategram from VB

Let's spend a little time looking at another similar example, where we post an Updategram, once again directly to the virtual root, but this time from a Visual Basic application.

Start Microsoft Visual Basic 6.0, and create a new Standard EXE project. Select Project | References and add a reference to Microsoft XML Parser 3.0 (msxml3.dll). Then double-click on the form and the following code to the Form_Load method:

```
Private Sub Form_Load()

    Dim objHTTP As New MSXML2.xmlHttp
    Dim objDoc As New MSXML2.DOMDocument
    Dim strUpdategram As String
```

```
    'Build the updategram template string
    strUpdategram = "<ROOT xmlns:updg=" & _
                    "'urn:schemas-microsoft-com:xml-updategram'>"
    strUpdategram = strUpdategram & "<updg:sync>"
    strUpdategram = strUpdategram & "<updg:after>"
    strUpdategram = strUpdategram & _
        "<Shippers CompanyName='VB Shippers' Phone='(509) 123-9999'/>"
    strUpdategram = strUpdategram & "</updg:after>"
    strUpdategram = strUpdategram & "</updg:sync>"
    strUpdategram = strUpdategram & "</ROOT >"

    'Load the updategram string into DOM document
    objDoc.loadXML strUpdategram

    'Check for Errors
    If objDoc.parseError.errorCode Then
        MsgBox "Error loading updategram. Exiting"
        End
    End If

    'POST the template
    objHTTP.open "POST", "http://localhost/TestUpdg", False
    objHTTP.setRequestHeader "Content-type", "application/xml"
    objHTTP.send objDoc


    'Results
    MsgBox objHTTP.responseText

End Sub
```

The above Visual Basic code uses the MSXML 3.0 `DOMDocument` and `xmlHttp` objects to post the Updategram directly to the virtual root. The posted Updategram simply inserts a new record into the `Shippers` table.

After creating the `xmlHttp` and `DOMDocument` object instances, the code builds the Updategram string, and then loads that string into the `DOMDocument` object. Then a little error checking code uses the `parseError` object to make sure that our Updategram is well formed. The `xmlHttp` object allows communication with the server. Internally it uses WinInet for HTTP communication. The remaining code opens the connection to the http://localhost/TestUpdg virtual root, sets the content type to `application/xml`, and finally posts the Updategram XML text to virtual root. Once again, `sqlisapi.dll`, the handler for `TestUpdg` virtual root, comes into the picture, and executes the Updategram.

When you run the project you should see the following message box:

Finally, let's look at some examples of executing Updategrams with ADO.

ADO and Updategrams

ADO's Command object has a property called Dialect. This property specifies how the Microsoft OLE DB Provider for SQL Server interprets the command text received from ADO, with the value of the Dialect property being a GUID. Starting with SQL Server 2000, the OLE DB Provider for SQL Server supports a new dialect called DBGUID_MSSQLXML ({5D531CB2-E6Ed-11D2-B252-00C04F681B71}) to execute XML templates. Since Updategrams are also XML templates, we can use this dialect to call Updategrams from ADO applications.

> *To learn more about ADO 2.6, refer to David Sussman's* ADO 2.6 Programmer's Reference *(ISBN 186100463X), also from Wrox Press.*

The basic steps for calling Updategrams from ADO are as follows:

- Make the ADO connection to the server
- Set the Command object's ActiveConnection and Dialect properties
- The Stream object is created and the Updategram XML text is copied to the input stream
- The input stream is assigned to Command object's CommandStream property
- The output stream is opened, and is set to receive any output data from the Updategram command execution
- Finally, the Execute method of the Command object is called, which in turn executes the Updategram, and copies the results to the output stream

Let's now look at the code to implement those steps. Once again, create a new Visual Basic 6.0 Standard EXE project. Select Project | References, and add a reference to Microsoft ActiveX Data Objects Library 2.6 (msado15.dll). Next, double-click on the form, and then add the following code to the Form_Load method:

```
Private Sub Form_Load()

   Dim objCmd As New ADODB.Command
   Dim objConn As New ADODB.Connection
   Dim objStreamIn As New ADODB.Stream
   Dim objStreamOut As New ADODB.Stream

   'Connect to server using SQL Server OLE DB Provider
   objConn.Provider = "SQLOLEDB"
   objConn.Open "server=(local); database=Northwind;" & _
                " uid=sa; pwd=sqlserver"

   Set objCmd.ActiveConnection = objConn

   'Build the Updategram template string
   strUpdategram = "<ROOT xmlns:updg=" & _
                   "'urn:schemas-microsoft-com:xml-updategram'>"
   strUpdategram = strUpdategram & "<updg:sync>"
   strUpdategram = strUpdategram & "<updg:after>"
   strUpdategram = strUpdategram & _
         "<Shippers CompanyName='ADO Shippers' Phone='(509) 123-9999'/>"
   strUpdategram = strUpdategram & "</updg:after>"
   strUpdategram = strUpdategram & "</updg:sync>"
   strUpdategram = strUpdategram & "</ROOT >"
```

```
    'Set the command dialect to DBGUID_MSSQLXML.
    objCmd.Dialect = "{5d531cb2-e6ed-11d2-b252-00c04f681b71}"

    'Open the input stream and write Updategram text to it
    objStreamIn.Open
    objStreamIn.WriteText strUpdategram
    objStreamIn.Position = 0

    'Set the CommandStream to point to input stream
    Set objCmd.CommandStream = objStreamIn

    'Open the return stream to receive results
    objStreamOut.Open
    objStreamOut.LineSeparator = adCRLF
    objCmd.Properties("Output Stream").Value = objStreamOut
    objCmd.Properties("Output Encoding").Value = "UTF-8"

    'Executing the Command (Updategram)
    objCmd.Execute , , adExecuteStream

    objStreamOut.Position = 0

    MsgBox objStreamOut.ReadText

End Sub
```

This code is an exact mapping of the steps outlined earlier to execute an Updategram using ADO's new `Dialect` property of the `Command` object, and once again, we can see that our example Updategram inserts a new record into the `Shippers` table.

Passing Parameters to Updategrams Using ADO

We can use XDR schemas with Updategrams executed using ADO, and this requires updating the Updategram text string to use the `mapping-schema` attribute with the `<sync>` element. It is also possible to pass parameters to Updategrams executed using ADO. Let's take a look at an example that illustrates passing parameters to Updategrams using ADO.

Create a new Visual Basic 6.0 Standard EXE Project. Select Project | References, and add a reference to Microsoft ActiveX Data Objects Library 2.6 (`msado15.dll`). Double-click on the form and add the following code to the `Form_Load` method:

```
Private Sub Form_Load()

    Dim objCmd As New ADODB.Command
    Dim objConn As New ADODB.Connection
    Dim objStreamIn As New ADODB.Stream
    Dim objStreamOut As New ADODB.Stream

    strCN = InputBox("Enter CompanyName:", "")
    strPH = InputBox("Enter Phone:", "")

    'Connect to server using SQL Server OLE DB Provider
    objConn.Provider = "SQLOLEDB"
    objConn.Open "server=(local); database=Northwind; uid=sa; pwd=sqlserver"

    Set objCmd.ActiveConnection = objConn
```

```
    'Build the updategram template string
    strUpdategram = "<ROOT xmlns:updg='urn:schemas-microsoft" & _
                    "-com:xml-updategram'>"
    strUpdategram = strUpdategram & "<updg:header>"
    strUpdategram = strUpdategram & "<updg:param name='CN'>"
    strUpdategram = strUpdategram & "</updg:param>"
    strUpdategram = strUpdategram & "<updg:param name='PH'>"
    strUpdategram = strUpdategram & "</updg:param>"
    strUpdategram = strUpdategram & "</updg:header>"
    strUpdategram = strUpdategram & "<updg:sync>"
    strUpdategram = strUpdategram & "<updg:after>"
    strUpdategram = strUpdategram & _
                    "<Shippers CompanyName='$CN' Phone='$PH'/>"
    strUpdategram = strUpdategram & "</updg:after>"
    strUpdategram = strUpdategram & "</updg:sync>"
    strUpdategram = strUpdategram & "</ROOT >"

    'Set the command dialect to DBGUID_MSSQLXML.
    objCmd.Dialect = "{5d531cb2-e6ed-11d2-b252-00c04f681b71}"

    'Open the input stream and write updategram text to it
    objStreamIn.Open
    objStreamIn.WriteText strUpdategram
    objStreamIn.Position = 0

    'Set the CommandStream to point to input stream
    Set objCmd.CommandStream = objStreamIn

    'Open the return stream to receive results
    objStreamOut.Open
    objStreamOut.LineSeparator = adCRLF
    objCmd.Properties("Output Stream").Value = objStreamOut
    objCmd.Properties("Output Encoding").Value = "UTF-8"

    'Append the parameter values
    objCmd.NamedParameters = True
    objCmd.Parameters.Append objCmd.CreateParameter("@CN", _
          adBSTR, adParamInput, Len(strCN) + 1, strCN)
    objCmd.Parameters.Append objCmd.CreateParameter("@PH", _
          adBSTR, adParamInput, Len(strPH) + 1, strPH)

    'Executing the Command (Updategram)
    objCmd.Execute , , adExecuteStream

    objStreamOut.Position = 0

    MsgBox objStreamOut.ReadText

End Sub
```

In this code, we begin by accepting the `CompanyName` and `Phone` fields from the user. The next change is in the Updategram string text to accept parameters (notice that we added `<header>` and `<param>` blocks to this example). Finally, using the `Command` object's `CreateParameter` and `Parameters.Append` methods, we added the parameter values to the Updategram. Once again, this Updategram also inserts a row into `Shippers` table.

Updategrams and Database Concurrency

Database concurrency issues arise when two or more processes (or users) try to interact with the same data at essentially the same time. To maintain database integrity in a multi-user environment, concurrent updates to data are handled by using either the pessimistic approach, or the optimistic approach.

With the **pessimistic** approach, a locking mechanism is used to prevent more than one application from accessing the same data at the same time. This approach is generally followed in high-transaction situations in which the application developer believes that such collisions are commonplace.

Optimistic concurrency derives its name from the optimistic assumption that collisions between transactions will rarely occur, and involves situations in which connections or client applications do not lock the data they are accessing.

Updategrams use the optimistic concurrency model, which ensures that data to be modified hasn't been changed by another transaction since it was read from the database. Updategrams make use of data inside the `<before>` block to compare it with the database field values, before applying the update, ensuring that both values match. As such, the `<before>` block plays an important role when it comes to concurrency.

If we were to just specify primary key field(s) in the `<before>` block, this would result in the lowest level of protection for concurrency issues, as a primary key is rarely (almost never) updated. So this approach is somewhat similar to a blind update.

Another option is to specify column(s) being updated in the `<before>` block, along with the primary key. This will ensure that the values that we are changing are not touched by some other transaction.

The third approach, which provides the highest level of protection, is to specify all the table columns in the `<before>` block. This will ensure that if any of the data column changed since we read the data, the update will not occur.

If the table has a column of data type `timestamp`, specifying this column in the `<before>` block gives the same level of protection as specifying all of the table columns. Remember that, if you are using a timestamp column, you'll have to associate an XDR schema with the Updategram, and properly specify the data type of the column as either `sql:datatype="timestamp"` or `dt:type="bin.base64"` or `dt:type="bin.hex"`, as timestamp values are stored in binary format.

The Limitations of Updategrams

While Updategrams have many things to offer, we believe that they are still in the preliminary stages of development, and are hoping that it is a technology that will grow and improve over time. Here are some of the limitations that Updategrams have today:

- Updategrams do not offer an easy solution if you wish to update or delete multiple rows. For instance, there is no easy shortcut to execute a modification similar to the following T-SQL statement:

  ```
  DELETE customers WHERE Region IS NULL
  ```

- Updategrams do not support modification across databases or servers.
- Sometimes the syntax becomes difficult to understand. For instance, the $ character is used for variables, and also to indicate explicit conversion when the XDR schema is not specified. Another example is how special characters are converted into _xHHHH_ notation.
- Updategrams do not natively support cascading deletes and updates; the cascading update/delete constraint needs to be set at database level, if cascading update/delete is desired.

Summary

This chapter focused on an important SQL Server XML feature – Updategrams, which was released as part of XML for SQL Server 2000 Web Release 1. XML Updategrams enable us to seamlessly and transparently update our database in real-time, with minimal programming, and maximum performance. Updategrams consist of blocks of special XML tags that describe what the data looks like now and what you want it to look like once the Updategram is executed.

We started with very simple examples for performing database modification operations, using implicit mapping. Then we talked about working with multiple rows and some special cases like dealing with identity and GUID columns, special characters handling etc.

To understand Updategrams better, it is important to know templates and annotated XDR schema well. We saw how we can pass parameters to Updategrams, and how we use XDR schemas to specify explicit mapping of Updategram elements and attributes/sub-elements to database tables (views) and columns, respectively.

We then studied a few examples of Updategrams being executed from HTML forms and from Visual Basic applications.

Finally, we discussed how Updategrams handle concurrent updates using the optimistic concurrency approach.

The next chapter will focus on yet another important SQL Server XML feature – Bulk Load, which was also made available as part of Web Release 1.

10

XML Bulk Load

XML Bulk Load is a new functionality for SQL Server 2000, which was first introduced as part of the Web Release 1 in January 2001.

> *Further information on where to find Web Release 1 and its installation can be found in Chapter 9, Updategrams.*

XML Bulk Load allows the importing of either well-formed or partly structured XML documents into a database. (**Partly structured** means that the file can be a fragment of an XML document as there is no need to have a top-level tag.) This is done using an annotated XDR schema to map the XML document onto the database schema, allowing it to be imported. The use of the annotated XDR schema also means that we are not limited to importing data into one table as with other forms of SQL Server bulk loads, such as the `bcp` utility or `BULK INSERT`.

XML Bulk Load's main strength is that it can be used to very quickly and efficiently drag large amounts of data into the database. This could be anything from a single record right up to millions of records.

To make the best use of this chapter you should already be familiar with:

- Annotated XDR schemas. For a review of these, please refer back to Chapter 5.
- Traditional SQL Server bulk load methods. We shall briefly go through this functionality, as many of the concepts are relevant to the new XML Bulk Load method.

Existing Bulk Insert Methods

With the advent of SQL Server 7.0, the `BULK INSERT` statement was introduced along with the bulk insert task in Data Transformation Services (DTS). Before version 7.0, the only method was to use the bulk copy program (`bcp`).

Data Transformation Services

DTS is perhaps the simplest and most commonly used method for importing data into SQL Server. It is also often used for importing and transforming data within other database systems, and can even be used with any other ODBC or OLEDB compliant database. With it, you can import a file into a table or view. As a very simple example using the `Northwind` database, create the following text file. Save it as `New Regions.txt` on your `C:\` drive. This file allows us to add three new regions for Europe, Asia, and South America:

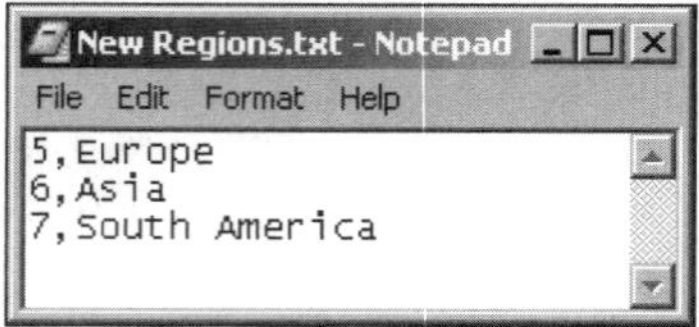

We can then create a new DTS package to perform the import. Right-click on the Data Transformation Services node in Enterprise Manager, and select New Package. Within this we create a new Microsoft OLE DB Provider for SQL Server connection, defining which server and database the file will be imported into. Then add a new Bulk Insert Task, which brings up the next dialog:

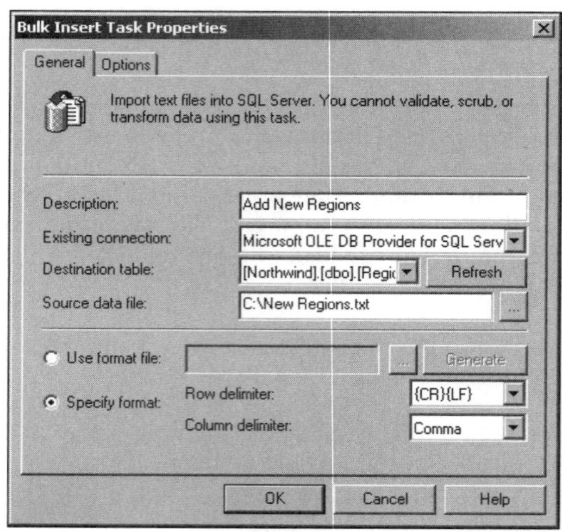

Fill in the Description, Destination table, Source data file, and Specify format options as shown here. Then, before pressing OK, take a look at the Options tab – various settings can be adjusted here to alter how bulk insert will perform. The most frequently used options are:

- Check constraints. By default, no constraints are checked when importing data, so ticking this box makes sure that the incoming data conforms to the rules that have been defined. This will slow the import down quite a bit.

- Enable identity insert. If the table that is being inserted into has an identity column then, normally, the identity values would be generated automatically on insert. However, by ticking this box, we tell SQL Server that the file we are importing from already has the identity values that you want to give to this column.
- Keep Nulls. Ticking this box overrides the use of defaults. Normally, if a field in the file has a `Null` value in it and the column that the value is going into has a default constraint, that constraint is applied. With this box ticked, the `Null` value is kept, rather than the default value for the column.
- Data file type. This has four options:
  - char – normal character text
  - native – indicates that the file was output from SQL Server by another bulk insert
  - widechar – Unicode data
  - widenative – as for native, but the output is in Unicode
- Insert batch size. The default value of 0 (zero) means that the whole file is imported within one transaction. You would normally change this value for one of two reasons:
  - The file is very large and causes the transaction log to fill. In this case, setting the batch size allows the transaction log to be emptied during the import to prevent it from filling.
  - Some of the data is known to be of suspect format. Setting the value to 1 (one) will then allow all of the correct rows to be inserted. Otherwise, one failed row will cause the whole batch to fail.

Once this is done, a package will be created like the one shown below. Running this package will import the rows from the file into the `Region` table.

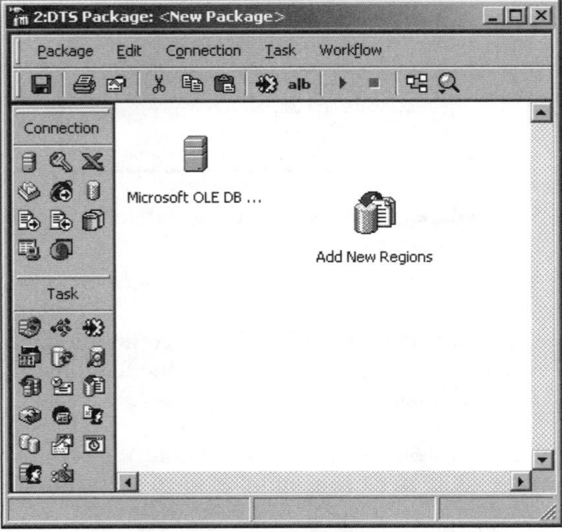

DTS provides many other ways of importing data into the database. These allow data to be validated, cleaned, and reformatted as it is loaded. For further details and a much more in-depth discussion, please see *Professional SQL Server 2000 DTS*, Wrox Press, ISBN 1861004419.

The bcp Utility

The bcp utility or bulk copy program is the oldest method of importing data into SQL Server. Nowadays, you will rarely see this utility used in anything but legacy code. Many DBAs have a love-hate relationship with this utility as it is a very important tool for importing data, but very often requires real effort to get it to work as required.

The bcp is a separate command line utility that takes a whole host of parameters, as shown below:

```
bcp {[[database_name.][owner].]{table_name | view_name} | "query"}
    {in | out | queryout | format} data_file
    [-m max_errors] [-f format_file] [-e err_file]
    [-F first_row] [-L last_row] [-b batch_size]
    [-n] [-c] [-w] [-N] [-V (60 | 65 | 70)] [-6]
    [-q] [-C code_page] [-t field_term] [-r row_term]
    [-i input_file] [-o output_file] [-a packet_size]
    [-S server_name[\instance_name]] [-U login_id] [-P password]
    [-T] [-v] [-R] [-k] [-E] [-h "hint [,...n]"]
```

The vast majority of the arguments are self-explanatory and we won't go into their details here. However, the main thing to watch out for when using them is that they are case sensitive – this utility did originate in the Unix world after all!

Let's develop the previous example and add in new territories to support the European region. We could import the following file of European countries into the Territories table:

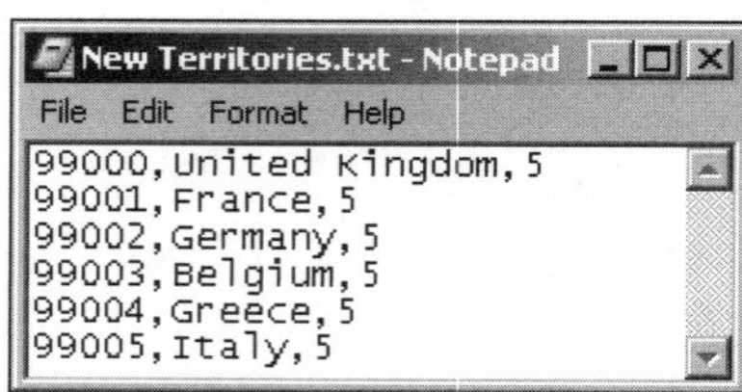

From the command line, we would execute the following statement to invoke the bcp utility:

```
bcp Northwind.dbo.Territories in "c:\New Territories.txt" -c -T -t,
```

This works by naming the table that the import is going to go into, followed by in to show that an import is happening rather than an export. We then name the file to be read along with its format. In this case, -c denotes that it is a character file.

-T is used to log onto SQL Server using a trusted connection. We could have used the -U and -P arguments instead to specify a valid user name and password.

Finally, -t, denotes that the file is comma separated, rather than the default tab separated that bcp expects.

We could have specified the -S argument to send the import to a remote server, but by excluding it from the parameter list we have used the default local server.

BULK INSERT

Finally, in our brief run-through of the traditional bulk load tools and utilities, we come to the `BULK INSERT` statement. `BULK INSERT` was introduced in SQL Server 7.0 as an alternative to using the `bcp` utility.

Its main advantage over `bcp` is that it is run as a statement by SQL Server and hence runs in-process. This makes it a little faster. In the past, if you wanted to perform a bulk data load from within a SQL statement, you would have had to use stored procedures like `xp_cmdshell` to execute the `bcp` utility.

Not surprisingly, therefore, the `BULK INSERT` statement takes an almost identical form to `bcp`, except that the arguments are given names that are far easier to remember:

```
BULK INSERT [['database name'.]['owner'].]{'table name'
FROM 'data file'}
     [WITH
      (
         [BATCHSIZE [= batch size]]
         [[,] CHECK_CONSTRAINTS]
         [[,] CODEPAGE [= 'ACP'|'OEM'|'RAW'|'code page']]
         [[,] DATAFILETYPE [={'char'|'native'|'widechar'|'widenative'}]]
         [[,] FIELDTERMINATOR [= 'field terminator']]
         [[,] FIRSTROW [= first row]]
         [[,] FIRE_TRIGGERS]
         [[,] FORMATFILE = 'format file path']
         [[,] KEEPIDENTITY]
         [[,] KEEPNULLS]
         [[,] KILOBYTES_PER_BATCH [= kilobytes per batch]]
         [[,] LASTROW [= last row]]
         [[,] MAXERRORS [= max errors]]
         [[,] ORDER ({column [ASC|DESC]}[,...n])]
         [[,] ROWS_PER_BATCH [= rows per batch]]
         [[,] ROWTERMINATOR [= 'row terminator']]
         [[,] TABLOCK]
      )
     ]
```

Continuing the same example again, we can import the next set of records. Now that we have our new territories, we need to assign a sales person to look after them. One of the sales people based in London is to be assigned to look after the European region, so we have a file to import as below:

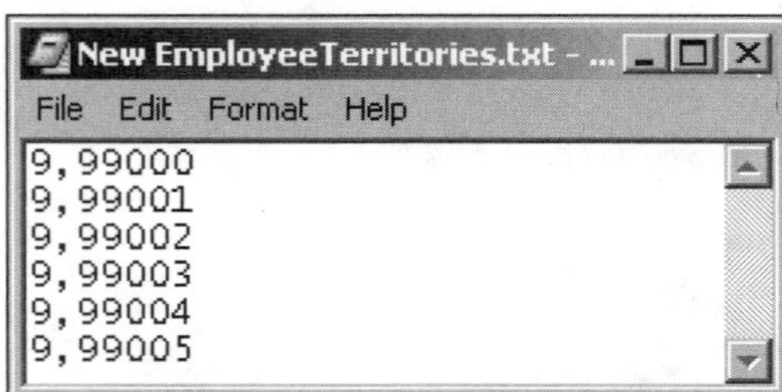

To import this file using the `BULK INSERT` statement, we would execute:

```
BULK INSERT Northwind.dbo.EmployeeTerritories
FROM 'C:\New EmployeeTerritories.txt'
WITH (FIELDTERMINATOR = ',')
```

This statement is fairly self-explanatory. The file `New EmployeeTerritories.txt` is imported into the `EmployeeTerritories` table using all default settings, with the exception that we specify that the file is comma delimited rather than tab delimited.

We have really only given a brief overview of these tools and utilities here, in order that you have at least a background understanding of them as many of the concepts used by XML Bulk Load are the same. They are covered in much greater detail in *Professional SQL Server 2000 Programming*, Wrox Press, ISBN 1861004486.

XML Bulk Load

Now that you have a background on how bulk loading has worked in general until now, we can turn to the specifics of XML Bulk Load.

XML Bulk Load is always run by invoking the `SQLXMLBulkLoad` object, setting the relevant properties, and then running its `Execute` method. So let's run through a simple example to show it in action, before we go into the details of what is going on behind the scenes and all of the options that you can tweak.

To keep things simple, we will just load some more countries into the `Territories` table, but this time for Asia. We have an XML document as follows:

```
<ROOT>
  <Territories>
    <TerritoryID>99100</TerritoryID>
    <TerritoryDescription>Thailand</TerritoryDescription>
    <RegionID>6</RegionID>
  </Territories>
  <Territories>
    <TerritoryID>99101</TerritoryID>
    <TerritoryDescription>Cambodia</TerritoryDescription>
    <RegionID>6</RegionID>
  </Territories>
  <Territories>
    <TerritoryID>99102</TerritoryID>
    <TerritoryDescription>Malaysia</TerritoryDescription>
    <RegionID>6</RegionID>
  </Territories>
  <Territories>
    <TerritoryID>99103</TerritoryID>
    <TerritoryDescription>India</TerritoryDescription>
    <RegionID>6</RegionID>
  </Territories>
  <Territories>
    <TerritoryID>99104</TerritoryID>
    <TerritoryDescription>Pakistan</TerritoryDescription>
    <RegionID>6</RegionID>
  </Territories>
</ROOT>
```

Save this as `Territories.xml` in a new folder called `C:\sqlxml\chapter10`. As we said earlier, XML Bulk Load takes this XML document and maps it onto the database using an annotated XDR schema. XDR schemas were described in detail in Chapter 5, so we won't elaborate on them here (other than for the specific restrictions on their use that are imposed by XML Bulk Load, but more of that later).

In order to load the XML document, we need to use the following annotated XDR schema:

```
<?xml version="1.0" ?>
<Schema xmlns="urn:schemas-microsoft-com:xml-data"
        xmlns:dt="urn:schemas-microsoft-com:xml:datatypes"
        xmlns:sql="urn:schemas-microsoft-com:xml-sql" >

   <ElementType name="TerritoryID" dt:type="string" />
   <ElementType name="TerritoryDescription" dt:type="string" />
   <ElementType name="RegionID" dt:type="int" />

   <ElementType name="root" sql:is-constant="1">
      <element type="Territories" />
   </ElementType>

   <ElementType name="Territories"  sql:relation="Territories" >
      <element type="TerritoryID"  sql:field="TerritoryID" />
      <element type="TerritoryDescription" sql:field="TerritoryDescription" />
      <element type="RegionID" sql:field="RegionID" />
   </ElementType>
</Schema>
```

Save this as `TerritoriesSchema.xml` in the same folder. To keep everything within SQL Server, we'll create a DTS package to perform this import. Create a new package in DTS and add an ActiveX Script Task to it. Add the following VBScript into the dialog so that it looks like this:

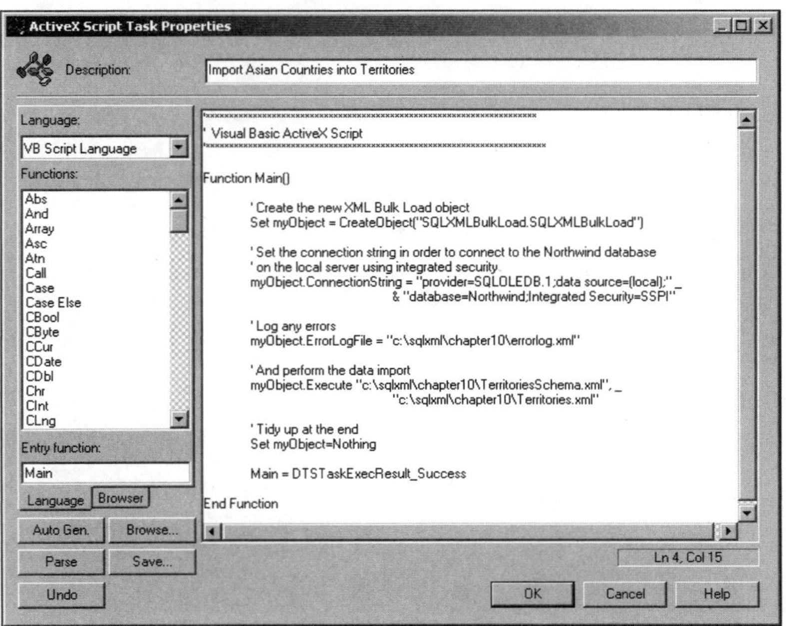

Click OK on this dialog to close it and then run the package. Once the package has run successfully, go to Query Analyzer and execute this SQL statement:

```
SELECT * FROM Territories
WHERE RegionID = 6
```

We can see that our new records have been imported:

```
TerritoryID                TerritoryDescription           RegionID
-------------------------- ------------------------------ ------------
99100                      Thailand                       6
99101                      Cambodia                       6
99102                      Malaysia                       6
99103                      India                          6
99104                      Pakistan                       6

(5 row(s) affected)
```

That's about as simple as we can get, but there are lots of ways in which we can change the behavior of the import. Before we see any more complicated examples, let's look at XML Bulk Load's object model.

The Bulk Load Object Model

The XML Bulk Load object model is very simple and consists of just the one object – `SQLXMLBulkLoad` – that has one method and fifteen properties.

As we will see, the vast majority of these properties are performing the same function as the parameters that we described in the initial sections on the traditional bulk loading methods. This is no coincidence as XML Bulk Load is calling them behind the scenes and, hence, we are really just manipulating them indirectly through this object model. In a way, you can think of the `SQLXMLBulkLoad` object as an XML wrapper around the normal `BULK INSERT` statement.

The Execute Method

The `Execute` method is the one and only method of the `SQLXMLBulkLoad` object. Understandably, it performs the actual process of the data load. It takes two parameters in the form of:

```
.Execute SchemaFileName, DataFileName | Stream Object
```

You pass the name and path of the annotated XDR schema, followed by the name and path of the XML document or an ADO 2.6 `Stream` object. This was illustrated in the example in the previous section.

Properties

The `SQLXMLBulkLoad` object has fifteen properties that can be set to affect how the bulk load performs.

BulkLoad

The `BulkLoad` property is used to indicate whether to perform the bulk load operation. This may initially sound like an odd thing to want to specify, but it allows for just the creation of the table objects, without actually having to load the data into them.

It takes either `True` or `False` values – if `True`, then the bulk load is performed. `True` is the default value.

CheckConstraints

The value of the `CheckConstraints` property determines which constraints are checked within the database during the load. These constraints include checking for violations of primary or foreign keys, or check constraints.

The default value is `False`, which means that constraints are not checked. This allows data to be loaded more quickly and without having to worry about loading parent records in before child records.

ConnectionString

The `ConnectionString` property takes a standard OLE DB connection string, of the same format that you would use in ADO. The usual components of the connection string are:

Component	Description
`provider=SQLOLEDB.1;`	The name of the OLE DB provider, SQL Server in this case.
`data source=servername;`	The name of the SQL Server that is to be connected to.
`database=databasename;`	The name of the database on the server.

plus one of the following:

Component	Description
`Integrated Security=SSPI;`	Used to connect using Windows authentication.
`uid=username; pwd=password;`	Used to connect using standard SQL Server security.

Putting all this together gives a connection string like:

```
myObject.ConnectionString = "provider=SQLOLEDB.1;data source=(local);" _
         & "database=Northwind;Integrated Security=SSPI"
```

ConnectionCommand

The `ConnectionCommand` property can be used as an alternative to the `ConnectionString` property that we just described. Instead of a connection string, this property takes an ADO `Command` object so, if you already have an open connection to your SQL Server database, you can use this instead of creating a new one.

A code fragment for its use looks like:

```
' Create the objects
Dim myConnection As New ADODB.Connection
Dim myCommand As New ADODB.Command
Dim myBulkLoad As New SQLXMLBulkLoad

' Make the connection
Set myConnection.ConnectionString = "provider=SQLOLEDB.1;" & _
    "data source=(local);database=Northwind;Integrated Security=SSPI"
myConnection.Open
```

```
' Set up the Command object for use
Set myCommand.ActiveConnection = myConnection

' Use the Command object's connection for bulk loading
myBulkLoad.ConnectionCommand = myCommand
```

If both the `ConnectionCommand` and `ConnectionString` properties are used, the one that is used last is the one in effect.

ErrorLogFile

The `ErrorLogFile` property is used to set the path and file name of a file that errors are written to during the bulk load. The file is deleted each time the XML Bulk Load is run and so, if no errors occur, the file is not created.

This property is used as:

```
myObject.ErrorLogFile = "C:\SQLXML\Chapter10\errorlog.xml"
```

The file can be saved as an `.xml` or `.txt` file, and will typically look something like:

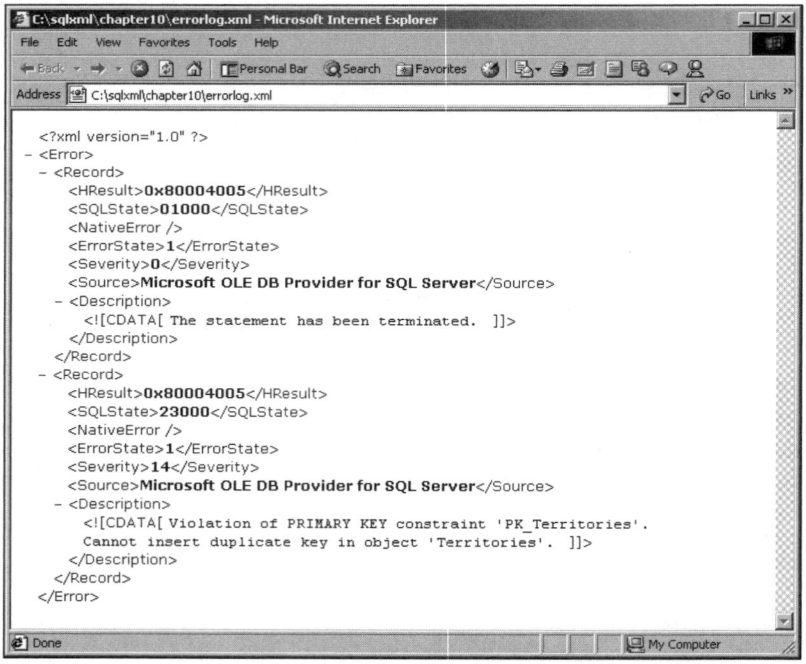

```
<?xml version="1.0" ?>
- <Error>
  - <Record>
      <HResult>0x80004005</HResult>
      <SQLState>01000</SQLState>
      <NativeError />
      <ErrorState>1</ErrorState>
      <Severity>0</Severity>
      <Source>Microsoft OLE DB Provider for SQL Server</Source>
    - <Description>
        <![CDATA[ The statement has been terminated. ]]>
      </Description>
    </Record>
  - <Record>
      <HResult>0x80004005</HResult>
      <SQLState>23000</SQLState>
      <NativeError />
      <ErrorState>1</ErrorState>
      <Severity>14</Severity>
      <Source>Microsoft OLE DB Provider for SQL Server</Source>
    - <Description>
        <![CDATA[ Violation of PRIMARY KEY constraint 'PK_Territories'.
        Cannot insert duplicate key in object 'Territories'. ]]>
      </Description>
    </Record>
  </Error>
```

ForceTableLock

The `ForceTableLock` property allows you to specify whether to put an exclusive table lock on to the table or tables that you are loading into. This can give a performance improvement, with the downside that nobody can use the tables when the bulk load is running. By default, this property is set to `False`, which does not put a table lock in place.

IgnoreDuplicateKeys

By default, the `IgnoreDuplicateKeys` property is set to `False`, which means that any attempt to insert a record that would cause a duplicate key to be created will fail. This then causes the XML Bulk Load operation to fail. In non-transacted mode this also means that some of the previous records may not be inserted. The different modes are described in the next section.

By setting the property to `True`, the XML Bulk Load operation does not fail. It recognizes that a duplicate key would be created and ignores the record without inserting it. Having the value set to `True` does, however, cause the import to run much slower as each record is committed as it is inserted.

KeepNulls

The `KeepNulls` property determines which value goes into fields in the table when no explicit value is given in the XML document or mapping schema.

This property is `False` by default, which means that any default constraints on the table are applied; otherwise `NULL` values are used. By setting the property to `True`, the default constraints are not applied and all fields have a value of `NULL` if their value is not specified.

KeepIdentity

The value of the `KeepIdentity` property determines how SQL Server handles identity columns.

When its default value of `True` is used, SQL Server takes the values that are passed from the XML document and uses these to populate the column, rather than letting the identity values be generated by SQL Server. When the property is set to `False`, SQL Server generates the identity values and ignores any values that are passed in from the XML document.

SchemaGen

The `SchemaGen` property is used to create the tables within the SQL Server database as part of the load process.

When set to `True`, the table schemas are generated from the annotated XDR schema using the names and data types that are specified within the mapping schema. When set to its default `False` value, no tables are created.

SGDropTables

The `SGDropTables` property is used in conjunction with the `SchemaGen` property, and drops the tables that the `SchemaGen` property then re-creates.

The default value of `False` does not drop the tables.

SGUseId

The `SGUseId` property is, again, used in conjunction with the `SchemaGen` property. When the `SchemaGen` property is set to `True`, this property is used to determine which fields make up the primary key of the table being created. If the property is set, it uses attributes with the `dt:type="id"` as the primary key. By default it is `False`.

TempFilePath

The `TempFilePath` property is only valid when the `Transaction` property is set to `True` and is used to override the default directory used for storing the temporary files created in this mode. Its default value is `NULL`, which means that the temporary directory specified in the `TEMP` environment variable is used.

To use this property, set its value along the lines of:

```
.TempFilePath = "C:\SQLXML\Chapter10"
```

Transaction

The `Transaction` property takes or returns a Boolean value and has a default value of `False`. It is used to set the transaction mode of the load, as described shortly.

XMLFragment

By default, the `XMLFragment` property is `False`, which means that the XML document being imported is expected to be well-formed with a single root node.

By setting the value to `True`, the document does not need to have this single root node.

Modifying the XML Bulk Load

In this section, we'll describe the various ways in which we can change the behaviour of the import – starting with the different modes that XML Bulk Load can run under.

Modes

There are two different ways that the XML Bulk Load can be executed: transacted and non-transacted. By default, it runs non-transacted, which is the simplest– but not necessarily the safest – way to go.

Transacted

Running in **transacted mode** guarantees that the whole import will either succeed or fail, by wrapping everything inside a transaction and either committing it or rolling it back at the end.

It does this by creating a temporary file for each table that the annotated XDR schema defines records going into. The import is then initially done into this file (or files). Once the initial step has been completed, the temporary files contain standard flat file import records, as we saw in the first sections of this chapter. These files are that which is actually imported into the database using the `BULK INSERT` statement.

Using transacted mode is best for when you need to safely import the records and cannot afford a table to be left in a partly loaded condition. However, transacted mode is slower to use, as it needs to effectively make two passes of the data to perform the import. Also, if the XML document is large, you will need to consider the extra overhead of keeping enough disk space free to hold the temporary files.

To use transacted mode, set the `Transaction` property of the `SQLXMLBulkLoad` object to `True` prior to the import. When setting the `Transaction` property to `True`, you must use the `ConnectionCommand` property rather than the `ConnectionString` property to make the database connection. This is because when using the latter it starts its own connection to the database and does not automatically commit transactions when the `Transaction` property is true.

> *Hopefully, future web releases will enable setting of the* `Transaction` *property to* `True` *when the* `ConnectionString` *property has been used.*

We could therefore change the previous example's VBScript, within the ActiveX Script Task, as follows:

```
Function Main()

   ' Create the new XML Bulk Load object
   Set myObject = CreateObject("SQLXMLBulkLoad.SQLXMLBulkLoad")
   Set myConnection = CreateObject("ADODB.Connection")
   Set myCommand = CreateObject("ADODB.Command")

   ' Set the connection string in order to connect to the Northwind
   'database on the local server using integrated security
   myConnection.ConnectionString = _
            "provider=SQLOLEDB.1;data source=(local);" _
            & "database=Northwind;Integrated Security=SSPI"
   myConnection.Open

   ' Set up the command object for use
   Set myCommand.ActiveConnection = myConnection

   ' Use the command object's connection for bulk loading
   myObject.ConnectionCommand = myCommand

   ' Log any errors
   myObject.ErrorLogFile = "c:\sqlxml\chapter10\errorlog.xml"
   myobject.Transaction  = True

   ' And perform the data import
   myObject.Execute "c:\sqlxml\chapter10\TerritoriesSchema.xml", _
                    "c:\sqlxml\chapter10\Territories.xml"

   ' Tidy up at the end
   Set myObject=Nothing
   Set myConnection = Nothing
   Set myCommand = Nothing

   Main = DTSTaskExecResult_Success

End Function
```

Note that you will need to delete the rows we created in the previous example before executing this modified package.

Non-Transacted

Non-transacted mode is the default mode used if you do not specify anything for the `Transaction` property. This mode is the exact opposite of transacted mode in that it does not guarantee that the whole XML document will either succeed or fail to load. It is therefore safest to use this mode when loading into empty tables. This way it doesn't matter if you need to empty the table and start the import again.

The main advantages of using non-transacted mode is that it is faster than transacted mode and less disk space is required as there are no temporary files. It loads the data straight into the tables in the database. Non-transacted mode also uses the `IRowsetFastLoad` interface to load the records, which means that it can load the data in a non-logged operation to gain even more speed.

To get the best import speeds, either import into an empty table without any indexes or into a table that contains a unique index. The former is the most efficient as there is no overhead creating any indexes. There is also less overhead in creating a unique index as opposed to a non-unique index.

> **Note that if you are importing binary data, you must use non-transacted mode.**

To use non-transacted mode in your code, either don't set the `Transaction` property or explicitly set it to `False`.

Loading into More than One Table

Given the correct annotated XDR schema, XML Bulk Load is capable of loading data into more than one table in a single pass of an XML document. There are, however, a few concepts that we need to explain before we show this in action.

Scope of Nodes

When a node enters scope and leaves scope determines when SQL Server makes a record ready for insertion into the table.

A node enters scope when its start tag is encountered. So, using our previous `Territories.xml` document, the node enters scope when `<Territories>` is read:

```
...
  <Territories>
    <TerritoryID>99100</TerritoryID>
    <TerritoryDescription>Thailand</TerritoryDescription>
    <RegionID>6</RegionID>
  </Territories>
...
```

The node leaves scope when the end tag is encountered, `</Territories>` in this case. In conjunction with the XDR schema, XML Bulk Load has built the record that is to be inserted and, at this point, in non-transacted mode sends it directly to be inserted into the table. In transacted mode it is added to the temporary file to be imported once all nodes have been read.

When the XML document is to go into more than one table, the scope works in basically the same way as when only one table is involved. For example, if we take the `Orders` and `Order Details` tables from `Northwind` (with a few fields removed for brevity), an XML document (`Orders.xml`) to load into these two tables simultaneously would look something like:

```
<ROOT>
   <Orders>
      <OrderID>12000</OrderID>
      <CustomerID>AROUT</CustomerID>
      <EmployeeID>9</EmployeeID>
      <OrderDate>2001-04-07</OrderDate>
      <RequiredDate>2001-04-30</RequiredDate>
      <ShipVia>4</ShipVia>
      <Freight>40.00</Freight>
      <ShipName>Around The Horn</ShipName>
```

```
        <ShipAddress>120 Hanover Sq</ShipAddress>
        <ShipCity>London</ShipCity>
        <ShipPostalCode>WA1 1DP</ShipPostalCode>
        <ShipCountry>UK</ShipCountry>
          <OrderDetails>
             <ProductID>4</ProductID>
             <UnitPrice>22.00</UnitPrice>
             <Quantity>100</Quantity>
          </OrderDetails>
          <OrderDetails>
             <ProductID>5</ProductID>
             <UnitPrice>21.35</UnitPrice>
             <Quantity>100</Quantity>
          </OrderDetails>
     </Orders>
  </ROOT>
```

In this case, the `Orders` node comes into scope first of all and remains in scope throughout, until its end tag is reached. The first `OrderDetails` node comes into scope with its start tag and out of scope with its end tag. The same happens with the second `OrderDetails` node. While these two nodes go in and out of scope the `Orders` node is still in scope. If you run a trace using SQL Profiler against this import, you will see that, although nodes are going in and out of scope, the records are going to the database slightly differently. The `Orders` record is sent first with one `BULK INSERT` statement and the two `Order Details` records are sent afterwards in a second `BULK INSERT`. This is to prevent the violation of referential integrity that would occur if we tried to insert order details for an order that didn't exist.

This document contains one order for two products. The annotated XDR schema (`OrdersSchema.xml`) to load this document looks like:

```
  <?xml version="1.0" ?>
  <Schema xmlns="urn:schemas-microsoft-com:xml-data"
          xmlns:dt="urn:schemas-microsoft-com:xml:datatypes"
          xmlns:sql="urn:schemas-microsoft-com:xml-sql" >
     <ElementType name="OrderID" dt:type="int" />
     <ElementType name="CustomerID" dt:type="int" />
     <ElementType name="EmployeeID" dt:type="int" />
     <ElementType name="OrderDate" dt:type="date" />
     <ElementType name="RequiredDate" dt:type="date" />
     <ElementType name="ShipVia" dt:type="int" />
     <ElementType name="Freight" dt:type="r8" />
     <ElementType name="ShipName" dt:type="string" />
     <ElementType name="ShipAddress" dt:type="string" />
     <ElementType name="ShipCity" dt:type="string" />
     <ElementType name="ShipPostalCode" dt:type="string" />
     <ElementType name="ShipCountry" dt:type="string" />
     <ElementType name="ProductID" dt:type="int" />
     <ElementType name="UnitPrice" dt:type="r8" />
     <ElementType name="Quantity" dt:type="int" />

     <ElementType name="root" sql:is-constant="1">
        <element type="Orders" />
     </ElementType>
```

```
    <ElementType name="Orders" sql:relation="Orders" >
       <element type="OrderID" sql:field="OrderID" />
       <element type="CustomerID" sql:field="CustomerID" />
       <element type="EmployeeID" sql:field="EmployeeID" />
       <element type="OrderDate" sql:field="OrderDate" />
       <element type="RequiredDate" sql:field="RequiredDate" />
       <element type="ShipVia" sql:field="ShipVia" />
       <element type="Freight" sql:field="Freight" />
       <element type="ShipName" sql:field="ShipName" />
       <element type="ShipAddress" sql:field="ShipAddress" />
       <element type="ShipCity" sql:field="ShipCity" />
       <element type="ShipPostalCode" sql:field="ShipPostalCode" />
       <element type="ShipCountry" sql:field="ShipCountry" />

       <element type="OrderDetails" >
          <sql:relationship
                 key-relation="Orders"
                 key="OrderID"
                 foreign-key="OrderID"
                 foreign-relation="[Order Details]" />
       </element>
    </ElementType>

    <ElementType name="OrderDetails" sql:relation="[Order Details]" >
       <element type="ProductID" sql:field="ProductID" />
       <element type="UnitPrice" sql:field="UnitPrice" />
       <element type="Quantity" sql:field="Quantity" />
    </ElementType>

</Schema>
```

The VBScript code to load this is pretty much identical to the previous example and, again, this can easily be run using DTS:

```
Function Main()

    ' Create the new XML Bulk Load object
    Set myObject = CreateObject("SQLXMLBulkLoad.SQLXMLBulkLoad")

    ' Set the connection string in order to connect to the Northwind
    ' database on the local server using integrated security
    myObject.ConnectionString = "provider=SQLOLEDB.1;data source=(local);" _
          & "database=Northwind;Integrated Security=SSPI"

    ' Log any errors
    myObject.ErrorLogFile = "c:\sqlxml\chapter10\errorlog.xml"

    ' And perform the data import
    myObject.Execute "c:\sqlxml\chapter10\OrdersSchema.xml", _
          "c:\sqlxml\chapter10\Orders.xml"

    ' Tidy up at the end
    Set myObject=Nothing

    Main = DTSTaskExecResult_Success

End Function
```

XDR Schema Restrictions

There are a few restrictions on what we can put into this annotated XDR schema, and on the way that we need to lay it out.

Specifying the Relationship Between Tables

When specifying the `sql:relationship` part of the annotated XML schema, it is important that it is put after the key field. This is to allow the key from the parent record – in this case the `OrderID` – to be used within the child record, without being explicitly put into either the schema or the XML document. Below is the correct way to lay out the schema – used in `OrdersSchema.xml` – with the `OrderID` element before the `sql:relationship`:

```
...
   <ElementType name="Orders" sql:relation="Orders" >
      <element type="OrderID" sql:field="OrderID" />
...
      <element type="OrderDetails" >
         <sql:relationship
                key-relation="Orders"
                key="OrderID"
                foreign-key="OrderID"
                foreign-relation="[Order Details]" />
      </element>
   </ElementType>
...
```

If we re-arrange the schema as below, to put the `OrderID` element after the `sql:relationship`, then it no longer works:

```
...
   <ElementType name="Orders" sql:relation="Orders" >
...
      <element type="OrderDetails" >
         <sql:relationship
                key-relation="Orders"
                key="OrderID"
                foreign-key="OrderID"
                foreign-relation="[Order Details]" />
      </element>
...
      <element type="OrderID" sql:field="OrderID" />
   </ElementType>
...
```

This restriction can be overcome, if necessary, by placing the key field within the child node, to give it an explicit value rather than inheriting it from the parent. You need to be careful when doing this though as the value within the child will always override any value that could be implicitly passed. So, even if you specified the schema correctly, as in the first case, but gave the child records an explicit key value, this would take precedence over the value being passed down from the parent.

Un-Supported Schema Annotations

The following annotations are not supported in the Web Release 1 version of XML Bulk Load:

- `sql:id-prefix`. This is not supported in that, if any prefixes are specified, they are removed before being passed to SQL Server.
- `sql:url-encode`. This is not supported.
- `sql:is-mapping-schema`. This annotation is not allowed.
- `sql:key-fields`. This annotation is allowed within the schema but is ignored by XML Bulk Load if used.
- `sql:idref`, `sql:idrefs`. XML Bulk Load ignores these annotations if they are found within the schema. This means that any records that use them will be ignored as well and not loaded.

Streaming

All the examples that we have used so far have been with a complete XML document. However, the way that XML Bulk Load actually works is to read part of the XML document at a time, rather than read the whole thing into memory to interpret it. If XML Bulk Load didn't work this way there would be real problems importing large XML documents in all but the largest memory equipped machines.

The side effect of this is that the XML document doesn't need to be well-formed. This means that it will quite happily load documents that don't have a single root node or even ones that come from an ADO `Stream` object.

To illustrate this, let's say that a customer (`VINET`) wants to make the same orders today that it made in 1996. We could write the query below, and put it into a stored procedure, to extract all the details of those orders. Rather than create an XML document that we then put through the XML Bulk Load, we can stream the results of this query directly through XML Bulk Load.

```
Create Procedure VINETOrders1996

   AS

SELECT Orders.OrderID,
       CustomerID,
       EmployeeID,
       OrderDate = '1 April 2001',
       RequiredDate = '10 April 2001',
       ShipVia,
       Freight,
       ShipName,
       ShipAddress,
       ShipCity,
       ShipRegion,
       ShipPostalCode,
       ShipCountry,
       ProductID,
       UnitPrice,
       Quantity
  FROM Orders
  JOIN [Order Details] OrderDetails
    ON Orders.OrderID = OrderDetails.OrderID
 WHERE CustomerID = 'VINET'
   AND OrderDate Between '1 Jan 1996' and '31 Dec 1996'
   FOR XML AUTO, ELEMENTS
```

Putting this query into the VBScript to perform the load gives the code below:

```
Function Main()

   ' Create the new XML Bulk Load object, the ADO connect,
   ' command, and stream
   Set myBLObject = CreateObject("SQLXMLBulkLoad.SQLXMLBulkLoad")
   Set myConnection = CreateObject("ADODB.Connection")
   Set myCommand = CreateObject("ADODB.Command")
   Set myStream = CreateObject("ADODB.Stream")

   ' Open connection to database to run query
   myConnection.ConnectionString = "provider=SQLOLEDB.1;" & _
      "data source=(local);database=Northwind;Integrated Security=SSPI"
   myConnection.Open

   ' Set up the command to stream out the query results
   Set myCommand.ActiveConnection = myConnection
   myCommand.CommandText = "exec VINETOrders1996"

   ' Stream the results
   myStream.Open
   myStream.LineSeparator = -1
   myCommand.Properties("Output Stream").value = myStream
   myCommand.Execute , , adExecuteStream
   myStream.Position = 0

   ' Set the connection string in order to connect to the Northwind
   ' database on the local server using integrated security
   myBLObject.ConnectionString="provider=SQLOLEDB.1;data source=(local);" _
         & "database=Northwind;Integrated Security=SSPI"

   ' Log any errors
   myBLObject.ErrorLogFile = "c:\sqlxml\chapter10\errorlog.xml"

   ' Let SQL Server override the identity values for OrderID
   myBLObject.KeepIdentity = False

   ' The FOR XML AUTO doesn't return a full document so we need to
   ' tell XML Bulk Load not to expect a single root node
   myBLObject.XMLFragment = True

   ' And perform the data import
   myBLObject.Execute "c:\sqlxml\chapter10\OrdersSchema.xml", myStream

   ' Tidy up at the end
   Set myBLObject = Nothing
   Set myStream = Nothing
   Set myCommand = Nothing
   Set myConnection = Nothing

   Main = DTSTaskExecResult_Success

End Function
```

As you can see, apart from creating the ADO stream at the beginning, the rest of the code is almost identical to before. The main difference is that the line where the bulk load object is executed now takes the ADO stream rather than an XML document. We also need to set the `XMLFragment` property to `True` as the stream doesn't contain the root tags.

Creating the Schema During the Import

We can also manipulate the tables within the database that we are loading into, as we are performing the load. As we load into them, we can:

- Create the tables
- Drop and recreate the tables

To create the table or tables as the import is happening, we use the `SchemaGen` property of the bulk load object. Setting this property to `True` has the effect of creating the tables that are defined within the annotated XDR schema, prior to the data being loaded in.

To show this in action, we are going to create a new table called `SubTerritories` that will hold a list of areas within a territory. We will then load into the table the areas within the United Kingdom. The XML document (called `SubTerritories.xml`) looks like this:

```
<ROOT>
  <SubTerritories>
    <SubTerritoryID>1</SubTerritoryID>
    <SubTerritoryDescription>London</SubTerritoryDescription>
    <TerritoryID>99000</TerritoryID>
  </SubTerritories>
  <SubTerritories>
    <SubTerritoryID>2</SubTerritoryID>
    <SubTerritoryDescription>South East</SubTerritoryDescription>
    <TerritoryID>99000</TerritoryID>
  </SubTerritories>
  <SubTerritories>
    <SubTerritoryID>3</SubTerritoryID>
    <SubTerritoryDescription>South West</SubTerritoryDescription>
    <TerritoryID>99000</TerritoryID>
  </SubTerritories>
  <SubTerritories>
    <SubTerritoryID>4</SubTerritoryID>
    <SubTerritoryDescription>East Anglia</SubTerritoryDescription>
    <TerritoryID>99000</TerritoryID>
  </SubTerritories>
  <SubTerritories>
    <SubTerritoryID>5</SubTerritoryID>
    <SubTerritoryDescription>Midlands</SubTerritoryDescription>
    <TerritoryID>99000</TerritoryID>
  </SubTerritories>
  <SubTerritories>
    <SubTerritoryID>6</SubTerritoryID>
    <SubTerritoryDescription>North West</SubTerritoryDescription>
    <TerritoryID>99000</TerritoryID>
  </SubTerritories>
  <SubTerritories>
    <SubTerritoryID>7</SubTerritoryID>
    <SubTerritoryDescription>Yorkshire</SubTerritoryDescription>
    <TerritoryID>99000</TerritoryID>
```

```
  </SubTerritories>
  <SubTerritories>
    <SubTerritoryID>8</SubTerritoryID>
    <SubTerritoryDescription>North East</SubTerritoryDescription>
    <TerritoryID>99000</TerritoryID>
  </SubTerritories>
  <SubTerritories>
    <SubTerritoryID>9</SubTerritoryID>
    <SubTerritoryDescription>Scotland</SubTerritoryDescription>
    <TerritoryID>99000</TerritoryID>
  </SubTerritories>
</ROOT>
```

The XDR annotated schema to do the actual loading (called `SubTerritoriesSchema.xml`) is as follows:

```
<?xml version="1.0" ?>
<Schema xmlns="urn:schemas-microsoft-com:xml-data"
        xmlns:dt="urn:schemas-microsoft-com:xml:datatypes"
        xmlns:sql="urn:schemas-microsoft-com:xml-sql" >

   <ElementType name="SubTerritoryID" dt:type="string" />
   <ElementType name="SubTerritoryDescription" dt:type="string" />
   <ElementType name="TerritoryID" dt:type="int" />

   <ElementType name="root" sql:is-constant="1">
      <element type="SubTerritories" />
   </ElementType>

   <ElementType name="SubTerritories" sql:relation="SubTerritories" >
      <element type="SubTerritoryID" sql:field="SubTerritoryID" />
      <element type="SubTerritoryDescription"
               sql:field="SubTerritoryDescription" />
      <element type="TerritoryID" sql:field="TerritoryID" />
   </ElementType>
</Schema>
```

The VBScript is almost identical to the previous examples, with the addition of the line to set the `SchemaGen` property:

```
Function Main()

   ' Create the new XML Bulk Load object
   Set myObject = CreateObject("SQLXMLBulkLoad.SQLXMLBulkLoad")

   ' Set the connection string in order to connect to the Northwind
   ' database on the local server using integrated security
   myObject.ConnectionString = "provider=SQLOLEDB.1;data source=(local);" _
         & "database=Northwind;Integrated Security=SSPI"

   ' Log any errors
   myObject.ErrorLogFile = "c:\sqlxml\chapter10\errorlog.xml"

   ' Create the SubTerritories table
   myObject.SchemaGen = True
```

```
    ' And perform the data import
    myObject.Execute "c:\sqlxml\chapter10\SubTerritoriesSchema.xml", _
         "c:\sqlxml\chapter10\SubTerritories.xml"

    ' Tidy up at the end
    Set myObject=Nothing

    Main = DTSTaskExecResult_Success

End Function
```

As you can see from the following diagram, the `SubTerritories` table has been created. However, because we used just a normal import annotated XDR schema, no primary key field was created and all the fields have been defaulted to the `nvarchar` data type:

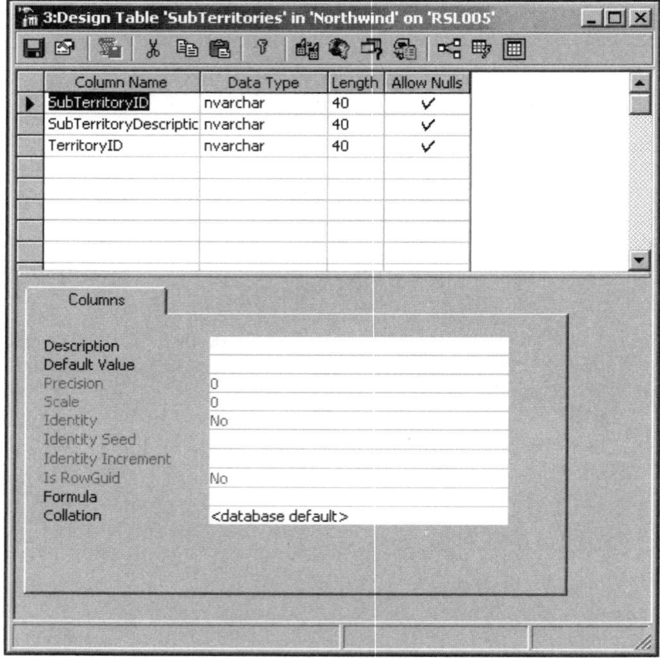

To get around this, we need to add some extra information to the annotated XDR schema, as highlighted below. We add a `sql:key` to specify that the `SubTerritoryID` is the primary key field, and then put `sql:datatype` against each element to specify the data type within SQL Server:

```
<?xml version="1.0" ?>
<Schema xmlns="urn:schemas-microsoft-com:xml-data"
        xmlns:dt="urn:schemas-microsoft-com:xml:datatypes"
        xmlns:sql="urn:schemas-microsoft-com:xml-sql" >

   <ElementType name="SubTerritoryID" dt:type="string" />
   <ElementType name="SubTerritoryDescription" dt:type="string" />
   <ElementType name="TerritoryID" dt:type="int" />
```

```
   <ElementType name="root" sql:is-constant="1">
      <element type="SubTerritories" />
   </ElementType>

   <ElementType name="SubTerritories" sql:relation="SubTerritories"
                sql:key-fields="SubTerritoryID" >
      <element type="SubTerritoryID" sql:field="SubTerritoryID"
                sql:datatype="int" />
      <element type="SubTerritoryDescription"
                sql:field="SubTerritoryDescription"
                sql:datatype="varchar(30)" />
      <element type="TerritoryID" sql:field="TerritoryID"
                sql:datatype="int" />
   </ElementType>
</Schema>
```

Unfortunately, the data types part of the element definition does not currently work in the XML Bulk Load from Web Release 1, even though the documentation indicates that this is one of the new features – so all your fields will still be created as `nvarchar(40)`.

As we have already created the `SubTerritories` table, we need to drop it first before we can re-create it. We need to use the `SGDropTables` property though, obviously, it only makes sense to use this in conjunction with the `SchemaGen` property – otherwise we wouldn't have any table to load our data into!

We therefore need to change the VBScript slightly to include the setting of this property:

```
Function Main()

   ' Create the new XML Bulk Load object
   Set myObject = CreateObject("SQLXMLBulkLoad.SQLXMLBulkLoad")

   ' Set the connection string in order to connect to the Northwind database
   ' on the local server using integrated security
   myObject.ConnectionString = "provider=SQLOLEDB.1;data source=(local);" _
         & "database=Northwind;Integrated Security=SSPI"

   ' Log any errors
   myObject.ErrorLogFile = "c:\sqlxml\chapter11\errorlog.xml"

   ' Create the SubTerritories table
   myObject.SchemaGen = True
   ' Drop the SubTerritories table prior to creating it
   myObject.SGDropTables = True

   ' And perform the data import
   myObject.Execute "c:\sqlxml\chapter11\SubTerritoriesSchema.xml", _
         "c:\sqlxml\chapter11\SubTerritories.xml"

   ' Tidy up at the end
   Set myObject = Nothing
   Set myStream = Nothing
   Set myCommand = Nothing
   Set myConnection = Nothing

   Main = DTSTaskExecResult_Success

End Function
```

Once this XML Bulk Load has been run, we can see that the primary key has been added to the `SubTerritoryID` column:

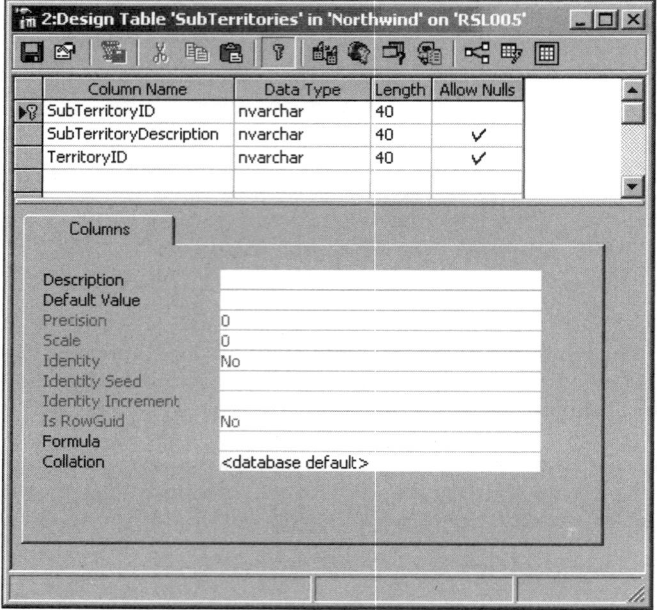

Summary

In this chapter we have seen how to use XML Bulk Load to import data into SQL Server from XML documents and streams.

Before going through the details of XML Bulk Load, we made a quick detour to give an overview of the other methods of bulk loading that SQL Server offers: DTS, `BULK INSERT`, and the `bcp` utility.

We showed how to import data into both one and multiple tables in one import, how to load from streams rather than from XML documents, and how to manipulate the underlying schema as we loaded the data.

We also described the XML Bulk Load object model and ran through the method and properties that are exposed by it.

Let's now turn our attention to how we can bring together all of the techniques we have covered so far in this book and show how best to put them into use.

SQL
XML

Enhancing Legacy Applications with XML

This case study will start with an existing client-server application rather than a completely new set of requirements. It is a fact of life that very few people want to throw out their existing systems every time a new language, feature, or opportunity presents itself. It is more likely that additional requirements have to be added to a system without breaking existing functionality. Legacy systems (in other words, systems that work and are providing benefits to users) are a fact of life, and one that XML in particular is well suited to dealing with, either in terms of application integration (trying to use all or parts of the present application as-is in new ways) or migration (trying to move the current application forward in a way that promotes further change).

The integration (and enhancement) of legacy applications using XML is a popular topic, and deserves an entire book devoted to it, rather than a brief case study. However, by working through this case study, some of the larger issues that are encountered in application integration will be uncovered and discussed, indeed, some of them may even be resolved. Please note that some of the techniques that would be used in "larger" environments (SOAP, BizTalk, industry standard XML vocabularies, Message Queuing) are all solutions of the "Sledgehammer, say hello to Mr. Nut" variety for the specific application we are attempting to enhance. The solution to any specific problem of course should be subject to a cost/benefit analysis and for another application any of these technologies may be an ideal fit.

The example we will use is very heavily Visual Basic/COM+ based to illustrate the scope and application of XML documents. SQL Server 2000 plays a secondary role in all of this purely because the amount of work required to generate XML documents in SQL Server is so small. This is actually one of the strongest selling points of SQL Server 2000 and a major reason why anyone developing XML-based applications would choose SQL Server 2000 over another database.

There are a number of proposed enhancements to our application, and we'll look at a simple implementation of each, and then we'll show you where other resources that will help achieve each particular enhancement can be found. Each of the enhancements is something that could reasonably be asked of an existing application, and each uses XML in the proposed solution for similar reasons.

In this case study we are going to discuss:

- The existing application and design
- Which SQL Server 2000 XML features we may be able to take advantage of, and how we use them
- How to incorporate these XML features in a way that promotes further flexibility
- Performance considerations of our proposed solution

All of the code referenced is available on the Wrox website for download. Because this is a "SQL Server 2000 XML" book rather than a generic programming book, we have attempted to keep the code generation walkthroughs to a minimum.

The Existing Application

Let's say that our existing application is a Win32 client-server application using the `Northwind` database within SQL Server and that we want to move to an N-tier solution running on Windows NT4 with MTS.

We'll be using the `Northwind` database that ships with SQL Server, as it's an example database that anyone with SQL Server should have, and because it's also adaptable to our requirements. The `Northwind` database does not have all of the stored procedures we would expect to find in a production system as installed, and as a result, where necessary, we'll need to add a few stored procedures, but we'll discuss these as we progress through the example.

The current functionality is accessed via a Win32 client (using stored procedures rather than embedded SQL statements), which also produces all of the reports that we use (again, all based upon stored procedures). The existing Win32 client will not be discussed in any great detail, although the assumption is that the functionality exposed in this client is in general sufficient (once the additional stored procedures we have to add are included) and all changes we are making are additional requirements.

We'll be changing the code in our client application as well, so for the purposes of this case study we will limit ourselves to examining the client code currently in place for adding a new customer.
At the moment, all data entry is carried out via the Win32 client. All reports are either viewed on screen or printed/faxed/e-mailed. There are several drawbacks to the way this application is written, and a brief summary of these is given here:

- "Simplistic" client-server design.
- Does not scale well.
- Presentation, business logic, and data access all reside in the same application – although hopefully (for the purpose of converting to n-tier) not the same set of routines.
- The client application and the database are tightly coupled (due to the extensive use of stored procedures) – we could not move the data over to Oracle (for example) without re-writing the application from the ground up.

The first point – that it has a "simplistic" client-server design is not necessarily a bad thing. This depends on the objective of the application. Not all applications warrant an n-tier design. Many 2-tier applications are faster and quicker to implement than their respective n-tier alternatives. The problem arises when a client-server design has to be extended … again … and again … and again. At some point, the design will "break" by which we mean lose relevance to the problem being addressed. So, we can either re-write parts of the application every time we have to modify the design, or we can look at ways to protect ourselves from the continual changes to our design. Two things that can help here are an N-tier design and XML.

Obviously, if we extend the functionality outside that of our existing application, then we would have to rewrite certain parts of our application. It is possible to rewrite the application in such a way as to minimize any further changes, if this is what we want. For the examples given (the data the user enters doesn't change substantially, but what we want to do with it does), this is the case – it may not always be.

Below is a list of additional pieces of functionality that we need to provide. Each of these could be addressed by either writing (or modifying) additional code, but what we will attempt to do is provide a proposed solution that is powerful enough to deal with these requirements and flexible enough to be extended in the future.

- Browser-based reporting
- Browser-based editing of information
- Additional functionality: automated re-ordering
- Additional functionality: targeted mailshots

Browser-Based Reporting

We have an existing application that can generate reports for us. However, we now have to provide these reports via a web browser. This could be for consistency with other applications we have or it could be so that customers can view their own order details across the Web.

The first issue we have to deal with when considering browser-based reporting is "do we need anything other than SQL Server 2000 (and the ISAPI extension it uses for XML support in IIS)?" It is possible to generate a complete web-based application from SQL Server 2000 using nothing other than XML generated by SQL Server, and XSLT that we have generated ourselves. This can be a very quick way to present data to the outside world. For example, if we have integration issues with another system that understands XML and HTTP, it is entirely possible that we can simply supply one URL, and the task is completed. Total time taken: about 5 minutes.

As an example, consider the following URL-based query, where `northwind` is the name of a virtual directory configured for SQL Server:

```
http://www.northwindtradersfictionalsite.com/northwind/?SQL=select+*+from+Orders+where+
shippeddate+=+'1998-05-05%2000:00:00.000'+FOR+XML+RAW&root=Order
```

This should result in an output that looks something like this:

```
<?xml version="1.0" encoding="utf-8" ?>
<Order>
    <row OrderID="11050" CustomerID="FOLKO" EmployeeID="8"
        OrderDate="1998-04-27T00:00:00" RequiredDate="1998-05-25T00:00:00"
        ShippedDate="1998-05-05T00:00:00" ShipVia="2" Freight="59.41"
        ShipName="Folk och fä HB" ShipAddress="Åkergatan 24" ShipCity="Bräcke"
        ShipPostalCode="S-844 67" ShipCountry="Sweden" />
    <row OrderID="11055" CustomerID="HILAA" EmployeeID="7"
        OrderDate="1998-04-28T00:00:00" RequiredDate="1998-05-26T00:00:00"
        ShippedDate="1998-05-05T00:00:00" ShipVia="2" Freight="120.92"
        ShipName="HILARION-Abastos"
        ShipAddress="Carrera 22 con Ave. Carlos Soublette #8-35"
        ShipCity="San Cristóbal" ShipRegion="Táchira" ShipPostalCode="5022"
        ShipCountry="Venezuela" />
</Order>
```

Now, if we modify our query to the following:

```
http://www.northwindtradersfictionalsite.com/northwind/?SQL=select+*+from+Orders+where+
shippeddate+=+'1998-05-05%2000:00:00.000'+FOR+XML+RAW&xsl=orders.xsl&root=Order
```

where the key change here is the addition of a stylesheet we have previously written (`orders.xsl`), we can very quickly produce web-formatted reports of high quality. This could be the subject of an entire chapter (and we have already discussed XSL in Chapter 2) so we will not go into any further detail here, other than to say that when using one or more queries, we can very quickly generate a SQL statement and corresponding XSL stylesheet that SQL Server 2000 can use to provide us with web reporting.

However, if we have a system that has potentially thousands of users, with advanced reporting requirements, we may need to look elsewhere. The proposed solution for this type of problem is an N-tier design.

This is not a book about COM, COM+, or .NET (or generic n-tier design for that matter). However, due to the nature of XML, the use of any of these gives us a degree of flexibility, and, due to Microsoft's inclusion of XML support in SQL Server 2000 and the external libraries such as MSXML, flexible solutions can be developed very quickly indeed.

Browser-Based Editing of Information

While it is possible to build a browser-based application using just the XML features within SQL Server 2000 to carry out the basic Create, Read, Update, and Delete (CRUD) functionality, we are currently more likely to use a mixture of Active Server Pages (ASP) and COM components using an n-tier design to supply this functionality (currently the most common approach using IIS). Within an n-tier design, an application is separated into three (or more) layers (or tiers). These are:

- A presentation layer
- A business logic layer
- A data access layer

The presentation layer is the GUI, web pages, and external APIs that we present to the world. The business logic layer is where the majority (ideally all) of the application specific logic of the application lies. The data access layer is not the database – it is how we access data. This of course leaves the database as an additional fourth tier.

At this point we'll include a quick definition of what component, object, and class mean within this case study – each of these has more than one meaning in the wider scheme of things:

- Component – a grouping of classes
- Class – a Visual Basic class
- Object – an instantiated (one we have created and are using in code) class

Each of our layers contains a number of components, and each component contains a number of objects (among other things). Each class can be a combination of data and behaviors. If we were to create a class called `cCustomer`, which enabled us to carry out the basic CRUD operations on individual rows within the `Customers` table of the `Northwind` database, what would it look like? While it is of course extremely bad practice to use the physical data model to derive our object design, an examination of the `Customers` table may be useful at this point:

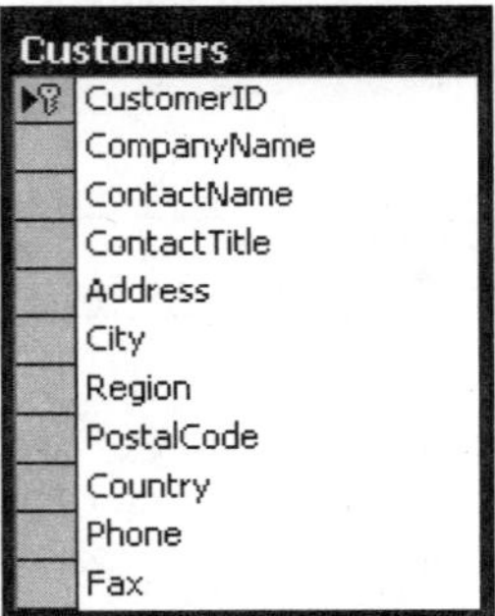

For the initial part of our discussion, all of the information we really need is supplied above, as we can see what the fields are, and what the primary key is. However, for later discussion, we will need to know slightly more about the structure of this table (field data types and lengths for example), so we'll include the DDL we would need to generate the table. The table is already present, so we don't need to actually generate this – it is just included for reference:

```
CREATE TABLE [dbo].[Customers] (
  [CustomerID] [nchar] (5) COLLATE Latin1_General_CI_AS NOT NULL ,
  [CompanyName] [nvarchar] (40) COLLATE Latin1_General_CI_AS NOT NULL ,
  [ContactName] [nvarchar] (30) COLLATE Latin1_General_CI_AS NULL ,
  [ContactTitle] [nvarchar] (30) COLLATE Latin1_General_CI_AS NULL ,
  [Address] [nvarchar] (60) COLLATE Latin1_General_CI_AS NULL ,
  [City] [nvarchar] (15) COLLATE Latin1_General_CI_AS NULL ,
  [Region] [nvarchar] (15) COLLATE Latin1_General_CI_AS NULL ,
  [PostalCode] [nvarchar] (10) COLLATE Latin1_General_CI_AS NULL ,
  [Country] [nvarchar] (15) COLLATE Latin1_General_CI_AS NULL ,
  [Phone] [nvarchar] (24) COLLATE Latin1_General_CI_AS NULL ,
  [Fax] [nvarchar] (24) COLLATE Latin1_General_CI_AS NULL
) ON [PRIMARY]
```

So, we can create an initial class called `cCustomer` that enables us to create, read, update, or delete any row within the `Customers` table. That class might look something like this, if we were to view it within Visual Basic's Object Browser:

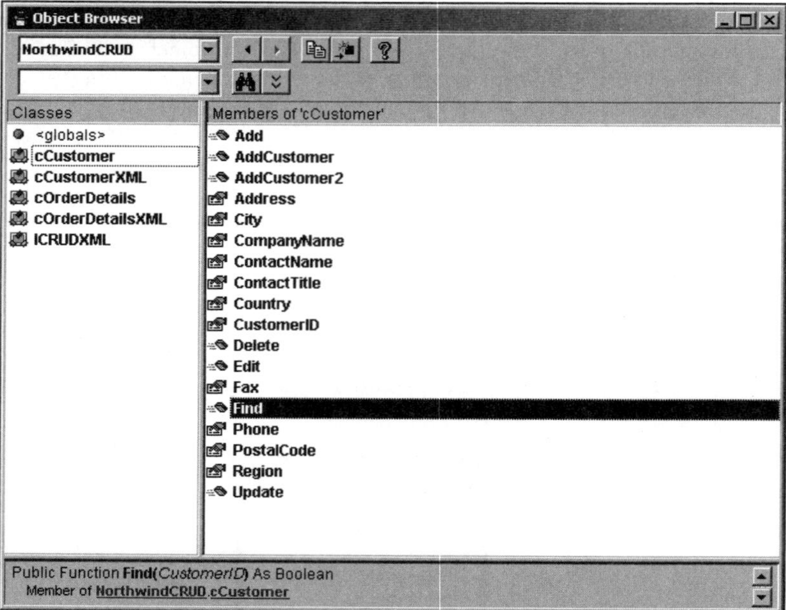

Don't worry about the other classes in the browser; we'll be discussing them later, for now, just look at the `cCustomer` class. Notice that there are a number of properties and methods within this object. There are properties for each attribute (field) a customer has, plus a number of methods relating to customer creation, updates, and deletion.

The following code fragment shows sample code for using this object to add a customer within an application. Note that we are assuming (solely for this example) that we have replaced some of our application's existing "add customer" code with the code shown here. This example is shown purely to highlight some of the problems associated with our initial object and is not intended to be our final solution, so we won't go through the steps required to generate this at this point:

```
Private Sub cmdAdd_Click()

On Error GoTo ERR_cmdAdd_Click

    Dim oCustomer As NorthwindCRUD.cCustomer

    Set oCustomer = CreateObject("NorthwindCRUD.cCustomer")

    With oCustomer
         .CustomerID = Me.CustomerID
         .CompanyName = Me.CompanyName
         .ContactName = Me.ContactName
         .ContactTitle = Me.ContactTitle
         .Address = Me.Address
         .City = Me.City
```

```
            .Region = Me.Region
            .PostalCode = Me.PostalCode
            .Country = Me.Country
            .Phone = Me.Phone
            .Fax = Me.Fax
            .Add
        End With

    EXIT_cmdAdd_Click:
        Set cCustomer = Nothing
        Exit Sub
    ERR_cmdAdd_Click:

        MsgBox "(" & Err.Number & ") " & Err.Description, vbInformation, _
            "Error Adding Customer"
        Resume EXIT_cmdAdd_Click

    End Sub
```

An additional benefit of having developed the above code at this stage is that if we wanted to add a web page that dealt with adding a customer, we have 50% of the code required already written – we simply write an ASP that uses this object.

Problems with the Initial Object Design

There are potential problems associated with this `cCustomer` class due to factors not immediately apparent upon viewing this code. These issues relate to flexibility, and the number of network roundtrips it requires to add a customer, retrieve a customer's information, or (possibly) edit a customer.

One way around this is to use ActiveX Data Object (ADO) disconnected recordsets in our application. This is a perfectly valid mechanism, and will be examined for performance related issues later in this case study. One of the other ways around this problem has been outlined (in a slightly different format) in *Visual Basic 6 Business Objects*, Wrox Press, ISBN 186100107X. Rather than passing all the fields in a separate format, we would declare a function similar to the one shown here:

```
    Function Add(ByVal CustomerInfo as String) As Boolean
```

A typical string we would pass-in, could be similar to this:

```
1.0,ALFKI,Alfreds Futterkiste,Maria Anders,Sales Representative,Obere
Str.57Berlin,NULL,12209,Germany,030-0074321,030-0076545,NULL
```

The format above is simply comma-separated values with all the fields relating to database fields with the exception of the first, which is a format version number.

If our `cCustomer` class checks the version of the information being passed-in against versions it is capable of dealing with this interface can be extremely flexible. For example, we could have a version 5.0 client talking with a version 1.0 `cCustomer` object, and although it may not be possible to execute any of the desired data operations (due to dramatic versioning differences), it is still possible to glean a useful output from such an interaction. You see, in causing a version 5.0 client to talk to a version 1.0 object, we can actually bring about certain other operations to help resolve the incompatibility issues between versions. For example, we could have the details passed to an object that can deal with version 1.0 (and hence alleviate the problem totally), or we could, if we were to choose to, generate an error message to be sent to the client that purveys useful information describing why the operation failed (as opposed to a generic "Sorry – this didn't work" message).

The only problem with the string format above is that we have to write code to support it. For example, we would have to write custom parsers to deal with data types, Null values, and for building-up and breaking-down the string. This isn't a great deal of code, but then we have to re-write, test, document, and maintain it (and we are, of course, planning on doing the last three of these) every time we wish to change the facilities of our parser. In addition, we then have to convert this data into a format that the database of our choice (in this case, SQL Server) can understand.

However, it is possible to pass strings round in a self-describing format that has a large set of tools freely available for use that we can use today – XML. Nothing within XML is revolutionary but it does bring a great deal of industry support (and less code to maintain as a result) that we can take advantage of.

Is XML Fast Enough for Our Purposes?

We are going to generate a number of tests to try and determine the relative performance of XML versus ActiveX Data Objects. Please bear in mind that some of these results will be dependant upon the hardware that the tests are running upon and the other loads that the machinery is under. All tests are available on the Wrox web site with additional instructions on how to set them up. We are not going to walk through every piece of code and describe how to start the Visual Basic IDE up for each and every test – there is enough information in this case study to build these tests from scratch if you want. Similarly, full code is available on the Wrox web site if you want it. For those that just want to look at the relative performance implications without a great deal of code walkthrough, here are the results.

Classes Required for Our Data Entry Test

Before we move onto a discussion of XML itself, we will examine what the performance implications of using XML within our application are likely to be. The machines used for this experiment are not servers, they barely qualify as desktop – but the relative figures are what is important for this discussion.

We can create a copy of the `Order Details` table from the `Northwind` database, called `tblOrderDetail`. We choose this table because it is a table that we would expect a reasonable amount of action on in a real-world situation. `Order Details` only has five fields, ideally we would have more, so as to amplify any reduction in the number of network roundtrips required to carry out an operation. As such, to observe a noticeable reduction in the number of network roundtrips any effect caused by our use of XML in this situation would need to be fairly pronounced.

The next thing we will do is create two separate classes: `cOrderDetails`, and `cOrderDetailsXML`. These classes would form part of our data access layer in a proposed N-tier design. These need to be created within an ActiveX DLL in the Visual Basic IDE. So start up Visual Basic and create a project of type ActiveX DLL.

Then make sure you have the ActiveX Data Objects Library loaded (the most recent one available and ideally no earlier than 2.5, due to the addition of `IStream`):

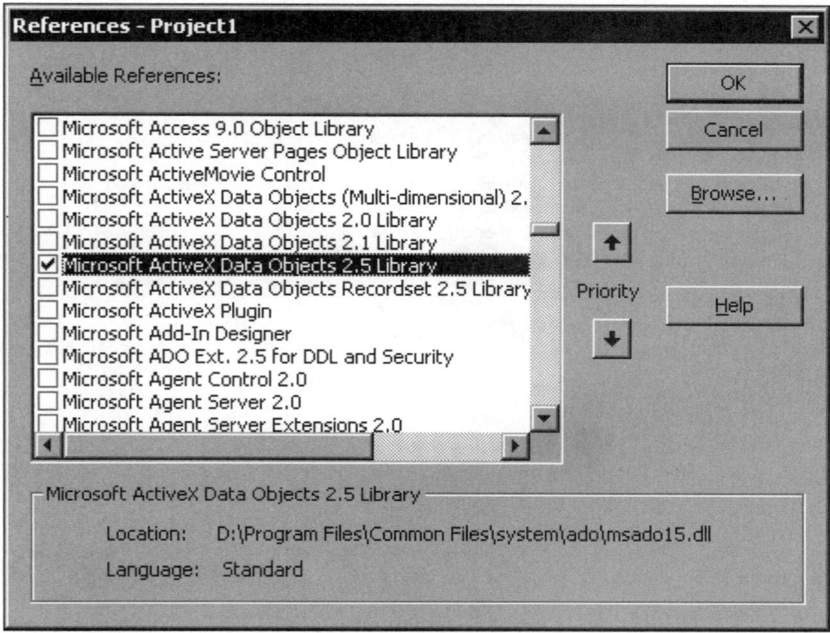

Rename the default class (`Class1`) to be `cOrderDetails`. The code for `cOrderDetails` is shown in the following code fragment:

```
Option Explicit

Public OrderID As Variant
Public ProductID As Variant
Public UnitPrice As Variant
Public Quantity As Variant
Public Discount As Variant

Private conn As ADODB.Connection
Private cmd As ADODB.Command

Private Const CONNECTIONSTRING = _
   "Provider=SQLOLEDB;Server=AO;Database=Northwind;UID=scott;PWD=TIGER"
'
'
'
Public Function Add() As Boolean

On Error GoTo ERR_Add

    Dim blnReturn As Boolean
    blnReturn = False

    Set conn = CreateObject("ADODB.Connection")
    Call conn.Open(getConnectionString())
```

```
    Set cmd = CreateObject("ADODB.Command")
    With cmd
        .CommandType = adCmdStoredProc
        .CommandText = "prcAddOrderDetail"
        .Parameters.Append cmd.CreateParameter( _
            "OrderID", adInteger, adParamInput, , OrderID)
        .Parameters.Append cmd.CreateParameter( _
            "ProductID", adInteger, adParamInput, , ProductID)
        .Parameters.Append cmd.CreateParameter( _
            "UnitPrice", adCurrency, adParamInput, , UnitPrice)
        .Parameters.Append cmd.CreateParameter( _
            "Quantity", adSmallInt, adParamInput, , Quantity)
        .Parameters.Append cmd.CreateParameter( _
            "Discount", adSingle, adParamInput, , Discount)
        .ActiveConnection = conn
        .Execute
    End With

    conn.Close

    Set cmd = Nothing
    Set conn = Nothing
    Add= True

End Function
'
'   Hard coded at present/change to one of
'
'       -   Registry entry
'       -   Suck out of active directory
'       -   local file
'       -   Generic config object
'
Public Function getConnectionString()

    getConnectionString = CONNECTIONSTRING

End Function
```

We are not incorporating error-trapping, validation etc. in this situation because this is purely a quick test to see how effective each type of interface will be. All that the above code does is provide simple properties to represent each field in the `Order Details` table, and provide an additional `Add` method that calls a stored procedure on the server to add a row. The stored procedure that we need is shown in the next code fragment, and is what you would expect to see:

```
CREATE PROCEDURE prcAddOrderDetail @OrderID int, @ProductID int,
                 @UnitPrice money, @Quantity smallint, @Discount real AS
INSERT tblOrderDetail
Values (@OrderID, @ProductID, @UnitPrice,@Quantity,@Discount)
```

The next class, `cOrderDetailsXML`, is a little more complicated. Here's the code:

```
Option Explicit

Implements ICRUDXML

Private conn As ADODB.Connection
Private cmd As ADODB.Command
```

```
Private Const CONNECTIONSTRING = _
   "Provider=SQLOLEDB;Server=AO;Database=Northwind;UID=scott;PWD=TIGER"


Private Function ICRUDXML_IXMLCreate(ByVal CreateXML As String) As String

    Set conn = CreateObject("ADODB.Connection")
    Call conn.Open(CONNECTIONSTRING)

    Set cmd = CreateObject("ADODB.Command")
    With cmd
        .CommandType = adCmdStoredProc
        .CommandText = "prcAddOrderDetailXML"
        .Parameters.Append cmd.CreateParameter _
                    ("XML", adWChar, adParamInput, 4000, CreateXML)
        .ActiveConnection = conn
        .Execute
    End With
    conn.Close
    Set cmd = Nothing
    Set conn = Nothing

    ICRUDXML_IXMLCreate = _
       "<AddOrderDetails><PROGID>NorthwindCRUD.cOrderDetailsXML" & _
       "</PROGID><Payload>" + CreateXML + "</Payload></AddOrderDetails>"

End Function
```

There are several differences – the first being this line:

```
Implements ICRUDXML
```

In this line we are implementing an interface to define what methods we can call. We will be going through this in more detail shortly.

Secondly, notice that we now have one call that accepts what we think is XML (as a string) and returns XML (as a string). The stored procedure associated with this class is also a little different from a normal stored procedure:

```
CREATE PROCEDURE prcAddOrderDetailXML @XML nvarchar(4000)  AS
DECLARE @iDoc int
EXEC sp_xml_preparedocument @idoc OUTPUT, @XML
INSERT INTO tblOrderDetail (OrderID, ProductID, UnitPrice, Quantity, Discount)
SELECT * FROM OPENXML (@iDoc,'/ROOT/OD',0) WITH (
         OrderID int,
         ProductID int,
         UnitPrice money,
         Quantity smallint,
         Discount real )

EXEC sp_xml_removedocument @idoc
```

This stored procedure uses a couple of the new XML features of SQL Server 2000 and it expects a string of the form:

```
<ROOT>
  <OD OrderID="10250" ProductID="41" UnitPrice="0" Quantity="10" Discount="0"/>
</ROOT>
```

If all goes according to plan when `prcAddOrderDetailXML` is executed, we should get a row added to `tblOrderDetail`, and a return value similar to this:

```
<AddOrderDetails>
    <PROGID>NorthwindCRUD.cOrderDetailsXML</PROGID>
    <Payload>
        <ROOT>
            <OD OrderID="10250" ProductID="41" UnitPrice="0"
            Quantity="10" Discount="0>
        </ROOT>
    </Payload>
</AddOrderDetails>
```

Running the Test

Next we need to build a test harness – something that will put both classes through their paces. The code for this is available on the Wrox website (`timing1.exe`).

The format for testing both classes is as follows:

- Create a local copy of the original `Order Details` table from the `Northwind` database
- For each row that we have, create either a `cOrderDetails` or `cOrderDetailsXML` object
- For each object, populate the object in the appropriate way and move on to the next row

We need to create a COM+ application to host our objects and run the test harness on another machine (since we are attempting to prove a reduction in network roundtrips will make our XML-based interface more efficient). We are measuring the time in seconds to completely copy over the entire `Order Details` table, row by row, to simulate actual use. Please notice, as has been said previously, this is not being carried out on high-end machinery, so don't expect fantastic absolute figures – it is relative performance we are interested in:

Test	cOrderDetails	cOrderDetailsXML
Initial test	72 (s)	78 (s)

As you can see, the extra overhead of packing the initial object into XML (plus the extra work at the SQL Server side to work with the XML document we have passed in) has actually degraded performance.

However, if we dig a little deeper into the physical setup, we discover that the network is not the bottleneck in our application – we have a 100Mbps switched network, and no other network traffic to speak of. So if we artificially generate moderate network traffic (using an application stress tool), we obtain the following results:

Test	cOrderDetails	cOrderDetailsXML
Moderate network load	265(s)	146(s)

This is a little better, and is more akin to what we expected to see. But what happens if we really load the network?

Test	cOrderDetails	cOrderDetailsXML
Heavy network load	371(s)	177(s)

Well, this is fairly convincing. If we put all the results together, we can see that using the `OPENXML` feature in SQL Server 2000 could potentially give us big performance improvements:

Test	cOrderDetails	cOrderDetailsXML
Initial test	72	78
Moderate network load	265	146
Heavy network load	371	177

Now the example given is fairly simplistic, and has no validation or error checking. If we assume that this type of object belongs in the data access layer, then all of the major validation should have been carried out at the business logic layer – so the approach is valid.

However, if we look at the stored procedure, we notice a side effect (intentional or otherwise). You see, other than the SQL Server limit of 4000 characters for a field of type `nvarchar`, there is nothing in the procedure that prevents us from passing in multiple order details in the same call. So if we re-write our test harness to request the entire `Order Details` table ordered by `OrderID`, we can send all `Order Details` records connected with a single `OrderID` in one operation – not an unreasonable usage. The results for this are given below:

Test	cOrderDetailsXML	cOrderDetailsXML(batch)
Initial test	78	36
Moderate network load	146	68
Heavy network load	177	81

So, we can see that if our applications pass us all `Order Details` associated with `OrderID 102050` in the following format:

```
<ROOT>
   <OD OrderID="10250" ProductID="41" UnitPrice="0" Quantity="10"Discount="0"/>
   <OD OrderID="10250" ProductID="51" UnitPrice="0.15" Quantity="35"
       Discount="0.15"/>
   <OD OrderID="10250" ProductID="65" UnitPrice="0.15" Quantity="15"
       Discount="0.15"/>
</ROOT>
```

We should get three additional rows, and a return value identical to the one here:

```
<AddOrderDetails>
    <PROGID>NorthwindCRUD.cOrderDetailsXML</PROGID>
    <Payload>
        <ROOT>
            <OD OrderID="10250" ProductID="41" UnitPrice="0" Quantity="10"
            Discount="0"/>
            <OD OrderID="10250" ProductID="51" UnitPrice="0.15" Quantity="35"
            Discount="0.15"/>
            <OD OrderID="10250" ProductID="65" UnitPrice="0.15" Quantity="15"
            Discount="0.15"/>
        </ROOT>
    </Payload>
</AddOrderDetails>
```

This would seem to be a fairly strong indicator that XML with SQL Server 2000 has a very large role to play – given the potential performance gains we may realize.

If we use XML as the structure for passing information around an n-tier application, ideally, the first question we should be asking is:

> "At what point in the system do I use XML?"

There are a number of possible answers and the tests we are carrying out will hopefully enable you to determine where the correct point in your own application lies. These include:

- Nowhere, binary formats are faster and I don't like angle brackets
- Nowhere, but we need to put it in because marketing insisted. Where it won't slow us down too much?
- It has a place delivering information to browsers and other applications, but that's about it
- Straight out of the database for cross platform interoperability
- Between the presentation and business logic tiers because they are physically separate
- Everywhere

We'll try to show that unless we are using massive data sets with complicated transforms or processing requiring extensive use of DOM, we may actually make some performance gains by using XML. In addition, the overall design of our application will be simpler and more extensible.

We have already examined the case of placing data into SQL Server, and have shown that using XML in that situation can potentially improve performance. The next case that we shall look at is an example of getting data out of SQL Server.

Test: Getting Data out of SQL Server

If we examine the three stored procedures below, all of which take a single input parameter (a `CustomerID`) and return the relevant `CompanyName`, we would expect performance to be relatively constant across all three stored procedures:

```
CREATE PROCEDURE dbo.prcCustomerInfo @CustomerID varchar(5) AS
SELECT
   CompanyName
FROM
   Customers
WHERE
   CustomerID = @CustomerID
GO
```

```
CREATE PROCEDURE prcCustomerInfoOUT @CustomerID varchar(5),
                 @MyCompanyName varchar(40) OUT AS
SELECT
   @MyCompanyName = CompanyName
FROM
   Customers
WHERE
   CustomerID=@CustomerID
GO
```

```
CREATE PROCEDURE prcCustomerInfoXML @CustomerID varchar(5) AS
SELECT
   CompanyName
FROM
   Customers
WHERE
   CustomerID = @CustomerID
FOR XML RAW
GO
```

If we again build a small test harness (`timings2.exe`) that calls each of these stored procedures for each customer in our `Customers` table, we obtain remarkably similar results for all methods. When we realize that we are only making 91 calls, and instead see just how many calls we can make in a five second interval, we obtain slightly more differentiated results. Obviously, in this case, the greater the number, the better the performance:

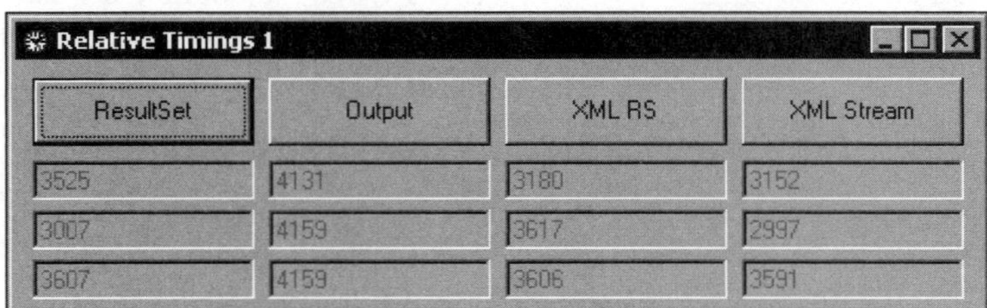

- ResultSet (or more properly recordset) uses the standard `prcCustomerInfo` and ADO code
- Output uses `prcCustomerInfoOUT` and standard ADO code
- XML RS uses `prcCustomerInfoXML` and standard ADO code to return this as a recordset
- XML Stream uses `prcCustomerInfoXML`, and uses streams to return the result we are interested in

Streams are a relatively new (ADO 2.5) feature, and enable us to take data out of SQL Server and quickly push it out to any other object that supports streams – the Microsoft XML Parser and the IIS Response object being two useful objects we can stream to. Sample code for all of these tests is available at the Wrox web site.

So, for small recordsets there doesn't appear to be a great deal of difference between any of the mechanisms outlined. What if (as in the code example above) we aren't after one small piece of information but a large recordset? An example of which would be a report with 2000+ line items? Is there any performance difference in such a situation?

As the following screenshot shows, there is a potential problem here. Using XML passed around as an ADO recordset is fairly fast, but `Streams` seem to be fairly slow. There is another issue arising here, which is specifically due to XML, which we affectionately call **XML bloat**. The additional information required in an XML representation of a recordset, compared to a binary representation such as ADO recordsets, rises as the amount of data we have to pass increases.

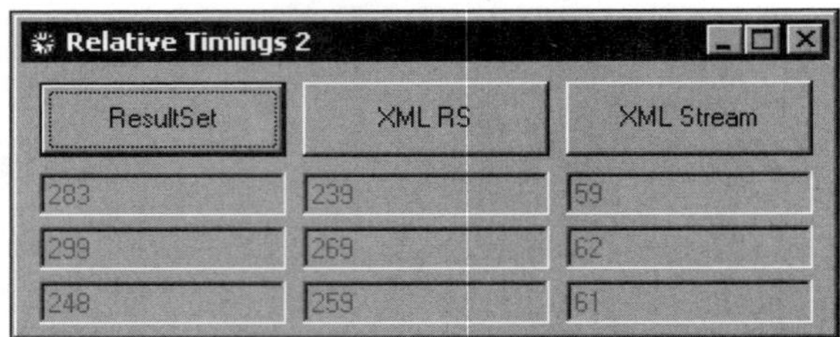

The `timings2` project exists to measure how efficient each method is at obtaining information from the database. We can see that an ADO recordset appears to be much more efficient, with the actual conversion of the data to XML being a secondary consideration. However, there is another issue here that has a big impact on overall performance, but not one that deals specifically with the database. We will be passing data around our application, and currently, there are two real methods for doing this. One is as XML in some form (we will use strings for now) and one is as disconnected recordsets. If we write two additional classes, one representing data as a string, and one using an ADO disconnected recordset, which is more efficient?

We generate two classes, and host them in a COM+ application. Each has only one method, representing either an XML string, or an ADO recordset. We then build a test harness that generates results of the appropriate type, and this passes the information back and forth across the network. Each test will be run three times, and in each case the queries used will be listed.

In the first example, we will use the queries:

```
SELECT * FROM Customers FOR XML RAW
SELECT * FROM Customers
```

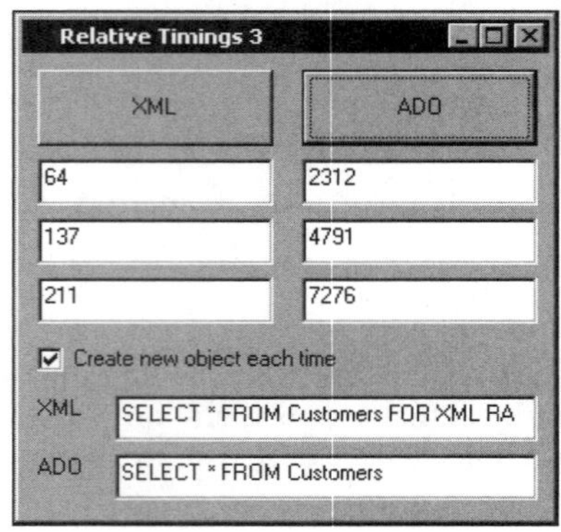

As we can see, the relative performance of passing information in an XML format is not great. But, if we limit the queries to a single row as shown here:

```
SELECT * FROM Customers WHERE CustomerID='ALFKI' FOR XML RAW
SELECT * FROM Customers WHERE CustomerID='ALFKI'
```

We can see that relative performance is a little better:

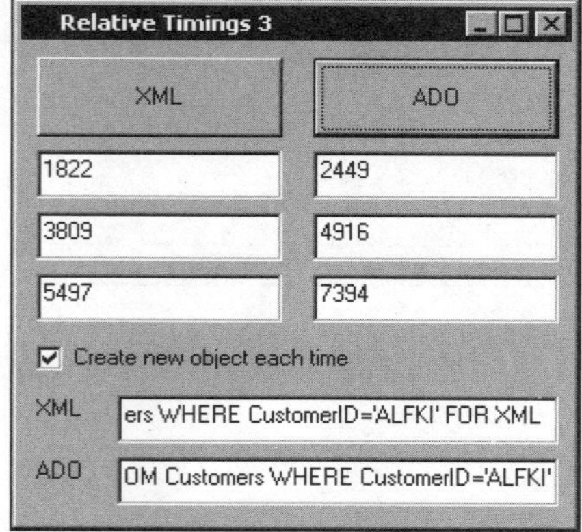

However, it is only when we really limit our queries that the results we get back would indicate XML has any real benefit:

```
SELECT CompanyName FROM Customers WHERE CustomerID='ALFKI'FOR XML RAW
SELECT CompanyName FROM Customers WHERE CustomerID='ALFKI'
```

With the associated result:

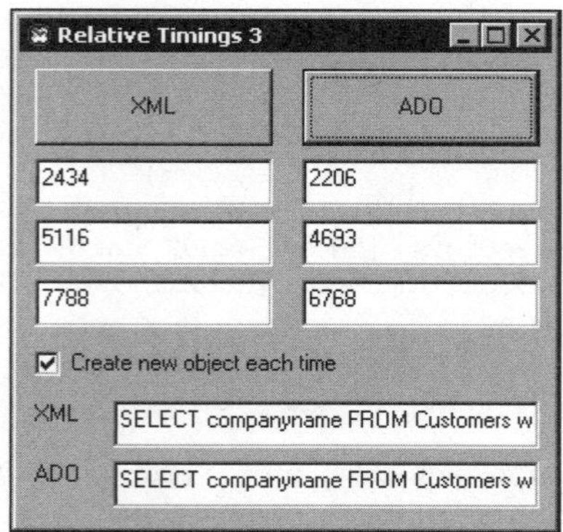

So, we can see from these examples that XML is not particularly well-suited to transferring large amounts of information about the network. In situations where we have small amounts of data, want flexibility, and are prepared to accept a small performance hit to obtain it, we should consider using XML. This is also a fair description of most COM/MTS or DNA applications – we don't want to be passing a lot of information around and we would like to achieve as much as possible with single method calls.

The Current Application

One obvious area in our application where we can use XML is therefore operations on a single row or small collection of rows – in other words, typical OLTP (online transaction processing) style operations. We will continue by extending our existing application for the example of adding an order, using XML and SQL Server 2000's new XML features in particular:

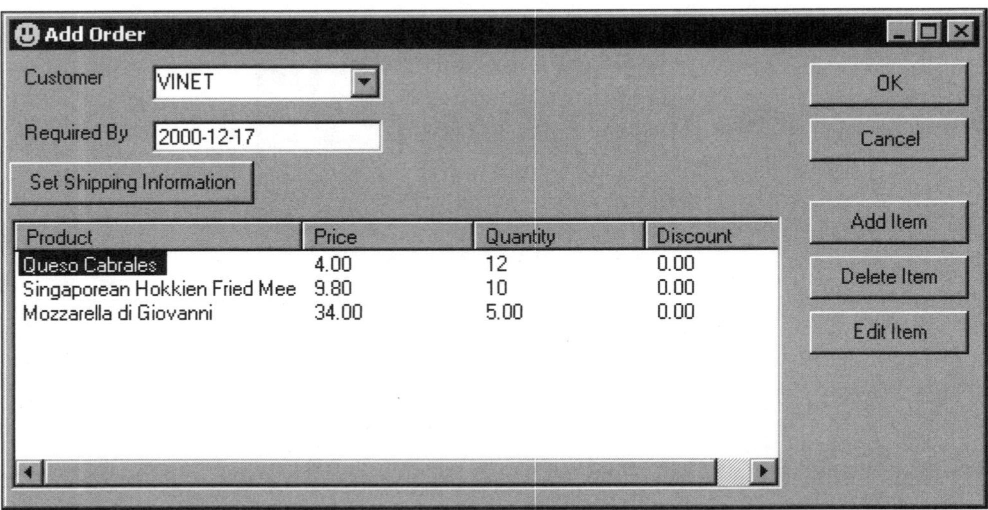

All we are interested in at the moment is what happens when the OK button is pressed. At present, our order is validated, and then created within the database, followed by each order detail. To use our XML-leveraging code, we must replace the existing client code behind the OK button with the code below:

```
Private Sub cmdOK_Click()

    Dim strXML As String
    Dim oAddOrder As XMLEventInterface.IXMLEvent

    strXML = GenerateOrderXML()
    Set oAddOrder = CreateObject("NorthWindEvents.AddOrderEvent")
    ValidateOutput (oAddOrder.XMLEvent(strXML))
    Set oAddOrder = Nothing

End Sub
```

Let's now consider the modifications necessary on the order submission process to leverage some of the capabilities of XML and SQL Server 2000.

First of all, we are going to develop a simple XML-based eventing mechanism to try and obtain some of the benefits we discussed earlier – the flexibility, ease of adding additional functionality and (in particular) deal with the way additional requirements rarely seem to add information, just require us to deal with it in different ways. To do this, we are also going to modify the stored procedure used to do order inserts to use SQL Server's OPENXML support.

Finally, we are going to look at how all this additional work makes some fairly interesting enhancements to our application quite simple. Specifically, we are going to touch on how we might extend the application to do restocking orders with some trading partner and how we might use this infrastructure to allow us to add mail-shot capabilities. Both of these extensions can be implemented without impacting the existing code base (once we have our initial XML eventing infrastructure in place).

- We have to create an interface called XMLEventInterface.IXMLEvent
- We have to create a class called NorthWindEvents.AddOrderEvent that implements this interface
- We have to generate an XML document based on our input and store it within strXML
- We get the results of the XMLEvent method on the NorthWindEvents.AddOrderEvent class and evaluate the results we get back

We will now deal with each of these in turn.

Interfaces

Interfaces are one (the preferred) way of designing COM objects. Rather than placing everything on the default interface, we can design a specific interface that we expect a group of objects to all support. An example at this point will help to illustrate this.

If we create an ActiveX DLL (with a project name of XMLEventInterface) with a single class (IXMLEvent), and the following code within the body of the class we have created, then we do not appear to have done anything particularly useful, it's just a prototype, but let's go a little bit further:

```
Public Function XMLEvent(ByVal EventString As String) As String
End Function

Public Function XMLEvent_Rollback(ByVal EventString As String) As String
End Function

Public Function XMLNotification(ByVal EventString As String)
End Function
```

We now create another ActiveX DLL project, NorthWindEvents that will implement this interface (we have to add a reference to the previous project XMLEventInterface for this to work), with (initially at least) a single class called AddOrderEvents. If we then add the following statement to the AddOrderEvents class:

```
Implements IXMLEVENT
```

we obtain three additional (private) methods – the same three that we defined previously in our interface (see screenshot). Note that with interfaces there is no inheritance of the implementation of functionality. Each class that implements the interface has to provide its own implementation. This is one reason why some programmers prefer delegation:

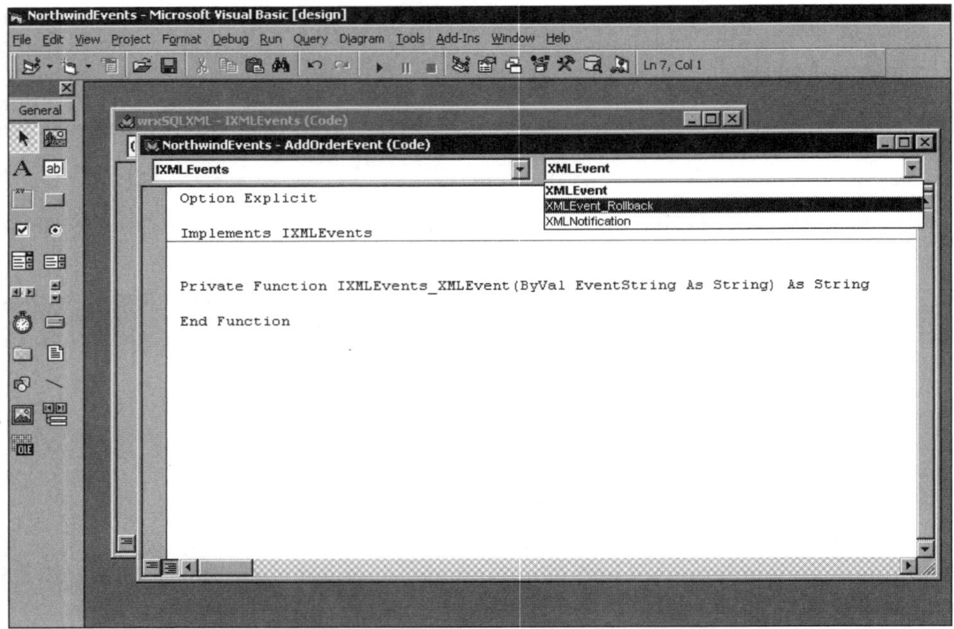

The XML we generate is based on the information we have supplied in the form. One example XML document is supplied below. Notice that this is obviously XML solely for the use of our application, and is structured to minimize the amount of work required to pass data between tiers, and into and out of the database:

```
<Northwind>
   <Header>
      <Version>
         <Major>1</Major>
         <Minor>0</Minor>
         <Revision>1</Revision>
      </Version>
   </Header>
   <Body>
      <AddOrder>
         <Order OrderID="" CustomerID="VINET" EmployeeID="5"
          OrderDate="1996-07-04 00:00:00.000"
          RequiredDate="1996-08-01 00:00:00.000"
          ShippedDate="1996-07-16 00:00:00.000" ShipVia="3"
          Freight="32.3800" ShipName="Vins et alcools Chevalier"
          ShipAddress="59 rue de l'Abbaye" ShipCity="Reims" ShipRegion=""
          ShipPostalCode="51100" ShipCountry="France">
            <OD ProductID="11" UnitPrice="14.0000" Quantity="12"
                Discount="0.0"/>
            <OD ProductID="42" UnitPrice="9.8000" Quantity="10"
                Discount="0.0"/>
            <OD ProductID="72" UnitPrice="32.0000" Quantity="5"
                Discount="0.0"/>
         </Order>
      </AddOrder>
   </Body>
</Northwind>
```

There are a few things to note about this document. Firstly, we have a structure that contains versioning information for the rest of the document, plus the body of the document contains all the information we require to create the new order in its entirety. We could achieve exactly the same ends using an XML namespace, but this would make our processing code a little more involved. For situations where we are sharing documents with others, or using industry-standard XML representations, using a namespace is absolutely the way to go. The versioning rules included are as follows.

Some Thoughts on Versioning

If we can process a major version and a document matches, we should continue. If the document has a lower version number, we will know either how to process it, or find an object that can. If the document has a higher major version number than we can deal with, attempt to locate an object that can deal with the document. Otherwise, an error is generated. A major version number should be incremented any time mandatory information is added to an XML document.

If we match major numbers but not minor, we can process the document but should expect either additional optional information or missing optional information that will not cause processing to fail.

Revision version numbers should be changed each time a document is changed, regardless of what has been changed. This can be either reset to zero every time we make a major or minor change, or just left as-is.

We should always include a version number of some sort, so that we know what we can and cannot do with this document. We will have to write this code ourselves, but it is absolutely vital that we are able to determine the exact version of any XML we are using. Even if we use a namespace, we will have to determine what we can and cannot do based on that namespace.

Before we create the main logic with the `AddOrderEvents` class, we should discuss what exactly we expect this class to do. We could put all the code required to parse and process our XML document within this class, but it would be almost as inflexible as our original client-server code, and slower into the bargain. If, on the other hand, the `AddOrderEvent` determines, based on what we are attempting to do (add an order), what objects could possibly be interested in this fact, and passes the information on to them, we have a much more flexible solution. We could achieve this through the COM+ event system, but that means our code wouldn't run on NT 4.0 machines. What we need is a method of determining what objects we need to create for this event, and then create each of them. This approach is extremely flexible, but works best for areas in which there are a number of disconnected processes associated with each event. Obviously, the synchronization of cancelled events, error conditions etc. have to be taken into account when writing objects that plug into this event-based model. One place we could store this object creation information is our existing SQL database, given that we have already paid for the software (and SQL Server is fairly good at storing data). This does move some of our business logic out of the business tier and straight into the backend, which leads to a blurring of responsibilities in the logical tiers we define. If we classify this information as application metadata then architecturally this becomes less of an issue. However, it is still a blurring of responsibilities between tiers and should be carefully examined.

We need to create a few objects and pieces of information on the SQL Server that we will be using shortly. The table `tblEvent` will hold a series of `ProgIDs` associated with each event we define, and the order in which we should run them:

```
CREATE TABLE tblEvent (
   EventName varchar(50) NOT NULL,
   VersionRequired int NOT NULL,
   Priority int NOT NULL,
   ProgID varchar(50) NOT NULL
)
```

We now need to define a stored procedure that can tell us what `ProgID`s we need for this event. The only other information required is which version(s) of the XML document we can support. If a component can only process (major) version 1 documents, and we receive a version 2 (or higher) document, there is generally very little point in trying to process it. The stored procedure below reflects this:

```
CREATE PROCEDURE prcListProgIDsForEvent @EventName varchar(50),@Version int AS
SELECT
   ProgID
FROM
   tblEvent
WHERE
   EventName = @EventName AND
   VersionRequired >= @Version
ORDER BY
   Priority ASC
```

The component that will actually process the XML and add the order to the database will be called `NorthWindEvents.ProcessAddOrder`, so let's add that to `tblEvent`:

```
INSERT tblEVENT VALUES ('AddOrder',1,1,'NorthWindEvents.ProcessAddOrder')
```

If we quickly use the stored procedure we have written previously:

```
EXEC prcListProgIDsForEvent 'AddOrder',1
```

```
ProgID
-----------------------------------------------
NorthWindEvents.ProcessAddOrder

(1 row(s) affected)
```

we see that when we attempt to add an order at the moment, the only object we will create is the `NorthwindEvents.ProcessAddOrder` class. The code for this `AddOrderEvents` class is shown below. We will go through this code although all following code examples have been cut short – all the techniques used have been demonstrated previously so there is little new to learn from them:

```
Option Explicit

Implements IXMLEvent
Private Const EVENTNAME As String = "AddOrder"
' Connection and command objects
Private conn As ADODB.Connection
Private cmd As ADODB.Command
```

```
Private Const CONNECTIONSTRING = _
   "Provider=SQLOLEDB;Server=AO;Database=Northwind;UID=scott;PWD=TIGER"

'   XML Document holders, filled during ParseDocumentVersion()

Private mintDocumentVersionMajor As Integer
Private mintDocumentVersionMinor As Integer
Private mintDocumentVersionRevision As Integer

'   2D array of strings to store ProgIDs and return codes
'   Eventually we may want to process each return here,
'   rather than at the top level
'
Private masProgIDReturn() As String
Private mblnHasEvents As Boolean
```

This is the main routine, and also where the two separate strands we have been pursuing really come together. The interface we have defined allows us to instantiate any number of objects that support this interface. The interface itself uses XML to provide a flexible and extensible approach.

If we walk through the initial version of this code we can summarize it as follows.

- The procedure `ParseDocumentVersion` determines we are using a version 1 document.
- The function `ListEvents` calls the stored procedure `prcListProgIDsForEvents` with the `@EventName` "`AddOrder`" and document version 1. We receive the following result back:

```
ProgID
----------------------------------------------
NorthWindEvents.ProcessAddOrder
```

This is then placed into a 2 x1 array like so:

(NorthWindEvents.ProcessAddOrder,??????)

where ?????? is the return value that this object generates.

Because all of the objects we call implement the `IXMLEvent` interface, we can use `CreateObject` with a variable `ProgID`, and still use the object we get back. Once we have finished with all our objects, we send the results back to the caller of this object:

```
Private Function IXMLEvent_XMLEvent(ByVal EventXML As String) As String

   Dim intLoop As Integer
   Dim oTemp As IXMLEvent
   Dim strProgID As String
   Dim strReturn As String

   Call ParseDocumentVersion(EventXML)
   Call ListEvents

   If mblnHasEvents Then
      For intLoop = LBound(masProgIDReturn, 2) _
         To UBound(masProgIDReturn, 2)
```

```
                strProgID = masProgIDReturn(1, intLoop)
                Set oTemp = CreateObject(strProgID)
                masProgIDReturn(2, intLoop) = oTemp.XMLEvent(EventXML)
                Set oTemp = Nothing
                strReturn = strReturn & masProgIDReturn(2, intLoop)
            Next intLoop
        End If

        IXMLEvent_XMLEvent = strReturn

    End Function
    '
    '   Parse passed in XML and populate class level variables
    '   Assuming only one version per document at present
    '
    Private Sub ParseDocumentVersion(ByVal pstrXML As String)

         Dim oXML As MSXML2.DOMDocument
         Dim oNodes as MSXML.IXMLDOMNodeList

        Set oXML =  new MSXML2.DOMDocument
        oXML.async = False
        If oXML.loadXML(pstrXML) Then
            Set oNodes = oXML.selectNodes("Northwind/Header/Version")
            mintDocumentVersionMajor = _
                oNodes.Item(0).selectSingleNode("Major").Text

            mintDocumentVersionMinor = _
                    oNodes.Item(0).selectSingleNode("Minor").Text

            mintDocumentVersionRevision = _
                    oNodes.Item(0).selectSingleNode("Revision").Text
        End If
        Set oNodes = Nothing
        Set oXML = Nothing

    End Sub
```

The above routine is our first encounter with the Microsoft XML parser and the DOM (Document Object Model) interface specifically. DOM has a (currently well-deserved) reputation for being both memory hungry and relatively slow. This, coupled with the fact that the latest version is not always universally available means DOM is not always the ideal choice for manipulating XML.

It has to be said in tests, the Microsoft XML Parser (MSXML) is one of the best and fastest. Timings on performance of MSXML go out of date faster than pretty much anything else, so check out both the Microsoft web site (http://msdn.microsoft.com/xml/default.asp) and www.xml.com (http://www.xml.com/pub/r/817 will be hopelessly out of date by the time this book gets published but is not a bad place to start on relative performance) for further information.

An additional factor here is the desire to minimize the new technologies we are showcasing – you may notice that the example above is fairly simplistic, and does not cover 1% of the functionality the Microsoft XML parser has. In real world applications, there is a lot of manipulation of XML by either DOM or another API called SAX (Simple API for XML), which is less memory intensive. If we are developing in any tier in the years to come, there is a very good chance we will be using one of these APIs.

```
'
'   Fill an Array with items of the form
'
'   (ProgID, ????)  where ???? will be the return value from the relevant ProgID
'
'   Uses prcListProgIDsForEvent
'
Private Function ListEvents()

    Dim rsTemp As ADODB.Recordset
    Dim intLoop As Integer

    Set conn = CreateObject("ADODB.Connection")
    Call conn.Open(CONNECTIONSTRING)
    mblnHasEvents = False
    Set cmd = CreateObject("ADODB.Command")
    Set rsTemp = CreateObject("ADODB.RecordSet")
    rsTemp.CursorLocation = adUseClient
    rsTemp.CursorType = adOpenStatic

    With cmd
        .CommandType = adCmdStoredProc
        .CommandText = "prcListProgIDsForEvent"
        .Parameters.Append cmd.CreateParameter("EventName", _
                           adVarChar, adParamInput, 50, EVENTNAME)
        .Parameters.Append cmd.CreateParameter("Version", _
                           adInteger, adParamInput, , _
                           mintDocumentVersionMajor)
        .ActiveConnection = conn
        Set rsTemp = .Execute
    End With

    ' Redim array and populate
    If Not (rsTemp.EOF Or rsTemp.BOF) Then
        mblnHasEvents = True
        ReDim Preserve masProgIDReturn(1 To 2, 1 To rsTemp.RecordCount)
        rsTemp.MoveFirst

        For intLoop = 1 To rsTemp.RecordCount
            masProgIDReturn(1, intLoop) = rsTemp.Fields("ProgID").Value
            rsTemp.MoveNext
        Next intLoop

    End If

     rsTemp.Close
    Set rsTemp = Nothing
    Set cmd = Nothing
    Set conn = Nothing

End Function
```

The sample code for the first of these objects (NorthWindEvents.ProcessAddOrder) is shown below:

```
Private Function IXMLEvent_XMLEvent(ByVal EventXML As String) As String

    Dim strCreateOrder As String
    Dim strOrderID As String
    Dim strOrderDetails As String

    Dim oOrder As ICRUDXML
    Dim oOrderDetails As ICRUDXML

    Dim strReturn As String

    strCreateOrder = GenerateOrderDocument(EventXML)

    Set oOrder = CreateObject("Northwind.Order")
    strOrderID = oOrder.Create(strCreateOrder)
    Set oOrder = Nothing

    '   Add the OrderID to the Order Details document
    strCreateOrderDetails = GenerateOrderDetails(strOrderID, EventXML)

    oOrderDetails = CreateObject("Northwind.OrderDetails")
    strOrderDetails = oOrderDetails.Create(strCreateOrderDetails)
    Set oOrderDetails = Nothing

    strReturn = "<ProcessAddOrder>" & strOrderID & strOrderDetails & _
                "</ProcessAddOrder>"
    IXMLEvent_XMLEvent = strReturn

End Function
```

As we can see, we take our AddOrder XML document, break out the necessary initial order information, and generate an OrderID. We then use this to populate an OrderDetails request similar to the one used in our test object cOrderDetails. We have changed the names here because this is a "production" system rather than our initial exploratory class.

A Web Page that Supports On-Line Ordering

Below is the HTML for a web page that enables us to add orders. Note that this is for testing purposes rather than actual use – the GUI is a little primitive. This page is a test harness for the placeorder.asp page outlined below, and would be replaced by an interactive JScript/DHTML page in reality. All this code is available via the Wrox website:

```
<HTML>
<HEAD>
<META NAME="GENERATOR" Content="Microsoft Visual Studio 6.0">
<TITLE></TITLE>
</HEAD>
<BODY>
```

```
<P>
<FORM action="http://ao/NorthwindWeb/placeorder.asp" method=post
      id=form1 name=form1>
<TEXTAREA id=TEXTAREA1 name=TEXTAREA1 style="HEIGHT: 183px; WIDTH: 547px">
&lt;Northwind&gt;
&lt;Header&gt;
&lt;Version&gt;
&lt;Major&gt;1&lt;/Major&gt;
&lt;Minor&gt;0&lt;/Minor&gt;
&lt;Revision&gt;1&lt;/Revision&gt;
&lt;/Version&gt;
&lt;Body&gt;
&lt;AddOrder&gt;
&lt;Order OrderID="" CustomerID="VINET" EmployeeID="5"
          OrderDate="1996-07-04 00:00:00.000"
          RequiredDate="1996-08-01 00:00:00.000"
          ShippedDate="1996-07-16 00:00:00.000"
          ShipVia="3" Freight="32.3800" ShipName="Vins et alcools Chevalier"
          ShipAddress="59 rue de l'Abbaye" ShipCity="Reims" ShipRegion=""
          ShipPostalCode="51100" ShipCountry="France"&gt;
&lt;OD ProductID="11" UnitPrice="14.0000" Quantity="12" Discount="0.0"/&gt;
&lt;OD ProductID="42" UnitPrice="9.8000" Quantity="10" Discount="0.0"/&gt;
&lt;OD ProductID="72" UnitPrice="32.0000" Quantity="5" Discount="0.0"/&gt;
&lt;/Order&gt;
&lt;/AddOrder&gt;
&lt;/Body&gt;
&lt;/Northwind&gt;
</TEXTAREA>
<INPUT id=submit1 name=submit1 type=submit value=Submit>
<INPUT id=reset1 name=reset1 type=reset value=Reset>
</FORM></P>

</BODY>
</HTML>
```

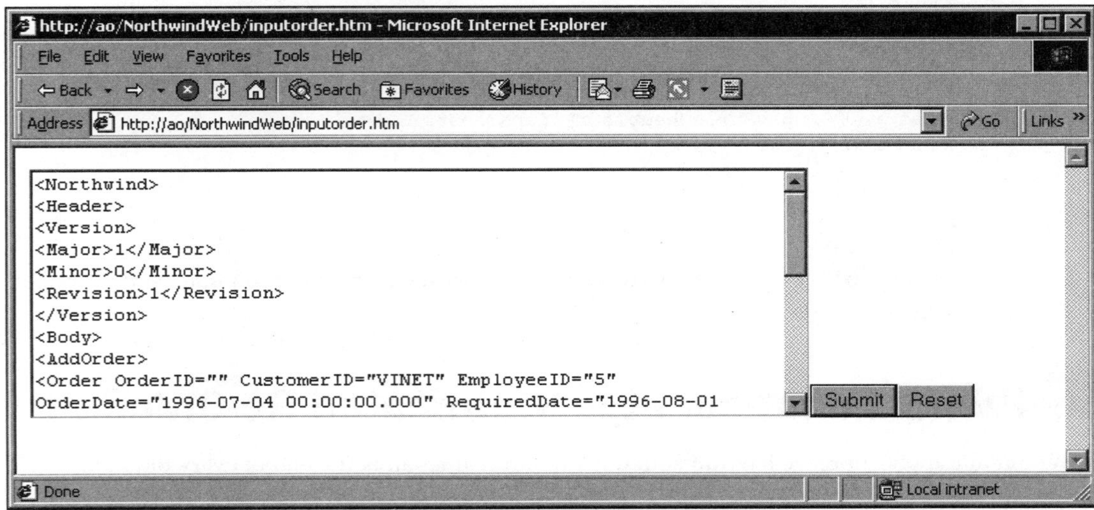
http://ao/NorthwindWeb/inputorder.htm - Microsoft Internet Explorer
File Edit View Favorites Tools Help
Back Search Favorites History
Address http://ao/NorthwindWeb/inputorder.htm
Go Links
<Northwind>
<Header>
<Version>
<Major>1</Major>
<Minor>0</Minor>
<Revision>1</Revision>
</Version>
<Body>
<AddOrder>
<Order OrderID="" CustomerID="VINET" EmployeeID="5"
OrderDate="1996-07-04 00:00:00.000" RequiredDate="1996-08-01
Submit
Reset
Done
Local intranet

This page takes the XML we have built-up, and submits it to a page called `placeorder.asp`. The source for this page is supplied below:

```
<HTML>
<HEAD>
<META NAME="GENERATOR" Content="Microsoft Visual Studio 6.0">
<TITLE></TITLE>
</HEAD>

<BODY>
<%dim x
set x = Server.createobject("NorthwindWeb.WebInterfaces")
Response.Write x.AddOrderEvent (Request.Form("TextArea1"), "AddOrderWeb.xsl")
set x = nothing
%>
<P></P>

</BODY>
</HTML>
```

Our existing objects are not used because we can't use these interfaces directly from an ASP page (although this changes in ASP.NET). The object `NorthwindWeb.WebInterfaces` is responsible for giving us access to the relevant objects and formatting the results, using a stylesheet we have passed in. Partial pseudocode for this class is shown here:

```
Public Function AddOrderEvent(ByVal pstrXML As String, ByVal pstrXSL As String)_
                As String

    Dim strReturn As String
    Dim oEvent As IXMLEvent

    '   Obtain the results from our AddOrderEvent
    Set oEvent = CreateObject("NorthWindEvents.AddOrderEvent")
    '   Process the XML result to see what we should be saying at this point
    strReturn = oEvent.XMLEvent(pstrXML)
    Set oEvent = Nothing
    strReturn = ValidateResult(strReturn)
    '   Apply stylesheet to result
    strReturn = ApplyStyleSheet(strReturn, pstrXSL)
    ' Send back results
    AddOrderEvent = strReturn

End Function
```

As we can see, the main body of this method is already written, leaving us to implement a number of supporting functions.

Additional Functionality – Automated Re-Ordering

Within our application, we have an additional report that is run at the end of every day. This report tells us what items we need to order, and will print off on a page-per-supplier basis, so that we can fax/e-mail the relevant suppliers with our needs.

However, we now have an additional requirement to our application – we want to re-order stock automatically as and when stock levels fall below their pre-defined levels, and we want to submit these orders to a Business to Business (B2B) exchange that uses a Microsoft BizTalk server.

The Microsoft BizTalk Framework is an XML framework for application integration and electronic commerce. Microsoft's BizTalk Server 2000 runs on Windows 2000 and is Microsoft's implementation of the framework, with functional extensions. BizTalk server allows you to quickly build Enterprise Integration systems and B2B exchanges. In this case, we are sending a BizTalk message to a URL that we assume is the entry point to a purchasing site.

> *Note that in reality, we would probably still want to order stock on a daily (or even weekly) basis. BizTalk even provides things such as operating windows, so we don't bother our suppliers every time we need to order an item. If you want to find out more about BizTalk, then check out* Professional BizTalk, *written by Stephen Mohr and Scott Woodgate and published by Wrox Press (ISBN 1861003293).*

So, we need to run a check every time we add an order. If we create a class (`NorthwindEvents.BiztalkOrder`) that implements the `IXMLEvent` interface we defined earlier on, there are two changes we need to make. The first is the following SQL statement that we have to issue against our `Northwind` database:

```
INSERT tblEVENT VALUES ('AddOrder',1,2,'NorthWindEvents.BiztalkOrder')
GO

EXEC prcListProgIDsForEvent 'AddOrder',1
```

```
ProgID
----------------------------------------------
NorthWindEvents.ProcessAddOrder
NorthWindEvents.BiztalkOrder

(2 row(s) affected)
```

The second piece of code we have to write is the actual `BiztalkOrder` class. This is slightly more involved, and an example implementation is given below. Parts of the code below are based on an example taken from the *Professional BizTalk* book that we've just recommended:

```
Private Function IXMLEvent_XMLEvent(ByVal EventXML As String) As String
    Dim strProducts As String
    Dim strBiztalkMessage As String
    Dim strReturn As String

    strReturn = "<BiztalkOrder/>"

    '   Get the Products in this order document
    strProducts = GetProducts(EventXML)

    ' Call the prcBiztalkOrder @ProductXML stored procedure that generate
    ' XML in the correct format for us to send straight out to our
    ' B2B exchange

    strBiztalkMessage = BiztalkMessageForProducts(strProducts)
    If LEN(strBiztalkMessage) >0 Then
       strReturn = SendBiztalk(strBiztalkMessage)
    End If

    IXMLEvent_XMLEvent = strReturn

End Function
```

The two other pieces of information we require here are the format of the stored procedure `prcBiztalkOrder` (which simply queries for products that we haven't currently re-ordered that are below their re-order level), in combination with the routine `BiztalkMessageForProducts` (based heavily on code from the BizTalk book mentioned) and the function `SendBiztalk` (included below).

One thing of note is that we are using the `XMLHHTP30` interface that is part of the MSXML library. This interface is intended for client side use and is safe for use within ASP.

```
Private Function SendBiztalk (ByVal pstrBiztalkMessage As String) As String

On Error GoTo ERR_SENDBIZTALK

     Dim oHTTP As XMLHTTP30

     Set oHTTP = CreateObject("XMLHTTP30")
     oHTTP.open "POST", strBiztalkURL
     oHTTP.setRequestHeader "Content-Type", "text/xml"
     oHTTP.send psrtBiztalkMessage

     strReturn = "<BiztalkOrder><BiztalkSendSuccess>" & pstrBiztalkMessage & _
                 "</BiztalkSendSuccess></BiztalkOrder>"

EXIT_SENDBIZTALK:
     Set oHTTP = Nothing
     SENDBIZTALK = strReturn
     Exit Function
ERR_SENDBIZTALK:
     strReturn = "<BiztalkOrder><BiztalkSendError>" & pstrBiztalkMessage & _
                 "</BiztalkSendError></BiztalkOrder>"
     Resume EXIT_SENDBIZTALK

End Function
```

Additional Functionality – Targeted Mailshots

We now have a problem – we've over-ordered on Grandma's Boysenberry Spread, and we really need to move this item. So what we want to do is e-mail every customer that makes a purchase with a targeted e-mail asking them if they would like to purchase a jar (or thirty). Notice that when the time comes to remove this rule, we can simply drop the entry in our table and we are done.

So, we need to run a check every time we add an order. So we create a class (`NorthWindEvents.MailshotValuedCustomer`) that implements the `IXMLEvent` interface we defined earlier on, and there are two changes we need to make. The first is the following SQL statement, which we again issue against the `Northwind` database:

```
INSERT tblEVENT VALUES ('AddOrder',1,3,'NorthWindEvents.MailshotValuedCustomer')
GO

prcListProgIDsForEvent 'AddOrder',1
```

```
ProgID
--------------------------------------------------------
NorthWindEvents.ProcessAddOrder
NorthWindEvents.BiztalkOrder
NorthWindEvents.MailshotValuedCustomer

(3 row(s) affected)
```

The second piece of code is to write the actual MailshotValuedCustomer class, and the implementation of the XMLEvent method of the IXMLEvent interface it supports. Pseudocode for which is supplied below, again full source code is available on the Wrox web site:

```
Private Function IXMLEvent_XMLEvent(ByVal EventXML As String) As String

    Dim strCustomer As String
    Dim strEmail As String
    Dim strReturn As String

    strReturn = "<Mailshot/>"

    '   Get the customerID
    strCustomer = GetCustomerID(EventXML)

    ' Determine the Email (if any) from this
    strEmail = EmailFromCustomerID (strCustomer) ' Any email address?

    If strEmail <> "" Then
        strReturn = SendMail(strEmail) ' Uses CDO
    End If

    IXMLEvent_XMLEvent = strReturn

End Function
```

Much of the functionality within the routines called here (with the exception of SendMail) has already been covered earlier in this case study – a combination of quick lookup functions (EmailFromCustomerID will return any e-mail address for our given customer) and returning the textual value of the correct element from a DOM (GetCustomerID) is all that is required. SendMail uses CDO to send a blanket e-mail to the e-mail address we have determined. As with all other examples included, the actual implementation of this functionality is not the important thing. It is the flexibility and ability to swap objects out of an event-based architecture that gives us real benefits.

Summary

We have covered a lot of ground in this case study, attempting to show where XML can bring benefit to our applications. If we use XML where it is appropriate (keeping an eye on performance trade-offs and ways to keep performance up) and keep examining the tools available (new versions of the XML parser come out on a regular basis and performance keeps going up) then it is possible to use XML in ways that enhance our applications without degrading performance.

As we have seen in the examples above, using XML has definite advantages. The flexibility and extensibility it gives us, combined with the polymorphic behavior we can use within COM and COM+ enable us to write extremely flexible and powerful applications. These factors, coupled with the increasing need to generate XML payloads for other applications (BizTalk, Web Services etc.), make SQL Server 2000 and its XML features an extremely powerful and easy to use tool. The main point to notice in all of these examples is just how little SQL Server code we are using, and how much of the overall functionality it is providing us with.

An Order Entry System Using VB and XML

In this case study, we'll develop a Visual Basic application demonstrating the exclusive use of XML to represent all the application data, which will be stored in standard relational form in a SQL Server 2000 database.

The application will be a very basic point-of-sale order entry system called XMLOrders. The actual functionality, data model, and business rules that are implemented by the program are not meant to be fully representative of a real-world working system. Instead, design choices have been made to deliberately expose you to particular techniques, tricks, and traps – to which solutions are offered. The result *is* a fully working application, but not one that you should treat as the final template for future developments.

XMLOrders provides software architects, systems analysts, and VB programmers with a framework on which to explore new ideas and techniques involving the use of XML. At the end of the chapter, indications are given as to how the XMLOrders project could evolve.

> **This case study will not include all of the code in the final working program, so access to the download source code is essential. The download package includes two versions of the whole project – one is the basic framework but without any code (`VB1`), and the other is the full system (`VB2`). In addition, all the SQL scripts and XML samples are included.**

Requirements

To build this application requires the following working environment:

- Win32 desktop (Windows 2000, SP1 or Windows NT 4.0 SP5)
- Microsoft Visual Basic 6.0 (SP4)
- Microsoft XML Parser 2.6, 3.0 or later
- Microsoft ADO 2.6
- Microsoft SQL Server 2000 (local or remote)
- Microsoft SQL Server 2000 client applications (Enterprise Manager, Query Analyzer, SQL Profiler)

Developers should be familiar with the following techniques:

- Creating ActiveX COM components in VB
- Using ADO to access SQL Server data
- Using Transact-SQL to write stored procedures

Program Specification

Let's assume we've been through the normal process of acquiring business requirements and performing a systems analysis, and have agreed with the user community what the functionality of the desired application program will be. We've also designed a prototype form that will demonstrate this functionality to the users. Hence, we are now at the stage where the functional and technical specifications have been signed-off. The aims of the program can be simply summarized as:

- Creation of a new sales order
- Modification of existing orders

The business rules that we will implement include:

- Orders can contain only products from the company product database
- There must be at least one product sold in every order
- Orders must be paid for in full by one or more accepted payment methods
- Commission earned on completed orders will be assigned to individual employees, and derives from the products sold
- Orders can only be modified on the same date they were created, since an external fulfillment and reconciliation process (not included) takes place overnight
- Customers are identified only by a simple freeform text field

User Interface Design

A simple UI (called `frmMain`) has been constructed. It comprises text boxes, combo boxes, a tab strip, command buttons, and a pair of MSFlexGrids.

UI design is not an issue that this chapter attempts to address, since it is beyond the scope of this book. The UI offered here is sufficient for the job in hand, and no more. Only minimal mention of the VB code relating to UI navigation and event handling will be provided, except where XML issues arise.

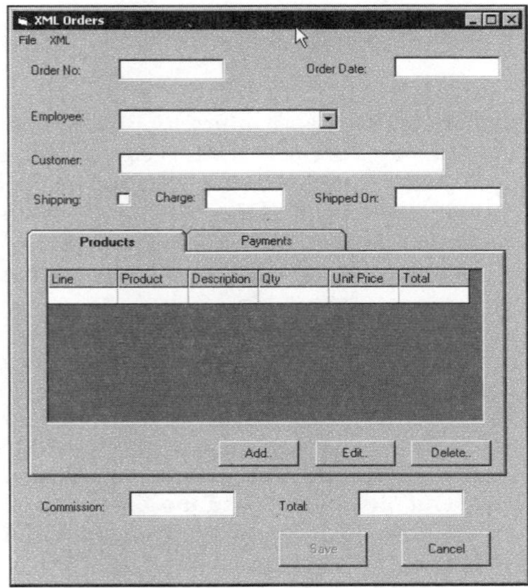

A few details on the form design:

- Tab order is set starting top-left and working down the form
- The Order Date, Shipped On, Commission and Total fields are `Locked`, their values being set programmatically (we could use labels instead, but they would require maintenance)
- Modification of data in the grids is done using subsidiary forms – these will be covered later

Database Design

The database structure that has been adopted is a wholly traditional, relational design to be implemented in SQL Server 2000, although it requires none of the new features of this version of SQL Server in terms of data types, constraints, relationships, etc.

The intention of using XML has had no effect on this design! The design consideration here is that we are *not* intending to store XML text within the database. Although SQL Server 2000 does provide facilities for querying and managing XML, its real forte lies with relational data, and there are currently no convincing arguments for abandoning all the benefits that the RDBMS offers, such as:

- Sophisticated query optimization
- A mature *standardized* SQL language
- A plethora of associated tools and technologies
- And last, but far from least, a rich and well-developed skill set in the development community

So, let's get started on the database. Here is the SQL script to build the tables.

Create the database, which is called `wroxdb`:

```
USE master
GO
CREATE DATABASE wroxdb
COLLATE SQL_Latin1_General_CP1_CS_AS
GO
```

The issue of SQL Server collations is the most significant point here; as you can see, we have specified a case-sensitive collation for this database. Because XML is case-sensitive, it makes sense to ensure that we treat our data accordingly. Using a case-insensitive collation will probably lead to bugs and unforeseen errors in the code that you develop. Of course, you may not always be able to make this choice – other systems that share the database may mean that a different collation cannot be avoided. It's not a showstopper, but a preference you should consider where possible.

> **The main issue with collation is in the XML that SQL Server generates – the names of all attributes will be derived automatically from the database schema definitions and the format of the `SELECT` query. In a case-insensitive database, regardless of the actual schema, the server allows your SQL queries to supply the names of tables and columns in any case format you choose. This possible inconsistency will almost certainly cause problems with the processing of the XML. If we use a case-sensitive collation, the server *enforces* the correct naming throughout all your SQL, and so helps to avoid this problem.**

The following Entity Relationship diagram shows the data we intend to work with:

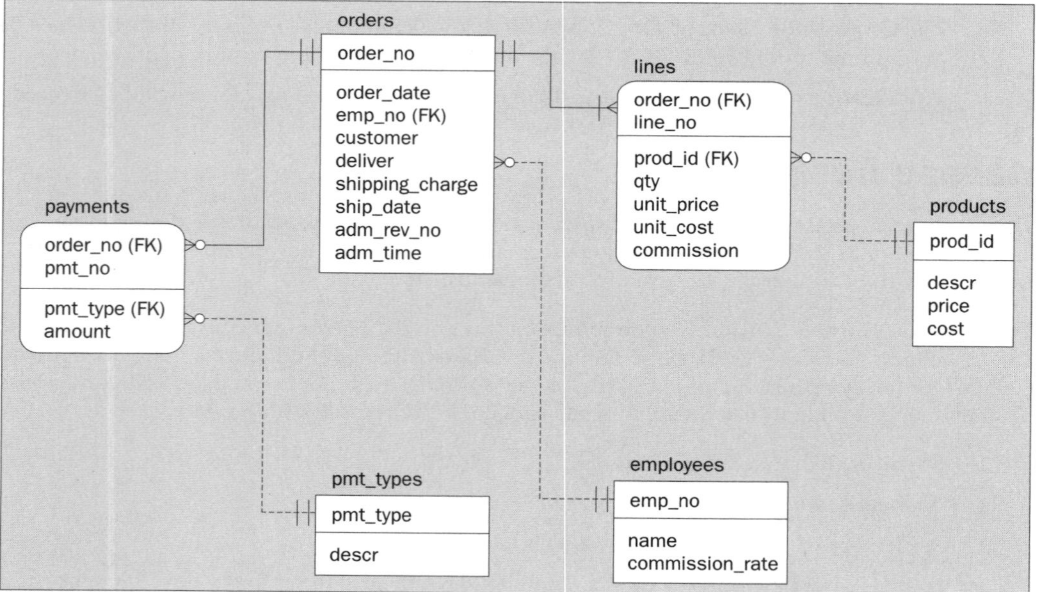

Note that we have chosen to use *lower-case* names throughout! This also assists in ensuring consistency throughout the system, and makes the manipulation of the XML more predictable.

The schema itself has enough complexity to ensure that our application must solve all of the typical issues that arise in developing OLTP solutions, but is suitably simplified to relieve you of the need to produce much repetitive code.

> **The remaining DDL code has been omitted from the chapter to save space – the whole database can be built from the `wroxdb.sql` script in the download.**

The orders Table

The core data of the XMLOrders system is held in the `orders` table:

Column	Type	Comments
`order_no`	`int`	The order number, uses an `IDENTITY` property to assign the unique number.
`order_date`	`datetime`	The date the order was raised – does not include a time component.
`emp_no`	`int`	The employee number to be assigned the sales commission. See the `employees` table.
`customer`	`varchar(30)`	May be blank.
`deliver`	`tinyint`	`0` = no delivery; `1` = to be delivered.
`shipping_charge`	`money`	Add this to the order total.
`ship_date`	`datetime`	May be `NULL`. Set by an external system!
`adm_rev_no`	`int`	Provides the mechanism for an optimistic concurrency locking strategy – this will be explained later.
`adm_time`	`datetime`	Records the time and date of the last change to the order.

`orders` has two child tables associated with it: `lines` and `payments`. Let's look at them next.

The lines Table

The `lines` table contains one row for every product purchased on each sales order.

Column	Type	Comments
`order_no`	`int`	The order number.
`line_no`	`smallint`	The line number within each order. Usually starting from one.
`prod_id`	`int`	The product identifier – see the `products` table.

Table continued on following page

Column	Type	Comments
qty	int	The quantity sold.
unit_price	money	The unit-selling price of this product at the time of sale *(prices may change)*.
unit_cost	money	The unit cost (to the vendor) of this product at the time of sale *(costs may change)*.
commission	money	The unit commission earned by the employee for this product (*commission_rate may change*).

We store price, cost, and commission figures in the `lines` table because, although they are derived from other referenced tables, they are not static values. We therefore need to preserve the figures computed at the time of raising the order.

The total price for a single order, order 1000 in this case, can thus be computed using the SQL expression:

```
SELECT o.order_no, shipping_charge + SUM(qty * unit_price) AS Total
FROM orders AS o INNER JOIN lines AS l
  ON o.order_no=l.order_no
WHERE o.order_no = 1000
GROUP BY o.order_no, shipping_charge
```

Whereas the total commission is:

```
SELECT SUM(qty * commission) AS Total_Commission
FROM lines
WHERE order_no = 1000
```

The payments Table

Each order has one or more payment records.

Column	Type	Comments
order_no	int	The order number.
pmt_no	smalli nt	The payment number within the order. Usually starting from one.
pmt_type	char(1)	The payment type – see the `pmt_types` table.
amount	money	The amount of money paid for this type.

The total value of the order can therefore also be computed using this SQL expression:

```
SELECT SUM(amount) AS Total_Payment
FROM payments
WHERE order_no = 1000
```

Obviously, we expect the totals arrived at from querying the `lines` table to exactly match those from the `payments` table.

The employees Table

The `employees` table contains the list of all valid employees. No order should exist on the system with an invalid or unknown employee (because of the foreign key we're going to place on the `orders` table).

Column	Type	Comments
`emp_no`	`int`	The employee number.
`name`	`varchar(30)`	The name of the employee.
`commission _rate`	`float`	The percentage rate of commission earned for each completed sale. In other words, a value of 2.0 means 2% commission against the value of goods.

Although commission_rate may be modified over time, our sample application does not currently provide the functionality to change this table.

The products Table

Every product available for sale must be defined in the `products` table:

Column	Type	Comments
`prod_id`	`int`	The product identifier.
`descry`	`varchar(50)`	The description of the product.
`price`	`money`	The selling price for one of this item.
`cost`	`money`	The cost price of one of this item.

Although prices and costs may be modified over time, our sample application does not currently provide the functionality to change this table.

The pmt_types Table

Each payment method requires an entry in the `pmt_types` table:

Column	Type	Comments
`pmt_type`	`char(1)`	The payment type code. This is the `PRIMARY KEY`.
`descry`	`varchar(15)`	A description.

Sample Data

Let's now insert some initial test data into the database, so we have something to play with. First, the reference tables:

```
-- employees
INSERT  employees
VALUES  (1,'Fred Brown',2.0)
INSERT  employees
VALUES  (2,'Bill Jackson',1.2)
INSERT  employees
VALUES  (3,'Charlie Watts',0.8)
GO

-- payment types
INSERT pmt_types
VALUES('C','Cash')
INSERT pmt_types
VALUES('R','Credit Card')
INSERT pmt_types
VALUES('D','Debit Card')
go

-- products
INSERT products
VALUES(100,'Bright red jacket',123.99, 88.0)
INSERT products
VALUES(101,'Black trousers',36.99, 24.55)
INSERT products
VALUES(201,'Men''s trainers',69.50, 48.12)
INSERT products
VALUES(202,'Ladies trainers',65.00, 41.40)
INSERT products
VALUES(301,'Cotton Socks',7.49, 5.30)
GO
```

As you can see, we've decided that our business is going to be selling articles of clothing.

Now to create a first order. Since we've decided to use an `IDENTITY` column for the order number, we need to do this in a single batch in order to use the `IDENTITY` value for order number in the child tables. Ultimately, of course, we'd place this kind of code inside a transaction to guarantee data integrity. If this is the first order created, then it should actually be order number `1000`.

```
-- sample order
DECLARE @ord int

INSERT orders (order_date,emp_no,customer,deliver,shipping_charge,
               adm_rev_no,adm_time)
VALUES ('2001-03-10', 1, 'Mrs Jane Smith', 1, $10, 2, GETDATE())
SELECT @ord = @@IDENTITY

INSERT lines
VALUES(@ord, 1, 101, 1, 36.99, 24.55, ROUND(36.99*0.02,2))
INSERT lines
VALUES(@ord, 2, 201, 2, 69.5, 48.12, ROUND(69.5*0.02,2))

INSERT payments
VALUES(@ord, 1, 'C', 185.99)
GO
```

Now we have a fully operational database to test our queries on during the program development.

The Application Architecture

The structure of the XMLOrders program is derived from fairly well established N-tier application architectures, such as Microsoft Windows DNA. If you are unfamiliar with this type of architecture then please see *Professional Windows DNA* by Wrox Press (ISBN 1861004451).

This case study demonstrates that the choice of adopting XML as the format for all data within the application code-space has a significant effect on the way in which our architecture evolves. How and where the XML is generated and manipulated becomes a key issue to resolve within the system design.

Let's see what our N-tier framework will look like for the XMLOrders application. The following diagram is a typical 3-layer class diagram from Visual Modeler, showing the basic components we intend to implement, albeit missing some of the methods and properties that we will eventually need:

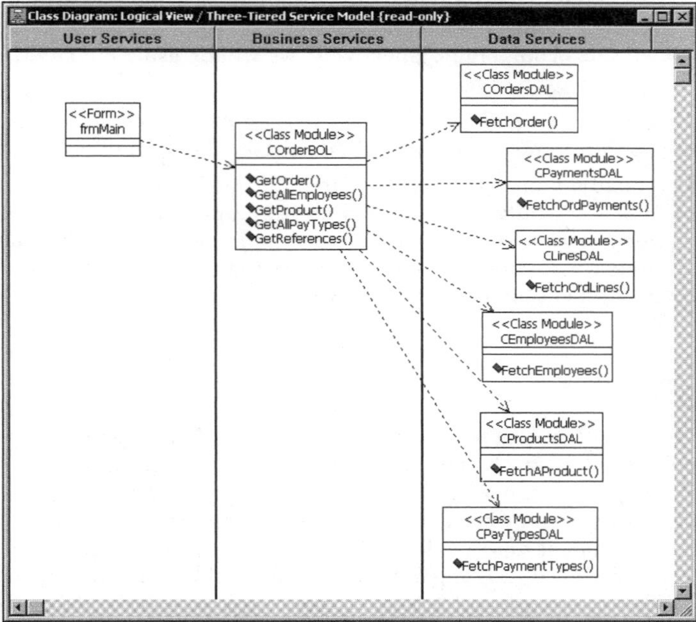

Normally we'd expect to perform a much more comprehensive analysis of the program requirements, resulting in a complete object model for the first phase of coding. For the purposes of this exercise, however, we want the application structure to evolve as we progressively solve the design problems that the development encounters.

Each of the tiers shown in the diagram will be built as a separate VB component, so our complete system will comprise three separate VB projects:

- `XMLOrders.exe` – the main client application
- `OrderBOL.dll` – the business object or services layer
- `OrderDAL.dll` – the data access layer

Let's just enumerate the design criteria for these applications:

- **XML data messaging** – all inter-component data messages must be passed as XML strings. If we are starting with XML output from SQL Server 2000, then clearly we do not want to convert the data into any other format or we lose the benefit of XML. Recordset objects are therefore banished!
- **Scalability** – all objects in the two DLL components will be designed to be **stateless.** This conforms to the requirements of a scalable application to create objects only when they are needed, and destroy them immediately after use. None of these objects will offer any property values – simple methods alone will provide the services we need.
- **Reusability** – the functionality of the service components should be as generic as possible. This will open up the possibility to develop other client applications, such as Web applications, for deployment to other user communities. Especially with regard to data fetch operations, we should not restrict the data content just because our current requirement may be limited.
- **Object-orientation** – you may have spotted already that the model above deviates from a more conventional OO model. Where, for example, are the `order` or `product` objects? The answer is that the rationalization brought about by using XML has made the need for **stateful** business objects less compelling. Effectively, we will be using the DOM to hold all application and session state information.
- **Database isolation** – we will use stored procedures exclusively for accessing SQL Server. This isolates the application from the physical database schema, and reduces dependencies.
- **Simplicity** – finally, it must be explained that this model is deliberately simplified for the purposes of this case study. In practice, a more complex model was used, breaking the business services layer into two by implementing Façade and Object Manager classes. However, this is an issue primarily for software architects, and does not fundamentally impact upon the development methodology described herein.

XML Design

Before we can start writing any code, we must define the XML data structures that the application will use. *This is extremely important!* Obviously, our XML structure will reflect the database schema that we have already defined although, in practice, the XML can be designed *before* the database schema is finalized. What quickly becomes apparent, especially in a team development environment, is that the specific format of each XML document must be defined and documented in advance, preferably according to standards defined within your own company. Ideally, this will include the development of standard XML schemas or DTDs in order to enforce the agreed rules, though we will not demonstrate this here.

The creation of sample XML files representing the typical data to be handled by the application provides the development team with vital documentation, and facilitates the segregation of work for the various system components, since each component interface deals primarily with XML strings. Therefore, the interface specifications for each component class can be agreed safely, without being troubled by compatability issues.

> **The (simplified) framework of this application sacrifices some of the benefits of standard OO design; data type enforcement and early-bound interface validation (via IntelliSense) are lost due to the choice of handling the XML data directly in application code. We will therefore be exposed to the possibility of undetected errors due to mistyped element or attribute names. Rigor in naming is the least we can do to protect against this.**

Attributes or Elements

The first choice we must make is whether to adopt an element or attribute structure.

Taking our `employees` record as an example, we can have either an attribute-based format:

```
<employee emp_no='1' name='Fred Brown' commission_rate='2.0000'/>
```

or an element-based format:

```
<employee>
   <emp_no>1</emp_no>
   <name>Fred Brown</name>
   <commission_rate>2.0000</commission_rate >
<employee>
```

In this case, there is no need to preserve the order of `<emp_no>`, `<name>`, and `<commission_rate>` child elements within `<employee>`, so they could equally well be structured as attributes. There are also performance arguments for using an attribute-based approach because of the shorter XML strings produced.

This is better demonstrated with a slightly more complex dataset. Let's use a query against our `wroxdb` database and compare the results of the different `FOR XML` formats available to us.

Here's a query that fetches the single payment record that we have inserted into the `payments` table, and includes a join to the `pmt_types` table to fetch the payment type description:

```
SELECT pmt_no, payments.pmt_type, descr, amount
FROM payments INNER JOIN pmt_types
ON payments.pmt_type = pmt_types.pmt_type
```

The three XML formats available to us are:

`FOR XML RAW`:

```
<row pmt_no="1" pmt_type="C" descr="Cash" amount="185.9900"/>
```

`FOR XML AUTO`:

```
<payments pmt_no="1" pmt_type="C" amount="185.9900">
  <pmt_types descr="Cash"/>
</payments>
```

`FOR XML AUTO, ELEMENTS`:

```
<payments>
  <pmt_no>1</pmt_no>
  <pmt_type>C</pmt_type>
  <amount>185.9900</amount>
  <pmt_types>
    <descr>Cash</descr>
  </pmt_types>
</payments>
```

Agreeing on a standard format and sticking to it will reduce the potential for confusion, troublesome bugs, and loss of productivity, but some applications may benefit from one form or another. Clearly, choosing a particular format is very much a choice that you must make within your own development organization.

For this case study, we have adopted a flat attribute-based format, as shown in the FOR XML RAW sample above. The reasons for this are:

- **Consistency** – using this format ensures that all values are returned as attributes, regardless of the data source. This makes the programming task easier for the developer, by requiring the same access methods for all data values.
- **Database schema independence** – using FOR XML RAW allows us effectively to mask the real source of the data from a query, since all values are returned as attributes within a single element, regardless of their origin. If, at some future time, we change the database schema, the XML will not need to change, and therefore our application will be unaffected. Of course, we can provide *more* attributes in a revised query but, until we need to make use of these new values, we do not need to modify the existing systems. This is one of the very significant benefits of adopting XML and the kind of architecture demonstrated in this case study.

The main drawback to the FOR XML RAW format lies with our inability to affect the element name – SQL Server 2000 imposes the row element name by default. This is not a particularly troublesome issue, although it would be if there were an enhancement to the query language to allow us to override it. Those of a more robust disposition might wish to evaluate the use of the EXPLICIT mode which is described in Chapter 3.

Data Values

Most of the values to be represented in our XML string can stay unaltered from the raw query results that SQL Server 2000 generates. There are two significant exceptions to this, which can be demonstrated by this simple query against wroxdb:

```
SELECT order_date, commission_rate
FROM orders AS o INNER JOIN employees AS e
ON o.emp_no = e.emp_no
WHERE o.order_no = 1000
FOR XML RAW
```

This returns the following XML:

```
<row order_date="2001-03-10T00:00:00"
   commission_rate="2.000000000000000e+000"/>
```

The XML generated by our query would benefit from having the results for the order_date and commission_rate attributes simplified. Let's consider these in turn.

Dates

One of the unfortunate omissions in SQL Server is not having a data type to represent pure dates without a time element. Instead, we have the datetime and smalldatetime types, which store both a date and time component, to differing degrees of resolution. However, most database applications have a requirement to store date values with a granularity of one day, and many are the novice SQL programmers who have been tripped up by this. If we store a date value with only the date component specified in a character string, SQL Server automatically sets the time component to zero, meaning midnight. This makes it safe for us to perform queries using date comparisons such as WHERE mydate = '10 Feb 2001' without worry.

It will benefit us to adopt an XML string format for dates that does not include a time component, but which to choose? The obvious candidate is the ISO standard YYYY-MM-DD, since this has the very significant benefit of being universally unambiguous, regardless of your local date display conventions (whereas adopting DD/MM/YYYY or MM/DD/YYYY is clearly asking for trouble, especially outside the US). Conveniently, SQL Server 2000 provides a suitable conversion to the ISO format, although we still need to truncate the output to remove the time component:

```
SELECT CONVERT(char(10), GETDATE(), 126)
```

Happily, VB also provides intrinsic conversions for this ISO format, using the `CDate()` or `Format()` functions. Of course, we will need to convert such dates to localized display formats when exposing them in the UI, as is demonstrated later. A secondary benefit of using this format is that it provides intrinsic sort and compare functionality. For example:

```
IF '2001-03-01' > '2000-12-31' THEN
```

For display-only datetime values that *do* hold a time component, such as the `adm_time` column on our `orders` table, it is a good idea to use a more literal conversion using style `113`, but truncating the milliseconds:

```
SELECT CONVERT(varchar(20), GETDATE(), 113)
```

This returns:

```
--------------------
17 Mar 2001 15:58:12
```

Floating Point Numbers

This is a simpler nut to crack. It's true that the default format used by `FOR XML` is a perfectly acceptable scientific notation, which will readily be understood by Visual Basic. However, for many systems we do not need the degree of precision that this represents.

In our sample application, the only float data we have is the `commission_rate`. It's perfectly reasonable in this context to restrict the resolution of the data to four decimal places, say, and thereby make another small saving in the size of XML we generate – for example:

```
SELECT LTRIM(STR(commission_rate,6,4)) AS commission_rate
```

Text Fields

We have no text data types in our sample application, but the issue of how they should be handled does warrant a mention, and should be covered by your XML design standards.

Because text data probably derives from free-form user entry, or possibly some form of document storage, it may be preferable to consider representing the contents in a CDATA section in your XML, rather than in an attribute, primarily because very long attribute strings will make the XML far less readable. However, this requires considerably more effort in order to persuade SQL Server 2000 to generate the correct XML output.

You may alternatively consider a different strategy. Instead of using FOR XML, try using VB and ADO to produce the output. This will cost in performance, but does mean you have total control.

XML Data Summary

We can now revise the query we first looked at, to see the standardized XML generated:

```
SELECT CONVERT(char(10), order_date, 126) AS order_date,
   LTRIM(STR(commission_rate,6,4)) AS commission_rate
FROM orders AS o INNER JOIN employees AS e
ON o.emp_no = e.emp_no
WHERE o.order_no = 1000
FOR XML RAW
```

This results in:

<row order_date="2001-03-10" commission_rate="2.0000"/>

This also offers an incidental but significant size reduction from 80 to 55 characters.

XML Sample Data

Now that we have agreed on a general standard for XML, we can see what the data that our XMLOrders application will deal with might look like. As discussed earlier, as part of the development methodology, it is worthwhile at this point to compose example XML files representing typical data that the application will process. These will help us focus on the way in which the program will handle the XML, and help to confirm the suitability of the chosen data in meeting the business requirements.

The benefit of this approach is that we do not need to finalize or build the data access components until we are confident that the data structures do indeed meet the requirements. We can produce a working prototype and fully test the front-end, merely by handcrafting the required XML.

As we work through the building of the XMLOrders application in the rest of the case study, we can put these ideas to the test.

For this application, we can expect to deal with four separate XML datasets.

Employees

Looking at the main application form shown earlier (frmMain), you may have spotted that a drop-down combo box has been adopted to enable a user to choose from the list of available employees. In the virtual world that our sample application lives in, we know that the number of available employees is small. If, in fact, we had to deal with a thousand employees, then a combo box would not be appropriate.

Since we have made this choice, we will need to populate the combo box from a suitable XML structure. Running the following query:

```
SELECT emp_no,
   name,
   LTRIM(STR(commission_rate,6,4)) AS commission_rate
FROM employees AS employee
FOR XML AUTO
```

gives a representative sample based on the values we originally inserted into wroxdb:

```
<employees>
   <employee emp_no='1' name='Fred Brown' commission_rate='2.0000'/>
   <employee emp_no='2' name='Bill Jackson' commission_rate='1.2000'/>
   <employee emp_no='3' name='Charlie Watts' commission_rate='0.8000'/>
</employees>
```

Note that we have used FOR XML AUTO in order to rename the elements to employee, rather than use FOR XML RAW and be stuck with row. Our XML standard represents a commitment to an output format, not how we use SQL to generate it. In general, AUTO is preferable provided that JOINs are not involved since it affords more control. Note also that we needed to alias the table name in order that the data elements were not called employees, which would clash with our chosen outer element name.

A big benefit for the developer of XML is its readable nature – it is therefore appropriate that care is taken over the seemingly trivial issue of naming. Element and attribute names should reflect the real-world nature of the content, rather than duplicating the names of database entities.

Of course, having made these choices, we must stick with them throughout the development process.

Payment Types

Just as for employees, we will need a list of all valid payment types, so here is the XML sample:

```
<pmt_types>
   <row pmt_type='C' descr='Cash'/>
   <row pmt_type='D' descr='Debit Card'/>
   <row pmt_type='R' descr='Credit Card'/>
</pmt_types>
```

And here is the SQL to get it – this time we're going to use FOR XML RAW and live with the row element names, just to demonstrate the technique:

```
SELECT pmt_type, descr
FROM pmt_types
FOR XML RAW
```

Products

Although we have only so far defined a handful of products for our products table, we want to assume that, in reality, we would have a very large number of products to handle. Fetching a list of all products has therefore been deemed too inefficient for this application. This is a choice affected in the real world by knowledge of the networking infrastructure, application deployment model, etc. However, it's a common choice, and we need to see what the implications of that choice would be.

Since we don't have a cache of all products, when a user wants to choose a product, the program will need to fetch all the details of that product in response to the user action. We therefore need to have an XML representation for a single product:

```
<product prod_id="101" descr="Black trousers" price="36.9900" cost="24.5500"/>
```

Here is the SQL query to fetch it:

```
SELECT *
FROM products AS product
WHERE prod_id=101
FOR XML AUTO
```

Orders

Unlike the other pieces of XML that we have produced, the data for orders in our application is hierarchical. It is therefore appropriate that the XML correctly represents this hierarchy. The current requirement for our XMLOrders application is only to process a single order at any time, so we need a sample of XML representing a single order record:

```
<order order_no='1000' order_date='2001-03-10' emp_no='1'
       customer='Mrs Jane Smith' deliver='1' shipping_charge='10.00'
       adm_rev_no='2' adm_time='12 Mar 2001 13:38:04'>
   <lines>
      <row order_no='1000' line_no='1' prod_id='101'
           descr='Black trousers' qty='1' unit_price='36.99'
           unit_cost='24.55' commission='0.74'/>
      <row order_no='1000' line_no='2' prod_id='201'
           descr='Men&apos;s trainers' qty='2' unit_price='69.50'
           unit_cost='48.12' commission='1.39'/>
   </lines>
   <payments>
      <row order_no='1000' pmt_no='1' pmt_type='C' descr='Cash'
           amount='185.99'/>
   </payments>
</order>
```

This can be constructed with a bit of work in Notepad, and the following simple queries:

```
SELECT order_no,
   CONVERT (char(10),order_date,126) AS order_date,
   emp_no, customer, deliver,
   CONVERT(varchar(10),shipping_charge) AS shipping_charge,
   CONVERT (char(10),order_date,126) AS ship_date,
   adm_rev_no, CONVERT(varchar(20),adm_time, 113) AS adm_time
FROM orders AS [order]
WHERE order_no=1000
FOR XML AUTO
```

```
SELECT order_no, line_no, l.prod_id, descr, qty,
   CONVERT(varchar(10),unit_price) AS unit_price,
   CONVERT(varchar(10),unit_cost) AS unit_cost,
   CONVERT(varchar(10),commission) AS commission
FROM lines AS l INNER JOIN products AS p
ON l.prod_id=p.prod_id
WHERE order_no=1000
FOR XML RAW
```

```
SELECT order_no, pmt_no, p.pmt_type, descr,
   CONVERT(varchar(10),amount) AS amount
FROM payments AS p INNER JOIN pmt_types AS t
ON p.pmt_type = t.pmt_type
WHERE order_no=1000
FOR XML RAW
```

The main point of note here is that we have chosen to join the `lines` and `products` tables in order to supply the product description in the data and, similarly, we have joined `payments` and `pmt_types` tables to supply the payment type description. These choices will make it easier for our application to process the XML, since all the information required to display the order details is encompassed in this XML package.

> *You may have spotted that our sample order XML does not include the* `ship_date` *attribute, even though the SQL specifically references it. This is because the default ship_date is* `NULL` *– this will be discussed further in the* Loading an Order *section.*

The deliberate exception is that we have *not* referenced the `employees` table by joining with `orders`; this will give us the opportunity to use our cached `employees` XML in order to provide the desired lookup for the program to display the employee name.

Building the XMLOrders Application

We are now ready to proceed with the coding of the various VB components. To create a version of XMLOrders yourself, open up `XMLOrders.vbg` in the `VB1` folder, and add the following code to `frmMain`. We start by declaring some module level variables, which will record the current state of the application, and hold the cached data. The `DOMDocument` objects will be explained as we meet them.

```
Public oRefDOM As DOMDocument ' DOM for reference data
Dim oDOM As DOMDocument       ' DOM for order data
Dim oNewDOM As DOMDocument    ' DOM for new data templates
Dim cCommis As Currency       ' total commission
Dim cShip As Currency         ' shipping charge
Dim cLines As Currency        ' total lines value
Dim cTotal As Currency        ' grand order total
Dim cPayments As Currency     ' total payments amount
Dim nMaxLineNo As Long        ' maximum line number
Dim nMaxPmtNo As Long         ' maximum payment number
Dim fCommisRate As Single     ' current employee commission rate
Dim bEditing As Boolean       ' edit mode flag

' Display conversion format for currency values
Const MONEY_FMT As String = "####0.00"
```

Startup

When the program starts, the first event we use to call code is `Form_Load` (normally we would use a Sub Main for program startup, but this has been omitted, for simplicity). In the `Form_Load` event, the first thing we do is invoke a local procedure called `InitGrids` to initialize the two FlexGrid controls:

```
'Add a call to InitGrids from Form_Load, and force the tab control to
'show the products grid

Private Sub Form_Load()
   Call InitGrids
   SSTab1.Tab = 0
End Sub

Private Sub InitGrids()

   With grdProducts
      .Cols = 6
      .Row = 0
      .Col = 0
      .ColSel = 5
      .Clip = "Line" & vbTab & "Product" & vbTab & "Description" & vbTab _
            & "Qty" & vbTab & "Unit Price" & vbTab & "Total"
      .Rows = 2
      .ColSel = 0
   End With

   With grdPayments
      .Cols = 4
      .Row = 0
      .Col = 0
      .ColSel = 3
      .Clip = "Pmt" & vbTab & "Type" & vbTab & "Description" & vbTab _
            & "Amount"
      .Rows = 2
      .ColSel = 0
   End With

End Sub
```

References DOM

oRefDOM is the first DOM object we will deal with. oRefDOM will be used for storing reference XML data. In XMLOrders, this means employees and payment_types. We wish to cache these values in order to provide a local source of data for validation, without requiring a round-trip to the database each time such a validation is required. Since the only stateful object in our model at this point is the main VB form, then this is where the DOM objects will have to live.

oRefDOM needs to be instantiated as soon as the program runs so, continuing on in the Form_Load procedure:

```
Private Sub Form_Load()
   Call InitGrids
   SSTab1.Tab = 0

   Set oRefDOM = New DOMDocument
   oRefDOM.async = False

End Sub
```

`DOMDocument` is the top-level object in the MSXML object architecture, into which we will load our XML.

> *Each new version of the DOM released by Microsoft has offered an alternative* `Document` *object – you may also have* `DOMDocument26` *or* `DOMDocument30`*. For our purposes, the basic* `DOMDocument` *will suffice. Microsoft offers a wealth of information on MSXML at* http://msdn.microsoft.com/xml*. Of course, you can choose to use other non-MS DOM implementations, but this will involve significant code change.*

The last line of code sets the `async` property of the `DOMDocument` object to `False`. This is vital, and ensures that our program code does not proceed onto the next statement until the DOM has been fully loaded.

To populate this DOM object, we will need to make a request via the `COrderBOL` object. The relationships between the different objects in our system at startup are best demonstrated using a UML sequence diagram:

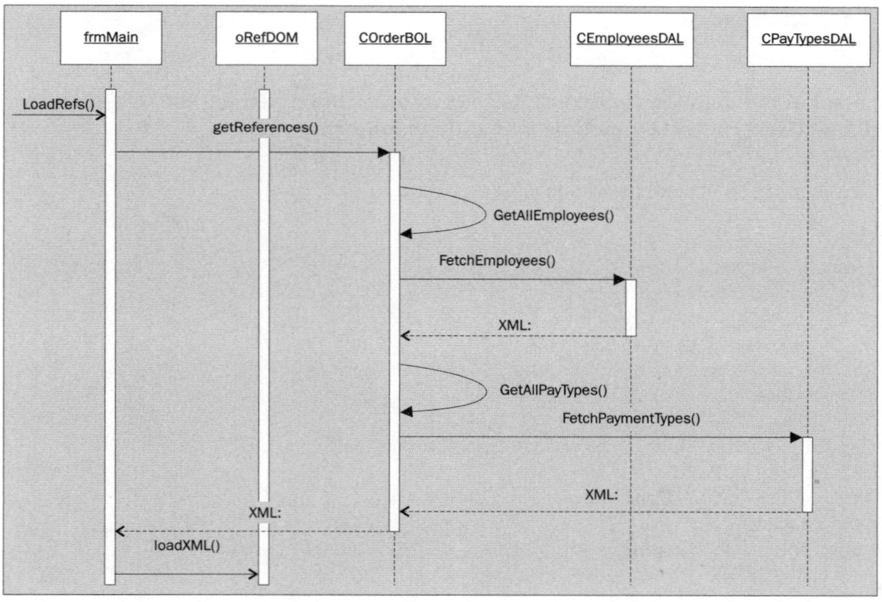

> *Even if you are not familiar with UML, you should find this diagram easy to follow. Time flows down the page. Messages are passed between the objects from left to right, with returned values shown as dashed lines in the opposite direction. The rectangular section (activity bars) in each object's timeline represents the period of time in which the object exists.*

From this diagram we can see that the first action that the `LoadRefs` procedure must accomplish is to create an instance of `COrderBOL` and invoke its `GetReferences` method (object instantiation is *implied* in the diagram by the start of the activity bar, rather than being shown as a separate program step). This will return the required data as an XML string to be loaded in our `oRefDOM` object. The diagram also shows that the `GetReferences` method in turn invokes internal calls (the looped-back arrows) to `GetAllEmployees` and `GetAllPayTypes`, so the task for `GetReferences` is to merge these two pieces of XML, as described earlier, into a single XML document.

So let's write the relevant code for LoadRefs:

```
Private Sub LoadRefs()
Dim oBOL As COrderBOL
Dim sXML As String

    Set oBOL = New COrderBOL

    sXML = oBOL.GetReferences
    oRefDOM.loadXML sXML

End Sub
```

and invoke it from Form_Load:

```
    Set oRefDOM = New DOMDocument
    oRefDOM.async = False
    Call LoadRefs
End Sub
```

Now we need to move to the OrderBOL project in order to implement the GetReferences method. Open up the COrderBOL class module and add the following code:

```
Public Function GetReferences() As String

Dim sXml As String
Dim oDom As DOMDocument
Dim oEl As DOMDocument

    On Error GoTo ErrHandler
    Set oDom = CreateObject("MSXML2.DOMDocument")
    oDom.loadXML "<refs></refs>"

    Set oEl = CreateObject("MSXML2.DOMDocument")
    oEl.async = False
    sXml = Me.GetAllEmployees
    oEl.loadXML sXml
    oDom.documentElement.appendChild oEl.documentElement

    sXml = Me.GetAllPayTypes
    oEl.loadXML sXml
    oDom.documentElement.appendChild oEl.documentElement

    GetReferences = oDom.xml
    Exit Function

ErrHandler:
    Err.Raise Err.Number, "COrderBOL.GetReferences", Err.Description

End Function
```

A number of points arise from this:

- We're using `CreateObject` here to instantiate the DOM, because ultimately the `COrderBOL` object might be running inside COM+, and it's well documented that VB's handling of the `New` operator does not always fit well within COM+ object management. We'll use `CreateObject` universally in the two DLL projects.
- We use the DOM to perform the XML merging, partly to show the technique, but it is equally possible to construct the final XML document using some simple string concatenation, for example:

```
GetReferences = "<refs>" & Me.GetAllEmployees _
              & Me.GetAllPayTypes & "</refs>"
```

- We've included a simple error handler, which merely passes any error back to the client. Since this code is inside a DLL component, which could be located on a separate computer, we should not attempt to alert the user to any errors – if they cannot be resolved internally then we pass them to the client to (hopefully) handle in an appropriately friendly manner.

  We'll soon see that error handling for DOMs doesn't follow the normal model (an XML error has to be inspected for, rather than trapped).

- The `appendChild` method call adds the given node as the next child of the parent node. In our case, the first use of `appendChild` adds the `employees` document as a child of the root, `<refs>`. The second use adds the `pmt_types` document as the second child of the root, in other words, as a sibling of `employees`.

Our resulting references DOM will therefore look something like this:

```
<refs>
  <employees>
    <employee emp_no='1' name='Fred Brown' commission_rate='2.0000'/>
    <employee emp_no='2' name='Bill Jackson' commission_rate='1.2000'/>
    <employee emp_no='3' name='Charlie Watts' commission_rate='0.8000'/>
  </employees>
  <pmt_types>
    <row pmt_type='C' descr='Cash'/>
    <row pmt_type='D' descr='Debit Card'/>
    <row pmt_type='R' descr='Credit Card'/>
  </pmt_types>
</refs>
```

For now, we can simulate the `GetAllEmployees` and `GetAllPayTypes` methods by hard-coding the XML strings. This postpones the need to build the `COrdersDAL` component (which we'll build later – in the *Data Access* section), until we have tested the interaction between our presentation and business objects tiers. This is often the stage in the development lifecycle that is most subject to change, especially if we are involving our potential users in the process. Experience shows that the earlier on in the lifecycle that we involve the user community, the more successful the final outcome will be, both for the users and for the development team.

So, our two procedures can now be added to `COrderBOL.cls`, merely using cut-and-paste from our sample XML files:

```
Public Function GetAllEmployees() As String

  GetAllEmployees = "<employees>" & vbCrLf _
  & "<employee emp_no='1' name='Fred Brown' commission_rate='2.0000'/>" _
  & vbCrLf _
  & "<employee emp_no='2' name='Bill Jackson' commission_rate='1.2000'/>" _
  & vbCrLf _
  & "<employee emp_no='3' name='Charlie Watts' commission_rate='0.8000'/>" _
  & vbCrLf _
  & "</employees>"

End Function

Public Function GetAllPayTypes() As String

   GetAllPayTypes = "<pmt_types>" & vbCrLf _
                 & "<row pmt_type='C' descr='Cash'/>" & vbCrLf _
                 & "<row pmt_type='D' descr='Debit Card'/>" & vbCrLf _
                 & "<row pmt_type='R' descr='Credit Card'/>" & vbCrLf _
                 & "</pmt_types>"

End Function
```

Note that we've made these methods `Public` – it's not strictly necessary for the current implementation since the only caller is the `GetReferences` method. However, these two methods return complete XML documents in themselves, so why not open up their possible use to other systems in the future?

XML Errors

If you've entered the above code correctly then you should find you now have a working application, albeit one which shows no visible signs that any code is at work. However, if you pause the program, you should be able to see that the `oRefDOM` object is correctly loaded by typing the ?oRefDOM.xml command in the Immediate window.

What if you have made a mistake in the code above? For instance, try leaving out the first < in the `GetAllEmployees` XML string. The error you then see will be a simplified error number 5:

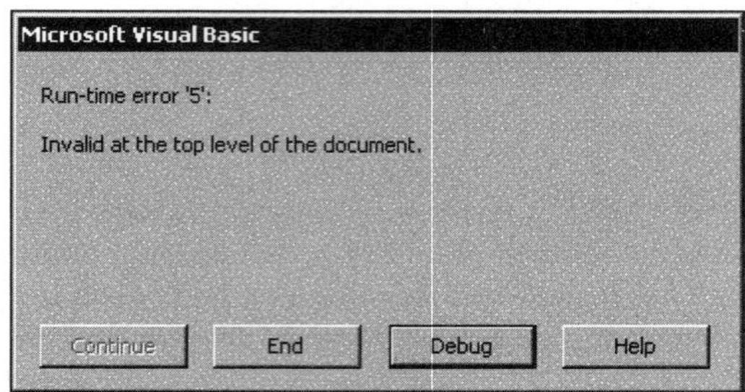

This is not exactly useful for tracing the problem!

We can improve on this by examining the ParseError properties of the DOM. Since we might expect to need similar functionality elsewhere in our application, we need to create a shared code module to hold the subsequent functions.

We now need to work with the module called XMLHelp.bas which is actually located in the VB1\Common folder. This module is placed in a separate folder so that it can be shared with the other projects in the system. Make sure that the XMLHelp.bas module is added to the OrderBOL and XMLOrders projects, and then add the following function to it which returns a much more explicit description of the error in your XML:

```
' return the ParseError in a readable format
Public Function GetDomError(ByRef oDom As DOMDocument) As String
   GetDomError = "XML Error: " & oDom.parseError.reason & vbCrLf _
            & "Line: " & oDom.parseError.Line & vbCrLf _
            & "Pos: " & oDom.parseError.linepos & vbCrLf _
            & "Source: " & oDom.parseError.srcText & vbCrLf
End Function
```

Now, change the error handler in GetReferences to detect the fact that one of our loadXML operations has failed, and report the problem:

```
ErrHandler:
   If oEl.parseError.errorCode <> 0 Then
      Err.Raise Err.Number, "COrderBOL.GetReferences", GetDomError(oEl)
   Else
      Err.Raise Err.Number, "COrderBOL.GetReferences", Err.Description
   End If
End Function
```

Now, if you run the program with the same mistake in the XML, you should see:

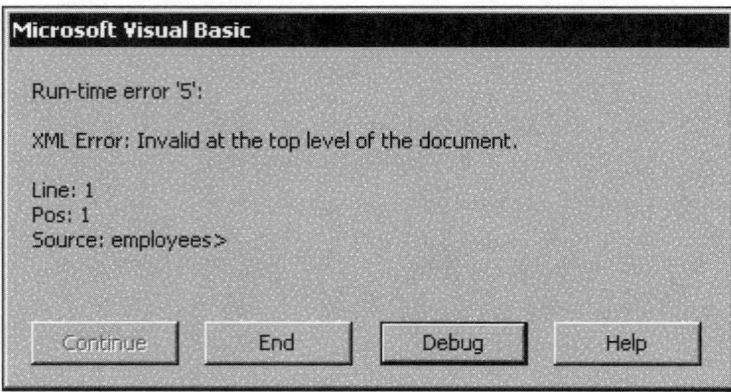

A considerable improvement – the Pos: 1 tells us quite explicitly that it's the first character in the employees tag which is problematic.

> **Although explicit error handling won't be shown throughout the rest of the chapter, it is clearly the preferred option to always reference ParseError after any loadXML operation.**

Returning to LoadRefs, we now need to populate the employee combo box with the employees data in our references DOM. Again, this provokes the need for a generic function, so add this function to populate any combo box to the XMLHelp.bas module:

```
' fill a combo box with the specified attribute values
Public Sub PopulateCombo(oNode As IXMLDOMNode, _
                         cboCombo As ComboBox, _
                         sPath As String, sAttrib As String)

Dim oElem As IXMLDOMNode
Dim oList As IXMLDOMNodeList

   cboCombo.Clear

   Set oList = FindNodes(oNode, sPath & "/@" & sAttrib)
   If oList Is Nothing Then Exit Sub
   For Each oElem In oList
       cboCombo.AddItem oElem.Text
   Next
End Sub
```

Note the call to the FindNodes procedure – this is a simple wrapper function for the selectNodes DOM method, to prevent any DOM errors feeding through due to invalid XPath specifications. So, add these procedures to XMLHelp.bas as well:

```
' find a single node using selectNodes syntax
Public Function FindNode(oRoot As IXMLDOMNode, sPath As String) As _
                         IXMLDOMNode

On Error GoTo errout
    Set FindNode = oRoot.selectSingleNode(sPath)
    Exit Function

errout:
    Set FindNode = Nothing
End Function

' find all matching nodes using selectNodes syntax
Public Function FindNodes(oRoot As IXMLDOMNode, sPath As String) As _
                          IXMLDOMNodeList

On Error GoTo errout
    Set FindNodes = oRoot.selectNodes(sPath)
    Exit Function

errout:
    Set FindNodes = Nothing
End Function
```

The first procedure, FindNode, returns a single node reference or Nothing if the search fails. The second procedure, FindNodes, returns a node list reference or Nothing if the search fails.

When using functions like these to query the DOM, a check that a node(s) was found (that is, Not Nothing) is vital to prevent run-time errors.

Both use standard XPath query syntax to find the matching record(s), if any exist.

Going back to the LoadRefs procedure in frmMain, we can complete the initialization process by populating the employees combo box:

```
    sXML = oBOL.GetReferences
    oRefDOM.loadXML sXML

    PopulateCombo oRefDOM.documentElement, cboEmp, _
                 "/refs/employees/employee", "name"
End Sub
```

This loads the combo box with the value of all the `name` attributes on the `employee` records. If you now run the program, you should see three names in the drop-down list, as shown:

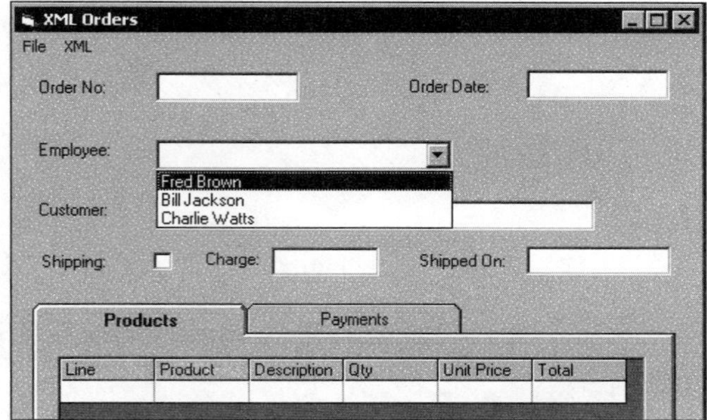

Viewing XML

We can anticipate that during the development cycle for this project we will frequently need to review the XML that we have been working with. In the final released application, you probably would not need this option available to your users, but it's very simple to add or remove. We are therefore going to add a second form to the XMLOrders program, called `frmXML`, and containing just a single multi-line text box.

We then expose a single `Public` property to take a reference to an existing DOM document, or any DOM node, and reformat the XML for display using a recursive function to descend the tree:

```
Public Property Set XMLDOM(oDOM As IXMLDOMNode)
   txtXML.Text = FormatXML(oDOM)
End Property
```

```
' build a new DOM as a copy of the original
Private Function FormatXML(oNode As IXMLDOMNode) As String
Dim oNew As DOMDocument
   If oNode Is Nothing Then Exit Function
   Set oNew = New DOMDocument
   oNew.loadXML oNode.xml
   FormatXMLDoc oNew, "   "
   FormatXML = oNew.xml
End Function
```

```
' recursive descent into each element node
Private Sub FormatXMLDoc(oDOM As IXMLDOMNode, ByVal sIndent _
                                    As String)
Dim oChild As IXMLDOMNode
Dim oNew As IXMLDOMNode
```

```
    If oDOM.childNodes.length > 0 Then
        For Each oChild In oDOM.childNodes
            FormatXMLDoc oChild, sIndent & sIndent
            If oDOM.nodeType = NODE_ELEMENT Then
                Set oNew = oDOM.ownerDocument.createNode(NODE_TEXT, _
                                            vbNullString, vbNullString)
                oNew.nodeValue = vbCrLf & sIndent
                Set oNew = oDOM.insertBefore(oNew, oChild)
                Set oNew = Nothing
            End If
        Next
        If oDOM.nodeType = NODE_ELEMENT Then
            Set oNew = oDOM.ownerDocument.createNode(NODE_TEXT, _
                                            vbNullString, vbNullString)
            oNew.nodeValue = vbCrLf & Left(sIndent, Len(sIndent) / 2)
            Set oNew = oDOM.appendChild(oNew)
            Set oNew = Nothing
        End If
    End If
End Sub
```

To use this new form, we must add some entries to the menu system on `frmMain`:

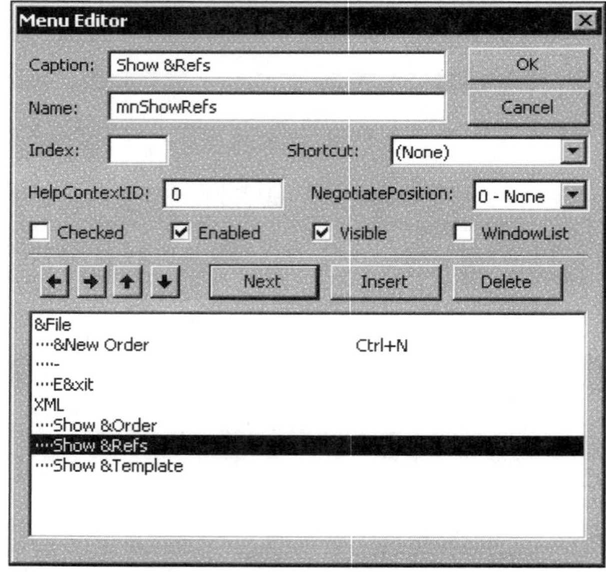

Now add the following code to `frmMain`:

```
Private Sub mnShowRefs_Click()
    frmXML.Show
    Set frmXML.XMLDOM = oRefDOM
End Sub
```

Running the program, we can now click the Show Refs option on the XML menu to see our references data:

XML

```
<refs>
  <employees>
    <employee emp_no="1" name="Fred Brown" commission_rate="2.0000"/>
    <employee emp_no="2" name="Bill Jackson" commission_rate="1.2000"/>
    <employee emp_no="3" name="Charlie Watts" commission_rate="0.8000"/>
  </employees>
  <pmt_types>
    <row pmt_type="C" descr="Cash"/>
    <row pmt_type="D" descr="Debit Card"/>
    <row pmt_type="R" descr="Credit Card"/>
  </pmt_types>
</refs>
```

We'll be able to employ the same technique to show the other sources of XML used by the application. The `frmXML` form is entirely portable to any other application that requires this functionality.

Loading an Order

We're now ready to start dealing with our orders data. As before, we're using the following UML sequence diagram to explain the process:

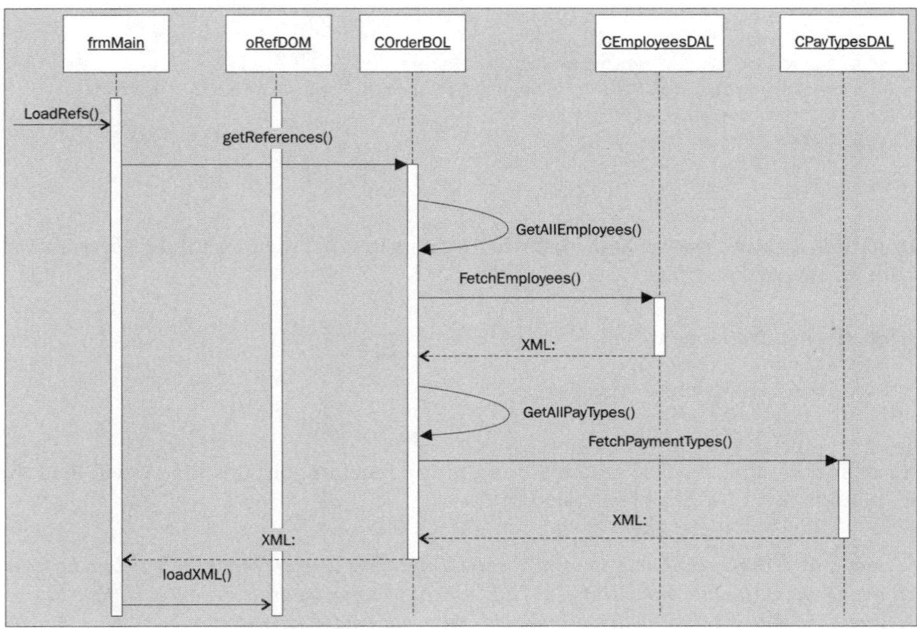

What does it show?

- The sequence is initiated by the user entering an order number in the `txtOrderNo` field.
- `txtOrderNo_Validate` calls the private `LoadOrder` function.
- `LoadOrder` instantiates `COrderBOL`, and invokes the `GetOrder` method.
- The `GetOrder` method on `COrderBOL` is tasked with assembling data from three separate sources: `COrdersDAL`, `CLinesDAL`, and `CPaymentsDAL`. This is very similar to the sequence we saw for the `GetReferences` method, so obviously we can use similar techniques to perform the task.
- As before, initially we will avoid implementing the Data Access Layer (DAL) objects by returning hand-coded XML from `GetOrder`, only this time we will do it in one piece (using the sample we created earlier).

In the `COrderBOL` class module, type the following code:

```
Public Function GetOrder(OrderNo As Long) As String

    ' hand-coded xml
    GetOrder = "<order order_no='1000' order_date='2001-03-10' emp_no='1'" _
             & " customer='Mrs Jane Smith' deliver='1' " _
             & " shipping_charge='10.00' adm_rev_no='2' " _
             & " adm_time='12 Mar 2001 13:38:04'>" & vbCrLf _
        & "<lines> " & vbCrLf _
        & "<row order_no='1000' line_no='1' prod_id='101'" _
           & " descr='Black trousers' qty='1' unit_price='36.99'" _
           & " unit_cost='24.55' commission='0.74'/>" & vbCrLf _
        & "<row order_no='1000' line_no='2' prod_id='201'" _
           & " descr='Men&apos;s trainers' qty='2' unit_price='69.50'" _
           & " unit_cost='48.12' commission='1.39'/>" & vbCrLf _
        & "</lines>" & vbCrLf _
        & "<payments>" & vbCrLf _
        & "<row order_no='1000' pmt_no='1' pmt_type='C' descr='Cash'" _
          & " amount='185.99'/>" & vbCrLf _
        & "</payments>" & vbCrLf _
        & "</order>"
End Function
```

If you think this is rather messy, and somewhat tedious to type, then a simpler *alternative* is to load the XML from an external text file:

```
Dim oDOM As DOMDocument
   oDOM.async = False
   oDOM.load App.Path & "\order.xml"
   GetOrder = oDOM.xml
```

In our `frmMain` module, we also create a `LoadOrder` function, but this time it will load the XML into a separate, module-level DOM object called `oDOM`.

We store each distinct set of data in separate DOM instances as there seems little to benefit from merging all the XML into one DOM. The chief benefit of using separate instances is that they segregate data that is being modified, and read-only data loaded for reference.

In `Form_Load`, we instantiate the other two DOM objects (we'll see more of `oNewDOM` later):

```
Private Sub Form_Load()
   Call InitGrids
   SSTab1.Tab = 0

   Set oRefDOM = New DOMDocument
   oRefDOM.async = False
   Set oDOM = New DOMDocument
   Set oNewDOM = New DOMDocument
   oDOM.async = False
   oNewDOM.async = False

   Call LoadRefs
End Sub
```

While we're looking at form loading, let's make sure our DOM objects are released when the application closes:

```
Private Sub Form_Unload(Cancel As Integer)
   Set oDOM = Nothing
   Set oRefDOM = Nothing
   Set oNewDOM = Nothing
End Sub
```

Now to get the order data deployed in `frmMain`, using the value of the `txtOrderNo` field (although our hard-coded XML will of course always return the same order details). Here's the `LoadOrder` procedure, which needs to be typed into `frmMain`:

```
Private Function LoadOrder() As Boolean
Dim oBOL As COrderBOL
Dim sXML As String

   Set oBOL = New COrderBOL

   sXML = oBOL.GetOrder(Val(txtOrderNo.Text))

   If Len(sXML) > 0 Then
      If Not oDOM.loadXML(sXML) Then
         MsgBox GetDomError(oDOM)
         Exit Function
      End If
   Else
      Beep
      MsgBox "Unknown Order No"
      txtOrderNo.SetFocus
      Exit Function
   End If

   Call UnPackOrder
   LoadOrder = True
   cmdSave.Enabled = True
   bEditing = True
End Function
```

As you can see, we've anticipated the case where no XML is returned by giving the user a simple **Unknown Order No** message. We call `LoadOrder` from the `Validate` event on `txtOrderNo` in `frmMain`:

```
Private Sub txtOrderNo_Validate(Cancel As Boolean)
Static bBusy As Boolean
   ' prevent double invocation
   If bBusy Then Exit Sub
   bBusy = True
   If Val(txtOrderNo.Text) > 0 Then
      Call LoadOrder
   End If
   bBusy = False
End Sub
```

Once we've loaded our `oDOM` object, we then need to call the `UnPackOrder` procedure (located in `frmMain`) to populate the form:

```
Private Sub UnPackOrder()
Dim oElem As IXMLDOMElement
Dim oEmp As IXMLDOMElement
Dim sEmpNo As String

   Set oElem = FindNode(oDOM.documentElement, "/order")
   With oElem
      txtOrderNo.Text = .GetAttribute("order_no")
      txtCustomer.Text = .GetAttribute("customer")
      txtOrderDate = XMLDateToField(.GetAttribute("order_date"))
      sEmpNo = .GetAttribute("emp_no")
      chkDeliver.Value = Val(.GetAttribute("deliver"))
      txtShipCharge.Text = .GetAttribute("shipping_charge")
      UpdateShipCharge
      ' may be null
      txtShipDate.Text = XMLDateToField(GetAttribute(oElem, "ship_date"))
   End With
   txtOrderNo.Enabled = False   ' prevent modifcation during Edit phase

   ' look up the employee name from emp_no
   Set oEmp = FindNodeByAttribute(oRefDOM.documentElement, _
                  "/refs/employees/employee", "emp_no", sEmpNo)
   If Not oEmp Is Nothing Then
      cboEmp.Text = oEmp.GetAttribute("name")
      fCommisRate = CSng(GetAttribute(oEmp, "commission_rate"))
   End If

   Call GetProducts
   Call GetPayments
End Sub
```

In `UnPackOrder`, we used `FindNode` to locate the topmost `<order>` element. We could just as easily use:

```
Set oElem = oDOM.childNodes(0)
```

If we are confident that our DOM will only ever contain a single `<order>` element at the root, then the `childNodes` method is acceptable and will be marginally more efficient. The chief disadvantage of this method lies with its implicitness – what is `childNodes(0)`? We can only tell by examining the DOM, whereas the `FindNode` method is self-explanatory. If our XML structure ever changes, the `FindNode` method would fail (rightly), whereas there will almost always be a `childNodes(0)`. However, it might not be what you expect.

We create an element object (`oElem`) since this gives us easy *named* access to the attributes:

```
With oElem
   txtOrderNo.Text = .GetAttribute("order_no")
   txtCustomer.Text = .GetAttribute("customer")
   txtOrderDate = XMLDateToField(.GetAttribute("order_date"))
   sEmpNo = .GetAttribute("emp_no")
   chkDeliver.Value = Val(.GetAttribute("deliver"))
   txtShipCharge.Text = .GetAttribute("shipping_charge")
   UpdateShipCharge
   ' may be null
   txtShipDate.Text = XMLDateToField(GetAttribute(oElem, "ship_date"))
End With
```

Attributes should always be referenced by name, rather than by `childNode` order. MSXML does not guarantee that the order of the attributes will remain the same throughout the lifetime of the DOM. It is therefore both unwise and unhelpful to other developers to use numbered offsets. Don't be tempted!

Date Values

We decided earlier that all dates in our XML will be represented in YYYY-MM-DD format – but we want the user to see dates in the format with which they are most familiar. We therefore need a further function in `XMLHelp` to perform the date conversion from YYYY-MM-DD to the local short date format (if the program allowed date changes, then we would also require a function to perform the conversion back the other way):

```
Public Function XMLDateToField(sYYMD As String) As String
   On Error Resume Next
   XMLDateToField = ""  ' empty string default
   If Len(sYYMD) = 10 Then
      XMLDateToField = Format(CDate(sYYMD), "Short Date")
   End If
End Function
```

NULL Values

So far, so good. However, when we come to the `ship_date` attribute, we encounter a problem – `ship_date` allows `NULL`, and `NULL` values are omitted as attributes in XML generated by the `FOR XML` statement. If we use the `GetAttribute` method of the DOM, an error will be raised if the underlying value is `NULL`, as is the case with the sample XML returned by `COrderBOL.GetOrder`. We would rather not have to handle such an error, and treat such a value as an empty string – so let's add a more friendly function to our `XMLHelp` module:

```
Public Function GetAttribute(oElem As IXMLDOMElement, Name As String) _
                              As String
Dim sValue As String

    ' if the attribute doesn't exist then return an empty string
    On Error Resume Next
    sValue = oElem.getAttributeNode(Name).Text
    GetAttribute = sValue
End Function
```

Now we can populate the `ship_date` field reliably, whether it is `NULL` or not (noting that `XMLDateToField` merely returns empty string values).

Cross References

You may have spotted in the code above that we have so far avoided dealing with employee number. We have retrieved the value of `emp_no` into a temporary variable `sEmpNo`:

```
sEmpNo = .GetAttribute("emp_no")
```

We need to relate `sEmpNo` to the entries in the drop-down combo box, that is, we need to find the matching name. This is where we need to perform a lookup against our reference DOM `oRefDOM` (from the `UnPackOrder` procedure):

```
' look up the employee name from emp_no
Set oEmp = FindNodeByAttribute(oRefDOM.documentElement, _
                  "/refs/employees/employee", "emp_no", sEmpNo)
If Not oEmp Is Nothing Then
   cboEmp.Text = oEmp.GetAttribute("name")
   fCommisRate = CSng(GetAttribute(oEmp, "commission_rate"))
End If
```

Note that there's a new generic function to add to the `XMLHelp` module:

```
' find a particular node by searching attribute values
Public Function FindNodeByAttribute(oRoot As IXMLDOMNode, Path As String, _
                        Attrib As String, Value As String) As IXMLDOMNode
Dim oEl As IXMLDOMNode
Dim sQuery As String
   Set FindNodeByAttribute = Nothing

   On Error GoTo errout
   ' search for first matching node using XPath query
   sQuery = Path & "[@" & Attrib & "='" & Value & "']"
   Set FindNodeByAttribute = oRoot.selectSingleNode(sQuery)
   Exit Function

errout:
    Err.Raise Err.Number, "FindNodeByAttribute", Err.Description
    Set FindNodeByAttribute = Nothing
End Function
```

As you can see, we once again use an XPath query to find what we are looking for. This time, however, we are not seeking an element by name alone – we want the element with a given attribute of a specific value. This function makes it easier on the developer by not requiring familiarity with the XPath syntax for matching attributes.

Unpacking the Children

Let's create a new procedure on `frmMain` called `GetProducts`, whose task is to unpack the `lines` elements in our order DOM. First, let's remind ourselves what the XML in `oDOM` looks like:

```
<order order_no='1000' order_date='2001-03-10' emp_no='1'
       customer='Mrs Jane Smith' deliver='1' shipping_charge='10.00'
       adm_rev_no='2' adm_time='12 Mar 2001 13:38:04'>
   <lines>
      <row order_no='1000' line_no='1' prod_id='101'
           descr='Black trousers' qty='1' unit_price='36.99'
           unit_cost='24.55' commission='0.74'/>
      <row order_no='1000' line_no='2' prod_id='201'
           descr='Men&apos;s trainers' qty='2' unit_price='69.50'
           unit_cost='48.12' commission='1.39'/>
   </lines>
...
```

Here's the `GetProducts` code, which will be responsible for populating the products grid, as well as compiling the various order totals:

```
Private Sub GetProducts()
Dim oList As IXMLDOMNodeList
Dim oElem As IXMLDOMElement
Dim nRows As Long
Dim j As Integer
Dim sRow As String
Dim cRowTotal As Currency
Dim nLineNo As Long

   grdProducts.Rows = 1
   sRow = ""
   cLines = 0
   cCommis = 0
   nMaxLineNo = 0
```

Build a node list of all line elements, and iterate through them using `For Each`:

```
   Set oList = FindNodes(oDOM, "/order/lines/row")
   nRows = oList.length
   If nRows > 0 Then
      For Each oElem In oList
         nLineNo = oElem.GetAttribute("line_no")
         If nLineNo > nMaxLineNo Then nMaxLineNo = nLineNo
         sRow = sRow & oElem.GetAttribute("line_no") & vbTab
         sRow = sRow & oElem.GetAttribute("prod_id") & vbTab
         sRow = sRow & oElem.GetAttribute("descr") & vbTab
         sRow = sRow & oElem.GetAttribute("qty") & vbTab
         sRow = sRow & oElem.GetAttribute("unit_price") & vbTab
```

Now we need to calculate the extended line total. Obviously, it would have been easy to provide this value by adding an expression to the SQL query, but we would still need this logic for processing local changes to the order:

```
            cRowTotal = CCur(oElem.GetAttribute("unit_price")) * _
                                  CInt(oElem.GetAttribute("qty"))
            cLines = cLines + cRowTotal
            sRow = sRow & Format(cRowTotal, MONEY_FMT) & vbCr
            cCommis = cCommis + (CCur(oElem.GetAttribute("commission")) * _
                                  CInt(oElem.GetAttribute("qty")))
         Next
```

sRow now contains all the data in Clip format for the grid, so we can now populate the products grid:

```
         grdProducts.Rows = nRows + 1
         With grdProducts
            .Row = 1
            .Col = 0
            .RowSel = .Rows - 1
            .ColSel = 5
            .Clip = sRow
            .Row = 1
         End With
      End If
      Call UpdateTotals
   End Sub
```

Now we can populate the totals fields on the form:

```
   Private Sub UpdateTotals()
      cTotal = cShip + cLines
      txtTotal.Text = Format(cTotal, MONEY_FMT)
      txtCommission.Text = Format(cCommis, MONEY_FMT)
      Call UpdateBalance
   End Sub
```

```
   Private Sub UpdateBalance()
      txtBalance.Text = Format(cTotal - cPayments, MONEY_FMT)

   End Sub
```

We also need to implement the UpdateShipCharge function, called by UnpackOrder:

```
   Private Sub UpdateShipCharge()
   Dim cNewShip As Currency

      If IsNumeric(txtShipCharge.Text) Then
         cNewShip = CCur(txtShipCharge.Text)
      Else
         cNewShip = 0
      End If
      cTotal = cTotal + (cNewShip - cShip)
      cShip = cNewShip
      UpdateTotals
   End Sub
```

The unpacking of the payments records can be done in a similar manner, so the code for `GetPayments` is not shown here, but is of course included in the download version. The one difference lies in the handling of the balance total – a calculated value representing the difference between the order total and the sum of all payments.

That completes the loading of the order header details. If you run the program now you can enter an order number – any number will do as long as it exists in the database – and the top half of the screen will be populated, the correct employee name will be displayed, and the products and payments grids will fill:

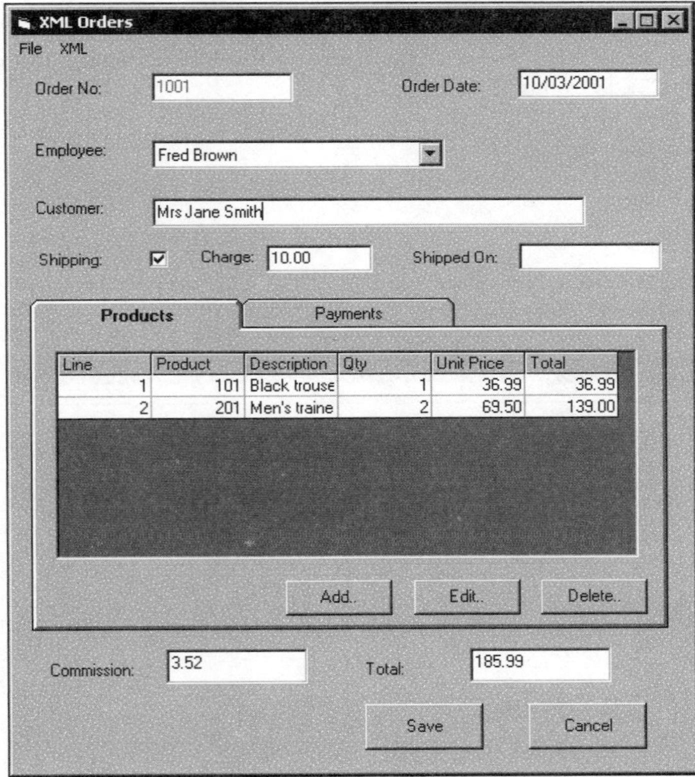

The associated Payments tab looks like this:

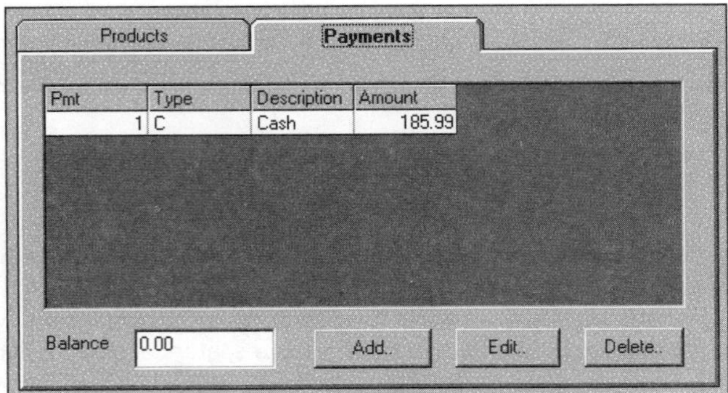

It only remains to provide some functionality to clear this data from the screen, and we have a simulation of a fully working prototype application, albeit currently only a read-only one. The `ClearAll` procedure performs the corollary to the `GetOrder` procedure, by clearing down all total values, and clearing all screen fields and grids. This is standard VB code, and for space reasons it is not shown here. `ClearAll` is of course invoked when we click the Cancel button:

```
Private Sub cmdCancel_Click()
    Call ClearAll
End Sub
```

Finally, we can review the XML in our DOM at any time using the `frmXML` form. Add this to the Show Order menu item's `Click` event:

```
Private Sub mnShowData_Click()
    frmXML.Show
    Set frmXML.XMLDOM = oDOM
End Sub
```

Now, if Show Order is selected for order number 1000, which we created at the beginning of this case study, `frmXML` will look like this:

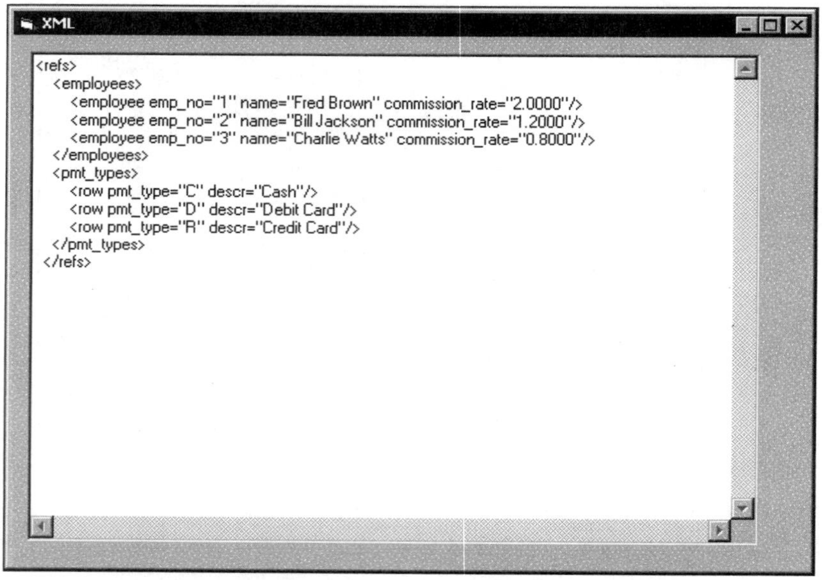

XML


```
<refs>
  <employees>
    <employee emp_no="1" name="Fred Brown" commission_rate="2.0000"/>
    <employee emp_no="2" name="Bill Jackson" commission_rate="1.2000"/>
    <employee emp_no="3" name="Charlie Watts" commission_rate="0.8000"/>
  </employees>
  <pmt_types>
    <row pmt_type="C" descr="Cash"/>
    <row pmt_type="D" descr="Debit Card"/>
    <row pmt_type="R" descr="Credit Card"/>
  </pmt_types>
</refs>
```


Data Access

Having successfully implemented all the code for our main screen (`frmMain`), using only the data and functionality inherent in the DOM, we can now proceed to look at the code to implement the data access tier classes. These objects will prove surprisingly simple to implement, and each requires very similar code, so once the few variations in functionality have been covered, creating new classes becomes mostly a copy-and-paste exercise where only the names of procedures, etc. need to be changed.

Let's go back to the beginning of our implementation exercise and start by providing real database access to retrieve the list of all employees. Go to the `OrderDAL` project and open up the `CEmployeesDAL` class module. The `FetchEmployees` method should return all the employee records:

```
Public Function FetchEmployees _
    (ConnStr As String, Optional Filter As String) As String
```

Note that the database's connection string (`ConnStr`) is to be passed in as a parameter. This is true for all the `OrdersDAL` classes – which server, database, and login ID we use to connect to the relevant SQL Server is a decision that should be external to the `DAL` components. Typically, it would be a function of the client application to determine these settings, depending upon a number of factors, such as client location, user ID, user role, etc. These issues are beyond the scope of this exercise and, as you will see, we take the simple choice of hard-coding the connection string in the `COrderBOL` component.

The `Optional Filter` parameter is just that – we have no need for it at present, but we include it in case a need arises.

We now create `Command` and `Stream` objects – note that we do not need any `Recordset` objects:

```
Dim cmd As ADODB.Command
Dim oStream As ADODB.Stream
Dim sXML As String
   On Error GoTo ErrHandler
   Set cmd = CreateObject("ADODB.Command")
   cmd.ActiveConnection = ConnStr
```

For now, let's just enter the required SQL query, which we've already used to create our XML samples:

```
   cmd.CommandType = adCmdText
   cmd.CommandText = "SELECT emp_no, name," _
            & " LTRIM(STR(commission_rate, 6, 4)) AS commission_rate" _
            & " FROM employees AS employee FOR XML AUTO"
```

Set up the `Stream` object to receive the output:

```
   Set oStream = CreateObject("ADODB.Stream")
   oStream.Open
   cmd.Properties("Output Stream") = oStream
```

Execute the command:

```
   cmd.Execute , , adExecuteStream
```

Extract the XML from the `Stream` and package it up for return by adding the outer `<employees>` element:

```
   sXML = oStream.ReadText
   sXML = "<employees>" & vbCrLf & sXML & vbCrLf & "</employees>"
   FetchEmployees = sXML
   Exit Function

ErrHandler:
   Err.Raise Err.Number, "CEmployeesDAL.FetchEmployees", Err.Description
End Function
```

To make use of this new functionality, we need to replace the hard-coded XML in the GetAllEmployees function in COrderBOL:

```
Public Function GetAllEmployees() As String
Dim oEmp As CEmployeesDAL

    Set oEmp = CreateObject("OrderDal.CEmployeesDAL")
    GetAllEmployees = oEmp.FetchEmployees(m_Conn)
End Function
```

m_Conn is the private connection string constant as discussed, declared at the module level in COrderBOL:

```
Private Const m_Conn = "Provider=SQLOLEDB; Data Source=(local); " _
                & "User ID=sa; Password=sa; Initial Catalog=wroxdb"
```

Obviously, you must change this as appropriate before attempting to use the COrderDAL classes. With that done, you should find the application still works as before, but now one small component of the XML is being derived from live SQL Server data.

SQL Errors

If an error occurs in any FOR XML query, SQL Server embeds the error details as a **Processing Instruction** (**PI**) within the XML stream. Although ADO may raise an error, this is not guaranteed, as can easily be demonstrated.

Add an x in front of the emp_no in the SELECT statement in CEmployeesDAL:

```
cmd.CommandText = "SELECT xemp_no, name," _
```

Now when you execute the program, set a breakpoint at the cmd.Execute line. Step into this and you should be at the ErrHandler, but this is not guaranteed (see below). Now, in the Immediate window, query the Stream object:

```
?oStream.ReadText
```

You should see the following:

```
<?MSSQLError HResult="0x80040e14" Source="Microsoft OLE DB Provider for SQL Server"
Description="Invalid column name 'xemp_no'."?>
```

> **There is a bug registered against ADO 2.6 that has important repercussions on error handling. The symptom is that the description for the SQL error is found to be blank. In addition, ADO does not always detect that a SQL error has occurred. At the time of writing, a work-around has been published by Microsoft. See Technet article *Q279760* at http://support.microsoft.com/support/kb/articles/Q279/7/60.ASP.**

To be safe, we add this code to check the XML returned, in case ADO has not raised an error. Insert this code into CEmployeesDAL after the extraction of the XML from the stream:

```
    sXML = oStream.ReadText
    ' check for MS Errors
    If InStr(sXML, "<?MSSQLError") > 0 Then
       Err.Raise vbObjectError + 1000, , sXML
    End If
    sXML = "<employees>" & vbCrLf & sXML & vbCrLf & "</employees>"
    FetchEmployees = sXML
    Exit Function
```

Stored Procedures

As stated at the outset, stored procedures are to be used exclusively for all data access, so let's now create a stored procedure to replace the `SELECT` query we executed in `FetchEmployees`:

```
CREATE PROCEDURE get_employees
AS

   SELECT '<employees>'

   SELECT emp_no,
      name,
      LTRIM(STR(commission_rate,6,4)) AS commission_rate
   FROM employees AS employee
   FOR XML AUTO

   SELECT '</employees>'
```

This is the same basic query, but we are now using SQL Server also to provide the outer `<employees>` element, instead of appending it in the VB code. It makes for better consistency if the generation of *all* the XML is performed inside SQL Server wherever possible.

Although a stored procedure incorporating three separate queries like this would generate three separate `Recordset` objects (if we were using `Recordsets`), when using the ADO `Stream` object, all output is collected into a single text stream so no special coding is required in VB to handle this.

We can now amend the `FetchEmployees` function to use the stored procedure – here's the whole of the code as revised for stored procedure execution – the changes are the highlighted lines:

```
Public Function FetchEmployees _
      (ConnStr As String, Optional Filter As String) As String
Dim cmd As ADODB.Command
Dim oStream As ADODB.Stream
Dim sXML As String

   On Error GoTo ErrHandler
   Set cmd = CreateObject("ADODB.Command")

   cmd.ActiveConnection = ConnStr
   cmd.CommandType = adCmdStoredProc
   cmd.CommandText = "get_employees"
   cmd.Prepared = False

   Set oStream = CreateObject("ADODB.Stream")
   oStream.Open
```

```
    cmd.Properties("Output Stream") = oStream

    cmd.Execute , , adExecuteStream
    sXML = oStream.ReadText

    ' check for MS Errors
    If InStr(sXML, "<?MSSQLError") > 0 Then
       Err.Raise vbObjectError + 1000, , sXML
    End If

    FetchEmployees = sXML
    Exit Function
 ErrHandler:
    Err.Raise Err.Number, "CEmployeesDAL.FetchEmployees", Err.Description
 End Function
```

Coding the remaining functions in the OrderDAL component is mostly going to involve a copy and paste job, changing only the name of the relevant stored procedure and the function name. This is certainly true of the FetchPaymentTypes function in the CPayTypesDAL class module, so we will not include the code here.

> *An alternative approach that could be explored is to use a common library routine to perform the stored procedure execution within each DAL function.*

The remaining four Fetch procedures (FetchOrder, FetchOrdLines, FetchOrdPayments, and FetchAProduct), however, each have the distinction that they require a single argument to be passed to the stored procedure, so let's look at the relevant code for just one of these.

Taking the FetchOrder function as our prototype, here's the stored procedure:

```
CREATE PROCEDURE get_order @ord int
AS
   SELECT xact='-',
      order_no,
      CONVERT (char(10),order_date,126) AS order_date,
      emp_no, customer, deliver,
      CONVERT(varchar(10),shipping_charge) AS shipping_charge,
      CONVERT (char(10),ship_date,126) AS ship_date,
      adm_rev_no, CONVERT(varchar(20),adm_time, 113) AS adm_time
   FROM orders AS [order]
   WHERE order_no = @ord
   FOR XML AUTO
```

You may have noticed that we've deviated a little from the agreed XML format for an order, and added an extra attribute, xact – this will be used for data maintenance control, and will be explained later when we start modifying orders. From now on, all the data elements for an order will carry this additional attribute.

> **One of the key features of adopting XML in the way that we have is that it is very amenable to this sort of change. Adding new attributes, or even element structures, will in no way damage the existing application code *providing* we have always used explicit named references to access its content.**

Here's the code for FetchOrder in COrdersDAL:

```
Public Function FetchOrder(ConnStr As String, OrderNo As Long) As String
Dim cmd As ADODB.Command
Dim oStream As ADODB.Stream
Dim param As Parameter
Dim sXML As String

   On Error GoTo ErrHandler
   Set cmd = CreateObject("ADODB.Command")

   cmd.ActiveConnection = ConnStr
   cmd.CommandType = adCmdStoredProc
   cmd.CommandText = "get_order"
   cmd.Prepared = False
```

Add the single, integer, and parameter:

```
   Set param = cmd.CreateParameter("ord", adInteger, adParamInput, , _
                                                           OrderNo)
   cmd.Parameters.Append param
```

and continue as before:

```
   Set oStream = CreateObject("ADODB.Stream")
   oStream.Open

   cmd.Properties("Output Stream") = oStream

   cmd.Execute , , adExecuteStream
   sXML = oStream.ReadText

   ' check for MS Errors
   If InStr(sXML, "<?MSSQLError") > 0 Then
      Err.Raise vbObjectError + 1000, , sXML
   End If

   FetchOrder = sXML
   Exit Function

ErrHandler:
   Err.Raise Err.Number, "COrdersDAL.FetchOrder", Err.Description
End Function
```

It's only going to take 5 or 10 minutes to apply the same process to the CLinesDAL, CProductsDAL, and CPaymentsDAL classes, and thereby complete the active data Fetch procedures.

The following list itemizes all of the DAL Fetch functions, the related stored procedures, and whether the code is included in this chapter or needs to be pasted in from the completed download sample:

VB Method	Stored procedure	Paste In
CEmployeesDAL.FetchEmployees	get_employees	No
CPayTypes.FetchPaymentTypes	get_paytypes	Yes
CProductsDAL.FetchAProduct	get_product	Yes
COrdersDAL.FetchOrder	get_order	No
CLinesDAL.FetchOrdLines	get_ord_lines	Yes
CPaymentsDAL.FetchOrdPayments	get_ord_payments	Yes

We can now return to `COrderBOL` and re-code the `GetOrder` function to assemble the hierarchical order document from the new `DAL` components:

```
Public Function GetOrder(OrderNo As Long) As String
Dim sXml As String
Dim oDOM As DOMDocument     ' master document
Dim oEl As DOMDocument      ' temporary child document
Dim oOrd As COrdersDAL
Dim oLine As CLinesDAL
Dim oPay As CPaymentsDAL

   Set oDOM = CreateObject("MSXML2.DOMDocument")
   oDOM.async = False
   Set oEl = CreateObject("MSXML2.DOMDocument")
   oEl.async = False
```

Request the order data and check that we actually found one:

```
   Set oOrd = CreateObject("OrderDal.CordersDAL")
   sXml = oOrd.FetchOrder(m_Conn, OrderNo)
   Set oOrd = Nothing

   ' did we get anything?
   If sXml = "" Then
      Exit Function
   End If

   ' set order as the root node
   oDOM.loadXML sXml
```

Now get the child elements for lines and payments:

```
   Set oLine = CreateObject("OrderDal.CLinesDAL")
   sXml = oLine.FetchOrdLines(m_Conn, OrderNo)
   Set oLine = Nothing
   ' add lines as a child of order
   oEl.loadXML sXml
   oDOM.documentElement.appendChild oEl.documentElement
```

```
    Set oPay = CreateObject("OrderDal.CPaymentsDAL")
    sXml = oPay.FetchOrdPayments(m_Conn, OrderNo)
    Set oPay = Nothing
    ' add payments as a child of order
    oEl.loadXML sXml
    oDOM.documentElement.appendChild oEl.documentElement

    GetOrder = oDOM.xml
End Function
```

After pasting in the remaining DAL functions and their related stored procedures, we then have a read-only application working with real SQL data, and it's time to turn our attention to data modification.

Modifying an Order

At this point, let's turn our attention to the new xact attribute that we added to our order XML. The principle behind this is to act as a marker for *all* modifications to data. The table below describes its use:

Value	Meaning
-	Initial unmodified value
U	Updated record
I	New, inserted record
D	Record marked for deletion

How we make use of the xact values is, of course, something that differs for each application and is dependant on the complexity of the data and how it changes, the functionality of the UI, the implementation of business rules, and the methods by which the SQL Server data is to be modified.

The XMLOrders application offers many forms of modification to the order data:

- Changes to header details such as customer, or shipping charge
- Addition, modification, and deletion of order lines
- Addition, modification, and deletion of payments

The download source contains working code for all these forms of change; here we can look at just one example to demonstrate the principles and techniques involved.

Let's load up our one and only order – order number 1000 – and increase the shipping charge from \$10.00 to \$15.00. To recognize this event, we will need to intercept the Validate event on the txtShipCharge field:

```
Private Sub txtShipCharge_Validate(Cancel As Boolean)
Dim cNewShip As Currency

    If IsNumeric(txtShipCharge.Text) Then
        cNewShip = CCur(txtShipCharge.Text)
```

```
    Else
       cNewShip = 0
    End If
    txtShipCharge.Text = Format(cNewShip, MONEY_FMT)
    SetOrderAttribute "shipping_charge", txtShipCharge.Text
    UpdateShipCharge
End Sub
```

All well and good but we need to update our running totals and, more importantly, we need to update the order DOM.

> *We* could *decide not to update the DOM until the user clicks on the* Save *button, but this is not a very practical choice. Updating the DOM as we go gives us the opportunity to apply any form of business rules validation at any time, since the DOM always represents the current state of the data in the application.*

So we'll add a procedure to `frmMain` to modify any attribute of the order record:

```
Private Sub SetOrderAttribute(Name As String, Value As String)
Dim oElem As IXMLDOMElement
    Set oElem = FindNode(oDOM.documentElement, "/order")

    oElem.setAttribute Name, Value
    If oElem.GetAttribute("xact") = "-" Then
       oElem.setAttribute "xact", "U"
    End If

End Sub
```

As you can see, we ensure that any change to the order record results in the `xact` attribute being altered also.

Because the shipping charge is added to the total value of the order, the running totals for the order are updated by the `UpdateShipCharge` procedure included earlier. This in turn causes the payments balance to be updated. If we've increased our order total by $5.00 (by increasing shipping charge to $15.00) then, of course, we will need to increase our payments accordingly.

Paste in the similar code for `chkDeliver_Validate` and `txtCustomer_Validate` to activate the other modifiable fields on `frmMain`. To handle changes to `Employee`, you will need to paste in the `cboEmp_Validate`, `GetEmployee`, `RecalculateCommissions`, and `CalculateCommission` functions in `frmMain`.

Changing Payments

The Payments tab on our main form shows three buttons – Add, Edit, and Delete – for the modification of payment records. We're going to use a small sub-form to make payment changes, so we'll add `frmPayments` to the XMLOrders project, and give it a drop-down combo box for the payment type, and a text box to enter the amount:

Here's the code for the Edit button on the `frmMain` Payments tab:

```
Private Sub cmdEditPay_Click()
Dim nPmtNo As Long

    grdPayments.Col = 0
    nPmtNo = Val(grdPayments.Text)
    If nPmtNo = 0 Then Exit Sub

    EditPayment nPmtNo

End Sub
```

This procedure calculates which payment record is to be edited by extracting the value of the first column in the payments grid. The user must click on the required grid row before clicking the Edit button or no action follows.

We might have chosen not to display the `pmt_no` in the grid, in which case we would have two alternatives:

- Hide the column, by setting its width to zero
- Omit the column and rely on the row order in the grid

The latter approach *might* work, but is always more dangerous, and means we must take extra precautions to keep the grid numbering consistent with the `pmt_no` values in our XML document.

Now we have identified the payment record we want to modify, let's look at the `EditPayment` procedure:

```
Private Sub EditPayment(PmtNo As Long)
Dim oEl As IXMLDOMElement
    Set oEl = FindNodeByAttribute(oDOM.documentElement,  _
                        "/order/payments/row", "pmt_no", CStr(PmtNo))
```

Here we have identified the matching element in our DOM. The intention is pass a reference to this element directly to the `frmPayments` form. We can then let the code in `frmPayments` use the element values as required – this is achieved by providing `frmPayments` with a `Public` property to save the DOM reference:

```
    Load frmPayments
    Set frmPayments.DomElement = oEl
    frmPayments.Show vbModal
```

This demonstrates an important principle of our design – `frmPayments` *encapsulates* the functionality for changes to payment records; passing in the DOM reference allows that object full scope to apply such changes.

Once the user has completed the payment changes required, the form will hide itself, thereby returning control to the `EditPayment` procedure. We then query a second `Public` property of the form to establish whether any changes were in fact made, in which case we will need to refresh the contents of our payments grid from the DOM, using the existing `GetPayments` procedure:

```
   If frmPayments.Dirty Then
SetOrderAttribute "adm_time", Now ' mark the order as Updated
GetPayments                       ' refresh the grid from the DOM
   End If

   ' now it's safe to Unload
   Unload frmPayments
End Sub
```

frmPayments

Let's now move onto the `frmPayments` code. First of all, we need to establish our private member variables to hold the DOM reference and the modification flag `m_Dirty`:

```
Private m_Elem As IXMLDOMElement
Private m_Dirty As Boolean
```

In the `Form_Load` event procedure, we need to populate the payment type combo box, using the same procedure we used for the employees in `frmMain`, and retrieving the values from the references DOM, `oRefDOM` (which we conveniently declared as `Public` in `frmMain` for this very purpose):

```
Private Sub Form_Load()
   ' load payment types combo
   PopulateCombo frmMain.oRefDOM.documentElement, cboPmt, _
                                       "/refs/pmt_types/row", "descr"

End Sub
```

We could have chosen not to unload the form after use, in which case the above code would only be executed once – the first time it is required. Either way, since we know that the list of payment types is small, the overhead is minimal.

On `Unload`, we should clean up the object reference to the order DOM:

```
Private Sub Form_Unload(Cancel As Integer)
   Set m_Elem = Nothing
End Sub
```

Next, we need to provide the public property to enable the DOM reference to the relevant payment record to be saved locally, and then extract the values for display on the form:

```
Public Property Set DomElement(ByRef thisEl As IXMLDOMElement)
   Set m_Elem = thisEl
   If GetAttribute(m_Elem, "descr") = "" Then
      cboPmt.ListIndex = 0
   Else
      cboPmt.Text = GetAttribute(m_Elem, "descr")
   End If
   txtAmount.Text = GetAttribute(m_Elem, "amount")
   m_Dirty = False
End Property
```

When the user changes either the payment type, or the amount, we need to set the `m_Dirty` flag, and provide a public property to expose it:

```
Private Sub cboPmt_Click()
   m_Dirty = True
End Sub
```

```
Private Sub txtAmount_Change()
   m_Dirty = True
End Sub
```

```
Public Property Get Dirty() As Boolean
   Dirty = m_Dirty
End Property
```

When the user clicks on the **Save** button, we must write the changed values into the DOM, not forgetting to update our `xact` attribute:

```
Private Sub cmdSave_Click()
Dim nType As Long
Dim sPmt As String
Dim oPmt As IXMLDOMElement

   If m_Dirty Then
      nType = cboPmt.ListIndex
      ' lookup the pmt_no
      Set oPmt = FindNodeByAttribute(frmMain.oRefDOM.documentElement, _
                           "/refs/pmt_types/row", "descr", cboPmt.Text)
      sPmt = GetAttribute(oPmt, "pmt_type")

      m_Elem.setAttribute "pmt_type", sPmt
      m_Elem.setAttribute "descr", cboPmt.Text
      m_Elem.setAttribute "amount", txtAmount.Text

      ' mark record for Update
      If m_Elem.GetAttribute("xact") = "-" Then
         m_Elem.setAttribute "xact", "U"
      End If
   End If
   Me.Hide
End Sub
```

Finally, if the user changes their mind and clicks the Cancel button, we need to reset the m_Dirty flag so that the EditPayment procedure can know that no changes have been made:

```
Private Sub cmdCancel_Click()
   m_Dirty = False
   Me.Hide
End Sub
```

Deleting a Payment

To delete a payment record, we choose to remove the element from the DOM (alternatively we could preserve the record and set xact = "D" if there was a benefit in functionality, such as an undo feature). The code for the cmdDelPay button is straightforward:

```
Private Sub cmdDelPay_Click()
Dim nPay As Long
Dim oElem As IXMLDOMElement
Dim oPay As IXMLDOMElement

   grdPayments.Col = 0
   nPay = Val(grdPayments.Text)
   If nPay = 0 Then Exit Sub

   Set oElem = FindNodeByAttribute(oDOM.documentElement, _
                      "/order/payments/row", "pmt_no", CStr(nPay))

   ' identify the parent payments element
   Set oPay = oElem.parentNode
   oPay.removeChild oElem

   If nPay = nMaxPmtNo Then nMaxPmtNo = nMaxPmtNo - 1
   SetOrderAttribute "adm_time", Now ' mark the order as Updated
   GetPayments    ' refresh the screen
End Sub
```

The process for modifying the product lines is comparable to that for payments, the main difference being that a run-time database lookup of product IDs is required, instead of using a combo box. Check the code in the additional frmLines module to see this.

Saving Changes

Having provided a number of ways to modify our order data, we are at last in a position to see how these changes will be relayed back to the SQL Server database. In a more conventional n-tier system, we would expect the updates to the various database entities to be performed by different DAL components, perhaps using COM+ to control the overall transaction. Something like this:

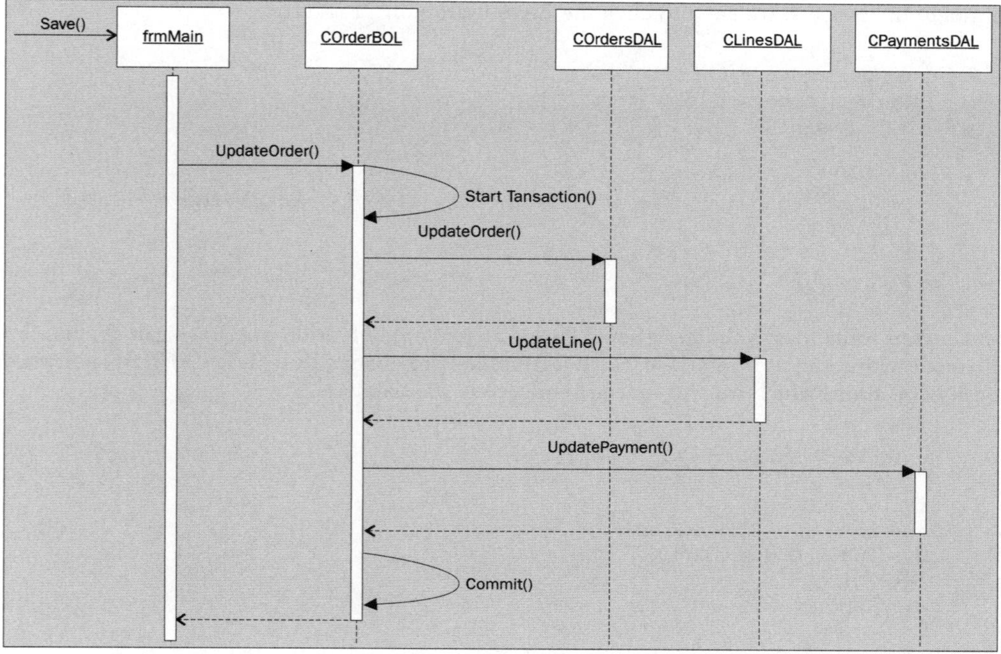

However, since we've adopted XML and we already have a hierarchical representation of a whole order, we can leverage SQL Server's OPENXML functionality to provide update functionality that is considerably simpler to implement, while retaining tight control over the transaction.

The following sequence diagram shows the actual model we will use: as you can see, it is much simpler:

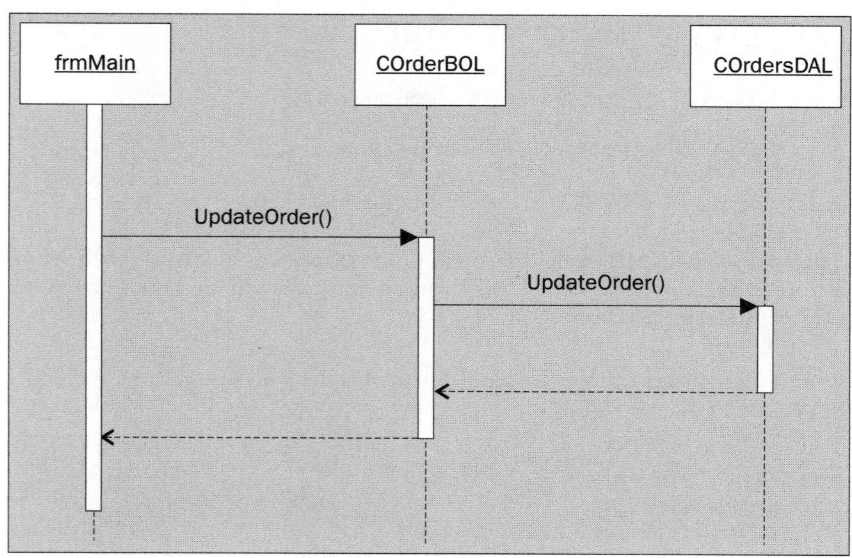

To initiate the process, we need to click the **Save** button on `frmMain`:

```
Private Sub cmdSave_Click()
Dim oBOL As COrderBOL
Dim sXML As String

   If cTotal <> cPayments Then
      MsgBox "You cannot save an Order until the Payments Balance is Zero"
      SSTab1.Tab = 1
      Exit Sub
   End If
```

We've added some local validation here. This is an example of a rule which we can deem safe to implement within the user interface, since it is unlikely to change over time – effectively it's a data integrity constraint which we will indeed reinforce in the database.

```
   Set oBOL = New COrderBOL

   sXML = oDOM.xml
   On Error GoTo ErrHandler
   oBOL.UpdateOrder sXML
   ClearAll
   Exit Sub

ErrHandler:
   MsgBox Err.Description
End Sub
```

As you can see, we pass the XML of the whole order down to the `COrderBOL` class, so here's our first pass at the `UpdateOrder` function:

```
Public Function UpdateOrder(sXml As String) As Boolean
Dim oOrd As COrdersDAL

   Set oOrd = CreateObject("OrderDal.COrdersDAL")

   UpdateOrder = oOrd.UpdateOrder(m_Conn, sXml)

End Function
```

Effectively, this passes the XML straight through to the `COrdersDAL` class – we'll return later to the above procedure to see how the business rules can be implemented. So here's the code for the `UpdateOrder` function in `COrdersDAL`:

```
Public Function UpdateOrder(ConnStr As String, sXML As String) As Boolean
Dim cmd As ADODB.Command
Dim param As Parameter

   UpdateOrder = False
   On Error GoTo ErrHandler
   Set cmd = CreateObject("ADODB.Command")

   cmd.ActiveConnection = ConnStr
   cmd.CommandType = adCmdStoredProc
```

```
    cmd.CommandText = "update_order"
    cmd.Prepared = False

    ' Set up parameter.
    Set param = cmd.CreateParameter("xml", adVarChar, adParamInput, 4000, _
                                                                    sXML)
    cmd.Parameters.Append param

    cmd.Execute , , adCmdStoredProc + adExecuteNoRecords
    UpdateOrder = True
    Exit Function

ErrHandler:
    Err.Raise Err.Number, "COrdersDAL.UpdateOrder", Err.Description
End Function
```

This all looks very recognizable from the earlier `Fetch` functions, the main difference being that this function passes the XML to the stored procedure as a single varchar `Parameter`.

> **Since a varchar in SQL Server 2000 has a maximum length of 8000 characters (or 4000 in Unicode), we must be careful about the size limits of our XML. However, SQL Server 2000 allows stored procedure parameters of type *text,* which effectively means there is no maximum limit, albeit you must design in this capability from the outset. For XMLOrders, we are in no danger of approaching the varchar limit.**

So now we need to code the `update_order` stored procedure. The approach that we are going to take is the rather brutal one of deleting all the related records for the order, and then re-inserting them from the XML. This has the benefit of code simplicity, but the risk that we create a *heavier* transaction than might be necessary (by deleting and re-inserting records that have stayed unchanged). You might like to try experimenting with different versions of this code to see how much difference a more targeted approach will make.

Using OPENXML

We start by getting SQL Server to instantiate a DOM from our XML using the `sp_xml_preparedocument` system procedure (note that the code for this stored procedure runs over the next couple of pages – so don't run this T-SQL yet):

```
CREATE PROCEDURE update_order @orderxml varchar(4000), @debug tinyint = 0
AS
DECLARE @hDoc int
DECLARE @ord  int
DECLARE @ret  int

   EXEC sp_xml_preparedocument @hDoc OUTPUT, @orderxml
   IF @debug=1 PRINT 'hDoc ' + CONVERT(varchar,@hDoc)

   SELECT @ord = x.order_no
   FROM  OPENXML (@hdoc, '/order', 1)
   WITH ( order_no                       int) AS x

   IF @debug=1 PRINT 'Updating Order ' + CONVERT(varchar, @ord)
```

Here, we've used OPENXML to extract the order number into an integer variable. (The optional @debug argument allows us to test the procedure more fully in Query Analyzer.) Now we can start the transaction:

```
BEGIN TRAN

   UPDATE orders
   SET order_date = x.order_date,
      emp_no = x.emp_no,
      customer = x.customer,
      deliver = x.deliver,
      shipping_charge = x.shipping_charge,
      adm_time=getdate(),
      adm_rev_no=x.adm_rev_no+1
   FROM  OPENXML (@hdoc, '/order', 1)
   WITH ( xact                           char(1),
         order_no                        int,
         order_date                      datetime,
         emp_no                          int,
         customer                        varchar(30),
         deliver                         tinyint,
         shipping_charge                 money,
         ship_date                       datetime,
         adm_rev_no                      int) AS x
   WHERE x.order_no = orders.order_no
   AND xact = 'U'
   IF @@error != 0 GOTO fail
```

Because we want to query the xact attribute, and this does not exist in the orders table, we need to use an explicit schema for this OPENXML statement.

In the download, you'll find a stored procedure – get_table_xml – that generates the equivalent schema code for any table.

There's a second reason that we used an explicit schema here. OPENXML, in the initial release of SQL Server 2000, does not map IDENTITY columns. If you execute:

```
SELECT * FROM OPENXML(@hDoc, '/order', 1) WITH orders
```

you will see that the order_no column is missing.

Now to process the lines records:

```
   DELETE lines
   WHERE order_no = @ord
   IF @@error != 0 GOTO fail

   INSERT lines
   SELECT order_no, line_no, prod_id, qty, unit_price, unit_cost,
               commission
   FROM  OPENXML (@hdoc, '/order/lines/row', 1)
   WITH ( xact                           char(1),
         order_no                        int,
         line_no                         smallint,
```

```
        prod_id                         int,
        qty                             int,
        unit_price                      money,
        unit_cost                       money,
        commission                      money) AS x
    WHERE xact <> 'D'
    IF @@error != 0 GOTO fail
```

We've specifically excluded the `xact='D'` records in this query, as an example, but if you look at the download source code for deleting lines or payments, we have chosen to remove the unwanted records immediately from the DOM – so `'D'` records will never be passed to this procedure.

And finally the payments:

```
    DELETE payments
    WHERE order_no = @ord
    IF @@error != 0 GOTO fail

    INSERT payments
    SELECT order_no, pmt_no, pmt_type, amount
    FROM  OPENXML (@hdoc, '/order/payments/row', 1)
    WITH  payments
    IF @@error != 0 GOTO fail
```

We're almost ready to commit, but first a sanity check on the whole package (this is the last section of the `CREATE PROCEDURE` for `update_order`):

```
    -- now check the sums
    EXEC @ret = validate_order @ord
    IF @ret <> 10 GOTO fail

  COMMIT TRAN
  IF @debug=1 PRINT 'COMMITTED'
  GOTO quit

fail:
  ROLLBACK TRAN
  IF @debug=1 PRINT 'ROLLED BACK'

quit:
  IF @debug=1 PRINT 'Releasing hDoc'
  EXEC sp_xml_removedocument @hDoc
GO
```

You'll get the SQL Server warning "Cannot add rows to sysdepends for the current stored procedure because it depends on the missing object 'validate_order'" when you load this procedure because we haven't yet loaded `validate_order`, which comes next.

DOM Handles

It's important to ensure that, however we exit the procedure, we always release the DOM by calling `sp_xml_removedocument`. SQL Server has a finite limit on the number of DOM handles it can create, and these are allocated from a global pool. It's therefore very easy to write a single misbehaving procedure that progressively uses up all available handles, at which point SQL Server will raise error 6224 on the next call to `sp_xml_preparedocument`. This will read:

XML document could not be created because server memory is low. Use sp_xml_removedocument to release XML documents.

It's true that DOM handles are released automatically when a session is closed, but with the possibility of object pooling, this may not be something you can rely upon.

The number of DOM handles you can have depends on the size of the XML and the memory available to SQL Server. The MSXML parser uses one-eighth of the total memory available to SQL Server and parsed documents are stored in the internal cache of SQL Server 2000. Books Online recommends running `sp_xml_removedocument` to prevent you from running out of memory.

It's rather unfortunate that this is not a configurable factor, like the procedure cache ratio in earlier versions of SQL Server. What happens to this one-eighth if you don't use any XML documents is not stated!

The following chart shows the results of a simple test on a test server, using two different sizes of XML, and three alternative memory configurations. It shows that system memory is by far the most important factor. While the numbers may look reasonable enough on many systems, they *could* represent a serious constraint for very high transactional systems. In effect, the number of DOM handles represents the maximum number of concurrent `OPENXML` statements that can be performed:

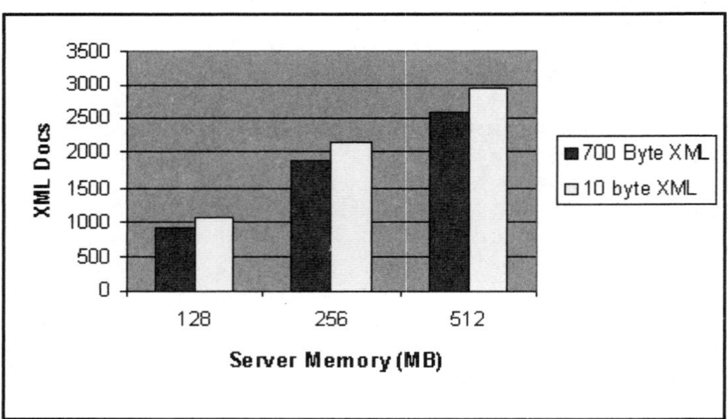

Data Validation

Getting back to our `update_order` stored procedure, you may have noticed that we included a call to another procedure called `validate_order`. The `validate_order` stored procedure gives us the opportunity to perform any other checks on the data not covered by the normal DRI constraints of the database tables. In our case, we want to make sure that the total payments equals the total value of the order:

```
CREATE PROCEDURE validate_order @order int
AS
DECLARE @pay_sum money
DECLARE @line_sum money
DECLARE @shipping money

    SELECT @shipping = shipping_charge
    FROM orders
    WHERE order_no = @order
```

```
    SELECT @line_sum = SUM(qty * unit_price)
    FROM lines
    WHERE order_no = @order


    SELECT @pay_sum = SUM(amount)
    FROM payments
    WHERE order_no = @order

    IF @pay_sum <> (@shipping + @line_sum)
       RAISERROR 99901 'Payments and Line totals do not match'
    ELSE
    BEGIN
       PRINT 'Order ' + CONVERT(varchar,@order) + ' validated'
       RETURN 10
    END
GO
```

The procedure returns a positive value of `10` if everything is OK. Any other value would cause the `update_order` transaction to rollback. We use a value of `10` since SQL Server will return `0` by default and negative values on error, and we want to ensure that we haven't exited the procedure by some unexpected route.

Concurrency

The issue that we have not yet resolved with this update process is concurrency control. In the definition of the `orders` table, we explained that the `adm_rev_no` column could be used to provide an optimistic locking strategy. We do not have room to cover this properly here, but a simple concurrency strategy could be implemented with a trigger and a rule saying that, whenever an `orders` record is updated, the value of the `adm_rev_no` column must always be *exactly one more* than the previous value. If two clients are viewing the same version of a record, and each submits an update to that version, the first one to be processed will succeed, and increment the `adm_rev_no`, whereas the second update should fail since it tries to set the revision to the value that already exists.

Creating New Data

So far, we've seen how to fetch existing data into the application as XML, and how to modify the XML before submitting changes back to the database. Of course, we also need to consider how to create new data records – at the orders, lines, or payments level. The key problem to solve here is not so much in submitting new XML records to SQL Server. The existing `update_order` stored procedure will happily handle any changes to the `lines` and `payments` tables as it stands, and creating a variation that does an `INSERT` instead of an `UPDATE` is a relatively trivial modification.

The main issue that we need to consider is how new XML records are generated by the application. One option would be to hard-code the order element structure, to be returned by a function in `COrderBOL`, for example:

```
Public Function GetTemplate() As String
  sXml = "<order><lines<row /></lines><payments><row /></payments></order>"
End Function
```

This would rely on the fact that the DOM `setAttribute` method call will add an attribute to an element if it does not already exist. There are limitations with this: what if we want more than one `lines` or `payments` record; how do we provide default values; what if the schema changes?

A better solution is that we create one more DOM to hold the XML template for each data record that the application needs to create, and that these records are provided in the first place by a SQL Server stored procedure. Let's start at the bottom this time, and look at the SQL to provide a definition of an empty record.

We cannot use `FOR XML` for this purpose. Without any data to select, it is not possible to persuade `FOR XML` to produce any output. Instead, we will need to craft the required XML in Transact-SQL code. However, we can at least start by basing our XML on the actual table schema. Here's a procedure that does just that, using the built-in `INFORMATION_SCHEMA` views provided by SQL Server:

```
CREATE PROCEDURE get_empty_xml @table varchar(30),
            @xml varchar(4000) OUTPUT,
            @alias varchar(30) = NULL
AS
DECLARE @colname varchar(30)
DECLARE @elem varchar(30)
DECLARE empty CURSOR
FOR
   SELECT substring(C.COLUMN_NAME,1,30) AS Colname
   FROM INFORMATION_SCHEMA.Columns C
   WHERE C.TABLE_NAME = @table
   ORDER BY C.ORDINAL_POSITION

   IF @alias IS NULL
      SELECT @elem = @table
   ELSE
      SELECT @elem = @alias

      SELECT @xml = '<' + @elem + ' xact=''I'''

OPEN empty

   WHILE 1=1
   BEGIN
      FETCH NEXT FROM empty INTO @colname
      IF @@FETCH_STATUS <> 0 break

      SELECT @xml = @xml + ' ' + @colname + '='''''

   END
   SELECT @xml = @xml + ' />'

CLOSE empty
DEALLOCATE empty
GO
```

Running this against our `orders` table:

```
DECLARE @xml varchar(4000)
EXEC get_empty_xml 'orders', @xml OUTPUT, 'order'
PRINT @xml
```

produces this output:

```
<order xact='I' order_no='' order_date='' emp_no='' customer='' deliver=''
      shipping_charge='' ship_date='' adm_rev_no='' adm_time='' />
```

Notes:

- We've automatically set xact to 'I', indicating that this will represent an inserted record
- We've used the @alias parameter to set the element name to order, rather than the default table name
- With a little extra work, it should be possible to insert default values from the table schema into the XML

We can now build a procedure to generate the three separate template records, embedded in a root <template> element:

```
CREATE PROCEDURE get_order_template @xmlout varchar(4000) OUTPUT
AS
DECLARE @xml varchar(4000)
DECLARE @tmp varchar(4000)

   EXEC get_empty_xml 'orders', @tmp OUTPUT, 'order'
   SELECT @xml = @tmp

   EXEC get_empty_xml 'lines', @tmp OUTPUT, 'row'
   SELECT @xml = @xml + @tmp

   EXEC get_empty_xml 'payments', @tmp OUTPUT, 'row'
   SELECT @xml = @xml + @tmp

   SELECT @xmlout = '<template>' + @xml + '</template>'
GO
```

Note that we have not created a hierarchical structure here – each element is at the same equivalent level in the template – so this template does not represent an order in itself, but provides the necessary building blocks to create an order.

This procedure returns the resulting XML in an OUTPUT variable – this enables us to avoid using a recordset to retrieve the XML text. Here's our new FetchOrderTemplate function in COrdersDAL:

```
Public Function FetchOrderTemplate(ConnStr As String) As String
Dim cmd As ADODB.Command
Dim param As Parameter
Dim sXML As String

   On Error GoTo ErrHandler
   Set cmd = CreateObject("ADODB.Command")

   cmd.ActiveConnection = ConnStr
   cmd.CommandType = adCmdStoredProc
   cmd.CommandText = "get_order_template"
   cmd.Prepared = False
```

```
    ' Set up output parameter.
    Set param = cmd.CreateParameter("xml", adVarChar, adParamOutput, 4000)
    cmd.Parameters.Append param


    cmd.Execute , , adCmdStoredProc + adExecuteNoRecords
    sXML = cmd.Parameters("xml").Value

    ' check for MS Errors
    If InStr(sXML, "<?MSSQLError") > 0 Then
       Err.Raise vbObjectError + 1000, , sXML
    End If

    FetchOrderTemplate = sXML
    Exit Function

ErrHandler:
    Err.Raise Err.Number, "COrdersDAL.FetchOrderTemplate", Err.Description
End Function
```

We could have decided that it would better suit the design framework if the template XML for each record were to be generated by the individual DAL components, and then merged together in `COrderBOL`*. Although slightly less efficient, this is the preferable approach, but we avoided it here for simplicity.*

Now we can insert this `GetTemplate` function in `COrderBOL`:

```
Public Function GetTemplate() As String
Dim oOrd As COrdersDAL
Dim sXml As String

    Set oOrd = CreateObject("OrderDal.COrdersDAL")
    sXml = oOrd.FetchOrdertemplate(m_Conn)
    GetTemplate = SetOrderDefaults(sXml)
    Exit Function
End Function
```

It's in here that any further modifications to the template records should take place before the XML is delivered to the client, hence the `SetOrderDefaults` function in `COrderBOL`:

```
Private Function SetOrderDefaults(sXml As String) As String
Dim oDOM As DOMDocument
Dim oEl As IXMLDOMElement

    Set oDOM = CreateObject("MSXML2.DOMDocument")
    oDOM.loadXML sXml

    ' access elements in turn
    Set oEl = oDOM.childNodes(0).childNodes(0)
    oEl.setAttribute "order_no", "-1"
    oEl.setAttribute "adm_rev_no", "1"
    oEl.setAttribute "order_date", Format(Now, "YYYY-MM-DD")
    oEl.setAttribute "deliver", 0
    oEl.setAttribute "shipping_charge", "0.00"
```

```
    ' lines
    Set oEl = oDOM.childNodes(0).childNodes(1)
    oEl.setAttribute "qty", "0"
    oEl.setAttribute "unit_price", "0.00"
    oEl.setAttribute "commission", "0.00"
    oEl.setAttribute "descr", ""

    ' payments
    Set oEl = oDOM.childNodes(0).childNodes(2)
    oEl.setAttribute "amount", "0.00"
    oEl.setAttribute "descr", ""

    SetOrderDefaults = oDOM.xml
End Function
```

The key points here are:

- Default the order date to the current system date.
- Set the adm_rev_no to 1.
- Set the order_no to -1. Since we are using an IDENTITY field for order_no, we will not have a valid order_no available until we submit the database INSERT.
- Add a descr attribute to the lines and payments records.

The end result will be an XML document something like this:

```
<template>
  <order xact="I" order_no="-1" order_date="2001-03-31" emp_no="" customer=""
                  deliver="0"    shipping_charge="0.00" ship_date="" adm_rev_no="1"
                  adm_time=""/>
  <row xact="I" order_no="" line_no="" prod_id="" qty="0" unit_price="0.00"
                  unit_cost="" commission="0.00" descr=""/>
  <row xact="I" order_no="" pmt_no="" pmt_type="" amount="0.00" descr=""/>
</template>
```

Just as we loaded the oRefDOM object during the program initialization phase, we should also do the same thing for our template records. If you look back at the code in the early part of the case study, you'll see we already have a DOM for this purpose:

```
Dim oNewDOM As DOMDocument
```

Now we just need to add these lines to the LoadRefs procedure, called during Form_Load, to establish this new DOM:

```
    PopulateCombo oRefDOM.documentElement, cboEmp, _
                  "/refs/employees/employee", "name"
    sXML = oBOL.GetTemplate
    oNewDOM.loadXML sXML
End Sub
```

To view the template from within XMLOrders, we just need to add some code to the event procedure behind the XML | Show Template menu item:

```
Private Sub mnShowNew_Click()
   frmXML.Show
   Set frmXML.XMLDOM = oNewDOM
End Sub
```

Add a Payment

Let's look at the code to implement the add payment functionality. This is triggered from the `cmdAddPay` button on the Payments tab:

```
Private Sub cmdAddPay_Click()
Dim oElem As IXMLDOMElement
Dim oNewElem As IXMLDOMElement
Dim oNewPay As IXMLDOMElement

   ' create new payments element and add it in the DOM
   Set oNewPay = oNewDOM.documentElement.childNodes(2).cloneNode(False)
```

We set `oNewPay` to be a clone of the existing template payment record. Then we insert into the main order DOM, using `appendChild` at the `payments` element:

```
   Set oElem = FindNode(oDOM, "/order/payments")
   Set oNewElem = oElem.appendChild(oNewPay)
   oNewElem.setAttribute "order_no", txtOrderNo.Text
   nMaxPmtNo = nMaxPmtNo + 1
   oNewElem.setAttribute "pmt_no", CStr(nMaxPmtNo)
```

We calculate the new payment number from the existing `nMaxPmtNo` variable and write this into the new element, along with the current order number. Now we can invoke the payments form using the same process that we have already seen for editing an existing payment:

```
   ' invoke Payments form
   EditPayment nMaxPmtNo
```

When this returns, we need to check whether useful data was actually added to the DOM. If the user clicked Cancel, then we need to remove this unnecessary element:

```
   If Val(GetAttribute(oNewElem, "amount")) <= 0 Then
      ' remove node
      oElem.removeChild oNewElem
      nMaxPmtNo = nMaxPmtNo - 1
   Else
      ' update grid
      GetPayments
   End If
End Sub
```

Again, with very similar code we can also implement the `cmdAddProd` functionality.

Create a New Order

One final demonstration of data generation. When we want to create a new order using the New Order menu option, the only code we need is this – the GetNewOrder function:

```
Private Sub GetNewOrder()
Dim oElem As IXMLDOMElement

    Set oElem = FindNode(oNewDOM, "/template/order")
    oDOM.loadXML oElem.xml
```

This creates our root element by transferring the XML from oNewDOM. We add the empty lines and payments elements as placeholders for when we start adding line and payment records. We do this using the addElement function in the XMLHelp module – you'll need to paste it in from the download source:

```
    addElement oDOM.documentElement, "lines"
    addElement oDOM.documentElement, "payments"
```

Our existing UnPackOrder procedure then populates the screen – every field being blank except the order date, and shipping charge (0.00):

```
    Call UnPackOrder
    cmdSave.Enabled = True
End Sub
```

When we come to save this new order, the only difference in the process is that the xact attribute on the order will have been set to 'I' not 'U', and this redirects the code to use COrdersDAL.CreateOrder which, in turn, invokes the insert_order stored procedure.

> **If you've been building the project as we go, this is a good point to switch to the full implementation in the download. If you examine this code, you will find that all the required modification functionality has been implemented using the techniques discussed above.**

Business Rules

The final issue to contemplate is regarding the implementation of business rules. This is always a somewhat contentious issue, partly because there is no simple solution that can be applied to all systems, and all designs. There is universal agreement that the one place you should not be coding rules is in the presentation or UI layer, simply because this can lead to much duplication of code and, inevitably, to anomalies and inconsistencies. One of the potential benefits of a decomposed framework such as that demonstrated here is that we should be able to re-use many of the components we have created in other contexts and applications.

It is sometimes argued that the best place to implement rules is either inside the database, or in the DAL. The primary benefits of this approach are:

- The lower down the object hierarchy we go, the easier it is to ensure that the rules cannot be circumvented – the perfect example of this would be in using SQL trigger code.
- Many rules may require further interrogation of the database and so can be performed more efficiently at the DAL.

The main arguments against this are:

- We require a round-trip to the database, down through two layers, to perform each validation. This might be acceptable for a web application; for a VB client application running across a WAN it would definitely not be good for obvious performance and responsiveness reasons.
- Many rules concern the relationships between different data entities – it breaks the concept of a tiered model if one DAL component needs to converse with other DALs to do its job.
- Many rules are application specific, and may depend on external factors which cannot easily be encapsulated in database code.

In this case study, we will put the business rules in the Business Objects Layer component (`COrderBOL`). The BOL should therefore expose any methods as `Public` to perform validation – either on individual values, on single records (such as a payment record), on sets of similar records (all payments), or on the whole document (order). Fortunately, we can easily extract from our order DOM details at whatever level is appropriate for passing to the relevant validation routine.

Each validation call would therefore require a roundtrip to the BOL, passing a suitable XML string as a parameter – this should be kept to the minimum necessary for the function concerned. Of course, if your BOL component is loaded locally on the client, then these round-trips will not be affected by network performance. The choice is yours.

In our XMLOrders application, we only have a single validation routine, which is linked into the `UpdateOrder` procedure. This procedure implements three rules:

- Orders with order dates in the past cannot be modified
- An order must have at least one product line
- The sum of payments must equal the order total

Here's the `Public` interface, taking XML as input:

```
Public Function ValidateOrder(XML As String) As Boolean
Dim oDOM As DOMDocument
   ODOM.loadXML XML
   ValidateOrder = ValidateOrderDOM (oDOM.documentElement)
End Function
```

Here's the `Private` function acting on a DOM element node, called from `UpdateOrder`:

```
Private Function ValidateOrderDOM(oOrd As IXMLDOMElement) As Boolean
Dim oList As IXMLDOMNodeList
Dim oElem as IXMLDOMElement
```

```
Dim cShip As Currency
Dim cLines As Currency
Dim cPay As Currency
Dim cTmp As Currency

   ValidateOrderDOM = False
   ' order date = Today
   If oOrd.GetAttribute("order_date") < Format(Now, "YYYY-MM-DD") Then
      Err.Raise vbObjectError + 2001, "COrderBOL.ValidateOrder", _
                     "Cannot modify an Order with a past Order Date"
      Exit Function
   End If

   ' cross check the totals
   cShip = CCur(GetAttribute(oOrd, "shipping_charge"))

   Set oList = FindNodes(oOrd, "/order/lines/row")
   If oList.length = 0 Then
      Err.Raise vbObjectError + 2002, "COrderBOL.ValidateOrder",  _
                       "An order must have at least one Product line"
      Exit Function
   End If
   For Each oElem In oList
      cTmp = CCur(oElem.GetAttribute("unit_price")) _
                    *  CInt(oElem.GetAttribute("qty"))
      cLines = cLines + cTmp
   Next

   Set oList = FindNodes(oOrd, "/order/payments/row")
   For Each oElem In oList
      cPay = cPay + CCur(oElem.GetAttribute("amount"))
   Next

   If cShip + cLines - cPay <> 0 Then
      Err.Raise vbObjectError + 2003, "COrderBOL.ValidateOrder", _
              "Payments total does not equal Lines total plus Shipping"
      Exit Function
   End If

   ValidateOrderDOM = True
End Function
```

Performance Considerations

We have seen in this case study that it is perfectly feasible to construct an n-tier application framework making full use of SQL Server 2000's XML features. Now we need to ask whether it is efficient, and how does it perform?

There are two key factors to which this application will be sensitive, and that differentiate it from other system designs:

- The size of the XML strings being passed between the application layers
- The resource overhead incurred by DOM instantiation and parsing

Bandwidth

It's a fact that XML is verbose – that's part of its attraction, especially to developers – but it does mean that choosing to ship data around the network in XML, instead of using a disconnected recordset, for example, inevitably incurs a perceptible performance cost.

The table below shows the comparative timings (in milliseconds) to load a 100 row by 6 column recordset into a VB application and to unpack each line into a grid, compared to loading and unpacking the same data using XML:

	RECORDSET (4.8kb)		**XML (11.8kb)**	
	Fetch	**Unpack**	**Fetch**	**Unpack**
Local	15	33	35	90
100MB LAN	17	33	38	90
2MB WAN	34	33	70	90

On average, XML requires between 100% to 200% more bandwidth than a recordset. We have tried to optimize our XMLOrders application by applying several implicit guidelines:

- Use a simple XML format. Don't add the overhead of database schema definitions which, in the main, you can do without.
- Make trips to the database as infrequent as possible, and capture as much information in one go as is necessary. With network packet sizes of, say 4kb, the extra size need not actually involve more packets, and larger packets place no extra burden on routers.
- Load reference data once only, on startup, and preserve it on the client.
- Don't try to cache everything – loading long lists (many hundreds of records) of reference data is unproductive, will delay program startup, and give the user a poor initial impression of responsiveness, although the use of **async** loading could alleviate this effect.

One interesting development that could help to alleviate network bandwidth issues is the freeware XMLZip product from xmlsolutions *– see for yourself at* *http://www.xmls.com/resources/xmlzip.xml?id=resources_xmlzip.*

DOM Parser

The cost of instantiating a DOM document can mostly be discounted – in this type of client application it's certainly not a major issue, although it could be where more process-oriented applications are concerned (for example, data transfer and transformation systems). However, it could be an issue in one of the other components, especially if high transaction volumes are involved. However, offset against this is the fact that we are not creating recordsets for every query – these pretty much cancel out. The one place where this overhead can be perceived to cost is in SQL Server itself.

We experimented with performing a single `UPDATE` against the `orders` table, comparing using `OPENXML` to using a normal SQL `UPDATE` statement, with all values passed as arguments to the stored procedure.

Run from Query Analyzer, the SQL `UPDATE` took 80ms for 100 iterations, whereas using `OPENXML` took 420ms. This seems a rather poor comparison, to say the least. However, performing the same test directly from a VB client, using ADO in the same manner as used in our XMLOrders application, the figures became 230ms versus 640ms – not brilliant, but not as dramatically bad. In any case, this still leaves individual updates as taking a negligible amount of time.

Using a 2-tier architecture across a 100Mbit Ethernet LAN gave average turn-round times for one transaction of 21ms versus 30ms using XML – clearly the network overhead of shipping the XML helps to flatten out the result.

Although there is clearly a deficit on the performance side for using XML, it is not such that it needs to impinge significantly on the user experience. However, it is always worth testing these factors in your own real-world environment.

> **In the download package, you will find the VB source for a simple program called `XMLPerf`, which was used to obtain the latter figures, and can easily be adapted for your own testing purposes. To run the program, you will first need to load the `perftest` stored procedure into `wroxdb`.**

Apart from the memory constraints governing the number of DOM handles that can be created by SQL Server, there may also be some scalability issues that conspire against using `OPENXML`.

What Next?

Now we've built a working application based exclusively on XML, we can start to explore the possibilities for further extensions to the program functionality, and the potential for re-use of some of the components that we have created.

The object model that would be employed in a real-world solution would be somewhat more elaborate than the one we have been working with in this case study. Discussion of this is mostly beyond the scope of this book, but you might like to consider these ideas:

- Interpose a persistent façade layer between the form and `COrdersBOL`, and then move the DOM objects and all related procedures from the form into the façade. Keep the façade object in the `EXE` code-space to minimize the calling overheads.
- Define a standard interface to be implemented by all of the DAL classes.
- Install the `DLL`s in COM+ Component Services.
- Investigate deploying the `XMLZip` compression technology.

If you are unhappy with the loss of *stateful* objects to represent the data now held in XML, consider building wrapper objects that isolate the DOM from the application. Microsoft MSDN magazine has published a VB project that takes an XML structure and generates a VB class module – see http://msdn.microsoft.com/msdnmag/issues/01/01/code/XMLWrap.exe.

As far as extending the functionality of the application, these are some of the possible avenues to explore:

- Add an option to send order details by e-mail, using XSL to transform the order
- Add a report option (for example an employee commission summary), using XSL to transform the XML
- Add a search facility to find orders using a variety of criteria (customer name, employee, order date range, etc.), encoding the search criteria in XML also
- Consider using XML data to define UI behavior; depending on the user's role and context, we could use XML to encode rules to determine which screen elements are visible and/or editable

Finally, in the area of re-use, consider the potential for developing a web application with some of the functionality of XMLOrders, using the existing `DLLs` as they stand. This could be done using ASP and XSL code to build the output HTML or, even better for IE5 users, load the XML into data islands and write DHTML to provide a more interactive user experience.

Summary

At the end of this case study, what have we learned? We've seen that the decision to make full use of the XML features of SQL Server 2000 in an n-tier application framework raises some significant issues – concerning application architecture, development methodology, and practical coding techniques. It also gives us some new areas of concern regarding performance and scalability.

On the other hand, the benefits of XML are more far-reaching. With a modicum of thought and planning, it is possible to build systems and components with more flexibility, extensibility, and re-usability than ever before. For developers, XML skills are fast becoming a prerequisite on your resume. Microsoft has already nailed its colors firmly to the XML mast with the .NET framework, and it's certain that the XML features of SQL Server will continue to evolve and improve.

The most tangible benefits found by the author's development team have been:

- XML *is* easy to generate, read, and discuss. It serves as excellent documentation in itself.
- Building the UI using patched XML delivers a working prototype very early in the lifecycle.
- State visibility – access to the XML at any time proves to be an excellent facility for debugging and testing.
- Greatly simplified data modification transactions using `OPENXML`.

The simple lessons from this case study can be summarized as:

- Set standards for XML content to cover naming, data formatting, etc.
- Define the XML early in the development lifecycle.
- Add a debug facility to view XML at any time.
- Use `OPENXML` when appropriate, but watch those document handles.
- If performance is likely to be an issue, then test and evaluate the options early on.

As we have seen, XML has a lot to offer – but it does come with some minor disadvantages, as do all new technologies.

SQL
XML

Creating an XML Reporting System

Reports help transform rows of data into presentable views of information. Unlike queries and data exports, these views are easier for users to understand. Reports are one of the most common features within applications; users rely on them to provide critical information. A reporting system allows for the creation of these reports. It provides an environment where the reports can be designed and generated to provide the users with a visual representation of information. From Crystal Reports to the Microsoft Access Reporting engine, it's hard to deny the important role these systems play within an organization.

Internet-based applications face a major challenge when it comes to reporting: there aren't many reporting systems that can integrate into Internet-based applications. So, developers are torn between generating reports in static HTML or using limiting extensions and add-ons for current reporting systems. These add-ons generally cause more problems than they fix; they often serve to increase the severity of the reporting systems. These systems present us with many serious issues, some of them linked to the inadequate client-server design of the system. Other issues concern limited manageability and lack of scalability.

In this case study we will address some of these limitations by using SQL Server 2000 XML capabilities, XML, XSL, Visual Interdev, and Active Server Pages (ASP) to create an XML reporting system. This system will not only be able to handle Internet reporting needs, but also the needs of other applications created in Visual Basic, C++, or Delphi. By the end of the case study we will:

- Understand some of the major issues with reporting systems
- Understand how the proposed XML reporting system can correct these issues
- Understand the design of the XML reporting system
- Know where key technologies are used within the system and how to use them
- Know how to transform XML documents using ASP
- Be able to access the reports with a web browser and Visual Basic
- Have a working foundation for an XML reporting system

What You Will Need for this Case Study

On our development computer we will need the following:

- Microsoft Visual Interdev
- Microsoft Data Access Components 2.6
- Internet Explorer 5 or higher
- Microsoft XML Parser 3.0
- Visual Basic 6.0

Our Internet server should consist of one of the following configurations:

- Internet Information Server 4.0 if running Windows NT 4.0 Server
- Peer Web Services 4.0 if running Windows NT 4.0 Workstation
- Internet Information Services if running Windows 2000

You should also have the Microsoft XML Parser 3.0 installed on the Internet Server. Finally, we will need the following items:

- SQL Server 2000
- A working knowledge of Visual Interdev, ASP, and ADO

> *You can learn more about ASP and ADO in* Beginning Active Server Pages 3.0, *Wrox Press, ISBN 1861003382.*

To further assist you, Wrox Press has a web site, found at http://www.wrox.com, that contains a range of resources, reference materials, and source code for this and other applications.

Gathering Requirements

This case study was not designed using a formal development process; however, we would like to emphasize the importance of gathering proper requirements if you decide to expand upon this case study. Imagine building a house without any blue prints; now imagine creating software without any requirements. No matter what methodology we choose to use, requirements still form the basic building blocks of the process. Give yourself time to gather requirements – they will make your development efforts a lot less frustrating.

The Major Issues Facing Reporting Systems

Applications created in Visual Basic, Delphi, and C++ have a variety of reporting systems to choose from, while Internet-based applications are left with only a few. With the popularity of Internet development still growing, most reporting systems have developed extensions to output reports to HTML. This 'square peg in a round hole' approach usually means lack of flexibility and scalability for developers. The lack of reporting systems options for Internet-based applications usually means that existing reporting systems must handle the load. It has been seen on more than one occasion that this has led development teams to rule out Internet development, even though it would have been the best solution for solving the problem.

This issue is very valid – why should we create an XML reporting system when we can create drag and drop reports with our existing reporting system? To answer that question we must first discuss some of the major issues with the existing reporting system, which are **inadequate client-server design**, **customization**, **maintenance**, and **cost**. Let's start by discussing the problems with the client-server design of reporting systems.

Client-Server Design

Most reporting systems issue a data request to the database server, and the results are returned to the engine on the client's machine where they are transformed into a viewable format. Both the reports and the engine generally reside on the client's machine, while the data resides on other servers within the organization. The diagram below depicts a typical client-server reporting system.

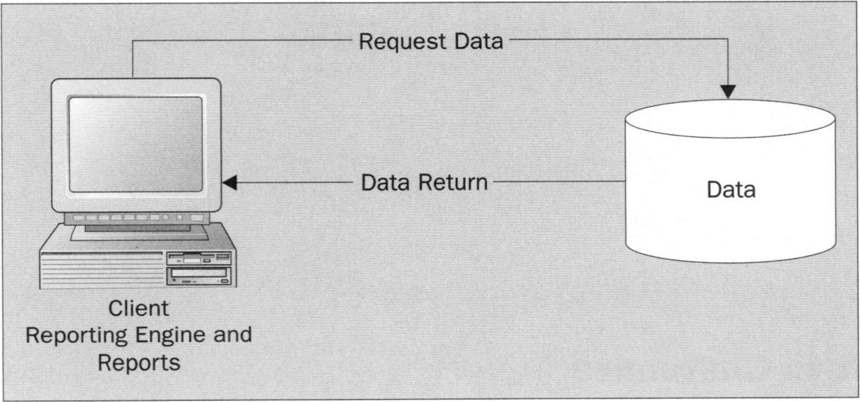

In many of these systems there is no way to separate the reports from the reporting engine. To further complicate matters, there is also no way to separate either component from the client's machine. These two components are usually included within the program file, which means that a new program file must be created each time a report is modified or created. There are reporting systems that allow us to create reports that can be saved independently of the executable file, but the reporting engine must still be installed on the user's machine or combined with the program file. These limitations affect the scalability of the reporting engine. What we are left with is a very fat client, which is difficult to manage and offers little flexibility for incorporating changes. This design also limits our reporting system to platform support by the software.

A better design for a reporting system would be to make the reporting engine and reports completely independent of the client's machine. This would remove a lot of complexity from the client and add flexibility and scalability to the system. We now would have the capability of positioning multiple reporting engines and report repositories throughout our organization. The following diagram depicts this solution.

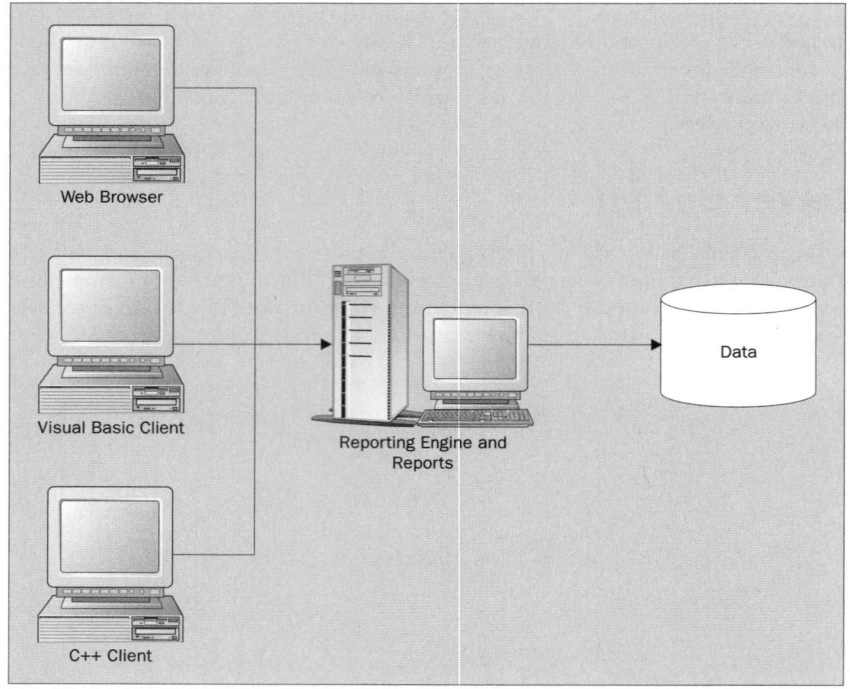

Difficult to Customize

The code that manages the reporting engine is for the most part hidden from the developer and generally consists of dynamic linked libraries (DLL) – countless hours have been lost trying to decipher these libraries. A better approach would be to create a reporting engine that is user friendly and leverages technology already used within our organization.

Maintenance

Reporting systems rely heavily on the client machine to host reports and the engine. Since these two critical components reside on the client machine, it adds complexity to the deployment and modifications. A better approach would be to centralize the reports and engine, allowing the users to access them from centralized locations. These locations would be easier to manage than hundreds of local client installs.

Licensing, Resources and Cost

There are systems that can address some of these common problems that we mentioned; however, they are usually accompanied with a huge price tag. Implementation also becomes an issue when we are dealing with enterprise reporting systems, as they generally take an extended period of time to deploy. Even when we have solved deployment problems, we are still tasked with training employees to operate and support yet another software application. A better approach would be to maximize the investment in current software applications and information systems.

How Can We Solve these Issues?

Our goal is to create a reporting system using the XML capabilities of SQL Server 2000, XSL, ASP, MDAC, and Visual InterDev. These technologies will allow us to create a 3-tiered reporting system that will be easy to maintain, provide scalability, and offer a low cost of ownership. The following diagram depicts the design of the reporting system and where the technologies will be applied.

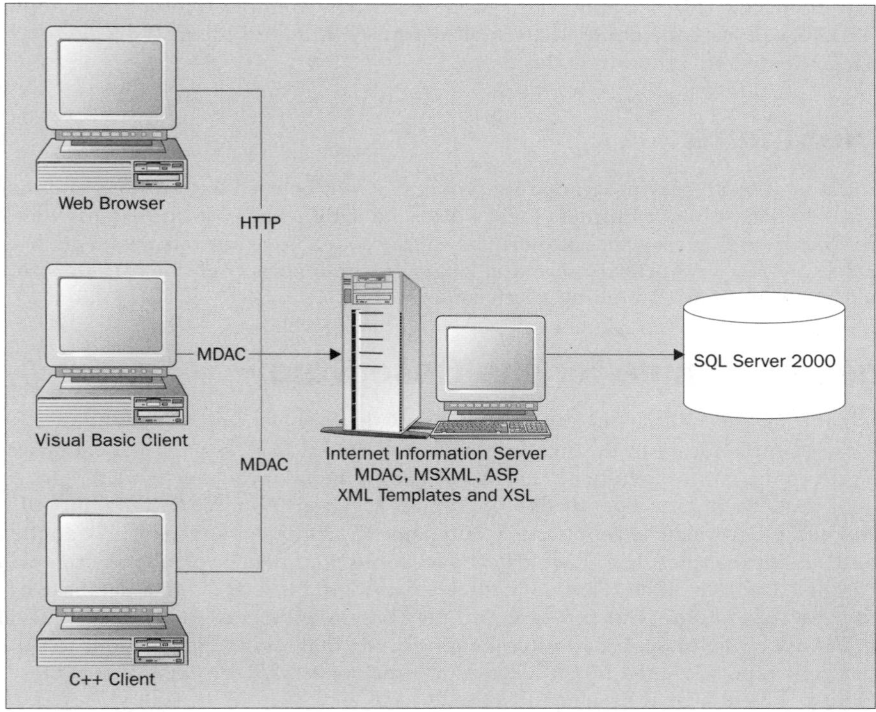

The following paragraphs discuss the roles of each core technology that will be used in the reporting system.

Visual Interdev

Visual Interdev will serve as our report designer: we will create our ASP, HTML, XSL stylesheets and any other files needed for the reports within this environment. By using Visual Interdev we can leverage an existing technology that is already in place in most organizations. We should also be able to enlist the talents of the Internet developers to help maintain the reporting system, removing some of the responsibility from the development staff.

Internet Information Server

Internet Information Server will serve as our reporting engine: its job will be to process user requests for reports. This will remove the reporting engine from the client's machine making it easier to manage. This approach also provides for greater scalability: we could easily cluster these servers to provide fault tolerance and faster reporting processing.

SQL Server XML Capabilities

By using the XML capabilities of SQL Server we can create XML templates and XDR schemas for our existing tables and views; these two components will serve as the data foundation for our reporting system. All reports will receive their data from XML templates that reference XDR schemas. This functionality allows us to take advantage of our existing database server. By using XML documents as our data providers, we can effectively share and combine data with external organizations with little or no customization. This will also allow our system to scale beyond the Internet. Any application capable of using MDAC will have the ability to view all reports within the system. We will create a Visual Basic client later in the case study to prove this point.

XSL StyleSheets

XSL provides us with an easy programming syntax that will be used to transform and manipulate the XML documents. Most of our business logic will reside within XSL stylesheets: this will open up our architecture by providing easy access to critical source code. Since our business logic will not consist of Visual Basic, C++, or a proprietary scripting language, the reports could be easy to maintain and distribute to other systems on multiple platforms.

A Business Example for the Case Study

To gain a better picture of how the reporting system will work, we will use the following scenario. A company has multiple locations throughout the United States. Each day these locations submit an activity report to the corporate office. This report allows the finance team to track sales, gross margins, and new accounts. Both the corporate and the remote locations require the capability of viewing activity information and other financial reports. The company implemented a spreadsheet application for viewing and submitting sales data. Each day the locations complete a spreadsheet template that is e-mailed to the corporate office. These e-mails are parsed and inserted into a database by an internally developed software solution. This software routinely breaks and needs four full-time developers to support it. We are going to design an Internet application that allows the locations to submit sales activity and view reports via the Internet. To satisfy the needs of other departments these reports must integrate into a current Visual Basic application as well.

To create this system we will complete the following steps.

- Create a Visual Interdev Project for our application
- Create the `SALES` database and tables, then load the data
- Create an XDR schema
- Create an XML template
- Create an XSL stylesheet
- Create the ASP and HTML files for the interface
- Prove that the reports can be accessed from Visual Basic

Creating the Visual Interdev Project

A zip file called `server.zip` accompanies this case study. It contains all the files needed for this case study. Within Visual Interdev create a new project called SALES. Copy the `server.zip` file to the newly created `sales` directory on your Internet server that Visual Interdev created for us as part of the project (you should find this folder under the root directory of your Internet server). Use a zip utility to extract the contents of this file to the `sales` directory. Your directory structure should now look like the following screen shot.

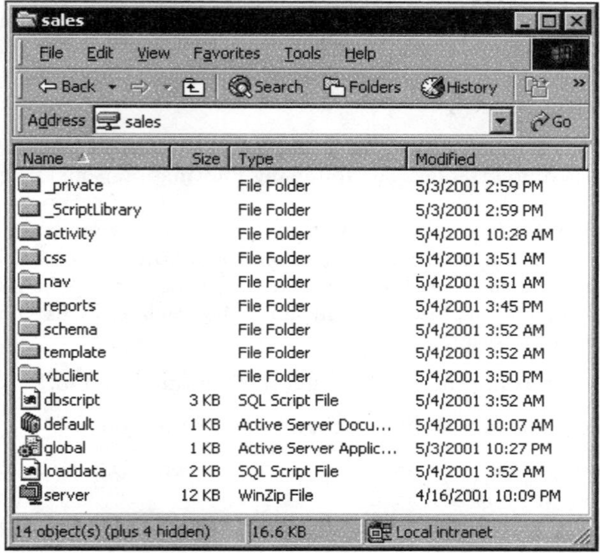

Creating the Database

We will create a simple SQL Server database for the application. We kept the design of the database simple to allow us to focus more on using the technologies rather than deciphering a complicated schema. The following diagram gives us a graphical view of the database.

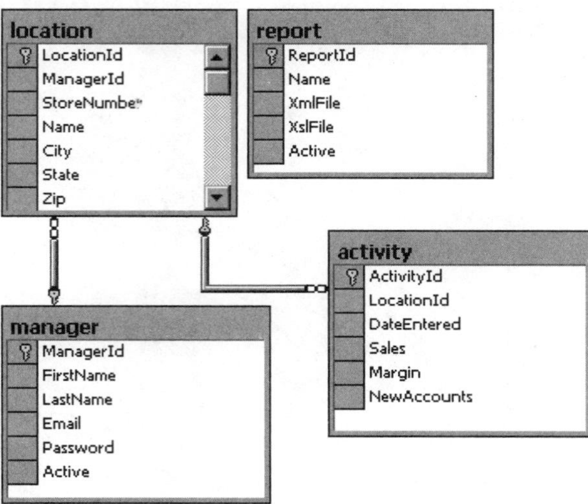

Executing the Database Creation Scripts

Within the project we will find two SQL Server scripts called `dbscript.sql` and `loadata.sql`. The `dbscript.sql` will create a database, called `SALES`, all the relevant tables, and a stored procedure. The `loaddata.sql` will populate the tables with data. Use the SQL Query Analyzer to open these files, or open them up within Visual Interdev and copy the text into the Query Analyzer – make sure you run `dbscript.sql` first.

Tables

The application consists of four tables. The following information is given about each table:

- **Report** – Contains information about reports available for viewing. Two key fields within this table are `XslFile` and `XmlFile`. These fields store the paths for the XML template file and XSL stylesheet used to create the report. If we set the `Active` field to N, this will stop the report from displaying within the application. This will allow us to make changes to the report without affecting the system.
- **Location** – Contains information about each reporting location.
- **Manager** – Contains information about a location manager.
- **Activity** – Contains the daily sales activity for a given location.

Stored Procedure

There is only one stored procedure used in the application. As we can see, not a lot of rocket science is going on here – it's a simple `INSERT` statement that will be called later from an ASP script.

```
CREATE PROCEDURE spACTIVITY_INSERT(
   @LocationId INT,
   @DateEntered DATETIME,
   @Sales MONEY,
   @Margin NUMERIC(18,0),
   @NewAccounts SMALLINT)
AS BEGIN
   INSERT INTO activity(
      LocationId,
      DateEntered,
      Sales,
      Margin,
      NewAccounts)
   VALUES(
      @LocationId,
      @DateEntered,
      @Sales,
      @Margin,
      @NewAccounts)
END
```

Creating the XDR Schema

Before we get started we should create a virtual directory named XMLSALES that can access the schema and template directories for the project. Configuring virtual directories is covered within Appendix A. We will not need this configuration in the production environment and our system will work correctly without performing these steps; we will only use it in development for debugging and instructional purposes. This functionality was not incorporated within the production reporting system, because it adds complexity. We also want to control the access to the system by using MDAC, specifically the Command and Stream objects. Developers are more familiar with these objects and they offer a smaller learning and implementation curve. As well as that, the virtual directories are yet another piece of software and point of failure that needs to be managed.

For the rest of the case study we will focus on one report called Daily Sales Activity. This report will show all sales activity for all locations. We will use an XDR schema file to define the layout for the XML document to be returned. One of the most appealing aspects of using XDR schemas above other SQL Server XML access capabilities is the amount of control we have over the document layout. This becomes extremely important when we are trying to perform XSLT and XPATH functions within our stylesheet. Some of these functions will not work on attributes, which are commonly returned with other access methods.

Your project contains a directory called schema; within this directory we will find a file called temdailysales.xml. Let's take a look at this file below.

```
<?xml version="1.0" ?>
<Schema
   xmlns="urn:schemas-microsoft-com:xml-data"
   xmlns:dt="urn:schemas-microsoft-com:datatypes"
   xmlns:sql="urn:schemas-microsoft-com:xml-sql">

<ElementType name="Manager" sql:relation="manager">
   <AttributeType name="Firstname" />
   <AttributeType name="Lastname" />
   <AttributeType name="Email" />

   <attribute type="Firstname" />
   <attribute type="Lastname" />
   <attribute type="Email" />
</ElementType>

<ElementType name="DateEntered" />
<ElementType name="Sales" />
<ElementType name="Margin" />
<ElementType name="NewAccounts" />

<ElementType name="Activity" sql:relation="activity">
   <element type="DateEntered" sql:field="DateEntered" />
   <element type="Sales" sql:field="Sales" />
   <element type="Margin" sql:field="Margin" />
   <element type="NewAccounts" sql:field="NewAccounts" />
</ElementType>

<ElementType name="Location" sql:relation="location" >
   <AttributeType name="Name" />
   <AttributeType name="City" />
   <AttributeType name="State" />
```

```
    <attribute type="Name" />
    <attribute type="City" />
    <attribute type="State" />

    <element type="Manager">
       <sql:relationship
          key-relation="location"
          key="ManagerId"
          foreign-key="ManagerId"
          foreign-relation="manager" />
    </element>

    <element type="Activity">
       <sql:relationship
          key-relation="location"
          key="locationId"
          foreign-key="locationId"
          foreign-relation="activity" />
    </element>
 </ElementType>

 </Schema>
```

Below we can see the first element within the file is called `Manager`; this element has an `sql:relation` to the `Manager` table. This element will have a `Firstname`, `LastName`, and `Email` attribute corresponding to fields within the table.

```
<ElementType name="Manager" sql:relation="manager">
  <AttributeType name="Firstname" />
  <AttributeType name="Lastname" />
  <AttributeType name="Email" />

  <attribute type="Firstname" />
  <attribute type="Lastname" />
  <attribute type="Email" />
</ElementType>
```

The second element in the file is the `Activity` element. This element contains all the daily sales activity for a given location. This element has an `sql:relation` to the `Activity` table; we need this element to contain other sub-elements and not attributes. It is easier to implement formatting on a node element; some functions will not work on attributes at all.

```
<ElementType name="DateEntered" />
<ElementType name="Sales" />
<ElementType name="Margin" />
<ElementType name="NewAccounts" />

<ElementType name="Activity" sql:relation="activity">
  <element type="DateEntered" sql:field="DateEntered" />
  <element type="Sales" sql:field="Sales" />
  <element type="Margin" sql:field="Margin" />
  <element type="NewAccounts" sql:field="NewAccounts" />
</ElementType>
```

The third and final element is called `Location`; it has an `sql:relation` to the location table. We will use the `Name`, `City`, and `State` fields from this table.

```
<ElementType name="Location" sql:relation="location" >
  <AttributeType name="Name" />
  <AttributeType name="City" />
  <AttributeType name="State" />

  <attribute type="Name" />
  <attribute type="City" />
  <attribute type="State" />

  <element type="Manager">
    <sql:relationship
      key-relation="location"
      key="ManagerId"
      foreign-key="ManagerId"
      foreign-relation="manager" />
  </element>

  <element type="Activity">
    <sql:relationship
      key-relation="location"
      key="locationId"
      foreign-key="locationId"
      foreign-relation="activity" />
  </element>
</ElementType>
```

In the above code we have nested the `Manager` and `Activity` elements within the `Location` element using an `sql:relationship`. This XDR schema will produce an easy to read XML document like the one below.

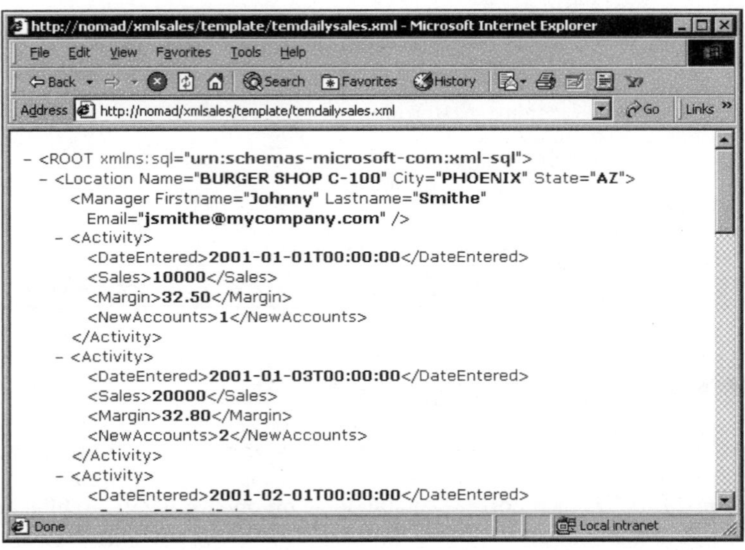

Creating the XML Templates

Within the TEMPLATE directory we will find a file called temdailysales.xml. This file, along with the XDR schema, will provide XML data for the reports. Let's take a look at temdailysales.xml.

```
<ROOT xmlns:sql="urn:schemas-microsoft-com:xml-sql">
   <sql:xpath-query mapping-schema="../schema/temdailysales.xml">
      /Location
   </sql:xpath-query>
</ROOT>
```

As we can see it is a very simple XML template that consists of an XPATH query utilizing the temdailysales.xml XDR schema file. If you have configured your virtual directory, try accessing the following URL using Internet Explorer.

```
http://YourServer/xmlsales/template/temdailysales.xml
```

You should receive results similar to the following screenshot.

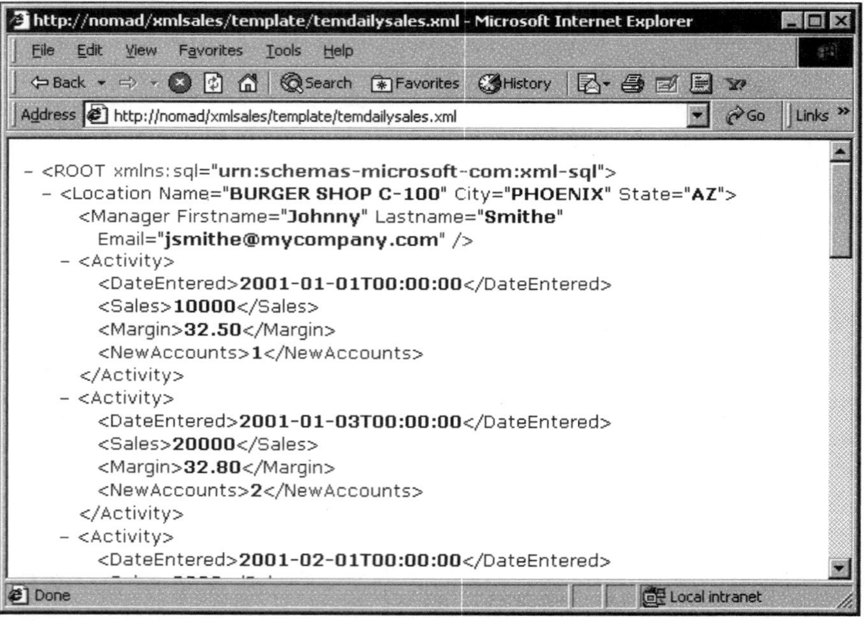

Creating the XSL StyleSheet

Most of our business logic will reside in XSL. This is a major difference from most reporting systems where logic is constructed using proprietary scripting languages, Visual Basic, or C++. This will allow us to construct a majority of our report processing logic on open software architecture. The programming syntax within XSL is similar to most common programming languages.

A common question at this point is "Why not use Cascading Style Sheets?" Cascading Style Sheets (CSS) is a client-side technology specifically designed for formatting HTML documents. A problem arises here because older browsers don't support XML. XSLT is better equipped to handling the formatting and transformation of XML documents, and they still allow us to incorporate CSS.

Within the `Reports` directory we will find a file called `dailysales.xsl`. This is the stylesheet we will use for both reports. Let's take a look at this file below.

```
<xsl:stylesheet
   xmlns:xsl="http://www.w3.org/1999/XSL/Transform" version="1.0">

<!-- main section starts -->
<xsl:template match="/">
   <HTML>
      <HEAD>
         <TITLE>Detail Sales Activity</TITLE>
         <!-- linking to a CSS -->
         <LINK rel="stylesheet" type="text/css"
            href="../../sales/css/sales.css" />
      </HEAD>
      <BODY>
         <!--creating the main table -->
         <TABLE bordercolor="#1e90ff" width="800" border="1" align="center">
            <TR bgcolor="#1e90ff">
               <TD class="report_header" align="center">Daily Sales
                  Report</TD>
            </TR>
            <!--applying the location template -->
            <xsl:apply-templates select="ROOT/Location"/>
         </TABLE>
         <A HREF="list.asp">Return to report list</A>
      </BODY>
   </HTML>
</xsl:template>
<!-- main section ends -->

<!--location template-->
<xsl:template match="ROOT/Location">
   <TR style="font-size:11pt;FONT-FAMILY:'Times New Roman';">
      <TD>
         <B><xsl:value-of select="@Name"/></B><BR />
         <xsl:value-of select="@City"/>, <xsl:value-of select="@State"/>
            <BR />

         <!--applying the manager template-->
         <I><xsl:apply-templates select="Manager" /></I><BR />
         <TABLE align="center">
            <TR>
               <TD width="100" align="left"><B>Date Entered</B></TD>
               <TD width="100"  align="right"><B>Sales</B></TD>
               <TD width="100" align="center"><B>New Accounts</B></TD>
               <TD width="100"  align="left"><B>Margin</B></TD>
            </TR>

            <!--applying the Activity template-->
            <xsl:apply-templates select="Activity" />
         </TABLE>
      </TD>
   </TR>
</xsl:template>
```

```
<!--Manager template -->
<xsl:template match="Manager">
   Store Manager: <xsl:value-of select="@Lastname" />, <xsl:value-of
      select="@Firstname" />
</xsl:template>

<!--Activity template -->
<xsl:template match="Activity">
   <xsl:for-each select=".">
      <TR>
         <TD align="left"><xsl:value-of
            select='substring(./DateEntered,1,10)' /></TD>
         <TD align="right"><xsl:value-of select='format-number(./Sales,
            "##,####.00")' /></TD>
         <TD align="center"><xsl:value-of select='format-
            number(./NewAccounts, "##,####")' /></TD>
         <TD align="left"><xsl:value-of select="./Margin" /></TD>
      </TR>
   </xsl:for-each>
</xsl:template>

</xsl:stylesheet>
```

This stylesheet represents the formatting instructions for our report; this is where we would put any additional business logic needed for formatting the report. Let's break apart the XSL stylesheet code so we can analyze it in more detail.

The code below is the first section of the stylesheet – we are basically creating a main table for the report to reside in. Once the table is created we apply the `ROOT/Location` template for additional processing.

```
<xsl:stylesheet
   xmlns:xsl="http://www.w3.org/1999/XSL/Transform" version="1.0">

<!-- main section starts -->
<xsl:template match="/">
   <HTML>
      <HEAD>
         <TITLE>Detail Sales Activity</TITLE>
         <!-- linking to a CSS -->
         <LINK rel="stylesheet" type="text/css"
            href="../../sales/css/sales.css" />
      </HEAD>
      <BODY>
         <!--creating the main table -->
         <TABLE bordercolor="#1e90ff" width="800" border="1" align="center">
            <TR bgcolor="#1e90ff">
               <TD class="report_header" align="center">Daily Sales
                  Report</TD>
            </TR>
            <!--applying the location template -->
            <xsl:apply-templates select="ROOT/Location"/>
         </TABLE>
         <A HREF="list.asp">Return to report list</A>
      </BODY>
   </HTML>
</xsl:template>
<!-- main section ends -->
```

The code for this `Location` template is shown below. Here we can see the core formatting for the report.

```
<!--location template-->
<xsl:template match="ROOT/Location">
   <TR style="font-size:11pt;FONT-FAMILY:'Times New Roman';">
      <TD>
         <B><xsl:value-of select="@Name"/></B><BR />
         <xsl:value-of select="@City"/>, <xsl:value-of select="@State"/>
            <BR />

         <!--applying the manager template-->
         <I><xsl:apply-templates select="Manager" /></I><BR />
         <TABLE align="center">
            <TR>
               <TD width="100" align="left"><B>Date Entered</B></TD>
               <TD width="100"  align="right"><B>Sales</B></TD>
               <TD width="100" align="center"><B>New Accounts</B></TD>
               <TD width="100"  align="left"><B>Margin</B></TD>
            </TR>

            <!--applying the Activity template-->
            <xsl:apply-templates select="Activity" />
         </TABLE>
      </TD>
   </TR>
</xsl:template>
```

Let's take a peek at what the report will look like once it is generated:

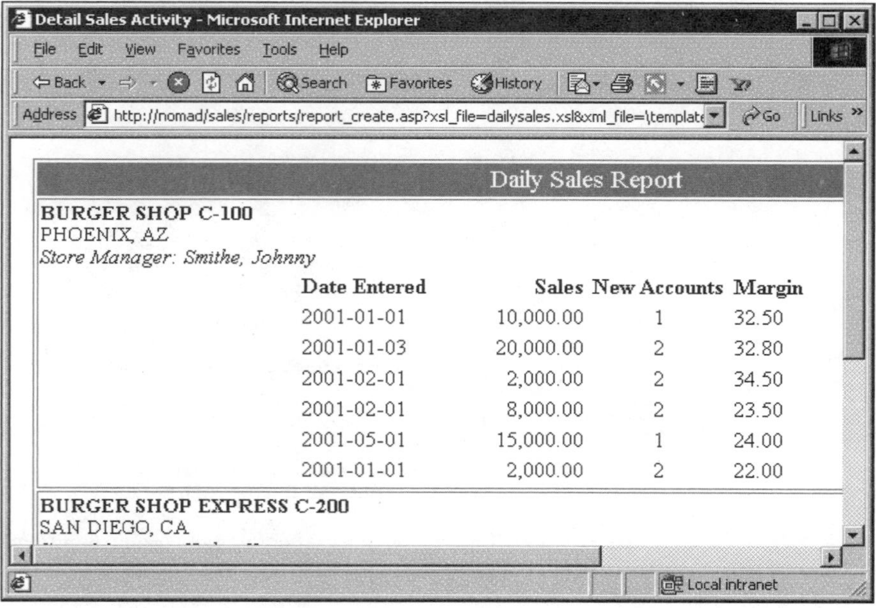

Creating the Interface

Now we are ready to create an interface for our system. We will use ASP, HTML, and a little JavaScript to build our interface. The list below provides information about each file that will be used in the interface. We will cover each one in detail in the following paragraphs.

- `nav/skeleton.asp` – serves as the foundation of the site. Provides a skeleton in which the content is to be placed.
- `default.asp` – the default page for our project. It mainly serves as a jump point.
- `activity/default.asp` – allows inputting of sales information into the system.
- `activity/insert.asp` – saves the sales information to the database.
- `css/sales.css` – a cascading stylesheet used for formatting the application.
- `reports/command_create.asp` – uses an ADO command and stream object to manipulate the XML document and XSL stylesheet on the web server.
- `reports/list.asp` – provides the user with a list of reports available within the system.
- `reports/prepare.asp` – retrieves information needed prior to transformation.

Our first file, `nav/skeleton.asp`, serves as a container for all other ASP pages. Almost every page references this as an include file. Let's take a look at the code below before we continue.

```
<%@ Language=VBScript %>
<HTML>
   <HEAD>
      <LINK rel="stylesheet" type="text/css"
         href="../../sales/css/sales.css">
      <TITLE>XML Reporting System</TITLE>
   </HEAD>
   <BODY onLoad="<%=strOnload%>">
      <TABLE border="0" align="center" cellpadding="0" width="800">
         <TR>
            <TD valign="top">
               <TABLE bgcolor="#1e90ff" height="23" border="0"
                  cellpadding="2" cellspacing="0">
                  <TR>
                     <TD align="center" width="100">
                        <A HREF="../../sales/default.asp"
                           class="menu_header">Home</A>
                     </TD>
                     <TD align="center" width="100">
                        <A HREF="../../sales/reports/list.asp"
                           class="menu_header">Reports</A>
                     </TD>
                     <TD align="center" width="100">
                        <A HREF="../../sales/activity/default.asp"
                           class="menu_header">Submit Sales</A>
                     </TD>
                     <TD align="center" width="500" class="menu_header">
                        XML Reporting System Case Study
                     </TD>
                  </TR>
```

```
                </TABLE>
            </TD>
        </TR>
    </TABLE>
    <TABLE border="1" bordercolor="#1e90ff"
        align="center" cellpadding="2" cellpadding="2" width="800">
        <TR>
            <TD width="100%"><%call content()%></TD></TR>
    </TABLE>
  </BODY>
</HTML>
```

This code formats the HTML structure for each page. The code below establishes the starting HTML elements, links in the stylesheet, and creates the menu.

```
<%@ Language=VBScript %>
<HTML>
   <HEAD>
      <LINK rel="stylesheet" type="text/css"
         href="../../sales/css/sales.css">
      <TITLE>XML Reporting System</TITLE>
   </HEAD>
   <BODY onLoad="<%=strOnload%>">
      <TABLE border="0" align="center" cellpadding="0" width="800">
         <TR>
            <TD valign="top">
               <TABLE bgcolor="#1e90ff" height="23" border="0"
                  cellpadding="2" cellspacing="0">
                  <TR>
                     <TD align="center" width="100">
                        <A HREF="../../sales/default.asp"
                           class="menu_header">Home</A>
                     </TD>
                     <TD align="center" width="100">
                        <A HREF="../../sales/reports/list.asp"
                           class="menu_header">Reports</A>
                     </TD>
                     <TD align="center" width="100">
                        <A HREF="../../sales/activity/default.asp"
                           class="menu_header">Submit Sales</A>
                     </TD>
                     <TD align="center" width="500" class="menu_header">
                        XML Reporting System Case Study
                     </TD>
                  </TR>
               </TABLE>
            </TD>
         </TR>
      </TABLE>
```

The second part of this code is listed below. It creates a table that will serve as the container for the other ASP pages. Each ASP has a method called `content()`, which is called each time `skeleton.asp` is referenced.

```
      <TABLE border="1" bordercolor="#1e90ff"
       align="center" cellpadding="2" cellpadding="2" width="800">
        <TR>
          <TD width="100%"><%call content()%></TD></TR>
      </TABLE>
    </BODY>
</HTML>
```

Our next file is default.asp, which is the startup file for our application. The code is standard ASP and HTML; however, let's take a look at this file so we can see how the skeleton.asp is referenced and the content() method is used. Any information that needs to be displayed must be contained within this method.

```
<%@ Language=VBScript %>
<%
Sub Content
%>
<TABLE>
   <TR>
      <TD class="table_header">XML Case Study</TD></TR>
   <TR>
      <TD>
         This is a small sample application to accompany the case
            study.<BR><BR>
      </TD>
   </TR>
   <TR>
      <TD class="table_header">Author Information</TD></TR>
   <TR>
      <TD>
         <A href="mailto:cwilson@harborviewsolutions.com">
            cwilson@harborviewsolutions.com.</A>
      </TD>
   </TR>
</TABLE>
<%End sub%>
<!-- #include file=./nav/skeleton.asp -->
<%Response.End%>
```

The screen shot below is the default.asp page contained within the skeleton.asp framework.

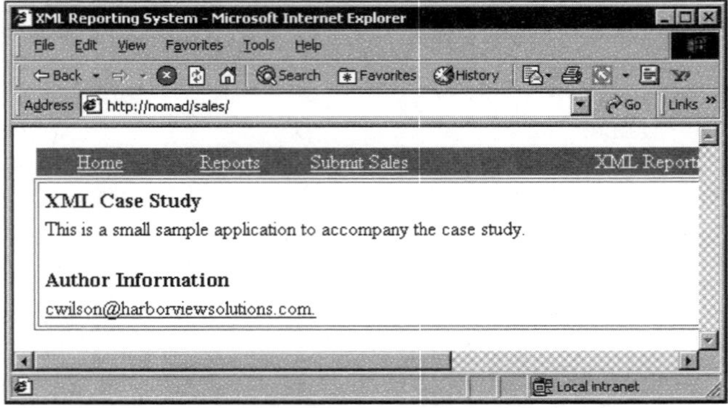

The next two files are located in the ACTIVITY directory. They are default.asp and insert.asp. default.asp presents a form that allows the user to submit daily sales information, as shown by the following screenshot:

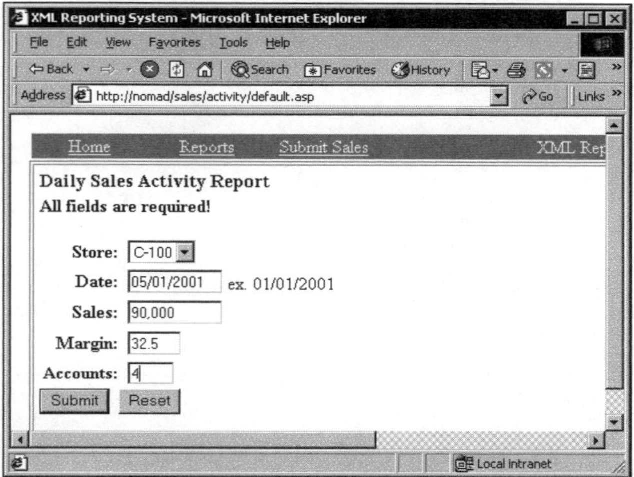

Upon submission, insert.asp is called to submit the information into the database using the stored procedure we created earlier. This code for this process is shown below.

```
<%@ Language=VBScript %>
<%
Sub Content
   Dim cmd
   Dim conn
   Dim strConnect

   'create connection
   strConnect = "Provider=SQLOLEDB.1;User id=sa;Password=;Initial
      Catalog=;Data Source=;"
   Set conn = Server.CreateObject("ADODB.Connection")
   conn.ConnectionString = strConnect
   conn.CommandTimeout = 30
   conn.open

   'create command
   Set cmd = Server.CreateObject("ADODB.Command")
   cmd.ActiveConnection = Conn
   cmd.CommandText = "spActivity_Insert"
   cmd.Prepared = True
   cmd.CommandType = adCmdStoredProc
   cmd.Parameters.Append _
   cmd.CreateParameter("@LocationId",adInteger,adparamInput,8,
      Request("flocationid"))
   cmd.Parameters.Append _
   cmd.CreateParameter("@DateEntered",adVarchar,adparamInput,15,
      Request("fdate"))
   cmd.Parameters.Append _
```

```
    cmd.CreateParameter("@Sales",adDouble ,adParamInput,8, Request("fsale"))
    cmd.Parameters.Append _
    cmd.CreateParameter("@Margin",adDouble ,adParamInput,8,
       Request("fmargin"))
    cmd.Parameters.Append _
    cmd.CreateParameter("@NewAccounts",adInteger ,adParamInput,8,
       Request("faccount"))
    cmd.Execute
%>
<table>
   <tr>
      <td>The data was inserted, try running the report to see if your
         numbers are in the list.</td>
   </tr>
</table>
<%
'cleanup
conn.Close
Set conn = nothing
Set cmd = nothing
End Sub
%>
<!-- #include file=../nav/skeleton.asp -->
<%Response.End%>
%>
```

Our next file, `sales.css` is located in the `CSS` directory; it's a cascading stylesheet that is used for formatting purposes through the application and XSL stylesheet.

The next three files are `list.asp`, `prepare.asp`, and `command_create.asp`, and they can be found in the `REPORT` directory. These files represent the reporting section of our application. Let's start with `list.asp` – the screenshot below shows the results of this file: it provides a list of active reports from the database.

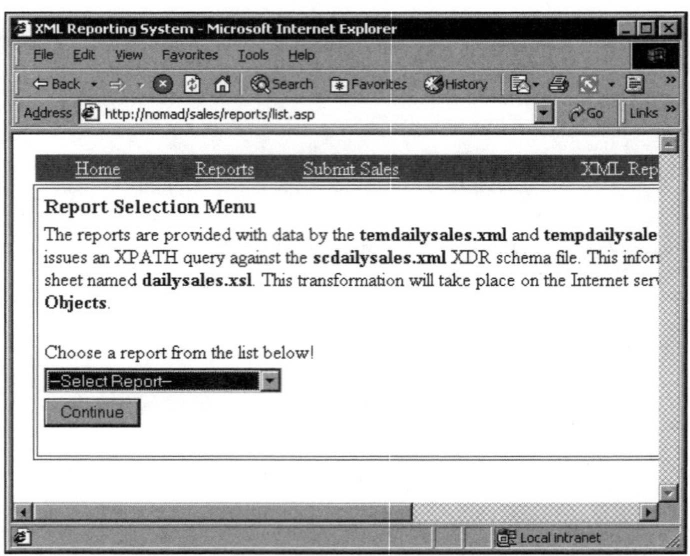

Our next file is prepare.asp. This file uses the freportid field from list.asp to query the database for the names of the XML template and XSL stylesheet files. When this information is obtained, we redirect the response command_create.asp. Take a look at prepare.asp below.

```
<%@ Language=VBScript %>
<%
   Dim conn
   Dim rs
   Dim strSQL
   Dim strXSL
   Dim strXML
   Dim strConnect

   'create the connection
   strConnect = "Provider=SQLOLEDB.1;User id=sa;Password=;Initial
      Catalog=;Data Source=;"
   set conn = Server.CreateObject("ADODB.Connection")
   conn.ConnectionString = strConnect
   conn.CommandTimeout = 30
   conn.open

   'create the rs
   set rs = Server.CreateObject("ADODB.Recordset")
   rs.ActiveConnection = conn
   strSQL = "SELECT XslFile, XmlFile FROM report WHERE ReportId = " &
     Request("freportid")
   rs.Open strSQL, ,adOpenStatic,adLockReadOnly

   'make sure we got our row
   If rs.recordCount > 0 Then
      strXML = rs("XmlFile")
      strXSL = rs("XslFile")
      conn.close
      Set conn = nothing
      Set rs = nothing
      Response.Redirect("command_create.asp?xsl_file=
         "&strXSL&"&xml_file="&strXML)
   Else
      conn.close
      Set conn = nothing
      Set rs = nothing
      Response.Write("Sorry but the report could not be displayed.")
   End If
 %>
```

Our next file is command_create.asp. This page is tasked with combing the XML document and XSL stylesheet to produce the report. At this point there are two common ways of transforming XML documents on the server side: we can use the Microsoft XML Parser, or we can use the ADO Command and Stream objects. The ADO Command and Stream objects were chosen because they are easier to work with. The Microsoft XML Parser can be used when we need more control over the XML document; however, we are managing our document with XSL stylesheets.

Another way to process the documents would be to send the XML document and XSL stylesheet to the client. Well, this puts us back into an environment that is difficult to manage: the client machines would be turned back into report servers. With all that said, let's take a look at the code for command_create.asp.

```
<%@ Language=VBScript %>
<%
   Dim conn
   Dim cmd
   Dim cmdXML
   Dim strTemp
   Dim strConnect

   'create the connection
   strConnect = "Provider=SQLOLEDB.1;User id=sa;Password=Initial
      Catalog=;Data Source=;"
   Set conn = Server.CreateObject("ADODB.Connection")
   conn.ConnectionString = strConnect
   conn.CommandTimeout = 30
   conn.open

   'create the XML stream
   Set cmdXML = CreateObject("ADODB.Stream")
   cmdXML.Open
   cmdXML.Charset = "ascii"
   cmdXML.Type = 1      'adTypeText
   strTemp = server.MapPath("../") & request("xml_file")
   cmdXML.LoadFromFile strTemp

   'create the command to connect the XML stream to
   Set cmd = CreateObject("ADODB.Command")
   Set cmd.ActiveConnection = conn
   Set cmd.CommandStream = cmdXML
   cmd.Dialect = "{C8B521FB-5CF3-11CE-ADE5-00AA0044773D}" 'DBGUID_DEFAULT
   cmd.Properties("Base Path") = server.MapPath(".")
   'set the results back to the response object
   cmd.Properties("Output Stream") = Response
   cmd.Properties("XSL") = request("xsl_file")
   cmd.Execute , , adExecuteStream

   'cleanup
   conn.Close
   Set conn = nothing
   Set cmdXML = nothing
   Set cmd = nothing
%>
```

In the first section of the code we create a connection. This connection will be used to access the data referenced within our XML template file. The snippet below shows this code.

```
   'create the connection
   strConnect = "Provider=SQLOLEDB.1;User id=sa;Password=Initial
      Catalog=;Data Source=;"
   Set conn = Server.CreateObject("ADODB.Connection")
   conn.ConnectionString = strConnect
   conn.CommandTimeout = 30
   conn.open
```

We then created a Stream object to load in our XML document. This snippet is shown below.

```
'create the XML stream
 set cmdXML = CreateObject("ADODB.Stream")
 cmdXML.Open
 cmdXML.Charset = "ascii"
 cmdXML.Type = 1       'adTypeText
 strTemp = server.MapPath("../") & request("xml_file")
 cmdXML.LoadFromFile strTemp
```

Next we create a Command object to start the transformation process. We must associate this object with an XML Stream object. Setting the CommandStream property to our XML Stream object does this.

```
'create the command to connect the XML stream to
 set cmd = CreateObject("ADODB.Command")
 set cmd.ActiveConnection = conn
 set cmd.CommandStream = cmdXML
```

Our next step is to tell the Command object where to find the XSL stylesheet that will be used for transformation. This is accomplished by setting the output stream and XSL properties.

```
 cmd.Dialect = "{C8B521FB-5CF3-11CE-ADE5-00AA0044773D}" 'DBGUID_DEFAULT
 cmd.Properties("Base Path") = server.MapPath(".")
 cmd.Properties("XSL") = request("xsl_file")
```

Once the transformation is complete, we must tell the Command object what to do with the object. We accomplish this be setting the output stream property:

```
 cmd.Properties("Output Stream") = Response
```

We are now left with the easy task of executing the command:

```
 cmd.Execute , , adExecuteStream
```

Put all these files together and we have an interface that allows users to submit sales and a reporting system that is flexible enough to handle any reporting task.

Accessing the Reporting System from VB

One of the appealing attributes of this system is that it can be accessed from within other applications. Any programming language capable of using MDAC will be able to access the reports created within the system. We will demonstrate this by using a very simple Visual Basic application that consists of a web browser control and button. You can also find code for this application within the VBCLIENT directory of the downloaded code. Let's take a look at this code.

```
Private Sub cmdLoadReport_Click()
   Dim conn As New ADODB.Connection
   Dim cmd As New ADODB.Command
   Dim cmdXML As New ADODB.Stream
   Dim cmdOutPut As New ADODB.Stream
   Dim strTemp As String
   Dim strConnect As String
   Dim strOutputFile As String
```

```
    'create the connection
    strConnect = "Provider=SQLOLEDB.1;User id=;Password=;Initial
       Catalog=;Data Source=;"
    conn.ConnectionString = strConnect
    conn.CommandTimeout = 30
    conn.open

    'create the XML stream
    cmdXML.open
    cmdXML.Charset = "ascii"
    cmdXML.Type = 1        'adTypeText
    strTemp = "C:\INETPUB\WWWROOT\SALES\TEMPLATE\TEMDAILYSALES.XML"
    cmdXML.LoadFromFile strTemp

    'create the command to connect the XML stream to
    Set cmd = CreateObject("ADODB.Command")
    Set cmd.ActiveConnection = conn
    Set cmd.CommandStream = cmdXML
    cmd.Dialect = "{C8B521FB-5CF3-11CE-ADE5-00AA0044773D}" 'DBGUID_DEFAULT
    cmd.Properties("Base Path") = "C:\INETPUB\WWWROOT\SALES\REPORTS\"
    cmd.Properties("XSL") = "dailysales.xsl"

   'Open the output stream and get ready to accept output
    cmdOutPut.open
    cmd.Properties("Output Stream") = cmdOutPut
    cmd.Execute , , adExecuteStream

    'Save the output to a file
    strOutputFile = "c:\sales.htm"
    cmdOutPut.SaveToFile strOutputFile, adSaveCreateOverWrite
    WebBrowser1.Navigate strOutputFile

    'clean up
    cmdXML.Close
    cmdOutPut.Close
    Set cmdOutPut = Nothing
    Set cmd = Nothing
    Set cmdXML = Nothing
    Set conn = Nothing
End Sub
```

You will notice that the paths to the XML and XSL files are hard-coded: this is because this is only a proof of concept application. If it was not, we could easily present the users with a list of reports and retrieve the XML and XSL file locations from the database. The code for this application should look extremely familiar, as it's basically the same code we are using within `command_create.asp`. If you run this application, you will get a report screen like the screen shot opposite:

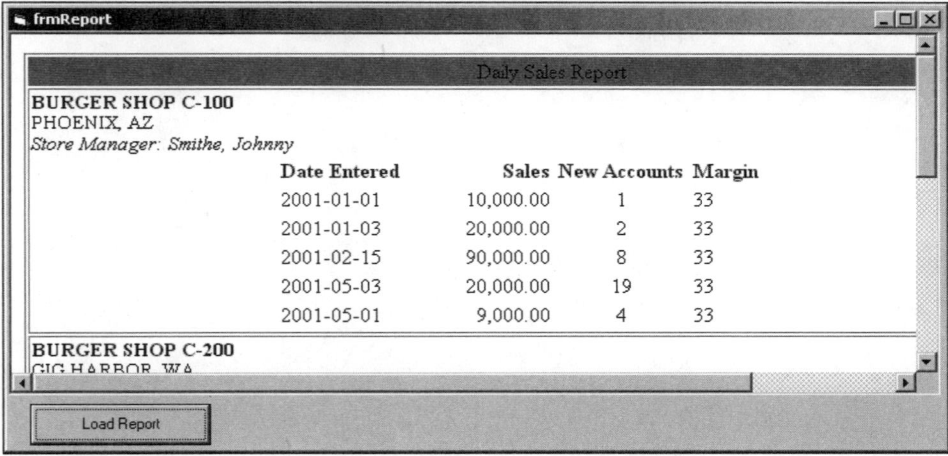

Summary

Hopefully this case study has spawned some new ideas and given you some insight into the ways of using SQL Server 2000 XML capabilities. At this point you should understand why reporting is so critical and how the technologies used within this case study can help you overcome some of these limitations.

SQL SQL SQL SQL SQL SQL
XML XML XML XML XML

SOAP

This case study will introduce you to the world of the **Simple Object Access Protocol** (**SOAP**). SOAP is an XML-based transfer method which can be initiated over the Hyper Text Transfer Protocol (HTTP) and is used to embed the information that we want to move around. Basically, we use SOAP to send messages encoded in XML from client to server, and vice-versa. The basic chain of events involved in this process is shown graphically below:

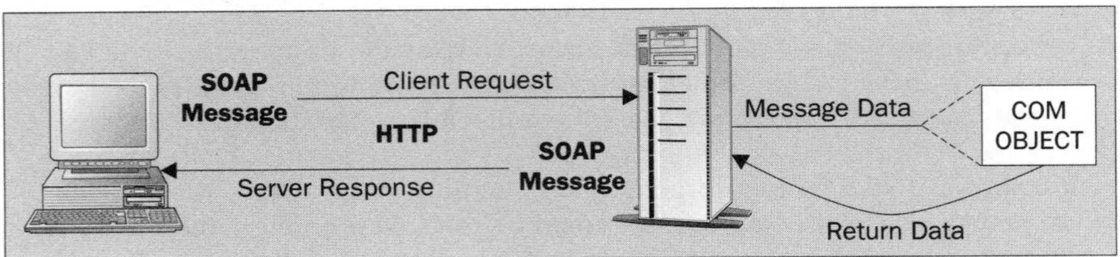

In the illustration above, the client – in this case a PC running some VB application – will generate a request for information, which can be provided by a COM component residing on an external server. The client generates this request by creating a SOAP message which specifies the component it wishes to call and any parameters that the component method might require. The message is then wrapped in an HTTP request and directed to the server via the Web. The server receives the request and uses the SOAP API to interpret the component and method to be invoked, along with any parameter information. The server executes the method and receives any returned data from the component. The server then wraps the response from the component method in a SOAP response message and sends it back to the client over HTTP. The client can then interpret the response message and continue processing.

An example of a SOAP request and response may help to clarify this. First, here is an example SOAP request:

```
<?xml version="1.0" encoding="utf-8"?>
<soap:Envelope xmlns:xsi="http://www.w3.org/2001/XMLSchema-instance"
 xmlns:xsd="http://www.w3.org/2001/XMLSchema"
 xmlns:soapenc="http://schemas.xmlsoap.org/soap/encoding/"
 xmlns:test="http://testsite/"
 xmlns:soap="http://schemas.xmlsoap.org/soap/envelope/">
  <soap:Body soap:encodingStyle="http://schemas.xmlsoap.org/soap/encoding/">
    <test:writemsg>
      <cMsg>Hello</cMsg>
    </tns:writemsg>
  </soap:Body>
</soap:Envelope>
```

Here is the subsequent response:

```
<?xml version="1.0" encoding="utf-8"?>
<soap:Envelope xmlns:xsi="http://www.w3.org/2001/XMLSchema-instance"
 xmlns:xsd="http://www.w3.org/2001/XMLSchema"
 xmlns:soapenc="http://schemas.xmlsoap.org/soap/encoding/"
 xmlns:test="http://testsite"
 xmlns:soap="http://schemas.xmlsoap.org/soap/envelope/">
  <soap:Body soap:encodingStyle="http://schemas.xmlsoap.org/soap/encoding/">
    <test: writemsgResponse>
      <Return>Hello</Return>
    </test: writemsgResponse>
  </soap:Body>
</soap:Envelope>
```

In the example above, the caller would send a request to the server to execute the `writemsg` method residing on `testsite`. As we can see, the message is encapsulated by the `soap:Envelope` tags. Within the envelope there are two distinct sections: the namespace information, which includes the namespace to be used to action our function call, and the portion encapsulated between the `soap:Body` tags.

The namespace section allows us to refer to information and methods from various sources. The information or method names from any of the sources could be referred to in the same way. Imagine two methods from different sources called `GetStock`. In order to prevent conflict, we can specify an alias for each of the sources and call the method we want by specifying the method's namespace, for example, `<a:GetStock>` or `<b:GetStock>`.

The portion between the `soap:Body` tags is called the **XML payload**. This is where the meta-information for the method call is held. The basic structure of the payload section is shown below:

```
<PayloadRoot>
  <MethodCall>
    <Parameter1>Parameter1 Value</Parameter1>
    <Parameter2> Parameter2 Value </Parameter2>
  </MethodCall>
</PayloadRoot>
```

The payload section holds all of the information required to execute the function, and the namespace section holds the reference to the method.

If the function is executed successfully, the server builds a response message that contains the results of the function. If the function fails, we can specify the error message or any other indicator to make the client aware of failure.

The response from the server is constructed in almost exactly the same way as the SOAP request. The message will again specify the method name, but the method call child elements will be the return data from the method call. If the method call succeeds, the SOAP response will look something like:

```
<PayloadRoot>
  <MethodCall>
    <Result>Success</Result>
  </MethodCall>
</PayloadRoot>
```

If the call fails, however, the response would be passed back like this:

```
<PayloadRoot>
      <MethodCall>
         <fault>
              <faultcode>400</faultcode>
            <faultstring>Bad Request</faultstring>
              <runcode>1</runcode>
         </fault>
      </MethodCall>
</PayloadRoot>
```

The `fault` tags encapsulate the error information from the method call. The `faultcode` and `faultstring` tags specify the error number and description, much like an `Error` object in VB would. The `runcode` tag holds a special code which specifies whether the call reached the target or not. The caller can then use this information to retry, or handle the error in some other way.

SOAP is a very powerful tool and, if used correctly, can handle a lot of the problems created by the hierarchy of disparate systems, which may contain critical systems belonging to collaborative companies. We can use SOAP to employ the functionality and information provided by these systems without having to replicate the services locally.

In this chapter, we are going to look at an excerpt of a real-world application which uses SOAP to perform messaging over HTTP. We will concentrate on the aspects of the application which enable the client to send SOAP messages over HTTP, and the code which allows the server to interpret this message and pass responses back to the client.

There will be quite a bit of code in this chapter and, to run the example, you will need to have the following resources:

- Microsoft SOAP Toolkit RC0 which can be downloaded free from http://www.msdn.microsoft.com/downloads/default.asp?URL=/code/sample.asp?url=/msdn-files/027/001/580/msdncompositedoc.xml
- IIS 5
- SQL Server 2000
- Visual Basic 6

We shall first look at an overview of the case study and explain our choice of implementation. We will then look at the code used to build the application. Finally, we will look at the client and server independently, and show how we can communicate between the two.

Problem Overview

A construction equipment rental company is looking for a system which would collate orders from a network of depots. The system should allow depot clerks to input orders for equipment, and should manage various tasks such as invoicing or the scheduling of product maintenance.

A central depot will collate all the orders and generate invoices when appropriate. These updates from the central depot will be filtered through to the appropriate depots nightly, via a dial-up connection.

Included in these updates are stock levels for all the products held by a depot *and* its neighboring depots. Each depot knows who its local depots are, and can look at the stock information for a product from these neighbors. The only downside about the way this would work is that the stock information for the neighboring depots is unreliable. A depot could hire out equipment after the updates from the central server have been posted to each of the depots.

We decide that the best way around this, both financially and functionally, is to manufacture real-time updates of stock levels from the client depots to the central depot. Table locks are used to ensure that information received from the central server is accurate at the time of the query. Due to the number of transactions per day (less than fifty), using a dial-up connection to the Internet and posting the updates using SOAP is very viable. A permanent connection to the Internet is too expensive and unjustifiable in terms of benefits and usage. It is this section of the application that we are going to concentrate on.

Below is a diagram of the area of the system dealing with updates and the retrieval of stock levels from local depots.

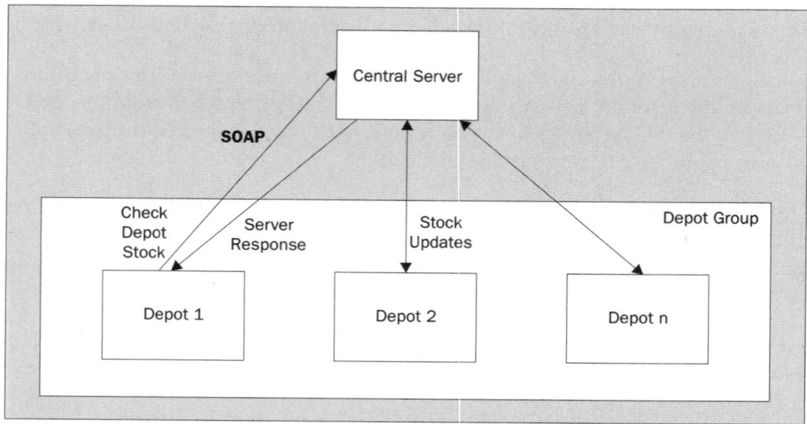

The diagram above only shows a very small part of stock maintenance. We will try to concentrate on the area of the depot management system that uses SOAP.

The code in the following sections will deal with the clients requesting stock levels from neighboring branches via the server. With all the clients updating the central depot in real-time, the levels of stock on the central depot will always be current.

First, we will look at the tasks that we want to perform across the Internet, and then we will look at the format of the messages that we need to generate to initiate these tasks. We can then design and code the server and client functionality needed to facilitate the SOAP conversation.

Functionality

To retrieve the stock level for a particular product from the central server, we need to pass the ID of the product and the ID of the depot from which we want to know the product's stock level.

The central depot has a SQL Server 2000 database to hold all of the data for the application. The client depots have Microsoft Data Engines (MSDEs) installed to hold relevant data, such as the local depots for stock allocation purposes.

The user will select a product and a local depot at the client's front-end. The user can then check the stock for that particular product at that particular depot.

The first thing that we need to do in our example is to set up the central depot SQL Server. We will create a database on SQL Server 2000 that we will call `Depot`. For our purposes, we can easily use one machine running SQL Server and IIS to run this application. We can get all the information from one database rather than creating two to hold the same data for this case study.

There are two tables involved in the checking of neighboring stock levels: `Product` and `Depots`. These tables exist on both the client depot MSDE and the central SQL Server.

In order to build up this case study's code as you work through the chapter, create the `Depot` database now. Then run the following SQL script which creates the `Product` and `Depots` tables and inserts some test data. For the purposes of anyone testing on an MSDE platform, the script is SQL Server 7 (MSDE) compatible:

```
CREATE TABLE [dbo].[Depots] (
   [DepotID] [int] NOT NULL ,
   [DepotName] [varchar] (30) NOT NULL ,
   [GroupID] [int] NOT NULL
) ON [PRIMARY]
GO

CREATE TABLE [dbo].[Product] (
   [ProductID] [int] NOT NULL ,
   [DepotID] [int] NOT NULL ,
   [ProductName] [varchar] (30) NOT NULL ,
   [ProductPrice] [decimal](18, 2) NOT NULL ,
   [ProductDesc] [varchar] (100) NULL ,
   [StockLevel] [int] NOT NULL
) ON [PRIMARY]
GO

INSERT Product(ProductID, DepotID, ProductName, ProductPrice,
               ProductDesc, StockLevel)
VALUES(1,1, '2 inch Drill', 12.11, '2 inch Drill bit', 3)

INSERT Product(ProductID, DepotID, ProductName, ProductPrice,
               ProductDesc, StockLevel)
VALUES(2,1, '3 inch Drill', 14.98, '3 inch Drill bit', 10)
```

```
INSERT Product(ProductID, DepotID, ProductName, ProductPrice,
               ProductDesc, StockLevel)
VALUES(3,3, '1/4 inch nails', 1.22, '100 1/4 inch nails', 120)

INSERT Product(ProductID, DepotID, ProductName, ProductPrice,
               ProductDesc, StockLevel)
VALUES(4,3, '1/2 inch nails', 1.89, '100 1/2 inch nails', 29)

INSERT Product(ProductID, DepotID, ProductName, ProductPrice,
               ProductDesc, StockLevel)
VALUES(5,1, 'D20 Spanner Set', 25.67, 'Spanners for the D20 Model', 2)

INSERT Product(ProductID, DepotID, ProductName, ProductPrice,
               ProductDesc, StockLevel)
VALUES(1,3, '2 inch Drill', 12.11, '2 inch Drill bit', 2)

INSERT Depots(DepotID, DepotName, GroupID)
VALUES(1, 'Glasgow', 1)

INSERT Depots(DepotID, DepotName, GroupID)
VALUES(2, 'London', 2)

INSERT Depots(DepotID, DepotName, GroupID)
VALUES(3, 'Edinburgh', 1)

INSERT Depots(DepotID, DepotName, GroupID)
VALUES(4, 'Manchester', 3)

INSERT Depots(DepotID, DepotName, GroupID)
VALUES(5, 'Birmingham', 3)
```

We will now look at what the server is expecting to receive from the client over the HTTP connection. The server is going to execute a SELECT statement over an ADO connection to retrieve the stock level. To do this, the server expects to receive a ProductID and a DepotID from the calling client.

Let's have a look at an example of the SOAP message that achieves this:

```
<?xml version="1.0" encoding="UTF-8" standalone="no"?>
   <SOAP-ENV:Envelope
      xmlns:SOAP-ENV="http://schemas.xmlsoap.org/soap/envelope/">
      <SOAP-ENV:Body>
         <SOAPSDK1:GetStock xmlns:SOAPSDK1="uri:Stock" >
            <ProductID>1</ ProductID >
            <DepotID >7</DepotID>
         </SOAPSDK1:GetStock>
      </SOAP-ENV:Body>
   </SOAP-ENV:Envelope>
```

So what does all that mean? Well, the header XML line should be pretty familiar by now and does not specify anything unique to SOAP. The <SOAP-ENV:Envelope> tag denotes the point at which the SOAP message begins and includes the SOAP namespace, which is used in subsequent tags.

The <SOAP-ENV:Body> tag is used to encapsulate the function to be called and the parameters to pass to the function. In the example above, the function is called GetStock and the parameters to be passed are ProductID (1) and DepotID (7). The source code for the GetStock function is shown later in this chapter.

Luckily, when we are writing the code to produce the message to send from client to server, the building of the SOAP message is more or less done for us. We use several functions to produce the tags that mark the start and end of the envelope and to add the function name and parameter values. We shall see the methods that we use to create these tags later when we discuss the client implementation.

First, though, let's look at the server side.

Server Implementation

On the server, we will need to build an ActiveX DLL to facilitate the reading of the SOAP message and the processing of the deconstructed message. In order to call this DLL from the client, we must set up an ASP page that simply creates an instance of the DLL and passes an ASP `Request` and `Response` object to the DLL for processing.

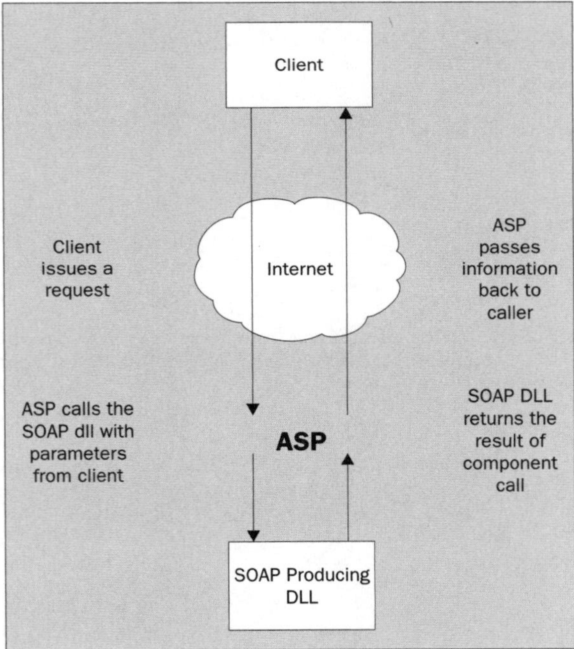

Let's go through the steps to set up the server side of the SOAP conversation. First, use IIS to create a virtual directory called `CheckGroupStock`. This directory should point to a specified directory which will hold the ASP (mentioned above) that will act as the messenger between the client and server. The VBScript code for the ASP is shown below. Save it as `CheckGroupStock.ASP` in the folder pointed to by the `CheckGroupStock` virtual directory:

```
<%
   Set CheckStock = Server.CreateObject("CheckGroupStock.clsCheckStock")
   CheckStock.Process Request, Response
%>
```

Nothing too taxing here. We simply create the object and then send the ASP's `Request` and `Response` objects to the `Process` sub of the `ClsCheckStock` object.

Let's now build the DLL to process the SOAP message, execute the function with the desired parameters, and return a SOAP message, via the ASP, back to the client for client-side processing.

Create a new ActiveX DLL project in Visual Basic 6. Call the project `CheckGroupStock`. Enter the following code into the default class, and rename this class `clsDatabase`:

```
Option Explicit

Private oADOCOnn As New ADODB.Connection

'Opens the connection to the database using the parameters provided.
Public Function bOpenDatabase(cConnectionString As String, cUserName As String _
                                          , cPassword As String) As Boolean
On Error GoTo badbOpenDatabase

oADOCOnn.Open cConnectionString, cUserName, cPassword
If oADOCOnn.State = 1 Then
    bOpenDatabase = True
Else
    bOpenDatabase = False
End If

Exit Function
badbOpenDatabase:
bOpenDatabase = False

End Function

'Generates a recordset to return from the cSQL string passed.
Public Function bRecordset(cSQL As String, rsIn As Recordset) As Boolean
On Error GoTo badbRecordset

Set rsIn = oADOCOnn.Execute(cSQL)

bRecordset = True

Exit Function
badbRecordset:
bRecordset = False

End Function

'Executes the cSQL string passed.
Public Function bExecute(cSQL As String) As Boolean
On Error GoTo badbexecute

oADOCOnn.Execute cSQL

bExecute = True

Exit Function
badbexecute:
bExecute = False

End Function
```

Now add another class module to the project. Call it `ClsCheckStock` and add the following code:

```
Option Explicit

'Namespace used in the returned message
Const STOCK_NS = "uri:Stock"

'Process function takes an ASP request and response object
'as parameters. Parses the SOAP message contained in the
'Request object and executes SELECT across ADO to retrieve
'stock level for a product and depot ID's contained in the
'SOAP request. Builds the SOAP message response which, on
'success, contains the stocklevel value in the stocklevel tag,
'or contains a standard SOAP Fault construct if not.
Public Sub Process(ByVal Request As ASPTypeLibrary.Request, _
                   ByVal Response As ASPTypeLibrary.Response)

    Dim Serializer As MSSOAPLib.SoapSerializer
    Dim Reader As MSSOAPLib.SoapReader
    Dim clsDatabase As New clsDatabase
    Dim rsLocal As ADODB.Recordset
    Dim bOK As Boolean, cSQL As String
    Dim iProductID As Integer
    Dim iDepotID As Integer
    Dim iStockLevel As Integer
    Dim cMethodName As String

    'For testing we are using the provided Depot database.
    Const CONNECTION_STRING = "Provider=SQLOLEDB;Server=(local);Database=Depot"
    On Error Resume Next

    'Open a new serializer object to build a SOAP message.
    Set Serializer = New MSSOAPLib.SoapSerializer
    If Err Then
        ServerFault Response, _
                    "Cannot create MSSOAP.SoapSerializer. " & _
                    Err.Description & "(0x" & Hex(Err.Number) & ")"
        Exit Sub
    End If

    'Open a new Reader object to parse the message.
    Set Reader = New MSSOAPLib.SoapReader
    If Err Then
        ServerFault Response, _
                    "Cannot create MSSOAP.SoapReader. " & _
                    Err.Description & "(0x" & Hex(Err.Number) & ")"
        Exit Sub
    End If

    'Load the SOAP message from the ASP Request Object.
    Reader.Load Request
    If Err Then
        ClientFault Response, "Cannot load request. " & Err.Description
        Exit Sub
    End If
```

```
'Retrieve the method name from the SOAP message.
'This is especially handy if you want to include
'more than one function in the DLL. You can select
'case on the method name passed and act accordingly.
cMethodName = Reader.RPCStruct.baseName
If Err Then
    ClientFault Response, _
                "Cannot get method name. " & _
                Err.Description
    Exit Sub
End If

'Get the product ID passed in.
iProductID = CInt(Reader.RPCParameter("ProductID").Text)
If Err Then
    ClientFault Response, _
                "Cannot get parameter A. " & _
                Err.Description
    Exit Sub
End If

'Get the Depot ID passed in.
iDepotID = CInt(Reader.RPCParameter("DepotID").Text)
If Err Then
    ClientFault Response, _
                "Cannot get parameter B. " & _
                Err.Description
    Exit Sub
End If

'Now that we have all the information we require, open
'a connection to the database.
bOK = clsDatabase.bOpenDatabase(CONNECTION_STRING, "sa", "")

'Build the SQL statement to execute on the database.
cSQL = "SELECT StockLevel FROM Product WHERE ProductID = " & iProductID & _
                " AND DepotID = " & iDepotID

'Execute the SQL passing back a recordset.
bOK = clsDatabase.bRecordset(cSQL, rsLocal)

'If ok, return the stock level, if not return -1 indicating error.
If bOK Then
    iStockLevel = CInt(rsLocal("StockLevel").Value)
Else
    iStockLevel = -1
End If

'Build the SOAP response message.
'Set the content type.
Response.ContentType = "text/xml"

'Initialize the serializer object we created earlier to
'the ASP response object passed in.
Serializer.Init Response
```

```
    'Specify the start of the envelope tags.
    Serializer.startEnvelope

    'Specify the start of the body tags.
    Serializer.startBody

    'Specify the start of a new element, in this case
    'we concatenate the method name & "response". We also
    'specify the namespace we are using.
    Serializer.startElement cMethodName & "Response", STOCK_NS

    'Specify the start of a new element, in this case the
    'result of the database read previously.
    Serializer.startElement "StockLevel", STOCK_NS

    'Set the value of the Stocklevel element to our result.
    Serializer.writeString CStr(iStockLevel)

    'End all the elements to close of the message.
    Serializer.endElement
    Serializer.endElement
    Serializer.endBody
    Serializer.endEnvelope

'Clean up
End Sub

Sub ServerFault(ByVal Response As ASPTypeLibrary.Response, _
                ByVal FaultString As String)
  ReturnFault Response, "Server", FaultString
End Sub

Sub ClientFault(ByVal Response As ASPTypeLibrary.Response, _
                ByVal FaultString As String)
  ReturnFault Response, "Client", FaultString
End Sub

Sub ReturnFault(ByVal Response As ASPTypeLibrary.Response, _
                ByVal FaultCode As String, _
                ByVal FaultString As String)

  On Error Resume Next

  Err.Clear

  Dim Serializer As MSSOAPLib.SoapSerializer

  Response.Status = "500 Internal Server Error"

  Set Serializer = New MSSOAPLib.SoapSerializer
  If Err Then

    Response.AppendToLog _
"Could not create SoapSerializer object. " & _
Err.Description
```

```
    Else

        Serializer.Init Response

        Serializer.startEnvelope
        Serializer.startBody
        Serializer.startFault FaultCode, FaultString
        Serializer.startFaultDetail
        Serializer.endFaultDetail
        Serializer.endFault
        Serializer.endBody
        Serializer.endEnvelope

    End If

  End Sub
```

To make this code compile into the correct DLL, you must add the following references:

- Microsoft Active Server Pages Object Library
- Microsoft ActiveX Data Objects 2.6 Library
- Microsoft SOAP Type Library
- Microsoft XML, v3.0

Let's go through `ClsCheckStock` above. There is a constant called `STOCK_NS` which specifies the namespace we use in the SOAP messages throughout the communication. We shall see this in the client application also. The `Process` sub itself takes two parameters – the ASP `Request` object, which contains the SOAP message, and the ASP `Response` object, which will contain the returned SOAP message.

We then declare our variables for processing, execution, and returning. Next, we create the objects to read and write SOAP messages. The `Serializer` object is used for the latter. The methods exposed by this object allow us to build up the SOAP message tags and values. The `Reader` object allows us to parse a SOAP message in a similar way to the XML DOM object, specifying elements to retrieve.

Now that the read and write objects have been created, we can load the SOAP message into the `Reader` object. The next section of code pulls the function name and the parameters from the message stored in the `Reader` object. We could use the function name to do a "select case on" if we wanted the DLL to perform multiple functions on a SOAP message but, since only one method is to be performed here, the function name is pretty redundant in this instance.

Everything is now in place for us to perform the database read via ADO, so we open the database, build the SQL to execute, execute the SQL returning a recordset, and – finally – set the `iStockLevel` variable to the stock level returned in the recordset. Note that this code is using a private class in the DLL to perform data access. The functions in the class are standard ADO calls to perform the opening of a database using connection information, and to execute a SQL statement that returns a recordset.

So we have the answer to the question posed in the SOAP message sent from the client. We now have to send the answer back to the client in a SOAP message via the `Response` object. This is where we use the `Serializer` object to build the response to the client.

First, we set the content type of the Response object to text/XML. Now we initialize the Serializer object with the Response object. This informs the Serializer object of the stream that the message is to be output to. We then build the SOAP message using the functionality provided by the Serializer object. We use a series of start and end methods to encapsulate the response from the server into a SOAP message.

When the execute method ends, processing returns to the calling ASP which has had its Response object set. Control then returns to the client and the client can interrogate the SOAP message contained in the Response.

The ServerFault, ClientFault, and ReturnFault subs handle any errors generated in processing the SOAP message. These subs are relatively straightforward and simply specify the error and where it originated – client or server. The error is then wrapped into a SOAP message in the same way as a valid response.

Once these two classes have been added to the CheckGroupStock project, and the correct references added, make the CheckGroupStock.dll (via the File menu) and register it as normal with regsvr32.exe.

Client Implementation

Now that the server has been set up to handle SOAP requests from the client, we can build the client application that will query the server for stock levels. The application presented here is a watered-down version of that which would ideally be built for the client. Its scope has been cut to highlight the SOAP functionality that we are interested in.

First, let's have a look at the simple screen that allows users to query stock:

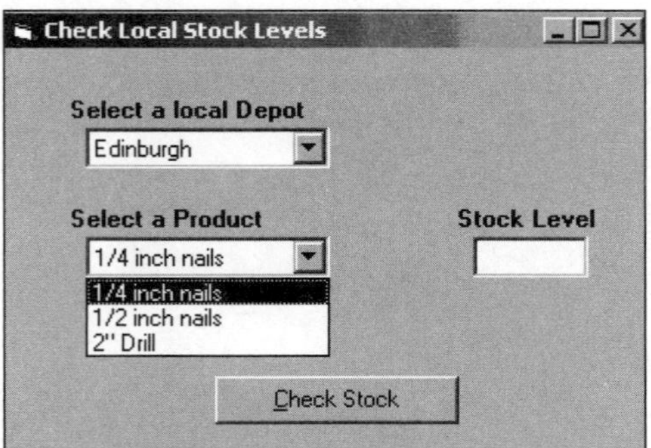

The user selects a depot from a list of depots local to it. The user then selects a product from the known list of products held in the selected depot. When the user clicks on Check Stock, the client builds the SOAP message with the appropriate values as parameters and waits for a response. When the response is received, the Stock Level text box is populated with the stock level value contained in the SOAP message returned.

Create a new Standard EXE project called CheckGroupStock_Client. Rename Form1 as frmMain. Add two combo boxes to the form (cboDepots and cboProducts), a command button (cmdCheck), and a text box (txtStockLevel). Arrange some labels and adjust captions so that the form looks like the previous screenshot.

This part of the application uses five classes which we will add shortly. The first is the database class (`clsDatabase`) used in the server DLL. The other four are product and depot classes, two for each. The `clsProduct` and `clsDepot` classes are basically the same, but access different objects in the database. The `clsProducts` and `clsDepots` classes are iterator classes for `clsProduct` and `clsDepot`, respectively. These hold collections of the underlying entity classes that describe an individual instance.

clsProduct

Add a class module to the project and call it `clsProduct`. Here is the code:

```
Private iProductID As Integer
Private iDepotID As Integer
Private cName As String
Private curPrice As Currency
Private cDesc As String
Private iStock As Integer
Private clsDatabase As New clsDatabase

Public Property Get ProductID() As Integer
   ProductID = iProductID
End Property

Public Property Get DepotID() As Integer
   DepotID = iDepotID
End Property

Public Property Get Name() As String
   Name = cName
End Property

Public Property Get Description() As String
   Description = cDesc
End Property

Public Property Get Price() As Currency
   Price = curPrice
End Property

Public Property Get Stock() As Integer
   Stock = iStock
End Property

'bGet retrieves a particular instance of the product by pulling the required
'information from the database and assigning the values to the property variables.
Public Function bGet(iProdID As Integer, iDepID As Integer) As Boolean
   Dim cSQL As String
   Dim rsLocal As ADODB.Recordset
   Dim bOK As Boolean

   bOK = bClear()

   cSQL = "SELECT * FROM Product WHERE ProductID = " & iProdID & _
          " AND DepotID = " & iDepID
```

```
    'Pass SQL string to an object method which returns the recordset
    'produced by the sql.
    bOK = clsDatabase.bRecordset(cSQL, rsLocal)

    If bOK Then
        If Not IsNull(rsLocal![ProductID]) Then iProductID = rsLocal!ProductID
        If Not IsNull(rsLocal![DepotID]) Then iDepotID = rsLocal!DepotID
        If Not IsNull(rsLocal![ProductName]) Then cName = rsLocal!ProductName
        If Not IsNull(rsLocal![ProductDesc]) Then cDesc = rsLocal!ProductDesc
        If Not IsNull(rsLocal![ProductPrice]) Then curPrice = rsLocal!ProductPrice
        If Not IsNull(rsLocal![StockLevel]) Then iStock = rsLocal!StockLevel
    End If

End Function

Private Function bClear() As Boolean

    On Error GoTo badbClear
    bClear = False
    iProductID = 0
    iDepotID = 0
    iStockLevel = 0
    cName = ""
    cDesc = ""
    curPrice = 0

    bClear = True
    Exit Function

badbClear:
    bClear = False
    Exit Function
End Function

Private Sub Class_Initialize()
    Dim bOK As Boolean
    bOK =clsDatabase.bOpenDatabase("Provider=SQLOLEDB;Server=(local);_
                                    Database=Depot", "sa", "")
End Sub
```

The clsProduct class allows us to store information related to a product stored in the database tables. In our project, we won't be using the bGet method as this allows the object to self-populate. What we want is a collection of these objects that we generate depending on the depot that a user selects. The properties of each of these instances will contain all the information we need.

clsProducts

The iterator class, clsProducts, allows creation and access to the instances of the underlying objects based on a depot. The code for clsProducts is shown here (add this to a new class module):

```
Private colProducts As New Collection
Private clsDatabase As New clsDatabase

Public Property Get GetCollection() As Collection
    Set GetCollection = colProducts
End Property
```

```
'The bGetProducts function builds a collection of product instances based
'on the filter in the cWhere parameter that will be used in the where clause.
Public Function bGetProducts (cWhere As String) As Boolean
Dim clsLocal As clsProduct
Dim cSQL As String
Dim bOK As Boolean
Dim rsLocal As ADODB.Recordset

On Error GoTo badbGetProducts

    If cWhere <> "" Then
        cSQL = "SELECT * FROM Product " & cWhere
    Else
        cSQL = "SELECT * FROM Product"
    End If


    'Retrieve a recordset from the database object using the cSQL created above.
    bOK = clsDatabase.bRecordset(cSQL, rsLocal)

    If bOK Then
        Do While Not rsLocal.EOF
            Set clsLocal = New clsProduct
            bOK = clsLocal.bGet(rsLocal("ProductID"), rsLocal("DepotID"))
            colProducts.Add clsLocal
            Set clsLocal = Nothing
            rsLocal.MoveNext
        Loop
    End If

bGetProducts = True
Exit Function

badbGetProducts:
    bGetProducts = False
    Exit Function

End Function

Private Sub Class_Initialize()
Dim bOK As Boolean
    bOK = clsDatabase.bOpenDatabase("Provider=SQLOLEDB;Server=(local);_
Database=Depot","sa", "")
End Sub

'Function used to populate the passed combo with the products from the collection
'of product classes, using the product ID as the identifier "itemdata"
Public Function bPopulateCombo (cboIn As ComboBox) As Boolean
   Dim iCount As Integer
   On Error GoTo badbPopulateCombo
   BadbPopulateCombo = false
   Do While iCount < colProducts.Count
      cboIn.AddItem (colProducts(iCount + 1).Name)
      cboIn.ItemData(cboIn.NewIndex) = colProducts(iCount + 1).ProductID
      iCount = iCount + 1
   Loop
```

```
    bPopulateCombo = True
    Exit Function

    badbPopulateCombo:
    bPopulateCombo = False
    Exit Function
End Function
```

Nothing too complicated here. The `clsProducts` iterator class purely holds a collection of the underlying product classes generated by the `bGetProducts` method. This method builds the SQL statement required to retrieve the products, based on the depot code if one has been passed. This then allows us to populate the combo box of products (`cboProducts`) using the `bPopulateCombo` method, which lists the available products for the selected depot.

clsDepot

The two depot classes are very similar, except for the SQL statements. Add a third class module, called `clsDepot`, and insert the following code:

```
Private iDepotID As Integer
Private cName As String
Private iGroup As Integer
Private clsDatabase As New clsDatabase

Public Property Get DepotID() As Integer
    DepotID = iDepotID
End Property

Public Property Get Name() As String
    Name = cName
End Property

Public Property Get Group() As Integer
    Group = iGroup
End Property

Public Function bGet(iID As Integer) As Boolean
Dim cSQL As String
Dim rsLocal As ADODB.Recordset
Dim bOK As Boolean

    bOK = bClear

    cSQL = "SELECT * FROM Depots WHERE DepotID = " & iID
    bOK = clsDatabase.bRecordset(cSQL, rsLocal)

    If bOK Then
        If Not IsNull(rsLocal![DepotID]) Then iDepotID = rsLocal!DepotID
        If Not IsNull(rsLocal![DepotName]) Then cName = rsLocal!DepotName
        If Not IsNull(rsLocal![GroupID]) Then iGroup = rsLocal!GroupID
    End If

End Function
```

```
Private Function bClear() As Boolean

On Error GoTo badbClear
iDepotID = 0
cName = ""
iGroup = 0

bClear = True
Exit Function

badbClear:
    bClear = False
End Function

Private Sub Class_Initialize()
Dim bOK As Boolean
    bOK =
clsDatabase.bOpenDatabase("Provider=SQLOLEDB;Server=(local);Database=Depot", _
                                    "sa", "")
End Sub
```

clsDepots

The fourth class module to add is for `clsDepots`:

```
Private colDepots As New Collection
Private clsDatabase As New clsDatabase

Public Property Get GetCollection() As Collection
    Set GetCollection = colDepots
End Property

Public Function bGetDepots(cWhere As String) As Boolean
Dim clsLocal As clsDepot
Dim cSQL As String, bOK As Boolean
Dim rsLocal As ADODB.Recordset

On Error GoTo badbGetDepots

    If cWhere <> "" Then
        cSQL = "SELECT DepotID FROM Depots " & cWhere
    Else
        cSQL = "SELECT DepotID FROM Depots"
    End If

    bOK = clsDatabase.bRecordset(cSQL, rsLocal)

    If bOK Then
        Do While Not rsLocal.EOF
            Set clsLocal = New clsDepot
            bOK = clsLocal.bGet(rsLocal("DepotID"))
            colDepots.Add clsLocal
            Set clsLocal = Nothing
            rsLocal.MoveNext
        Loop
    End If
    bGetDepots = True
    Exit Function
```

```
badbGetDepots:
    bGetDepots = False
End Function

Private Sub Class_Initialize()
Dim bOK As Boolean
    bOK =
clsDatabase.bOpenDatabase("Provider=SQLOLEDB;Server=(local);Database=Depot", _
                                    "sa", "")
End Sub

Public Function bPopulateCombo(cboIn As ComboBox) As Boolean
Dim iCount As Integer
On Error GoTo badbPopulateCombo

    Do While iCount < colDepots.Count
        cboIn.AddItem (colDepots(iCount + 1).Name)
        cboIn.ItemData(cboIn.NewIndex) = colDepots(iCount + 1).DepotID
        iCount = iCount + 1
    Loop

bPopulateCombo = True
Exit Function

badbPopulateCombo:
bPopulateCombo = False

End Function
```

The fifth and final class to add to the project is the same `clsDatabase` that we saw in the server-side project.

frmMain

These five classes are used by the main form to populate the combo boxes with appropriate values. The main form itself holds the method that generates the SOAP message to send to the server. Let's look at `frmMain` now.

When the user clicks the command button, the item data values of the combo boxes are passed to the `Execute` method. This function uses these parameters to build the SOAP message to send to the server. Here's the code behind `frmMain`:

```
Private clsDepots As New clsDepots
Private clsProducts As New clsProducts
Const DEPOT_ID = 1
Const GROUP_ID = 1
Private Const END_POINT_URL =
"http://localhost/CheckGroupStock/CheckGroupStock.asp"
Private Const STOCK_NS = "uri:Stock"

Private Sub cboDepots_Change()
Dim bOK As Boolean
```

```
    bOK = True

    If bOK Then
        bOK = clsProducts.bClear
        bOK = clsProducts.bGetProducts("WHERE DepotID = " &
cboDepots.ItemData(cboDepots.ListIndex))
    End If

    If bOK Then
        cboProducts.Clear
        bOK = clsProducts.bPopulateCombo(cboProducts)
    End If

End Sub

Private Sub cboDepots_Click()
Dim bOK As Boolean

    bOK = True

    If bOK Then
        bOK = clsProducts.bClear
        bOK = clsProducts.bGetProducts("WHERE DepotID = " & _
                cboDepots.ItemData(cboDepots.ListIndex))
    End If

    If bOK Then
        cboProducts.Clear
        bOK = clsProducts.bPopulateCombo(cboProducts)
    End If

End Sub

Private Sub cmdCheck_Click()
Dim iDepotID As Integer, iProductID As Integer

    iDepotID = cboDepots.ItemData(cboDepots.ListIndex)
    iProductID = cboProducts.ItemData(cboProducts.ListIndex)

    txtStockLevel = CStr(Execute("", iProductID, iDepotID))

End Sub

Private Sub Form_Load()
Dim bOK As Boolean
Dim cWhere As String

    cWhere = "WHERE GroupID > 0 AND DepotID > 0"
    bOK = clsDepots.bGetDepots(cWhere)

    If bOK Then
        bOK = clsDepots.bPopulateCombo(cboDepots)
    End If
```

```
End Sub
'Calls the SOAP DLL created earlier using the product ID
'and the depot ID to retrieve the stock levels.
Private Function Execute(ByVal Method As String, _
                         ByVal iProductID As Integer, _
                         ByVal iDepotID As Integer) As Integer

    'Create the objects required to Connect, build the SOAP message
    'and read the results.
    Dim Serializer As SoapSerializer
    Dim Reader As SoapReader
    Dim ResultElm As IXMLDOMElement
    Dim FaultElm As IXMLDOMElement
    Dim Connector As SoapConnector

    'Set up the connector as an HTTP connector object
    Set Connector = New HttpConnector
    'Sets the ENDPointURL property on the connection to the
    'asp page we created earlier to call the DLL.
    Connector.Property("EndPointURL") = END_POINT_URL
    Connector.Connect

    'Specifies the SOAP action. Not really utilized here as
    'there is only one method we wish to use.
    Connector.Property("SoapAction") = "uri:" & Method

    'Instantiate the serializer object.
    Set Serializer = New SoapSerializer
    'Initiate the serializer with the connectors input stream.
    Serializer.Init Connector.InputStream
    'Indicate the start of the SOAP message.
    Connector.BeginMessage

    'Creates the <SOAP:Envelope> Tag
    Serializer.startEnvelope
    'Creates the <SOAP:Body> Tag
    Serializer.startBody
    'Build the function call
    Serializer.startElement Method, STOCK_NS, , "m"
    Serializer.startElement "ProductID"
    Serializer.writeString CStr(iProductID) 'ProductID parameter
    Serializer.endElement
    Serializer.startElement "DepotID"
    Serializer.writeString CStr(iDepotID) 'DepotID Parameter
    Serializer.endElement
    Serializer.endElement
    'Creates the </SOAP:Body> Tag
    Serializer.endBody
    'Creates the </SOAP:Envelope> Tag
    Serializer.endEnvelope

    'Signal the end of the message.
    Connector.EndMessage

    'Instantiate the reader object
    Set Reader = New SoapReader
    'Load the result from the connector into the reader object
    Reader.Load Connector.OutputStream
```

```
        'Check for a fault element <Fault>
        If Not Reader.Fault Is Nothing Then
            MsgBox Reader.faultstring.Text, vbExclamation
        Else
            'If no fault then set the result of the method to the
            'returned value (RPCResult)
            Execute = CDbl(Reader.RPCResult.Text)
        End If
    End Function
```

Let's concentrate on the `Execute` method, as the other events and functions are pretty standard. This method will look pretty familiar as it is almost exactly the same as that used to produce the SOAP return message on the server side. There are some important differences though, so let's go through them.

We have created an `HTTPConnector` object in this function. The `HTTPConnector` object is derived from the `SOAPConnector` object, which specifies the bindings used by a particular protocol to communicate using SOAP messaging. In our case, the protocol is HTTP, so the `HTTPConnector` object is used. For reference, the available protocols are as follows:

- HyperText Transfer Protocol (HTTP)
- Simple Mail Transfer Protocol (SMTP)
- File Transfer Protocol (FTP)

We specify the `EndPointURL` property of the `SOAPConnector` object to point to the URL of the ASP page we created earlier – in our case http://localhost/CheckGroupStock/CheckGroupStock.asp.

Next, we initiate the connection. We do this by executing the `Connect` method of the `HTTPConnector` object. To complete setting up the connector, we need to specify the connector's `SOAPAction` property. This specifies the operation to be performed. In our case, we have set this to the namespace URI used throughout the application.

We can now set up the `Serializer` object. This works slightly differently as we now set the `Serializer`'s initialization parameter to the connector's `InputStream`. This is because the SOAP message will be sent via the HTTP connector, whereas, in the case of the server, the response object was storing the message for us.

If we now set the `Connector.BeginMessage` property to signal the start of a SOAP message, we can build up the SOAP message using the parameters passed in and the various `Serializer` methods to build up the message. When the message is ready to go, we set the `Connector.EndMessage` to signal the end of the SOAP message and initiate communication with the server through the ASP page specified as the `EndPoint`.

When the client receives a response, a reader object is used to load the returned SOAP message from the server. The returned message is stored in the `Connector`'s `OutputStream` object.

If the `Reader.Fault` value does not contain any data, then the transaction has been successful and we can query the response. If not, we can pull the fault string from the message to see what went wrong.

We can use the `RPCResult` property of the `Reader` to retrieve the response from the server if the transaction has completed successfully. This property retrieves the first child of the `Body` element of the SOAP message. In our case, this would hold the stock level of the product and depot combination we specified originally.

If all goes well, the UI is updated accordingly:

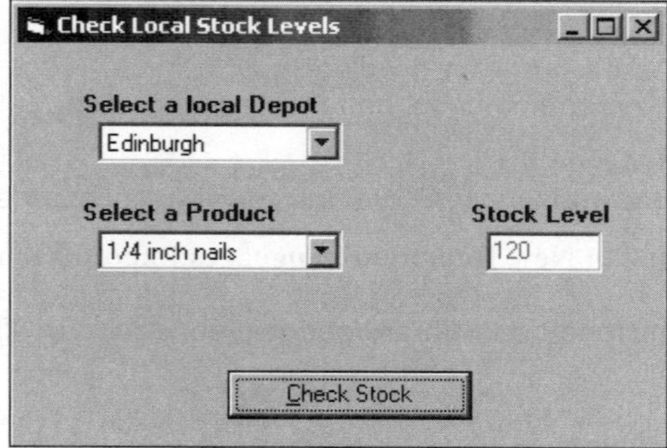

As we can see, the stock level has been updated from the server. This process can be executed as many times as the user wants.

Before trying it for yourself, be sure to add the same four references that we used in the server-side project to the client project.

SOAP and Firewalls

Sometimes firewalls will not let SOAP requests through the security barrier to be handled by the server. This is due to the configuration of the firewall as regards what is to be submitted to the server through its configured HTTP ports.

The best solution to this problem is to set up a filter on the firewall that checks the HTTP request coming in for a `SOAPAction` header. For example:

```
SOAPAction: "http://myserver/test"
```

This could be used to allow the firewall to identify the request's intention. If the field was omitted, blank, or contained an invalid URL, the firewall would not allow the request to pass.

The Future of SOAP

The scalability of SOAP's functionality is impressive. Because of this, SOAP has been harnessed by Microsoft to help power Web Services on the .NET Framework. Web Services will be the Next Big Thing. They allow an application's functionality to be exposed over the Web using XML and SOAP, and leveraged by other applications – think of them as Web pages for computers.

Here are some SOAP and Web Services resources:

- SOAP
  - Detailed SOAP overview for developers at:
    http://msdn.microsoft.com/xml/general/soapspec.asp
  - A four minute movie(!) at:
    http://www.soapwebservices.com/articles/what_is_soap.asp
  - SOAP Toolkit 2.0: New Definition Languages Expose Your COM Objects to SOAP Clients:
    http://msdn.microsoft.com/library/periodic/period01/Toolkit20.htm
- Web Services
  - Microsoft Web Services home page at:

    http://msdn.microsoft.com/webservices/

It will be interesting to watch where the harnessing of remote functionality will lead. Could we end up with Function Farms? People paying to send messages to your server which takes the messages, processes them, and returns responses to clients. We could also be looking forward to completely platform independent development if everyone knows the predefined way to communicate using SOAP. We watch and wait...

SQL
Server
XML

A .NET Case Study

This chapter presents a case study in which a Visual Studio 6.0 application is migrated to Microsoft.NET (Visual Studio.NET and the .NET Framework). The Visual Studio 6.0 application used a variety of SQL Server 2000 features (`FOR XML` and `OPENXML`) that facilitate working with XML. The basic premise is that an application implemented using VB Script, ATL, COM using C++, and ASP will be migrated to Visual Studio.NET, C#, ASP.NET, and ADO (that's right ADO and not ADO.NET). Specifying ADO and not ADO.NET is a logical decision. Moving to .NET will require significant changes be made to any application. By not modifying the database API used (ADO), the upgrade process is clearly simplified. Emphasis can instead be place on improving and enhancing the existing application using SQL Server 2000's XML features. SQL Server 2000 and its XML features represent a stable technology. Providing enhancements using a proven technology minimizes risk.

The Project

The product developed by our case-study company is a set of business objects and web reporting tools that are used by the `Northwind` database. Currently, the project utilizes:

- SQL Server 2000 in order to make use of the XML features of this database. This XML support was originally added to the project to facilitate the importing and exporting of data from our business objects and to simplify displaying data on the web.
- `FOR XML` queries to retrieve data including `RAW`, `AUTO`, and `EXPLICIT` modes.
- `OPENXML` to insert data.
- ADO and a mix of SQL commands and stored procedures to access SQL Server 2000.

- C++ in process COM servers to perform all business tier functionality (data retrieval and inserting).
- ASP and server-side VB Script to access the business tier.
- ASP and server-side VB Script directly access the database.
- A variety of client-side scripting techniques in order to display the XML.

The basic layout of our legacy project is as follows:

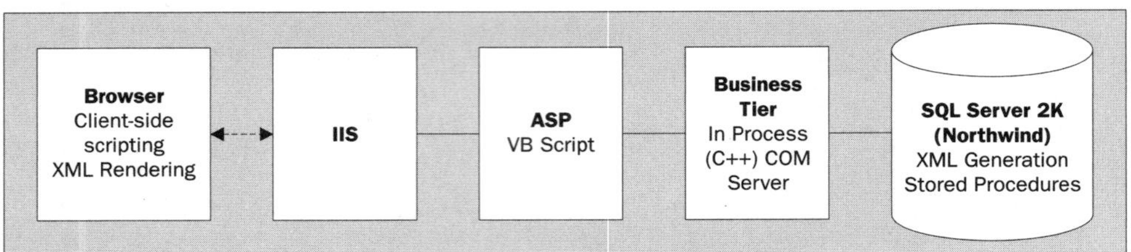

The next release of the project will consist of:

- Better optimized SQL queries. Certain queries presently in the product were not implemented in an efficient manner. By exploring tradeoffs of using each mode of `FOR XML` the queries will be better optimized. Additionally, the type of access performed by ADO will be modified to increase performance.
- Migration of all data access to business objects. Every developer out there has experienced the pitfalls associated with letting SQL development and database access be handled at every tier of an application.
- Migration of all C++ COM objects to C# classes. Presently there are a variety of memory leaks and COM objects leaks (un-released pointed) in the business objects. C# provides a way to clean up these leaks and greatly simplifies the development process.
- Migrate from ASP to ASP.NET. At present the migration will not seek to exploit advanced ASP.NET features. By migrating now it will be simpler to extend the application in the future to use the cross-browser and mobile features of ASP.NET.

After .NET migration the project will appear as follows:

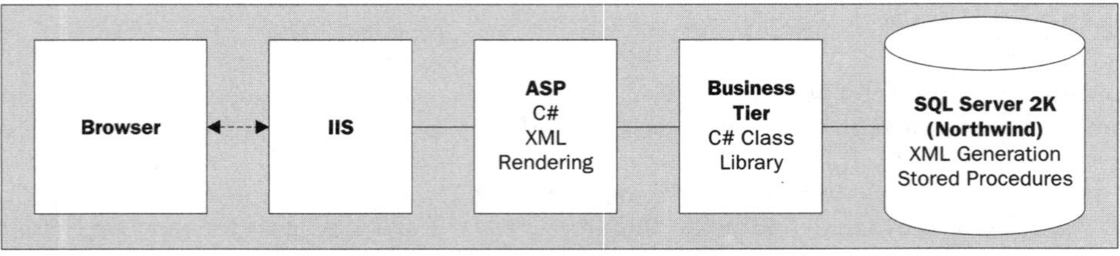

The specific projects being migrated are:

- `TheLegacyBusTier` (ATL, C++, in-process COM Server) is being migrated to `BusTierDotNet` (C#, class library).
- `TheLegacyClient` (ASP, server-side VB Script, client-side XML rendering) is being migrated to `TheClientDotNet` (ASP.NET, server-side C#, client-side XML rendering).

SQL Performance and Optimization

Before migrating the legacy application to .NET a review was made of how SQL Server's XML support was used by this project and how performance could potentially be enhanced. The basic areas investigated were:

- Is there a significant performance advantage in using a stored procedure over straight SQL specified in the source code?
- Is there an advantage in using one form of `FOR XML` over another (`RAW`, `AUTO`, or `EXPLICIT`)?
- What is the cost associated with using `XMLDATE` to retrieve schema information?

FOR XML Performance

While performing a review on the legacy version of the project, a particular `FOR XML` query was flagged as a candidate for optimization. This query is utilized in stored procedure, `GetEmpTerrRegExpV1`. A portion of this stored procedure is as follows with … used to indicate portions excluded for brevity (see script, `PerfAuto01.sql`, to view the stored procedure in its entirety):

```
CREATE PROCEDURE GetEmpTerrRegExpV1
    @preTag NVARCHAR(40), @postTag NVARCHAR(40) AS
SELECT @preTag
SELECT 1 AS Tag,
       0 AS Parent,
       Firstname AS [EmployeeTable!1!FirstName],
       LastName AS [EmployeeTable!1!LastName],
       ' ' AS [EmployeeTerritoriesTable!2!TerritoryID],
       NULL AS [EmployeeTerritoriesTable!2!TerritoryDesc],
       0 AS [RegionTable!3!RID],
       NULL AS [RegionTable!3!RDesc]
FROM Employees

UNION ALL

SELECT 2, 1 …
UNION ALL

SELECT 3, 2,…
FOR XML EXPLICIT

SELECT @postTag
```

The basic idea of this stored procedure is to:

- Display a tag before the XML document is generated using parameter, `@preTag` (`SELECT @preTag`)
- Display a `FOR XML` query generated using `EXPLICIT` mode
- Display a tag after the XML document is generated using parameter, `@postTag` (`SELECT @postTag`)

The rationale for using FOR XML EXPLICIT is to dictate a specific XML data hierarchy using the Tag and Parent schema columns or to specify per-column data transforms using directives such as element, xml, xmltext, and cdata. Stored procedure, GetEmpTerrRegExpV1, is approximately fifty lines of text yet generates a standard hierarchy and uses no directives to transform the data. An excerpt from this hierarchy is as follows:

```
<EmployeeTable FirstName="Steven" LastName="Buchanan">
    <EmployeeTerritoriesTable TerritoryID="02903" TerritoryDesc="Providence">
        <RegionTable RID="1" RDesc="Eastern"/>
        <RegionTable RID="2" RDesc="Western"/>
        ...
    </EmployeeTerritoriesTable>
```

The alias for each table name in this query appears as an element (EmployeeTable, EmployeeTerritoriesTable, and RegionTable). The columns associated with each database table are represented by attributes (FirstName, LastName, etc.). This specific behavior is precisely the default behavior of a FOR XML AUTO query. In fact, this lengthy FOR XML EXPLICIT query could actually be rewritten using FOR XML AUTO.

The GetEmpTerrRegAutoV1 stored procedure uses FOR XML AUTO and generates the same output as the GetEmpTerrRegExpV1 stored procedure. This stored procedure is implemented as follows:

```
CREATE PROCEDURE GetEmpTerrRegAutoV1
    @preTag NVARCHAR(40), @postTag NVARCHAR(40) AS
SELECT @preTag

SELECT EmployeeTable.Firstname AS FirstName,
       EmployeeTable.LastName AS LastName,
       EmployeeTerritoriesTable.TerritoryID AS TerritoryID,
       RTRIM(T.TerritoryDescription) AS TerritoryDesc,
       RegionTable.RegionID AS RID,
       RTRIM(RegionTable.RegionDescription) AS RDesc
FROM Employees AS EmployeeTable,
     EmployeeTerritories AS EmployeeTerritoriesTable,
     Territories AS T,
     Region AS RegionTable

WHERE EmployeeTable.EmployeeId = EmployeeTerritoriesTable.EmployeeID AND
      EmployeeTerritoriesTable.TerritoryID = T.TerritoryID

ORDER BY EmployeeTable.LastName,
         EmployeeTable.FirstName,
         EmployeeTerritoriesTable.TerritoryID,
         E.RID
FOR XML AUTO
SELECT @postTag
```

Of interest in the GetEmpTerrRegAutoV1 stored procedure is the use of function RTRIM on columns TerritoryDescription and RegionDescription. These columns are both of type NCHAR, a fixed size, Unicode string. RTRIM removes the spaces that pad each string out to be fixed length. RTRIM, makes the XML document generated much more readable.

A C# application, PerfTestDotNET01, was developed that compared the performance of the FOR XML EXPLICIT and FOR XML AUTO implementations of this query. The results of running PerfTestDotNET01 are as follows:

	Pass	Number of Iterations	Time (seconds)
FOR XML EXPLICIT	1	1000	28.55
FOR XML EXPLICIT	2	1000	28.57
FOR XML AUTO	1	1000	27.26
FOR XML AUTO	2	1000	27.60

The previous performance results were each run twice (Pass 1 and Pass 2). Running the test multiple times is a safety measure designed to ensure that each reading is accurate. If Pass 1 was radically different then Pass 2, the test would have to be rerun.

The `FOR XML AUTO` query runs approximately 3.5% faster than the `FOR XML EXPLICIT` query. This number will clearly differ depending on the query executed. This difference makes intuitive sense. Remember that a `FOR XML EXPLICIT` query generates a rowset referred to as a Universal Table. This Universal Table ultimately generates the XML document. In order to view the contents of the Universal Table, execute the `FOR XML EXPLICIT` query but do not specify, `FOR XML EXPLICIT`. The first four columns and four rows of our queries Universal Table is as follows:

```
Tag  Parent  EmployeeTable!1!FirstName                 EmployeeTable!1!LastName
----- ---------  -----------------------------------------  -------------------------------------
1    0       Steven                                    Buchanan
2    1       Steven                                    Buchanan
3    2       Steven                                    Buchanan
3    2       Steven                                    Buchanan
```

What is significant about the Universal Table is that it shows the `Tag` and `Parent` columns. `FOR XML EXPLICIT` queries process additional columns and can perform per-column data manipulation. The result of this is a slight performance overhead.

The decision made as part of the migration was to change to the `FOR XML AUTO` query. The performance improvement was one reason to migrate as was the plain fact that it is simpler to read a `FOR XML AUTO` query.

Comparing the relative performance of each flavor (`RAW`, `AUTO`, and `EXPLICIT`) of `FOR XML` query is taken one step further by SQL script file, `Performance03.sql`. This SQL script file defines three stored procedures that each generate the same XML document. These stored procedures are defined as follows:

- `GetCustomersRawV3` – retrieves an XML document using `FOR XML RAW`
- `GetCustomersAutoV3` – retrieves an XML document using `FOR XML AUTO`
- `GetCustomersExplicitV3` – retrieves an XML document using `FOR XML EXPLICIT`

The following `FOR XML AUTO` query is the same query executed by stored procedure, `GetCustomersAutoV3`:

```
SELECT CustomerID, CompanyName, ContactName, Address, City, Region,
       PostalCode, Country, Phone
FROM Customers AS row
ORDER BY CustomerID
FOR XML AUTO
```

Remember that each row returned by a FOR XML RAW is contained in an element named, row. Notice in the previous query the use of the alias in the FROM clause, FROM Customers AS row. This is how the AUTO version of the query generates the same document as the RAW version of this query. The EXPLICIT version of this query sets the containing element using a per-column alias such as CustomerID AS [row!1!CustomerID].

The Visual Basic 6.0 application, Performance03, executes each of these three flavors of stored procedures over a number of iterations. The performance numbers generated by this application are as follows:

FOR XML type	Number of Iterations	Pass 1 (secs)	Pass 2 (secs)
RAW	10,000	125	125
AUTO	10,000	125	126
EXPLICIT	10,000	128	129

Notice once again that each performance measurement test was run twice (Pass 1 and Pass 2). The results of Pass 1 supported validity of the results of Pass 2. For a query this simple, there is approximately a 2.4% difference separating RAW and AUTO mode from the slower EXPLICIT mode. Basically, Performance03 confirms what we could have guessed. EXPLICIT mode is the slowest form of FOR XML query because it supports the generation of complex XML documents through the fine-tuning of the data hierarchy and per-column manipulation.

Stored Procedures

Every SQL Server developer recognizes the performance benefits in using stored procedures instead of placing SQL directly in source code. The advantage of using stored procedures with FOR XML-style queries is both a performance and ease of use issue. An alternate form of query must be specified in order for ADO to directly use FOR XML queries. This alternative form of query is referred to as a template query. This query is not specified using an ADO Command object's CommandText property but is instead specified using an ADO Stream object and setting the value of a Command's CommandStream property. The Command object's Dialect property in turn has to be set to "{5D531CB2-E6Ed-11D2-B252-00C04F681B71}". This GUID value is actually defined in SQL Server's OLE DB 2.6 header file, sqloledb.h.

Before making the decision to migrate from queries placed directly in the source code to stored procedures, the performance gain of this move had to be measured. Clearly if the performance gain would be a percent or two then it might not be worth the risk of changing code that already works.

Performance01 contains code that executes a FOR XML AUTO query as a command placed in source code and then executes the same SQL query as a stored procedure. Actually, there are two different mechanisms used to execute the FOR XML AUTO query directly from the source code: early binding to ADO objects and late binding to ADO objects. The merits of early binding (good) versus late binding (bad) are not directly germane to this case study. Still, we are measuring performance and trying to determine if we should risk modifying the code in order to achieve better performance. It just so happens that a novice developer wrote our legacy application using FOR XML AUTO queries placed directly in the source code in conjunction with late binding ADO objects.

The subroutine, `RunCommandLateBinding`, of `Performance01` demonstrates the way not to write this code. Developers interested in the correct way to handling object binding with `FOR XML AUTO` queries placed directly in the source code should take a look at the `RunCommand` subroutine of `Performance01`. The subroutine called `RunStoredProc` demonstrates the same `FOR XML` query executed from within the `GetEmpTerrRegAutoV2` stored procedure. The code associated with our late binding subroutine, `RunCommandLateBinding`, is as follows:

```
Private Sub RunCommandLateBinding(count As Integer, startTime, _
            conn As Connection, timeToPrint As Boolean)
' count -- the current interation we are one
' conn - connection to SQL Server 2000
' startTime -- the time we started processing the first subroutine
'             call to RunCommandLateBinding
' timeToPrint -- last iteration so display performance information

    ' this is late binding
    Dim streamIn, streamOut, cmd
    ' This should have been implemented as follows to utilize
    ' early binding:
    ' Dim streamIn As New Stream
    ' Dim streamOut As New Stream
    ' Dim cmd As New Command

    Set streamIn = CreateObject("ADODB.Stream")
    Set cmd = CreateObject("ADODB.Command")
    Set streamOut = CreateObject("ADODB.Stream")

    streamIn.Open
    streamIn.WriteText strQuery, adWriteChar
    streamIn.Position = 0

    Set cmd.CommandStream = streamIn
    Set cmd.ActiveConnection = conn
    cmd.Dialect = "{5D531CB2-E6Ed-11D2-B252-00C04F681B71}"

    cmd.CommandText = _
        "<ROOT xmlns:sql='urn:schemas-microsoft-com:xml-sql'>" & _
        "<sql:query>" & _
          "SELECT EmployeeTable.Firstname AS FirstName, " & _
            "EmployeeTable.LastName AS LastName, " & _
            "EmployeeTerritoriesTable.TerritoryID AS TerritoryID, " & _
            "RTRIM(T.TerritoryDescription) AS TerritoryDesc, " & _
            "RegionTable.RegionID AS RID, " & _
            "RTRIM(RegionTable.RegionDescription) As RDesc " & _
          "FROM Employees AS EmployeeTable, " & _
            "EmployeeTerritories AS EmployeeTerritoriesTable, " & _
            "Territories AS T, " & _
            "Region As RegionTable " & _
          "WHERE EmployeeTable.EmployeeId = " & _
            "EmployeeTerritoriesTable.EmployeeID AND " & _
            "EmployeeTerritoriesTable.TerritoryID = T.TerritoryID " & _
          "ORDER BY EmployeeTable.LastName, " & _
            "EmployeeTable.FirstName, " & _
            "EmployeeTerritoriesTable.TerritoryID, " & _
            "E.RID " & _
```

```
            "FOR XML AUTO" & _
        "</sql:query></ROOT>"

    streamOut.Open
    cmd.Properties("Output Stream") = streamOut
    cmd.Execute , , adExecuteStream

    streamOut.Position = 0
    If timeToPrint Then
        endTime = Time
        Text1.Text = Text1.Text & _
              "SQL Text (late binding), Iterations: " & count & _
              ", Seconds: " & DateDiff("s", startTime, endTime) & _
              vbCrLf
        'streamOut.ReadText (adReadAll)
    End If

    Set cmd = Nothing
    Set streamOut = Nothing

End Sub
```

In the previous source code, the `Command` object's `CommandText` property is set to the same `FOR XML AUTO` query executed when comparing `AUTO` and `EXPLICIT` performance.

The results of comparing a `FOR XML AUTO` query called using 1) early-bound COM objects, 2) late-bound COM objects, and 3) from within a stored procedure is as follows:

SQL Type	Number of Iterations	Pass 1 (secs)	Pass 2 (secs)
SQL text (early binding)	10,000	132	132
SQL command (late binding)	10,000	138	137
Stored procedure	10,000	119	119

The question we were ultimately answering was, "Does it make sense to upgrade this code to use stored procedures when we migrate to C#?" The performance difference between late-bound COM objects executing the query and a stored procedure executing the query is approximately 13.3 percent. The performance between early-bound COM objects executing the query and a stored procedure executing the query is 9.8 percent.

Don't be concerned if the performance measuring application (a Visual Studio .NET, C# application), `PerfTestDotNET01`, runs more slowly than this latest performance measurement application written in Visual Basic 6.0. The C# application was developed using a pre-release version of Visual Studio .NET and a pre-release version of the .NET Framework. Microsoft's emphasis was on developing .NET features first (in the Beta releases) followed by performance (in the final release).

Our next generation application will use SQL Server 2000 XML features in conjunction with ASP.NET. Part of the impetus for this migration is the fact that ASP.NET does not use scripting languages therefore such applications can use early binding to ADO COM objects.

XMLDATA Performance

Thus far our migration from Visual Studio 6.0 to .NET has been limited to evaluating the choices originally made with respect to how to optimally manipulate XML using SQL Server 2000. There is one final issue to be resolved before determining how the SQL should be modified to facilitate better performance in the new version of the project.

Certain `FOR XML` queries in the legacy application use the `FOR XML` option, `XMLDATA`, to pre-pend a schema to the XML document generated. The underlying database and hence the XML schema generated with each `FOR XML` query is stable. Not changing the database schema means that the XML schema does not need to be generated each time a `FOR XML` query is executed. Instead, the XML schema could be attached manually to the beginning of the XML document generated.

This idea sounds like a reasonable way to improve performance but a bit of investigation is in order before it is adopted as standard in the next version of our application. The downside to this approach would occur in the event that the database schema change or that SQL Server adopted a different XML schema representation. In May of 2001, the World Wide Web Consortium (www.w3.org) announced, "XML Schema Becomes a Recommendation". Clearly the standards body that oversees XML is adopting a standard months after SQL Server 2000 shipped. This could ultimately affect SQL Server and the XML schemas generated using the `FOR XML` option, `XMLDATA`.

The SQL script file, `Peformance04.sql`, contains a stored procedure called `GetCustomersAutoV4`. This stored procedure takes a single parameter, `@getSchema`. The following settings are permissible for this parameter:

- `@getSchema` set to `1` – a `FOR XML` query is executed using option `XMLDATA`.
- `@getSchema` set to `2` – the schema generated by option `XMLDATA`, is pre-pended to the `FOR XML` query. This query is executed without specifying option `XMLDATA`.
- otherwise – the `FOR XML` query is executed without specifying option `XMLDATA`.

The `GetCustomersAutoV4` stored procedure is defined as follows (where … indicates portions excluded for brevity):

```
CREATE PROCEDURE GetCustomersAutoV4
    @getSchema Integer AS
    If @getSchema = 2 SELECT '<Schema … </Schema>'

    If @getSchema = 1
       SELECT CustomerID, CompanyName, ContactName,
            Address, City, Region, PostalCode, Country, Phone
       FROM Customers AS row
       ORDER BY CustomerID
       FOR XML AUTO, XMLDATA
    Else
       SELECT CustomerID, CompanyName, ContactName,
           Address, City, Region, PostalCode, Country, Phone
       FROM Customers AS row
       ORDER BY CustomerID
       FOR XML AUTO
```

The FOR XML query executed is identical (save for the XMLDATA caveat) to the query previously demonstrated by the GetCustomersAutoV3 stored procedure. The application that calls the GetCustomersAutoV4 stored procedure under each of these scenarios is Peformance04. The performance results generated by this application are as follows:

Execution Scenario	Number of Iterations	Pass 1 (secs)	Pass 2 (secs)
No schema	10,000	118	118
Manually applied schema	10,000	120	121
XMLDATA generated schema	10,000	123	123

To use XMLDATA or not to use XMLDATA is a question that is best answered by determining if the performance gain achieved exceeds the risk of database and/or XML schema change? It is approximately 1.6% faster to pre-pend a schema manually than to retrieve one using XMLDATA. There is very little reward to using the manual schema approach so it is best (in most applications) just to use the XMLDATA option. The execution time for XMLDATA will vary from query to query, but it is never likely to degrade performance by more than a percentage point or two.

The XML documents generated by our case study's application do not use the XMLDATA option. This was simply a feature not needed for our application. As we have demonstrated, XMLDATA was not excluded for reasons of performance.

Business Tier

The legacy business tier is an in-process COM server, TheLegacyBusTier. Visual C++ 6.0 and ATL were used to develop this in-process COM server. The objects in this COM server needed to be accessed from Active Server Pages using VBScript, so the type of interface exposed by each object is dual. Each interface exposed by the business tier's COM objects (ICustomer, IOrder, and IShipper) is derived from IDispatch. This COM server contains the following COM objects:

- Customer – retrieves information pertaining to Northwind's customers. The form of data access used by this object was ADO in conjunction with SQL commands specified in the source code. The queries make use of FOR XML. This business option will be migrated to C# and will use stored procedures to retrieve XML documents.
- Order – retrieves information pertaining to Northwind's orders. The form of data accessed used by this object was ADO in conjunction with stored procedures. The queries make use of FOR XML to retrieve XML documents. This business option will be migrated to C#.
- Shipper – retrieves and inserts information pertaining to Northwind's shippers. The data retrieval queries make use of FOR XML. The insertion of data is performed using XML and a stored procedure that makes use of OPENXML. This business option will be migrated to C#, and delete and update functionality will be added courtesy of OPENXML.

XML Retrieval, Legacy Application

For the sake of brevity, only crucial portions of the TheLegacyBusTier COM objects will be examined in detail. The first object examined is the Order object. This object retrieves XML pertaining to customers using FOR XML-style queries. XML data could have been generated using ADO's native support (the Recordset object's Save method to a file or stream). ADO's support for XML is not nearly as feature rich as that provided by SQL Server 2000's FOR XML queries.

The FOR XML-style queries associated with the Order object are executed by the GetOrdersAuto stored procedure. This stored procedure is defined as follows:

```
CREATE PROCEDURE GetOrdersAuto @customerID NVARCHAR(40) AS
  SELECT '<ROOT>'
  IF LEN(@customerID) > 0
    SELECT OrderID, CustomerID, EmployeeID
    FROM Orders
    WHERE CustomerID LIKE (@customerID+'%')
    FOR XML AUTO
  ELSE
    SELECT OrderID, CustomerID, EmployeeID
    FROM Orders
    FOR XML AUTO
  SELECT '</ROOT>'
```

If GetOrdersAuto's input parameter, @customerID, has a length of zero then SELECT * is executed. If this input parameter contains a string then the same query is executed but the WHERE clause limits the query using LIKE, as in CustomerID LIKE (@customerID+'%'). In the GetOrdersAuto stored procedure, the XML generated by FOR XML AUTO is not contained in a single root element. By design the XML document the stored procedure generates will be contained in an element, <ROOT>. In order to ensure this, a SELECT '<ROOT>' precedes the FOR XML AUTO query and a SELECT '</ROOT>' follows the FOR XML AUTO query. Using Query Analyzer to execute this stored procedure results in the following:

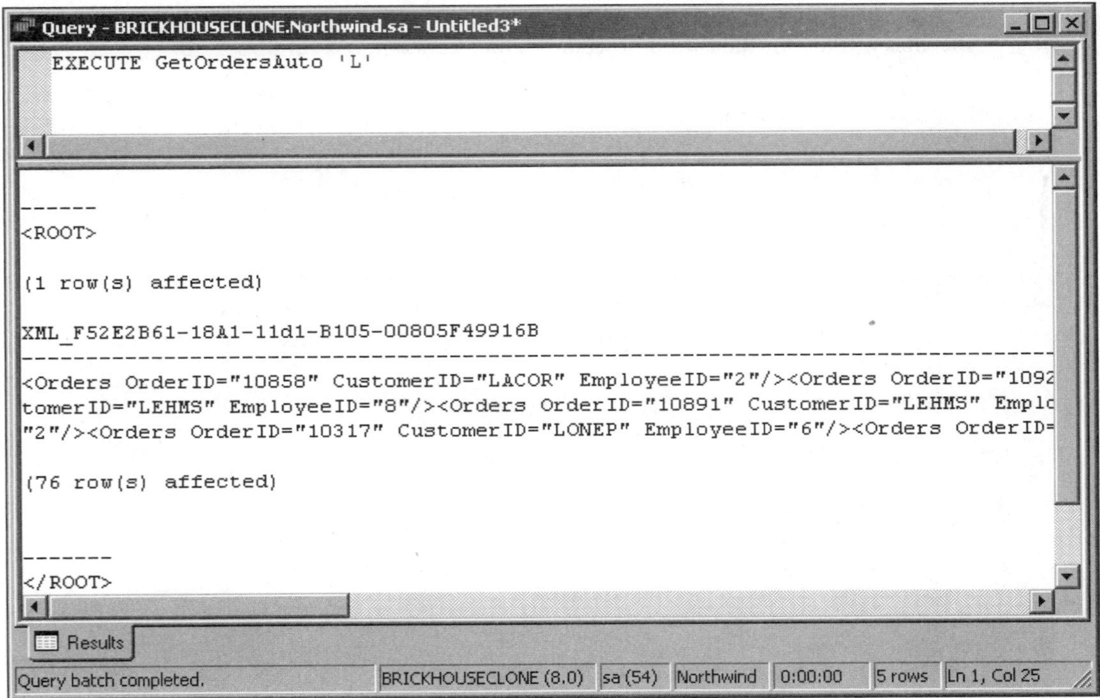

Each Order object exposes interface, IOrder (see TheLegacyBusTier.idl):

```
interface IOrder : IDispatch
{
    [propget, id(1), helpstring("property CustomerIDPrefix")]
        HRESULT CustomerIDPrefix([out, retval] BSTR *pVal);
    [propput, id(1), helpstring("property CustomerIDPrefix")]
        HRESULT CustomerIDPrefix([in] BSTR newVal);
    [id(2), helpstring("method Get")]
        HRESULT Get([retval, out] BSTR *pbstrOrders);
};
```

The CustomerIDPrefix property sets a data member, m_bstrCustomerIDPrefix, inside class COrder. The value of the m_bstrCustomerIDPrefix data member is passed as a parameter to the GetOrdersAuto stored procedure. The XML representation of Orders is retrieved using the Get method.

The tasks performed by the Get method include:

- Opening a connection to SQL Server's Northwind database using an ADO Connection object (spConnection->Open).
- Creating a command that refers to the GetOrdersAuto stored procedure (spCommand->put_CommandType(adCmdStoredProc) and spCommand->put_CommandText(CComBSTR(L"GetOrdersAuto"))).
- Assigning a parameter to the command (spParameter->put_Value(vParmValue)) that specifies a value for the stored procedure input parameter, @customerID.
- Setting up a stream to be used to retrieve the XML document generated by the query (spStreamOut->Open).
- Associating this command with a stream that will be receiving the XML document (spPropertyOutputStream->put_Value(vStreamOut)).
- Executing the query (spCommand->Execute).

A simple macro called HR provides a quick way to check the return code of each method called by Get. This macro checks the value of an HRESULT and if an error is detected, returns the value of the HRESULT. This macro is defined as follows and is implemented in the header file, stdafx.h:

```
#define HR(hrExpression) if (FAILED(hr = hrExpression)) return hr;
```

The Get method is implemented as follows (see Order.h):

```
STDMETHOD(Get)(BSTR *pbstrOrders)
{
    CComBSTR bstrConn;
    CComPtr<_Connection> spConnection;
    CComPtr<_Command> spCommand;
    CComPtr<_Stream> spStreamOut;
    CComPtr<Properties> spProperties;
    CComPtr<Property> spPropertyOutputStream;
    HRESULT hr = S_OK;
    CComVariant vtParamNotFound;
```

```
    *pbstrOrders = NULL;
    vtParamNotFound.vt = VT_ERROR;
    vtParamNotFound.scode = DISP_E_PARAMNOTFOUND;
    bstrConn = L"PROVIDER=SQLOLEDB;DATA SOURCE=localhost;"
               L"DATABASE=NorthWind;USER ID=sa;PASSWORD=sa;";
    HR(spConnection.CoCreateInstance(__uuidof(Connection)));
    HR(spConnection->Open(bstrConn,
                          NULL,
                          NULL,
                          adConnectUnspecified));
    HR(spCommand.CoCreateInstance(__uuidof(Command)));
    HR(spCommand->put_CommandType(adCmdStoredProc));
    HR(spCommand->putref_ActiveConnection(spConnection));

    CComVariant vParmName = ::SysAllocString(L"@customerID");
    CComPtr<Parameters> spParameters;
    CComPtr<_Parameter> spParameter;
    CComVariant vParmValue;

    HR(spCommand->put_CommandText(CComBSTR(L"GetOrdersAuto")));
    vParmValue.vt = VT_BSTR;
    V_BSTR(&vParmValue) = m_bstrCustomerIDPrefix.Copy();
    HR(spCommand->get_Parameters(&spParameters));
    HR(spParameters->get_Item(vParmName, &spParameter));
    HR(spParameter->put_Value(vParmValue));
    spParameter = 0;
    spParameters = 0;

    VARIANT vStreamOut;
    long lSize;
    CComVariant vRecordsAffected = 0L;

    HR(spCommand->get_Properties(&spProperties));
    HR(spProperties->get_Item(CComVariant(CComBSTR(L"Output Stream")),
                              &spPropertyOutputStream));
    HR(spStreamOut.CoCreateInstance(__uuidof(Stream)));
    HR(spStreamOut->Open(vtParamNotFound,
                         adModeUnknown,
                         adOpenStreamUnspecified,
                         NULL,
                         NULL));

    ::VariantInit(&vStreamOut);
    vStreamOut.vt = VT_DISPATCH;
    V_DISPATCH(&vStreamOut) = spStreamOut;
    HR(spPropertyOutputStream->put_Value(vStreamOut));
    HR(spCommand->Execute(&vRecordsAffected,
                          NULL,
                          adExecuteStream,
                          NULL));

    HR(spStreamOut->get_Size(&lSize));
    HR(spStreamOut->ReadText(lSize, pbstrOrders));
    spCommand = 0;
    spPropertyOutputStream = 0;
    spProperties = 0;
    HR(spConnection->Close());
    spConnection = 0;

    return hr;
}
```

Of interest within the source code for the `Get` method was a line of code that did not appear:

```
spParameters->Refresh();
```

The `Refresh` method is associated with a `Command` object's `Parameters` collection. This method queries the underlying database's catalog and fills in the individual `Parameter` objects found in the `Parameters` collection. Querying the database's catalog represents an undesirable performance overhead. The OLE DB Provider for SQL Server automatically sets up the `Parameter` objects without requiring that `Refresh` be called. Don't be fooled! The database catalog was queried. With the SQL Server OLE DB provider we were not allowed to choose whether or not to call `Refresh`.

Object Insertion (OPENXML), Legacy Version

The in-process COM server, `TheLegacyBusTier`, exposes the following interface for its `Shipper` object:

```
interface IShipper : IDispatch
{
    [propget, id(1), helpstring("property CompanyNamePrefix")]
        HRESULT CompanyNamePrefix([out, retval] BSTR *pVal);
    [propput, id(1), helpstring("property CompanyNamePrefix")]
        HRESULT CompanyNamePrefix([in] BSTR newVal);
    [id(2), helpstring("method Insert")]
        HRESULT Insert([in] BSTR bstrShippers);
    [id(3), helpstring("method Get")]
        HRESULT Get([retval, out] BSTR *pbstrShippers);
    [id(4), helpstring("method Delete")]
        HRESULT Delete([in] BSTR bstrShippersPrefix);
};
```

The `Insert` method takes as an input an XML document where shippers (element, `Shippers`) are represented by a series of attributes (`CompanyName` and `Phone`). The motivation for demonstrating XML data insertion should be clear from the simplicity of these two columns. Neither `CompanyName` nor `Phone` is a foreign key, so data insertion is simple to demonstrate and test. An example of XML data that can be inserted by the `Shipper` object's `Insert` method is:

```
<SHIPPERS CompanyName="Blue Parrot Freight" Phone="(408) 555-1234"/>
<SHIPPERS CompanyName="S. Norman's Express " Phone="(650) 555-5678"/>
<SHIPPERS CompanyName="Silly Walk Shippers" Phone="(415) 555-9876"/>
```

The stored procedure that supports the insertion of data by the `Shipper` object is `InsertShippers`. This stored procedure uses `OPENXML` to insert data. `InsertShippers` is defined as follows:

```
CREATE PROCEDURE InsertShippers @xmlDoc VARCHAR(4000) AS
DECLARE @xmlDocIndex INT
DECLARE @RetVal INT
-- leave extra room for <ROOT> and </ROOT>
DECLARE @xmlDocInternal VARCHAR(4014)

IF '<ROOT>' != LEFT(LTRIM(@xmlDoc), 6)
    SELECT @xmlDocInternal = '<ROOT>'+@xmlDoc+'</ROOT>'
ELSE
    SELECT @xmlDocInternal = @xmlDoc
```

```
EXECUTE sp_xml_preparedocument @xmlDocIndex OUTPUT, @xmlDocInternal

-- 1 is ATTRIBUTE-centric mapping
-- If the XML was generated with FOR XML's ELEMENTS directive
-- then we specify 2 (ELEMENT-centric mapping)
INSERT Shippers
SELECT CompanyName, Phone
FROM OPENXML(@xmlDocIndex, N'/ROOT/SHIPPERS',1)
WITH Shippers

EXECUTE sp_xml_removedocument @xmlDocIndex

SELECT @RetVal = 1
RETURN @RetVal
```

InsertShippers requires that the data contain a root element, <ROOT>. If no <ROOT> element is included in the input XML (input parameter, @xmlDoc) then a <ROOT> element is generated by this code:

```
IF '<ROOT>' != LEFT(LTRIM(@xmlDoc), 6)
    SELECT @xmlDocInternal = '<ROOT>'+@xmlDoc+'</ROOT>'
ELSE
    SELECT @xmlDocInternal = @xmlDoc
```

Before an XML document can be processed with OPENXML it must be parsed and made ready for consumption by SQL. OPENXML is discussed in detail in Chapter 4. The process of parsing an XML document and making it ready for consumption is handled using SQL Server's sp_xml_preparedocument stored procedure. This stored procedure returns a handle to the processed document that must later be freed using SQL Server's sp_xml_removedocument stored procedure call. The parsing of the XML document is performed in InsertShippers as follows:

```
EXECUTE sp_xml_preparedocument @xmlDocIndex OUTPUT, @xmlDocInternal
```

The document handle opened by sp_xml_removedocument is passed into OPENXML for processing. OPENXML opens a rowset using the parsed XML document. This rowset is then inserted into the Shippers table. The SQL handling this task is as follows:

```
INSERT Shippers
SELECT CompanyName, Phone
FROM OPENXML(@xmlDocIndex, N'/ROOT/SHIPPERS',1)
WITH Shippers
```

Only the CompanyName and Phone columns of the Shippers table are selected for insertion. The primary key for the Shippers table, ShipperID is not selected. This is because ShipperID is an IDENTITY column and therefore SQL Server generates a unique ID each time a row is inserted. The parameters passed to OPENXML can be broken down as follows:

- *document* – document handle (@xmlDocIndex) returned by a call to sp_xml_preparedocument.
- *rowpattern* – identifies the nodes to be processes as rows. This pattern (N'/ROOT/SHIPPERS') is why this stored procedure ensures that the XML document is contained in a root element, <ROOT>.

- *flags* – a 1 (the flag used above) indicates that the data resides in XML attributes. A 2 indicates that the data resides in XML elements. An 8 causes unconsumed SQL to be copied to an overflow location. Chapter 3 presents an example of how to retrieve such overflow data.
- WITH [*schema declaration* | *tablename*] – this parameter is used by InsertShippers to specify the Shippers table.

Once processing of the XML document has been completed, the document must be released using sp_xml_removedocument. It is actually the handle that is released. This is the same handle initially returned by sp_xml_preparedocument. The releasing of the XML document handle is performed in InsertShippers as follows:

```
EXECUTE sp_xml_removedocument @xmlDocIndex
```

InsertShippers is ultimately called by the Shipper object's Insert method. We have already demonstrated how to call a SQL Server stored procedure call from ADO using C++ so the code associated with Insert is not particularly enlightening.

A Visual C++ 6.0 console application, TheLegacyBusTest, demonstrates using the Shipper object's IShipper interface to Get, Delete, and Insert data. The form that the data takes can be seen by examining the contents of BSTR, bstrDataWrite (see example below from source file, TheLegacyBusTest.cpp):

```
HRESULT TestShipper(bool bAttachRoot)
{
    HRESULT hr = S_OK;
    CComPtr<IShipper> spIShipper;
    CComBSTR bstrData;
    CComBSTR bstrCustomerIDPrefix = L"ZZ";
    // ShipperID is autogenerated so it can be left as zero
    CComBSTR bstrDataWrite;

    if (bAttachRoot)
    {
        bstrDataWrite = L"<ROOT>";
    }

    bstrDataWrite +=
        L"<SHIPPERS ShipperID=\"0\" CompanyName=\"ZZSpeedy Express\" "
            L"Phone=\"(503) 555-9831\"/>"
        L"<SHIPPERS ShipperID=\"0\" CompanyName=\"ZZUnited Package\" "
            L"Phone=\"(503) 555-3199\"/>"
        L"<SHIPPERS ShipperID=\"0\" CompanyName=\"ZZFederal Shipping\" "
            L"Phone=\"(503) 555-9931\"/>";
    if (bAttachRoot)
    {
        bstrDataWrite += L"</ROOT>";
    }

    HR(spIShipper.CoCreateInstance(__uuidof(Shipper)));
    HR(spIShipper->Insert(bstrDataWrite));
    bstrData.Empty();
    HR(spIShipper->Get(&bstrData));
    bstrData.Empty();
```

```
        HR(spIShipper->Delete(bstrCustomerIDPrefix));
        HR(spIShipper->Get(&bstrData));
        bstrData.Empty();

        spIShipper = 0;

        return hr;
    }
```

Mixing Legacy COM Objects with .NET

This section presents how to access COM objects from any .NET language. Before we get started, recall that the .NET version of our application will use the legacy COM objects found in ADO. ADO is an extremely rich suite of COM objects. There are certain intricacies to be examined when using the legacy COM objects from a .NET application. To simplify moving to .NET we are going to migrate the business tier in two phases:

- Phase 1 – develop a C# client that calls the legacy business tier (`TheLegacyBusTier`'s `Customer`, `Order`, and `Shipper` COM objects). The actually C# client demonstrated is a test application. This approach is adopted because the interfaces exposed by the COM objects, `Customer`, `Order` and `Shipper`, are much simpler than the interfaces exposed by ADO.
- Phase 2 – migrate `TheLegacyBusTier` (COM, C++, and ADO) to `TheBusTierDotNet` (ADO, C#, and a C# class library). This migration will include the C# code accessing the legacy COM objects found in ADO.

Phase 1 – Business Tier Migration

For reasons of performance we used early binding in order to access ADO. The .NET Framework provides a utility (`TlbImp.exe`) that allows .NET applications to access legacy COM objects using early binding. This is achieved by using the COM server's type library (an unmanaged type library) in order to generate a proxy .NET assembly (.NET metadata). It is this "proxy .NET assembly" that allows .NET clients to access legacy COM objects. A diagram of how this legacy access is achieved is as follows:

`TlbImp` takes a type library as an input and by default generates a proxy .NET assembly (a type of DLL that acts as a managed wrapper and can be called by a managed language). The name of this proxy .NET assembly can be specified using `TlbImp`'s parameter, `/out`. For our Phase 1 migration, the proxy .NET assembly will be named `TheLegacyBusTierPhase1.dll`. We execute `TlbImp` from the command-line as follows:

```
D:\wrox\TheLegacyBusTier>tlbimp TheLegacyBusTier.tlb
/out:TheLegacyBusTierPhase1.dll
```

```
TlbImp - TypeLib to .NET Assembly Converter Version 1.0.2204.21
Copyright (C) Microsoft Corp. 2000.  All rights reserved.
Typelib imported successfully to TheLegacyBusTierPhase1.dll
```

.NET developers are used to XCOPY deployment (all assemblies are copied into a location as part of installation). Legacy COM DLL cannot just be copies. Even under .NET, COM servers must be registered. The DLL generated, `TheLegacyBusTierPhase1.dll`, uses conventional means in order to call the objects specified in `TheLegacyBusTier.tlb`. If the Debug version of business tier is built and registered, this version of the legacy COM server is loaded. Visual Studio.NET will not be able to actually debug this code. If the Release version of the business tier is built and registered, then this version is loaded whenever legacy COM objects are accessed.

> **If, for any reason, the type library is modified (for example, say the version of ADO changes or a new flag is added to an integer parameter), the `TlbImp` utility must be run again in order to generate a new proxy .NET assembly. Unless `TlbImp` is run again, the previously generated proxy .NET assembly will be unaware of the changes to the type library. This is not a violation of the immutability of COM objects and their interfaces. It is perfectly legal to add a new COM object to a type library (for example, ADO adding a `Stream` object) or to add a new enumeration value.**

In order to test the viability of accessing legacy COM objects from C#, a C# console application will be developed. This console application, `TheBusTierTestPhase1`, is created using Visual Studio.NET. In order for this application to access the legacy business tier, we need to access the Project | Add Reference menu option in Visual Studio.NET. The following dialog will be displayed:

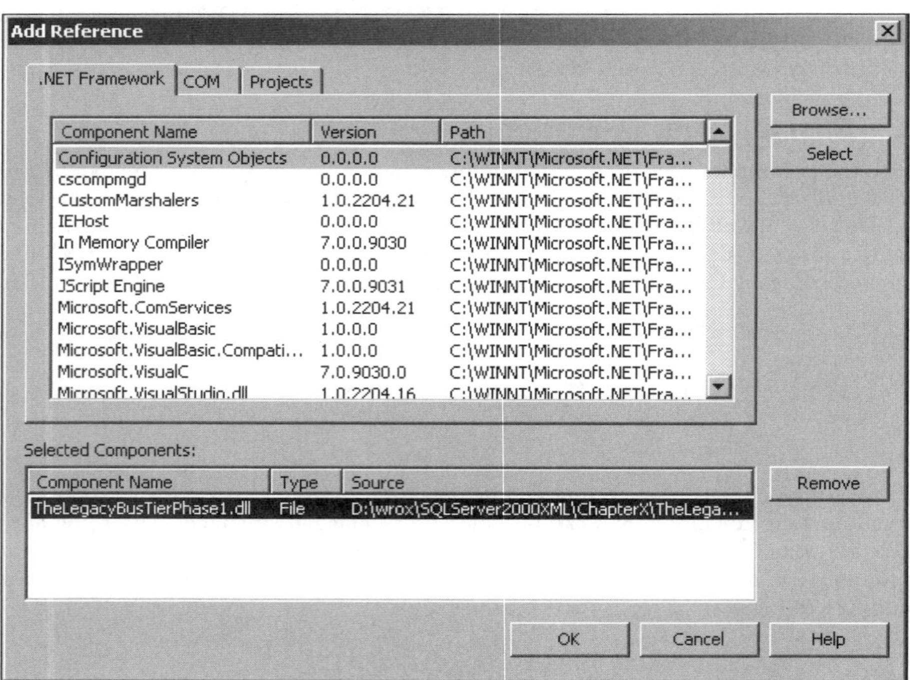

Using the Browse button and the dialog it displays, we navigate to the location of the proxy .NET assembly, `TheLegacyBusTierPhase1.dll`. Once this DLL is selected, Visual Studio.NET's Solution Explorer window will contain a reference to `TheLegacyBusTierPhase1` (shown in the following dialog under, References):

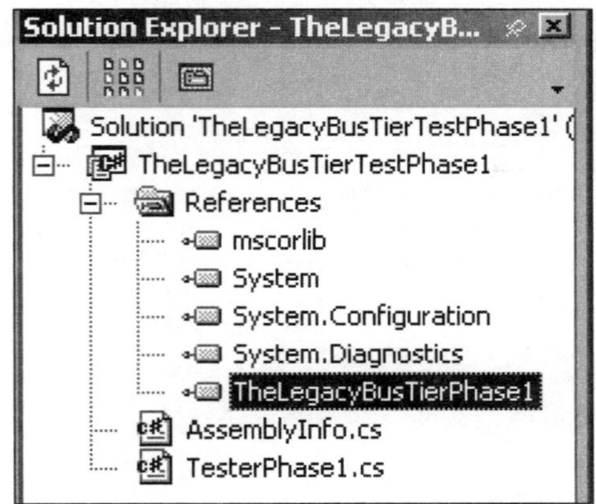

In .NET, every assembly is wrapped in a namespace. The IDL file used to create the COM server, `TheLegacyBusTier` (`TheLegacyBusTier.idl`), specifies a namespace of `THELEGACYBUSTIER` by using the IDL `library` attribute. In order to more easily access the contents of this namespace, the following line of code is added to our C# source file, `Class1.cs`:

```
using THELEGACYBUSTIER;
```

The `Main` method of class, `TheBusTierTestPhase1`, fully tests each legacy COM object:

```
public static int Main(string[] args)
{
    try
    {
        Customer customer = new Customer();
        string strCustomers = "";
        string strNamePrefix = "L";

        strCustomers = customer.Get();
        customer.NamePrefix = strNamePrefix;
        strCustomers = customer.Get();

        string strOrders = "";
        string strCustomerIDPrefix = "LET";
        Order order= new Order(); // New Order is a great band

        strOrders = order.Get();
        order.CustomerIDPrefix = strCustomerIDPrefix;
        strOrders = "";
        strOrders = order.Get();
        Console.WriteLine(strOrders);

        Shipper shipper = new Shipper();
        string shipDataOut = "";
        string strShipDataIn =
          "<SHIPPERS ShipperID=\"0\" CompanyName=\"ZZSpeedy Express\" "+
            "Phone=\"(503) 555-9831\"/>"+
          "<SHIPPERS ShipperID=\"0\" CompanyName=\"ZZUnited Package\" "+
            "Phone=\"(503) 555-3199\"/>"+
          "<SHIPPERS ShipperID=\"0\" CompanyName=\"ZZFederal Shipping\" "+
            "Phone=\"(503) 555-9931\"/>";
```

```
            shipper.Insert(strShipDataIn);
            shipDataOut = shipper.Get();
            shipper.Delete("ZZ");
        }

        catch(System.Runtime.InteropServices.COMException comException)
        {
            Console.WriteLine(comException.ToString());
        }

        catch(System.Exception exception)
        {
            Console.WriteLine(exception.ToString());
        }

        return 0;
    }
```

From a programming perspective using a simple legacy COM object in a C# application is fairly simple. That's right, the words "programming" and "simple" in the same sentence!

Within the `Main` method we made a point of catching exceptions from the `System.Runtime.InteropServices` namespace of type, `COMException`. This type of exception is thrown if the COM objects we are interoperating with return an error value. Each time a proxy .NET assembly is used to access a legacy COM object, this exception will have to be handled.

There is one minor caveat with respect to the previous example code that is worth mentioning, namely that C# parameter types (`in`, `ref`, and `out`) do not directly map to their legacy IDL counterparts, `in` and `out`). Recall that in IDL each `Get` method was specified as containing an `out` and `retval` attribute. For example, `IShipper`'s `Get` method is defined as:

```
    [id(2), helpstring("method Get")]
        HRESULT Get([retval, out] BSTR *pbstrShippers);
```

In the test application, `TheBusTierTestPhase1`, the `IShipper Get` method is called as follows:

```
    strOrders = order.Get();
```

Consider the case where `IShipper`'s `Get` method does not specify attribute `retval` with respect to its lone parameter. An example of how `TheLegacyBusTier.idl` would be changed is as follows:

```
    [id(2), helpstring("method Get")]
        HRESULT Get([out] BSTR *pbstrShippers);
```

When the test application, `TheBusTierTestPhase1`, called `IShipper Get` method the code would take the following form:

```
    shipper.Get(ref shipDataOut);
```

C# defines three types of parameters to methods:

- default – a parameter with no qualifier is considered to be an input-only parameter
- `ref` – a `ref` parameter must be initialized by the caller and can be changed by the method to which this parameter is passed
- `out` – an `out` parameter does not need to be set by the caller and can be set by the method called

Why the C# review? Because we specified the `out` attribute in IDL! This tells any marshaling supported by IDL generated type library or IDL generated proxy/stub that this parameter needs only be marshaled in one direction, out. Our C# code had to initialize each `string` passed to `Get` (`Order`, `Customer`, or `Shipper`) and had to pass each `string` as type `ref`. Specifying `out` in C# results in a compilation error.

This is just a friendly heads-up as to the issues you will encounter during migration. ASP developers recognize why the `retval` attribute was specified. This is how scripting retrieves `out` parameters, specifically an `out` parameter per property or method.

Phase 2 – Business Tier Migration

The first phase of migrating our application's business tier was more of a "proof of concept" than an actual migration. The second phase of business tier migration requires that the in-process COM server written in C++ be rewritten as a C# class library. Turning to Visual Studio.NET we create a new Class Library type Visual C# Project. The class library is called `TheBusTierDotNet`, and uses the `TheBusTierDotNet` namespace. The following screenshot demonstrates using Visual Studio.NET to set up a class library:

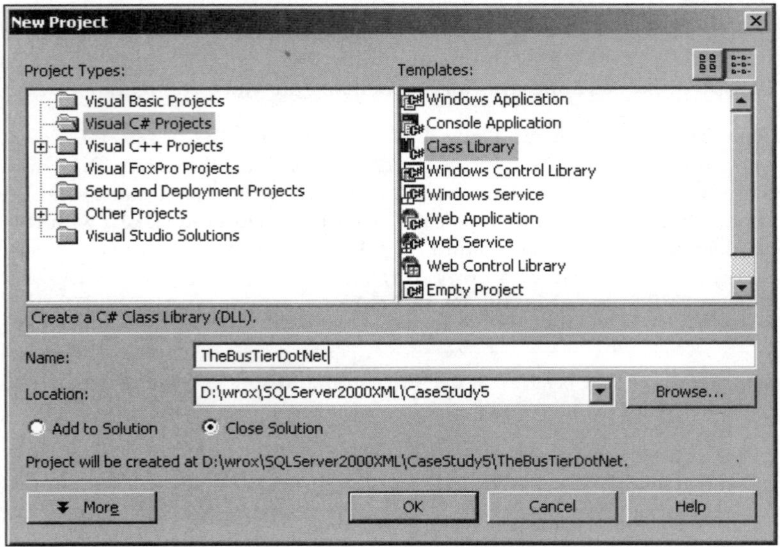

The trick now is to allow the `TheBusTierDotNet` class library to access the ADO COM objects. `TlbImp` could again be called from the command-line in order to generate a proxy .NET assembly that can access ADO. Once again, we will add a reference to our project:

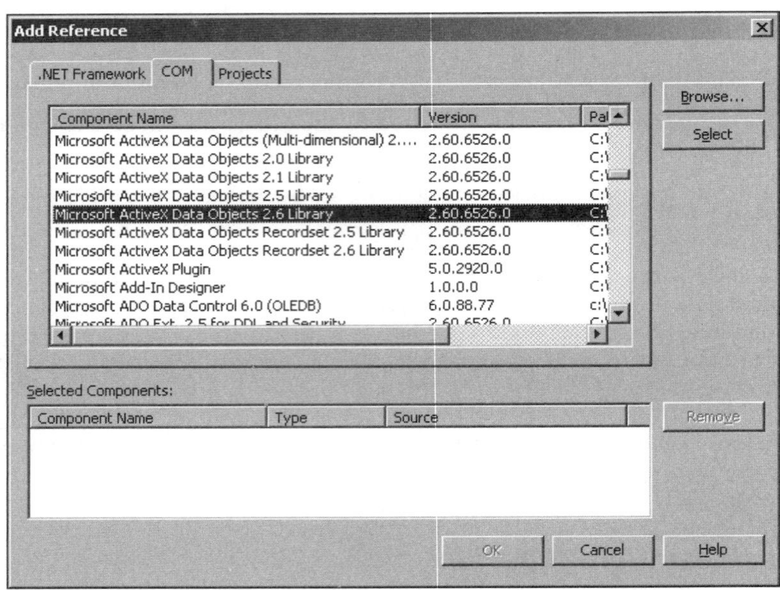

There is one crucial piece of information that you cannot see in the above dialog, namely the path associated with Microsoft ActiveX Data Objects 2.6 Library. This path specifies the DLL that contains this version of ADO. The DLL is actually `msado15.dll`. This DLL always contains the latest version of ADO. Don't let the version number 15 fool you!

Notice in the Add Reference dialog that the COM tag is selected and the legacy COM object, Microsoft ActiveX Data Objects 2.6 Library is highlighted. By selecting this library we are running `TlbImp` from Visual Studio.NET. The name of the proxy .NET assembly generated is the same as the namespace used by ADO, `ADODB.dll`. This DLL is created in the `TheBusTierDotNet\bin\debug` or `TheBusTierDotNet\bin\release` directory, depending on which configuration is built (debug or release).

If we had not specified a name during Phase 1 of the migration, the proxy .NET assembly generated would have been called `THELEGACYBUSTIER.dll`. That's right, the proxy .NET assembly for the legacy in-process COM server, `TheLegacyBusTier.dll`, would have been a DLL with the same name. This happens because file names are case insensitive. Different DLLs with the same name are bad, dangerous, risky and, in general, unkind. The DLLs associated with each version of ADO are not called `ADODB.dll`, so Phase 2 can in no way overwrite the legacy in-process COM server (original DLL) with the proxy .NET assembly (the proxy DLL).

The lesson then, is that it is safer to use the command-line version of `TlbImp.exe`.

There is one major benefit experienced when calling `TlbImp` from Visual Studio.NET's IDE. Recall that the proxy .NET assembly generated is stored in a directory that could be considered transient in nature, `.\bin\debug` or `.\bin\release`. The contents of this type of directory are typically not stored under source code control. The Visual Studio project that called `TlbImp` to generate the reference to a legacy COM server recognizes the transient nature of its own build directories (`.\bin\debug` or `.\bin\release`). For this reason, `TlbImp` is run as part of the build process. If the proxy .NET assembly is deleted, it will be rebuilt. This includes updating the proxy .NET assembly to reflect changes in the original type library.

Now that we have a reference to ADODB.dll, we will simplify things but specifying C#'s using keyword with respect to ADO's namespace, ADODB. The line of code is added to each source file that uses ADO as follows:

```
using ADODB;
```

Our legacy COM object (Order) exposed an interface called IOrder. In Visual Studio.NET, select Project | Add Class..., this dialog will be displayed:

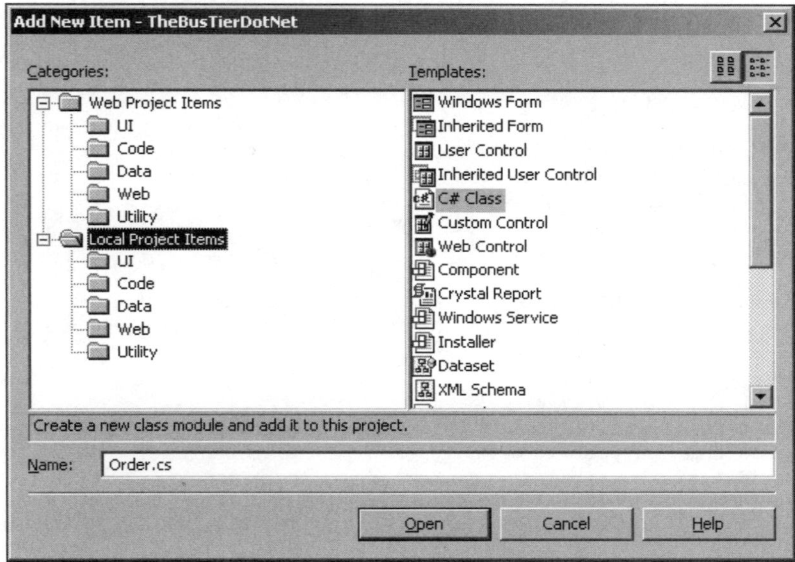

Select Local Project Items and C# class from the dialog. The name of the new class is Order.cs. Once the Open button is clicked, we can repeat this process for new classes named Customer.cs and Shipper.cs.

The legacy IOrder interface contained a read/write property, CustomerIDPrefix. The source file Order.cs is updated to included a C# property of the same name:

```
public string CustomerIDPrefix
{
    get
    {
        return strCustomerIDPrefix;
    }
    set
    {
        strCustomerIDPrefix = value;
    }
}
```

In C#, the get keyword is analogous to the propget IDL attribute found in the legacy IDL file, TheLegacyBusTier.idl and the set keyword is analogous to the propput IDL attribute used in TheLegacyBusTier.idl.

What remains is to translate the C++ Get method (approximately seventy lines of C++ code) found in the C++ header file, Order.h, to C# in Order.cs. We've mentioned the number of lines of code here for a reason. A savvy COM developer recognizes that seventy lines of C++ ADO development should result in significantly fewer lines of VB code. In order for C# to appeal to C++ developers it must look, taste, and smell like C++. At the same time, it should be easier to code in C# than in C++. Fewer lines of code is a reasonable metric for measuring how much simpler a language is to use. Please, do not at this stage mention Perl, APL, or some such incredibly terse language. We are comparing C++ to C#, and indirectly to VB.

The C# implementation of the Order.Get method is as follows (the source file is order.cs):

```
public void Get(out string strOrders)
{
    string strConn;
    Connection connection = new Connection();
    Command command = new Command();
    Stream streamOut = new Stream();
    Object emptyObject1 = new Object();
    Object emptyObject2 = new Object();

    strConn = "PROVIDER=SQLOLEDB;DATA SOURCE=localhost;" +
              "DATABASE=NorthWind;USER ID=sa;PASSWORD=sa;";
    connection.Open(strConn,
                    null,
                    null,
                    (int)ConnectOptionEnum.adConnectUnspecified);
    command.CommandType = CommandTypeEnum.adCmdStoredProc;
    command.ActiveConnection = connection;
    command.CommandText = "GetCustomersAuto";
    command.Parameters["@customerID"].Value = CustomerIDPrefix;
    streamOut.Open(System.Reflection.Missing.Value,
                   ConnectModeEnum.adModeUnknown,
                   StreamOpenOptionsEnum.adOpenStreamUnspecified,
                   "",
                   "");
    command.Properties["Output Stream"].Value = streamOut;
    command.Execute(ref emptyObject1,
                    ref emptyObject2,
                    (int)ExecuteOptionEnum.adExecuteStream);
    strOrders = streamOut.ReadText(streamOut.Size);

    connection.Close();
}
```

The C# implementation of the Order.Get method takes about thirty lines of code to implement. Recall that in C++ this took seventy lines of code. Some of the code savings can be attributed to lines of code such as:

```
command.Parameters["@customerID"].Value = CustomerIDPrefix;
```

This single line of code calls the Command object's Parameters property, the Parameters collection's get_Item method, and the Parameter object's Value property. An error in any of these calls results in an exception being raised. When only return codes are being examined (as in our C++ implementation) each COM method or property takes a single line of code.

A nice feature of C# is available when using legacy COM objects, namely that each enumeration value must be qualified. A C# enumeration value is specified as follows: EnumType.EnumValue. This "type then value" qualification prevents name conflicts between enumeration values within the same namespace. This feature of C# is demonstrated when methods such as Connection.Open are called using parameter such as ConnectOptionEnum.adConnectUnspecified (see the fourth parameter). This value of the fourth parameter of the Open method just indicates that there are no special options specified with opening the connection.

Legacy Client Tier

The client tier of our legacy project is composed of Active Server Pages. For the .NET version of the project, ASP.NET will be used. The legacy client tier is implemented as a Visual Interdev 6.0 project, TheLegacyClient. The project contains a variety of ASP files but of particular interest because of how they display XML documents are:

- ShipperList.asp – legacy Shipper object's XML displayed as a list
- CustomerTable.asp – legacy Customer object's XML displayed as a table
- OrderRecordset.asp – legacy Order object's XML displayed using a client-side ADO recordset

There are two other ASP files worth mentioning. One of these is CovertForPerformance.asp. This file contains a FOR XML query (a template query) that is executed using ADO Connection, Command, and Stream objects. At the beginning of this chapter there was a discussion as to the performance associated with using ADO, with late binding in conjunction with executing a FOR XML query. The name of this ASP file, CovertForPerformance, states what should take place to improve performance, namely the FOR XML query should be removed and a stored procedure should be executed instead.

The other ASP file of interest is AStoredProcDemo.asp. This second ASP file is what CovertForPerformance.asp should be converted into in order to improve performance. This file also demonstrates the FOR XML EXPLICT query that should be converted to FOR XML AUTO for reasons of performance. Both of these ASP files call ADO using server-side scripting (VBScript). In reality, both of these ASP files should call the business tier directly instead of going straight to the database.

Both of these ASP files use ADO objects. In support of this both ASP files include file, adovbs.inc. This file contains all the information necessary for an active server page to call ADO using server-side scripting.

Legacy Client Tier, Customer

The legacy ASP file CustomerTable.asp displays the XML generated for the Customer object. This XML is generated using FOR XML AUTO as part of the GetCustomersAuto stored procedure. This stored procedure is not called directly by the Active Server Page but is instead called indirectly by using the business tier's Customer object and its Get method. The XML is displayed in table form. Demonstrating this, CustomerTable.asp is as follows:

```
<%@ Language=VBScript %>

<HTML>

<HEAD>
```

```
<%
    Set customer = Server.CreateObject("TheLegacyBusTier.Customer")
    Dim strCustomer

    strCustomer = customer.Get
    Response.Write "<XML ID='CustomersDataIsland'>"
    Response.Write strCustomer
    Set customer = Nothing
    Response.Write "</XML>"
%>

<META NAME="GENERATOR" Content="Microsoft Visual Studio 6.0">
</HEAD>

<BODY>

<TABLE DATASRC="#CustomersDataIsland" BORDER=1>
  <TR><TH>Customer ID</TH>
         <TH>Company Name</TH>
         <TH>Contact Name</TH></TR>
  <TR>
    <TD><SPAN DATAFLD="CustomerID"></SPAN></TD>
    <TD><SPAN DATAFLD="CompanyName"></SPAN></TD>
    <TD><SPAN DATAFLD="ContactName"></SPAN></TD>
  </TR>
</TABLE>

</BODY>
</HTML>
```

The server-side scripting portion of the Active Server Page implemented by `CustomerTable.asp` performs the following tasks:

- Create a COM object of type, `Customer`:

```
Set customer = Server.CreateObject("TheLegacyBusTier.Customer")
```

- The data island created with the HTML page is set to ID, `CustomersDataIsland`:

```
Response.Write "<XML ID='CustomersDataIsland'>"
```

  It would be cleaner to let the business object generate the containing tag. We'll defer this enhancement until the next release of the product.

- Retrieve the XML associated with the customers:

```
strCustomer = customer.Get
```

- Write this XML directly to the ASP `Response` object:

```
Response.Write strCustomer
```

The HTML generated by CustomerTable.asp performs the following task:

- The XML data island created is associated with a table:

```
<TABLE DATASRC="#CustomersDataIsland" BORDER=1>
```

- The elements of the XML data island are displayed as rows of the table, for example:

```
<TD><SPAN DATAFLD="CustomerID"></SPAN></TD>
```

A portion of the XML generated by the Active Server Page, CustomerTable.asp, is as follows:

```
<Customers>
        <CustomerID>ALFKI</CustomerID>
        <CompanyName>Alfreds Futterkiste</CompanyName>
        <ContactName>Maria Anders</ContactName>
</Customers>
<Customers>
        <CustomerID>ANATR</CustomerID>
        <CompanyName>Ana Trujillo Emparedados y helados</CompanyName>
        <ContactName>Ana Trujillo</ContactName>
</Customers>
```

The following is an example of the page displayed by CustomerTable.asp:

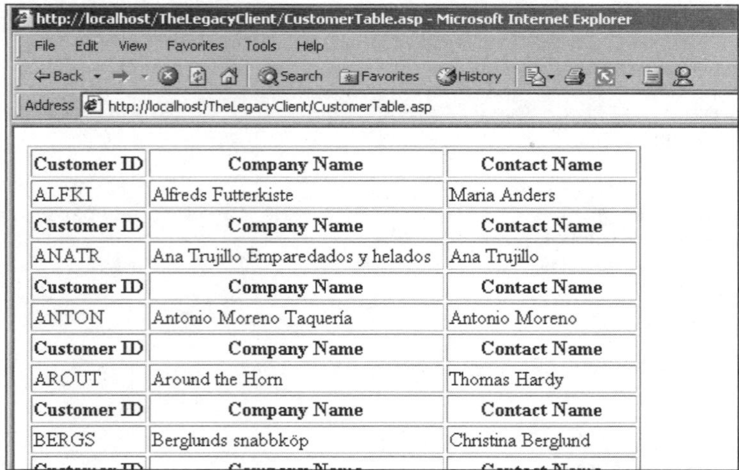

Legacy Client Tier, Shippers

The legacy ASP file ShipperList.asp displays the XML generated for the Shippers object. This XML is generated using FOR XML RAW as part of the GetShippersRaw stored procedure. This stored procedure is not called directly by the Active Server Page but is instead called indirectly by using the business tier's Shipper object's Get method. The XML is displayed in list form (client-side script to generate HTML). Demonstrating this, ShipperList.asp is as follows:

```
<%@ Language=VBScript %>

<HTML>

<SCRIPT language="VBScript" For="window" Event="onload">

   Dim xmlDocument
   Dim rootNode, childNode
   Dim xmlData

   Set xmlDocument = ShippersDataIsland.xmlDocument
   xmlDocument.resolveExternals=false
   xmlDocument.async=false

   Set rootNode = xmlDocument.documentElement
   For each childNode in rootNode.childNodes
      xmlData = document.all("MyDataList").innerHTML
      document.all("MyDataList").innerHTML = _
          xmlData & _
          "<LI>" & _
          childNode.getAttribute("ShipperID") & _
          ", " & _
          childNode.getAttribute("CompanyName") & _
          ", " & _
          childNode.getAttribute("Phone") & _
          "</LI>"
   Next

</SCRIPT>

<HEAD>
<%
    Set shipper = Server.CreateObject("TheLegacyBusTier.Shipper")
    Dim strShipper

    strShipper = shipper.Get
    Response.Write "<?xml version="1.0" ?><XML ID='ShippersDataIsland'>"
    Response.Write strShipper
    Set shipper = Nothing
    Response.Write "</XML>"
%>

<META NAME="GENERATOR" Content="Microsoft Visual Studio 6.0">
</HEAD>
<BODY>

<UL id=MyDataList></UL>

</BODY>
</HTML>
```

The server-side scripting portion of the Active Server Page implemented by `ShipperList.asp` performs the following tasks:

- Create a COM object of type, `Customer`:

```
Set shipper = Server.CreateObject("TheLegacyBusTier.Shipper")
```

- The data island created with the HTML page is set to ID, `ShippersDataIsland`:

```
Response.Write "<?xml version="1.0" ?><XML ID='ShippersDataIsland'>"
```

- Write this XML directly to the ASP `Response` object:

```
Response.Write strShipper
```

When the HTML page is loaded, client-side script is executed:

```
<SCRIPT language="VBScript" For="window" Event="onload">
```

This script performs the following steps:

- Retrieves the data island in an XML document:

```
Set xmlDocument = ShippersDataIsland.xmlDocument
```

- Retrieves the data associated with the root node, `<ROOT>`:

```
Set rootNode = xmlDocument.documentElement
```

- Traverses each child element, `<Row>`, within the document:

```
For each childNode in rootNode.childNodes
```

- For each child element, the attributes are associated with the document being displayed (the list). This document is named, `MyDataList` and an example of attribute retrieval is as follows: `childNode.getAttribute("ShipperID")`.

The HTML generated by `ShipperList.asp` simply relies on the client-side script to generate the list displayed. The key line of HTML, `<UL id=MyDataList></UL>`, specifies that ID associated with the list created by the client-side script. The XML generated by `ShipperList.asp` is as follows:

```
<ROOT>
    <row ShipperID="1" CompanyName="Speedy Express" Phone="(503) 555-9831"/>
    <row ShipperID="2" CompanyName="United Package" Phone="(503) 555-3199"/>
    <row ShipperID="3" CompanyName="Federal Shipping" Phone="(503) 555-9931"/>
</ROOT>
```

The following is an example of the page displayed by `ShipperList.asp`:

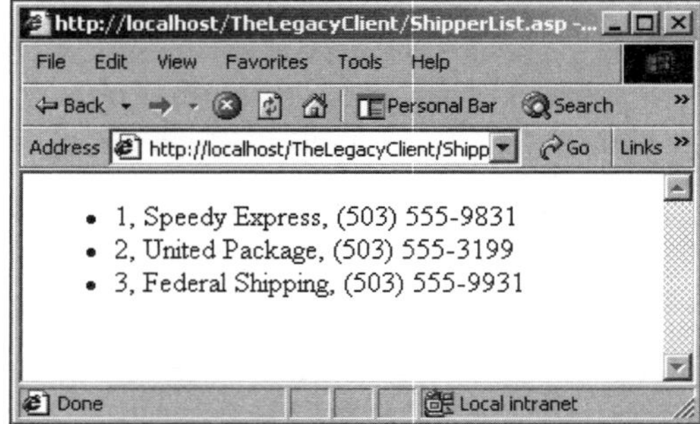

Legacy Client Tier, Order

The legacy ASP file `OrderRecordset.asp` displays the XML generated for the `Order` object. This XML is generated using `FOR XML AUTO` as part of the `GetOrdersAuto` stored procedure. This stored procedure is not called directly by the Active Server Page but is instead called indirectly by using the `Get` method of the business tier's `Order` object. The XML is using a client-side ADO recordset. The contents of `OrderRecordset.asp` are as follows:

```
<%@ Language=VBScript %>

<HTML>

<HEAD>
<%
    Dim order
    Dim strOrder

    Set order = Server.CreateObject("TheLegacyBusTier.Order")
    strOrder = order.Get
    Response.Write "<?xml version="1.0" ?><XML ID=OrdersDataIsland>"
    Response.Write strOrder
    Set order = Nothing
    Response.Write "</XML>"
%>

<META NAME="GENERATOR" Content="Microsoft Visual Studio 6.0">
</HEAD>
<BODY>

<P>Order ID:
  <SPAN DATASRC="#OrdersDataIsland" DATAFLD="OrderID"></SPAN></P>
<P>Customer ID:
  <SPAN DATASRC="#OrdersDataIsland" DATAFLD="CustomerID"></SPAN></P>
<P>Employee ID:
  <SPAN DATASRC="#OrdersDataIsland" DATAFLD="EmployeeID"></SPAN></P>

<INPUT TYPE=BUTTON
      VALUE="Previous OrderID"
      onclick="OrdersDataIsland.recordset.movePrevious()">
<INPUT TYPE=BUTTON
      VALUE="Next OrderID"
      onclick="OrdersDataIsland.recordset.moveNext()">

</BODY>
</HTML>
```

The server-side scripting portion of the active server page implemented by `OrderRecordset.asp` performs basically the same tasks as the server-side scripting for `ShipperList.asp` and `CustomerTable.asp`. The XML data island created by `OrderRecordset.asp` is named `OrdersDataIsland`.

The HTML generated by `OrderRecordset.asp` creates two buttons (Previous OrderID and Next OrderID) that traverse the recordset associated with the XML data island, `OrdersDataIsland`. Recall that the Previous OrderID button was created as follows:

```
<INPUT TYPE=BUTTON
       VALUE="Previous OrderID"
       onclick="OrdersDataIsland.recordset.movePrevious()">
```

The attributes associated with each individual `Orders` element are displayed. Each attribute is displayed based on the current element within the data island, `OrdersDataIsland`. For example, the `OrderID` attribute is displayed as follows:

```
<P>Order ID:
  <SPAN DATASRC="#OrdersDataIsland" DATAFLD="OrderID"></SPAN></P>
```

A portion of the XML generated by `OrderRecordset.asp` is as follows:

```
<ROOT>
    <Orders OrderID="10248" CustomerID="VINET" EmployeeID="5"/>
    <Orders OrderID="10249" CustomerID="TOMSP" EmployeeID="6"/>
    <Orders OrderID="10250" CustomerID="HANAR" EmployeeID="4"/>
    <Orders OrderID="10251" CustomerID="VICTE" EmployeeID="3"/>
    ...
</ROOT>
```

The following is an example of the page displayed by `OrderRecordset.asp`:

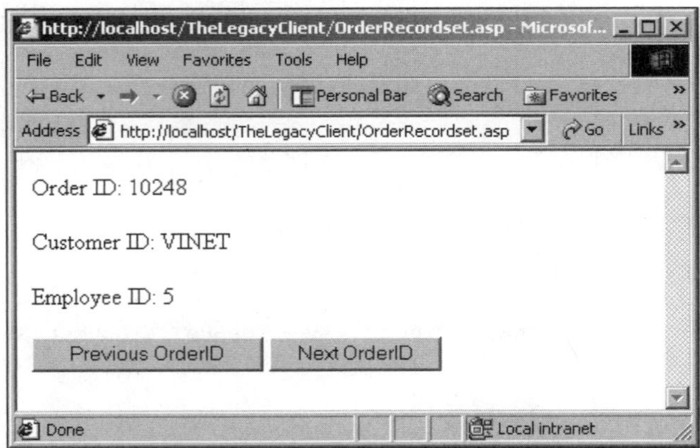

Each time Next OrderID is clicked on, the next `Orders` element becomes the current offset within the recordset. The attributes of this current element (`OrderID`, `CustomerID`, and `EmployeeID`) are then displayed. When the Previous OrderID button is clicked on, the previous `Orders` element becomes the current offset within the recordset. The attributes of this current element are then displayed.

.NET Client Tier

The intent of the .NET version of our client tier was not to utilize every snazzy, whiz-bang feature of ASP.NET. A simple mapping was attempted between each ASP file and its ASP.NET counterpart. The .NET client tier can be found in ASP.NET project, `ClientDotNet`. The ASP.NET files of interest in this project are:

- `ShipperList.aspx` – displays the .NET version of `Shipper` object's XML as a list. This ASP.NET file is the counterpart of the ASP file called `ShipperList.asp`.
- `CustomerTable.aspx` – displays the .NET version of `Customer` object's XML as a table. `OrderRecordset.asp`'s legacy counterpart is `CustomerTable.asp`.
- `OrderRecordset.aspx` – displays the .NET version of `Order` object's XML using a client-side recordset. It should be no surprise that `OrderRecordset.aspx` is a first cousin of `OrderRecordset.asp`.

When the .NET client tier project was created it did not initially reference the business tier, `TheBusTierDotNet`. This should not come as a surprise since Visual Studio.NET is a fantastic tool but it is certainly not psychic. The business tier, `TheBusTierDotNet`, needed to be referenced from the Version 3 client using Visual Studio.NET's **Project** menu.

It is important to note that no screen shots are provided of the .NET client tier. The reason for this is because the appearance of the GUI did not change between the ASP version (Visual Interdev 6.0) and the ASP.NET version (Visual Studio.NET). The same HTML and client-side scripting is used in both versions. The server-side was the only piece upgraded (ASP to ASP.NET).

.NET Client Tier, Shippers

The ASP.NET file, `ShippersList.aspx`, displays the XML generated for the .NET `Shippers` object. The fact that `ShippersList.aspx` is a clone of legacy ASP file, `ShippersList.asp`, is demonstrated by examining the contents of `ShippersList.aspx`. The contents of `ShippersList.aspx` are as follows:

```
<%@ Page language="c#" Description="ShipperList" %>
<%@ Import Namespace="TheBusTierDotNet" %>

<HTML>

<SCRIPT language="C#" runat=server ID=Script1>

void Page_Load(Object sender, EventArgs EvArgs) {

    TheBusTierDotNet.Shipper shipper = new TheBusTierDotNet.Shipper();
    string strShipper;

    shipper.Get(out strShipper);
    Response.Write("<?xml version='1.0' ?><XML ID='ShippersDataIsland'>");
    Response.Write(strShipper);
    Response.Write("</XML>");
}
</SCRIPT>
```

```
<SCRIPT language="VBScript" For="window" Event="onload">

   Dim xmlDocument
   Dim rootNode, childNode
   dim xmlData

   Set xmlDocument = ShippersDataIsland.xmlDocument
   xmlDocument.resolveExternals=false
   xmlDocument.async=false

   Set rootNode = xmlDocument.documentElement
   For each childNode in rootNode.childNodes
      xmlData = document.all("MyDataList").innerHTML
      document.all("MyDataList").innerHTML = _
          xmlData & _
          "<LI>" & _
          childNode.getAttribute("ShipperID") & _
          ", " & _
          childNode.getAttribute("CompanyName") & _
          ", " & _
          childNode.getAttribute("Phone") & _
          "</LI>"
   Next

</SCRIPT>

<BODY>
   <span id="Message" runat=server/>
</BODY>

<UL id=MyDataList></UL>

</HTML>
```

The start of this file indicates the language used by the server-side scripts (C#):

```
<%@ Page language="c#" Description="ShipperList" %>
```

The namespace of Version 3's business tier was referenced by the second line of `ShippersList.aspx`:

```
<%@ Import Namespace="TheBusTierDotNet" %>
```

When an ASP.NET page is loaded, the `Page_Load` event is fired. Correspondingly, the `Page_Unload` event is fired when a page is unloaded. `ShippersList.aspx` contains a C# handler for the `Page_Load` event. This server-side code (notice we didn't say "server side scripting") is implemented as follows:

```
 void Page_Load(Object sender, EventArgs EvArgs) {

//**Set shipper = Server.CreateObject("TheLegacyBusTier.Shipper")
    TheBusTierDotNet.Shipper shipper =
         new TheBusTierDotNet.Shipper();
//**Dim strShipper
    string strShipper;
```

```
//**strShipper = shipper.Get
    shipper.Get(out strShipper);
//**Response.Write " <?xml version='1.0' ?><XML ID='ShippersDataIsland'>"
    Response.Write("<?xml version='1.0' ?><XML ID='ShippersDataIsland'>");
//**Response.Write strShipper
    Response.Write(strShipper);
//**Response.Write "</XML>"
    Response.Write("</XML>");
}
```

Did we mention that this is compiled code and not scripting?

The C# code that handles the `Page_Load` event is shown above. The C# code is interlaced with the VBScript code from the legacy Active Server Page, `ShipperList.asp`. The VBScript code is delineated by C#-style comments. Clearly migration from ASP to ASP.NET was not particularly taxing for our crack team of developers. The remainder of ASP.NET file, `ShipperList.aspx`, is identical to the corresponding region of ASP file, `ShipperList.asp`.

A VB.NET implementation would be nearly identical to our previous VBScript implementation. Based on the previous source code excerpt, the C# implementation is not that far removed from the VB implementation (regardless of the flavor of VB).

Notice that `ShipperList.aspx` still contains a client-side VBScript. When the document is loaded (`onload` event) this VBScript code is executed. Leaving the client-side alone made practical sense. Our application resides on a set of servers that was upgraded to support the .NET Framework and its corresponding technologies. The crack MIS staff at our mythical company are in no position to upgrade every client machine to support .NET. There are too many older machines out there that just aren't worth upgrading. It is simpler to only upgrade the piece that you have the most control over, the server-side.

.NET Client Tier, Customers

The pattern exhibited in mapping from ASP Shippers to ASP.NET Shippers holds for each object upgraded. The pattern is basically this:

- Convert all server-side code from VBScript to C#
- Leave everything else alone

The ASP.NET file, `CustomerTable.aspx`, is as follows:

```
<%@ Page language="c#" Description="CustomerTable" %>
<%@ Import Namespace="TheBusTierDotNet" %>


<html>

<SCRIPT language="C#" runat=server ID=Script1>

void Page_Load(Object sender, EventArgs EvArgs) {

    TheBUsTierDotNet.Customer customer =
        new TheBusTierDotNet.Customer();
    string strCustomer;
```

```
    customer.Get(out strCustomer);
    Response.Write("<?xml version='1.0' ?><XML ID='CustomersDataIsland'>");
    Response.Write(strCustomer);
    Response.Write("</XML>");
}
</SCRIPT>

<body>
   <span id="Message" runat=server/>
</body>

<BODY>

<TABLE DATASRC="#CustomersDataIsland" BORDER=1>
  <THEAD><TH>Customer ID</TH>
        <TH>Company Name</TH>
        <TH>Contact Name</TH></THEAD>
  <TR>
    <TD><SPAN DATAFLD="CustomerID"></SPAN></TD>
    <TD><SPAN DATAFLD="CompanyName"></SPAN></TD>
    <TD><SPAN DATAFLD="ContactName"></SPAN></TD>
  </TR>
</TABLE>

</BODY>

</html>
```

The C# implementation of the `Page_Load` is directly derived from `CustomerTable.asp`'s server-side VBScript. The mechanism used to display the customer's XML data island, `CustomersDataIsland`, is identical in `CustomerTable.asp` and `CustomerTable.aspx`.

.NET Client Tier, Orders

The relationship between `OrderRecordset.aspx` and `OrderRecordset.aspx` follows a familiar pattern. `OrderRecordset.aspx`, is as follows:

```
<%@ Page language="c#" Description="OrderRecordset" %>
<%@ Import Namespace="TheBusTierDotNet" %>

<HTML>

<SCRIPT language="C#" runat=server ID=Script1>

void Page_Load(Object sender, EventArgs EvArgs) {

    TheBusTierDotNet.Order order = new TheBusTierDotNet.Order();
    string strOrder;

    order.Get(out strOrder);
    Response.Write("<?xml version='1.0' ?><XML ID='OrdersDataIsland'>");
    Response.Write(strOrder);
    Response.Write("</XML>");
}
</SCRIPT>
```

```
<BODY>
   <span id="Message" runat=server/>

<P>Order ID: <SPAN DATASRC="#OrdersDataIsland" DATAFLD="OrderID"></SPAN></P>
<P>Customer ID: <SPAN DATASRC="#OrdersDataIsland" DATAFLD="CustomerID"></SPAN></P>
<P>Employee ID: <SPAN DATASRC="#OrdersDataIsland" DATAFLD="EmployeeID"></SPAN></P>

<INPUT TYPE=BUTTON
       VALUE="Previous OrderID"
       onclick="OrdersDataIsland.recordset.movePrevious()">
<INPUT TYPE=BUTTON
       VALUE="Next OrderID" \
       onclick="OrdersDataIsland.recordset.moveNext()">

</BODY>
</HTML>
```

Summary

The idea of this case study was to demonstrate a commonplace application – commonplace code to provide practical solutions. The basic ideas presented included that:

- Using SQL Server's `FOR XML` construct is relatively simple
- Once XML is generated it is not that difficult to display (list, table or recordset)
- Using SQL Server' `OPENXML` to insert code into the database is relatively simple
- Moving to Visual Studio.NET and the .NET framework facilitates simplicity

It is a rare occurrence in software development to upgrade technology yet experience less complexity. Hopefully it was demonstrated that the migration from C++ to C# reduces complexity and was a relatively painless process. Jumping from VB to C# should in no way cause mortal terror. Similarly, features of the .NET Framework are designed to make development less difficult. Those late nights of tracking down memory leaks and un-released COM objects are hopefully behind us thanks to GC (garbage collection). Calling legacy COM objects from a .NET application is straightforward. This "straightforwardness" also applied to ADO. Even migrating from ASP to ASP.NET was trouble free. Then again we kept the feature set implemented to a minimum.

This case study demonstrated the great new features of SQL Server (`FOR XML` and `OPENXML`). This case study also showed that developers should not be intimidated or overwhelmed by Microsoft's .NET initiative. C# and .NET might actually make life easier. Haven't we said that with every technology we embraced? Have we said that about every new technology before we used it on a large-scale application?

Creating and Configuring Virtual Directories

In this appendix we will show you how to configure a virtual directory using Internet Information Services (IIS) ready for use by SQL Server. This then allows the use of XML templates, XPath queries, and SQL queries from directly within the URL of the web site.

Configuring the virtual directory can be done either through the IIS Virtual Directory Management for SQL Server utility, or programmatically through a set of objects. Both methods set up SQL Server's XML ISAPI filter within the web site and it is this that interfaces to SQL Server.

Web Release 1 of XML for SQL Server was released in January 2001 and updated and enhanced various parts of the virtual directory functionality. We'll also show how to install this, and what these enhancements give you.

IIS Virtual Directory Management Utility

Let's begin by discussing the system requirements, installation steps, and steps required to create a virtual directory for the IIS Virtual Directory Management utility for SQL Server 2000. Then we'll discuss the changes that have taken place with Web Release 1.

System Requirements

On the hardware side, the use of virtual directories by SQL Server does not require any special system requirements above those already required by the SQL Server installation.

However, there are some additional software requirements:

- Internet Information Server 4.0 if running Windows NT 4.0 Server
- Peer Web Services 4.0 if running Windows NT 4.0 Workstation
- Internet Information Services 5.0 if running Windows 2000

If you find that you need to install any of these prerequisites, this can be done through Control Panel | Add/Remove Programs.

If you are running Windows NT 4.0, the Microsoft Management Console must be updated to version 1.2. This is already installed in Windows 2000. At the time of writing MMC 1.2 does not appear to be downloadable from the Microsoft site but is available on the Technet discs.

If you are running Windows 2000 Professional, the Administrative Tools also need to be installed. This can be done using the `adminpak.msi` install file that can be found either on the Windows 2000 Server CD-ROM, or within the `System32` folder of a server install.

Installation

The IIS Virtual Directory Management utility is actually already installed as part of the default SQL Server 2000 installation, and there are no options for configuring during the SQL Server installation of this utility.

Creating the Virtual Directory

The IIS Virtual Directory Management for SQL Server utility can be accessed by selecting the Configure SQL XML Support in IIS menu option, which can be found at Start | Programs | Microsoft SQL Server.

Once the utility has started, you will be presented with a screen similar to the one shown below. The exact options that are shown will depend upon which web sites are already configured on the computer:

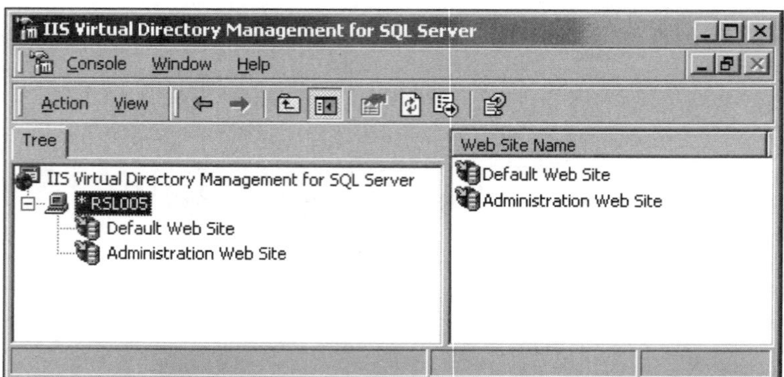

By default there are up to two web sites, depending on the version of Windows that you are running. The Administration Web Site is used for configuring IIS and so isn't used for any standard web sites. Details of how to create a web site are discussed in a later section.

If we wished to create a new virtual directory in a given web site, we could simply use the New | Virtual Directory option invoked by right-clicking on the desired web site. In this case we are going to use the Default Web Site.

A dialog appears, enabling us to set the properties of the new virtual directory. This dialog has six different tabs: General, Security, Data Source, Settings, Virtual Names, and Advanced. Let's have a look at each one of these in detail.

The General Tab

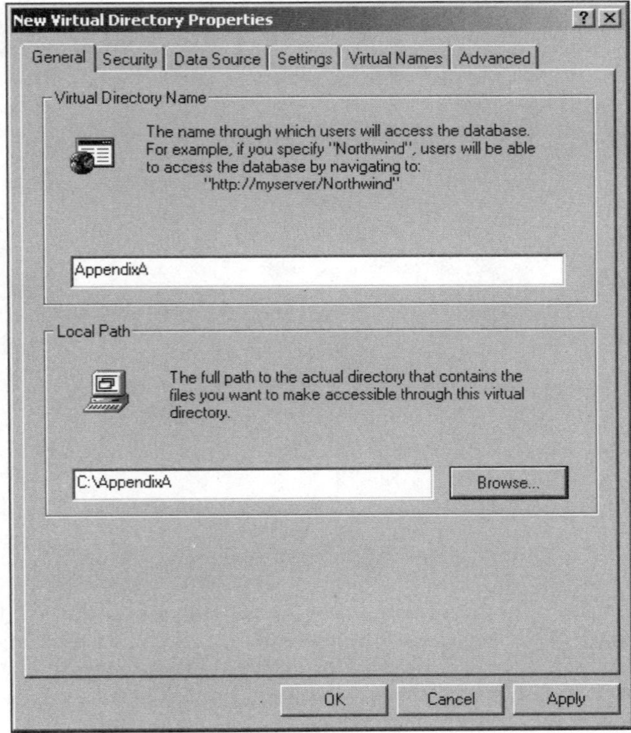

The General tab consists of two parts. The first half allows the configuration of the virtual directory name. This is the name that appears within the site. Here we have called it AppendixA, so that if later on it is running from the local machine, it can be referenced by the URL: http://localhost/AppendixA.

The second half of the tab enables us to configure where we actually want to store the XML files that we will create. We can specify any folder on the local machine, and IIS will then create a mapping between the virtual directory and the physical folder, so that it knows where to look for the files. For simplicity, we have given them both the same name, but there is no need for this.

Note that at this stage you will need a suitable folder to map to, in this case we'll assume you have created a new folder called `AppendixA` on your `C:\` drive.

The Security Tab

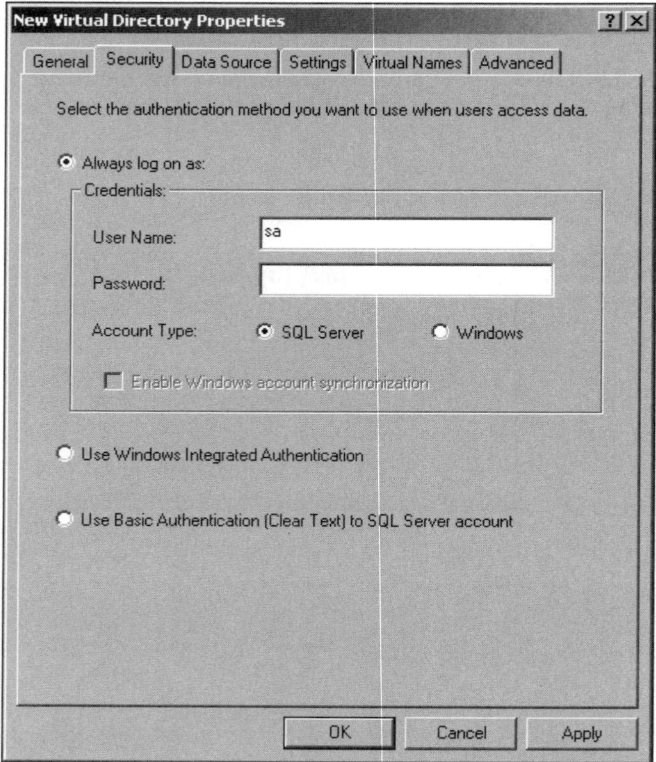

The Security tab is used to configure how SQL Server will be accessed. The three options are:

- Always log on as. With this option, a user name and password are to be given. These can be either a standard SQL Server account that will be authenticated by SQL Server, or a Windows NT/2000 account that is authenticated using Windows authentication. If a Windows account is to be used, we can also select to enable account synchronization. This means that if the password is changed, it will be automatically changed here too.
- Use Windows Integrated Authentication. This option is usually used on an intranet and is where the login details of the user who is accessing the web site are used to connect to SQL Server to perform the query. This will therefore not work on a web site that uses anonymous log-ins.
- Use Basic Authentication. When using this mode, the web site first tries to log in using the anonymous account of the site. If this fails, the user is prompted for a valid SQL Server login and password. There is a risk in using this method in that the user name and password will be transmitted as plain text and could therefore be captured by a network monitoring tool.

Normally you will use the first option with either a standard SQL Server or Windows account as this is more secure than using basic authentication.

The Data Source Tab

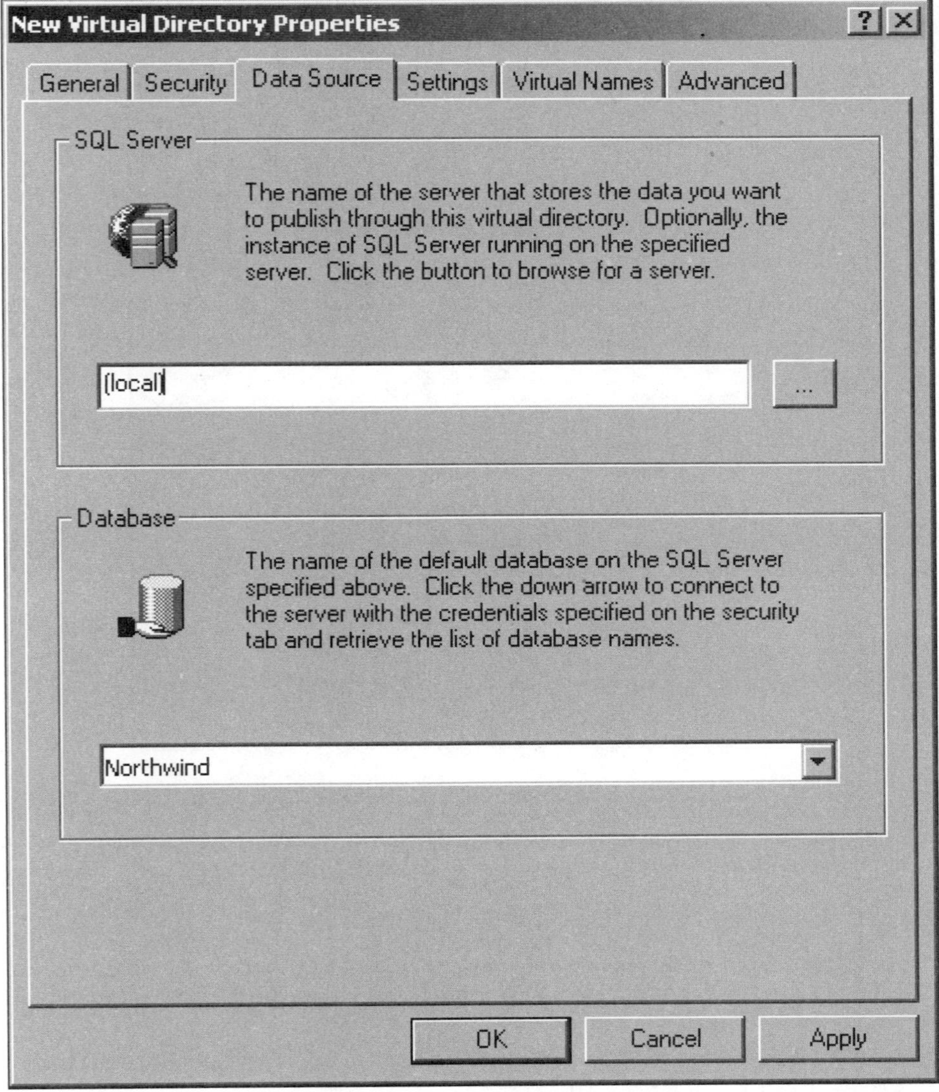

The Data Source tab is used to control which SQL Server database is connected to when running queries on this directory.

Simply specify the name of the SQL Server, or if connecting to the same server, as here, (local). Once the server is chosen, you can then select a database that is held on that server. Note that a connection is made to discover the list of databases when you click on the drop-down box, so the Security tab must have been filled in with valid information for this to work.

The Settings Tab

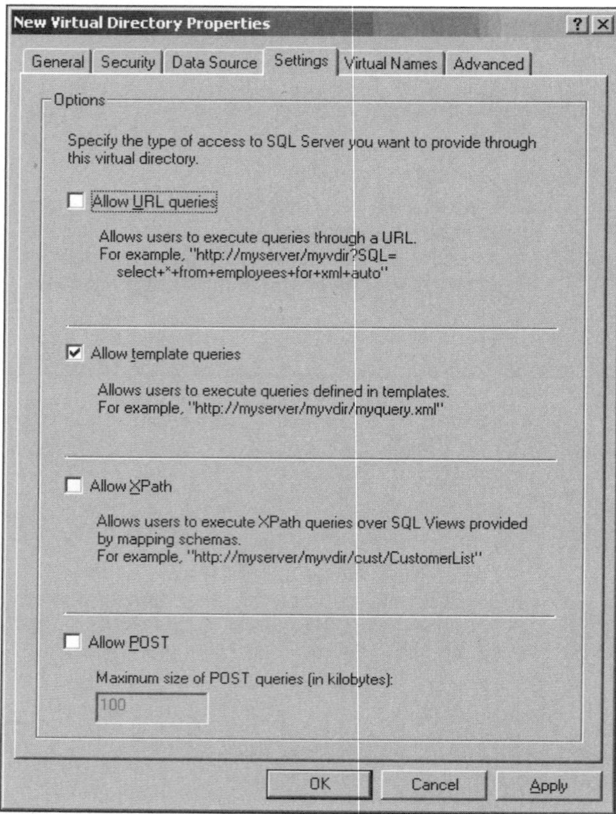

The Settings tab allows the enabling and disabling of different types of queries. Careful consideration of the security implications of enabling options should be weighed against the benefits of the functionality offered.

The four available options are:

- Allow URL queries. By default, this option is unchecked, and should only ever be used in the least sensitive or non-production environments. It allows the use of SQL queries directly within the URL such as:

  http://localhost/AppendixA?sql=SELECT+EmployeeID,+FirstName,+LastName+

  FROM+Employees+FOR+XML+AUTO&root=ROOT

  As you can see, this query is just a `SELECT` but we could have just as easily put a `DROP DATABASE` statement in there instead.

- Allow template queries. This is the only option that is selected by default, and allows templates to be set up to perform queries. This abstracts the details of the query from the URL so that the web site user cannot talk directly to the database, and so is much safer to perform. See Chapter 7 for more details of template queries.

- Allow XPath. This option allows the use of XPath queries against the database. For more details, see Chapter 8.

- Allow POST. This option allows the passing of data into the database in the form of an HTTP form `POST` rather than just running a query against it. Once this option is enabled, you can also specify the maximum size of the post.

> **Note that this tab has changed with Web Release 1. See the *Web Release 1 Changes* section later in this appendix for details.**

The Virtual Names Tab

The Virtual Names tab is used to configure virtual names for database objects, templates, and mapping schemas for XPath queries. These are used as a further abstraction of the physical query files from the URL of the web page. Three types of virtual name can be created:

- dbobject – a database object. This references the database that is specified on the Data Source tab and is used when putting queries directly within the URL.
- schema – a mapping schema for use by XPath queries. See Chapter 8 for more details on XPath queries.
- template – a template file for use by template queries. See Chapter 7 for details of XML template queries.

To create a new virtual name, click on the New button to bring up the following dialog box:

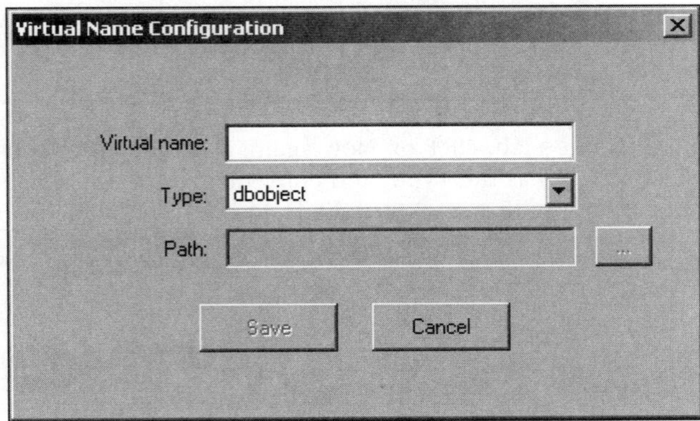

In this dialog box, enter the virtual name that you want to use, and select the type of object that this virtual name will hold. For schemas and templates you will also need to specify the path to the folder that the files will go in. This will be a folder under the Local Path that we specified on the General tab. Note that the path is not validated, so it may be safer to browse to the directory, as this will avoid any typing mistakes.

A Quick Example of Setting up Virtual Names

Let's have a look at an example. Say we wanted to set up a virtual directory called `Northwind` for submitting XPath queries against the `Northwind` sample database. Let's have a look at how we'd go about doing this…

Select Start | Programs | Microsoft SQL Server | Configure SQL XML Support in IIS. In the tree control on the left of the window, double-click on the name of the machine that your SQL Server uses, and then right-click on Default Web Site in the expanded view that appears, select New | Virtual Directory.

Now, on the General tab of the New Virtual Directory Properties dialog, enter Northwind as the Virtual Directory Name, and as the default database on the Data Source tab.

On the Security tab, specify a login that will allow read access to the `Northwind` sample database of your SQL Server installation. Next, on the Settings tab, check the Allow XPath box.

On the Virtual Names tab, click on New, and enter dbobject in the Virtual name field of the dialog that appears. Keep dbobject (the default type) as the Type field parameter, and click on Save:

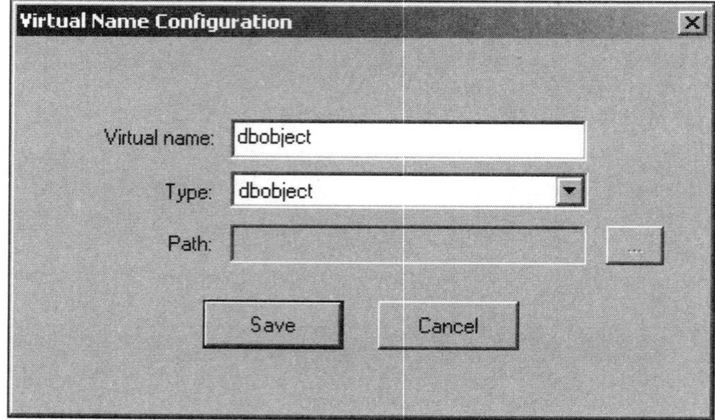

Now, back on the Virtual Names tab, click on New again, and then enter schema into the Virtual name field of the dialog, select schema as the Type, and enter the path to the schema (C:\inetpub\Northwind\schema in this case) into the Path box. Save your work once again:

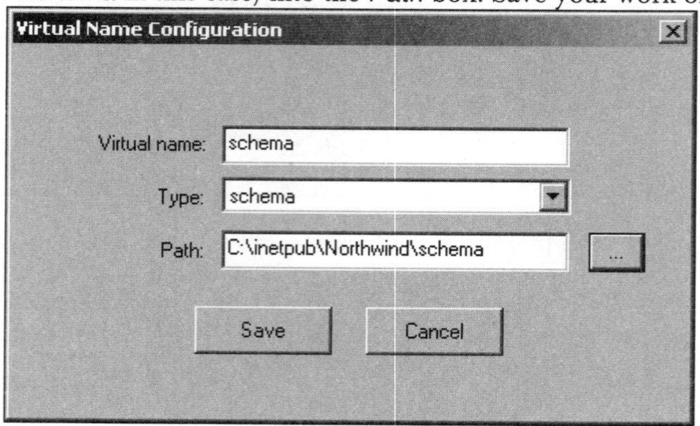

Your final dialog should look similar to that shown in the following screenshot, so click on OK to finish the process:

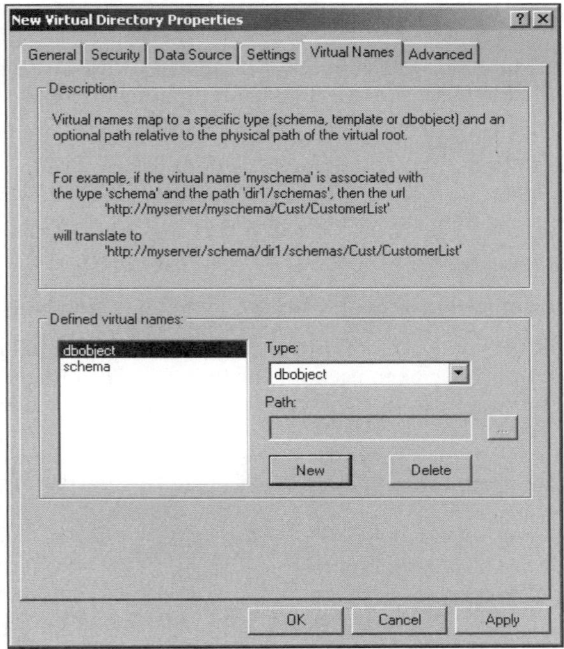

The Advanced Tab

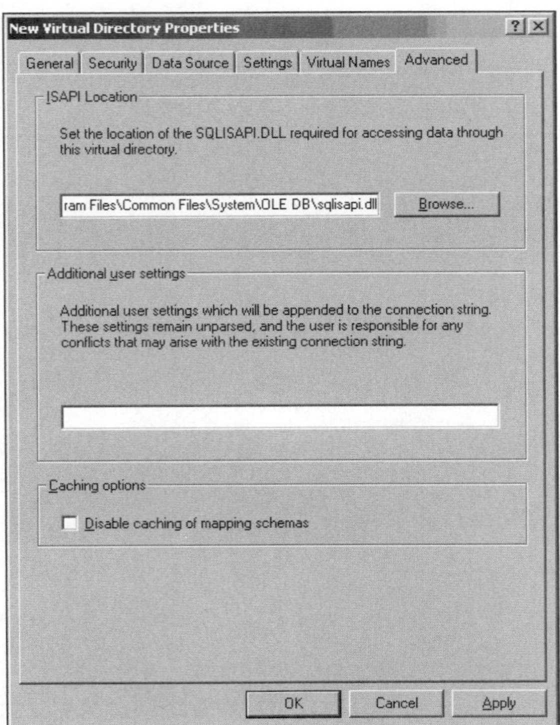

The Advanced tab provides three options, which you will rarely need to touch:

- ISAPI Location. The XML web support is contained within an ISAPI DLL. This option allows the location of the file to be altered. By default it points to the location in which it was installed.
- Additional user settings. This allows extra settings to be passed in the connection string. For example, if you had a slow or busy link, you could put the following string into this text box to increase the length of time allowed to connect to SQL Server:

  ```
  ConnectionTimeOut=60
  ```

  Any other valid connection string parameter could be passed here.
- Caching options. Normally, in order to improve performance, mapping schemas are cached in memory once they have been used for the first time. You might check this option to disable caching if your server was low on memory or if the mapping schemas were used infrequently.

Note that as with the Settings tab, this tab has changed with Web Release 1 – see the next section for details.

Web Release 1 Changes

Two of the tabs (Settings and Advanced) within the New Virtual Directory Properties utility have changed in Web Release 1, and we'll look at these changes next.

The Settings Tab

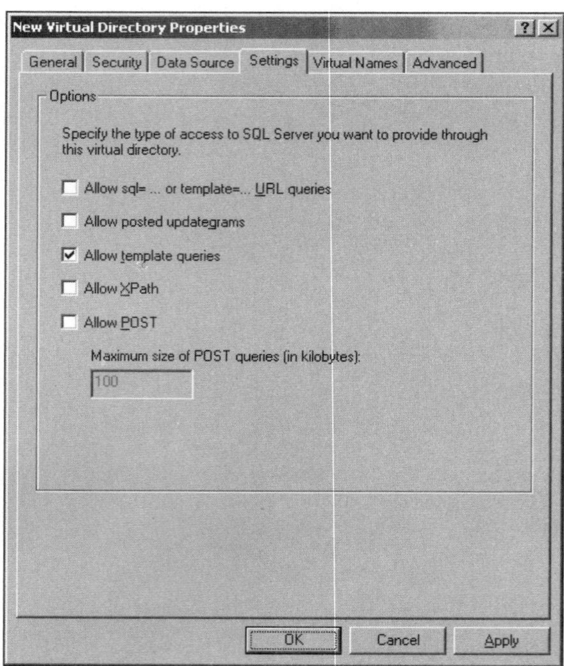

The general layout of the Settings tab has changed, although the only real change in terms of functionality is the addition of the Allow posted updategrams option. This is to support the new Updategrams feature that is also introduced in this web release. For more details of Updategrams, see Chapter 9.

The Advanced Tab

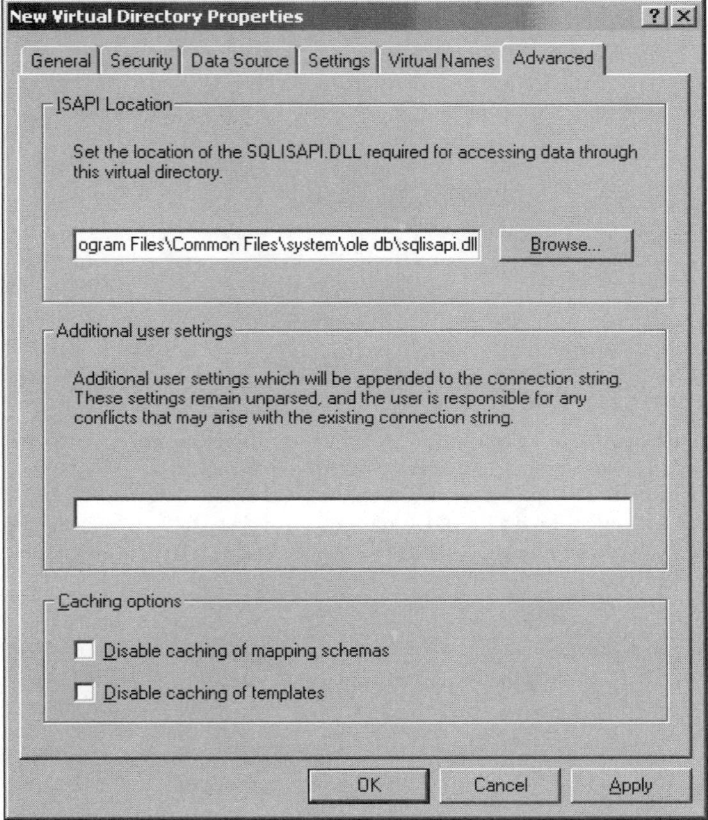

Again, there is only a minor change to the functionality of the Advanced tab, and that is to add the Disable caching of templates option. Template caching is a new feature introduced in Web Release 1, which can improve the performance of template queries by caching them in memory following their first use. You might want to disable their caching if your server is low on memory, or if you only use templates infrequently so that there is little benefit from caching them in memory.

Programming Virtual Directory Management

As well as the IIS Virtual Directory Management for SQL Server utility, Microsoft also supplies an object model that you can program against, to create and modify virtual directories. This object model is what the utility uses to create the virtual directory, and so it won't be a surprise to see that is closely mirrors what we have already seen.

The Object Model

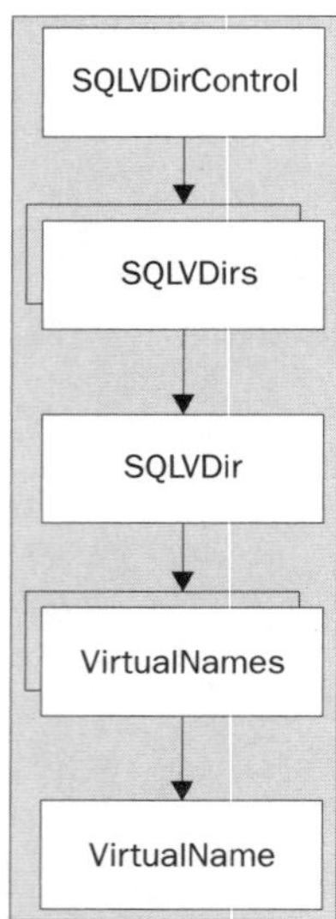

The IIS Virtual Directory Management for SQL Server object model consists of a hierarchy of five objects. Only the top-level object, `SQLVDirControl`, is exposed publicly. All of the other objects must be referenced through it. The object model is referenced as the **Microsoft SQL Virtual Directory Control 1.0 Type Library** and uses the DLL named `sqlvdir.dll`, which is installed within the main SQL Server 2000 installation folder:

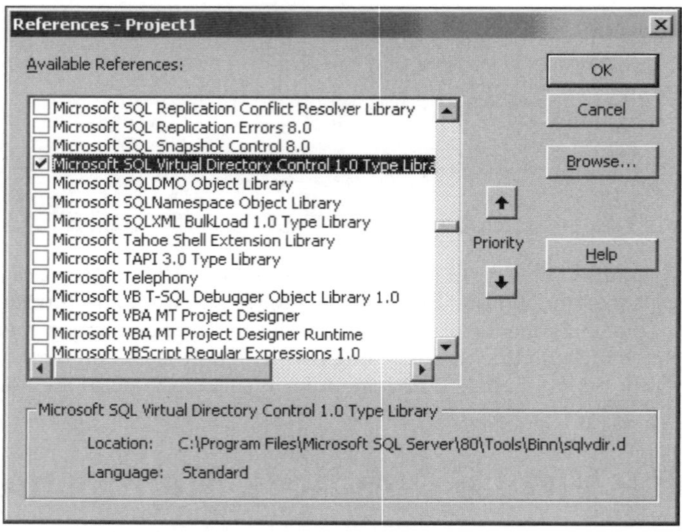

Within VB code, the top-level object is referenced as `SQLVDirControl`. If you are using `CreateObject` to instantiate this object from a web page, you should use the format `CreateObject("SQLVDir.SQLVDirControl")`.

The SQLVDirControl Object

The `SQLVDirControl` object is the top-level object of the model, which is used to connect to the IIS server, and bring back a collection of virtual directories. It has the following three methods.

The Connect Method

The `Connect` method is used to make a connection to a web server ready to configure the virtual directories. It takes two optional parameters:

- *`szServer`* – the server name of the web server being connected to.
- *`szWebSite`* – the web site number on the server. This can be found by looking in the **metabase** of the server.

The `Connect` method is called in the following way:

```
mySQLVDirControlObject.Connect "myIISServer", "1"
```

Where `myIISServer` is the computer name of the web server and `1` is the number of the web site.

If you want to connect to the local web server's default web site, do not pass either of these parameters.

> **The metabase is where IIS stores its configuration information and is similar in use to the registry. Knowledge Base article Q232068, describes the MetaEdit utility that can be used for viewing and editing the metabase. This utility is un-supported, and editing the metabase can be as dangerous as editing the registry, so use with extreme care.**

The Disconnect Method

The `Disconnect` method terminates the connection to the web server specified in the `Connect` method.

The SQLVDirs Method

The `SQLVDirs` method returns a `SQLVDirs` collection object, thereby enabling access to the rest of the object hierarchy, as described in the following section. The following code shows how to use this object from within Visual Basic:

```
Function CreateVirtualDirectory()

    ' Set up the objects ready for use
    Dim objVDir As New SQLVDirControl
    Dim objSQLVDirs As Object

    ' Connect to the local web server
    objVDir.Connect

    ' Retrieve the SQLVDirs collection
    Set objSQLVDirs = objVDir.SQLVDirs

    ' Tidy up at the end
    objVDir.Disconnect

End Function
```

Error handling has been omitted from this function to make the code more readable and show the use of the object model more clearly.

The SQLVDirs Collection Object

The SQLVDirs object holds a collection of SQLVDir objects that in turn are references to a virtual directory. Let's take a look at a couple of the methods of the SQLVDirs object.

The AddVirtualDirectory method

The AddVirtualDirectory method is used to create a new virtual directory on the server. It takes one parameter for the name of the virtual directory.

The following code adds to the previous code to show the creation of a new virtual directory called AppendixAProg:

```
Function CreateVirtualDirectory ()

    ' Set up the objects ready for use
    Dim objVDir As New SQLVDirControl
    Dim objSQLVDirs As Object
    Dim objSQLVDir As Object

    ' Connect to the local web server
    objVDir.Connect

    ' Retrieve the SQLVDirs collection
    Set objSQLVDirs = objVDir.SQLVDirs

    ' Create a new virtual directory
    Set objSQLVDir = objSQLVDirs.AddVirtualDirectory("AppendixAProg")

    ' Tidy up at the end
    objVDir.Disconnect

End Function
```

Note that the objSQLVDirs and objSQLVDir variables are declared as type Object and are therefore late bound. This is because they are not exposed directly by the object model and can't be referenced directly.

The RemoveVirtualDirectory Method

The RemoveVirtualDirectory method is used to remove an existing virtual directory. It also takes the single parameter of the name of the directory to be removed.

Other Methods of SQLVDirs

In addition to the methods listed above, the SQLVDirs object also supports the standard collection methods: Clone, Count, Item, Next, Reset, and Skip.

The SQLVDir Object

The SQLVDir object is the main object used for configuring the different aspects of the virtual directory. It has a single method, VirtualNames.

The VirtualNames Method

The `VirtualNames` method returns a `VirtualNames` collection object. This is used for configuring the virtual names for templates, mapping schemas, and database objects. This method takes no parameters.

In addition to this single method, the `SQLVDir` object also has numerous properties.

The AdditionalSettings Property

The `AdditionalSettings` property sets the additional connection string as on the Advanced tab of the utility.

The AllowFlags Property

The `AllowFlags` property is a bit mask for allowing the different settings as described on the Settings tab of the utility. It is also used for setting the caching options on the Advanced tab.

The valid values equivalent to the Settings tab options are:

Value	Description
1	URL queries
8	Templates
64	XPath queries
128	Post
512	Updategrams (introduced in Web Release 1)

The valid caching options are:

Value	Description
256	Don't cache schemas
1024	Don't cache templates (introduced in Web Release 1)

The DatabaseName Property

The `DatabaseName` property sets the database name as on the Data Source tab of the utility.

The DLLPath Property

The `DLLPath` property is the path to the SQL ISAPI DLL used by the XML web support for SQL Server.

The EnablePasswordSync Property

The `EnablePasswordSync` property is used in conjunction with the `UserName`, `Password`, and `SecurityMode` properties (discussed further down), and if set, allows IIS to synchronize password changes to the Windows account specified by the `Name` property.

The Name Property

The `Name` property is the name of the virtual directory.

The Password Property

The `Password` property takes the password for the user account specified in the `UserName` property. For obvious security reasons, this property is write-only.

The PhysicalPath Property

The `PhysicalPath` property describes the path to the folder on the local drive that will hold the files for the virtual directory.

The PostSize Property

The `PostSize` property takes the maximum size of the data that can be passed to SQL Server in a `POST` query.

> *This property is new in Web Release 1 and is undocumented in Books Online or the Web Release Help.*

The SecurityMode Property

The `SecurityMode` property sets one of the four authentication methods as described on the Security tab of the utility. Valid values are:

Value	Description
1	SQL Server login
2	Windows login using a fixed account
4	Basic authentication
8	Windows Integrated login

The ServerName Property

The `ServerName` property sets the SQL Server name as on the Data Source tab of the utility.

The UserName Property

The `UserName` property takes a string value for the name of the SQL Server or Windows user account that will be used to connect to SQL Server.

Continuing with Our CreateVirtualDirectory Function

To continue building the virtual directory we can add the following code to that shown previously to configure the virtual directory:

```
Function CreateVirtualDirectory()

    ' Set up the objects ready for use
    Dim objVDir As New SQLVDirControl
    Dim objSQLVDirs As Object
    Dim objSQLVDir As Object
```

```
    ' Connect to the local web server
    objVDir.Connect

    ' Retrieve the SQLVDirs collection
    Set objSQLVDirs = objVDir.SQLVDirs

    ' Create a new virtual directory
    Set objSQLVDir = objSQLVDirs.AddVirtualDirectory("AppendixAProg")

    ' Use integrated security
    objSQLVDir.SecurityMode = 8

    ' Use the Northwind database on the local server
    objSQLVDir.ServerName = "(local)"
    objSQLVDir.DatabaseName = "Northwind"

    ' Set the physical path
    objSQLVDir.PhysicalPath = "C:\AppendixA"
    objSQLVDir.AdditionalSettings = "ConnectionTimeout=60"

    ' Tidy up at the end
    objVDir.Disconnect

End Function
```

The VirtualNames Collection Object

The `VirtualNames` object holds a collection of `VirtualName` objects. These are used to control the names of the database, schema, and template objects as on the Virtual Names tab of the utility. Amongst others, this object has two notable methods.

The AddVirtualName Method

The `AddVirtualName` method is used to create a new virtual name. It takes three parameters:

- `Name` – the name of the virtual name.
- `Type` - the type of virtual name to create; database object, schema, template.
- `Path` – this parameter is only valid for schema and template types and is the path to the folder where the files of this type are stored.

The RemoveVirtualName Method

The `RemoveVirtualName` method removes a specified virtual name. It takes one parameter, the name of the virtual name to remove.

Other Methods of the VirtualNames Collection

In addition to the above methods, this object also supports the standard collection methods: `Clone`, `Count`, `Item`, `Next`, `Reset`, and `Skip`.

The VirtualName Object

The `VirtualName` object is the bottom-most object in the object hierarchy.

The Name Property

The Name property describes the name of the virtual name.

The Path Property

The Path property is the physical path to the folder that holds the files for the virtual name. This is only valid for schema and template types.

The Type Property

The Type property specifies the type of virtual name that the object is. Valid values are:

Value	Description
1	Database object
2	Schema
4	Template

Finishing the CreateVirtualDirectory Function

To finalize the code for creating our new virtual directory, we need to add the code to create a new virtual name, and then modify its type (just to illustrate the use of the final object). We have also added some extra code at the end to finally tidy all the objects up and release them:

```
Function CreateVirtualDirectory()

    ' Set up the objects ready for use
    Dim objVDir As New SQLVDirControl
    Dim objSQLVDirs As Object
    Dim objSQLVDir As Object
    Dim objVirtualNames As Object
    Dim objVirtualName As Object

    ' Connect to the local web server
    objVDir.Connect

    ' Retrieve the SQLVDirs collection
    Set objSQLVDirs = objVDir.SQLVDirs

    ' Create a new virtual directory
    Set objSQLVDir = objSQLVDirs.AddVirtualDirectory("AppendixAProg")

    ' Use integrated security
    objSQLVDir.SecurityMode = 8

    ' Use the Northwind database on the local server
    objSQLVDir.ServerName = "(local)"
    objSQLVDir.DatabaseName = "Northwind"

    ' Set the physical path
    objSQLVDir.PhysicalPath = "C:\AppendixA"
    objSQLVDir.AdditionalSettings = "ConnectionTimeout=60"

    ' Add a new template virtual name
    Set objVirtualNames = objSQLVDir.VirtualNames
    Set objVirtualName = _
    objVirtualNames.AddVirtualName("template", 4, "C:\AppendixA\template")
```

```
        ' Change the newly created virtual name to a schema
        objVirtualName.Name = "schema"
        objVirtualName.Type = 2
        objVirtualName.Path = "C:\AppendixA\schema"

        ' Tidy up at the end
        objVDir.Disconnect

        Set objVirtualName = Nothing
        Set objVirtualNames = Nothing
        Set objSQLVDir = Nothing
        Set objSQLVDirs = Nothing
        Set objVDir = Nothing

    End Function
```

The example above uses Visual Basic to create the virtual directory, but we could have used VBScript instead. We could then use utilities like Windows Scripting Host to run the script as an administrator without having to rely on writing a VB program. The code to do this is almost identical with the main change being that the `SQLVDirControl` object is created differently:

```
        ' Set up the objects ready for use
        Set objVDir = CreateObject("SQLVDIR.SQLVDirControl")

        ' Connect to the local web server
        objVDir.Connect

        ' Retrieve the SQLVDirs collection
        Set objSQLVDirs = objVDir.SQLVDirs

        ' Create a new virtual directory
        Set objSQLVDir = objSQLVDirs.AddVirtualDirectory("AppendixAProgVBS")

        ' Use integrated security
        objSQLVDir.SecurityMode = 8

        ' Use the Northwind database on the local server
        objSQLVDir.ServerName = "(local)"
        objSQLVDir.DatabaseName = "Northwind"

        ' Set the physical path
        objSQLVDir.PhysicalPath = "C:\AppendixA"
        objSQLVDir.AdditionalSettings = "ConnectionTimeout=60"

        ' Add a new template virtual name
        Set objVirtualNames = objSQLVDir.VirtualNames
        Set objVirtualName = _
        objVirtualNames.AddVirtualName("template", 4, "C:\AppendixA\template")

        ' Change the newly created virtual name to a schema
        objVirtualName.Name = "schema"
        objVirtualName.Type = 2
        objVirtualName.Path = "C:\AppendixA\schema"

        ' Tidy up at the end
        objVDir.Disconnect
```

```
        Set objVirtualName = Nothing
        Set objVirtualNames = Nothing
        Set objSQLVDir = Nothing
        Set objSQLVDirs = Nothing
        Set objVDir = Nothing
```

To use this, save the code as `SQLVDir.vbs`. When run, it creates a new virtual directory called `AppendixAProgVBS`.

Best Practices

This section gives you a few quick tips on what you should consider doing to make the best use of IIS when using it with SQL Server:

- Keep all folders and files on an NTFS partition, and make sure that only read access is given to them and only to the minimum number of accounts. This then helps prevent unauthorised users from changing the contents of any of the files.
- Use Windows security using the anonymous option to connect to SQL Server. This ensures that no passwords are stored in the registry or metabase.
- Make sure that you have all the latest security patches applied for IIS. These can be downloaded at:

  http://www.microsoft.com/windows2000/downloads/default.asp

  For Windows 2000 or for Windows NT at:

  http://www.microsoft.com/NTServer/all/downloads.asp
- Follow the guidelines published by Microsoft regarding the setting up of a secure web site. The latest version of this is in Technet, and can currently be viewed online at:

  http://www.microsoft.com/technet/security/iis5chk.asp
- Consider subscribing to the Microsoft security newsletter to stay informed of future problems and available patches. Details of how to subscribe to this can be found at:

  http://www.microsoft.com/technet/security/notify.asp

SQL SQL SQL SQL SQL SQL SQL
server
XML XML XML XML XML XML

B

Microsoft XML View Mapper 1.0

Simply put, the Microsoft XML View Mapper is a tool that allows us to create XML View schemas from SQL Server 2000 database schemas. It is a visual development environment that maps relationships between a SQL schema and an XDR schema. However, it was developed to support the XML functionality added to SQL Server 2000. Therefore, it does not support the earlier versions of SQL Server such as SQL Server 6.x and SQL Server 7. Database schemas must be generated from SQL Server 2000. All schemas used must be well-formed XML documents, or document items may have to be manually edited to bring them into conformance.

As with many of Microsoft's development tools, we organize our work into projects. Within a project, we can create one or more maps. Each map defines the relationship between a single SQL schema and a single XDR schema. "Drag-and-drop" technology is used extensively to establish the mappings. Once we create a map, we test and export the XML View schema.

In this appendix, we will discuss how to:

- Check the system requirements needed to use XML View Mapper
- Get the software
- Install the software
- Examine the software architecture
- Start XML View Mapper
- Tour the visual development environment
- Use the on-line documentation
- Troubleshoot

- Perform batch conversions
- Use the built-in utilities
- Customize the development environment

Getting the XML View Mapper

At the time this appendix was written, you could only get this tool by downloading it from the Microsoft MSDN Web. It was not contained in the April 2001 release of MSDN Library.

System Requirements

The software tool will not load if your machine does not meet certain requirements. The installation script checks your hardware resources and software environment and halts if one of the prerequisites does not exist, or is an unsupported version. Before heading off to the MSDN web site, you should verify that your system meets the following requirements.

Software Requirements

The required software environment includes:

- Microsoft Windows 2000, all editions
- SQL Server 2000
- MSXML 3.0 is needed to use one of the utility programs

Hardware Requirements

The minimum hardware requirements are:

- 10 megabytes (MB) of available disk space
- 64 megabytes (MB) RAM is minimum, 128 MB is recommended
- A Pentium 166 megahertz (MHz), or higher

Networking

If you want to refer to external schemas you will need an Internet connection.

Administration

To install XML View Mapper, you must have Administrator rights, or have the Administrator install it for you.

Downloading the Software

The download file size is approximately 4.5 megabytes (MB). Download the software by going to the MSDN SQL Server Developer Center at http://msdn.microsoft.com/sqlserver and selecting SQL Server Downloads entry in the table of contents menu in the left pane of the page, SQL Server XML View Mapper 1.0 and then clicking on the Download icon to start the download process. While this URL was valid at the time this appendix was written, it may change overtime. If so, search the Downloads section at http://msdn.microsoft.com.

> **If you have a beta version of XML View Mapper, we recommend that you remove it before the installation of the Version 1 software. Do not remove the beta software using the Remove option of the InstallShield Wizard. Instead, click the Start button, point to Settings, click Control Panel, double-click Add/Remove Programs, select the beta version of XML View Mapper from the list and click the Remove button.**

Installing the XML View Mapper

Using the installation wizard, we can:

- Install XML View Mapper
- Modify an existing installation
- Repair an existing installation
- Remove an existing installation

You cannot use the Modify or Repair options to upgrade to a newer version. Again, to perform an upgrade, the safest approach is to remove the current version using the Add/Remove Programs application in Control Panel.

Installing XML View Mapper

If there is no existing installation of XML View Mapper, Setup will offer you two installation options: Complete or Custom.

The Complete setup option creates an installation that includes all features, and installs the software at the default location of `C:\Program Files\Microsoft SQL Server XML Tools\XML View Mapper`. The Custom setup option allows you to select the features that want to install and change the default location for the software files. In general, you should consider using the Complete setup option.

Performing an Installation – Complete Option

Now, let's go through the process of installing XML View Mapper on a system using the Complete option. As a quick reminder, you must have Administrator rights to install the software.

The first screen that you see when you double-click on setup.exe is the Welcome to the InstallShield Wizard for Microsoft SQL Server XML View Mapper. Click the Next button to continue the installation process. Up pops the ubiquitous End-User License Agreement. Select the option button to accept the terms, and then click the Next button to continue the installation process. The Setup Type screen is displayed as shown below:

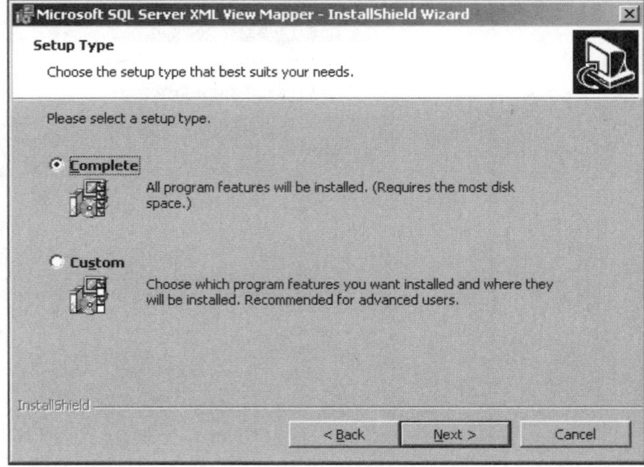

At this point, you should select the Complete installation option. Using this option, the wizard will perform a complete installation in the default folder structure. Click Next to proceed. The installation script will prompt you with Ready to Install the Program. Click Install to move forward with the installation. A series of progress bars are displayed as the installation script copies files, creates shortcuts, updates the registry, and so on. Finally, the installation script will announce its completion by displaying the InstallShield Wizard Completed screen. Click the Finish button to finish the installation process.

What Was Installed and Where Did It Go?

So, after all those screens and all that disk activity, what software was loaded and where did the installation script put all those files? The Complete option installs the software at the default location of `C:\Program Files\Microsoft SQL Server XML Tools\XML View Mapper`.

The `XML View Mapper` folder contains the following controls, files, folders, and libraries:

- A `samples` folder
- `XMLMapper.exe` – Application file
- `xmlsqlmp.chm` – Compiled HTML Help file
- A ReadMe file
- Four OCXs
- Eight DLLs

The following five folders are created as children of the `samples` folder and each folder contains sample files:

- `Customers`
- `MultiNameSpace`
- `OrderForm`
- `Orders`
- `SampleSchema`

Modifying, Repairing and Removing XML View Mapper

Once there is an existing installation of XML View Mapper on your system, subsequent executions of the Setup wizard will allow you to modify, repair, or remove the software as shown in the following figure:

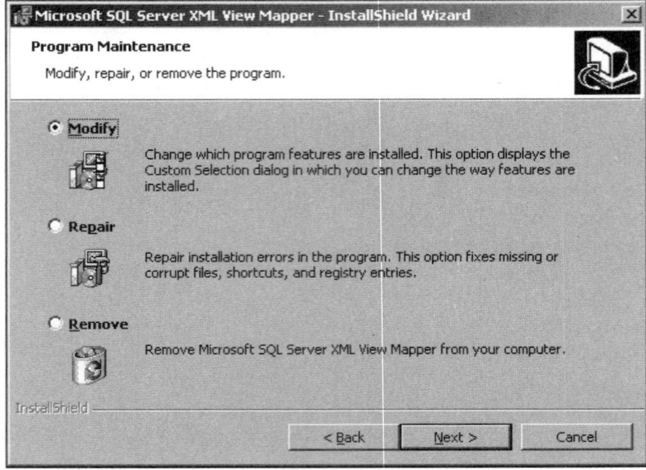

Modify an Existing XML View Mapper Installation

The Modify installation option allows you to change which program features are installed. If you select this option, it will open the Custom Setup dialog box. Initially, all features are selected by default. You cannot change the location or select a different program group using this option.

Repair an Existing XML View Mapper Installation

The Repair option is used to repair installation errors in the program. It addresses missing or corrupt files, shortcuts, and registry entries. Corrupt files are replaced and registry entries are corrected.

Remove an Existing XML View Mapper Installation

The Remove option is used to remove XML View Mapper from your computer. It removes the registry entries, the program group, and all files that Setup originally installed. However, it will not remove data files that you have created while using the tool. Remember, when upgrading from a previous version, do not use the Remove option. Remove the current version using the Add/Remove Programs application in Control Panel.

Now, that we have successfully installed XML View Mapper on our system let's take quick look at its architecture.

XML View Mapper Architecture

XML View Mapper is a project-based visual development environment. You use it to import a SQL Server 2000 database schema and a corresponding XDR schema defined for that database schema. XML View Mapper will create a SQL module from the SQL database schema and an XDR module from the XDR schema. Next, you use the Map Editor to view (and modify if required) the maps created between tables, views and/or columns in the SQL module, and ElementTypes, elements, and local attributes in the XDR schema by the tool based on the input schemas. Once these mappings have been completed, they can be validated by the tool and tested with appropriate XPath queries. After validation and testing is completed, a revised XDR schema and a new XML View schema are exported.

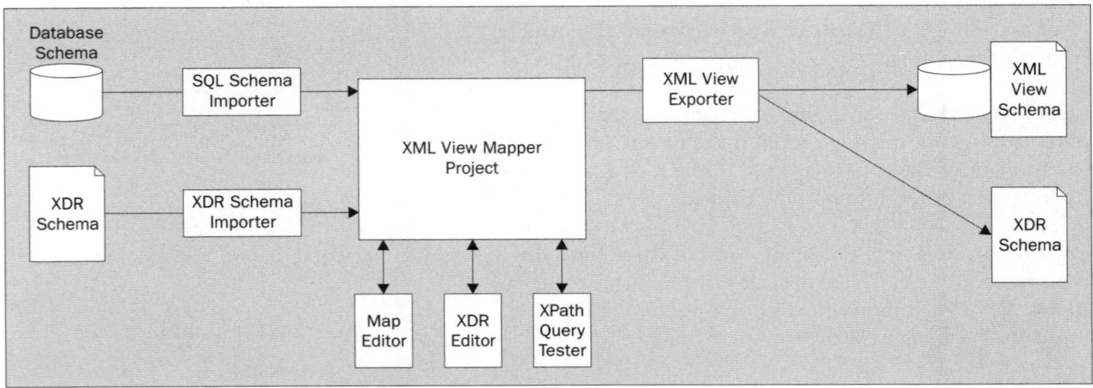

After this whirlwind tour of XML View Mapper, let's review each of its major components in some detail.

Data Inputs

Database Schemas

The definition of tables, views, and any constraints for a database is called a **database schema**. As a reminder, we can only use XML View Mapper to import database schemas that are defined in SQL Server 2000.

SQL Schema Importer

The SQL Schema Importer creates a SQL module from a database schema created for SQL Server 2000. During the import process, XML View does a lot behind the scenes. It analyzes the structure of the database and makes decisions on what is placed in the SQL module.

SQL modules can be imported in the visual development environment, or using a command file. Command files will be covered in an upcoming section.

XDR Schema

An XML-Data Reduced (XDR) schema is a special-purpose XML document written in the XDR language, which is proprietary to Microsoft. It defines the structure of other general-purpose XML documents and any constraints that apply to the XML items. XDR schemas are covered in Chapter 5.

XDR Schema Importer

To add an XDR module to a project, we use the XDR Schema Importer. It will take an XDR schema file and create the XDR module. `xml-sql` notations are used to create initial mappings which can be reviewed and adjusted using the Map Editor.

XDR modules can be imported using the visual tool, or using a command file.

The Project Explorer

The Project Explorer is the part of XML View Mapper that we will use to assemble and work with the project modules and files.

The Project Explorer organizes modules into a tree structure where the root node of the tree is the project name. Under the root is a set of folders, one for each of three types of module in our project.

When you start a new project, each of these modules will be empty. As the project development process takes place each module will be populated with appropriate files, as shown:

Data Outputs

XML View Exporter

The role of the XML View Exporter is to create an XML View schema file from a map module that you have created. The XML View schema is the principle output format of the tool. The resulting XML View schema file can be used for issuing XPath queries from other programs.

XML View Schema

An XML View schema is one of the two outputs from XML View Mapper. It is generated during the export process from the current map module and takes into account all `xml-sql` annotations. The relationship is one XML View from one map module. The output is stored in Microsoft's proprietary semantic modelling format (SMF).

XDR Schema

The other output of the XML View Mapper is the XDR schema.

Two Editors and a Tester

Map Editor

You use the Map Editor to graphically define and edit mapping between items in the SQL schemas such as tables, views, and columns to corresponding items in the XDR schema such as ElementType, elements, and local attributes.

XDR Editor

To view the mapping created during the import process, use the XDR editor. When using the editor, modules are present in XML format. At this point, you can make appropriate changes to modules and store the result. In addition, access to the XPath Query Tester is provided through the editor for the editing-testing cycle.

XPath Query Tester

The XPath Query Tester enables you to run a test XPath query against the XML View schema that you are designing. When you start the XPath Query Tester, the currently selected map module is exported to a temporary XML View schema file, which is used by the XPath Query Tester. You can then type XPath queries in terms of the XML View schema.

Starting XML View Mapper

The XML View Mapper is launched in any of three ways, using:

- The Start menu (via Start | Programs | Microsoft SQL Server XML Tools | XML View Mapper)
- A program association
- A command line prompt

Using a Program Association

We can launch XML View Mapper using a **program association**. Simply put, a program association is a relationship that is created between a filename extension and the application that typically runs that file. File associations are usually established during the installation process for an application. However, they can be manually changed using an operating system tool. XML View Mapper uses the `.smp` extension to designate a project file.

You open a project using a program association by opening Windows Explorer, navigating to the folder for your project and double-clicking on the `.smp` file for the project that you want to open. For example to open the Microsoft bundled `SampleSchema1` project in your `samples` folder you would select the `SampleSchema1.smp` file (the other files shown in the folder are part of the project; there will be more on file types later in *XML ViewMappes Files* this appendix).

Using a Command Line Prompt

We can also use the command line prompt to open a project. In the command prompt, navigate to the location of the XML View Mapper (if you performed a Complete installation, this is `C:\Program Files\Microsoft SQL Server XML Tools\XML View Mapper`), and type the name of the XML View Mapper executable, followed by a project file name. The fully qualified file name must be enclosed in quotation marks as follows:

```
XMLMapper "C:\Program Files\Microsoft SQL Server XML Tools\XML View
Mapper\MyFiles\MyProject.smp"
```

In this example, `XMLMapper` is the name of the executable for XML View Mapper and `MyProject.smp` is the name of the project file.

The command line prompt is most commonly used when we want to perform a batch conversion of schema files or if you are a die-hard command line fan. So, if you are a die-hard command line fan, or expect to be doing a large number of batch conversions, consider using a custom installation to place the XML View Mapper folder structure closer to a root directory on one of your drives.

A Guided Tour of XML View Mapper

Now, let's take a tour of the XML View Mapper's visual development environment. If it is not open, restart the XML View Mapper from the Start menu and make the selection to create a new project. At this point you should see the following screen:

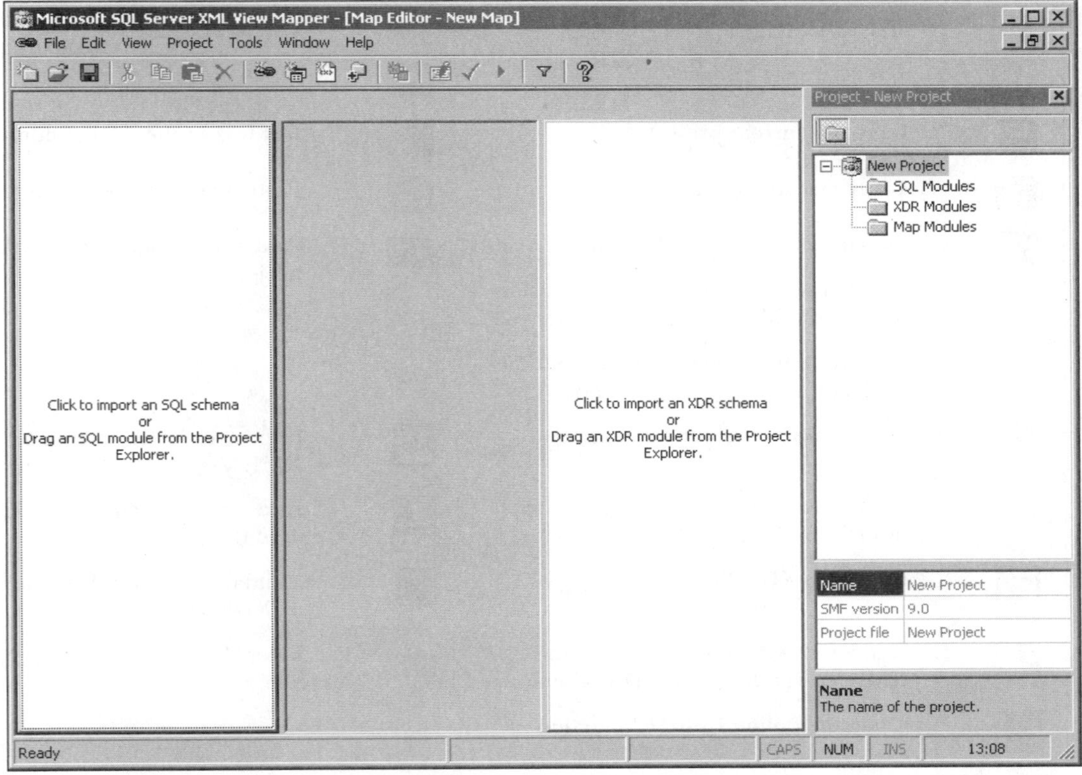

XML View Mapper's visual development environment consists of:

- A menu bar located below the window title
- A toolbar located below the menu bar
- A Map Editor window consisting of three vertical panes:
  - **a.** A SQL schema pane
  - **b.** A mapping pane
  - **c.** An XDR schema pane
- A Project Explorer window located on the right

The Toolbar

You will find that the XML View Mapper's toolbar uses icons common to most Microsoft Windows applications plus some icons that are specific to the XML View Mapper application. Tooltips are provided for each icon on the toolbar if you ever get stuck. The toolbar icons are described in the table overleaf:

Icon	Use to ...	Icon	Use to ...
	Create a new project.		Open an existing project.
	Save the current project.		Cut text in the XDR Editor.
	Copy text in the XDR Editor.		Paste text in the XDR Editor.
	Delete text (in the XDR Editor). Delete the selected mapping or custom join (in the Map Editor). Remove the selected module from the project (in the Project Explorer).		Add a new map module to the project.
	Import a SQL Server schema.		Import an XDR schema or XML View schema.
	Add an existing SQL, XDR, or map module to the project.		Add a custom join to the SQL module.
	Open the XDR Editor.		Validate the XML View schema or XDR schema.
	Run a test XPath query against the XML View schema or XDR schema.		Filter the display of mapping lines.
	Open the online Help (*F1* function key).		

The Menu Bar

You will find the standard menu selections of File, Edit, View, Tools, Window, and Help plus the application-specific Project menu. For a new project, you will find that many of the menu items are disabled and will only become enabled as you create your project.

Keyboard Shortcuts

XML View Mapper supports a wide variety of keyboard shortcuts. It supports the standard Microsoft Windows keyboard shortcuts. Many of these are shown as part of the drop-down menu items (for example *Ctrl+C* for copy). In addition, it provides a series of application-specific keyboard shortcuts to perform common operations in XML View Mapper. A complete explanation of these shortcut keys can be found in the online help document in an article called Keyboard Shortcuts in XML View Mapper.

General Access Keyboard Shortcuts

Some of the general access keyboard shortcuts are shown in the following table:

Keyboard Shortcut	Use to ...
F1	Show the Help window for the selected or active item.
Ctrl+R	Go to the Project Explorer.
F4	Open and go to the property sheet for an item selected in the XDR schema pane, mapping pane, or SQL schema pane of the Map Editor.
F5	Open the XPath Query Tester.
Alt+F4	Close the property sheet if open and return to the main window, or close XML View Mapper.
Ctrl+Tab or *Ctrl+F6*	Go to the next module window or the XDR Editor.
Shift+Ctrl+Tab or *Shift+Ctrl+F6*	Go to the previous module window or the XDR Editor.
Tab while in the Map Editor window	Move between the SQL schema pane, mapping pane, and XDR schema pane.
Enter while in the Project Explorer	Open a module window, or open or close a folder.
Shift+F10, or the *Application* key (which is near the right *Ctrl* key)	Show the right-click menu for the selected item.
* on the number pad	Fully expand the selected branch in the Project Explorer or a pane of the Map Editor.
Delete	Delete a custom join (from the SQL schema pane), remove a module (from the Project Explorer), or delete a mapping (from the mapping pane).
Ctrl+N	Create a new XML View Mapper project.
Ctrl+O	Open an existing XML View Mapper project.
Ctrl+S	Save changes to the selected module.
Ctrl+Enter after selecting a schema item and *Tab*ing to the other schema pane	Create a mapping line.
Ctrl+K	Change the selected ElementType to a constant ElementType or remove the `is-constant` setting.
Ctrl+M	Change the selected XDR schema item to Do not map or remove the Do not map setting.

The Project Explorer Window

Now, let's compare the Project Explorer windows for a new blank project and a sample project provided with XML View Mapper:

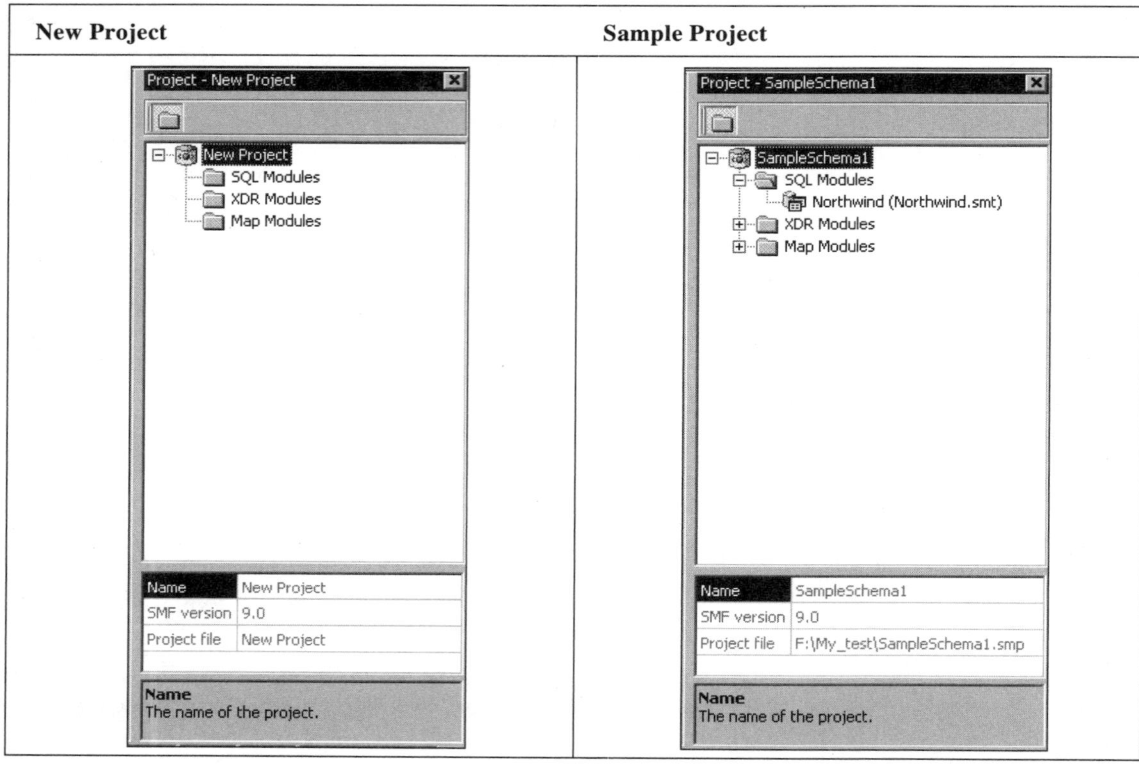

The left figure shows the Project Explorer for a new project; the default name is New Project. It appears in three places in the Project Explorer: the title bar, the root element for project, and in the Name grid area at the bottom of the window. You can change the name of the project when you save it.

The main window displays the basic tree structure for the new project consisting of:

- New Project icon (root)
- SQL Modules folder
- XDR Modules folder
- Map Modules folder

Initially, each of these folders is empty for a new project. As you develop your project you add files to each of these folders.

The figure on the right displays the Project Explorer for a sample project, or your project as you develop it. First, let's look at the changes in the main window. The name of the project is SampleSchema1. This name is also reflected in the Project Explorer's title bar and the Name grid area. The interconnection lines from the root icon to each of the module types in the tree structure have changed to include + and – icons. The + icon indicates that a folder contains additional files, which can be viewed by clicking on this icon. In the figure on the right, you'll see a file called Northwind.smt. This file is a SQL module (stored in SMF format). File types and extensions are discussed in the *XML View Mapper Files* section later in this appendix. Clicking the – icon reverses the process.

Finally, let's look at the grid at the bottom of the Project Explorer. Again, the name of the project is displayed next to Name. Project file indicates that this project is located in F:\My_test\SampleSchema1.smp. Finally, what is SMF version? SMF stands for Semantic Modeling Format and it is a file format that tags file contents with semantic values. SMF is a non-published file format that is used internally by several Microsoft products.

XML View Mapper Schemas & Modules

When you use XML View Mapper, you will work with the following schemas and modules:

Schema/Module	Description
SQL Schema	Represents a complete definition of the tables, views, and constraints of a SQL Server database.
SQL Module	Represents a SQL Server 2000 database schema definition in SMF that includes internal information used for transformations and mapping within XML View Mapper. It can include all or part of a database schema. However, it cannot encompass more than one schema.
XDR Schema	A special-purpose XML document written in the XDR language, which defines the structure of other general-purpose XML documents and any constraints that apply to the XML items.
XDR Module	Created when XML View Mapper imports an XDR schema. It represents an XDR schema definition in SMF that includes internal information used for transformations and mapping within XML View Mapper. An XDR module includes all of an XDR schema. It cannot include a subset, and it cannot include definitions from more than one schema.
Map Module	Represents the design-time version of an XML View schema. It displays a set of mapping definitions between an XDR module and a SQL module. The XML View schema is generated from this module.
XML View Schema	Represents the output of XML View Mapper. It is an XDR schema that includes `xml-sql` annotations that associate SQL schema items with XDR schema items.

XML View Mapper Files

An XML View Mapper project consists of a number of different file types and extensions. Each of these is listed in the following table:

Extension	Sample File	Description
`.smp`	`Order.smp`	The project file for an XML View Mapper project.
`.smt`	`Northwind.smt`	The SQL module that contains definitions of tables and views from the `Northwind` sample database. This must be the version installed with SQL Server 2000. This file type is created when you import the Northwind SQL schema.
`.smx`	`Order-xdr.smx`	An XDR module that contains schema definitions from the `Order.xdr` schema file. This file is created when you import `Order.xdr`.
`.smm`	`Order.smm`	A map module that contains `xml-sql` annotations that associate XDR module items with SQL module items.
`.xdr`	`Order.xdr`	An XDR schema file that includes element-based and attribute-based content.
`.xml`	`Order.xml`	The XML View schema that is exported from XML View Mapper.

The Map Editor Window

The **Map Editor** is the three-paned window in the middle of the XML View Mapper. The three vertical panes are a SQL schema pane (left), a mapping pane (center pane), and an XDR schema pane (right). For a new project, each of these panes is empty. You can have multiple Map Editor windows open at one time. However, all active instances always work with the current Project Explorer.

The Map Editor opens when you start XML View Mapper or when you double-click a file in one of the module folders in the Project Explorer. Double-clicking a file in either the SQL modules or XDR modules folders will open the Map Editor but only populate its corresponding pane with a schema. However, double-clicking on a map module will populate all three panes: the SQL and XDR schema panes plus the mapping pane.

The Map Editor is used to graphically define and edit mappings between items in SQL modules and XDR modules. The SQL schema pane shows the tree view of the SQL module. The mapping pane contains mapping lines joining SQL schema items and XDR schema items. The XDR schema pane shows a tree view of the XDR module. The two schema panes can scroll independently of each other but the mapping pane is always stationary. The contents of the mapping pane change as nodes are expanded and contracted.

The Tools | Option menu item is a tabbed control that is used to filter mapping lines, and set the mapping line colors and styles. This menu is discussed in the *Customizing XML View Mapper* section towards the end of this appendix.

The SQL Schema Pane

The **SQL schema pane** is used to view properties for SQL schema items, to add a join, or to select an item to map to an XDR schema.

The following table contains the icons used in the SQL schema pane:

Icon	Meaning	Icon	Meaning
	SQL schema		Custom join
	Table		View
	Mapped table		Mapped view
	Provisional table		Column
	Provisional mapped table		Mapped column
	Join		Provisional column
	Provisional join		Provisional mapped column

Now, let's open a sample project included with the XML View Mapper, so open the `SampleSchema1.smp` file in your `samples\SampleSchema1` folder. Next, open a SQL schema by double-clicking on the Northwind.smt file in the SQL Modules folder. This will place the schema file in the left pane of Map Editor as shown in the next figure:

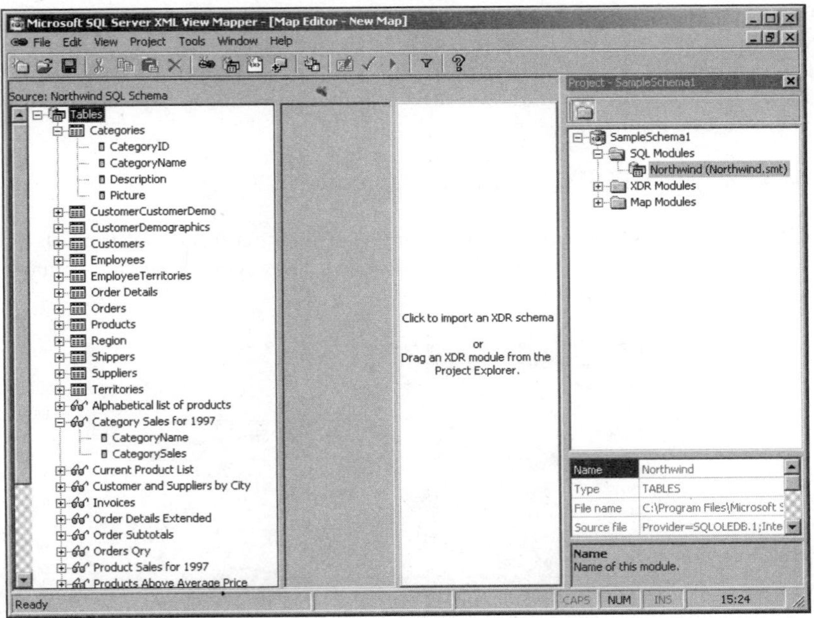

Looking at the left pane, you can see:

- The SQL schema's icon at the root of the hierarchy is denoted as Tables
- A series of SQL Server tables, including the Categories table, which is expanded to show the columns contained in that table
- A series of SQL Server views, including the Category Sales for 1997 view, which is expanded to show the columns contained in the view
- Of course, a set of horizontal and vertical scrollbars

SQL Schema Properties

A properties dialog box can be displayed for any of the items in the SQL schema pane and is opened in one of three ways: by selecting the item in the SQL schema pane and pressing *F4,* or by selecting the item, right-clicking in the SQL schema pane, and clicking on Properties, or alternatively by selecting the item and selecting Properties from the View menu.

The properties dialog allows us to view the following properties of SQL schema items:

- Root node (for example the topmost node in the SQL schema)
- Table nodes
- Table column nodes
- View nodes

A property box for a SQL schema item will consist of one or more of the following tabs depending upon the item:

- None
- A SQL Schema tab
- A Mappings tab – an optional tab that will only appear if the SQL schema item can participate in a mapping

Now let's take a look at a typical property sheet for a column node.

From the SQL Schema tab, you can see that it provides information about the CustomerID column in the Customers table of the schema. The data type is string, the column is the primary key, it cannot contain nulls, and it is not provisional:

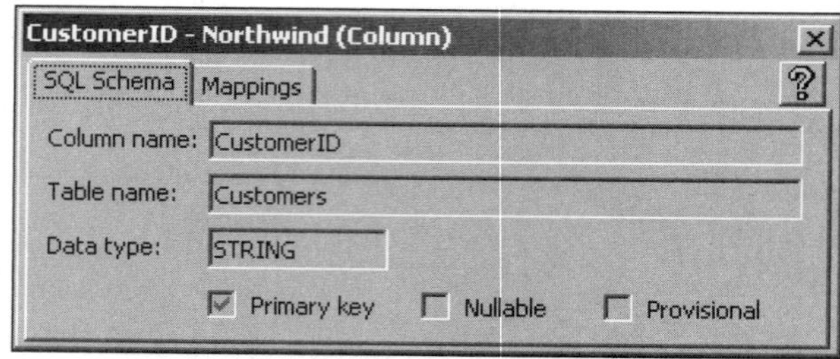

From the Mappings tab below, you can see that there are two mappings between the SQL schema and the XDR schema. The first mapping is from the `Orders` table to the Order element. What is not shown is that this element is a child element of the `Customer` ElementType. The second mapping is from the `Orders` table to the Order ElementType:

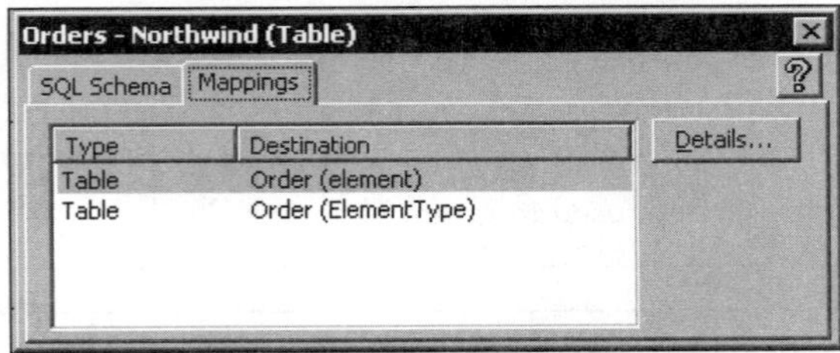

Note that all the properties displayed in the properties dialog are read-only and that the look of the dialog will vary depending upon the SQL schema item selected. The online help documentation has a series of help topics on the various properties for the SQL schema.

The XDR Schema Pane

Now, let's move to the right and look at the **XDR schema pane**. The XDR schema pane of the Map Editor is used to view the properties for an XDR schema, create a join, or to select an item to map to a SQL schema.

The icons for the XDR Schema Pane are segregated into four groups and are displayed in the next set of tables:

XDR ElementType Node Icons

Icon	Meaning
	ElementType
	Mapped ElementType
	ElementType that needs to be mapped
	ElementType with a Do not map setting
	Constant ElementType (has a `sql:is-constant` annotation)

XDR Element Nodes

Icon	Meaning
	Element
	Mapped element
	Element that needs to be mapped
	Element with a Do no map setting
	Annotation element (a user-specified annotation that is an element)

XDR Other Node Types

Icon	Meaning
	Schema
	Namespace
	Description text
	Group, used to group elements

XDR AttributeType Nodes

Icon	Meaning
	AttributeType
	Attribute
	Mapped attribute
	Attribute that needs to be mapped
	Attribute with a Do not map setting
	Local attribute (represents an AttributeType and attribute that are contained in the same ElementType)
	Mapped local attribute
	Local attribute that needs to be mapped
	Local attribute with a Do not map setting

Let's open an XDR schema by double-clicking on the SampleSchema1-xdr.smx file in the Project Explorer window. This will place the XDR schema file in the right pane of Map Editor as shown in the figure (note that the SQL schema in the SQL schema pane will disappear as the XDR schema opens):

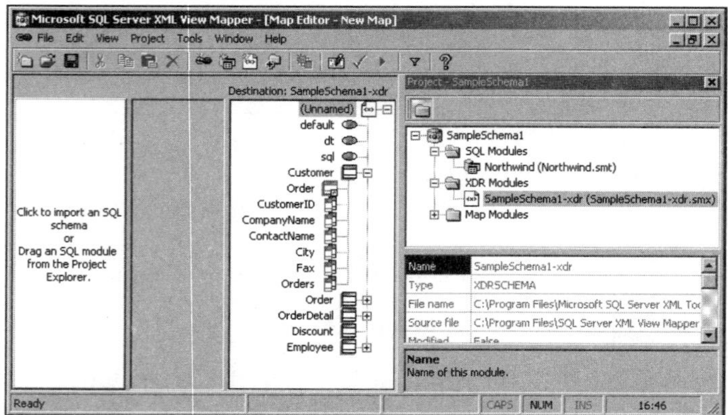

Looking at the XDR schema pane, you can see:

- The schema name – (Unnamed).
- Three namespaces – default, dt, and sql.
- A series of XDR ElementType nodes – Customer, Order, OrderDetail, Discount, and Employee. Note that the Customer XDR ElementType consists of an Order element and six local attributes called CustomerID, CompanyName, ContactName, City, Fax, and Orders.

XDR Schema Properties

XDR schema item properties can be viewed in the same manner as SQL schema item properties, by selecting the XDR item in the XDR pane and pressing the *F4* key, or by selecting the XDR item, right-clicking in the XDR pane, and clicking on Properties, or finally by selecting the XDR item and selecting Properties from the View menu. Each of these methods will display the appropriate dialog box for the XDR item selected.

The tab structure for the XDR dialog box is similar to one for SQL schema and contains the tabs shown in the following table:

Dialog Box Tab	Description and Typical Usage
XDR	The contents of this tab vary with the type of XDR item selected. Some of the most common properties include: Name, Data type, Default (value), Required, and Source file. You can change the values in an XDR tab using the XDR Editor.
SQL	The contents of this tab vary with the type of XDR item selected. Some of the most common properties include: Use SQL data type, URL encoding, and Use CDATA. This tab appears for XDR schema items that are contained in a map module in a project. You can change the values in the SQL tab directly on the tab itself.
Mappings	This tab shows mapping information such as the type of mapping, the source SQL schema item, and navigation details (if applicable). This tab appears for any XDR or SQL schema item that can take part in a mapping.
Values	This tab provides a list of valid values for attributes. This tab appears for any attribute that uses the enumeration data type.

Let's take a look at the property dialog box for the CustomerID local-attribute XDR item. From the XDR tab, you can see that name of the XDR item is CustomerID, it has no default value, its data type is id, and it is not required:

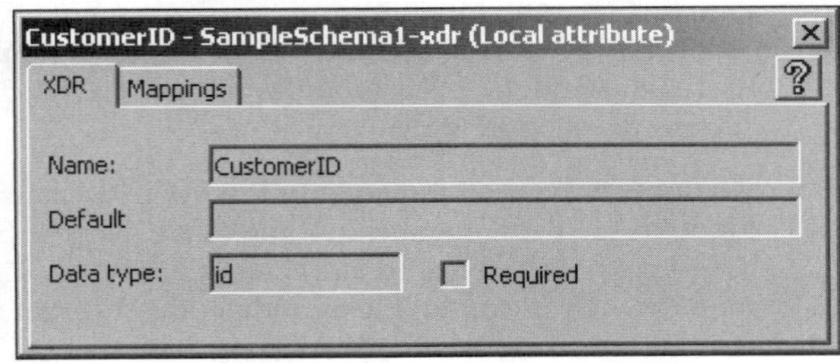

From the Mappings tab, we can see that there are no mappings shown to this local attribute. However, when we open a mapping file any mapping created to this local attribute would be visible in this tab (as shown previously):

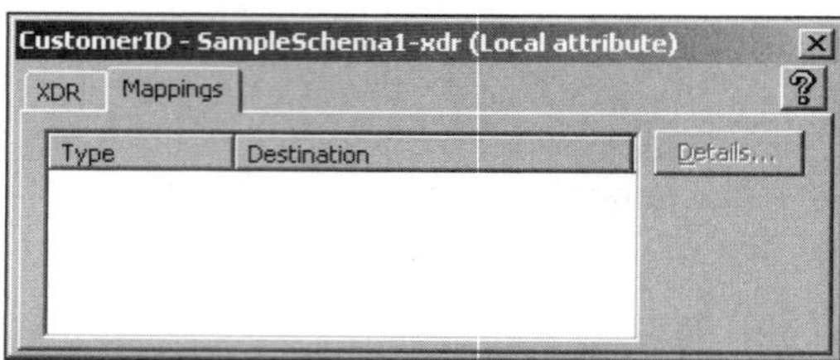

Note that all the properties displayed in the properties dialog are read-only.

Module Operations

When working with modules in your project, you will routinely perform the operations listed in the following table:

Module Operation	"How To" Plus Things to Watch out for
Adding a module	Right-click in the Project Explorer and select Add Module, or select Add Module from the Project menu. The Add Module dialog box will open, allowing you to: ❑ Add a SQL module, XDR module, or map module to your project ❑ Import a SQL schema ❑ Import an XDR schema ❑ Add an existing SMF module This operation places the module file that you have added in the appropriate folder of the current project.
Removing a module	Select Remove Module from the Project menu, or right-click a module name and then select Remove Module. You can only remove one module at a time. If a module is part of a map module, you must remove the map module first. This process removes the module from your project but not your hard drive, so don't forget to remove the old module file using Windows Explorer.
Refreshing a module	Right-click the module in Project Explore and then select Refresh Module, or select Refresh Module from the Tools menu. You should refresh a module after making additions or deletions to it. You can refresh individual SQL or XDR modules but a more efficient approach is to refresh the map module.
Renaming a module	Right-click the module name in Project Explorer and then select Save Module As. Type the new module name, use the Save as type list to select the proper file extension, and then select Save. This saves a copy of the module. As with removing a module, don't forget to remove the old module file using Windows Explorer.

Module Operation	"How To" Plus Things to Watch out for
Saving a module	Select Save Module from the File menu, or right-click a module name and then select Save Module. Modules must be saved before you can save a project.
Viewing a module	Double-click on the module name in the Project Explorer. You can also drag a module from the Project Explorer to the appropriate pane in the Map Editor.

Database Connection

When you start a new project, the first operation is to import a SQL schema. You do this by clicking on the empty SQL schema pane, or selecting Import SQL Schema from the Project | Add Module menu item. This will bring up Data Link Properties dialog box that you use to establish a connection to the database:

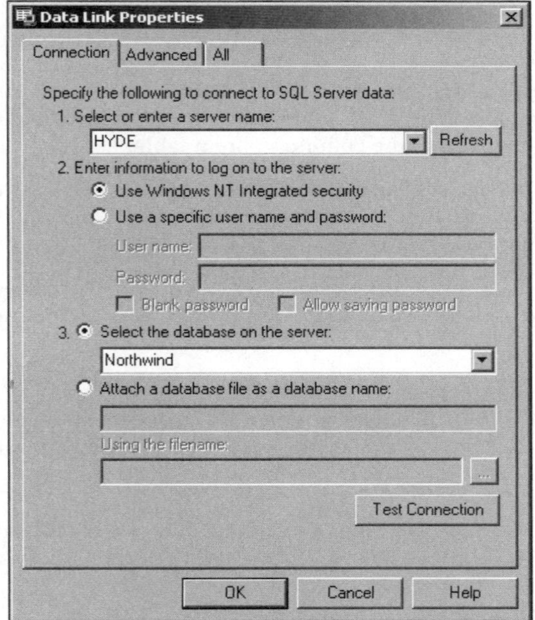

You use the Connection tab to specify a server, select the type of security, select a database on the server, and test the connection. The Advanced tab is used to set the timeout, and the access permissions. The All tab allows you to display and edit the properties of the connection.

Mapping

Before looking at the mapping pane for our example, let's take a look how XML View Mapper displays the various mappings between SQL schema items and the XDR schema items, the various mapping types, and the use of line color and style to display these mappings.

Table Mapping

Table mappings connect a SQL table with a corresponding XDR item. There are three types of table mappings:

- **Explicit (without a navigation path)** – this mapping approach shows all mapping lines that represent associations between SQL tables and XML items that have been specified in the XDR schema.
- **Explicit (with a navigation path)** – this mapping approach shows all mapping lines that represent associations between SQL tables and XML items that have been specified in the XDR schema, when the item's parent is mapped to a table other than the column's parent table.
- **Implied** – this mapping approach shows all lines that automatically connect a SQL table with an XDR item, for database tables and XDR item that have the same name.

Column Mapping

We use column mappings to show all mapping lines that connect a SQL table column with an XDR item. Here again, are the same three mapping types:

- **Explicit (without a navigation path)** – This mapping shows all lines that represent associations between SQL columns and XML items that have been specified in the XDR schema, if the item's parent is mapped to the column's parent table.
- **Explicit (with a navigation path)** – This mapping shows all lines that represent associations between SQL columns and XML items that have been specified in the XDR schema, when the item's parent is mapped to a table other than the column's parent table.
- **Implied** – This mapping shows all lines that automatically connect a SQL columns with an XDR item, for database column and XDR items that have the same name.

Overflow Mapping

When records are inserted into a database from an XML document using `OPENXML`, all unconsumed data can be stored in a special column normally called an **overflow column**. This data is typically XML-tagged data.

To illustrate this, let's take a look at a simple example. First, we create a table `Employee` and enter a single data row as follows:

```
CREATE TABLE Employee (
   EmployeeID     VARCHAR(10),
   EmployeeName   VARCHAR(20),
   OverFlowData   NVARCHAR(150))
Go

INSERT INTO Employee  VALUES (
   'EMP01',
   'Joe Bagadonuts',
   N'<xyz><address>100 Main Street, AnyTown, AnyState USA</address></xyz>')
Go
```

In this example, the unconsumed data, the XML-tagged address information, is stored in the overflow column of the `Employee` table. Later, when an XPath query is executed against the mapped schema, the XML-tagged address information is added to the XML document that is returned by the query. The complexity of the XML-tagged data can include subelements and their descendants and this will return more data in the XML document.

The `sql:overflow-field` attribute is used to specify the column in the table that contains the overflow data as shown below:

```
<?xml version="1.0" ?>
<Schema xmlns="urn:schemas-microsoft-com:xml-data"
        xmlns:dt="urn:schemas-microsoft-com:datatypes"
        xmlns:sql="urn:schemas-microsoft-com:xml-sql">
  <ElementType name="Employee" sql:overflow-field="OverflowData" >
    <AttributeType name="CustomerID" />
    <AttributeType name="ContactName" />

    <attribute type="EmployeeID" />
    <attribute type="EmployeeName"/>
  </ElementType>
</Schema>
```

Note that the name of the overflow column in this example is `OverFlowData`.

Overflow mapping occurs when you map a SQL table or view to an XDR ElementType, and then map the overflow column in the same table to the same XDR ElementType. There can only be one overflow mapping for each ElementType. The mapped overflow column cannot be mapped to any other XDR item. The ElementType content type is restricted to `eltOnly`, `mixed`, or `empty` and it cannot have a `dt:type` attribute.

Mapping Line Representation: Colors and Styles

XML View Mapper uses color-coded mapping lines to indicate what type of SQL item is mapped, and mapping line styles indicate mapping categories. The following table describes the default color codes and line styles:

Mapping Type	Node Types Mapped	Default Line Color
Table mapping	Table (or view) to ElementType or element	Black ____________________ — — — — — — -
Column mapping	Column to ElementType, element, or attribute	Blue ____________________ — — — — — — -
Overflow mapping	Column to ElementType	Red ____________________

Black, blue, and red lines are used to represent table mapping, column mapping, and overflow mapping respectively. A solid line is used to represent an explicit mapping. A dashed line is used to represent an explicit mapping with a navigation path. A dotted line is used to represent an implied mapping.

It is possible to customize both the color and style of your mapping lines. This is discussed in the section *Customizing XML View Mapper* later in this appendix.

Mapping Examples

Now, let's look at some examples of table, column, and overflow mappings. In each of the examples, take note of the use of the special symbol to indicate mapped SQL and XDR items:

Table Mapping Examples

A table mapping line is normally shown as a black line. Depending upon the type of mapping, the line style may be solid or dashed. Table mapping types include: implied mapping, explicit mapping to an ElementType, and explicit mapping to an element.

Implied Table Mapping

An implied table mapping uses a dotted black line to map a SQL table that has the same name as an XDR ElementType. In this example, an implied mapping exists between the Categories table and the Categories XDR ElementType. It was created during the import process because the name of the Categories XDR element matches the name of the Categories SQL table:

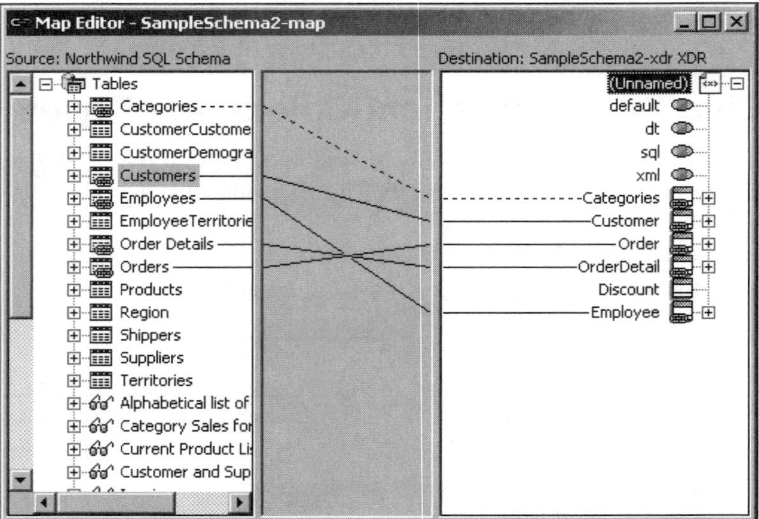

Explicit Table Mapping

An explicit table mapping uses a solid black line to map a SQL table or view and an XDR ElementType or element. In this example, an explicit mapping exists between the Customers table and the Customer XDR ElementType:

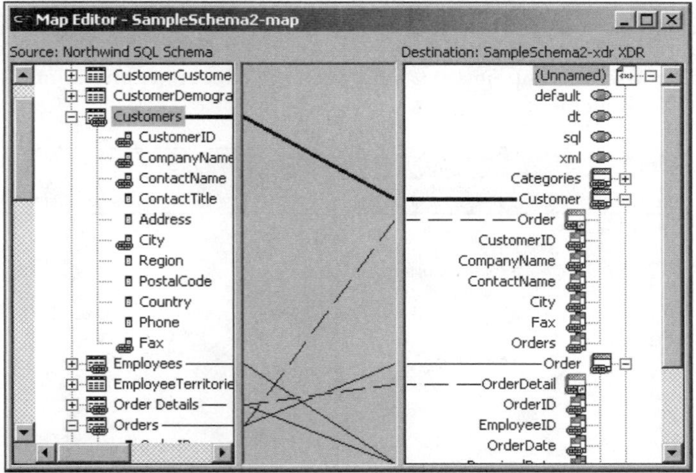

Column Mapping Examples

A column mapping line is normally shown as a blue line. Depending upon the type of column mapping, the line style may be solid or dashed. Column mappings types include: implied column mapping to an attribute, explicit column mapping to an ElementType, explicit column mapping to an element, and explicit column mapping to an attribute.

Implied Column Mapping

An implied column mapping exists whenever a column in either a SQL table or view is mapped to an XDR element and they share a common name. This type of mapping is shown with a dotted blue line. In this example, an implied column mapping exists between the ProductID column in the Order Details table and the ProductID Local attribute in the OrderDetail XDR ElementType. The implied mapping is formed during the import process because the table Order Details and the XDR ElementType both contain descendants called ProductID:

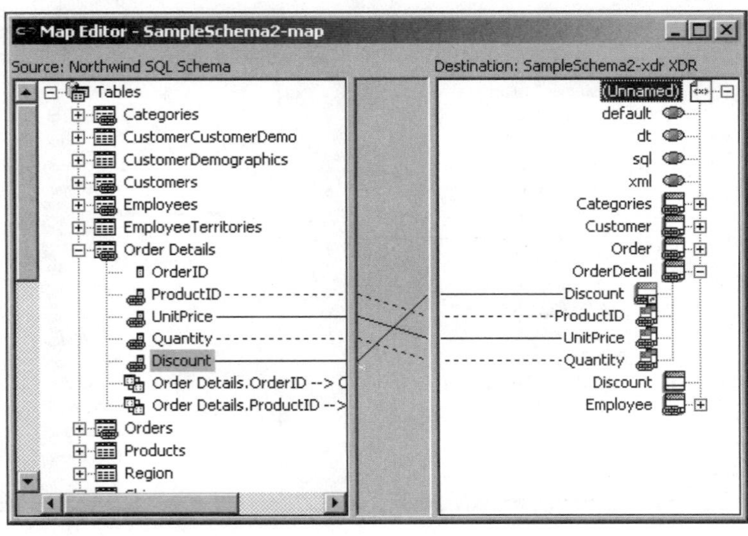

Explicit Column Mapping

An explicit column mapping uses a solid blue line to map a table column to an XDR item. In this example, an explicit column mapping exists between the Discount column of the Order Details table and the Discount XDR element:

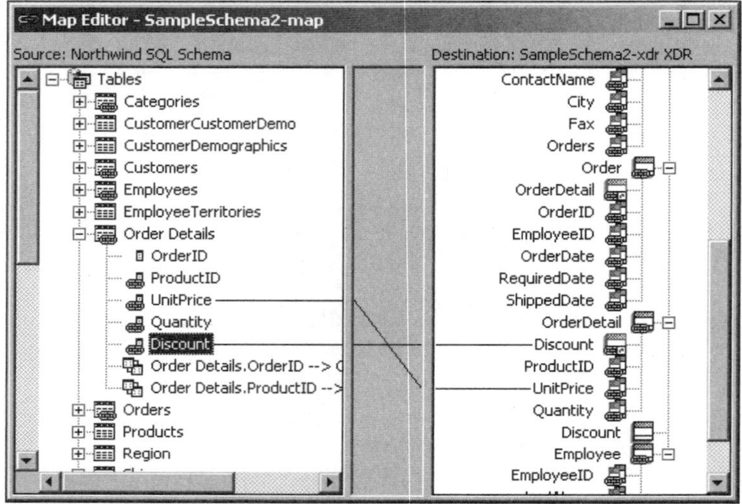

Explicit Mapping with Navigation Example

A mapping that requires a navigation path uses a dashed line. This mapping type is used to map a SQL table to an XDR element, a SQL column to an XDR element, or a SQL column to an XDR attribute. In this example, an explicit mapping with navigation exists between the Orders table and the Order XDR element of the Customer XDR ElementType:

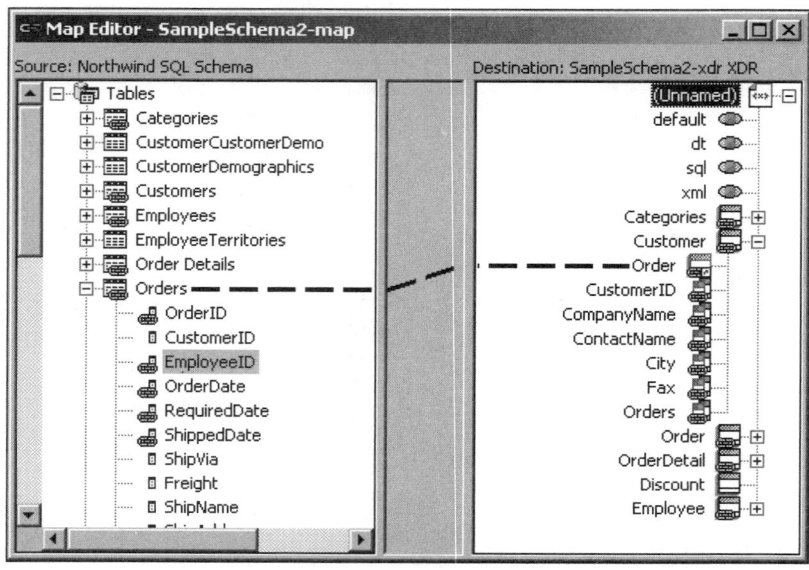

Overflow Mapping Example

As a quick review, this type of mapping occurs when you map a SQL table or view to an XDR ElementType and then map a column in the same table to the sample ElementType. Overflow mapping uses a solid red line. In this example, an overflow mapping exists between the OverflowData column of the Customers table and the Customer XDR ElementType:

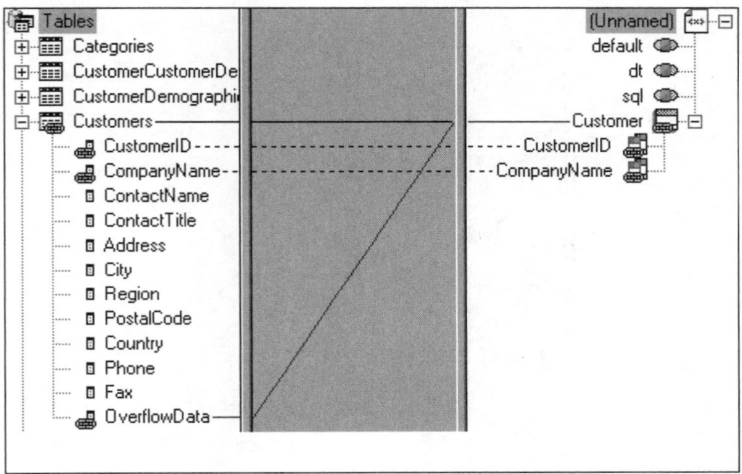

The sample schema (`SampleSchema1.xml`) supplied with XML View Mapper does not contain an overflow mapping.

More on Mapping

You can find more information on mapping in the online help documentation article entitled Examples of Each Type of Mapping Line. For each mapping type, the article provides a link to a help topic that contains the following information:

- A Map Editor diagram for the specific mapping
- A description of the specific mapping
- The resulting `xml-sql` annotations
- A resulting XML View schema
- A "step-by-step" procedure to create the specific mapping

In addition to this article, the online help documentation contains numerous other articles on mapping.

The Mapping Pane

Now that we have looked at the left and right panes of the Map Editor and the basics of mapping, let us return to our example to view the mappings between SQL schema and XDR schema pane items.

Open the project's map file by double-clicking on the file (SampleSchema1-map.smm) in the Project Explorer. When you open a mapping file, XML View Mapper populates all three vertical panes of the Map Editor as follows: there will be a SQL schema in the left pane, an XDR schema in the right pane, and the mappings in the center pane as shown:

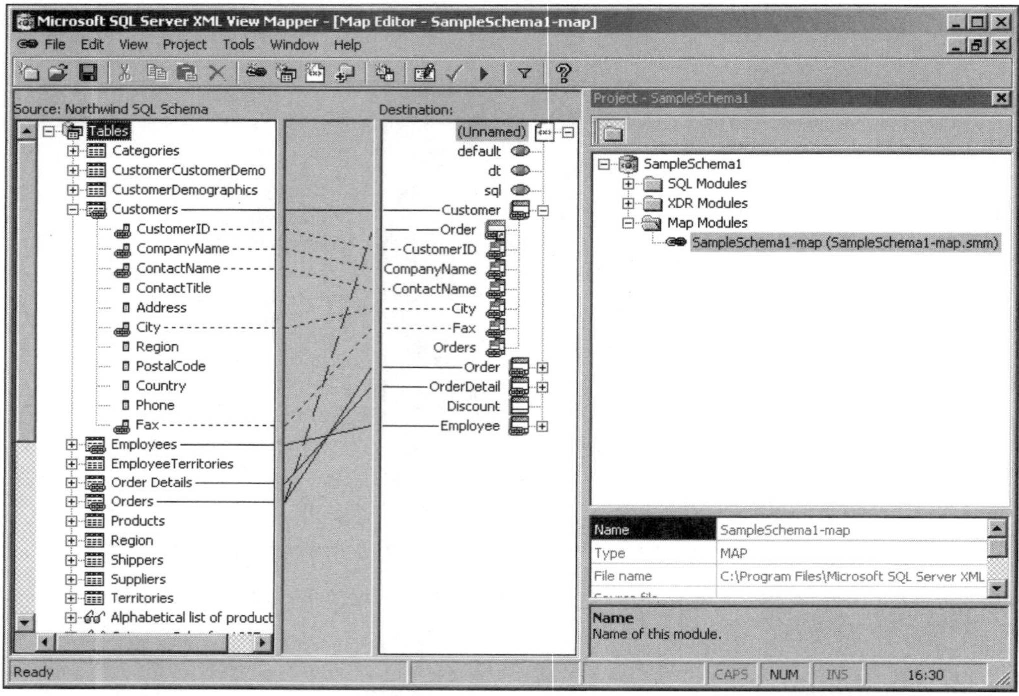

SQL schema pane items mapped include:

- Four mapped tables – Customers, Employees, Order Details, and Orders
- Five mapped columns for the Customers table – CustomerID, CompanyName, ContactName, City, and Fax

XDR schema pane items mapped include:

- Four XDR mapped ElementTypes – Customer, Employee, OrderDetail, and Order
- One mapped element – Order
- Five XDR mapped Local attributes – CustomerID, CompanyName, ContactName, City, and Fax

The mapping pane displays the following mappings for the SampleSchema1-map.smm map file:

Source SQL Schema	Destination XDR Schema	Mapping Type
Customers (table)	Customer (ElementType)	Explicit table mapping represented by a solid black line.
Customers.CustomerID (column)	Customer.CustomerID (attribute)	Implied column mapping represented by a dotted (blue) line.
Customers.CompanyName (column)	Customer.CompanyName (attribute)	Implied column mapping represented by a dotted (blue) line.
Customers.ContactName (column)	Customer.ContactName (attribute)	Implied column mapping represented by a dotted (blue) line.
Customers.City (column)	Customer.City (attribute)	Implied column mapping represented by a dotted (blue) line.
Customers.Fax (column)	Customer.Fax (attribute)	Implied column mapping represented by a dotted (blue) line.
Orders (table)	Customer.Order (element)	Explicit table with a navigation path represented by dashed black line.
Employees (table)	Employee (ElementType)	Explicit table mapping represented by a solid black line.
Order Details (table)	OrderDetail (ElementType)	Explicit table mapping represented by a solid black line.
Orders (table)	Order (ElementType)	Explicit table mapping represented by a solid black line.

Controlling Mapping Line Visibility

The mapping lines shown in this example are just a subset of all the lines defined for this map file. XML View Mapper provides you with a number of options in the View menu to control the visibility of mapping lines:

Menu Item	Used To ...
Reveal All Mappings	Selectively expand both SQL and XDR trees to make all mapped items visible, reset all filters so no mapping lines are filtered out, and show all hidden mappings.
Hide All Mappings	Remove the display of all mapping lines without affecting how the two trees are expanded.
Unhide All Mappings	Display all hidden mapping lines without affecting how the two trees are expanded.
Expand All Mappings	Selectively expand both trees to show all mapping lines that are not set to Hidden.

Table continued on following page

Menu Item	Used To ...
Show Pending Mappings	Selectively expand the XDR tree to show all XDR nodes that need to be mapped before executing an XPath query.
Expand All	Expand all nodes in the current tree.
Collapse All	Collapse all nodes in the current tree.
Expand Node Mappings	Selectively expand both trees to show all mapping lines that connect to the selected node's children.

Mapping Line Properties

The properties dialog box for mapping lines is opened in one of three ways:

- Select a mapping line in mapping pane and press *F4*
- Select a mapping line, right-click in the mapping pane, and select Properties
- Select a mapping line and then select Properties from the View menu

From the Mapping tab, you can see that the origin for the mapping line is the CustomerID column of the Customers table. The destination for the line is the CustomerID attribute of the Customer ElementType. Notice that the title bar indicates that this is an Implied Column Mapping:

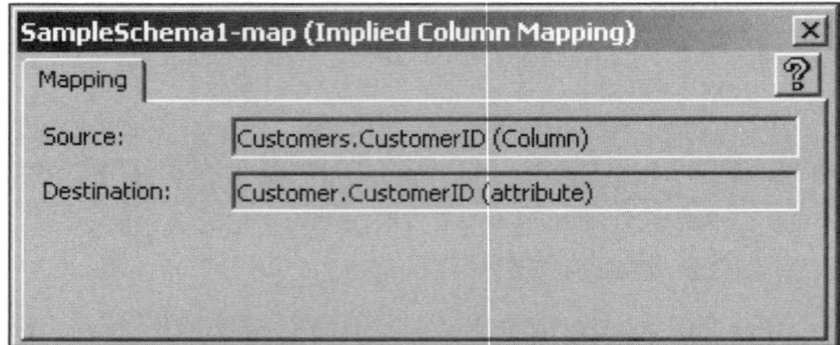

The XDR Editor

The **XDR Editor** is used to view and edit XML tagging corresponding to a map module or an XDR module. It enables you to preview an XDR schema as a file stored in memory and manually makes changes to the schema before exporting it as a file on the drive.

You can access the XDR editor in a number of ways:

- Right-click on a map module or an XDR module file in the Project Explorer and then select the XDR Editor menu item
- If the Map Editor is populated:
    - **a.** Select the XDR Editor menu item from the Tools menu
    - **b.** Right-click anywhere in the Map Editor window and then select the XDR Editor menu item

In the XDR Editor, these modules are presented in XML format as shown here. Changes that you make to the XML tags and definitions are subsequently stored with the module:

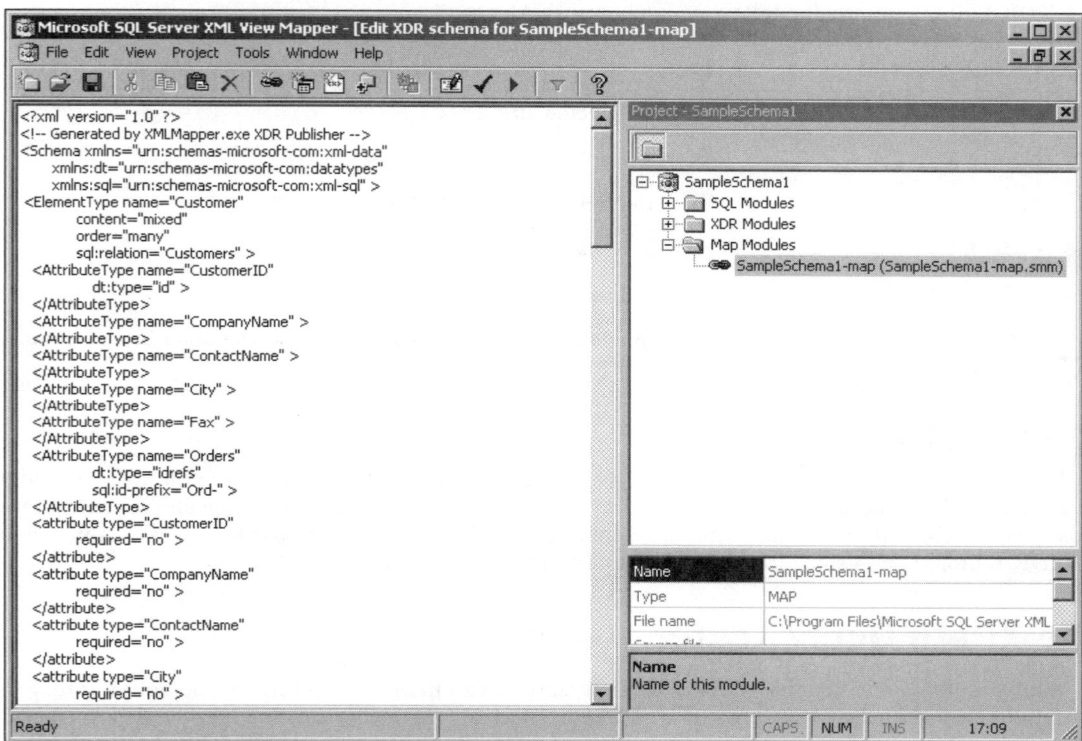

Auto-completion

The XDR Editor completes strings as follows:

You Type	Resulting String	You Type	Resulting String
`<E`	`<ElementType name="`	`</A`	`</AttributeType>`
`</E`	`</ElementType>`	`<a`	`<attribute type="`
`<e`	`<element type="`	`</a`	`</attribute>`
`</e`	`</element>`	`<g`	`<group`
`<A`	`<AttributeType name="`	`</g`	`</group>`

Keyboard Shortcuts

The XDR Editor supports the following keyboard shortcuts:

Use this Shortcut	To
Ctrl+X	Cut the selected string
Ctrl+C	Copy the selected string
Ctrl+V	Paste the string from the buffer
Ctrl+F	Find or replace a string
Ctrl+A	Select all text in the file
Ctrl+Z	Undo the last action, such as deleting one character or a selection block

XDR Validator

The **XDR Validator** checks the syntax of XML View or XDR schema whenever you save your edits or manually check the schema. You can check your schema by clicking on the blue check mark on the tool bar or by selecting the Tools | Validate Schema menu item. These options are only available when the XDR Editor is open since the Validator is part of the editor software.

The XPath Query Tester

While testing and validating your XML View schema can help you determine whether your map definitions are successful and ready to be exported as an XML View schema file, the **XPath Query Tester** enables you to specify SQL Server queries to be executed against your XML View schema. These queries are specified in the XML Path Language (XPath). At this point in the development process, the tester converts an XPath query into a SQL query and it is executed against the SQL schema.

Before issuing an XPath query, make sure that your XML View schema meets the following criteria:

- It has at least one defined mapping
- It meets the completeness rules for mappings listed in the next section

Completeness Rules

Before you can issue an XPath query, you must meet the mapping completeness requirements for the XDR schema items that are involved in the query. To be complete, every ElementType, element, and attribute (or local attribute) in the map module must fulfill one of the following conditions:

- The XDR item is implicitly mapped
- The XDR item is explicitly mapped
- The XDR item is marked Do not map
- The XDR item is marked `is-constant`

You can identify elements or attributes that do not meet the completeness rules because they are designated as Pending Mapping nodes and are shown with a yellow circle with an exclamation point.

Using the XPath Query Tester

In an open project, you can launch the XPath Query Tester in any one of the following ways:

- Pressing the *F5* keyboard shortcut
- Selecting XPath Query Tester option from the Tools menu
- Right-clicking on a `.map` file in the Project Explorer and then selecting XPath Query Tester

The first window displayed shows the schema file that was loaded successfully:

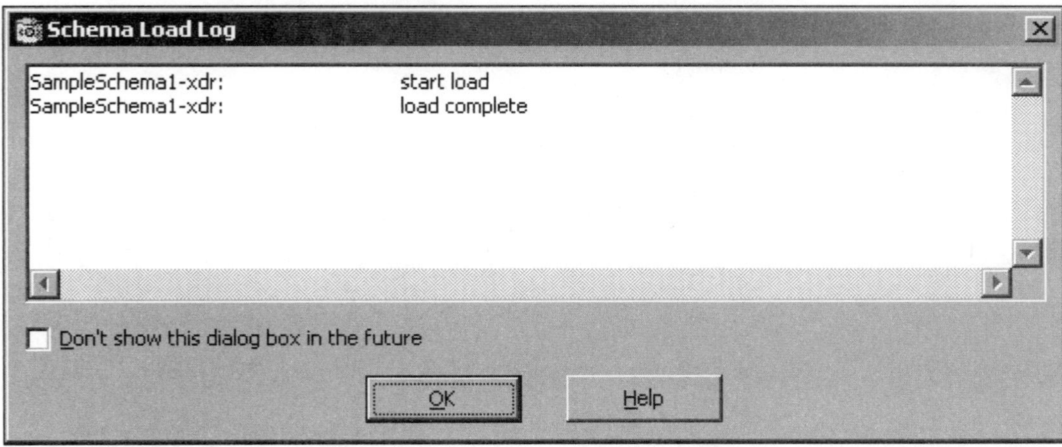

Click on OK to continue the process. Next, you will see the XPath Query Tester screen, which is used to execute XPath queries. To execute a query you must have an active connection to a SQL database. In this example, a connection exists to the Northwind database using the localhost. Type your XPath query into text box as shown below and click on Execute (don't forget that XPath queries are case-sensitive):

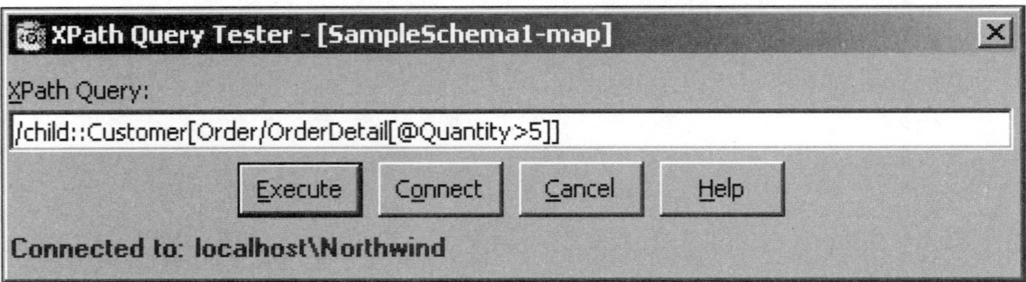

Internet Explorer displays the results of the query in XML format as shown:

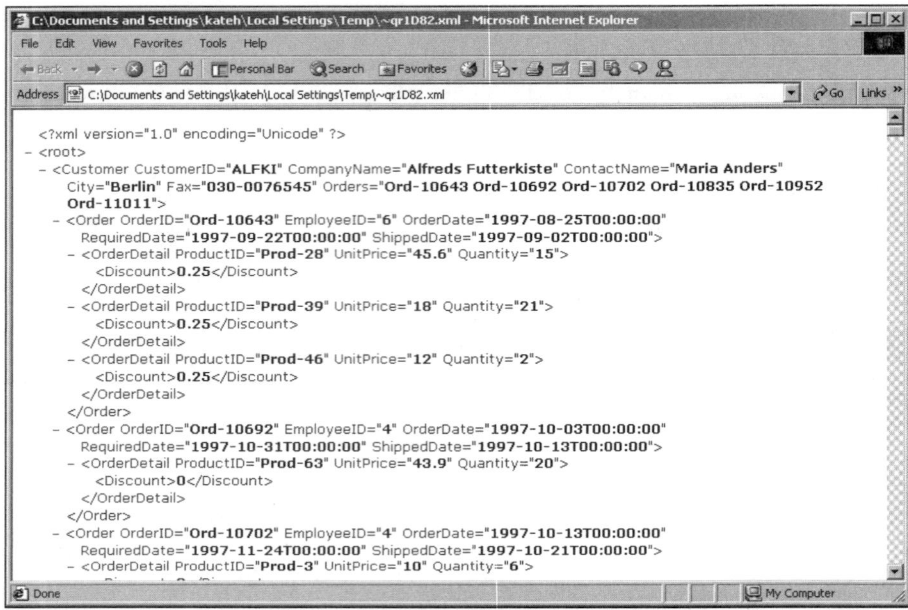

Using the Online Documentation

XML View Mapper provides an extensive and comprehensive online HTML Help file. You can press *F1* at any time to get context-sensitive help related to the current window, pane, or dialog box. Pressing *F1* is the same as clicking the Help button in a dialog box or clicking the ? button in a window or on a toolbar. Microsoft provides you with context-sensitive help for the following topics:

- SQL schema pane of the Map Editor
- Mapping pane of the Map Editor
- XDR schema pane of the Map Editor
- Project Explorer
- XDR Editor
- All dialog boxes
- All message boxes

Batch Conversion of Schemas Using a Command File

In this section, we will look at creating a **command file** to perform batch conversions of schemas. Command files can be used to perform many of the functions that are done in the visual environment. The command file is created using one or more of the command file elements. The completed command file is executed at the operating system's command prompt.

Command File Elements

The elements that can be used in a command file include:

Command element	Used to ...
COMMANDS	Contain the root element of an XML View Mapper command file.
LOG	Save parsing error messages to a log file.
CREATE_EMPTY	Create an empty module.
IMPORT_XDR	Import an XDR schema file as an XDR module.
IMPORT_DB	Import a database schema from a database as a SQL module.
EXPORT_XDR	Export an XDR module as an XDR schema file.
EXPORT_XAS	Export a map module as an XML View schema file.

First, let's look at each of these elements, its attributes (if any), and any things to watch for when using the element. Command element names and attributes are case-sensitive and most specified as uppercase.

The COMMANDS Element

The `COMMANDS` command element is the root element of a command file. It is the container for the command file elements. This element is required and has no attributes. Your command file must have a single `COMMANDS` element.

The syntax for using the `COMMANDS` element is:

```
<COMMANDS> </COMMANDS>
```

Now, let's start our sample command file. We will call the file `MyCommandFile.xml`. For simplicity, we will place it in the folder `C:\sample_command` to minimize the path length at the command line.

> **Since a command file is an XML document, you can use an XML tool (for example Internet Explorer 5.0 or later) to flag basic typing mistakes or syntax errors.**

We start out command files as follows:

```
<?xml version="1.0" encoding="utf-8" ?>
<COMMANDS>
   Place command elements here!
</COMMANDS>
```

The first line of our file is an XML declaration used to maintain compatibility with World Wide Web Consortium (W3C) specification. It is not required for the proper operation of XML View Mapper.

The LOG Element

We use the LOG command element to create an error log file to store messages that are generated while running the subsequent commands in the commands file. While a file can contain multiple LOG elements, each LOG element must contain a single FILE attribute and a single LEVEL attribute. If the file does not exist, it will be created. If it exists, the existing file will be replaced with the new file. Path information is case-insensitive. If the path contains a space, it must be enclosed in quotation marks.

The LOG element has the following attributes:

Attribute Description	Used to ...
FILE	Specify the full path and file name of the error log file.
LEVEL	Determine which types of errors to include in the log file. Valid values are: ❑ TYPE_ERROR – error messages ❑ TYPE_WARNING – warning and error messages ❑ TYPE_LOG – error, warning and log messages

The syntax for the LOG command is:

```
<LOG FILE={full path and file name} LEVEL={level}/>
```

Next, let's add a LOG command element to our sample command file as follows:

```
<?xml version="1.0" encoding="utf-8" ?>
<COMMANDS>
   <LOG FILE="C:\sample_command\errorlog.txt" LEVEL="TYPE_LOG"/>
</COMMANDS>
```

This file will create a log file called errorlog.txt in folder c:\sample_command as specified by the FILE attribute. The LEVEL attribute specifies that all errors, warning, and log messages will be saved in the file. If you opened the error log file at this point, you would see the following text information:

```
*** File Opened at 4/23/2001 3:14:43 PM***
*** File Closed at 4/23/2001 3:14:43 PM***
```

This entry indicates when the command file opened to create the log file and when the command file closed.

The CREATE_EMPTY Element

We use the CREATE_EMPTY element to create one or more of the three module types: XDR, SQL, and map. Just like the LOG element, if you specify the name of a file of module that already exists, the existing file will be overwritten.

The CREATE_EMPTY element has the following attributes:

Attribute Description	Used to ...
NEW_XDRSCHEMA	Specify the full path and file name for a new XDR module.
NEW_SQLSCHEMA	Specify the full path and file name for a new SQL module.
NEW_MAP	Specify the full path and file name for a new map module.

The syntax for CREATE_EMPTY is:

```
<CREATE_EMPTY NEW_XDRSCHEMA={full path and file name}/>
```

Now let's add the CREATE_EMPTY command element to our command file to create the three empty module files as follows:

```
<?xml version="1.0" encoding="utf-8" ?>
<COMMANDS>
   <LOG FILE="C:\sample_command\errorlog.txt" LEVEL="TYPE_LOG"/>
   <CREATE_EMPTY
      NEW_XDRSCHEMA="C:\sample_command\my_xdr.smx"
      NEW_SQLSCHEMA="C:\sample_command\my_sql.smt"
      NEW_MAP="C:\sample_command\my_map.smm"/>
</COMMANDS>
```

Each of the three files created using CREATE_EMPTY uses an XML structure and can be viewed with Notepad, Internet Explorer, or any development tool such as Visual Interdev 6.0. Each file forms a template that is populated when a complete command file is executed.

The IMPORT_XDR Element

Use the IMPORT_XDR element to create an XDR module from an XDR schema. Like the IMPORT_DB element, if the module exists, it will be updated, preserving its existing schema information, whenever possible. Both of these attributes are required. In addition, you must use the EXISTING_SQLSCHEMA and EXISTING_MAP attributes to preserve xml-sql annotations in the output XDR module.

The attributes for the IMPORT_XDR element include:

Attribute Description	Used to ...
IN_XDR	Specify the full path and file name of the XDR module to use as input.
OUT_XDRSCHEMA_MODULE	Specify the full path and file name of the output XDR module.
EXISTING_SQLSCHEMA	Specify the full path and file name of the SQL schema module.
EXISTING_MAP	Specify the full path and file name of the map module.

While a command file can contain multiple IMPORT_XDR elements, each IMPORT_XDR element can only contain a single IN_XDR attribute and a single OUT_XDRSCHEMA_MODULE attribute.

The syntax for the IMPORT_XDR command is:

```
<IMPORT_XDR
    IN_XDR={full path and file name}
    OUT_XDRSCHEMA_MODULE={full path and file name}
    EXISTING_SQLSCHEMA={full path and file name}
    EXISTING_MAP={full path and file name}/>
```

The syntax for the IMPORT_XDR command shown in the initial online documentation is incorrect and a bug report has been accepted by Microsoft and may be repaired by the time you read this appendix, or download the tool. The incorrect syntax is shown below for reference:

```
<IMPORT_XDR
    IN_XDR={full path and file name}
    OUT_XDRSCHEMA_MODULE={full path and file name}/>
    EXISTING_SQLSCHEMA={full path and file name}
    EXISTING_MAP={full path and file name}/>
```

Our next step in developing our command file is to create an XDR module based on a predefined XDR schema file. We will use the ever popular Northwind database and a sample schema file SampleSchema1.xml. We need to include the EXISTING_SQLSCHEMA and EXISTING_MAP attributes since this sample schema contains xml-sql annotations. Our command file now looks as follows:

```
<?xml version="1.0" encoding="utf-8" ?>
<COMMANDS>
   <LOG FILE="C:\sample_command\errorlog.txt" LEVEL="TYPE_LOG"/>
   <CREATE_EMPTY
      NEW_XDRSCHEMA="C:\sample_command\my_xdr.smx"
      NEW_SQLSCHEMA="C:\sample_command\my_sql.smt"
      NEW_MAP="C:\sample_command\my_map.smm"/>
   <IMPORT_XDR
      IN_XDR="C:\sample_command\SampleSchema1.xml"
      OUT_XDRSCHEMA="C:\sample_command\my_xdr.smx"
      EXISTING_SQLSCHEMA="C:\sample_command\my_sql.smt"
      EXISTING_MAP="C:\sample_command\my_map.smm"/>
</COMMANDS>
```

Schema Error

The SampleSchema1.xml file provided in the download as a sample has a syntax problem as of April 2001. Microsoft has accepted a bug report and this problem may be repaired by the time you read this appendix, or download the tool.

The original code section reads:

```
<ElementType name="OrderDetail" sql:relation="[Order Details]"
                                sql:key-fields="OrderID ProductID">
   <AttributeType name="ProductID" dt:type="idref"  sql:id-prefix="Prod-" />
   <AttributeType name="UnitPrice"/>
   <AttributeType name="Quantity" />
```

```
    <attribute type="ProductID" />
    <attribute type="UnitPrice" sql:field="UnitPrice" />
    <attribute type="Quantity" />

    <element type="Discount"  sql:field="Discount"/>
</ElementType>

<ElementType name="Discount" dt:type="string"
             sql:relation="[Order Details]"/>
```

The issue is how `Discount` is defined in the original schema. It is defined as an `ElementType` in a separate statement and is being referenced as an undeclared element in the `OrderDetail ElementType` statement. It should have been defined as an attribute type for `OrderDetail`. Two basic changes are required to correct the code. First, the `ElementType` declaration for `Discount` should be dropped. Second, an `attribute` declaration should be added. This requires the addition of `<AttributeType name="Discount" />` and `<attribute type="Discount" sql:field="Discount" />` statements as shown below:

```
<ElementType name="OrderDetail" sql:relation="[Order Details]"
                                sql:key-fields="OrderID ProductID">
    <AttributeType name="ProductID" dt:type="idref" sql:id-prefix="Prod-" />
    <AttributeType name="UnitPrice"/>
    <AttributeType name="Quantity" />
    <AttributeType name="Discount" />

    <attribute type="ProductID" />
    <attribute type="UnitPrice" sql:field="UnitPrice" />
    <attribute type="Quantity" />
    <attribute type="Discount" sql:field="Discount"/>
</ElementType>
```

The IMPORT_DB Element

Use the `IMPORT_DB` command element to import a SQL schema and create a SQL module using the schema definitions. Unlike the `LOG` and `CREATE_EMPTY` elements, if the SQL module currently exists, it is refreshed preserving its existing schema information. When a module is refreshed, it is synchronized with its underlying SQL or XDR schema to adjust for changes. We will discuss the refresh process in more detail in a later section of this appendix.

The `IMPORT_DB` element has the following two required attributes:

Attribute Description	Used to ...
`IN_DATABASE`	Specify the database connection string.
`OUT_SQLSCHEMA_MODULE`	Specify the full path and file name of the output SQL module.

While a command file can have any number of `IMPORT_DB` elements, each one can only contain one `IN_DATABASE` and one `OUTSQLSCHEMA_MODULE` attributes.

The syntax for the IMPORT_DB command element is:

```
<IMPORT_DB
IN_DATABASE={database connection string}
OUT_SQLSCHEMA_MODULE={full path and file name}/>
```

Now, let's continue the process of building our sample command file by adding the IMPORT_DB element:

```
<?xml version="1.0" encoding="utf-8" ?>
<COMMANDS>
   <LOG FILE="C:\sample_command\errorlog.txt" LEVEL="TYPE_LOG"/>
   <CREATE_EMPTY
      NEW_XDRSCHEMA="C:\sample_command\my_xdr.smx"
      NEW_SQLSCHEMA="C:\sample_command\my_sql.smt"
      NEW_MAP="C:\sample_command\my_map.smm"/>
   <IMPORT_XDR
      IN_XDR="c:\sample_command\SampleSchema1.xml"
      OUT_XDRSCHEMA_MODULE="C:\sample_command\my_xdr.smx"
      EXISTING_SQLSCHEMA="C:\sample_command\my_sql.smt"
      EXISTING_MAP="C:\sample_command\my_map.smm"/>
   <IMPORT_DB
      IN_DATABASE="Provider=SQLOLEDB;User ID=sa;Initial
      Catalog=Northwind;Data Source=localhost"
      OUT_SQLSCHEMA_MODULE="C:\sample_command\my_sql.smt"/>
</COMMANDS>
```

Using the IMPORT_DB command element, we created an OLEDB connection to the Northwind database on the localhost server using the default User ID of sa. Then, we created the SQL module my_sql.xml and stored it in folder C:\sample_command.

Check Point

So where are we at this point? First, we created an error log file using the LOG command element. Next, we used the CREATE_EMPTY command element to create the empty files for the SQL, XDR, and map modules. Finally, we used the IMPORT_XDR and IMPORT_DB command elements to create the XDR and SQL modules respectively. Now, we have an XDR module file, SQL module file, and a map module file based on the imported XDR schema file and the database schema.

Now, there are a number of approaches that we to take at this point. The first approach is to create a new project, add the three module files to the project, review and change mapping as needed, save the map file, and then perform the export. The second direction is to use an existing map file and continue with the command file development. This approach is good for minor changes to schemas or tables. The final approach is to accept the derived map file and continue with the development of our command file, which we will do.

The EXPORT_XDR Element

Use the EXPORT_XDR element to create an XDR schema from an existing XDR module. Like other command elements, if the schema currently exists it will be refreshed to reflect new or changed information.

The two required attributes for the EXPORT_XDR element are:

Attribute Description	Used to ...
IN_XDRSCHEMA_MODULE	Specify the full path and file name of the source XDR module
OUT_XDR	Specify the full path and file name of the exported XDR schema

While a command file can contain multiple EXPORT_DB elements, each one can only contain a single IN_XDRSCHEMA_MODULE attribute and a single OUT_XDR attribute.

The syntax for the EXPORT_XDR command is:

```
<EXPORT_XDR
    IN_XDRSCHEMA_MODULE={full path and file name}
    OUT_XDR={full path and file name}/>
```

Now, let's continue with our sample command file, by adding the EXPORT_XDR command element to export an XDR schema file based on our XDR module as follows:

```
<?xml version="1.0" encoding="utf-8" ?>
<COMMANDS>
   <LOG FILE="C:\sample_command\errorlog.txt" LEVEL="TYPE_LOG"/>
   <CREATE_EMPTY
      NEW_XDRSCHEMA="C:\sample_command\my_xdr.smx"
      NEW_SQLSCHEMA="C:\sample_command\my_sql.smt"
      NEW_MAP="C:\sample_command\my_map.smm"/>
   <IMPORT_XDR
      IN_XDR="c:\sample_command\SampleSchema1.xml"
      OUT_XDRSCHEMA_MODULE="C:\sample_command\my_xdr.smx"
      EXISTING_SQLSCHEMA="C:\sample_command\my_sql.smt"
      EXISTING_MAP="C:\sample_command\my_map.smm"/>
   <IMPORT_DB
      IN_DATABASE="Provider=SQLOLEDB;User ID=sa;Initial
      Catalog=Northwind;Data Source=localhost"
      OUT_SQLSCHEMA_MODULE="C:\sample_command\my_sql.smt"/>
   <EXPORT_XDR
      IN_XDRSCHEMA_MODULE="C:\sample_command\my_xdr.smx"
      OUT_XDR="C:\sample_command\my_xdr_schema.xml"/>
</COMMANDS>
```

The EXPORT_XAS Element

Use this command element to create an XML View schema from an existing map module that you have created using the visual development environment. Recall that the map module contains complete information about a SQL module, an XDR module, and all the mappings between them.

The two required attributes for EXPORT_XAS are:

Attribute Description	Used to ...
IN_MAP_MODULE	Specify the full path and file name of the map module that has the SQLSCHEMA_TO_XDRSCHEMA map element
OUT_XDR	Specify the full path and file name of the XDR schema to be exported

While a command file can contain multiple EXPORT_XAS elements, each one can only contain a single IN_MAP_MODULE attribute and a single OUT_XDR attribute.

The syntax for the EXPORT_XAS command is:

```
<EXPORT_XAS
    IN_MAP_MODULE={full path and file name}
    OUT_XDR={full path and file name}/>
```

Finally, we can complete our sample command file by adding the EXPORT_XAS command element to create an XML View schema based on the map module as follows:

```
<?xml version="1.0" encoding="utf-8" ?>
<COMMANDS>
   <LOG FILE="C:\sample_command\errorlog.txt" LEVEL="TYPE_LOG"/>
   <CREATE_EMPTY
      NEW_XDRSCHEMA="C:\sample_command\my_xdr.smx"
      NEW_SQLSCHEMA="C:\sample_command\my_sql.smt"
      NEW_MAP="C:\sample_command\my_map.smm"/>
   <IMPORT_XDR
      IN_XDR="c:\sample_command\SampleSchema1.xml"
      OUT_XDRSCHEMA_MODULE="C:\sample_command\my_xdr.smx"
      EXISTING_SQLSCHEMA="C:\sample_command\my_sql.smt"
      EXISTING_MAP="C:\sample_command\my_map.smm"/>
   <IMPORT_DB
      IN_DATABASE="Provider=SQLOLEDB;User ID=sa;Initial
      Catalog=Northwind;Data Source=localhost"
      OUT_SQLSCHEMA_MODULE="C:\sample_command\my_sql.smt"/>
   <EXPORT_XDR
      IN_XDRSCHEMA_MODULE="C:\sample_command\my_xdr.smx"
      OUT_XDR="C:\sample_command\my_xdr_schema.xml"/>
   <EXPORT_XAS
      IN_MAP_MODULE="C:\sample_command\my_map.smm"
      OUT_XDR="C:\sample_command\my_xas_schema.xml"/>
</COMMANDS>
```

Running a Command File

Once we have completed our command file, we can execute it using the operating system's command prompt. Let's take a look at how we can run the command file MyCommandFile.xml at the command line.

We can use the XMLMapper with the /? switch to display a "help-type" dialog box for command line usage:

```
C:\Program Files\Microsoft SQL Server XML Tools\XML View Mapper\XMLMapper /?
```

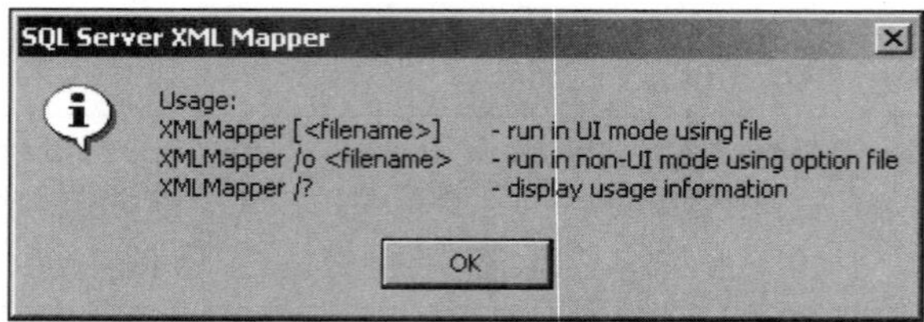

From the following dialog box, we can see that there are two basic ways to run XMLMapper from the command line:

- Run in UI (Visual Development environment) mode. The [ ] indicates that supplying a filename is optional. This method allows us to open XML View Mapper or an XML View Mapper project from the command line.
- Run a command file outside the user interface.

To run a command file, we use the /o switch:

```
C:\Program Files\Microsoft SQL Server XML Tools\XML View Mapper\XMLMapper /o
"C:\sample_command\MyCommandFile.xml"
```

Commands in the command file are processed sequentially from top to bottom. To verify the results of a batch operation, view the error log. A typical error log is shown in a later section on the Error Log.

Refreshing Modules

While we were exploring the command file elements, we ran across the concept of refreshing an existing module. We refresh a SQL or XDR module in our project to reflect changes that have occurred in the associated underlying SQL or XDR schema after project completion.

There are two ways to refresh a module:

- Write a command file to perform the refresh
- Use the visual development environment

You can always refresh a SQL module. In contrast, you can only refresh an XDR module imported from a disk or saved at least once.

Write and Use a Command File

You can create simple command files to refresh one or both of the module types using the appropriate IMPORT_DB, IMPORT_XDR, and EXPORT_XDR command elements in the command file.

Use the Visual Development Environment

To refresh a SQL module and/or XDR module for a project, open its project file. Right-click the module in the Project Explore and then click Refresh Module. You can use a map module to gain access to both modules. An alternative method is clicking the Refresh Module on the Tools menu.

Don't Forget Mapping

The process of refreshing one or both of the modules may not be the total solution to keeping your project up-to-date. After refreshing the modules, consider the mapping between the SQL module and XDR module. Do you need to drop mappings? Do you need to add mappings? Do you need to change mapping types? If so, adjust the mappings using the Map Editor and save the updated map module. The next step is to create a new XML View schema and XDR schema files using either the visual development environment, or a command file.

The XML View Mapper Utilities

The XML View Mapper includes a set of utilities that we can use to generate new modules from existing modules of a different type or from other schema formats. The conversion and generation tools in the XML View Mapper are available on the Tools menu, as menu items in the Utilities submenu.

Convert DTD to XDR

The DTD to XDR conversion utility enables us to convert a Document Type Definition (DTD) file to an XDR schema. Since XML View Mapper does not support DTD files directly, the conversion process puts the DTD into a format used by XML View Mapper. When a conversion utility such as this is used for the first few times, you should review its output to verify that the results are what are expected. The online help documentation provides a detailed help topic on the "step-by-step" use of the DTD to XDR utility.

Generate XDR Module

The Generate XDR Module menu item will only be enabled if your project contains a SQL module as this conversion utility generates an XDR module from a SQL module. The generated XDR module represents an XDR schema in an attribute-oriented format. It does not produce `xml-sql` annotations. Once you convert a module, it can be used to create a map module, define mappings, and generate XML View schemas. XDR ElementType names cannot contain spaces so underscore characters replace any spaces in the names of SQL items. The online help documentation provides a detailed help topic on the use of this utility.

Derive XDR Schema from XML Document

The Derive XDR Schema from XML Document menu item provides us with the ability to derive XDR schema from an XML data file. The XDR file can then be imported into a project automatically or manually. The help topic titled Deriving an XDR Schema from an XML Data File provides a step-by-step guide to using this utility. Before you use this utility, we recommend that you read this article to understand the conversion rules built into the utility and how it handles multiple namespaces.

Troubleshooting

The XML View Mapper provides a series of messages, a set of Frequently Asked Questions (FAQs), a set of best practices, and a trouble log to assist you in using it.

Messages

XML View Mapper provides three types of messages: errors, warnings, and informational messages. You can find the description for any of these messages in the XML View Mapper online help under Contents | Troubleshooting | Messages. Three subsections are available Errors, Warnings, and Informational Messages corresponding to the three types of messages.

Errors

Error messages indicate a condition that prevented the software from completing an action or process. The possible error messages are:

- A join must have at least one condition line
- File does not exist or is unreadable
- Invalid column name
- Invalid project file
- Schema: relationship expected on <XDR item>
- sql_relationship annotation <annotation> is not defined for the table <table> that is mapped to the parent ElementType
- The data types of the selected objects are incompatible

Warnings

Warning messages are displayed when the software detects conditions that are not expressly unsupported, but may indicate a problem or potential problem in the future. There is only one possible type of warning message:

- Schema <XDR module> cannot be modified while it is open in the XDR Editor. Switch to XDR Editor for <XDR module>?

Informational Messages

Information messages reveal details about an action or process. The possible informational messages are:

- Ambiguous mapping
- Cannot create an explicit mapping between a column and an element whose referenced ElementType has content other than textOnly
- Cannot establish a database connection. Do you want to create a new database connection?
- Existing Mapping: A mapping already exists between <SQL item> and <XDR item>
- Incompatible Data Types: <SQL item> is of type <data type> and <XDR item> is of type <data type>
- Incompatible node types: <SQL item> is a <SQL node type> and <XDR item> is an <XDR node type>
- No database connection established
- Overflow-field mapping ignored on textOnly ElementType
- sql:relation annotation dropped on ElementType <name> because it has textOnly content
- sql:relation annotation dropped on ElementType <name> because sql:relation annotation is not specified
- Unmapped Parent Element Type: Children of <item> cannot be mapped unless <item> is mapped

XPath Query Errors

XPath Query Error: prefixes any XPath query error. These errors are documented separately in SQL Server Books Online. You should search its online documentation for the article Errors in XPath Queries for descriptions of these errors.

FAQs

The list of FAQs provided in the online help documentation is sparse at best and not very useful. Specifically, there are only two basic questions and answers (*Why are some items mapped, and others not?* and *Mapping lines are not visible, even after I click Expand All Mappings on the View menu. How do I make them visible?*), perhaps this will improve with future versions of XML View Mapper.

Best Practices

The Best Practices section of the online help documentation is slightly better. It provides us with the following four recommendations developed by Microsoft on how to use XML View Mapper:

- Importing into an empty Map Editor
- Using tables and views in a SQL module
- Arranging editors and windows
- Viewing mapping lines

Error Log

The XML View Mapper log file is a record of program activity. It contains an entry for every warning, error, or informational message that occurs. We can view the log file using any text editor including Notepad or WordPad. The default log file is named `Logger_errorlog.txt` and is located in the `C:\Program Files\Microsoft SQL Server XML Tools\XML View Mapper` folder if you performed the standard installation.

Now, let's take a look at an error log that was produced during the process of developing our command file:

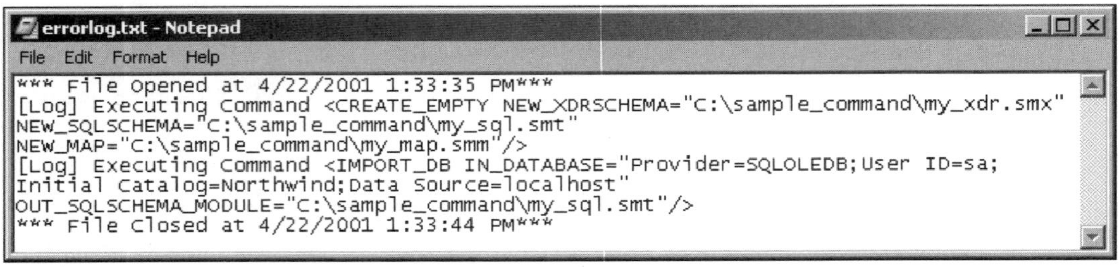

errorlog.txt - Notepad

File Edit Format Help

```
*** File Opened at 4/22/2001 1:33:35 PM***
[Log] Executing Command <CREATE_EMPTY NEW_XDRSCHEMA="C:\sample_command\my_xdr.smx"
NEW_SQLSCHEMA="C:\sample_command\my_sql.smt"
NEW_MAP="C:\sample_command\my_map.smm"/>
[Log] Executing Command <IMPORT_DB IN_DATABASE="Provider=SQLOLEDB;User ID=sa;
Initial Catalog=Northwind;Data Source=localhost"
OUT_SQLSCHEMA_MODULE="C:\sample_command\my_sql.smt"/>
*** File Closed at 4/22/2001 1:33:44 PM***
```

If we observe the entries in the log file, we see the following:

- The command file that caused the log entries opened at 4/22/2001 at 1:33:35 PM.
- The first log entry, denoted by `[Log]`, was the result of executing `CREATE_EMPTY` element. It successfully created the three empty module files.

- The second log entry was the result of executing the `IMPORT_DB` element. It successfully created a SQL module.
- The command file closed at 4/22/2001 at 1:33:44 PM.
- The execution of this command file took 9 seconds.

To customize the log file see the *Customizing XML View Mapper* section later in this appendix.

Error Log Dialog Box

The Error Log dialog box provides error messages when you are working with modules. It only appears when there is an error loading, importing, or exporting a file. All messages appearing in this dialog box are appended to the error log file. Each messages consists of: Error message, reason, and line number of the file being processed. All other errors, warnings, and informational messages will appear in message boxes.

Other Sources

In addition to these topics, you can find additional information in MSDN, the Microsoft Development Network at http://msdn.microsoft.com.

Customizing XML View Mapper

We can customize our XML View Mapper environment by selecting Options from the Tools menu. This will bring up the Tool Options dialog box which contains four command buttons and tab strip with four tabs: General, Mapping Filter, Mapping Format, and Error Log:

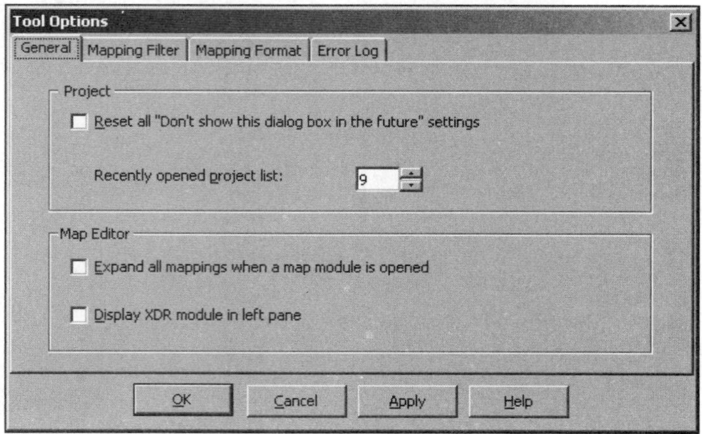

The General Tab

Use the General tab to set the options for the overall XML View Mapper environment. This tab is normally selected when the tab strip is opened.

The Project Section

If you have ever checked a box called Don't show this dialog box in the future and wished you had, this option in the Project section will undo that in XML View Mapper. Selecting the checkbox will restore those dialog boxes. One example is the Welcome to XML View Mapper dialog box.

Use the spin control to set the number of previously opened projects that will be listed at the bottom of the File menu. The range is from one through nine.

Map Editor

The Map Editor configuration section consists of two checkboxes that we can use to control how a project will be displayed in the Map Editor when it is opened.

If you select the checkbox corresponding to Expand all mapping when a map module is opened, the tool will automatically expand all branches that contain mappings when a project is opened. This makes all mappings visible immediately, rather than initially showing only the top-level mappings between tables and elements.

The Display XDR module in left pane option allows you to reconfigure the pane arrangement of the Map Editor by swapping the positions of the SQL schema and the XDR schema panes. The mapping pane will always remain in the center of the Map Editor.

The following figure shows result of selecting both of the Map Editor options:

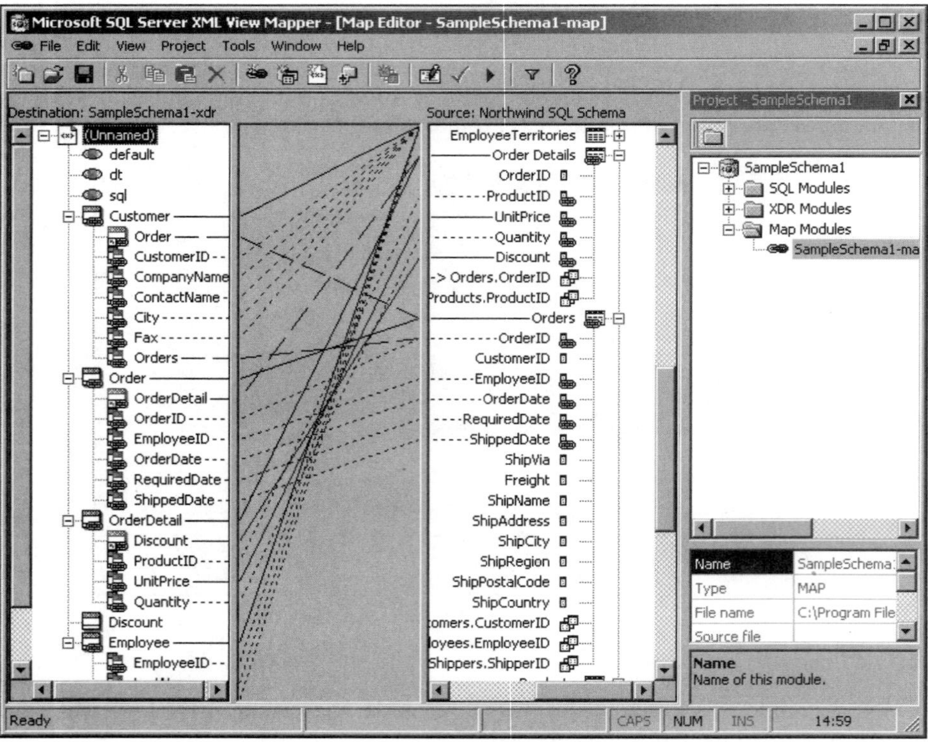

The Mapping Filter Tab

The Mapping Filter tab is used to control which types of mapping lines are shown in the mapping view:

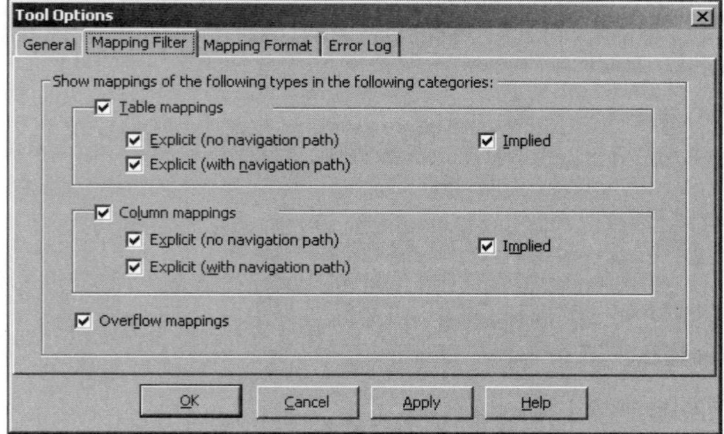

These settings are the defaults for all Map Editors in the current and future sessions. The mapping options fall into three distinct categories:

- Table mappings
- Column mappings
- Overflow mappings

In addition, we can set options to display table and column mapping based on the type of mapping: explicit without a navigation path, explicit with a navigation path, and implied.

The Mapping Format Tab

The Mapping Format tab allows us to customize mapping line color and styles:

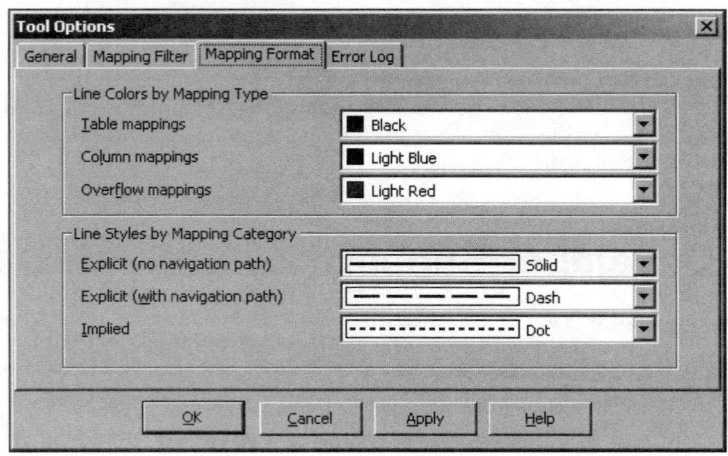

Set the mapping line color for each mapping type by selecting the desired color from the drop-down boxes associated with table mappings, column mappings, and overflow mappings. There are fifteen predefined colors to choose from. Normally, you should specify different colors for each mapping type.

We can also customize the mapping line style for each mapping type by selecting the style from the drop-down boxes associated with explicit (no navigation path) mapping, explicit (with navigation path), and implied mapping. There are five different line styles to choose from: solid, dash, dot, dash-dot, and dash-dot-dot. Again, you would normally select different line styles for each mapping category.

Once you have clicked on OK or Apply these settings will apply to all projects and sessions.

The Error Log Tab

The Error Log tab is used to customize error logging by allowing us to select the types of errors to track in the log file and to set the error log's path. When you select this tab, you will see the following:

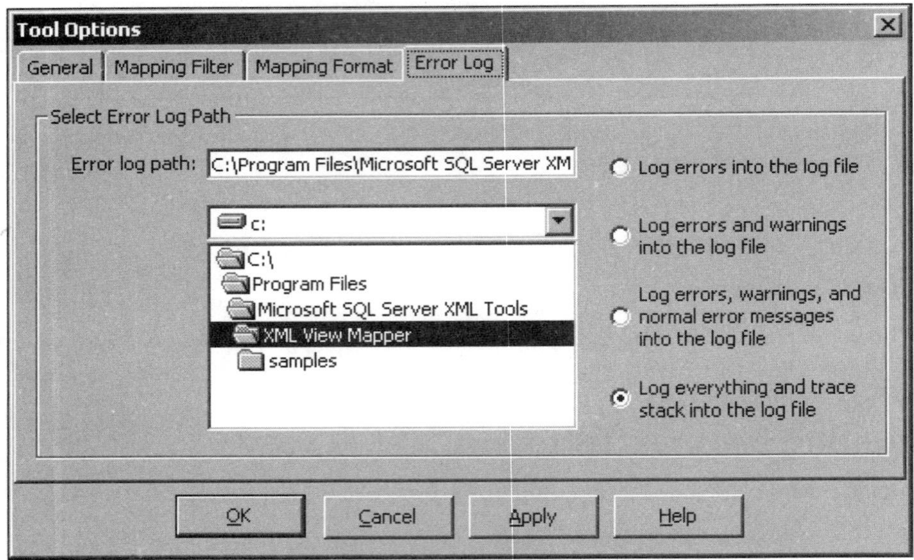

The single line text box, drop-down box, and directory viewer are used to specify the location of the error log file. We can also decide the specific information logged in the event of an error by selecting one of four option buttons on the right. As seen in the tab, the logged information can range from basic errors to a log everything plus the stack trace.

Microsoft Developer Support for XML View Mapper

As pointed out throughout this appendix, there are some inconsistencies in the documentation and sample code. As of the April 2001 release, searching the MSDN Library CD-ROM did not return any hits for the tool name. In a similar manner, searches on the MSDN Web for XML View Mapper using "exact phrase" only returned a link to the download page.

While Microsoft's fee-based developer support operation provides 24 x 7 support for SQL Server 2000, the support for XML View is more limited. The number of engineers familiar with the tool is a subset of SQL Server support engineers. These engineers currently work a Monday to Friday schedule.

In fairness to Microsoft, this may change by the time you read this appendix, or later as the use of the tool widens among developers.

The best source of support at the time of writing is the MSDN online newsgroup called sqlxml.viewmapper, which can be viewed via a Web-based newsreader at:

http://msdn.microsoft.com/newsgroups/default.asp

The sqlxml.viewmapper newsgroup is located under Web Development | XML/XSL.

Web Release 2 – Beta 1

The Web Release 2 – Beta 1 Version of SQL Server 2000 was made available for download on Microsoft's web site on April 30, 2001. As with all betas, Web Release 2 – Beta 1 is subject to change prior to final release. Several new enhancements are included in Web Release 2, as described below:

- **Annotated XDR Schema Enhancements**: The `sql:datatype` annotation initially only supported text, ntext, image, and binary data types. It now supports all the SQL Server built-in data types (but not user-defined data types or synonyms). The `sql:datatype` annotation also supports precision and scale.
- **Annotated XSD Schema Support**: A major enhancement included in Web Release 2 – Beta 1 is support for XSD Schema Definition (XSD). Previously, only XDR was supported. Now, XSD support is introduced with the same annotations as XDR, with minor differences. XSD annotations allow you to map the XSD schema to database tables and columns and create XML views of relational data. Furthermore, XPath queries can be run against those XML views to query the database and return records in an XML format.
- **Client-Side XML Formatting Support**: Previously, the formatting of an XML document from a rowset generated by a query was always performed on the server. Now, the rowset generated by the query can also be processed on the client. There are times when processing on the client is advantageous. One advantage of client-side support is the ability to execute stored procedures server-side while transforming the rowset into XML client-side. Another advantage is that you can now run queries against SQL Server 7.0 and retrieve XML, even though there is no built-in XML functionality with SQL Server 7.0. In the past, queries returning data as XML could only be run against SQL Server 2000.
- **Enhanced XML Template Support:** The `client-side-xml`, `nullvalue`, and `is-xml` template attributes are introduced. The `client-side-xml` attribute allows you to specify client-side or server-side XML formatting. The `nullvalue` attribute allows you to specify that a null value can be passed as the parameter value. The `is-xml` value indicates whether the parameter is XML. In addition to these new attributes, template caching is introduced to improve performance and new limitations on template parameters are introduced.
- **Enhanced Virtual Directory Management for SQL Server**: New options have been added to the IIS Virtual Directory Management Utility.
- **New OLE DB Provider – SQLXMLOLEDB**: The SQLXMLOLEDB provider is introduced to support client-side and server-side XML formatting of the rowsets generated.

Index

A Guide to the Index

The index is arranged hierarchically, in alphabetical order, with symbols preceding the letter A. Most second-level entries and many third-level entries also occur as first-level entries. This is to ensure that users will find the information they require however they choose to search for it.

A

D

E

F

M

N

O

P

Q

T

U

V

W

X

Wrox writes books for you. Any suggestions, or ideas about how you want information given in your ideal book will be studied by our team. Your comments are always valued at Wrox.

Free phone in USA 800-USE-WROX
Fax (312) 893 8001

UK Tel. (0121) 687 4100 Fax (0121) 687 4101

Professional SQL Server 2000 XML - Registration Card

Name ______________________

Address ______________________

____

____

____

City ____________ State/Region ____________

Country ____________ Postcode/Zip ____________

E-mail ______________________

Occupation ______________________

How did you hear about this book? ____________

- ☐ Book review (name) ____________
- ☐ Advertisement (name) ____________
- ☐ Recommendation ____________
- ☐ Catalog ____________
- ☐ Other ____________

Where did you buy this book? ____________

- ☐ Bookstore (name) ____________ City ____________
- ☐ Computer Store (name) ____________
- ☐ Mail Order ____________
- ☐ Other ____________

What influenced you in the purchase of this book?

- ☐ Cover Design
- ☐ Contents
- ☐ Other (please specify) ____________

How did you rate the overall contents of this book?

- ☐ Excellent ☐ Good
- ☐ Average ☐ Poor

What did you find most useful about this book? ____________

What did you find least useful about this book? ____________

Please add any additional comments. ____________

What other subjects will you buy a computer book on soon? ____________

What is the best computer book you have used this year?

____

Note: This information will only be used to keep you updated about new Wrox Press titles and will not be used for any other purpose or passed to any other third party.

5466 **Check here if you DO NOT want to receive support for this book** ☐ **5466**

NB. If you post the bounce back card below in the UK, please send it to:

Wrox Press Ltd., Arden House, 1102 Warwick Road,
Acocks Green, Birmingham B27 6BH. UK.

Computer Book Publishers

NO POSTAGE
NECESSARY
IF MAILED
IN THE
UNITED STATES

BUSINESS REPLY MAIL
FIRST CLASS MAIL PERMIT#64 CHICAGO, IL

POSTAGE WILL BE PAID BY ADDRESSEE

WROX PRESS INC.,
29 S. LA SALLE ST.,
SUITE 520
CHICAGO IL 60603-USA